An Advanced Introduction to

CW00925682

This book is an advanced introduction ͟ͅ ͟͟͟͟͟͟ this crucial component of human language through the lens of the 'Meaning-Text' theory – an approach that treats linguistic knowledge as a huge inventory of correspondences between thought and speech. Formally, semantics is viewed as an organized set of rules that connect a representation of meaning (semantic representation) to a representation of the sentence (deep-syntactic representation). The approach is particularly interesting for computer assisted language learning, natural language processing and computational lexicography, as our linguistic rules easily lend themselves to formalization and computer applications. The book combines abstract theoretical constructions with numerous linguistic descriptions, as well as multiple practice exercises that provide a solid hands-on approach to learning how to describe natural language semantics.

Igor Mel'čuk is Professor Emeritus of linguistics at the University of Montreal, Québec, Canada. One of the pioneers of Machine-Translation research, he launched, together with A. Zholkovsky, the Meaning-Text linguistic approach – a universal linguistic theory.

Jasmina Milićević is Associate Professor of linguistics at Dalhousie University in Halifax, Nova Scotia, Canada. She is co-author of the three-volume *Introduction à la linguistique* (2014) with Igor Mel'čuk.

An Advanced Introduction to
Semantics

A Meaning-Text Approach

Igor Mel'čuk
University of Montreal

and

Jasmina Milićević
Dalhousie University

CAMBRIDGE
UNIVERSITY PRESS

CAMBRIDGE
UNIVERSITY PRESS

University Printing House, Cambridge CB2 8BS, United Kingdom

One Liberty Plaza, 20th Floor, New York, NY 10006, USA

477 Williamstown Road, Port Melbourne, VIC 3207, Australia

314–321, 3rd Floor, Plot 3, Splendor Forum, Jasola District Centre, New Delhi – 110025, India

79 Anson Road, #06–04/06, Singapore 079906

Cambridge University Press is part of the University of Cambridge.

It furthers the University's mission by disseminating knowledge in the pursuit of education, learning, and research at the highest international levels of excellence.

www.cambridge.org
Information on this title: www.cambridge.org/9781108481625
DOI: 10.1017/9781108674553

First published 2020

Printed in the United Kingdom by TJ International Ltd, Padstow Cornwall

A catalogue record for this publication is available from the British Library.

ISBN 978-1-108-48162-5 Hardback
ISBN 978-1-108-72304-6 Paperback

Contents

Figures

Tables

Preface

First things first: What kind of book is this? Well, this is a textbook, an introduction to linguistic semantics; but it is an **advanced** introduction to the field, and it requires a certain degree of application on the part of the reader. (However, as we shall see, it is structured in a way that makes it easier to navigate than it might seem at first.) Apart from this, the book has the following two main "distinctive features":

- It adopts a view of semantics as a component, or module, of the linguistic system, whose functioning is simulated by a corresponding linguistic model. Language is considered to be a set of rules that establish correspondences between meanings and their possible expressions, and the lion's share of this correspondence is taken care of by the semantic module. This is the approach put forward by the Meaning-Text linguistic theory and its language models, called, predictably, Meaning-Text models.
- It is organized around a system of rigorous notions, specified by about eighty mathematical-like definitions. (Some of the notions that will be introduced are semanteme, semantic actant, communicative dominance, lexical function.) This system is deductive, consistent and formal; therefore, our exposition is also deductive and (strives to be) logically consistent.

Four salient characteristics of the Meaning-Text approach, reflected in the way the present textbook is organized, need to be mentioned.

1. Its emphasis on **formal modeling** of languages and their fragments implies, among other things, the elaboration and use of formal languages for the representation/description of semantic facts. (This makes the proposed linguistic descriptions suitable for applications in natural language processing and language teaching.) Accordingly, several kinds of formalism will be used in the book: semantic networks for representing meanings of sentences and lexical units; dependency trees for representing the syntactic structure of sentences; lexical functions for representing lexical relations; and rules of various types for representing semantic operations (such as lexicalization of an initial semantic structure or synonymous paraphrasing).
2. It prioritizes **synthesis** over analysis. That is to say, it models speech **production**, as opposed to speech understanding; the latter has been the focus of most mainstream approaches to semantics. It takes the viewpoint of the Speaker (rather than the Addressee); in this way, synonymy, in

particular paraphrase, is placed at the center of semantic research. All linguistic phenomena discussed are consistently presented from the Speaker's perspective.

3. It is based on **relational** representations – it considers relations, in the first place, dependency relations, among linguistic units as the main organizing factor in language, and, therefore, in semantics. (Most current linguistic approaches are focused on classes and constituency.) This is why we will have a lot to say about semantic and deep-syntactic dependencies in this book.

4. It is **lexicon-centered** – it attaches paramount importance to the lexicon and its modeling, and has developed for this purpose a special kind of dictionary, the *Explanatory Combinatorial Dictionary*, which is a pivotal element of the semantic module. Therefore, the description of lexical units – their meaning, cooccurrence and groupings within the lexicon – takes center stage in this textbook.

Let it be emphasized that we deal exclusively with synchronic semantics; historical (= diachronic) semantics is not even touched on. Within synchronic semantics we cover both propositional semantics – the representation and description of the meanings of sentences and the semantic relations between them – and lexical semantics – i.e., the representation and description of lexical meanings and semantic-lexical relations, the emphasis being squarely on the latter. It goes beyond propositional semantics in that it considers information structure (topic–comment distribution, focus assignment, etc.), usually treated as belonging to pragmatics, as an integral part of semantic description. However, the following important domains of synchronic semantics are left outside our scope:

*   Morphological semantics is not considered; the representation of semantic inflectional meanings, for instance, verbal voice, mood, tense and aspect in English, etc. is discussed sporadically, to the extent that these meanings appear in the linguistic representations under discussion.
*   Semantic phenomena are considered up to the level of sentences, to the exclusion of text/discourse semantics.
*   No systematic review of other approaches to semantics is offered; where appropriate, pointers to the work done in frameworks close to ours – such as *Natural Semantic Metalanguage* and *Frame Semantics* – are provided.

A few words about the organization of the textbook are in order. The main text consists of twelve chapters, divided into three parts: Part I – Fundamentals (Chapters 1–2), Part II – Meaning in Language and Its Description (Chapters 3–9), and Part III – Meaning-Text Model of Semantics (Chapters 10–12).

Chapter 1 characterizes semantics as part of language viz. a branch of linguistics and broadly presents our frame of reference, Meaning-Text linguistic theory and its language models. Chapter 2 introduces some basic linguistic notions necessary for the discussion of semantics to follow. Chapter 3 is dedicated to the main *persona dramatis* of this book – linguistic meaning. Chapter 4 considers lexical meanings, expressed as lexical items of various types, and Chapter 5, the main tool for describing them – the lexicographic definition. Chapters 6 and 7 are reserved, respectively, for semantic-lexical relations (such as synonymy, antonymy, intensification, nominalization, etc.) and their formal modeling by means of lexical functions. Chapter 8 describes the overall organization of the lexical stock and a particular type of dictionary used within Meaning-Text theory to model it, the *Explanatory Combinatorial Dictionary*. Chapter 9 is about sentential meaning and semantic relations between sentences (paraphrase, implication, and so on). Chapter 10 is dedicated to the linguistic representation that serves as the input for the application of semantic rules: the semantic representation. Chapter 11 deals with the deep-syntactic representation, the output of semantic rules. Finally, Chapter 12 presents semantic rules, responsible for the mapping between semantic and deep-syntactic representations of linguistic expressions.

Each chapter contains a "Further Reading" section, with pointers to the essential titles related to the topic of the chapter.

The textbook also features:

- An appendix presenting some mathematical and logical notions (sets, operations, relations, formal languages, etc.) widely used in linguistics.
- Exercises with a detailed key (available at www.cambridge.org/meaning-text).
- Bibliographic references
- Indexes:
  - Index cum glossary of notions and terms, containing succinct characterizations of the most salient elements of the notional and terminological system used in the book.
  - Index of definitions. The book introduces scores of new terms, or old terms used in novel ways, that are defined when they first occur. They are presented here in order of appearance.
  - Index of languages from which linguistic examples are drawn.
  - Index of lexical units and semantemes (= lexical meanings) exemplified or otherwise treated in the book.

Before we place the reader in a *tête-à-tête* with the book, a word of caution is in order. As we said at the outset, this is not an easy introduction; it cannot be read linearly. But language itself is not linear! In language, everything is interconnected, so you will need to navigate back and forth. To give just one example, before studying lexical functions, in Chapter 7, it would be useful to read about the linguistic representation in which they are used, that is, the deep-syntactic structure, which is dealt with in Chapter 11. We have provided lots of cross-references to help you with the task.

Acknowledgments

We extend our heartfelt thanks to Lidija Iordanskaja for her attentive reading of the manuscript and a host of modifications it underwent as a result, which greatly improved the accuracy and clarity of our formulations.

Our most profound gratitude goes to Ian Mackenzie for hunting down a number of mistakes and correcting several less-than-felicitous formulations, as well as for his merciless editorial interventions, which went a long way towards making the language and style of the book "more English."

We are very grateful to Stephanie Doyle-Lerat for her editorial suggestions, which have made our text lighter and more elegant.

And we say a cordial "Thank you" to two anonymous readers of the Cambridge University Press.

Symbols, Abbreviations and Writing Conventions

Symbols

$\mid C$	condition part of a linguistic rule
L	a particular language
L	a particular lexical unit
«L»	a particular fictitious lexeme (in the deep-syntactic structure)
L('X')	a particular lexical unit L expressing the meaning 'X'
$\ulcorner L_1 \ldots L_n \urcorner$	a particular idiom $L_1 \ldots L_n$
L_1–**morph**→L_2	L_2 depends on L_1 morphologically
L_1–**sem**→L_2	L_2 depends on L_1 semantically
L_1–**synt**→L_2	L_2 depends on L_1 syntactically
$L_1 \longleftrightarrow L_2$	L_1 and L_2 are co-referential ⟨= L_1 and L_2 have the same referent⟩
NB	important but tangential (= logically not necessary) information
Q	underlying question (used to determine the Rheme and the Theme of a sentence)
r	a particular syntactic dependency relation
R	Rheme (communicative value)
R$_{\text{DSynt}}$	Deep-Syntactic Rheme (communicative value)
R$_{\text{Sem}}$	Semantic Rheme (communicative value)
s	a particular linguistic sign
's'	the meaning of **s**; the signified of a linguistic sign **s**
'$\underline{s}$'	the communicatively dominant component of a meaning
/s/	the segmental signifier of a linguistic sign **s**
'σ'	a particular semanteme
'$\tilde{\sigma}$'	a particular configuration of semantemes
$\Sigma_{\mathbf{s}}$	the syntactics of a linguistic sign **s**
T	Theme (communicative value)
T$_{\text{DSynt}}$	Deep-Syntactic Theme (communicative value)
T$_{\text{Sem}}$	Semantic Theme (communicative value)
X	a linguistic expression
$*X$	an ungrammatical linguistic expression
$^?X$	an incorrect or dubious linguistic expression
$^{\#}X$	a pragmatically deficient or semantically anomalous linguistic expression
X ⟨Y⟩	Y, a variant of X

X | Y   Y, conditions of use of X
X ⊃ Y   set X includes Y as a subset
X ∩ Y ≠ Λ   sets X and Y have a non-empty intersection
X ∩ Y = Λ   sets X and Y have an empty intersection ⟨= X and Y are disjoint⟩
X ⇔ Y   correspondence between linguistic entities X and Y of two adjacent
                 representation levels ⟨= 'X corresponds to Y and vice versa'⟩
X ≡ Y   X and Y are exactly equivalent
X ≅ Y   X and Y are quasi-equivalent
X → Y   X implies/entails Y ⟨= Y is an implication/entailment of X⟩
$\{x_i\}$ a set of elements x_i
⟨x, y, ..., z⟩   an ordered set of elements x, y, ..., z
⟦'X'⟧   a presupposed semantic component 'X'
//x   a fused element x of the value of a lexical function
x-   a radical or a prefix
-x   a suffix
1, 2, 3   pronominal/verbal person 1, 2, 3
I, II, ..., VI   DSynt-actants **I, II, ..., VI**
Ø   zero sign (= sign whose signifier is empty)
Λ   the empty set
⊕   operation of linguistic union
⚠   directly relevant important information
☞   explanations concerning conventions and notations

Abbreviations

-A   actant
A ⟨= ADJ⟩ adjective (part of speech)
ACC   accusative (grammeme of nominal/adjectival case)
ACT   active (grammeme of verbal voice)
ADV   adverb (part of speech)
APPEND   the **appenditive** deep-syntactic relation
ART   article
ATTR   the **attributive** deep-syntactic relation
CDN   communicatively dominant node (of a semantic configuration)
CLAUS   clausative (part of speech)
colloq.   colloquial (stylistic label)
COMPAR   comparative (grammeme of adjectival/adverbial degree of
           comparison)
compar   comparative (conjunction; value of a syntactic feature)
COORD   the **coordinative** deep-syntactic relation
COND   conditional (grammeme of verbal mood)
CONJ   conjunction (part of speech)
D-   deep (sublevel of linguistic representation)

DAT	dative (grammeme of nominal/adjectival case)
DEF	definite (grammeme of nominal determination)
DET	determiner (syntactic class of lexemes)
DirO	Direct Object
dir-obj	the **direct-objectival** surface-syntactic relation
DSyntA	deep-syntactic actant
DSyntS	deep-syntactic structure
DSynt-AnaphS	deep-syntactic anaphoric structure
DSynt-CommS	deep-syntactic communicative structure
DSynt-ProsS	deep-syntactic prosodic structure
DSyntR	deep-syntactic representation
ECD	*Explanatory Combinatorial Dictionary*
FEM	feminine (a grammeme of adjectival/verbal gender)
fem	feminine (gender; value of a syntactic feature of a noun)
FUT	future (grammeme of verbal tense)
GP	Government Pattern
iff	if and only if
impers	impersonal (value of a syntactic feature)
IND	indicative (grammeme of verbal mood)
IndirO	Indirect Object
indir-obj	the **indirect-objectival** surface-syntactic relation
INDEF	indefinite (grammeme of nominal determination)
INF	infinitive (grammeme of verbal finiteness)
intrans	intransitive (value of a syntactic feature of a verb)
LDOCE	*Longman Dictionary of Contemporary English*
LF	lexical function
LU	lexical unit
lit.	literal
liter.	literary (stylistic label)
MASC	masculine (grammeme of adjectival/verbal gender)
masc	masculine (gender; value of a syntactic feature of a noun)
MTM	Meaning-Text model
MTT	Meaning-Text theory
MWLD	*Merriam-Webster's Learner's Dictionary*
N	noun (part of speech)
NEU	neuter (grammeme of adjectival/verbal gender)
neu	neuter (gender; value of a syntactic feature of a noun)
NOM	nominative (grammeme of nominal/adjectival case)
NUM	cardinal numeral (part of speech)
OblO	Oblique (= Prepositional) Object
obl-obj	the **oblique-objectival** surface-syntactic relation
OED	*Oxford English Dictionary*
PART	participle (grammeme of verbal finiteness)
PASS	passive (grammeme of verbal voice)

PAST	past (grammeme of verbal tense)
PERF	perfective (grammeme of verbal aspect)
pers	personal (value of a syntactic feature)
PL	plural (grammeme of nominal/adjectival/verbal number)
PREP	preposition (part of speech)
PRES	present (grammeme of verbal tense)
pron	pronominal (value of a syntactic feature)
-R	representation (linguistic)
RefS	referential structure
RhetS	rhetorical structure
S-	surface (sublevel of linguistic representation)
-S	structure
Sem-	semantic
SemA	semantic actant
Sem-CommS	semantic-communicative structure
SemS	semantic structure
SemR	semantic representation
SG	singular (grammeme of nominal/adjectival/verbal number)
SSyntA	surface-syntactic actant
SSyntR	surface-syntactic representation
SSyntS	surface-syntactic structure
SyntRel	syntactic relation
SyntR	syntactic representation
subj	the **subjectival** surface-syntactic relation
Synt-	syntactic
trans	transitive (value of a syntactic feature of a verb)
V	verb (part of speech)
vulg.	vulgar (stylistic label)

Fonts

- Linguistic examples are in *italics*
- Textual glosses are in roman and between 'semantic quotes.'
- Interlinear glosses are in roman
- Lexical units are in UPPER CASE: APPLE, LEAVE, FOR, etc.
- Grammemes ⟨= inflectional values⟩ are in UPPER CASE: PAST, PL(URAL), etc.
- Derivatemes are in *HELVETICA ITALICS UPPER CASE*: '*ONE WHO* [does L]' (*read+er* from *read*$_L$, *teach+er* from *teach*$_L$).
- The names of lexical functions are in Courier New: S_0, Magn, Oper$_1$, etc.
- Semantic labels are in Courier New: fact, event, manufactured object, etc.

- At their first mention (and sporadically where it is deemed useful), technical terms are in Helvetica: antonymy, dependency, semanteme, etc.

Lexicographic Numbers

When citing English lexical units, we use, when necessary, lexicographic, or sense-distinguishing, numbers: $BABY_{(N)}\mathbf{1}$, $CHANGE_{(V)}\mathbf{1}$, $FILE_{(N)}\mathbf{3}$, $LIE_{(V)}{}^2\mathbf{1}$, ⌐MAKE SENSE⌐$\mathbf{1}$, etc. For the most part, these numbers are taken from LDOCE Online (www.ldoceonline.com), but with an important modification. Unlike LDOCE, we do not use the numbers in superscript to indicate the part of speech of lexical units; thus, instead of writing LIE^2 for the verb (*to lie through one's teeth*) and LIE^3 for the noun (*to tell lies*), as LDOCE does, we write $LIE_{(V)}{}^2\mathbf{1}$ and $LIE_{(N)}$. We use numbers in superscript exclusively to distinguish homophonous vocables (= phonologically identical but semantically unrelated lexical items), such as $LIE_{(V)}{}^1$ (*I need to lie[1] down.* | *I know where the problem lies[1]2.*) and $LIE_{(V)}{}^2$ (*Don't lie[2]1 to me.* | *Statistics can often lie[2]2.*). At times we also use our own lexicographic numbers (our lexicographic-numbering system will be introduced in Ch. 8, *2.3.2*).

Phonemic/Phonetic Symbols

More or less obvious symbols are not listed.

C′	palatalized consonant C
V̄	long vowel V
Ṽ	nasal vowel V
æ	high-front open unrounded vowel [Eng. *cat*]
c	voiceless alveolar affricate [It. *grazie* 'thanks', Ger. *zwei* 'two']
č	voiceless palatoalveolar affricate [Eng. ***church***]
ð	voiced interdental fricative [Eng. ***the***]
e	mid-front closed unrounded vowel [Fr. *fée* 'fairy']
ɛ	mid-front open unrounded vowel [Fr. *fait* 'fact']
j	voiced palatal fricative [Eng. ***year***]
l	voiced palatal lateral approximant [Sp. ***lluvia*** 'rain', It. *veglio* 'old']
ŋ	voiced velar nasal [Eng. *young*]
ɲ	voiced palatal nasal [Sp. *niña* 'girl', Fr. *peigne* '[a] comb']
o	mid-back closed rounded vowel [Fr. *peau* 'skin']
ɔ	mid-back open rounded vowel [Eng. *law*]
ø	mid-front closed rounded vowel [Fr. *queue* 'tail']
œ	mid-front open rounded vowel [Fr. *cœur* 'heart']
q	voiceless uvular stop
ɾ	voiced alveolar flap [Am. Eng. *rider*]
š	voiceless dental sibilant fricative [Eng. ***shy***]
u	high-back closed rounded vowel
ü	high-front rounded vowel [Fr. *lune* 'moon']
θ	voiceless interdental fricative [Eng. ***think***]
w	voiced rounded labiovelar fricative [Eng. ***we***]
x	voiceless velar fricative [Ger. *Bach* 'stream']
ž	voiced dental sibilant fricative [Eng. *treasure*]
ȝ	voiced palatoalveolar affricate [Eng. *jam*]
ʔ	glottal stop
ʕ	voiceless pharyngeal stop [Arabic *'ain*]

Part I

Fundamentals

1   Semantics in Language and Linguistics

This chapter – together with Ch. 2 – sets the scene for everything that follows. It briefly characterizes semantics and its place in language and general linguistic theory (Section *1*), and then presents the framework of our own approach to semantics, namely, Meaning-Text linguistic theory and its functional models of languages (Section *2*).

1   Semantics and Its Place in Language and Linguistics

The English noun SEMANTICS has its (remote) origin in the Ancient Greek noun SĒMA 'sign', so that, etymologically, *semantics* roughly means 'handling of signs'.[1] (In this book, we will see the root **sem-** on fairly numerous occasions.) Today, the term *semantics* denotes both a specific component of language and the linguistic discipline that studies this component. In most cases the context helps resolve this ambiguity; however, when the context is insufficient, we will use subscripts:

- semantics$_1$ is a component of a particular language;
- semantics$_2$ is a branch of linguistics – that is, a linguistic discipline – that studies different particular semantics$_1$.

---

[1] In its turn, SĒMA goes back to the Proto-Indo-European root ***dheye-** 'see, contemplate' (the asterisk indicates, as is a rule in diachronic linguistics, that this form is not attested in a language, but is reconstructed). This root underlies, among other things, the noun ZEN (as in *Zen Buddhism* – via Sanskrit and Chinese); literally, SĒMA means 'what is seen'.

To characterize semantics as a component of language – that is, semantics$_1$ – we must first characterize the notion of language.

> **Definition 1.1:** Natural Language
> A (natural) language **L** is a set of rules encoded in the brains of its speakers that establish a correspondence between meanings of **L** and their expression, or texts of **L**.

The terms *meanings* and *texts* are used here in a special, technical sense. For the time being, let us say that a meaning is an informational content that can be verbalized in the given language – according to Roman Jakobson, meaning is "something conceivable and translatable." Thus, meaning is understood here in the narrowest way possible – strictly as **linguistic** meaning (on the opposition linguistic [= "shallow"] ~ real [= "deep"] meaning, see Ch. 3, *1.2*). A text is material support for the meaning, a fragment of speech of any length – again, in R. Jakobson's terms, "something immediately perceptible," for instance, an acoustic or graphic string. As for linguistic rules, at this stage you may think of a rule as an instruction telling you how some linguistic items – meanings, words, phrases, speech sounds, etc. – should be manipulated in speech production and understanding. More formally, a linguistic rule is an expression of the form $X \Leftrightarrow Y \mid C$, where X is some content, Y the expression for this content, $\Leftrightarrow$ means 'corresponds to' and C is the set of conditions under which a given correspondence holds. On linguistic rules in general, see Ch. 2, *1.6.2*, and on semantic rules in particular, Subsection *2.3* below.

The correspondence between linguistic meanings and their expression is extremely complex (this will be illustrated in due course) and has to be established in stages that correspond to different language components. Besides semantics, these are syntax (responsible, roughly, for sentence structure), morphology (word structure) and phonology (sound and intonation patterns of words and sentences). The semantic component of language **L** will be called **L**'s semantics$_1$; it fulfills the task of linking the meanings of **L** to the "deepest" form of their expression that could be viewed as the skeleton, or understructure, of future phrases, clauses and sentences (Ch. 2, *2.1*). Thus, a semantics$_1$ is necessarily that of a particular language: semantics$_1$ of English, Russian, Swahili, Nez Perce, etc. (The tasks of semantics$_1$ will be stated in a more precise way in Subsection *2.3*, after some necessary concepts have been introduced.)

Semantics$_2$, on the other hand, is a branch of linguistics that develops the conceptual tools and other formal means necessary to construct the (rules of) semantics$_1$ of individual languages; in other words, semantics$_2$ is general semantics. Semantics$_2$ also deals with questions such as the nature of linguistic meaning, the semantic properties of linguistic units, and types of relations between those units.

NB: The dichotomy "component of language ~ corresponding linguistic discipline" exists at all levels of linguistic description; thus, we distinguish syntax$_{1/2}$, morphology$_{1/2}$ and phonology$_{1/2}$.

To make the distinction "semantics$_1$ ~ semantics$_2$" more tangible, let us see, first, what kinds of questions arise when one studies semantics$_1$, and then compare these with those that come up in semantics$_2$.

If you work on semantics$_1$ of, say, English, you will have to answer questions like these:

- How can a given "simple" (= non-complex) meaning be expressed in English? (By simple meanings, or semantemes, we understand the meanings of lexical units [LUs]; see Ch. 4, *2*.) For instance, how is the meaning 'X takes too much time to do something because X does not want to do it' expressed in this language? Some possible answers: *X drags X's feet* (in doing something); *X is stalling* (something); *X is procrastinating*. The same questions have to be answered in a systematic and coherent way for all simple meanings of English, which are, as we will see later (Ch. 2, *1.6.2*, Footnote 5), about a million!

- What is the meaning of the LU FREAK OUT, as in *I freaked out when I realized that I had bird flu*, and how is this meaning to be represented? Here is a suggestion: 'person X freaks out over fact Y' = 'X becomes very upset, which is caused**1** by fact Y adversely impacting X, this possibly causing**1** X to lose self-control'.[2] Again, the same questions have to be answered for all LUs of English, that is, as we have just said, for about a million of these.

- What other English LUs and expressions is FREAK OUT related to? In what way are they related? For instance, synonymous verbs and expressions: *flip out, lose it, lose one's cool ⟨composure⟩, fly off the handle …*; antonymous verbs and expressions: *keep one's shirt on, keep calm, keep one's cool …*; adjectives characterizing someone who freaked out: *freaked-out, upset, anxious, afraid …*; and so on.

- By what English sentence(s) can a given meaning be expressed? Or, inversely, what is the meaning that a given English sentence expresses?

And this is not the end of the story: in addition to having to provide answers to these and many other similar questions, the researcher must come up with formal rules that model the answers in a sufficiently parsimonious and elegant way. In fact, linguists are supposed – among other things – to formulate the rules that allow for computing the correct expressions for any meaning of English, and vice versa; this includes establishing links not only between LUs and their meanings, but also between English sentences and their meanings – a daunting task, given the fact that the number of possible sentences is infinite.

---

[2] 'Cause**1**' stands for a non-agentive, non-voluntary causation: 'be the cause of'.

But if you work on semantics$_2$ (= general semantics), the questions you will face are very different:

- In terms of which units and which relations can one describe the meaning of a lexical unit or a sentence of any given language?
- How are our semantic descriptions to be structured and organized?
- Which notions are necessary and sufficient to describe semantic phenomena?
- Which substantial and formal constraints should be imposed on semantic descriptions?
- What is the optimal form of rules that associate linguistic meanings to their expressions?

And so on.

 Semantics$_1$ is not "just another component" of a linguistic system: it occupies within it a special place because language is above all a communication tool – that is, a means for conveying meaning.

Meaning properties of linguistic expressions determine in large part their syntactic behavior and influence their morphology. Thus, the meaning of an LU L is predictive of the number of L's semantic actants ($\approx$ obligatory participants in the situation denoted by L), as well as of the collocations it can form (on collocations, see below, *2.2.3*, point 3). For instance, 'catastrophe' is, roughly, 'an event that causes great damage to someone or something'. Therefore, the noun CATASTROPHE must have at least one semantic actant X, which denotes this someone or something that undergoes the catastrophe and which is featured in collocations like *a catastrophe befell ⟨happened to⟩ X* and *X suffered a catastrophe*. At the same time, because the meaning of CATASTROPHE contains the component 'damage', we can expect it to form collocations with intensifiers, like *great ⟨grand, huge⟩ catastrophe*. All this clearly shows that semantics$_1$ has a place of choice within the description of a language.

Consequently, semantics$_2$, which supplies all the tools and terms for dealing with the semantics$_1$ of different languages, constitutes a discipline which is the very foundation of linguistics.

Linguistic semantics$_2$ is a very young science, much younger than linguistics itself, which is fairly young in comparison with most sciences.

REMARK. We are not claiming, of course, that linguistic inquiry started with the advent of linguistics as an autonomous and full-blown discipline. On the contrary: Aristotle's analytic lexicographic definition has been around since the fourth century BC; Panini's description of Sanskrit grammar, still amazing even by today's standards, is about 2500 years old; and Arabic grammarians – among them, for instance, the brilliant Sibawayhi – created a coherent syntactic theory in the eighth century AD; etc. We are just saying that linguistics as a unified science in the modern sense of the word is one of the youngest sciences.

For a long time, linguistics was centered around phonology and morphology, because these disciplines manipulate the most observable, "superficial" data; syntax came to the fore only in the 1940s, and linguistic semantics$_2$ picked up steam a couple of decades later. Semantics$_2$ was first practiced by philosophers and logicians, who to this day continue to be interested in fundamental questions of semantics$_2$, such as the nature of linguistic meaning and its links with thought, meaning expressibility and meaning representation. In fact, formal languages that linguists use today to represent meaning are based on formalisms invented by logicians. Because of the close links between meaning and thought, other sciences – psychology, cognitive science, Artificial Intelligence, and so on – have a vested interest in the study of meaning and, especially, linguistic meaning.

Within linguistics itself, semantics$_2$ was for a long time treated as a poor cousin of other linguistic disciplines, in part because of the extreme complexity of semantic$_1$ data. Today, however, this trend has finally been reversed, and there is an abundance of studies dedicated to various aspects of the discipline. A renewed interest in linguistic meaning has drawn linguists towards the study of the meaning of words, i.e., lexical semantics. This in turn has given a new impetus to lexicology, the linguistic discipline that studies LUs of a language in their semantic and syntactic aspects. Since a set of all lexical descriptions for a given language constitutes a dictionary of this language, it is only normal that linguists have started paying more attention to lexicography, whose task is to compile dictionaries. This expansion of modern semantics is due to the fact that its role has been strengthened by certain major applications of linguistics: on the one hand, natural language processing (e.g., machine translation and automatic text generation) and on the other hand, language learning and teaching. This is quite understandable: in both domains, the main objective is the transmission of meaning.

There is currently a plurality of approaches to semantics: Formal Semantics, Generative Semantics, Cognitive Semantics, Frame Semantics and Natural Semantic Metalanguage, to mention just the most current ones. They make use of very different conceptual tools, which are not easily "intertranslatable." We cannot offer here an overview of these differences and will limit ourselves to presenting a single point of view: that of Meaning-Text theory. However, we will provide pointers towards, and cursory comparisons with, approaches similar to our own.

2 Doing Semantics with Meaning-Text Linguistic Theory

We could succinctly characterize Meaning-Text linguistic theory [MTT] by laying out two of its crucial properties:

- It is synthesis-oriented – that is, it aims at speech production (rather than speech understanding); as a result, MTT concentrates on the description of how meaning is expressed by the corresponding texts. (For more on this, see Subsection *2.2.3* below.)
- It is dependency-based – that is, all semantic and syntactic representations it uses are conceived in terms of dependency relations (see Ch. 2, *1.3*).

MTT is a framework for the construction of functional models of languages, with a strong formal flavor, implying recourse to various formalisms: semantic networks, syntactic trees, lexical functions, paraphrasing rules, and so on. It has good potential for applications in natural language processing and language learning and teaching.

We will start by presenting the basic tenets of the Meaning-Text theory and the architecture of its language models (*2.1* & *2.2*); we will then restate in a formal way the tasks of semantics₁, informally described above (*2.3*); we will conclude by situating Meaning-Text linguistic models within an overall model of human linguistic behavior (*2.4*).

2.1   Language as Meaning-Text Correspondence

From a functional viewpoint, language allows a speaker to express meanings by texts and, conversely, to extract meanings from texts. We can say that language establishes a correspondence between a set of meanings and a set of texts; this statement can be represented as follows (curly brackets "{ ... }" symbolize a set; see Appendix, *1*):

Language correspondence

$$\{\text{Meanings}\} \underset{\text{language}}{\Longleftrightarrow} \{\text{Texts}\}$$

Language correspondence is bi-directional. If considered in the direction from meaning to text, we are dealing with linguistic synthesis, or speech production: {Meanings} ⟹ {Texts}. And if the correspondence is considered in the opposite direction, we are looking at analysis, or speech comprehension: {Texts} ⟹ {Meanings}. Linguistic synthesis and analysis correspond, respectively, to the activity of the two participants of the speech act: the Speaker and the Addressee.

 The noun SPEAKER is ambiguous: 'someone who speaks language **L**' and 'someone who is speaking (now)' ≈ 'someone who is saying this'. To distinguish these two senses, we will write *Speaker* with the capital *S* when we wish to name the main participant of a speech act – 'someone who is saying this'. (The same holds for *Addressee*.)

The meaning ~ text correspondence has a very important property which determines the structure of language and, consequently, the structure of linguistics.

> **NON-UNIVOCITY OF LANGUAGE CORRESPONDENCE**
> The correspondence {Meanings} ⇔ {Texts} is not a one-to-one correspondence: a meaning can correspond to several texts, and a text can correspond to several meanings.

Two simple illustrations:

(1) a. **Meaning**: 'individual living permanently in Montreal'
⇔ **Text 1**: [*an*] *inhabitant of Montreal*
⇔ **Text 2**: [*a*] *Montrealer*

b. **Meaning**: 'I ask you to give me some salt' [at the table, during a meal]
⇔ **Text 1**: *Could you pass (me) the salt?*
⇔ **Text 2**: *Pass the salt, please.*
⇔ **Text 3**: *The salt, please.*

(2) a. **Text**: *window*
⇔ **Meaning 1**: 'opening in the outer wall of a room, designed for letting in light and air'
⇔ **Meaning 2**: 'part of the image on a computer screen, designed for displaying data of a certain type'

b. **Text**: *Giant poster sale* [on a sign advertising a sale]
⇔ **Meaning 1**: 'a sale of very large posters'
⇔ **Meaning 2**: 'a very large sale of posters'

The above examples illustrate two basic phenomena observed in natural languages: synonymy (1a–b) and equinomy (2a–b). Synonymy is the relation between two linguistic expressions that have the same meaning but different physical forms; equinomy is the relation between two linguistic expressions that have different meanings but the same physical form (see Ch. 9, *2.4*, Definition 9.8).

> **NB:** Instead of speaking of two equinomous expressions **E** and **E′**, in linguistic literature it is more current to say that the expression **E** is ambiguous between two meanings '**E**' and '**E′**'; this is actually an abbreviation for *expression **E**'s signifier coincides with the signifier of another expression, **E′**, whose meaning '**E′**' is different from '**E**'*. Unlike synonymy and equinomy, ambiguity is not a relation: it is a property of an expression that corresponds alternatively to more than one meaning; this is why we need the new term of *equinomy*. However, alongside *equinomy*/*equinomous expressions*, we will use the terms *ambiguity*/*ambiguous expression* for their familiarity and commodity. Note that equinomy covers both homonymy and polysemy (Ch. 6,

1.3.1): if two expressions have identical signifiers and different signifieds (that is, if they are equinomous), their signifieds can be either unrelated, in which case the expressions in question are homonymous, or related, in which case they are polysemous.

Synonymy and equinomy, in conjunction with other factors which will be addressed later, make the study of language extremely complex.

Let us now see how linguistics sets out to model, from an MTT viewpoint, the correspondence characterized above.

2.2   Modeling Meaning-Text Correspondence

We will start by discussing the method favored by the Meaning-Text approach for describing the aforesaid language correspondence: namely, the construction of functional models of language (*2.2.1*). Then we will underscore the stratificational (= multi-stratal) character of these models, in particular that of the Meaning-Text Model (*2.2.2*). We will conclude by invoking the reasons for which Meaning-Text modeling of language adopts linguistic synthesis as the preferred direction – i.e., the viewpoint of the Speaker rather than that of the Addressee (*2.2.3*).

2.2.1   Functional Models of Language

The meanings and texts of a given language are directly accessible to its speakers: meanings are accessible thanks to introspection (ideally, a speaker knows what he wants to say), and texts – thanks to perception. Therefore, meanings and texts constitute linguistic data, language facts observed by linguists and used by them in order to construct their model and check its functioning.

Let us emphasize the following crucial fact:

> Linguistics does not study meanings and texts in their psychoneurological and physical reality; rather, it studies their symbolic representations, written in terms of different formal languages (Appendix, *4*), which reflect different aspects of linguistic phenomena under study (see below, *2.2.2*).

A representation of the studied object must be isomorphic (Appendix, *3.3*) to this object in the relevant aspect(s); this means that the elements of the representation must entertain the same relations among themselves as the corresponding source elements of the represented object. (We will have more to say on this topic in Ch. 9, *1.3* & *2.4.4* and Ch. 10, *2.2*.) As will be seen below, modern linguistics makes use of different formal representational languages, such as semantic networks, syntactic trees, morphological/phonological/phonetic strings, etc.

> REMARK. All sciences have recourse to symbolic representations, and symbolic representations are also widely used in everyday life. For instance, one can buy and sell gold without possessing or even seeing the actual bullion but by means of certificates that stand for it.

The representation of language correspondence given at the beginning of Section *2* can now be made more precise:

LANGUAGE CORRESPONDENCE (bis)

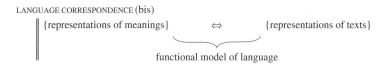

{representations of meanings}   ⇔   {representations of texts}

functional model of language

While meanings and texts are directly accessible to speakers, the correspondence between them – the rules which link them and which constitute language proper – is not: speakers are entirely unconscious of language rules and unable to "exteriorize" them (unless they are specially trained to do so). Therefore, the only way linguists have to describe this correspondence is to **simulate** it by means of a logical device – a system of rules written by them. This device must be able to do the same thing a speaker does: on the one hand, it must produce, for a given meaning, all possible texts which carry this meaning and are thus more or less synonymous; on the other hand, the device must extract from a given text the meaning it encodes (or the meanings, if the text is ambiguous). This device is called a linguistic model. So a model of language **L** is made up of rules (written by the researcher) that establish correspondences between representations of meanings of **L** and of texts of **L** (and vice versa), in the same way speakers of **L** do.

The system of rules that constitute a linguistic model has two important properties.

- First, this is a symbolic, or abstract, model (as opposed to a "physical" model, such as an airplane model used as a child's toy, for instance). A symbolic model manipulates symbols and symbols only; it is this type of model that interests us in this textbook. This very important notion of symbolic model has been borrowed from hard sciences like physics, chemistry and cosmology, on the one hand, and economy, geology and biology, on the other; cf. the model of the atom, of the universe, of the economic development of a country, etc.
- Second, the use of such models is characteristic of hypothetical-deductive approaches: starting from a certain number of postulates about language, a model is constructed which simulates the way the language functions. Thus,

one of the postulates of our linguistic model is that language ensures the correspondence between meanings and texts (as explained above).

A model of language **L** must be built in such a way that its validity – that is, its capacity to take into account all observable data of **L** – can be confirmed or invalidated; in other words, the model must be falsifiable. For instance, the model would be falsified if, because of a missing or imprecise rule, it produced an incorrect – unacceptable – text from a given correct meaning. This would force the researcher to "go back to the drawing board" and correct the error.

Thanks to functional models, linguistics acquires an experimental aspect. Thus, it is possible to test a model, for instance, by having it produce sentences for the selected meanings and then analyzing the results.

2.2.2   The Stratificational Character of Language Models

In principle, it is possible to conceive of a linguistic model whose rules would directly link meanings to texts; however, such rules would be prohibitively complex, in particular because of synonymy and equinomy. Let us consider the reasons for this, from the viewpoint of linguistic synthesis.

On the one hand, as we already know, a given meaning can give rise to several more or less synonymous texts. On the other hand, producing each of those individual texts takes several distinct operations, each highly complex in its turn. Thus, the Speaker must: (1) choose the words which correspond well to the meaning that he wants to express; (2) arrange these words in an appropriate linear order; (3) inflect them (e.g., put nouns in the singular or the plural, the verbs in the right mood and tense, etc.); (4) stress them; (5) supply the string of words thus obtained with appropriate pauses and intonations; and, finally, (6) pronounce them correctly.

The task of the Speaker is Herculean! And so is the task of a linguist who wants to describe language correspondence.

In order to reduce the complexity of language description, most modern linguistic approaches use stratificational models. A stratificational model presupposes several levels of linguistic representation, and its rules are organized in a modular fashion: each representation level reflects a specific aspect of the organization of a verbal message, and the rules of the same nature are grouped into sets of manageable size, called modules, which operate between representations of adjacent levels. This allows the linguist to proceed step by step and take the difficulties inherent to text synthesis (and analysis) one at a time. An outline of a typical stratificational linguistic model is given in *Figure 1.1*:

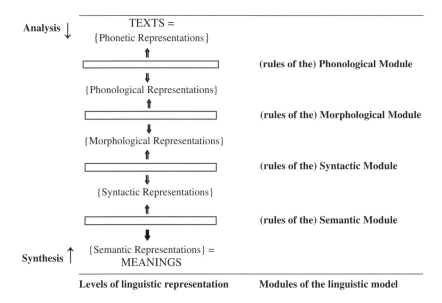

Figure 1.1 A stratificational linguistic model of the Meaning-Text type (abridged view)

Let us characterize the representations and modules of a linguistic model.

1. The semantic representation [SemR] describes the meanings of verbal messages. A (complex enough) meaning represented by means of a SemR can be expressed by several synonymous or near-synonymous sentences. To put it differently, a SemR always represents a family of more or less synonymous sentences, i.e., paraphrases.[3] (This is why the expression *the SemR of this (individual) sentence* is, strictly speaking, inaccurate.)
2. The syntactic representation [SyntR] reflects the organization of a sentence corresponding to the starting SemR in terms of hierarchical relations between the words it is made up of (closer to the surface, the words will be grouped into phrases and clauses).
3. The morphological representation [MorphR] specifies the linear arrangement of clause elements, i.e., linear order of individual words, appropriately inflected and organized into prosodic groups.
4. The phonological representation [PhonR] shows the organization of the sounds of the sentence: phonemes (a phoneme being a set of non-distinctive

---

[3] Other linguistic representations are also representations of families of synonymous sentences, but the number of synonymous sentences on higher (= closer-to-surface) levels is much smaller: the closer we are to the surface, the lesser the variability of linguistic forms.

phones, i.e., language sounds), and prosodemes (a prosodeme is a set of non-distinctive prosodies, i.e., stresses, intonations and pauses). This representation is traditionally called phonological, or broad, transcription.

5. The phonetic representation [PhonetR] represents the organization of the acoustic aspect of the sentence in terms of phones, symbols of real sounds, and prosodies, symbols of real stresses, intonations and pauses. This is actually a phonetic, or narrow, transcription.

The formalisms for writing linguistic representations are graphs of particular types: the SemR is a network (= a connected, directed and labeled graph), the SyntR is a tree (= a network subjected to additional constraints), while the MorphR, the PhonR and the PhonetR are strings (= trees subjected to additional constraints). These formalisms, further described in Ch. 2, *1.6.1*, are illustrated in *Figure 1.2*; the letters labeling the nodes of the graphs represent linguistic entities – semantemes, lexical units, morphemes, or phonemes, and the labels of the arcs are the dependency relations (Ch. 2, *1.3*) holding between linguistic units.

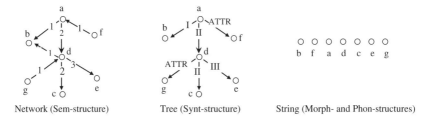

Network (Sem-structure)   Tree (Synt-structure)   String (Morph- and Phon-structures)

Figure 1.2 Basic formalisms used to write linguistic representations

Let us now turn to the task that each of the four modules of a linguistic model is supposed to fulfill:

• The semantic module, or semantics, establishes a correspondence between SemRs (= the meanings) and SyntRs, constructing, for a given SemR, all SyntRs that correspond to it (that is, are capable of expressing it).

• The syntactic module, or syntax, establishes a correspondence between SyntRs and MorphRs, constructing, for a given SyntR, all MorphRs that correspond to it.

• The morphological module, or morphology, establishes a correspondence between MorphRs and Phon(ological)Rs, constructing, for a given MorphR, all PhonRs which correspond to it.

• The phonological module, or phonology, establishes a correspondence between PhonRs and PhonetRs (= the texts), producing, for a given PhonR, all corresponding PhonetRs.

This modular organization of rules corresponds to traditionally recognized levels of language organization. These are the four basic components of language that are the object of synchronic linguistics:[4]

SEMANTICS – SYNTAX – MORPHOLOGY – PHONOLOGY

> REMARK. Phonetics, which describes the correspondence between PhonetRs and real sounds and deals with physical (articulatory and acoustic) aspects of speech, lies beyond the limits of linguistic study proper. It represents one of the two interfaces of the linguistic model with other models of human linguistic behavior, the second interface being that which models the transition "conceptual representations ⇔ meaning representations." For more on this interface, which is the domain of so-called conceptics, see Subsection *2.4*.

In *Figure 1.1* we have represented a typical stratificational linguistic model; the concrete model that we will adopt in this book – the Meaning-Text Model – is even more stratified, in two respects.

• First, a Meaning-Text Model [MTM] recognizes, at each major representational level except the semantic one, two sublevels called deep and surface. Thus, there is a deep-syntactic representation and a surface-syntactic representation, and so on. A **deep sublevel** is oriented towards the meaning – that is, towards the content the Speaker wants to express; its task is to explicitly reflect the relevant informational distinctions. A **surface sublevel** is oriented towards the text – that is, towards the form in which the content is expressed; its task is to explicitly reflect all relevant formal distinctions. Here is an illustration of how this works at the syntactic level of representation. At the deep-syntactic sublevel, the choice has to be made between major syntactic constructions; for instance, the sentences *The President **decided** to accept the proposal* vs. *The President **made a decision** to accept the proposal*, while having the same semantic structure, have different deep-syntactic structures. At the surface-syntactic sublevel, the choice concerns the specific formal means to implement a syntactic construction; for instance, the phrases *the decision **by the President*** vs. *the **Presidential** decision* have the same deep-syntactic structure, but different surface-syntactic structures.

This architecture of an MTM is designed to ensure the best possible interface between utterance representations of different levels and, therefore, maximally simplify the transitions between them. An MTM thus presupposes seven levels of representation: SemR, Deep- and Surface-SyntR, Deep- and Surface-MorphR, Deep- and Surface-PhonR. Accordingly, it contains

---

[4] While synchronic linguistics studies language "here and now," diachronic linguistics studies its historical development. In this book we are concerned exclusively with synchronic semantics.

six modules, or sets of rules: semantics, deep syntax, surface syntax, deep morphology, surface morphology, deep phonology.

- Second, each of the seven representations is a set of formal objects, called structures, comprising a basic structure, which reflects the central linguistic entity of the given level, and peripheral structures, which supply additional information – communicative, prosodic, stylistic, etc. – about the basic structure. Formally, a linguistic representation [-R] of a given level appears as an ordered set (Appendix, *1*) of structures [-S]:

$$R = \langle _{basic}S, \,_{peripheral}S_1, \,_{peripheral}S_2, \,..., \,_{peripheral}S_n \rangle.$$

This abstract formula will be made more concrete as we go along.

2.2.3   Language Modeling from Meaning to Text: Primacy of the Speaker

The correspondence between meanings and texts is bi-directional and can be described either in the direction of linguistic synthesis (from meaning to text) or in the direction of linguistic analysis (from text to meaning). These two ways of describing language are logically equivalent; however, there are many reasons, provided by language itself, to prefer linguistic synthesis – i.e., the viewpoint of the Speaker. Here are three of these reasons.

1   Language itself has a preference for the viewpoint of the Speaker
To realize this, one needs only consider some well-known properties of natural languages.

First, all languages have a word meaning 'to speak', while virtually none has a special word with the meaning 'to understand speech' (the verb meaning 'understand' applies to understanding of anything).

Second, in language **L**, to express the meaning 'be a speaker of **L**', one says *speak* **L**, rather that *understand* **L**: *speak English*, Fr. *parler français*, Rus. *govorit´ po-russki*.[5] Moreover, these expressions are often idiomatic: cf. Fr. *parler français*, but *comprendre le français* 'understand the French' ⟨*comprendre français*⟩ or Fr. *dire en français* 'say in French' ⟨*dire français*⟩.

---

[5] This is not universally true: some languages express the meaning 'use language …' by verbs meaning 'hear', 'know' or 'understand'. Thus:

(i) Ewe (Ghana; ⌜*sè ... gòmè*⌝ is an idiom meaning 'understand')

Nyè+mé +**sè**	*Èvè+gbè*	*o,*	*gake*	*mè+***sè**	*nyà*	*si*	*nè+gblɔ*	*la*	*gòmè*
1SG NEG **hear**	Ewe language	NEG	but	1SG **hear**	word	which	2SG say	DEF	under

'I don't speak Ewe, but I understood what you said'.

(ii) Georgian: *Kartuli icit?* lit. 'Georgian you$_{PL}$.know?'

(iii) Necaxa Totonac (Mexico): *Wix katzīya? tutunaku?* 'You$_{SG}$ know Totonac?'

(iv) Eastern Penan (Borneo): *Iah jam ha' Penan* 'He/she understands language Penan'.

1. Angular brackets "⟨ … ⟩" indicate either an ordered set, as above, *2.2.2*, p. 16, or variants: $X ⟨Y⟩$ means that Y is a variant of X.
2. The symbol "*" (= asterisk) preceding an expression means that this expression is incorrect.

Third, the lexical meaning 'I' and the configuration of grammatical meanings FIRST-PERSON, SINGULAR [1.SG] have a special status in all languages of the world: the Speaker has a much more prominent role than the Addressee (second person), and even more so than the non-participant in the speech act (third person). The meaning 'I' and the semantic grammmemic configuration 1.SG have many special properties, which they do not share with any other semantic configuration. Therefore, the following hierarchy of pronominal persons and numbers can be established:

$$1.SG > 1.NON\text{-}SG > 2 > 3$$

This hierarchy has various manifestations in the lexical stock, as well as in the grammar, of a language. Thus, all languages have lexical signs whose signified includes an obligatory reference to the Speaker: **I** 'person who says *I*' (that is, the author of this speech act), **here** 'place where I am when I say *here*', **now** 'the moment when I say *now*', etc. Signs of this type, known as shifters (Jespersen 1923: 12; Jakobson 1957 [1971]), play a very important role, in particular in the structuring of inflectional categories (Ch. 2, *3.2.1*). In contrast, there are no linguistic signs whose meaning has to be defined exclusively with respect to the Addressee. More than this, it is the Speaker who identifies his Addressee by calling him **you** – which means that the meaning 'you' is based on the meaning 'I'. Or, to take an example from grammar, in Japanese and some other languages, the verbs denoting interior physiological or psychological states of a person – such as 'be.hungry', 'be.afraid', 'need', 'want' – can be used in declarative sentences only in the first-person singular, since it is only I who can know whether I am hungry, etc. Thus, a Japanese speaker cannot construct a sentence meaning literally 'She needs to leave' (he can without any problems produce a sentence with the meaning 'I need to leave'); instead, he has to add to the verb in the third person the suffix **-gar-**, meaning 'show the signs of' (so that 'She needs to leave' becomes in Japanese literally '≈ She seems to need to leave').

2   Text synthesis is a more linguistic task than text analysis
Linguistic synthesis, at least in an ideal case, requires only that the Speaker, who possesses all the information necessary to construct his text, use his linguistic knowledge – i.e., knowledge having to do exclusively with the way he manipulates language. In contrast, given the vagueness and ambiguity of the majority of texts, analysis requires that the Addressee not only have this same linguistic knowledge, but also extralinguistic knowledge: real-world

knowledge, logical capacities, common sense, etc. In other words, if we want to focus on linguistic problems as such, it is preferable to study language from the viewpoint of text synthesis.

Caution: We do not claim that the greater logical complexity of linguistic analysis with respect to synthesis necessarily corresponds to a greater psychological complexity of speech understanding with respect to speech production. We reserve our judgment on the issue.

3   Some linguistic phenomena can be better observed from the viewpoint of synthesis

This is the case, for example, with collocations, expressions of a particular type to be considered later (Ch. 4, *2.2.2.1*, Ch. 6, *2* and Ch. 7, *2.2*), which we will illustrate for the time being with three examples: ***make** a mistake*, ***do** a favor*, ***take** a walk*. Collocations, which are very frequent in texts, are much more difficult to produce than to understand. A foreigner learning English could easily erroneously say, for instance, **do a mistake, *make a favor, *launch a party* or **throw an air-raid*, but he would have no difficulty in grasping the meaning of the correct expressions. This shows that the relevance and difficulty of the study of collocations becomes obvious only if we adopt the perspective "from meaning to text."

> As a result, in this book, we will describe all semantic phenomena starting from meaning, rather than from text.

Put succinctly, the central question in our approach to language is *How can the meaning 'σ' be expressed in language **L**?*, rather than *What can a text T of **L** mean?* An important corollary of this way of seeing things is that synonymy has a central place in our descriptions, while equinomy (or ambiguity) is left aside.

2.3   Tasks of the Semantic Module of a Meaning-Text Linguistic Model

As a component, or module, of language **L**, semantics$_1$ is responsible for the first phase of the "meaning $\Rightarrow$ text" correspondence. More precisely:

> Semantics$_1$ links each complex meaning of **L** to an initial form of its linguistic expression – the syntactic structure of future phrases, clauses and sentences.

In technical terms, semantics$_1$ consists of a lexicon (descriptions of all lexical units of **L**) and a grammar (a specific subset of grammatical rules of **L**). A Meaning-Text model of semantics$_1$ operates with a dictionary of a particular type, called an *Explanatory Combinatorial Dictionary*, or ECD (described in Ch. 8, *2*). Using the information on LUs stored in the ECD, the grammar establishes a correspondence between a given semantic representation and all deep-syntactic representations of sentences that express the meaning encoded by this semantic representation (these two representations will be considered, respectively, in Ch. 10 and Ch. 11); this is illustrated symbolically in *Figure 1.3*.

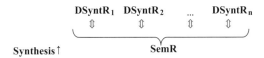

Figure 1.3 Linguistic representations serving as the input and the output of the semantic module of an MTM

Formally speaking, there are two basic linguistic rule types: transition, or correspondence, rules, operating between fragments of representations of adjacent levels, and equivalence, or paraphrasing, rules, operating between fragments of representations belonging to the same level (for a substantive classification of the rules, see Ch. 12, *Figure 12.2*, p. 311). Schematically, the structure of a Meaning-Text semantic module looks like *Figure 1.4*.

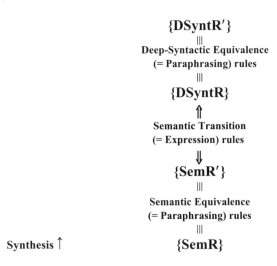

Figure 1.4 Semantic module of an MTM

By way of illustration, we will give the relevant representations and some of the semantic rules involved in the production of sentences (3a–c), which are mutual paraphrases. All the representations and rules shown are maximally simplified, and the way they are constructed is not explained (there will be plenty of time for this later!); this first illustration is just to help the reader get the gist of the approach.

(3) a. *This noise makes me unable to think.*
     b. *This noise prevents me from thinking.*
     c. *Because of this noise I am not able to think.*

The Semantic Structure serving as a starting point for the synthesis of these – and many other – sentences, henceforth the initial SemS, is given in the left-hand part of *Figure 1.5*.

The initial SemS represents the core propositional meaning of the above sentences, or their semantic invariant (Ch. 3, *1.1*). Taking the semanteme 'cause1' as the starting point, the initial SemS reads literally as follows: 'this noise causes1 that I am not able to think [about something], the moment of causing1 being now'.[6]

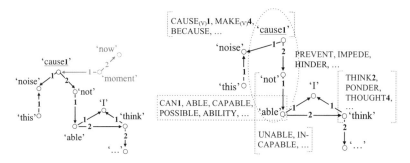

Figure 1.5 The initial SemS of the underlying sentences in (3) and some of its possible lexicalizations

This is a fairly simple, rather "shallow" SemS, which nonetheless offers many realization possibilities, as shown in the right-hand part of *Figure 1.5*.

> **NB:** Some of these potential realizations are not exactly synonymous (THINK2 and PONDER do not mean exactly the same thing, nor do PREVENT and HINDER, etc.) and thus give rise to approximate (a.k.a. near- or quasi-)paraphrases; see below for examples. In our approach such paraphrases are not only allowed, but indeed preferred over exact paraphrases, since they represent the paraphrase type most frequently used in actual language production. For a typology of paraphrases, see Ch. 9, *2.1.2*.

Concrete lexicalizations (roughly, selection of LUs and phrases expressing semantemes and their configurations) and the corresponding arborizations (selection of syntactic constructions forming the skeletons of future sentences) depend crucially on the communicative orientation the Speaker wants to give to the initial SemS – in the first place, on what he wants to present

---

[6] The meaning configuration 'the moment of causing1 being now', to be implemented as verbal inflection (present tense), will be omitted from the subsequent semantic representations.

as the Rheme ($\approx$ comment, or what is communicated), and what he wants to present as the Theme ($\approx$ topic, or what the Rheme is stated about) of his message.

Before we start describing the production of the selected sentences, it is worth indicating some other potential realizations of the initial SemS:

(4) a. *This noise impedes my thinking.*
     b. *This noise hinders my ability to think.*
     c. *This noise makes it impossible for me to think.*
     d. *Because of this noise it is impossible for me to think*
     e. *Because of this noise it is not possible for me to think.*
     f. *Because of this noise I cannot think.*

These are fairly close paraphrases of sentences (3a–c); for comparison, here are some more remote ones, whose SemSs are different from the initial SemS (albeit quasi-equivalent):

(5) a. *With such noise, how am I even supposed to think?*
     b. *With this kind of noise, thinking is not an option ⟨you can forget about thinking⟩.*
     c. *It's so noisy here my brain just isn't working.*

This abundance of realizations of a relatively simple semantic structure illustrates what we call the paraphrastic potential of our meaning representations (Ch. 10, *1:* 258 & *4.2*).

Generally speaking, the semantic part of the synthesis of a sentence proceeds in four stages:

1. Construction of the initial semantic representation [SemR], by pairing the initial SemS with a semantic-communicative structure [Sem-CommS], which traces the Speaker's "itinerary" through the propositional semantic space of the initial SemS. In our examples, the Sem-CommS consists of the rhematic ~ thematic division of the initial SemS, with the indication, in each division, of the communicatively dominant node (Ch. 10, *3.1.1*), i.e., the semanteme which sums up the meaning of the entire division and is its "minimal paraphrase."

2. Meaning-preserving modifications of the initial SemR, which may include expansions/reductions of the initial SemS or the removal/addition of some semantemes, as well as changing some parameters of the Sem-CommS. These operations are performed by semantic (quasi-)equivalence rules, i.e., semantic paraphrasing rules; their result is a "pre-lexicalized" semantic representation, called reduced SemR, which is mapped onto the deep-syntactic representation [DSyntR].

3. Construction of the deep-syntactic representation for the sentence under production.

NB: To simplify our discussion, we will show only how the basic structure of the DSyntR – the deep-syntactic structure [DSyntS] – is constructed.

The main operations involved here are the previously mentioned lexicalization and arborization, performed by semantic transition rules: in a nutshell, these rules map semantemes onto deep LUs, and "translate" semantic and communicative dependency relations into deep-syntactic dependency relations.

4. Once the DSyntS of the sentence is constructed, it may be subject to meaning-preserving modifications by means of paraphrasing rules, which perform (quasi-)synonymic substitutions of specific lexical-syntactic configurations in the DSyntS, based on lexical relations such as synonymy, antonymy, nominalization, etc.

Let us now see how these operations are applied in the synthesis of sentences (3a–c).

☞ $\mathbf{R_{Sem}}$ and $\mathbf{T_{Sem}}$ stand for Semantic Rheme and Semantic Theme, respectively; the communicatively dominant node [CDN] of $\mathbf{R_{Sem}}/\mathbf{T_{Sem}}$ is underscored; the shading indicates a   lexicalization zone   – that is, the semanteme configuration earmarked to be realized as one LU.

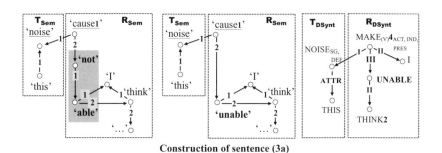

Construction of sentence (3a)

Figure 1.6 Partial representations of sentence (3a) manipulated by the semantic module of an MTM

The initial SemR of sentence (3a) (*This noise makes me unable to think.*) has 'this–1→noise' as its $\mathbf{T_{Sem}}$, the rest of its SemS being the $\mathbf{R_{Sem}}$, with 'cause1' as the CDN. (The sentence is an appropriate answer to the underlying question "What about this noise?"; on underlying questions as a means of eliciting the semantic theme of an utterance, see Ch. 10, *3.1.2.1*.) The semanteme configuration 'not–1→able' in $\mathbf{R_{Sem}}$ is marked as a possible lexicalization zone.

The reduced SemR of our sentence is constructed using the following expansion/reduction semantic paraphrasing rule (Ch. 12, *2.1.1.1*), a part of the lexicographic definition of the lexeme UNABLE (the rule is applied from right to left):

'[X is] unable [to do Y]' = '[X is] not able [to do Y]'

Here we see a semantic configuration (in the SemS of the sentence under synthesis) being matched with the signified of an LU (described in the dictionary), namely UNABLE, which will be selected for insertion into the DSyntS of the sentence.

Now semantic transition rules take over to build the DSyntS of sentence (3a). Lexicalization rules (see Ch. 12, *1.1*) finish semanteme-to-lexeme mappings (note the distinctive lexicographic numbers accompanying some lexemes): 'cause**1**' $\Leftrightarrow$ MAKE$_{(V)}$**4**; 'unable' $\Leftrightarrow$ UNABLE; etc. Arborization rules (Ch. 12, *1.3*) select MAKE$_{(V)}$**4**, the image of the CDN of the $\mathbf{R_{Sem}}$ of the Reduced SemR of (3a), as the top node of the DSynt-tree and construct the branches of the tree. For example, one such rule treats the semantic relation **1** and matches it, under specific conditions, to the deep-syntactic relation **I** (the future syntactic subject or the adnominal complement); see the transition 'cause**1**–**1**→noise' $\Leftrightarrow$ MAKE$_{(V)}$**4**–**I**→NOISE between the reduced SemR and DSyntS of (3a). Another arborization rule takes this same semantic relation and "translates" it, of course under a set of different conditions, into the deep-syntactic **ATTR(IBUTIVE)** relation; this is what we see in the transition 'this–**1**→noise' $\Leftrightarrow$ THIS←**ATTR**–NOISE above. And so forth.

Note that a DSyntS contains only full LUs, thus excluding structural (= syntactically induced) LUs. For this reason, the preposition TO introducing the complement of the adjective UNABLE does not appear in the DSyntS of (3a). (The same is true also for all syntactically induced inflectional values, such as verbal person/number, for instance.)

Suppose that (for whatever reason) we want to reformulate sentence (3a); we can do this, for example, by applying to the node UNABLE in its DSyntS the following, very simple, lexical-syntactic paraphrasing rule (Ch. 12, *2.2*), stating that any LU L can be replaced by its synonym:

L ≡ Syn(L).

This rule allows us to replace UNABLE$_{[L]}$ by INCAPABLE$_{[Syn(L)]}$; the resulting DSyntS, minimally different from that of sentence (3a), will be implemented by the sentence *This noise makes me **incapable**$_{[Syn(UNABLE)]}$ of thinking*.

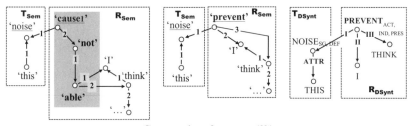

Construction of sentence (3b)

Figure 1.7 Representations of sentence (3b) manipulated by the semantic module of an MTM

The initial SemR of sentence (3b) (*This noise prevents me from thinking.*) is identical to that of sentence (3a), except that here a different semanteme configuration within the **R_Sem**, 'cause1–2→not–1→able', is marked as a potential lexicalization zone. That is, we are now looking for a single lexical meaning that matches this specific semanteme configuration. A good candidate appears to be 'prevent', whose decomposition is given in the left-hand part of *Figure 1.8*; the right-hand part of *Figure 1.8* shows how this decomposition fits the initial SemR of sentence (3b).

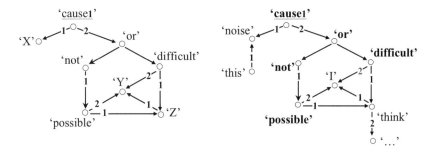

Figure 1.8 Decomposition of the semanteme 'prevent' and its matching with the initial SemR of (3b)

This is not an exact match: the semanteme 'prevent', whose decomposition literally reads as 'X causes1 that Z(Y) is difficult or impossible for Y', is richer than the meaning configuration present in the initial SemR; plus, it contains the semanteme 'possible', quasi-conversive with respect to 'able': '[to do Z is] possible [for Y]' ≅ '[Y is] able [to do Z]'. These are, however, acceptable differences, which do not alter the initial meaning too much. Therefore, the configuration 'cause1–2→not–1→able' in the initial SemR of (3b) is replaced by 'prevent' to construct the reduced SemR of this sentence, which is then treated by transition semantic rules similar to those mentioned in the preceding example, eventually yielding DSyntS of (3b).

If we wanted to reformulate sentence (3b), we could use, among others, the following lexical-syntactic paraphrasing rule (for the precise formulation of the rule, see Ch. 12, *2.2.2.2*):

$$L \equiv \texttt{Anti}(L) + NOT$$

This rule describes an antonymic substitution; it specifies that an LU L can be replaced (in the DSyntS) by a lexical configuration consisting of this L's antonym and the negative lexeme NOT. In our case, the rule allows for the substitution *prevent ~ not allow*$_{[\texttt{Anti}(PREVENT)]}$; see *Figure 1.9*.

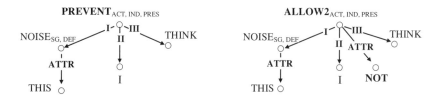

Figure 1.9 DSyntS of sentence (3b) and an equivalent DSyntS

Other examples of the application of this rule: *stay ~ not leave*; *condone ~ not oppose*; *disobey ~ not obey*; etc.

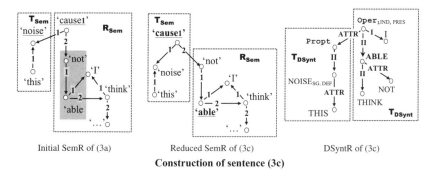

Construction of sentence (3c)

Figure 1.10 Representations of sentence (3c) manipulated by the semantic module of an MTM

The construction of sentence (3c) (*Because of this noise I am not able to think.*) starts from the initial SemR of sentence (3a), which undergoes two modifications.

1. A communicative restructuring takes place (by application of a semantic-communicative quasi-equivalence rule that we will not cite here): the

boundary between **T**$_\text{Sem}$ and **R**$_\text{Sem}$ is moved in such a way that 'cause1' becomes the CDN of the **T**$_\text{Sem}$ and 'able' the CDN of the **R**$_\text{Sem}$. Sentence (3c) is therefore an approximate communicative paraphrase of the other two sentences; it answers a different underlying question: "What effects does this noise have on you?" In the transition towards the DSyntS of (3c), this modification of the communicative structure triggers the inversion of subordination (or head switching) with respect to the DSyntS of sentence (3a); cf. *make* ['cause1 to be']–I→*unable* ~ *be.unable*–ATTR→*because* ['caused by...'].

2. The semantemes 'not' and 'able' are to be lexicalized separately.

The construction of the SSyntS of sentence (3c) involves some transition rules different from those seen so far. Since the CDN of the **R**$_\text{Sem}$ (supposed to give the top node of the corresponding DSynt-tree) is not a verb, it is necessary to "verbalize" it – for instance, by means of the support verb Oper$_1$ (this is a lexical-functional notation; for lexical functions, see Ch. 7). An arborization rule, described in Ch. 12, *1.3.1*: p. 323, takes care of the transition 'able'**R**$_\text{Sem}$ ⇔ Oper$_1$–II→ABLE. Since 'cause1' is now the CDN of **T**$_\text{Sem}$, subordinated to the CDN of **R**$_\text{Sem}$, it is implemented (by a lexicalization rule not cited here) as the LF Propt, subsequently realized as BECAUSE. The other semantic transition rules needed to construct the DSyntS of sentence (3c) are the same ones used in the construction of the DSyntSs of the other two sentences.

Finally, some lexical-syntactic paraphrasing can take place, if desired, to reformulate sentence (3c). For instance, the following rule is applicable:

$$L_{(V)} \equiv \text{Oper}_1(A_1(L_{(V)})) + A_1(L_{(V)})$$

The rule describes a synonymic substitution: a verbal LU $L_{(V)}$ can be replaced by a lexical-syntactic configuration made up of the deverbal adjective characterizing the first deep-syntactic actant of the verb $L_{(V)}$ ('such that he/it does L') and the support verb for this adjective (the linking verb [to] BE). In our case, the rule (applied from right to left) gives $can_{L_{(V)}}$ ~ $be_{\text{Oper}_1(A_1(L)_{(V)})}$ $able_{A_1(L_{(V)})}$; see *Figure 1.11*.

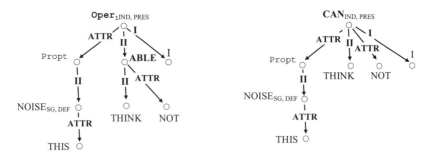

Figure 1.11 DSyntS of sentence (3c) and an equivalent DSyntS

Other examples of this rule's application: *want* ~ *be willing*; *know* ~ *be aware*; *suffice* ~ *be sufficient*; etc.

 If you feel somewhat intimidated by this illustration, please be reminded that doing science is not a walk in the park, yet it can be equally fun, if you are up to the challenge. Once you have gone through the textbook and the exercises, you will not only find the above representations and rules much easier to "digest" but will be able to write them yourself – and enjoy it!

2.4   The Meaning-Text Model within a General Model of Linguistic Behavior

By way of concluding this introductory chapter, let us emphasize and explain the following fact:

> A Meaning-Text Model of a language does not cover the entirety of linguistic behavior of its speakers.

A Meaning-Text Model starts with a semantic representation SemR and ends with a phonetic representation PhonetR – two formal symbolic objects. But where do the SemRs come from and where do the PhonetRs go to?

To answer the first part of the question, the input SemR is constructed by the Speaker based on some informational content that he intends to verbalize. At present, it is not known for sure how this content is represented in the Speaker's mind. However, it can be safely assumed that there is a level of representation deeper than the SemR at which the situation to be talked about is specified more or less independently of the linguistic means that will be used to verbalize it. This is the conceptual representation [ConceptR] – roughly, a network composed of discrete concepts as language-independent as possible and the relations between them. Thus, the content of a text ("what to say") is determined at a prelinguistic – conceptual – representation level; the linguistic levels of representation, starting with the SemR, and the rules operating between them, are responsible only for the realization of this content (for "how to say"). In this connection, see Ch. 3, *1.2*, where the opposition between "deep," or "real," meaning and linguistic meaning is discussed. The mapping of concepts onto linguistic meanings, i.e., the {ConceptRs} ⇔ {SemRs} transition, is performed by the rules of the conceptual module, or the conceptics, a vital component of the global model of linguistic behavior, but external to the Meaning-Text Model.

REMARKS

1. And the ConceptRs – where do they come from? They are constructed from raw psychological and physiological data by a mechanism that performs discretization of the perceived continuous extralinguistic world. This mechanism, the Reality ⇔ ConceptR

submodel, is of course the most complex part of the whole model of human cognitive behavior. However, it lies completely outside of linguistics and is left out of this book.

2. Human conceptualization of reality is an extremely complex and multifaceted problem, studied by different disciplines: Cognitive Science, Psychology, Neurology, Philosophy, Artificial Intelligence, Computer Science, etc. It has engendered an enormous amount of literature; for some pointers, see Further Reading.

To give the reader an idea of what such a mapping looks like, here is a maximally simplified illustration from the domain of natural language processing, where the use of conceptual representations has been a practical necessity. Suppose that we want to automatically generate weather forecasts for the general public. First, we need to make a list of concepts relevant for conveying information about the weather, such as probability of precipitation, rainfall, sudden drop in temperature, significant wind change, wind chill factor, nebulosity, state of the sky, and so on. Using these concepts, we could represent the contents that we eventually want to be verbalized by natural language texts, for example:

ConceptR 1: probability of rain: 100%; duration: 8am-2pm

ConceptR 2: state of the sky: 1 (a value on the scale from $1_{[\text{min. nebulosity}]}$ to $5_{[\text{max. nebulosity}]}$)

We would then need some rules linking these concepts to linguistic meanings, in our case the meanings of English, which would allow us to construct a number of corresponding SemRs. Applying these rules to ConceptR 1, we could get, for instance, the following SemRs: 'Rain is expected today', 'A wet day is ahead', 'Don't forget your umbrella', etc. And their application to ConceptR 2 could yield the SemRs 'The sky will be clear', 'Expect a cloudless sky', 'No clouds in sight', etc. From the semantic representations, constructed by conceptics, the linguistic realization system (which means a Meaning-Text model) would take over and produce the corresponding texts. As we just saw, one and the same ConceptR can be expressed by conceptually equivalent but semantically non-equivalent, i.e., non-synonymous, SemRs; this demonstrates that content planning belongs to a deeper-than-linguistic representation level.

And now to the second part of the question, the fate of the output PhonetR: it is turned into an actual acoustic string by the Speaker. The transition {PhonetRs} ⇔ {real articulated sounds} is performed by a system of rules that is called phonetics. Phonetics, as we said, does not belong to the Meaning-Text model, since it has to deal with articulatory or acoustic – that is, non-discrete – entities.

To conclude, with all its complexity, semantics$_1$ is but a small fragment of linguistic correspondence, which is itself a part of something larger and more complex.

Further Reading

Some foundational texts on language: Sapir 1921 [2004]; Saussure 1916 [2013]; Jakobson 1960 and 1971.

Introductions to general semantics: Cruse 2011; Goddard 2011; Saeed 2011; Löbner 2013; Zimmermann & Sternefeld 2013; Lappin & Fox 2015; Akmajian *et al.* 2017: 215–259.

An introduction to English semantics: Cummins & Griffiths 2016.

Meaning-Text theory: Steele 1990; Kahane 2003; Mel'čuk 2016.

Semantics Meaning-Text-style: Mel'čuk 2012b, 2013 and 2015.

Different approaches to meaning: [Formal Semantics] Portner & Partee 2002; [Generative Semantics] Jackendoff 1992; [Cognitive semantics] Lakoff 1988; [Frame Semantics] Fillmore 2006; [Natural Semantic Metalanguage approach] Wierzbicka 1980 and Goddard & Wierzbicka 2014; Weinreich 1961 represents an original approach, which is still of interest, more than half a century later.

Conceptual representation: Barsalou *et al.* 1993; [neurological perspective] Kiefer & Pulvermüller 2012.

2   Some Basic Linguistic Notions

"Language is a system in which everything is interconnected," as Ferdinand de Saussure said. Consequently, it is impossible to talk about semantics without having recourse to several notions belonging to other linguistic domains.

These notions are rather general and, for this reason, difficult to define; as a result, in an introductory textbook of semantics we can offer only approximate, sometimes rather rough, characterizations for many of these. (For mathematical and logical notions widely used in linguistics, in particular in semantics, see Appendix, p. 345*ff.*)

The necessary notions are presented in three blocks: general linguistic notions (Section *1*), syntactic notions (Section *2*), and morphological notions (Section *3*).

1   General Linguistic Notions

Six groups of notions will be introduced: linguistic sign and related notions (*1.1*), the two axes of speech production (*1.2*), linguistic dependency (*1.3*), linguistic significations (*1.4*), linguistic expressive means (*1.5*), and basic formalisms for representing linguistic phenomena (*1.6*).

1.1   Linguistic Sign and Related Notions

The most important of all linguistic notions is, beyond any doubt, the linguistic sign. All other notions used in linguistics are derived from it. This notion, introduced by Ferdinand de Saussure (Saussure 1916 [2013]), is presented here in a developed and more rigorous form (Mel'čuk 1982: 40*ff*).

1.1.1   The Notion of Linguistic Sign

> **Definition 2.1:** Linguistic Sign
> A linguistic sign **s** is a triplet **s** = $\langle$'s' ; /s/ ; $\Sigma_s\rangle$, where 's' is the signified of **s**, /s/ is the signifier of **s**, and Σ_s is the syntactics of the pair $\langle$'s' ; /s/$\rangle$.

In what follows, we will often omit the adjective *linguistic* and speak simply of *signs* – since no other type of sign is considered in this book.

NOTATIONS

1. The name of a sign is printed in **boldface**: **apple**, **apple-**, **drink**, **-s**, **-ing**, **re-**, **-able**. In the name of the sign the hyphen does two things. It either identifies a radical (or a stem): thus, the radical **apple-** is opposed to the wordform **apple** = **apple+Ø$_{SG}$** (with a zero suffix of the singular). Or else it identifies an affix, specifying its type: a hyphen which precedes an affix means that it is a suffix (**-s**), and one which follows it shows that it is a prefix (**re-**). For these notions, see Section *3*.

2. Signifieds that are genuine meanings appear between semantic quotes: 'apple', 'drink', 'if'; signifieds that are inflectional values (= grammemes) are in SMALL CAPS: PL(ural), PRES(ent), PASS(ive).

3. Graphic signifiers are in *italics*: *apple*, *drink*, *if*; phonic signifiers are given in phonemic transcription – between slanted brackets, or slashes: /ǽpl/, /drínk/, /íf/.

Signified

Most often, the signified of a sign is a "chunk" of meaning; the signified of the sign **dog**$_{(N)}$**I.1**, for instance, is the meaning 'domestic animal … whose functions are to keep company with its owner, protect a place …'.

As stated in "Symbols, Abbreviations and Writing Conventions," p. xxi, lexicographic, or sense-distinguishing, numbers accompanying LUs come from LDOCE Online: www.ldoceonline.com. However, we allow ourselves to modify the corresponding definitions and introduce our own lexicographic numbers if we deem LDOCE numbers not entirely adequate.

The signified can also be an inflectional value, for example, the signified ACC (= the accusative case). It can even be empty, as is the signified of the English sign **it**$_{(Pron, impers)}$ in **It** *is raining* or **It** *is necessary to leave*; a sign of this type is an empty sign.

Here are three signs having the signifieds of these three types:

dog$_{(N)}$**I.1-** = ⟨'domestic animal …'   ; /dɔ́g/   ; Σ = radical, nominal …⟩

Hung. **-t** = ⟨ACC(usative)   ; /t/   ; Σ = suffix, nominal, non-pronominal …⟩

               [NOM *lány* /lāɲ/ 'girl' ~ ACC *lányt* /lāɲt/, as in '[I see a] girl']

it = ⟨Λ   ; /ít/   ; Σ = wordform, noun, pronominal, 3, SG …⟩

☞   Λ stands for the empty set (Appendix, *1*).

Two signs can have identical signifieds; thus, the signifieds of the signs **cougar** and ⌐**mountain lion**⌐ coincide: 'a large wild cat living in the mountains …'. Such signs are synonymous (Ch. 5, *1.1.1*). However, following from the definition of sign, a sign cannot, of course, have two or more signifieds.

Signifier

In the prototypical case, the signifier of a sign is a string of phonemes, for instance /báˈsɪkəl/. A string of phonemes is called a segment; therefore, a signifier that is a string of phonemes is segmental. But other types of signifiers are known, too – non-segmental signifiers: prosodies and operations, such as reduplications, alternations and conversions. Thus, in the sentence *John left?* the signifier of the signified INTERROG(ation) is a particular intonation contour; in the verbal wordform **sprang** the signifier of the signified PAST is the alternation /ɪ/ ⇒ /æ/. (The corresponding sign is the apophony $\mathbf{A}_{\text{PAST}}^{/ɪ/⇒/æ/}$.)

A signifier, like the signified, can be empty. Thus, the signifier of the English sign SG$_{\text{nominal}}$ ("nominal singular") seen in the wordform [*a*] **car** is empty – that is, it does not contain phonemes: [*a*] *car*+$\boldsymbol{\varnothing}$ vs. [*two*] *car*+*s*); a sign having an empty signifier is called a zero sign and is denoted by the symbol "$\boldsymbol{\varnothing}$".

Here are the corresponding signs:

bicycle-	= ⟨'a vehicle with two wheels ...'	; /báˈsɪkəl/;	Σ = radical, nominal ...⟩
$\mathbf{A}_{\text{PAST}}^{/ɪ/⇒/æ/}$	= ⟨PAST	; /ɪ/ ⇒ /æ/ ;	Σ = apophony, applies to Vs marked "A$^{/ɪ/⇒/æ/}$", ...⟩
-$\boldsymbol{\varnothing}_{\text{SG}}$	= ⟨SG	; Λ;	Σ = suffix, nominal, ...⟩

Two signs can have identical signifiers, such as the radicals of the noun **firm**$_{\text{(N)}}$ (*a manufacturing firm*) and the adjective **firm**$_{\text{(ADJ)}}$ (*a firm answer*). Such signs are equinomous; it is generally accepted to speak of their ambiguity. But, again, a sign cannot have two or more signifiers.

Syntactics

The syntactics of a sign **s** specifies the combinatorial properties of **s** – its capacity to combine with other signs – that cannot be deduced from its signified or its signifier; these are the idiosyncratic properties of **s**.

For example, one of the combinatorial properties of the French noun **eau** 'water' is its grammatical gender. To correctly use this sign in combination with other signs, you have to know that this noun is feminine: cf. the ungrammaticality of **l'eau froid*$_{\text{SG, MASC}}$ /frwa/, where the masculine adjective does not agree in gender with the noun; the correct form of the adjective is *froide* /frwad/. The grammatical gender of **eau** cannot be deduced from its signified: **eau** could have well been masculine, as is the corresponding Arabic noun (*māʔ bārid*+$\varnothing_{\text{SG, MASC}}$ ⟨*māʔ bārid+*a*$_{\text{SG, FEM}}$⟩ lit. 'water cold', with the adjective in the masculine form), or neuter, as in German (*das*$_{\text{NEU}}$ *Wasser*) and Modern Greek (*tó*$_{\text{NEU}}$ *húdōr*, **colloq**. *tó*$_{\text{NEU}}$ *neró*). The signifier /o/ of the sign **eau** does not allow us to deduce its gender, either, because signs with similar signifiers may very well be of masculine gender (**sceau** / so/ 'seal [mark that shows the legal authority ...]', **seau** /so/ 'bucket', **sot** / so/ 'fool', etc.).

> REMARK. The incompatibility of the noun **eau** with the verb **manger** 'eat' (#*J'ai mangé de l'eau* 'I have eaten some water') or with the indefinite article **une** (**J'ai bu une eau* 'I have drunk a water') is a property deducible from its signified, whose central component is 'liquid' (something that cannot be eaten or counted). The obligatory

elision of the vowel of the definite article before the noun **eau** (*l'eau* and not **la eau*) is a property deducible from its signifier, which starts with a vowel, since in French the final vowel of an article is elided before the initial vowel of the following wordform. Such properties need not be specified in the syntactics of a sign. In contrast, the impossibility of eliding the article before nouns such as [*la*] *hauteur* 'height' or [*la*] *une* 'the first (page of a newspaper)' does not follow from their phonemic signifiers /otœr/ or /ün/ and therefore has to be mentioned in the syntactics of such nouns.

☞   The symbol "#" marks semantically anomalous sentences (see Ch. 9, *1.1*); "*" is the symbol of ungrammaticality.

The syntactics of a sign is made up of features, each feature admitting particular values. Here is a sample of syntactic features (they are shown in parentheses, subscripted to "their" sign):

- Type of sign: *dog*-(radical) vs. *dogs*(wordform)
- Part of speech (see *2.2* below): *down*(V) vs. *down*(N) vs. *down*(ADV); Fr. *verger*(N) 'garden' vs. *verser*(V) 'pour'; *entrer*(V) 'enter' vs. *entrée*(N) 'entrance'; Fr. *ferme*(N) '[a] farm' vs. *ferme*(ADJ) 'firm'
- Nominal gender: Fr. *table*(fem) 'table' vs. *meuble*(masc) 'piece of furniture'; Fr. *fille*(fem) 'girl' vs. Ger. *Mädchen*(neu) 'girl' vs. Gr. *korítsi*(neu) 'girl' vs. Irish *cailín*(masc) /kál'īn'/ 'girl'
- Verbal conjugation group: Fr. *finir*(IInd) 'finish' vs. *partir*(IIIrd) 'leave' (*Ils finiss+ent* 'They finish' vs. *Ils part+ent* 'They leave')
- Defective paradigm: the noun INFORMATION(SG only) does not have the plural form (**these informations*), while Fr. INFORMATION can be pluralized without difficulty: *ces informations*PL; on the contrary, the French noun FUNÉRAILLES(PL only) has no singular: **une funéraille*, but the English FUNERAL has both numbers: *a funeral* vs. *funerals*. Cf. as well Fr. *Nous *frions* 'we fry' vs. *Nous rions* 'we laugh' or Rus. *ajvá* 'quince' ~ **ájv*PL.GEN vs. *slíva* 'plum' ~ *slív*PL.GEN.

> **NB:** 1. A paradigm of a lexeme is the set of all its inflectional forms.
> 2. Note that the English nouns of the type AIRCRAFT or DEER have both numbers, whose forms are, however, identical: *an aircraft* ~ *these aircraft*.

- Collocations – phraseologized expressions in which the lexeme in question imposes the choice of another lexeme for the expression of a particular meaning. Consider, for instance, the different behavior of nouns *favor* vs. *mistake* or *caution* vs. *attention*: you DO *a favor*, but you MAKE *a mistake*; similarly, you USE *caution*, but you PAY *attention*. (On collocations, see Ch. 4, *2.2.2.1*, Ch. 6, *2* & Ch. 7, *2.2*.)

Two signs can, understandably, have identical syntactics, but a single sign cannot have two or more different syntactics, just as it cannot have two signifieds or two signifiers.

1.1.2   Reference and Denotation of a Linguistic Sign

Generally speaking, a sign used by a Speaker in an utterance is mentally linked to something external to this utterance: to an object X or a state of affairs X in the world, called the referent of the sign; the sign points to its referent X, or refers to X. Thus, the sign **armchair** used in the utterance *This armchair is comfortable* refers to a specific piece of furniture located in the Speaker's environment and having the properties that allow him to call it an **armchair** (you can sit in it, it has a particular shape, etc.).

As an element of extralinguistic reality, the referent of a sign is exterior to the sign itself, and it is important not to confound it with the signified of the sign. The signified is an integral component of a sign, independent of the sign's use in speech, a piece of neurological reality in the speaker's brain. The referent is a piece of physical reality in the outer world. To show the independence of the two notions – a sign's signified vs. a sign's referent – let us consider the following facts:

- Some signs never have referents: only a sign with a non-empty signified that is a chunk of meaning is potentially a referring sign; for instance, **building**, **pen**, **tiger**, **red**, **lovely**, **run**, **Moon**, etc. are referring signs. Structural, or grammatical, signs, whose signifieds are indications of particular syntactic links (between words in a sentence), are not referring; governed prepositions, as in *secretary **to** the Minister, tell Y **from** Z, wrap one's brain **around** Y, reliance **on** Y*, etc., are examples of non-referring signs.
- A referring sign does not refer in every case of its use. Thus, a complex sign consisting of "normal" referring signs can have no referent: for instance, the sign **the biggest integer**, even though it has a clear meaning (= an obvious signified), does not have a referent, since there is no such thing as "the biggest integer."
- While some signs have just one possible referent, such as **Sun**, **Moon**, **Earth**, **Canada**, a typical referring sign has an infinite set of potential referents. Thus, the signified of a sign and its referent are not in one-to-one correspondence: the signified is an inherent, permanent feature of a sign, while the sign's referent is its contingent, provisional "partner." Each time it is used in speech, the noun **armchair**, with the signified 'a seat for one person with a back and armrests', can have a different referent; for instance, its two occurrences in the expression *this armchair here and that armchair there* refer to two different objects. Conversely, two distinct non-synonymous signs, which have different signifieds, can have the same referent: we can refer to the same object calling it **armchair** on one occasion and **seat**, or

even **this piece of furniture**, on another. The hackneyed examples of this phenomenon are the expressions *Sir Walter Scott* ~ *the author of "Waverley"* or *Morning Star* ~ *Evening Star* (the planet Venus).

The ability to refer is conferred to a (referring) sign by its signified. The signified of a referring sign **s** corresponds in a one-to-one way to a set of real-world things called the denotation of **s**. (This set can be a singleton, i.e., a one-element set, such as the denotation of the nouns **Sun**, **Pacific**, **Spain**, etc., or infinite, such as the denotation of the nouns **leaf**, **girl**, **rain**, etc. All intermediate cases are also possible.) The denotation of **s** embraces all **s**'s potential referents. When used in an utterance the sign **s** specifies just one particular thing or a well-defined group of things contained in its denotation; this is **s**'s referent. (The crucial distinction between sign and its denotation/reference was established by Gottlob Frege: Frege 1892.)

> REMARK. Our characterization of the notion of referent is simplistic: it covers only the most common cases, as illustrated above. But what could be the referents of signs like **yeti**, **Popeye**, **intergalactic wars**, **eternal life**, etc., since these beings and facts exist only in our imagination? And do expressions whose denotations are abstract concepts, such as *my reputation*, *this love*, *the meaning of the universe*, have referents? Problems of this kind are dealt with by philosophy and logic and are far from being solved.

Based on the relation between a referring sign and its referent in a given utterance, reference is characterized by two features: definiteness and specificity.

Definiteness. The referent of the sign **s** in a given utterance is:

1. Definite if, and only if [iff], it is fully (= uniquely) identifiable for both the Speaker and the Addressee (*Give me this **apple**!*).
2. Weakly definite iff it is identifiable for the Speaker, but not for the Addressee (*A **friend** of mine gave me this book.*).
3. Indefinite iff it is not identifiable either for the Speaker or for the Addressee (*I want an **apple**.*).

Specificity. The referent of the sign **s** in a given utterance is:

1. Specific iff it is an individual entity or fact (*She wants to marry a **Russian**, who her parents don't know.*).
2. Generic iff it is a class of individuals or facts (*She wants to marry a **Russian** – any Russian.*).

These features are logically independent, so their crossing engenders six types of referent:

a. Definite specific referent	: *This **response** kept the moderates in line.*
b. Definite generic referent	: *This response can keep the **moderates** in line.*
c. Weakly definite specific referent	: *A **friend** of mine arrived.*
d. Weakly definite generic referent	: *I love some **friends** of mine.*
e. Indefinite specific referent	: *I need a **clove of garlic**.*
f. Indefinite generic referent	: *I am sure there are **people** who like **garlic**.*

Reference has close links with many important linguistic phenomena; thus, it is related, on the one hand, to the communicative opposition of Givenness (Ch. 10, *3.1.2.2*) and, on the other hand, to the inflectional category of determination (in English, and many other languages, expressed by articles). However, we cannot go into further detail about this.

1.1.3   Compositionality of Complex Linguistic Signs

When we look at the way the components of a complex linguistic expression are selected by the Speaker (this is the paradigmatic perspective, see *1.2*), we can say that a typical complex linguistic expression is free – that is, the selection of any of its components is in no way constrained by any individual, idiosyncratic property of any other component. Thus, in the sentence *The pet looked healthy and joyful*, the speaker is able to choose each word as he likes, as long as it corresponds to the meaning he wants to express. This means that almost every word of the sentence can be replaced by any of its (near-)synonyms without affecting the grammaticality: e.g., *The animal appeared in good health and cheerful*. The number of free complex expressions in a language is infinite – that is what unlimited productivity of a linguistic system means.

Compositionality has to do with the way signs combine with one another (this is the syntagmatic perspective, *1.2*) in order to produce free expressions. Language allows for an unlimited number of free expressions to be built from a finite number of simple signs. For this to be possible, the simple signs must be united into complex signs according to some sufficiently general rules; in other words, the resulting expressions must be compositional. If a complex linguistic sign is compositional, all of its components – its signified, its signifier and its syntactics – are compositional. A compositional sign **AB** can be presented as **AB** = **A** ⊕ **B**; this formula symbolizes the concept of compositionality.

     The symbol "⊕" stands for linguistic union, a very general operation that unites signs of a language by uniting their corresponding components in order to construct wordforms, phrases, clauses, and sentences (see *2.1*). The operation ⊕ is implemented by a set of rules, specific for each language.

In what follows, for simplicity's sake, we will limit the discussion to the compositionality of signifieds, i.e., semantic compositionality.

Semantic compositionality of a complex linguistic expression **AB** means that its meaning, 'σ', can be represented using only the meanings of the expressions which compose it: the sign **A** with the meaning 'A' and the sign **B** with the meaning 'B', so that 'σ' = 'A ⊕ B'. Put differently, the union of the meanings of the expressions making up a compositional expression ['A' ⊕ 'B'] is equal to the meaning of the union of these expressions ['A ⊕ B']; symbolically: 'A' ⊕ 'B' = 'A ⊕ B'.

> REMARK. The meaning of a linguistic expression can be compared to the weight of a physical body, which is also a compositional property: if we weigh two objects separately and then add their weights, we will obtain the same result as if we had weighed them together. But beauty, for instance, is not a compositional property: the beauty of two identical objects taken together is not twice the beauty of these objects considered separately.

If we know the meaning of the phrase [*a*] *gray car*, and those of the words *gray* and *car*, we can represent the meaning 'gray car' as 'gray' ⊕ 'car' = 'gray ⊕ car'. But, knowing the meaning of the phrase *red tape* 'bureaucratic rules that are unnecessary and prevent things from being done easily', we cannot represent it by trying to express the component 'official rules' by *tape*, and the component 'that are unnecessary ...' by *red*, because those words do not mean that: they cannot be used with these meanings outside of the expression *red tape*. The phrase *red tape* is thus not semantically compositional: it is an idiom, which is a type of phraseme (Ch. 4, *2.2.2.1*).

1.2   Paradigmatic vs. Syntagmatic Relations between Linguistic Signs

In order to produce an utterance, the Speaker has to manipulate linguistic signs, and he does this along two axes: paradigmatic axis and syntagmatic axis.

On the one hand, the Speaker has to **select** the signs he wants to use. Linguistic signs, stored in his brain, are interconnected via multiple links, which allow him to browse through the signs in search of those he would prefer to use in a given situation. Sign selection happens on the paradigmatic axis.

On the other hand, due to the oral nature of language, the signs that make up an utterance are pronounced in a linear sequence. Each selected sign has to **be combined** with other signs – that is, at least be linearly positioned with respect to other signs in the utterance. This is not done arbitrarily: the linear position of a sign encodes, perhaps indirectly, its semantic links with other signs. The proper linearization of linguistic signs occurs on the syntagmatic axis. (For simplicity's sake, we ignore prosodic and morphological marking here.)

As one can see, the construction of an utterance by the Speaker implies two "orthogonal" operations: the selection of signs from the inventory of available signs and the combination of selected signs. Selection of signs is performed based on their relations in the mental lexicon, i.e., according to paradigmatic relations; combination of signs is carried out based on their relations in text; i.e., according to syntagmatic relations. (These two major types of relations in natural language were established by F. de Saussure.)

Paradigmatic Relations

These are relations between linguistic signs stored in the brain of the Speaker (relations *in absentia*, because these signs will not all be present in the utterance produced); they allow the Speaker to select the signs he needs. For example, the sign [to] **sleep** is paradigmatically related to the signs **[a] sleep, insomnia, dream, bed, bedroom, snore**, etc., in the sense that any one of them, in principle, can be used instead of **sleep**, in a given speech situation and in accordance with the Speaker's needs and goals. This is not replacement in the literal sense, but rather a choice of the most appropriate sign. For example, instead of saying "Excuse me, I'm going to sleep.", you can say "Excuse me, I'm going to bed." (A restaurant menu offers a good parallel: for dessert, you can choose between a cup of coffee, cheese or a cake; either of the three elements can be chosen, even though they do not, strictly speaking, replace one another.)

The following are the major classes of interlexemic paradigmatic relations (more precisely, lexical-semantic relations between linguistic expressions, Ch. 6, *1*):

1. synonymy: *understand P ~ realize (that) P ~ get (that) P*
2. antonymy: *remember ~ forget, absent ~ present, near ~ far*
3. conversion: *buy ~ sell, husband ~ wife, after ~ before*
4. (semantic) derivation: *buy ~ buyer, absent ~ absence, [to] attack ~ [an] attack*

Syntagmatic Relations

These are relations between linguistic items used by the Speaker in speech (relations *in praesentia*); they ensure the appropriate combination of linguistic items into grammatical expressions. For instance, an article and the noun which follows it form a phrase "ART + N," which in its turn can combine with other phrases into larger units: clauses and sentences. Here, we are dealing with the relations between units co-existing side by side in an utterance.

Syntagmatic relations are of two main types: hierarchical or oriented (antisymmetric), relations, and equivalence (symmetric) relations. Hierarchic syntagmatic relations are further divided into structural and linear relations.

- Structural hierarchical syntagmatic relations are dependencies of three types: semantic, syntactic and morphological; see immediately below, Subsection *1.3.*
- Structural linear syntagmatic relations are precedence relations: they determine the linear order of linguistic signs – what precedes (or follows) what. Linear order is one of the four expressive means of natural languages (the other three being structural words, prosody and inflection); see Subsection *1.5.*

- Equivalence syntagmatic relations are, for instance, co-reference relations: in an utterance, they link LUs referring to the same fact or entity (e.g., the lexemes JOHN and HIS in the sentence *John used this argument in **his** proof* are co-referential); cf. Subsection *1.1.2* above.

1.3   Linguistic Dependency

Dependency is one of the core notions of the Meaning-Text approach to language. (In fact, this approach can be essentially characterized as relational, since it considers relations – in particular, dependency relations – as an essential factor of linguistic organization.)

> **Definition 2.2:** Linguistic Dependency
> Linguistic dependency is a hierarchic (= antisymmetric) syntagmatic relation between two lexical units in a sentence *S* or two semantemes in the semantic structure of *S*, one called governor and the other dependent.

> **NB:** Here and below, we use the term **sentence** *pour fixer les idées*, but what is said about sentences is true also of any utterance smaller than a sentence.

A lexical unit L of language **L** is either a word taken in a well-defined sense (= a lexeme) or a non-compositional multiword phraseologized expression, also taken in a well-defined sense (= an idiom); see *1.4* below.

A linguistic dependency will be represented by an arrow: $L_{1[governor]} \rightarrow L_{2[dependent]}$. This relation is hierarchical in that the governor controls the linguistic behavior of the dependent: for instance, its presence in the sentence, linear placement, inflectional form, etc.

1.3.1   Types of Linguistic Dependency

Three major types of linguistic dependency are distinguished: semantic dependency, syntactic dependency and morphological dependency.

> **Definition 2.3:** Semantic Dependency
> Semantic dependency is dependency between either two semantemes 'L_1' and 'L_2' that stand in a "predicate ~ argument" relation or two corresponding lexical units in a sentence, L_1 and L_2: the governor (= predicate) determines the presence and the nature of the dependent (= argument) in the sentence.

A meaning of an LU corresponds to a predicate in the logical sense (see Appendix, *5.2*) iff it is "incomplete," i.e., iff it requires other meanings – its arguments – to be expressed along with it. Thus, the meaning 'sleep' is incomplete without the specification of the being that sleeps, 'love' requires an indication of the person who feels love and the person being loved, and so on.

REMARK. Another term used to designate an argument of a predicate, and absolutely synonymous with the latter, is semantic actant; cf. Ch. 3, *3.2.2*, where semantic actants are characterized, to see why we prefer the latter term.

The notation "L_1–**sem**→L_2" means that 'L_2' is an argument of the predicate 'L_1'; in the predicate calculus notation (Appendix, *5.2*), this can also be written as 'L_1'('L_2') or, for short, '$L_1(L_2)$'. For example, semantic dependencies between the (meanings of the) LUs of the sentence *This cute kitten runs fast* are as follows:

'run–**sem**→kitten'; 'this–**sem**→kitten'; 'cute–**sem**→ kitten'; 'fast–**sem**→run'.

The set of semantic dependencies holding between the meanings of the LUs of a sentence constitute the semantic structure of that sentence. On semantic dependency relations, see Ch. 3, *3.2*, and on semantic structures of sentences, Ch. 10, *2*.

> **Definition 2.4:** Syntactic Dependency
> Syntactic dependency is a dependency between two LUs in a sentence, L_1 and L_2, such that one, for instance, L_1, called the governor of L_2, determines the syntactic distribution – i.e., types of external syntactic links – of the whole phrase L_1–**synt**→L_2.

L_1 is also called the head of the phrase L_1–**synt**→L_2.

Saying that a phrase L_1–**synt**→L_2 has the same distribution as its head L_1 means that the former can be used in the same syntactic contexts as the latter. For example, the phrase *cute kitten*, consisting of an adjective and a noun, is appropriate in the same syntactic contexts where just the noun *kitten* alone can be used ([*the*] **kitten** *runs* ~ [*the*] **cute kitten** *runs*; *I see* [*the*] **kitten** ~ *I see* [*the*] **cute kitten**, etc.), but does not fit into contexts appropriate for the adjective ([*the*] **cute** *kitten* vs. *[*the*] **cute kitten** *kitten*). Moreover, the noun can be used without the adjective, but the converse is not true.[1] Thus, the noun is the syntactic governor of the adjective and the head of the ADJ + N phrase; in our case, this is written KITTEN$_{(N)}$–**synt**→CUTE$_{(ADJ)}$. (Note that the direction of the arrow joining **kitten** and **cute** at the syntactic level is the opposite to what it is at the semantic level; more on this below.)

> REMARK. The terms *governor* and *head* are related but quite distinct. The head of a phrase is not the governor of the phrase: the head of the

---

[1] To be sure, English (like many other languages) has constructions in which an adjective does not syntactically depend on a noun, but rather on a verb: for instance, *The kitten is/became cute*. However, these constructions are possible only with a particular type of verb – the copula and several similar verbs – which links the adjective to the noun. This makes matters more complex, but does not contradict our statement.

phrase is inside the phrase, while its governor is exterior to the phrase. In our example, *kitten* is the head of the phrase *cute kitten*, but the governor of this phrase is the verb *runs*.

The set of syntactic dependencies holding between the LUs of a sentence taken together with these LUs constitutes the syntactic structure of that sentence. As mentioned in Ch. 1, *2.2.2*, we distinguish two sublevels of representation in syntax: deep and surface sublevels. For deep-syntactic dependency relations and deep-syntactic structure, see Ch. 11, *2*.

> **Definition 2.5:** Morphological Dependency
>
> Morphological dependency is a dependency between two LUs in a sentence, L_1 and L_2, such that at least some inflectional values of one, for instance, L_2, called target (= morphological dependent), are imposed by the other, L_1, which is the controller (= morphological governor).

Inflectional values, or grammemes, are obligatory – that is, language-imposed – grammatical significations; see *3.2*.

In our sample sentence, the verb **runs** depends morphologically on the noun **kitten**, whose grammatical person and number it "copies": in English, a finite verb in the present indicative agrees in person and number with its subject. Therefore, we write

controller   target

KITTEN_{SG}—**morph**→$\text{RUN}_{3,\ SG}$

Similarly, the adjective THIS depends morphologically on the noun KITTEN (THIS agrees with KITTEN_{SG} in number).[2]

Morphological dependency manifests itself either as agreement or government. Examples of agreement were just given; as an illustration of government, we can mention a preposition that controls the case of the dependent noun (as in Ger. *Bücher für*$_{(PREP)}$ *Kind+er*$_{PL}$+$\mathbf{\varnothing}_{\mathbf{ACC}}$ 'books for children', where FÜR 'for' requires a noun in the accusative), or a verb that controls the case of its nominal complements (as in Serb. *pomagati ljud+ima*$_{PL.\underline{\mathbf{DAT}}}$ lit. '[to] help to.people').

---

[2] The pronominal adjectives THIS and THAT are the only pluralizable adjectives in English and thus the only ones that can depend morphologically (on a noun). Other English adjectives, as indeed adjectives in many languages (that have them), are invariable with respect to number. Cross-linguistically speaking, it is also possible for a noun to depend morphologically on the adjective that modifies it; this happens, for instance, in Iranian languages, in the so-called "izafet construction": cf. Persian KETAB 'book', ǯALEB 'interesting', and *ketab+e ǯaleb* lit. 'book interesting', where a modifying adjective requires the modified noun to add the suffix **-e**, known as *izafet*, which marks on the noun the presence of a modifier.

The three major types of linguistic dependency are logically independent of each other and can combine in a sentence in all possible ways. Thus, dependencies of different types holding between two LUs in a sentence can go in the opposite direction. In the sentence *This cute kitten runs*, the verb governs the noun semantically and syntactically, but is itself governed by it morphologically; the pronominal adjective THIS governs the modified noun semantically, but depends on it syntactically and morphologically (see *Figure 2.1*).

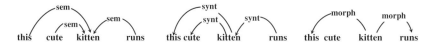

Figure 2.1 Three types of linguistic dependency between the lexemes of the sentence *This cute kitten runs*

Semantic and syntactic dependencies are universal in two respects. First, there is no language without semantic and syntactic dependencies between LUs of a sentence. Second, in every non-elliptical sentence each LU is semantically linked to at least one other unit and all units are related – two by two – by direct syntactic dependencies, so that a connected structure results. By definition, a sentence cannot contain an LU that is completely unrelated to its other LUs semantically and syntactically (such a string would be incoherent). Morphological dependency, however, is not universal, also in two respects. On the one hand, some languages, such as Vietnamese and Mandarin Chinese, do not have inflectional morphology at all; on the other hand, sentences of a language that does have inflection can contain LUs that are not linked morphologically to other LUs. Thus, an invariable word, like a preposition or an adverb in English, does not depend morphologically on other words in the sentence.

1.3.2 Major Dependency Roles

A dependency relation can be considered from the viewpoint of the dependent member, i.e., taking into account the role that the dependent plays with respect to the governor.

At the **semantic level**, there is just one type of dependent: a semantic actant (or semantic argument) of a lexical meaning 'L' (which corresponds to a predicate in the logical sense).

At the **syntactic level**, there are two major types of dependents: syntactic actants of an LU L and L's modifiers/circumstantials (in a broad sense). "Syntactic actant vs. syntactic modifier/circumstantial" is one of the most fundamental oppositions in the domain of syntax.

We distinguish deep- and surface-syntactic actants; only the former are directly relevant in a textbook on semantics (Ch. 11, *2.3*). In most cases, the deep-syntactic actants of an LU L correspond to its semantic actants.

Surface-syntactic actants are defined inductively: starting from prototypical SSynt-actants (such as the subject and the direct object in the case of verbs), all L's dependents that sufficiently resemble the prototypical ones according to some relevant syntactic properties are also recognized as its actants.[3] Actants are closely linked to L's lexicographic definition and are an integral part of L's syntactic frame, or Government Pattern (see *1.3.3*); they tend to be expressed in a way that is idiosyncratic, i.e., not fully foreseeable. In other words, their expression is contingent upon the governing L. In contrast, modifiers/circumstantials are free adjuncts, and their expression is usually regular, and independent of the lexical identity of the governing L.

1.3.3   Valence, Diathesis and Government Pattern

The term *valence* came into linguistics from chemistry, where it refers to the capacity of atoms to bind with other atoms and form molecules. Analogously, some LUs are capable of binding with some other LUs, i.e., they can enter into dependency relations with other LUs in a sentence to form larger linguistic structures.

> **Definition 2.6:** Semantic Valence of a Lexical Unit
> The semantic valence of an LU L is the set of all L's semantic actants –
> i.e., the set of L's semantic dependents filling the actantial slots in L's
> lexicographic definition.

The alternative term is the argument structure of L.

Examples

The verb [to] SELL (*John sold his car yesterday*) has a semantic valence of 4: 'person **X** sells entity or service **Y** to person **Z** for money **W**'. The noun IDEA (*John's idea to move house*) has a semantic valence of 2: 'person **X's** idea to perform action **Y**'.

> **Definition 2.7:** Passive Syntactic Valence of a Lexical Unit
> The passive syntactic valence of an LU L is the set of all syntactic
> constructions into which L can enter as a dependent.

The alternative term is the syntactic distribution of L (see Definition 2.4).

L's passive syntactic valence is described in terms of parts of speech (see *2.2* below), as well as the syntactic features of L and those of its governor. For example, the passive syntactic valence of an English nominal lexeme includes the following syntactic roles (the list is, of course, not exhaustive): (1) the subject of a finite verb (*The **sun**←**subjectival**–is shining.*); (2) the attribute of the

---

[3] For instance, in *John wrote **me** a poem*, the element *me*, which does not correspond to a Sem-actant of 'write', is considered to be its SSynt-actant – the indirect object – by analogy with such sentences as *He gave **me** an apple*, etc.

copula (*Max is*–**copular**–*[a]→teacher.*); (3) the direct object of a transitive verb (*write*–**direct-objectival**–*[an]→article.*); (4) an apposition of another noun (*my friend*–**naming-appositive→Collins**).

> **Definition 2.8:** Active Syntactic Valence of a Lexical Unit
> The active syntactic valence of an LU L is the set of all syntactic constructions into which L enters as the governor of its actantial dependents, a.k.a. complements.

Examples

The active syntactic valence of the verb [to] SELL (*John sold his car yesterday.*) includes the following constructions: subjectival (N_X *sells*), the direct-objectival (*sells* N_Y), the indirect-objectival (*sells to* N_Z or *sells* N_Z [N_Y]) and the oblique-objectival (*sells for* NUM N_W), the dependent members of these constructions expressing the corresponding semantic actants of the verb. The active syntactic valence of the noun IDEA includes the subjectival-adnominal construction (N_X's *idea*/[*an*] *idea of* N_X) and the oblique-objectival construction (*idea to* V_{INF-Y}); their dependent members express the noun's semantic actants.

> **Definition 2.9:** Diathesis of a Lexical Unit
> The correspondence between the semantic actants of an LU L and its deep-syntactic actants is called the diathesis of L.

This correspondence, otherwise known as linking, is by no means trivial (i.e., one-to-one). Thus, while the adjective FAITHFUL1 (*politicians faithful to their word*) has two semantic actants ('X_{who} faithful to Y_{what}'), it has only the deep-syntactic actant **II** (corresponding to 'Y', while the element corresponding to 'X' becomes its governor in syntax); cf.:

	FAITHFUL1, adjective		
Semantic actants	**X**'who'	**Y**'to what'	} Diathesis
Deep-syntactic actants	–	**II**	

L's basic, or lexicographic, diathesis (specified in L's Government Pattern (GP); definition immediately below) corresponds to the basic, or lexicographic, form of L.[4] The basic diathesis can undergo modifications, which are the source of many important semantic and syntactic phenomena: grammatical voices, lexical conversion, verbal derivation, etc.

---

[4] The lexicographic form of an LU L is its simplest, least marked form. Thus, verbs are entered in the dictionary in the form of the active infinitive, and in a language that does not have infinitives, in the 3rd person singular active past form (Arabic) or 1st person singular active present form (Bulgarian). An adjective in a morphologically rich language is given in the masculine, singular, nominative form, etc.

Definition 2.10: Government Pattern of a Lexical Unit
The Government Pattern of an LU L is a specification of L's basic diathesis, as well as of the surface-syntactic constructions and morphological means implementing L's deep-syntactic actants.

Here is the Government Pattern of the adjective FAITHFUL1:

$\mathbf{X}_{\text{'who'}}$	$\mathbf{Y}_{\text{'to what'}}$
	II
————	**–oblique-objectival**→*to* N

[*woman*$_X$] *faithful to her principles*$_Y$

This GP indicates that the Sem-actant X of FAITHFUL1 is not expressible as an actant in syntax (because it becomes the syntactic governor of the adjective) and that the Sem-actant Y is expressed by an oblique object – the prepositional phrase with TO.

The illustration in *Figure 2.2* will help the reader grasp the Government Pattern formalism and the correspondence between semantic and deep-syntactic actants it specifies.

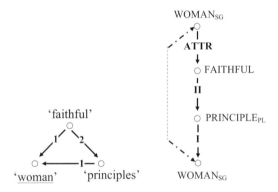

Figure 2.2 The representations of the phrase *[a] woman faithful to her principles* at the semantic and deep-syntactic levels

For more on the Government Pattern, see Ch. 8, *2.2.3*.

1.4   Major Types of Linguistic Significations

A rough definition of linguistic signification would be as follows: any informational content that can be carried by linguistic signs; significations include genuine meanings, syntactic information, communicative information, rhetorical information, etc.

Linguistic significations can be classified along three logically independent axes:

Axis 1: Lexical significations vs. grammatical significations

Lexical significations bear mostly on, or are about, the extralinguistic world; they are rather concrete, and numerous (about a million in the language of a modern society; see below, *1.6.2*, Footnote 7) and constitute an open set. Here are several lexical significations of English: 'like' (*like a madman*), 'piece' (*a piece of wood*), 'narrow' (*a narrow lane*), 'interest$_{(V)}$' (*This interests me.*), 'interest$_{(N)}$' (*without interest*), 'die' (*die from a heart attack*), etc. They are genuine meanings; in language **L** they are expressed by full LUs of **L**.[5] Thus, the lexical significations cited above are expressed by the lexemes LIKE$_{(CONJ, compar)}$, PIECE$_{(N)}$, NARROW$_{(ADJ)}$, INTEREST$_{(V)}$, INTEREST$_{(N)}$ and DIE$_{(V)}$. A lexical signification can also be expressed by an idiom; for instance the idiom ⌐KICK THE BUCKET⌐ expresses the same signification as the lexeme DIE (plus flippancy of the Speaker towards the dying person; and, of course, a different register).

☞   Idioms are indicated by raised half-brackets: ⌐…⌐.

A lexical signification – that is, a chunk of meaning expressed by a full LU – is also called a lexical meaning, or a semanteme. The semanteme is the basic semantic unit in natural languages (Ch. 3, *3.1*).

Grammatical significations bear on lexical significations and are rather abstract; in a given language, they are not numerous (a few hundred, at most) and constitute a closed set. Grammatical significations are a motley collection: some are meanings – that is, configurations of semantemes (which is the case for most derivatemes) or correspond to clusters of meanings (semantically full grammemes, such as PLURAL), while some others represent various types of combinatorial (= cooccurrence) information. *Table 2.1* gives some examples of grammatical significations.

Table 2.1 Grammatical significations: an illustration

Derivatemes (see *3.2.2*)	'person who does [L]' [*eat*$_L$+*er*] Sp. 'small and pleasant [L]' [*arbol*$_L$+*it*+*o* 'small and pleasant tree']
Grammemes (see *3.2.1*)	(nominal) PLURAL (*chair*+*s*, *teeth*) INDEFINITE (*a chair*) PAST [tense] (*talk*+*ed*, *sang*); FUTURE [tense] (*will work*) ACCUSATIVE [case] (Lat. *aquil*+*am* 'eagle')
Syntactic relations, deep and surface	–**ATTR**→, …; –**prepositional**→, …
Communicative values	**THEME** (marked by Jap. *-wa* or Kor. *-nin/-in*)

[5]   In some – rather infrequent – cases, a lexical signification can be expressed by a meaningful syntactic construction: see Ch. 11, *2.2.3*, p. 290).

In language **L**, grammatical significations are expressed by the grammatical means of **L**, namely by morphological means – affixes and morphological operations (such as apophonies), and by syntactic (= non-morphological) means – structural (= grammatical) LUs. The derivatemes and grammemes cited above are expressed by suffixes and by the morphological operation of apophony (the grammeme PLURAL in *teeth* is expressed by the apophony $A_{PL}^{/u/\Rightarrow/i/}$ and the grammeme PAST in *sang* by the apophony $A_{PAST}^{/ı/\Rightarrow/æ/}$, or else by structural words (the article A/AN and the auxiliary WILL). Syntactic relations are expressed by syntactic constructions, and the communicative value THEME is realized by a suffix (in our example; however, in most languages theme is expressed by word order).

Axis 2: Semantic significations vs. syntactic significations

Semantic significations correspond to genuine meanings and are freely chosen by the Speaker. For instance, the configuration of semantemes 'X uses X's resources in order to cause**2** that Y, who wants to do Z, can successfully do Z' is a semantic signification (= a chunk of meaning); it can be expressed by the lexeme $HELP_{(V)}$, or, if the Speaker chooses, by its near-synonyms $AID_{(V)}$ or $ASSIST_{(V)}$. These are, then, lexical-semantic significations. Similarly, the configuration of semantemes '[P] before now' is a semantic signification that the Speaker will choose if he wants to talk about an event 'P' as taking place in the past, while expressing 'P' as a verb. This is a grammatical – more precisely, inflectional – semantic signification.

> REMARK. The Speaker's freedom in choosing linguistic units needs to be qualified when it comes to inflectional significations. In English, tense **must** be expressed with each verb (no choice here!), but whether this will be the present, the past or the future is up to the Speaker. For more on this, see *3.2*.

Syntactic significations do not correspond to genuine meanings. Rather than being freely chosen by the Speaker, they are imposed on him by his language – to express syntactic and morphological dependencies and convey other grammatical information. Thus, governed prepositions and conjunctions (*insist **on**, dream **of**, demand **that**, wonder **whether**,* etc.) express lexical-syntactic significations, while, for instance, markers of adjectival agreement with the modified noun (Fr. [*histoire*$_{(fem)}$+s_{PL}] *intéressantes*+e_{FEM}+s_{PL} 'interesting [stories]') express grammatical (in this case, inflectional) syntactic significations.

Axis 3: Morphological significations vs. non-morphological significations

A morphological signification is expressed within the wordform on whose stem it bears – that is, synthetically; a non-morphological signification is expressed outside the wordform on whose stem it bears – that is, analytically. Thus, the passive of a verb is expressed in Latin by a suffix within the verbal wordform, while in English, the passive marker is a form of the auxiliary verb BE combined with the past participle of the lexical verb:

(1) a. Lat. *Urbs*$_{NOM}$ *a hostibus*$_{ABL}$ *oppugnā+ba*$_{IMPF}$+*t*$_{3.SG}$+***ur***$_{PASS}$. ~
    b. Eng. *The city was **being** attack+ed by the enemies.*

Another good example is the expression of definiteness in Scandinavian languages – morphological (by a suffix) and in English – non-morphological (by an article):

(2) a. Swed. *stol*   *stol*+Ø$_{SG}$+***en***   *stol*+*ar*$_{PL}$+***na***
    b. Eng. *chair*   ***the*** *chair*+Ø$_{SG}$ ***the*** *chair*+*s*$_{PL}$

Combined, the three classification axes give a total of eight classes of logically possible linguistic significations. Four of these classes are relevant to semantics; they are indicated in the following table, along with linguistic sub-disciplines that study them. (As we announced in the *Preface*, morphological semantics will not be explored in any detail in this book.)

Table 2.2 Linguistic significations studied by semantics

Class of linguistic significations relevant to semantics	Linguistic sub-discipline that studies them
Lexical-semantic morphological significations	lexical semantics
Lexical-semantic non-morphological significations	
Grammatical semantic morphological significations	morphological semantics
Grammatical semantic non-morphological significations	

1.5   Linguistic Expressive Means

The linguistic expressive means of language **L** are the totality of devices that **L** has at its disposal to express meanings and the structural organization of texts of **L**. There are just four possible types of linguistic expressive means: LUs, linear order, prosody, and inflection (see *3.3* below). The first three of these are universal: all languages use them; in contrast, there are quite a few languages that do not use inflection (among others, Yoruba, Thai, Mandarin Chinese, Vietnamese).

Each of the four types of expressive means can be used in one of the following two ways:

1. In a semantic capacity, to express a meaning directly; such a means has its source in the semantic representation (of the corresponding text).
2. In a syntactic (= non-semantic) capacity, to mark a syntactic role, without direct correspondence with elements of the semantic representation.

Table 2.3 illustrates the four types of linguistic expressive means.

Table 2.3 Linguistic expressive means

Linguistic expressive means	in a semantic capacity	in a syntactic capacity
Lexical units	RAIN, ʰKICK THE BUCKETʼ, BLUE, WHEN, WITHOUT, etc.	THAT (*think **that** P*), WHICH (*the hypothesis **which**...*), ON (*depend **on***), BE (***is** intelligent*), PAY (***pay** attention*), etc.
Linear order	Expresses the communicative structure; e.g.: *This*FOCALIZED *I do not know* vs. *I do not know this.*	Marks syntactic constructions: ART + N, PREP + N, CONJ + CLAUSE, etc.
Prosody	Expresses affirmation, interrogation, exclamation; irony, sarcasm; tenderness; emphasis; etc.	Marks breath groups, etc.
Inflection	Expresses nominal number and definiteness; voice, mood, aspect and tense of the verb; the degree of the adjective	Marks agreement and government

We have presented the linguistic expressive means in the order that corresponds to their importance: lexical units > linear order > prosody > inflection.

LUs constitute the most important expressive means because all other means act upon them, as it were. Linear order comes before prosody because the latter can only be superimposed on a linearized sequence. Inflection is the most limited expressive means because it is absent from many languages and does not appear in all the sentences of a language that does have it. By their physical nature, these means are not equal, either: some are used preferentially in a semantic capacity (e.g., LUs), while others rather in a syntactic capacity (e.g., linear order).

1.6   Basic Formalisms for Representing Linguistic Phenomena

We now turn to the formalisms used in the Meaning-Text approach to write linguistic representations of utterances (*1.6.1*) and linguistic rules that establish correspondences between these representations (*1.6.2*).

1.6.1   Linguistic Representations

At this point, we will present only the formalisms used to construct the basic structures of linguistic representations at the semantic, syntactic and morphological levels, leaving the peripheral structures aside (for the contrast "basic vs. peripheral structure," see Ch. 1, *2.2.2*, p. 16). These structures – the (semantic) network, the (deep- and surface-syntactic dependency) tree, and the (morphological) string – are graphs of particular types.

A **graph** is a set of points, called vertices, or nodes, linked by lines, called edges. The nodes represent the elements of a set, and the edges represent the relations between these elements. Generally speaking, the nodes of a graph are not linearly ordered; the physical disposition of the nodes on paper is therefore irrelevant.

The graphs considered in linguistics are:

1. Connected, i.e., there is a path – a series of edges – between any two nodes.
2. Directed, i.e., each edge is assigned an arrow, indicating the hierarchy between the two nodes it connects; an edge supplied with an arrow is called an arc.
3. Labeled, i.e., all nodes and all arcs are supplied with labels specifying their linguistic nature. (However, see below for a caveat concerning strings.)

From a formal viewpoint, the graph representing a semantic structure is a **network**: a fully connected, fully directed and fully labeled graph without further constraints. The nodes of a semantic network are labeled with lexical meanings (= semantemes) of a language, and its arcs bear distinctive numbers indicating the relations between a predicative meaning and its arguments.

A syntactic structure is formally a **tree** – that is, a network satisfying the following two conditions:

1. Each of its nodes receives no more than one arc (it either has a unique governor or no governor at all).
2. There exists one and only one node that receives no arc (= does not have a governor); this node is called the top node, or the head, of the tree.

The nodes of a syntactic tree are labeled with LUs and its arcs (a.k.a. branches) with the names of syntactic dependency relations. The nature of these labels depends on which sublevel we are dealing with: at the deep-syntactic sublevel, the nodes are labeled with deep LUs, and the branches with deep-syntactic relations; at the surface-syntactic sublevel, the respective labels are surface lexemes subscripted with semantic inflectional characteristics, and surface-syntactic relations.

Finally, the deep-morphological structure is a **string** – that is, a particular case of a tree such that each of its nodes allows for only one leaving arc – that is, each governor has only one dependent. In other words, there is no branching. In a string, the arcs and their labels, which are always identical, are omitted; the dependency relation that exists between the nodes is in fact the precedence relation, indicated by their linear order. To put it simply, a string is a linear sequence of lexemes.

The nodes of a morphological string are labeled with lexemes supplied with all necessary inflectional characteristics, i.e., with all their grammemes. In other words, the DMorphS of a sentence is an ordered sequence of DMorph-representations of all its wordforms.

Figure 2.3 shows the basic structures representing the organization of the sentence *I like swimming a lot* 'I very much like swimming' at the semantic, deep- and surface-syntactic and deep-morphological levels.[6]

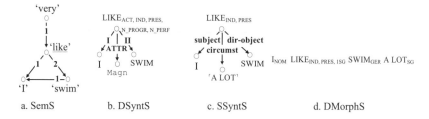

a. SemS   b. DSyntS   c. SSyntS   d. DMorphS

Figure 2.3 Structures of the sentence *I like swimming a lot* at different representation levels

The first two of these structures will be revisited, respectively, in Ch. 10 and Ch. 11.

1.6.2   Linguistic Rules

Linguistic rules come in several types, of which we will introduce the most common one here: transition linguistic rules.

> **Definition 2.11:** Transition Linguistic Rule
> A transition linguistic rule is an expression of the form X ⇔ Y (| *C*), where X is instantiated by some linguistic content and Y by what expresses this content; the bi-directional double arrow means 'corresponds to', and *C* represents the set of conditions (possibly empty) under which the correspondence in question is valid.

If read from left to right, a linguistic rule means 'X is expressed by Y (under conditions *C*)'; read from right to left, it means 'Y expresses X (under conditions *C*)'.

In this book, the term *rule* is used strictly in its technical sense, as it was just defined. Here are three examples of transition linguistic rules (for English).

A lexicalization semantic rule		
'manufactured object designed for people X to sleep in ...'	⇔	**bed-**

The indicated meaning can be expressed by the radical of the English noun $BED_{(N)}1$ – that is by the lexical sign

$$bed\text{-} = \langle \text{'bed'}; \text{/béd/}; \Sigma = \text{radical, nominal } ... \rangle \,.$$

---

[6] Pronounced with a different prosody, namely with a pause after *like* (*I like | swimming a lot*), this string expresses a different meaning: 'I like to swim frequently'. This corresponds to a different SemS, which, instead of 'very' bearing on 'like', has 'much' bearing on 'swim'. Its DSyntS and SSyntS are also different from the ones in *Figure 2.3*.

A morphologization semantic rule

'more than one'	$\Leftrightarrow$	PLURAL

The semanteme configuration 'more than one' can be expressed by the inflectional signification (= grammeme) PLURAL (which, on a closer-to-surface level will be expressed by the morpheme {PLURAL}.

A linearization syntactic rule

$L_{1(N)}$–determinative→$L_{2(determ)}$	$\Leftrightarrow$	$L_{2(determ)} + \ldots + L_{1(N)}$

In English, a determiner precedes the determined noun, from which it can be separated by some other lexical elements (this is shown by "..."): *the*$_{(det)}$ *child*$_{(N)}$, *a*$_{(det)}$ ***gentle*** *child*$_{(N)}$, *these*$_{(det)}$ ***big and promising*** *projects*$_{(N)}$, etc.

A Meaning-Text model of a language is a set of modules, each module being a set of rules operating between representations of utterances at two adjacent levels. In this book we are interested in the rules of the semantic module, or for short, semantic rules, which operate between semantic and deep-syntactic representations; semantic rules were introduced in Ch. 1, *2.3* and will be discussed in Ch. 12.

The concept of linguistic rule calls for two important comments having to do with the generality of rules and their relation to linguistic signs.

Generality of linguistic rules

From Definition 2.11 it follows that a linguistic rule can be more or less general. A rule can even be individual, such that X and Y can each be instantiated by a single element; all lexical rules and most of the morphological rules are of this type, like the lexicalization and morphologization semantic rules above. On the other hand, a rule can have absolute generality; the linearization syntactic rule above is such a rule, because it applies to all nouns and all determiners of English. Between the two extremes, there are numerous intermediate cases. For instance, the adverb ENOUGH is linearly positioned after the adjective it modifies, contrary to all other adverbs: *big enough* vs. *sufficiently big*; the corresponding rule manipulates a single element, the adverb in question, and an open set of adjectives. Rules that are sufficiently general are called productive.

Linguistic rules and linguistic signs

A linguistic sign (as introduced in Subsection *1.1*) can be considered as a particular type of transition rule. More specifically, the signified 's' constitutes the left-hand part (= X) of this rule, and its signifier /s/ and syntactics Σ_s, taken together, its right-hand part (= Y). The semantic rules 1 and 2, given above as examples, are such rules.

According to a long-standing tradition, it is customary to speak separately about lexical **signs** and grammatical **rules**. This is also a pedagogically handy distinction: it allows us to sketch the general structure of language in a simple and graphic way, keeping apart the lexicon and the grammar.

Language is a set of two very unequal subsets: a set of simple signs and a set of rules. Simple linguistic signs are of two types:

1. Lexical signs (counting several hundred thousand[7]) correspond to lexemes and idioms; they constitute the lexical stock, or the lexicon, of language **L**.
2. Grammatical signs (several hundred) correspond to affixes and morphological operations; they belong to **L**'s grammar. The grammar (i.e., semantic + syntax + morphology + phonology) includes, along with grammatical signs, around one thousand grammar rules, which manipulate linguistic signs and produce more complex expressions: these rules combine radicals and affixes into wordforms, wordforms into phrases, phrases into clauses, and the latter into sentences (see *2.1*).

Table 2.4 Language = lexicon + grammar

<table>
<tr><th colspan="3">Language</th></tr>
<tr><th>Lexicon</th><th colspan="2">Grammar</th></tr>
<tr><th>– Lexical Signs –</th><th>– Grammatical Signs –</th><th>– Grammatical Rules –</th></tr>
<tr>
<td>chair, go, limited, around, ⌐red tape¬, ⌐pull [N_Y's] leg¬, ⌐as if¬</td>
<td>-s, -ed, -er, anti-, re-, $\mathbf{A}_{PL}^{/u/\Rightarrow/i/}$ (*tooth ~ teeth*), $\mathbf{A}_{PAST}^{/\text{I}/\Rightarrow/æ/}$ (*spring ~ sprang*)</td>
<td>

Semantic rules
'σ₁'–1→'σ₂' ⇔ L('σ₁')–I→L('σ₂') | L('σ₁') is a verb not in the passive

Syntactic rules
ADJ←modif–N ⇔ ADJ +...+ N (*interesting book*)
PREP–prepos→N ⇔ PREP +...+ N (*for John*)

Morphological rules
{PL} ⇔ +/z/ |__ /Vowel/ or /Voiced Consonant/

Phonological rules
/t/ ⇔ [tʰ] | **not** /s/__ **and** __ /V́/ [*potato*]
   ⇔ [t] | /s/__ **or not** __ /V́/ [*stand, potato*]

</td>
</tr>
</table>

The main difference between lexicon and grammar lies in the degree of generality of corresponding descriptions. The lexical stock contains elements

---

[7] This number (about a million) is a rough upper estimate, obtained in the following way. *American College Dictionary* has 135,000 entries, with an average of 2.5 wordsenses per entry, which gives a total of 340,000 wordsenses. To this we need to add idioms, "buried" in the entries of their lexical constituents. Moreover, divisions of lexical items into wordsenses are often too coarse in this dictionary; with the necessary adjustments, we can easily reach more that 500,000 wordsenses. If we consider French, *Le Petit Robert* contains some 60,000 entries and 150,000 wordsenses (2.5 per entry on the average). With the idioms and additional wordsenses due to a more precise analysis, we reach the same number of wordsenses as in English: ≈ 500,000. A similar situation exists in other languages. A lexicographic wordsense corresponds to one lexical sign (a lexeme or an idiom). It is thus justified to posit 1,000,000 lexical signs as the upper limit for a language.

that do not lend themselves easily to a generalized description: each of them requires a description of its own. As a result, the description of the lexical stock is not fully systematic. (True, LUs form systems, but, in spite of this, each LU has to be described separately.) In contrast, the grammar works by generalizations; its rules manipulate classes of LUs, rather than single units. Rules of grammar, even when they are described individually, show in their behavior a degree of regularity and systematicity that one never sees with lexical units. Of course, this is but an idealization: there are many regularities in the lexical stock and many exceptions to the rules of grammar; however, in order to get a clear picture, it is useful to think of these two aspects of language in this way, i.e., as consisting of a lexicon (= system of individual lexical signs) and a grammar (= system of general grammatical rules).

2   Syntactic Notions

Syntactic notions will be presented in two groups: basic syntactic units (*2.1*) and major syntactic classes of lexical units, or parts of speech (*2.2*).

2.1   Basic Syntactic Units

We distinguish four basic syntactic units: (1) wordform, the minimal unit manipulated by syntactic rules (and also the maximal unit of morphology); (2) phrase; (3) clause and (4) sentence, which is the maximal unit of syntax.

   Since all syntactic units are particular cases of utterance, we will start by characterizing this latter concept.

2.1.1   Utterance

> **Definition 2.12**: Utterance
> An utterance is a linguistic expression that is more or less autonomous: it can appear between two major pauses, can constitute a prosodic unit, and its internal structure is governed by linguistic rules; an utterance is perceived by speakers as "something that exists in the language."

> **NB:** Strictly speaking, this is not a real definition, but rather an informal characterization. This cannot be otherwise, given the great generality of the notion of utterance.

   An utterance can be a wordform, a phrase, a clause, or a sentence. Linguistic expressions smaller than an utterance are parts of wordforms (morphs such as the prefix **re-** in *retake* or the suffix **-ed** in *answered*); they cannot be used alone in ordinary speech, outside of metalinguistic statements.[8] A linguistic expression can also be larger than an utterance, for example a sequence of sentences forming a paragraph.

---

[8] They, however, are *texts* in the technical sense used in the MTT; see Ch. 1, *1*.

2.1.2 Wordform

> **Definition 2.13:** Wordform
>
> A wordform is a segmental sign that is more or less autonomous and not
> representable in terms of other (previously established) wordforms.

NB: This definition is inductive:[9] it presupposes establishing some obvious,
or clear-cut, wordforms and then using these to define other, less obvious,
ones. (We'll see in an instant what "obvious" means here.)

Informally, a wordform is a minimal chunk of speech: it cannot be broken
up into other chunks of the same type, that is, into other wordforms. At the
same time, it is sufficiently autonomous, which means one of the following
two things: (1) Either, in principle, it can be used alone (between two major
pauses), in which case we are dealing with an obvious wordform, e.g., **book**,
interesting, **read**, **speaks**, **little**, **boys**. (2) Or it cannot be used alone but can
be separated from an obvious wordform by (at least) another obvious one, e.g.,
the English articles **a/the** are separable in this way: *a very interesting* book; *the
most interesting and useful* book. The wordforms like these, whose identity is
(more or less) "stable" and "permanent," are called language wordforms.

There is also a different type of wordform, called speech wordform; "unsta-
ble" and "transient," speech wordforms are produced dynamically – in actual
speech – by some syntactic rules applied to language wordforms. Stock examples are amalgams such as Fr. **à le** 'to the' ⇒ **au** /o/, resulting from an obligatory
fusion of the preposition À with the article LE, and splittings such as Ger. *Ich
mache das Fenster **auf***'I open the window', a result of an obligatory separation
of the prefix **auf-** from the radical **mach-** of the verb AUFMACHEN '[to] open'
and its positioning at the end of the clause (MACHEN alone means 'make').

Prototypically, a language wordform is a particular inflectional form of a
lexeme; for instance, the wordforms **speak**, **speaks**, **spoke**, **spoken**, **speaking**,
etc. are inflectional forms of the lexeme SPEAK$_{(V)}$ (*John spoke at the meeting.*). In contrast, a speech wordform does not belong to a lexeme.

A wordform is a simple sign because it does not contain other wordforms
within itself; but in languages with sufficiently rich morphology, a wordform
is in most cases a non-elementary sign, that is, it can be represented in terms of
morphs and/or other signs, cf.: *definition+s*, Rus. *zaščiščaj+ušč+ix+sja* 'of those

---

[9] An inductive, or recursive, definition specifies a set {X} of elements {x$_1$, x$_2$, ..., x$_n$} in two
 steps: (1) It gives – by a list – a small number of entities that are declared elements of {X};
 they constitute the induction base. (2) It specifies the rule that allows for adding to {X}
 other elements similar to the elements of the base: this is the induction step. The other major
 definition type, most often used in this textbook, is the deductive definition: a set {X} of
 elements {x$_1$, x$_2$, ..., x$_n$} is defined as a subset of a previously defined set {Y}, called common
 genus – by formulating the properties (specific differences) that characterize the elements of
 {X}, but not the elements of the set {Y} – {X}.

who are defending themselves [PL.GEN]',[10] *geese = goose-* $\oplus$ $\mathbf{A}_{\mathrm{PL}}^{/i/\Rightarrow/u/}$, etc. (An elementary sign – see *3.1.1* – is necessarily simple, while the converse is not true.)

> REMARK. Compound nouns, such as Ger. *Ost+frankreich* 'Eastern France' or *Sprach+geschichte* lit. 'language history', do not contain two complete wordforms, but two stems. Thus, 'East' in German is *Osten*, not *Ost-*, and 'language' is *Sprache*, not *Sprach-*. Of course, a radical can "physically" coincide with a wordform; e.g., in the English wordform *book* the radical is *book-*. Yet, notionally, these two entities are distinct.

2.1.3   Phrase

> **Definition 2.14:** Phrase
> A phrase is an utterance that consists of syntactically linked word-forms supplied with an appropriate prosody and is perceived by the speakers as a unit of their language, but that does not necessarily constitute a complete unit of communication.

NB: 1. As a limiting case, a phrase can consist of one wordform.
     2. Some phrases can constitute a sentence and thus be a complete unit of communication: *John arrived. | It depends. | Wow! | No way.*

Examples: *sequence*; *a sequence*; *syntactically linked wordforms*; *of syntactically linked wordforms*; *a sequence of syntactically linked wordforms*.

A phrase of **L** always manifests a particular syntactic construction of **L** (or several syntactic constructions).

Stretching the terminology a bit, we also use the term *phrase* – a convenient abbreviation – for a structural representation of an actual phrase. Thus, for instance, we can speak of the "ADJ + N" phrase, meaning the set of phrases like *intelligent child*, *expensive houses*, *former minister*, *blue sky*, etc.

2.1.4   Clause

> **Definition 2.15:** Clause
> A clause is a phrase that contains a finite verb with its actants or is syntactically equivalent to such a phrase (that is, it has the same syntactic distribution).

A finite verb V_{FIN} is a form of a verb that obligatorily expresses the mood – indicative, imperative, subjunctive, etc.; in many languages, it also expresses

---

[10] This wordform impressed Lewis Carrol (a.k.a. Charles Dodgson, the author of *Alice's Adventures in Wonderland*), who wrote in his travel diary while on a trip to Russia: "[the word] *zashcheeshchayooshcheekhsya* (of those who protect themselves) is impossible to utter." Alice herself would, of course, say "Curiouser and curiouser!"

the tense – present, past, future (but this is not obligatory: in Chinese or Vietnamese it does not).

Finite forms of a verb are opposed to its non-finite forms. Here are several finite and all non-finite forms of the verb SING.

- Some of its finite forms: [*I, you, we, they*] *sing*; [*he/she*] *sings*; [*I*] *am singing*; [*you*] *have sung*; [*we*] *will sing*; *Sing!*; [*if he*] *had sung*; [*they*] *have been sung*; [*it*] *was sung*; [*it*] *will be sung*; etc.
- All of its non-finite forms: (infinitives) *sing*; [*to*] *have sung*; [*to*] *be sung*, [*to*] *have been sung*; (participles and gerunds) *singing*; *having sung*; *being sung, having been sung*.

> **NB:** In principle, a non-finite verbal form can express tenses or even person/ number distinctions. For instance, in Hungarian and Portuguese the infinitive expresses the person and number of the actor: Hung. *Kell menn+em* 'Is. necessary to.go-**I**'. vs. *Kell menn+iük* 'Is.necessary to.go-**they**'; Port. *É necesario ir+mos* 'Is necessary to.go-**we**'. vs. *É necesario ir+em* 'Is necessary to.go-**they**'. However, a non-finite form cannot express the mood.

A clause can be a constituent part of a sentence or constitute a (simple) sentence by itself.

Examples: *when John arrives, …*; *… that I will be visiting Boston with my kids*; *John and Mary study at the University of Montreal. | In reality, the three are closely related.*

> **NB:** Definition 2.15 rules out the concept of **non-finite clause*; in our framework, this is a *contradictio in adjecto*. What are commonly called "non-finite clauses" (namely, infinitive- and gerund-headed expressions such as *to play on computers* and *playing on computers*) are considered here simply to be special types of phrases.

2.1.5   Sentence

> **Definition 2.16:** Sentence
> A sentence is a maximal utterance that typically consists of clauses and is a complete unit of communication.

A sentence is crucially characterized by one of the sentence-specific prosodies (particular to each language): declarative, interrogative and exclamative.

Two or more sentences represent a sequence of utterances. A simple sentence consists of just one clause. The sentence you just read constitutes an example of this.

This definition covers only prototypical sentences – those that constitute descriptive utterances (such that they communicate in the technical sense – i.e., contribute information in a syntactic form that allows for negation and questioning; on communication vs. signaling as a manner of transmitting information by means of language, see Ch. 10, *3.2.1.5*). However, all languages also have various so-called minor-type sentences, which do not contain finite verbs – that is, do not consist of clauses: *Yes!* | *How nice!* | *Down with taxes!* | *Wham!* | *Of course*. These are non-descriptive, more precisely, signalative utterances (such that they do not communicate, in the technical sense alluded to above, but rather signal the emotional state of the Speaker, his attitudes, and so on).

The sentence is the upper limit for syntactic dependencies between word-forms; wordforms from different sentences can be connected only by anaphoric links, which are not dependencies.

As indicated in the *Preface*, in this book we will consider semantic phenomena up to the level of sentences, to the exclusion of discourse semantics.

2.2 Major Syntactic Classes of Lexical Units, alias Parts of Speech

According to their syntactic properties, LUs of a language fall into a number of major syntactic classes, traditionally known as parts of speech: noun, verb, adjective, adverb, and so on. Members of a given syntactic class share many important syntactic properties, namely the ability to play the same or similar syntactic roles in a sentence. Thus, in English, a "bare" noun (i.e., a noun without a preposition) can be: the subject of the Main Verb (*The* **baby**$_{(N)\text{-Subject}}$ ⌜*woke up*⌝$_{(V)\text{-MV}}$. | *The* **rain**$_{(N)\text{-Subject}}$ *is*$_{(V)\text{-MV}}$ *falling.*); the direct object of a transitive verb (*in order not to* ⌜*wake up*⌝$_{(V)}$ *the* **baby**$_{(N)\text{-Dir-Object}}$; *liking*$_{(V)}$ *the* **rain**$_{(N)\text{-Dir-Object}}$); the object of a preposition (*the sleep of the* **baby**$_{(N)\text{-Prep-Object}}$; *insist on the* **departure**$_{(N)\text{-Prep-Object}}$); etc. This means that the syntactic behavior of an LU is to a great extent conditioned by its syntactic class. To put it differently, the same (or similar) syntactic rules apply to (almost) all members of the given class, which allows for a compact formulation of rules and important generalizations.

Some syntactic classes are open: LUs are easily added to and subtracted from them in the process of the historical development of the language. Some other syntactic classes are closed and rather limited in size: they very rarely accept additions or subtractions in membership. The LUs belonging to an open class are most often those that express lexical meanings; they can be considered prototypical LUs. Those in a closed syntactic class either express grammatical meanings or are semantically empty; they are atypical LUs. The distinction between LUs of open and closed syntactic classes is also known as the distinction "lexical words ~ grammatical words."

As can be seen from what immediately follows, each closed syntactic class of LUs represents a subclass of an open class; thus, copular and auxiliary verbs are a subclass of verbs; pronominal nouns, a subclass of nouns, etc.

Major syntactic classes of LUs (= parts of speech) are disjoint: no LU can belong to more than one major class. English LUs fall into the following major syntactic classes.

OPEN CLASSES (≈ "lexical words")

- Verbs: LIVE$_{(V)}$, DIE$_{(V)}$, HELP$_{(V)}$, KNOW$_{(V), ...}$; ⌐HAVE BUTTERFLIES⌐$_{(V)}$, ⌐KICK THE BUCKET⌐$_{(V)}$, ⌐BITE [Y's] HEAD OFF⌐$_{(V)}$, ...
- Nouns: LIFE$_{(N)}$, DEATH$_{(N)}$, HELP$_{(N)}$, KNOWLEDGE$_{(N)}$, SAND$_{(N)}$, OATS$_{(N)}$, JOHN$_{(N)}$, MONTREAL$_{(N)}$, ⌐RACE AGAINST TIME⌐$_{(N)}$, ⌐BLACK BELT⌐$_{(N)}$, ⌐LAME DUCK⌐$_{(N)}$, ...
- Adjectives: RED$_{(A)}$, SHORT$_{(A)}$, INTELLLIGENT$_{(A)}$, BEAUTIFUL$_{(A)}$, ...; ⌐SECOND TO NONE⌐$_{(A)}$, ⌐IN STITCHES⌐$_{(A)}$, ...
- Adverbs: SLOWLY$_{(ADV)}$, FAST$_{(ADV)}$, HARD$_{(ADV)}$ (*It was raining hard.*), INTERMITTENTLY$_{(ADV)}$; ⌐FROM RAGS TO RICHES⌐$_{(ADV)}$, ⌐TOOTH AND NAIL⌐$_{(ADV)}$, ...
- Clausatives (≈ expressions, mono- or multi-lexemic, such that each constitutes a clause): YES$_{(CLAUS)}$, WOW$_{(CLAUS)}$, ⌐THE CAT IS OUT OF THE BAG!⌐$_{(CLAUS)}$, ...

OPEN CLASSES (≈ "grammatical words")

- Copula verbs: BE$_{(V, cop)}$, BECOME$_{(V, cop)}$
- Auxiliary verbs: BE$_{(V, aux)}$, DO$_{(V, aux)}$, HAVE$_{(V, aux)}$
- Pronominal verbs [= pro-verbs]: DO$_{(V, pron)}$ ([*Do you agree?*] *Yes, I do.*)
- Pronominal nouns [= pronouns]: I$_{(N, pron, pers)}$, IT**I.1**$_{(N, pron, pers)}$ (*It* [e.g., the book] *is here*), IT**II**$_{(N, pron, impers)}$ (*It snows*), WHO$_{(N, pron, interr)}$?, NOTHING$_{(N, pron, neg)}$, ⌐NO MATTER WHO⌐$_{(N, pron)}$
- Pronominal adjectives [= determiners]: A$_{(ART)}$, THE$_{(ART)}$; THIS$_{(ADJ, pron, demonstr)}$; MY$_{(ADJ, pron, poss)}$; WHICH?$_{(ADJ, pron, interr)}$, WHICH$_{(ADJ, pron, rel)}$
- Pronominal adverbs: HERE$_{(ADV, pron, demonstr)}$, THERE$_{(ADV, pron, demonstr)}$, WHERE?$_{(ADV, pron, interr)}$, ⌐NO MATTER HOW⌐$_{(ADV, pron)}$, NEVER$_{(ADV, pron, neg)}$

Special subclasses of adverbs:
- Prepositions: ON**6** (*right on the border*), BY**2** (*travel by train*), ⌐ACCORDING TO⌐**3** (*Everything was done according to plan.*)
- Conjunctions: AND**I.1** (*John and Mary*), BUT**II.3**, THAT**1**, IF**1**
- Particles: EVEN, ALSO, ONLY, NOT

In addition to sharing many syntactic properties, members of a major syntactic class also share some semantic and (in languages that have morphology) morphological properties.

Semantic properties of LUs are much less predictable from their major syntactic class membership. It is often said that verbs denote actions or events, that nouns denote objects and substances, and adjectives – properties (these are semantic classes; see Ch. 8, *1.2*). Even if this is true for prototypical members of these syntactic classes, verbs can very well denote properties, there are many nouns denoting actions, many adjectives denoting entities, and so on;

cf.: *John **lacks**(V)* [property] *courage*. | *This is a crazy **race**(N)* [action]. | ***vehicular**(ADJ)* [entity] *accident* ['vehicular' = 'vehicle']. However, a verb can never denote an entity (an object, a substance, a person, etc.): verbs only denote facts.

In contrast, morphological properties of LUs are largely predictable from their major syntactic class membership. Thus, all English verbs (with full, i.e., non-defective, paradigms) are inflected for mood, tense, perfectivity (perfect vs. non-perfect), aspect (progressive vs. non-progressive), person and number; transitive verbs, in addition, are inflected for voice. All English nouns inflect for number (singular or plural) and definiteness (indefinite ~ definite ~ non-definite).

3   Morphological Notions

In this section, we sketch the definitions of some basic morphological signs – signs that make up wordforms (*3.1*); we characterize inflectional and derivational significations, i.e., significations that are most often expressed within wordforms (*3.2*); and we describe the two basic morphological mechanisms by which the forms of lexemes are constructed and new lexemes are produced: inflection and word formation (*3.3*).

3.1   Morphological Signs

3.1.1   Elementary Sign

> **Definition 2.17:** Elementary Sign
> An elementary sign of language **L** is a sign that is not representable in terms of other signs of **L**.

English signs such as **house-**, **write-**, **-ed**, **re-**, etc. are elementary; in fact, they are morphs, see immediately below.

3.1.2   Segmental Sign

> **Definition 2.18:** Segmental Sign
> A segmental sign is a sign whose signifier is a segment – a string of phonemes.

English signs such as **a**, **house-**, **write-**, **-ed**, **re-**, etc. are segmental; the signs **house**, **houses**, **brick houses**, **beautiful brick houses** are also segmental (they are all complex signs). However, the English apophony $A_{\text{PAST}}^{/ɪ/ ⇒ /æ/}$ (as in **spit** ~ **spat**, **sing** ~ **sang**, etc.) is not a segmental sign, nor is English morphological conversion of the type [the] **oil** ~ [to] **oil**, [the] **sand** ~ [to] **sand**, etc.

3.1.3   Morph

> **Definition 2.19:** Morph
> A morph is an elementary segmental sign.

Morphs constitute the vast majority of elementary signs of a language. (The remaining are non-segmental elementary signs: apophonies, reduplications, morphological conversions.)

A morph can either be a simple, i.e., non-derived and non-compound stem, also called radical (**house-, write-**), or an affix (**re-, -ed**).

3.2   Inflectional and Derivational Significations

As already mentioned (*1.4*), inflectional and derivational significations are the major subtypes of grammatical significations relevant to semantics.

3.2.1   Inflectional Significations and Inflectional Categories

Inflectional significations, or grammemes, such as PLURAL, DEFINITE, ACCUSA-TIVE, INDICATIVE, FUTURE, etc. characterize LUs of a given part of speech. Their expression is obligatory and highly regular with all LUs belonging to this part of speech. For example, each English noun has to be either in the singular or the plural, on the one hand, and definite, indefinite or non-definite, on the other. Each English verb must be characterized as being in the indicative, subjunctive, conditional or imperative; if in the indicative, it has to be either in the present, the past or the future; moreover, it is either perfective or non-perfective and either progressive or non-progressive. A Latin noun needs to be put into an appropriate case: nominative, accusative, dative, and so on. Mutually opposed grammemes are united into inflectional categories: the grammemes PLURAL$_{(N)}$ and SINGULAR$_{(N)}$ form the category of nominal number of English; PRESENT, PAST and FUTURE constitute the category of verbal tense in that language; Latin cases form the category of nominal case; and so forth.[11]

Two types of grammemes are distinguished:

1. Semantic grammemes, also called deep grammemes, correspond to seman-tic significations (or to values of semantic–communicative oppositions). In English, these are the grammemes of number and determination for the noun, the grammemes of voice, mood, perfectivity, aspect and tense for the verb, and the grammemes of degree of comparison for the adjective. For more on deep grammemes, see Ch. 11, *2.3*.
2. Syntactic, alias surface, grammemes do not correspond to semantic significa-tions; they are induced by syntactic phenomena of agreement and government. Typical syntactic grammemes are those of adjectival agreement with the noun in gender and number or nominal class (lacking in English but present in a

---

[11] Inflectional categories are of course language-specific (for example, unlike Latin, the English noun does not have case). Grammeme membership in a given inflectional category is language-specific as well (thus, Arabic has nominal number, like English, but with an additional grammeme: DUAL; cf. *kitāb* 'one book' ~ *kitābāni* 'two books' ~ *kutub* 'more than two books').

host of other languages – Romance, Slavic, Baltic, Semitic, Bantu, Wolof, etc.), and verbal agreement in person and number with the subject.

Grammemes are normally expressed within a wordform (Ch. 2, *2.1.2*), that is, by morphological means like affixes (suffixes, prefixes, etc.) and apophonies (meaningful alternations: substitutions of type *-oo* ⇒ *-ee* as in *goose ~ geese* or *-i-* ⇒ *-a-* as in *sing ~ sang*); in this case we speak of synthetic, or morphological expression. Grammemes can also be expressed by separate wordforms, this type of expression being called analytic, or non-morphological; for instance, auxiliary verbs in compound tenses express the grammemes of voice, mood, perfectivity, aspect and tense analytically (while the lexical meaning of the verb is expressed by the participle or the infinitive).

3.2.2   Derivational Significations

Derivational significations, or derivatemes, are neither obligatory (unlike grammemes, they do not necessarily form categories) nor necessarily regular; however, they resemble grammemes in that they are expressed by the same type of linguistic means: affixes and different morphological operations.

A derivateme can be a chunk of genuine meaning – a configuration of semantemes, for instance:

- 'person who does [L]', as in *read+**er*** from *read*$_L$, *teach+**er*** from *teach*$_L$, *particip+**ant*** from *participate*$_L$, etc.
- 'apply Y to Z', as in *[to] oil Z* from *[the] oil*$_Y$ (*He was oiling the machinery.*), *[to] hammer Z* from *[the] hammer*$_Y$, *[to] bomb Z* from *[the] bomb*$_Y$, etc.

However, some derivatemes are not meanings but syntactic significations: 'relative [to L]' (that is, an adjectivalization of the noun L: *space ~ spat+**ial***) or 'action [L]' (that is, a nominalization of the verb L: *move ~ move+**ment***).

3.3   Two Basic Morphological Mechanisms: Inflection and Word Formation

A morphological mechanism is a set of rules which, using some morphological expressive means, construct wordforms of language **L**. As we said above, there are two basic morphological mechanisms: inflection and word formation.

Inflection produces wordforms belonging to the same lexeme L, namely inflectional forms of L; they all carry the same lexical signification but express different inflectional – i.e., obligatory, or grammatical – significations. Inflectional forms of L are semantically compositional and formally regular; normally, they exhibit no phraseologization in either the signified or the signifier. Cf., for instance, the inflectional forms of the French lexeme INTELLIGENT$_{(ADJ)}$ 'intelligent':

intelligent+Ø$_{MASC}$+Ø$_{SG}$	**intelligent**+Ø$_{MASC}$+**s**$_{PL}$
intelligent+**e**$_{FEM}$+Ø$_{SG}$	**intelligent**+**e**$_{FEM}$+**s**$_{PL}$

Each of these forms has been constructed by putting together the radical **intelligent**- and the corresponding suffixes; the signified of each one is a regular sum of the signifieds of its components, and so is the signifier. Thanks to their regularity, the inflectional forms of lexemes need not be stored in the dictionary. Inflection is thus a purely synchronic and fully productive mechanism.

Example: inflectional paradigm of the Latin noun AMICUS$_{(N, masc, 2nd declension)}$ 'male friend'

	SINGULAR	PLURAL
NOMINATIVE	amic+us	amic+i
GENITIVE	amic+i	amic+orum
DATIVE	amic+o	amic+is
ACCUSTIVE	amic+um	amic+os
ABLATIVE	amic+o	amic+is
VOCATIVE	amic+e	amic+i

Word formation produces new lexemes out of the existing lexemes of a language. There are two major word formation types:

• Derivation, which adds a morphological means expressing a derivateme to the stem of a lexeme to produce a derived stem belonging to another lexeme.
• Compounding, which puts together the stems of two lexemes to produce a compound stem, also belonging to another lexeme.

Unlike inflection, which can only be synchronic, word formation can either be synchronic (actively used in speech and not confined to the dictionary – that is, semantically compositional and formally regular), or diachronic (no longer actively used and confined to the dictionary; it is non-compositional and/or irregular). Only synchronic word formation is a morphological mechanism, which has a constructive role in language **L**. The exclusive task of diachronic word formation is to characterize lexemes stored in the dictionary of **L**.

Examples of word formation

Synchronic derivation: (by prefix) PHILOSOPHICAL ~ ANTI-PHILOSOPHICAL 'that is against philosophy', CLERICAL ~ ANTI-CLERICAL 'that is against clergy'; (by suffix) DEFEND ~ DEFENDABLE 'that can be defended', EXCUSE$_{(V)}$ ~ EXCUSABLE 'that can be excused'; (by conversion) OIL$_{(N)}$ ~ OIL$_{(V)}$ 'to apply oil (to something)', HAMMER$_{(N)}$ ~ HAMMER$_{(V)}$ 'to apply a hammer (to something)'.

Diachronic derivation: (formally regular) RE**TAIN**, CON**TAIN**, DE**TAIN**, but there is no radical *tain; (formally irregular) PERFECT ~ PERFEC**TION** vs. STRONG ~ STREN**GTH** vs. MAGNIFICENT ~ MAGNIFICE**N**CE, or RICH ~ RICH**NESS** vs. ABUNDANT ~ ABUNDA**N**CE.

<u>Synchronic compounding</u>: Ger. WINTER 'winter' and ZEIT 'time' ~ WIN-
TERZEIT 'winter.time', STUDIEN 'study$_{(N)}$' and ZEIT 'time' ~ STU-
DIENZEIT 'study.time', KRIEG 'war' and ZEIT 'time' ~ KRIEGSZEIT
'war.time'.

<u>Diachronic compounding</u>: Ger. HOCHZEIT lit. 'high.time' = 'wedding',
ZEITWORT lit. 'time.word' = 'verb'.

During sentence synthesis, synchronic derivation and compounding are
involved in the operation of lexicalization (selection of LUs to express, at the
deep-syntactic level, some configurations of semantemes specified at the
semantic level of representation); see Ch. 12, *1.1*.

Further Reading

Linguistic sign: Saussure 1916 [2013]: 65–78; Mel'čuk 1982: 40–41 and Mel'čuk
2006a: 384–388.

Reference and denotation of linguistic signs: Cruse 2011, 382–401; Reimer &
Michaelson 2017.

Types of linguistic dependency and their possible combinations: Mel'čuk 2016:
195–197.

Linguistic significations: Jakobson 1957 [1971].

Valence and argument structure: Levin & Rappaport Hovav 2005; Matthews 2007. See
also Further Reading for Chapters 8 (Structure of an ECD Entry – Government Pattern)
and 11/12 (Semantic Actants/Deep-Syntactic Actants).

Sentence: Quirk *et al.* 1985 [2010]: 717–799.

Parts of speech: Hengeveld 1992.

Morphological signs: Mel'čuk 2006a: 383–403.

Inflection and word formation: Bauer 2004.

Part II

Meaning in Language and Its Description

3   Linguistic Meaning

As we know from Ch. 1, *2.3*, semantics$_1$ links linguistic meanings to corresponding linguistic expressions, or texts in our technical sense (in their "initial form" – that is, in the form of their deep-syntactic structures). From a Meaning-to-Text perspective, meaning is the starting point for semantic mechanisms. Therefore, it is natural to begin with a discussion of linguistic meaning.

This chapter covers four topics: the nature of linguistic meaning (Section *1*), meaning representation (Section *2*), semantic units and semantic relations (Section *3*) and, finally, semantic decomposition (Section *4*).

Before we start, a remark is in order. Natural language expresses meaning by two basic types of linguistic entity: words and sentences. In an important sense, **words are primary** – their number is finite, they are stored in the brains of speakers and constitute building blocks of sentences.

> **NB:** The primacy of words is not contradicted by the fact that most words have to be described not in isolation but within a propositional form – for instance, *X meets Y*, *X's gift to Y*, etc. (see *4.1* below), which is sentential by nature. (Think of an individual and his relation to society: it is individuals that make up a society, but an individual cannot be fully characterized outside his social network.)

For this reason, we have to begin with words and describe the process of their "coalescing" into sentences: the Meaning-Text model synthesizes sentences out of words starting from, and being guided by, a given semantic representation. These considerations determine the order of our presentation in the following chapters: Chapters 4–8 are dedicated to word-level semantics and Chapter 9 to sentence-level semantics.

1   The Nature of Linguistic Meaning

Semantics is about meaning; linguistic semantics is about linguistic meaning. But what is linguistic meaning? Or, at least, what is the meaning of a given linguistic expression? These questions are far from being new; they can be, and have been, answered in many different ways. The diversity of answers is partly due to the fact that linguistics is not the only science dealing with these questions: philosophy, psychology, cognitive science, Artificial Intelligence, etc. also try to define linguistic meaning. And they do so according to necessarily different perspectives. On the other hand, this diversity can be explained by a plurality of approaches within linguistics itself, as mentioned in Ch. 1, *1*: 7. As will be seen immediately below, our construal of linguistic meaning hinges upon the notion of synonymy, fundamental to language and linguistics.

1.1   Linguistic Meaning as the Invariant of Paraphrases

The proposed characterization of linguistic meaning is based on an intuitive perception of **the same** (= **identical**) **meaning**, a notion that is simpler than the notion of meaning *tout court*. Thus, consider sentences (1):

(1) a.   *Max spilled the beans.*
    b.   *Max told the secret (to everybody).*
    c.   *Max gave away the information that he was supposed to keep to himself.*

If you ask an English speaker "What is the meaning of sentence (1a)?", he will probably say that it means more or less the same thing as sentence (1b). In other words, he will answer by using an English expression that, according to him, has the same meaning as, or is a paraphrase of, (1a), but is somehow easier to understand. In order to explain the meaning of (1b), the Speaker will, again, suggest a paraphrase thereof, something like (1c); etc.

 If we want to stay within the confines of language, the only way to describe the meaning of a linguistic expression **E** is to give a paraphrase of **E**.

From this, Definition 3.1 follows:

> **Definition 3.1:** Linguistic Meaning (= The Meaning of a Linguistic Expression)
> The meaning of an expression **E** of language **L** is a formal description of the invariant of paraphrases of **E** – that is, a description of the meaning of all the expressions of **L** having the same meaning as **E**.
>
> **NB:** An invariant of a class is a property that is held by all elements of this class and that remains unchanged when transformations of a certain type are applied to the elements.

The notion of 'meaning' is thus derived from that of 'same meaning'.

In order to clarify the notion of meaning based on the identity of meanings, we can draw a parallel with the parameters of physical objects, such as weight (Reichenbach 1947: 210*ff*). The definition of the meaning 'weight' within naïve (= everyday) physics is based on the meaning of 'same weight', determined by a measuring instrument – a kind of scales, which need not be very sophisticated: one's arms can be used for the purpose. Weight is the only property common to all objects of the same weight; cf. a kilo of feathers and a kilo of iron. The "scales" used in the case of linguistic meaning are speakers' linguistic intuitions. The precision of the measure may vary – be more or less exact – as a function of the particular needs of the speaker in a given speech situation (cf. the essentially approximate nature of synonymy, to be discussed in Ch. 5, *1.1.1* and Ch. 9, *2.1*).

The intuitive notion of the identity of meaning underlies a speaker's lexical knowledge; for him, it is much easier to determine whether **E**' has the same meaning as **E** (= whether **E**' is a paraphrase of **E**) than to come up with a description of the meaning of **E**'. In fact, paraphrase judgments can be compared to judgments of grammaticality: speakers know whether an expression of their language is grammatical or not even if they have never studied grammar; such ability is part of linguistic competence. This explains the importance we attach to linguistic intuition and, in particular, to linguistic paraphrase (Ch. 9, *2.1*).

The common meaning of all paraphrases of **E**, or their **semantic invariant**, is presented by one of these paraphrases having special properties. This is an expression **Ê** that conforms to certain formal rules for writing meaning representations – the same rules that lexicographic definitions of LUs must obey (Ch. 5, 2). According to these rules:

- The meanings of '**E**' and '**Ê**' are identical ('**E**' = '**Ê**'), i.e., **Ê** is an exact paraphrase of **E**.
- Lexical elements used in **Ê** are disambiguated (by means of lexicographic numbers; for simplicity's sake, we allow ourselves not to use these numbers where the intended sense is clear from the context).
- **Ê** expresses the minimal semantic decomposition of **E**, which means that (1) **Ê** consists of lexical elements whose meanings are simpler than the meanings of the elements making up **E** and (2) that these elements are the least decomposed possible; for details, see Subsection *4.1.1* below.

Such a representation of the meaning of **E** – that is, by **Ê** – is called the canonical representation of '**E**'. For example, the canonical representation of the meaning of sentence (2a) is given in (2b):

(2) a. **E**: *John has been in Halifax since yesterday.*
   b. **Ê**: 'The human male named John is located at this moment in the city named Halifax, having begun to be located there the day that immediately preceded today'.

A canonical representation of the meaning of **E** is not necessarily an idiomatic paraphrase of **E**. It is not intended to be one: its *raison d'être* is to allow for comparisons with other expressions and provide a measure of semantic similarity between these expressions and **E**.

Sentence (2a) has of course other paraphrases, which are not considered canonical representations of its meaning, since they do not conform to the rules above. Thus, the sentences in (3) do not present semantic decompositions of the meaning of (2a):

(3) *It's been a day since John arrived in Halifax. | John came to Halifax yesterday.*

So far, our examples have illustrated meaning representation of sentences; however, nothing prevents us from using the same technique for the description of the meaning of LUs. A canonical representation of the meaning of an LU L is in fact L's lexicographic definition; construction of lexicographic definitions, a major task of lexical semantics, will be considered in Ch. 5.

1.2   Linguistic (= "Shallow") Meaning vs. Real (= "Deep") Meaning

If the linguistic meaning, the primary object of semantic study, is something that can be described only by a linguistic paraphrase, then this meaning is rather "shallow": it is **literal meaning**, accessible to speakers exclusively through knowledge of the language.

What we mean by linguistic meaning is 'non-pragmatic, non-extralinguistic, non-encyclopedic meaning'. Thus, we do not exclude figurative, or metaphorical, lexical meanings and consider such items as lexicalized metaphors[1] and idioms (Ch. 4, *2.2.2.1*) an integral part of speakers' lexical knowledge. Furthermore, we include in linguistic meaning the specification of speakers' communicative and stylistic intentions (cf. Subsection *1.3*, the aspects of linguistic meaning).

Linguistic meaning must be carefully distinguished from real, or "deep," meaning, whose apprehension requires recourse to extralinguistic knowledge and logical capacities. Simplifying things somewhat, we can reduce this distinction to the opposition between the "meaning of words" (*What does the expression **E** mean?*) and the "meaning of things" (*What did the Speaker mean by **E**?*) To illustrate, let us compare the sentences in (4) from the viewpoint of their linguistic (= "shallow," or literal) meaning and their "deep" meaning.

(4) a.   *It's garbage day tomorrow.*
     b.   *Get the garbage to the curb!*

The linguistic meanings of these sentences are very different: the first one means, roughly, 'I am communicating to you that tomorrow is the day when the garbage is disposed of' and the second, 'I am signaling that I want you to put the garbage at the place on the curb designated for its pickup'. However, they can be pragmatically equivalent, since both can be used for the same purpose: to make the Addressee take the garbage out. In other words, in an appropriate situation, they can have the same "deep" meaning.

The "deep" meaning can be seized through the behavior of the people participating in an exchange; it can be communicated even without recourse to language, by means of a drawing or a gesture, for instance. In contrast, linguistic meaning can be grasped and conveyed only through the perception and manipulation of linguistic items. The meaning that is the target of linguistics is in fact an interface between speech and "deep" meaning. That is why linguistic semantics is a study of the links between linguistic meaning and its expression; investigation into the links between linguistic meaning and extralinguistic

---

[1] A lexicalized metaphor is part of language – a word or a set phrase whose metaphorical meaning is interpretable in the same way by all members of a speech community, with no help from context; for instance, FOX**II** 'cunning person' in *John is a fox*, derived from FOX**I** 'animal' via the corresponding lexicographic connotation (Ch. 5, *4*) of the latter. A free metaphor, on the contrary, is not part of language – it is a one-time creation by an individual speaker, open to different, context-dependent interpretations; for instance, *John is a spider* can be understood to mean, alternatively, 'John is very patient', 'John is persistent', 'John is malicious/cruel', and so on. These are all possible connotations of SPIDER 'animal' (via the corresponding components of its definition, namely 'web weaving' and 'insect catching'), but they are not yet stable enough and accepted by the entire speech community. On metaphorical meaning extensions, see Ch. 6, *1.3.1*.

reality falls outside of the scope of linguistics as such. This fact has two corollaries for the way we approach meaning.

- First, we leave aside factors linked to encyclopedic knowledge and logical capacities that do not have direct repercussions on language.

Encyclopedic knowledge

(5) a. *The author of* The Wings of the Dove *was born in 1843.*
     b. *Henry James Jr. was born in 1843.*

The sentences in (5) convey the same information, provided one knows that it was Henry James who wrote the novel in question. However, their linguistic meanings are different: 'the author of *The Wings of the Dove*' ≠ 'the person named Henry James', even if these meanings have the same referent (Ch. 2, *1.1.2*).

Logical capacities

(6) a. *The price of gas jumped from one to two dollars.*
     b. *The price of gas suddenly doubled – it is now two dollars.*

Just like the sentences in the previous example, those in (6) have the same informational content, which can be established by means of a rudimentary arithmetic calculation. Meanwhile, their linguistic meanings are different: 'jump from one to two dollars' ≠ 'double'.

Sentences like those in (5) and (6), whose semantic equivalence is based on encyclopedic knowledge or logical capacities (calculus, deduction, etc.), are cognitive paraphrases. This type of paraphrase will not be considered in the present book.

- We do not consider pragmatic knowledge (of the context of the speech situation, its participants, etc.) or linkage of meanings to their referents; these factors do have repercussions on language, but are excluded for simplicity's sake.

Pragmatic knowledge

This type of knowledge plays a role in example (4): to establish the equivalence between sentences (4a) and (4b), encyclopedic information is required: "garbage cans have to be emptied." But this is not all; it is also necessary to take into account the speech situation and the relations between its participants in order to be able to interpret a simple statement in (4a) as a request expressed in (4b). This is pragmatic knowledge.

Referential identification

By referential identification we mean the linking of linguistic meanings used in an utterance to their referents – the corresponding facts and entities of the extralinguistic world. A meaning can be referential (= have a referent) or not; its referent can be definite specific, non-definite specific, definite generic, etc., as illustrated in Ch. 2, *1.1.2*, example (1). Here is another series of examples:

(7) a. **Definite specific reference**
Fr. *Je cherche **la maison** de mes amis*
lit. 'I look.for **the house** of my friends'.

b. **Non-definite specific reference**
Fr. *Je cherche **une maison** qui $a_{\text{INDICATIVE}}$ un jardin*
lit. 'I look.for **a house** that **has** a garden'.

c. **Non-definite non-specific reference**
Fr. *Je cherche **une maison** qui $ait_{\text{SUBJUNCTIVE}}$ un jardin*
lit. 'I look.for **a house** that **would.have** a garden'.

d. **Definite generic reference**
*The vocabulary of **a third grader** ⟨= **third graders**⟩ is relatively poor.*

e. **Non-definite non-specific reference vs. definite specific reference**
Rus. *V konce koridora stojal+$o_{\text{NEU.SG}}$ pjat' škafov$_{\text{PL}}$*
lit. 'At end of.corridor **was**.standing [some] five wardrobes'.
vs. *V konce koridora stojal+i_{PL} pjat' škafov$_{\text{PL}}$*
lit. 'At end of.corridor **were**.standing [**the**] five wardrobes'.

By using the indicative mood in the relative clause modifying the noun *maison* 'house' in (7b), the Speaker signals that he believes that a house having this characteristic exists (= the noun *maison* has a specific, albeit non-definite, referent), while by using the subjunctive in (7c), he signals that he is not sure about the existence of such a house (= *maison* may not have a referent at all). In (7d), the phrase *a third grader* is used in a generic way – to refer to an entire class of individuals, rather than to a specific individual. In a generic context, the semantic contrast between nominal singular and plural is neutralized: the phrase *an N* can mean 'every N', and it thus becomes equivalent to *all Ns*. Finally, the form of the verb in the Russian sentence in (7e), more precisely, verbal agreement with the subject *škaf* 'wardrobe', indicates the referential status of the latter: the singular neuter agreement is an indication of non-definite non-specific reference (≈ 'some five wardrobes'), whereas the plural agreement points to definite specific reference (≈ 'those five wardrobes [being talked about]').

The referential status of a meaning can have consequences for its expression, namely, by influencing pronominalization and ellipsis, the choice of articles, of verbal mood, etc. For this reason, a semantic representation must be supplied with pointers towards the referents of the corresponding meanings (cf. the referential structure of a semantic representation, Ch. 10, *1.*) These pointers come from a deeper representation level – the conceptual representation (Ch. 1, *2.4*), a language-independent representation of a real-word state of affairs that can be communicated verbally or otherwise. Referential pointers are introduced into the semantic representation – a representation of the meaning of linguistic expressions selected to talk about the state of affairs in question – by the rules that ensure the transition between these two representation levels.

The fact that we leave out the above-mentioned phenomena does not of course mean that we consider them irrelevant for linguistic communication; quite the opposite – after all, it is the "deep" meaning that is the true *raison d'être* of linguistic exchange. However, a description of such phenomena is not among the tasks of a strictly linguistic model; it falls within the scope of a larger model: that of overall human linguistic behavior, of which the linguistic model is only a part.

What we just said goes to illustrate the central methodological principle of the Meaning-Text approach:

> **Principle of maximum distinction of different aspects of phenomena under study**
>
> We distinguish and separate as much as possible different aspects of the linguistic phenomena being studied in order to better describe them individually before giving a synthetic account of the links they entertain.

1.3 Three Aspects of Linguistic Meaning: Propositional, Communicative and Rhetorical Meaning

Three aspects of linguistic meaning can be distinguished: propositional, communicative and rhetorical.

Propositional meaning is the semantic content proper of a linguistic expression: it is the meaning that targets the state of affairs described by this expression – that is, entities and facts in the world, as well as the relations between them, including the Speaker's interior states, such as his thoughts, attitudes, desires, etc. This meaning is called propositional because it can be described by means of logical propositions. (A logical proposition is an expression that, thanks to its form, can have a truth-value, i.e., be true or false in a given extra-linguistic world; see Appendix, *5.1* and Ch. 9, *1.2*.)

Communicative and rhetorical meanings are not part of the propositional content; rather, they characterize the way in which this content is "packaged" for communication by the Speaker.

Communicative meaning has to do with the specification of the Speaker's communicative intentions. It is, in a sense, the Speaker's itinerary through the "propositional space" of his utterance: what he wants to mention first and what will come later, what he wants to present as given or as new, what he wants to foreground or background, what he will assert or presuppose, etc.

Finally, rhetorical meaning is a specification of the Speaker's stylistic intentions: whether he wants his utterance to be neutral, formal, colloquial, poetic, ironic, etc.

As an illustration, let us consider the sentences in (8) as possible answers to the underlying question (Ch. 10, *3.1.2.1*) *What do you think of the last municipal election results?*

(8) a. **formal**   *The matter is of no consequence to me.*
     b. **neutral**   *It is all the same to me.*
     c. **colloquial**   *I couldn't care less.*

These three sentences express the same propositional meaning: 'I am communicating that the fact in question [the results of the municipal election] is not important for me'. However, they differ with respect to the communicative dimension of meaning since the first two sentences are about the fact itself and the way it affects the Speaker, and the last one is about the Speaker and the way he reacts to the fact. Rhetorically, these sentences belong to different styles, identified by usage labels **formal**, **neutral** and **colloquial**.

Each utterance can be characterized in terms of these three dimensions of meaning; they are modeled by means of three different structures constituting a semantic representation. (A semantic representation contains yet another structure – the referential structure; thus, it is formed of a total of four structures; see Ch. 10, *1*.)

2   Meaning Representation

In order to study the way in which linguistic meanings are expressed in natural language, they first have to be represented in some well-defined formal way. In other words, semantics needs a formal language (or several formal languages) for representation of meaning, something like a "semantic transcription." (For the notion of formal language, see Appendix, *4*.)

> The same is true for all other linguistic phenomena. Each level of linguistic representation requires its own formal language: syntactic trees for the syntactic level, morphemic/morphic strings for the morphological level, and phonemic/phonetic transcriptions for the phonic level.

Two major types of meaning representations are used in linguistics: representations based exclusively on an artificial logical language and representations based on a natural language.

Semantic Representations Based on an Artificial Language

Among artificial languages used to represent meaning, the language of propositional calculus and the language of predicate calculus (Appendix, *5*), which came into linguistics from logic, have the most general currency. The obvious advantage of logical languages is their precision and explicitness; however, they are not expressive enough for linguistic purposes.

The language of propositional calculus has at least three drawbacks: (1) it does not allow the representation of the internal semantic structure of a proposition; (2) it does not make it possible to state semantic equivalences between atomic propositions; and (3) the logical connectors of propositional calculus are semantically poorer than the corresponding linguistic items; to give just one example, the English conjunction AND can mean not only 'and' (= logical conjunction "∧"), as in *John left and Mary stayed*, but also 'and then' [temporal succession], as in *He got up and left*.

The language of predicate calculus, much more powerful than that of propositional calculus, is, nevertheless, also hardly adequate to capture all the complexities of natural language semantics. Its two main drawbacks are:

- its linear notation, leading to a heavy use of co-referential indices, which reduces readability; and
- the impossibility of representing communicative information in a simple enough way (oppositions such as Rheme ~ Theme, focalized ~ non-focalized, etc.).

Semantic Representations Based on a Natural Language

Language-based semantic representations are written in a semantic metalanguage, which is a well-defined subset of a natural language, (at least, ideally) exempt from synonymy and ambiguity, thus guaranteeing the univocity of the description.

> REMARK. A metalanguage is a language used to describe another language, called the object language. A metalanguage used by linguists to describe language **L** (which they speak) is a part of **L**; iin other words, a linguistic metalanguage is a subset of its object language. This situation – coincidence of the object of study with the means used to describe this object – creates considerable difficulties for linguistics, because the distinction between its metalanguage and its object language may become fuzzy and lead to confusion. One of the corollaries is that linguistics, even more than other sciences, has to rely on a rigorous and coherent conceptual system and precise terminology.

"Natural" representations have a long tradition, especially in philosophy, e.g., the famous *Characteristica Universalis*, of G. W. Leibnitz (seventeenth century), but also in modern linguistics, e.g., the *Natural Semantic Metalanguage* of A. Wierzbicka (see below, *4.1.3*). Lexicographers routinely use defining languages, sometimes taking the form of controlled vocabularies, to write dictionary definitions; two well-known examples are *Basic English* and the controlled vocabulary of *Longman Dictionary of Contemporary English*.

In the Meaning-Text approach, propositional meaning is represented by means of a special metalanguage specific to each object language (in other words, English, French, Russian, etc. have different semantic metalanguages). The semantic metalanguage for a natural language **L** is a hybrid: in its vocabulary, it is based on **L**, and in its syntax, on the universal formal language of semantic networks (Ch. 2, *1.6.1*), a simplified version of the language of predicate calculus. These metalanguages are used to represent the meanings of both sentences and LUs of the corresponding natural language. (Meanings of LUs are also represented – when it is convenient – in a verbal, or textual, form, equivalent to a semantic network; this is done in lexicographic definitions.)

Meaning representations will be further discussed in Section *4* below, as well as in Ch. 5 (representation of the meaning of LUs), Ch. 9, *1.3* and *2.1.4* and Ch. 10 (representation of the meaning of sentences).

3   Semantic Units and Semantic Relations

Linguistic meaning is described in terms of discrete semantic units – semantemes (*3.1*) and semantic dependency relations between them (*3.2*).

3.1   Semantemes

Let us consider language **L** and concentrate on its semantics. The basic semantic unit of the semantic metalanguage we will use for **L**'s description is a semanteme.

> **Definition 3.2:** Semanteme
> A semanteme is a lexical meaning – that is, the signified of a full lexical unit of **L**.

The concept of lexical unit will be characterized in detail in Ch. 4, *2*; here, it suffices to say that an LU is, roughly, one particular sense of what is traditionally called a "polysemous word" (or vocable, in our terminology, Ch. 8, *1.1*).

As has already been mentioned, an LU is either a lexeme, e.g., $LOVE_{(V)}1$ (*I love you, Mary!*) and $LOVE_{(V)}3$ (*I love carrots.*), or an idiom, e.g., ⌜RED TAPE⌝ (*The new rules should help cut red tape for farmers.*) and ⌜SHOOT THE BREEZE⌝ (*Well, no time to shoot the breeze.*). Each LU whose signifier is identical to the signifier of another LU described in the dictionary of **L** is supplied with a lexicographic number, which can also be used to identify the corresponding semanteme. Thus, when we write '$love_{(V)}1$', we identify this semanteme as the signified of the lexeme $LOVE_{(V)}1$.

Since an LU is actually not a linguistic sign but a (particular) set of signs (cf. Ch. 4, *2.1*, Definition 4.1 [lexeme]), it is formally incorrect to speak about the signified of an LU: one should say instead *the signified common to all wordforms/phrases that belong to an LU*. However, throughout this book, we use this shortcut for the sake of brevity. The same is true for the expressions *the signifier ⟨the syntactics⟩ of an LU*, by which we actually mean 'the signifier ⟨the syntactics⟩ of the stem common to all the elements of this LU'.

Here are some English semantemes: 'love$_{(V)}$**3**', '˹red tape˺', 'friend**1**' (*You are my best friend.*), 'friend**5**' (*the friends of the museum*), 'vehicle**1**' (*Have you locked your vehicle, Sir?*), 'liberty**2**' (*liberties such as freedom of speech*), 'nice**2**' (*a nice guy*), 'yesterday**I**' (*yesterday's meeting*), 'yesterday**II**' (*the great champions of yesterday*), 'after**1**' (*after lunch*), 'here**1**' (*Come here!*), 'here**2**' (*Spring is here at last.*), etc.

There is no one-to-one correspondence between the semantemes and the LUs of a given language.

On the one hand, while a semanteme necessarily corresponds to an LU, the converse is not true: there are LUs that do not correspond to any semanteme – that is, they appear in a sentence without having their direct sources in the corresponding meaning representation. These are so-called grammatical words (Ch. 2, *2.2*), or structural LUs. Some of these are inherently empty, such as substitute pronouns (***They*** *will be considered later.* | *the soup **that** Mary cooked*) and the conjunction THAT (*I know **that** Mary has cooked this soup.*); some others become empty in particular contexts: governed prepositions and conjunctions (*count **on** somebody*, *be faithful **to** somebody*; *ask **whether**…*).

On the other hand, a semanteme or a configuration of semantemes can describe a grammeme (Ch. 2, *3.2.1*) or a derivateme (Ch. 2, *3.2.2*). For example, one of the meanings of the nominal plural grammeme (expressed by the suffix -**s** in *book*+**s**, *mother*+**s**, etc.) is represented as 'more than one' (*The boy**s** were eating apples.*); the Agent derivateme, expressed by the suffix -**er** in *read*+**er**, *work*+**er**, etc., appears in a SemS as 'a person who does …'; etc. That is why we have to stress that a semanteme is the signified of a **full** LU of the language under consideration.

Semantemes, together with semantic dependencies, are the only linguistic items that can appear in Meaning-Text semantic structures, which represent the propositional meaning of utterances. This method of description ensures the homogeneity of semantic representations.

3.1.1   The Language-Specific Character of Semantemes

In the previous subsection, the notion of semanteme was illustrated with examples from English, but such examples can be taken from any other language.

Each language has its own unique stock of full LUs, and therefore of semantemes, even if considerable overlaps exist between different stocks. The language-specific character of semantemes is reflected in the following three aspects of meaning organization.

Relations Between Semantemes and the Extralinguistic World

As is well known, every language presents a unique conceptualization of the world; this phenomenon is often referred to as specific articulation of extralinguistic reality, which is "built into" a language and which it imposes on its speakers. Here are three examples.

The Serbian noun LUK corresponds in English to both ONION and GARLIC; it is normal to ask *Daj mi taj luk* 'Give me that *luk*' to refer either to an onion or to a clove of garlic lying on a kitchen table. To indicate precisely which of the two vegetables one has in mind, either the adjective *crni* 'black' or *beli* 'white' is added (this gives the correspondences *crni luk* ≡ *onion* and *beli luk* ≡ *garlic*[2]).

The English noun GLASS 'drinking container' covers a conceptual zone that Russian divides among at least these five nouns:

STAKAN	'transparent cylindrical	glass designed to drink cold beverages and tea'
RJUMKA	'small transparent stemmed	glass designed to drink alcoholic beverages'
BOKAL	'transparent cylindrical stemmed	glass designed to drink wine'
STOPKA	'very small	glass designed to drink spirits'
FUŽER	'transparent conical stemmed	glass designed to drink champagne'

The French adverb BEAUCOUP corresponds semantically to two English adjectives, MANY and MUCH: *beaucoup de pommes* lit. 'much of apples' ≡ *many apples* ('big number' [of countable discrete objects]); *beaucoup de neige* lit. 'much of snow' ≡ *much snow* ('big quantity' [of uncountable continuous substance]).

We could give more examples, but it must already be clear that each language chooses its own way to draw distinctions between different entities and different facts of the world.

The Structural Complexity of Semantemes

Languages differ widely in the quantity of information that they can "squeeze" into their semantemes. Thus, in the domain of motion verbs, English can pack into a single semanteme much more meaning than Spanish can. In an English ~ Spanish parallel text having the same number of occurrences of motion verbs (165), there are 47 different LUs in English but only

---

[2] It is not contradictory to say in Serbian *crveni crni luk* lit. 'red black onion' = 'red onion', as it is not contradictory to say *green blackboard* in English.

26 in Spanish; if we consider also English verbs with postverbal particles (*sneak **out***, *sneak **up***, etc.), the number of English motion verbs jumps to 125, which is almost 5 times that of the Spanish ones (Slobin 1996). This is explained by the fact that within a single semanteme English easily combines semantic components that encode (1) the motion itself, (2) the means of locomotion, (3) the orientation and (4) the manner of moving (e.g., CRAWL OUT); such a combination is impossible in Spanish.[3] To see this, it is enough to compare three English sentences containing motion verbs with their Spanish equivalents:

(9) a. *He **stomped** from the house.* ~ ***Salió*** *de la casa* 'He got out of the house'.
     b. *The women **drifted down** the street.* ~ *Las mujeres **siguieron** calle abajo* 'The women continued (walking) down the street'.
     c. *Mrs. Tranter **rustled** forward.* ~ *Mrs. Tranter **se adelantó*** 'Mrs. Tranter came.forward'.

Due to the lower complexity of verbal semantemes in Spanish, each Spanish sentence in (9) carries less information than the corresponding English one: namely, the manner of motion is omitted, so that in (9a), the Spanish translation lacks the meaning 'stepping heavily', in (9b), the meaning 'slowly and without purpose' is omitted, and in (9c), the meaning 'producing the sound of rustling' is not taken into account. If a Spanish speaker wanted to keep all the information present in the original English sentences, he would have to add words and thus make the translations awkward.

Another example of different possible "semanteme packaging" is provided by English and Russian motion verbs. Unlike English, Russian verbal semantemes must incorporate information on both the manner of motion – on foot or using some transportation means – and the medium of travel: on land, on water, or in the air. Thus, the English verb *come*, neutral with respect to the manner of motion and to the medium traveled in (it is possible to *come* somewhere on foot, on a bike, in a car, by boat, on a plane, etc.), does not have a direct correspondent in Russian. In this language, *come* corresponds, as the case may be, to one of the following verbs: *pri+jti* 'come on foot' vs. *pri+exat´* 'come by using a ground transportation means' [bike, car, train, horseback, …] vs. *pri+plyt´* 'come in a watercraft' [boat, raft, …] vs. *pri+letet´* 'come in an aircraft' [plane, chopper, airship, …]. (The prefix PRI- indicates the orientation towards the Speaker, and the verbal radical specifies the means of motion; *priplyt´* and *priletet´* mean also 'come by swimming/flying' [speaking, for instance, of a fish or a bird].)

---

[3] Following L. Talmy (1985), such "packaging" of specific semantic components within a signified of a lexical unit is commonly referred to as lexical conflation.

The Obligatory Character of Some Semanteme Configurations

The case of motion verbs that we just saw is a good example of obligatory or, on the contrary, impossible cooccurrence of semantemes within the signified of an LU in different languages. As another example of this phenomenon, let us consider the way different languages construct expressions of time.

The meaning 'It is 13 minutes to 5 (o'clock)' [= 16:47], perfectly normal in English, is ill-formed in French (and in Russian), since in French you do not say *Il est treize minutes jusqu'à cinq* (*heures*), but rather *Il est cinq heures moins treize* (*minutes*) lit. 'It is 5 o'clock less 13 minutes'; thus, here French expresses a different (albeit pragmatically equivalent) meaning. In German, you say something more similar, but not identical, to English: Ger. *Es ist dreizehn vor fünf* 'It is 13 before 5', which means that German and English construe this meaning in a parallel way.

What we just said has the following important corollary:

> Meaning-Text semantic structures, which handle language-specific semantemes and their configurations, are language-specific. However, the basic formalism used to draw semantic structures, the semantic network (Ch. 2, *1.6.1* and Ch. 10, *2.1*), is cross-linguistically valid.

3.1.2 Two Major Classes of Semantemes: Semantic Predicates and Semantic Names

From the viewpoint of their logical nature, semantemes are divided into two major classes: semantic predicates and semantic names.

A semantic predicate (Appendix, *5.2*) is an "incomplete," or "binding," meaning: when used by the Speaker, it requires that some other meanings, called its arguments, be expressed alongside it. For example, the meaning 'love' requires the indication of who loves whom/what and cannot be defined without these two arguments. So, to represent *Mary loves John*, we write 'love(Mary; John)', where 'Mary' and 'John' are the arguments of the predicate 'love'. If we want to talk about a predicate without specifying its arguments, these must still be represented – as variables X, Y, Z, etc.: 'love(X; Y)'. A predicate cannot be used without – at least implicit – instantiation of its arguments: it is in this sense that a predicate meaning is incomplete. And it is binding because it binds its arguments into a structure by connecting them.

The term predicate was borrowed from logic, where it has a long-standing tradition; in linguistics, a parallel terminology is used. If an LU L has a predicate meaning and another LU L′ expresses, in a given sentence, an argument of the predicate 'L', so that we have 'L(L′)', we say that L′ is a semantic actant of L. In other words, an argument of the predicate 'L' corresponds to a semantic actant of the LU L – and vice versa. The term semantic actant is thus an absolute synonym of argument. However, *actant* is a more general term, because it can also be used to refer to governed dependents at

the syntactic level: in addition to semantic actants, we distinguish two further actant types – deep-syntactic actants and surface-syntactic actants. This
is why, in a linguistic discussion, we prefer to talk about *semantic actants*,
rather than *arguments*.

The term *predicate* (as illustrated above) is two-way ambiguous.
On the one hand, as a "semantic part of speech," predicates contrast
with semantic names (see immediately below); in this sense, the
term *predicate* designates a class of semantemes. On the other hand,
as "elements of the semantic expression," predicates contrast with
arguments: in this case, the term *predicate* indicates a structural role
within a semantic structure. In 'I saw John leave' the semantemes
'see' and 'leave' are predicates in the first sense, but at the same time
the semanteme 'see' is also the predicate in the second sense (that is,
the semantic governor) of the predicate 'leave', which is its argument.

Semantic predicates denote `facts`. For instance:

`events`	'explosion of $_{\text{entity}}$X'; 'death of $_{\text{being}}$X'
`actions`	'$_{\text{person}}$X breaks $_{\text{object}}$Y USING $_{\text{object}}$Z'; '$_{\text{person}}$X gives $_{\text{object}}$Y TO $_{\text{person}}$Z'
`states`	'$_{\text{person}}$X [is] happy'; 'love OF $_{\text{person}}$X FOR $_{\text{person}}$Y'; 'sorrow of $_{\text{person}}$X BECAUSE.OF $_{\text{fact}}$Y'
`processes`	'$_{\text{entity}}$X grows BY $_{\text{quantity}}$Y'; 'deterioration OF $_{\text{state}}$X'
`relations`	'$_{\text{person}}$X [is] older THAN $_{\text{person}}$Y BY $_{\text{quantity}}$Z'; '$_{\text{entity}}$X precedes $_{\text{entity}}$Y IN $_{\text{sequence}}$W'
`properties`	'$_{\text{entity}}$X [is] solid'; 'solidity OF $_{\text{entity}}$X'; '$_{\text{entity}}$X [is] red'

  Left subscripts in `Courier New` font are semantic labels, taxonomic char-
acterizers used to describe in a general way the meanings of LUs and indicate
semantic types of their actants. Semantic labels, which are important tools of
lexicographic description, will be characterized in Ch. 8, *1.2*.

Semantic predicates are typically expressed by verbs, adjectives, adverbs,
conjunctions and prepositions, but also by nouns ('death', 'marriage', 'war',
'beauty', 'property', etc.).

Among semantic predicates, a particular type is distinguished: connectors,
which correspond to logical operations (Appendix, *2*). These are, in particular,
semantemes 'and' (expressing the logical conjunction "∧," e.g., 'John will invite
Peter **and** Mary') and 'or' (expressing the logical disjunction "∨," e.g., 'John
will invite Peter **or** Mary'). At the semantic level, these two semantemes represent what is called coordination (Ch. 11, *2.3*) in syntax. They are special in the

sense that they both admit a theoretically unlimited number of arguments that all fulfill the same semantic role and, for this reason, cannot be distinguished.

> **NB:** Note a particularly inconvenient homonymy of terms: conjunction in the logical sense, which is a logical operation/operator (= connector) "Λ," and conjunction in the syntactic sense (*and*, *or*, *but*, *that*, *when* ...), which is a part of speech (Ch. 2, *2.2*).

A semantic name is a complete and non-binding meaning; it cannot have arguments. Semantic names denote classes of objects (in a very broad sense, including `physical objects`, `landscape elements`, `substances`, `living beings`, `persons/people`), for example: 'pebble', 'river', 'sand', 'bird', 'Jonas'. A semantic name can be expressed only by a noun.

In addition to predicates and semantic names, natural language extensively uses another, hybrid, class of semantemes: quasi-predicates. Quasi-predicates denote entities, but, nevertheless, have arguments (= semantic actants). This is possible because a quasi-predicate denotes an entity associated with specific functions or usage, and it is the corresponding situation that provides its arguments. For instance, 'train DRIVEN BY $_{\text{people}}$X AND DESIGNED TO TRANSPORT $_{\text{people/entities}}$Y FROM $_{\text{place}}$Z TO $_{\text{place}}$W' denotes a physical object manipulated by a team of people X and used to transport passengers/goods Y from place Z to place W.

Quasi-predicates are expressed exclusively by nouns; for example:

`professionals`	'teacher OF $_{\text{information}}$Y TO $_{\text{people}}$Z AT $_{\text{institution}}$W'
`humans entertaining specific relations with other humans`	'mother OF $_{\text{person}}$Y'
`artwork`	'film CREATED BY $_{\text{person}}$X CONCERNING $_{\text{facts}}$Y FOR $_{\text{people}}$Z'
`substances designed for a particular use`	'medication OF $_{\text{person}}$X FOR.TREATING $_{\text{illness}}$Y (PRESCRIBED.BY $_{\text{person}}$Z)'
`body parts`	'leg OF $_{\text{person}}$X'
`parts [in general]`	'wall OF $_{\text{building}}$X'

> A quasi-predicate can have the Sem-actant Y ⇔ **2** without having the Sem-actant X ⇔ **1**. This happens when the meaning that could be its Sem-actant X is, so to speak, incorporated into it. Thus, 'mother of Y' is 'woman who ⌜gave birth⌝ to Y'; here the meaning 'woman' fills in the Sem-actant slot X of ⌜give birth⌝.

For the purposes of manipulating semantic networks, quasi-predicates can be assimilated to genuine predicates, since they have similar formal properties: both the predicates and quasi-predicates have arguments, which is crucial for their semantic description.

3.2 Semantic Dependency Relations

With each of its arguments, a predicate entertains a semantic dependency relation, which is a particular case of linguistic dependency. Both of these notions were introduced in Ch. 2, *1.3.2*; for convenience, we will restate here the definition of semantic dependency:

> **Definition 3.3 (= 2.3):** Semantic Dependency
> Semantic dependency is dependency between either two semantemes 'L_1' and 'L_2' that stand in a "predicate ~ argument" relation or two corresponding lexical units in a sentence, L_1 and L_2: the governor (= predicate) determines the presence and the nature of the dependent (= argument) in the sentence.

A semantic dependency will be noted as follows:

$$L_{1[governor]}\text{--}\mathbf{sem}\rightarrow L_{2[dependent]}.$$

3.2.1 Properties of Semantic Dependency

Like any binary relation, a semantic dependency relation can be characterized, from a logical viewpoint, according to the properties of reflexivity, symmetry and transitivity (Appendix, *3.2*).

a. Semantic dependency is an antireflexive relation, since no predicative meaning 'σ' can be its own argument:

b. It is also an antisymmetric relation, since a predicative meaning 'σ_1' that has another predicative meaning 'σ_2' as its argument cannot itself be the argument of 'σ_1':

> **NB:** Cases like 'I know that he knows that I know…' do not contradict the antisymmetry of semantic dependency, since they represent infinite regression, which is a semantic absurdity.

c. Finally, semantic dependency is a non-transitive relation, since the meaning 'σ_1' with an argument 'σ_2', which in its turn has an argument 'σ_3', may or may not have 'σ_3' as an argument – as a function of the meaning 'σ_1'. (Note that in the two previous cases the identity of the meanings involved is irrelevant.) Compare, respectively, a well-formed semanteme configuration in (i) *Paul is able to leave*, illustrating a case of transitivity of semantic dependency, and an ill-formed one in (ii) *John hates Paul's leaving*, which illustrates a case of its antitransitivity:

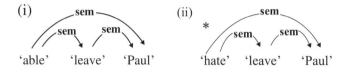

In (i), the Sem-dependency is transitive, because 'Paul' depends on 'leave', 'leave' depends on 'able', and 'Paul' also depends on 'able'. But in (ii), 'hate' controls an antitransitive semantic dependency, because 'Paul' depends on 'leave', 'leave' depends on 'hate', but 'Paul' does not, and cannot, depend on 'hate': John does not hate Paul! (However, In *John hates Paul for leaving*, 'Paul' does depend on 'hate', and also on 'leave', which in its turn depends on 'hate', so that in this – different – configuration the semantic dependency controlled by 'hate' is transitive.)

   This logical characterization of semantic dependency relation is very helpful when it comes to learning how to draw semantic networks.

3.2.2   Semantic Actants

When speaking of a predicate, it is normal to mention its arguments, but, as we explained in *3.1.2* above, in the case of a semanteme expressing a predicate (= predicative semanteme), we prefer to use the term semantic actant. Semantic actants were informally characterized in Ch. 2, *1.3.2*; here is a formal definition of the term.

> **Definition 3.4:** Semantic Actant
> A semantic actant of a predicative semanteme 'σ_1' is another semanteme 'σ_2' that is an argument of the predicate 'σ_1': '$\sigma_1(\sigma_2)$'; a semantic actant of a predicative LU L_1 is another LU L_2 that corresponds to an argument of the predicate 'L_1'.

   Thus, it is possible to speak about *predicative semantemes* and *predicative LUs*, as well as about *semantic actants of a semanteme* 'σ_1' and *semantic actants of an LU* expressing this semanteme, i.e., semantic actants of L('σ_1').

   For each predicative semanteme 'σ' it is necessary to determine the number of semantic actants that 'σ' controls and indicate the hierarchy of these actants – by assigning them actantial numbers; this amounts to specifying what is called the actantial structure of 'σ' (or of the LU L('σ')). In order to do so, it is necessary to proceed to a semantic decomposition of 'σ', which is the only procedure that allows us to see "who does what to whom with what"; see *4.2.1* below.

Semantic actants of 'σ'/L('σ') are predicted by the lexicographic definition of L; in other words, they are semantically obligatory. An LU deprived of one of its semantic actants [SemAs] can no longer be used to name the corresponding situation. Here is an illustration:

GIVE   '$_{person}$X **gives** $_{object}$Y TO $_{person}$Z'
SELL   '$_{person}$X **sells** $_{object}$Y TO $_{person}$Z FOR $_{amount}$W'
LEND   '$_{person}$X **lends** $_{object}$Y TO $_{person}$Z FOR $_{period}$P'
RENT   '$_{person}$X **rents** $_{object}$Y TO $_{person}$Z FOR $_{amount}$W FOR $_{period}$P'

As we can see, SELL has an additional SemA in regard to GIVE: the sum of money exchanged; LEND has an additional SemA in regard to SELL, corresponding to the lending period, but has no SemA corresponding to the price; finally, RENT has an additional SemA in regard to LEND – the renting price.

Note that the syntactic expressibility of L's SemAs is independent of the obligatory presence of the corresponding actantial slots in the L's meaning: the expression of a SemA can be obligatory, optional or even blocked. Thus, in English, the SemA X of SLEEP$_{(V)}$ must be expressed with a finite form of the verb, but the expression of SemAs Z and W of BUY$_{(V)}$ is optional: *John bought a house* is a perfectly normal sentence; even the expression of SemA Y can be omitted in some contexts: *I am buying!* It is natural to express the SemA Y of WIDOW ('[X,] widow of Y'): *his/John's widow, the widow of President Kennedy*; however, with WIDOWER, this SemA is practically blocked (a Google search [2019.06.14] shows that *widower of Y* is 26 times less frequent than *widow of Y – the widower of Amelia Earhart, George Putnam* feels forced).

As mentioned in Ch. 2, *1.3.2*, actants (unlike modifiers) tend to be idiosyncratic, in both their organization and their expression.

On the one hand, the actantial structure of an LU L cannot be completely deduced from L's meaning. Semantically close LUs can have a different number of SemAs; for instance, SELL$_{(V)}$ and COST$_{(V)}$ denote the same situation of transfer of property, but with COST(V) it is impossible to express the participant that corresponds to SemA **1** of SELL$_{(V)}$: *Granny sold the vase to the Duke for a small fortune* vs. *The vase cost the Duke a small fortune *to ⟨*to the benefit of⟩ Granny*. Thus, we have '$_{person}$X sells $_{object}$Y to $_{person}$Z for $_{amount}$W' vs. '$_{object}$Y costs $_{person}$Z $_{amount}$W'.

On the other hand, two semantically related LUs with the same number of SemAs belonging to the same semantic types can differ in the way these actants are expressed in syntax. This is the case, for instance, with conversive verbs TEACH**1** '$_{person}$X teaches $_{subject/skill}$Y to $_{person}$Z' and INSTRUCT '$_{person}$X instructs $_{person}$Y in $_{subject/skill}$Z': *They* *teach religion*$_{\text{DirObj}}$ *to children*$_{\text{IndirObj}}$ vs. *They instruct children*$_{\text{DirObj}}$ *in religion*$_{\text{OblObj}}$.[4] To make the matter even more complex, L's SemAs do not always correspond one-to-one to its deep-syntactic actants (which, in their turn, correspond to surface-syntactic actants), even though this is generally the case. Quite often, this correspondence is more involved, so that what is an actant at one representation level can become a modifier at another (for more on the opposition "actant ~ modifier (in a broad sense)," see Ch. 11, *2.3*). For these reasons, the actantial structure of an LU L and the way the actants are expressed at different representation levels need to be explicitly indicated (as part of L's lexicographic description); in our framework this is done by means of the formalism known as the Government Pattern (GP) (Ch. 2, *1.3.3* and Ch. 8, *2.2.3*).

4   Semantic Decomposition

Most meanings of a language are not atomic but constitute configurations of simpler meanings – so to speak, semantic molecules. Therefore, it is possible to describe the internal structure of a linguistic meaning – by means of semantic decomposition. This is a fundamental operation, comparable to decomposition of substances into molecules, molecules into atoms, atoms into elementary particles, and elementary particles (which are thus not quite elementary!) into quarks. Semantic decomposition makes the discrete nature of linguistic meaning apparent: the meaning of a linguistic expression is not an unanalyzable amalgam; it is composed of clearly identifiable units, organized into a hierarchical structure.[5]

4.1   How Is Semantic Decomposition Done?

Let us start by giving three examples of semantic decomposition, involving, respectively, a semantic name, a quasi-predicate and a genuine predicate. Note that predicate semantemes are not defined in isolation, but rather within an expression that includes variables representing their semantic actants; such an expression is called propositional form (Appendix, *5.2*).

'west'   ≈ 'direction from any place towards the place where the sun ⌐goes down⌐'

'X, Y's spouse' ≈ 'person X married to person Y'

---

[4]   INSTRUCT = Conv$_{132}$(TEACH); on the lexical relation of conversion and its description in terms of lexical functions, see Ch. 6, *1.1* and Ch. 7, *2.1.1*.
[5]   Semantic decomposition was introduced into modern semantics by Anna Wierzbicka; in what follows, we will refer to her work on more than one occasion.

'X obeys Y'   ≈ 'living being X <u>behaves</u> in a such way as to comply with demands
                  of living being Y concerning X'

The blocs of meanings making up a semanteme are its semantic components. The central component, which in this case is also the communicatively
dominant component (underlined), is the generic term of the decomposition, of
which the meaning being defined is a particular case. The remaining components constitute specific differences of this particular meaning with respect to
other, related, meanings.

A semantic decomposition of this type is equivalent to a meaning representation by means of a semantic network (Ch. 2, *1.6.1*). Thus, the decomposition
of the meaning 'west' given above can also be represented by means of the
semantic network in *Figure 3.1*.

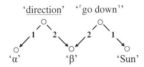

Figure 3.1 Decomposition of the semanteme '*west*'

4.1.1   Basic Rules of Semantic Decomposition

Semantic decomposition is performed according to strict rules, which will be
presented in Ch. 5, *2*. Here, we will limit ourselves to a cursory characterization.

Semantic decomposition of a meaning 'σ' has to be done only in terms of
meanings simpler than 'σ'. 'Simpler', when speaking of meaning, does not have
a psychological connotation (i.e., 'easier to understand'); it is just a technical term:

> A meaning 'σ₁' is simpler than a meaning 'σ₂' iff the decomposition of
> 'σ₂' contains 'σ₁', but the converse is not true.

Thus, 'obey' contains 'behave', but 'obey' cannot be used in the definition
of 'behave': obeying is a particular case of behaving, but behaving is by no
means a particular case of obeying.

Semantic decompositions must use simpler meanings because this is the only
way to avoid vicious circles, or circularity, in the system of definitions (within a
dictionary). A definition of term A that uses term B, which in its turn is defined
by A, is a flagrant example of circularity. Thus, there is a direct vicious circle
if we define, as is done in LDOCE, ANXIETY2 as 'the feeling of being very
worried about something' and WORRY2 as 'the feeling of being very **anxious** about something'. In many cases, circularity is more indirect – that is, it
becomes apparent only after recursive decomposition of the meanings involved.

Semantic decomposition is **recursive**, i.e., can be iterated until we reach
the level of semantic primitives – "atomic" meanings, such as 'something',
'no', 'time', 'be.located [at a place]', etc., that cannot be described in terms of

simpler linguistic meaning of the same language. This raises the question of the depth of decomposition.

In our framework, the depth of semantic decomposition is determined by the Maximal Block Rule (Ch. 5, *2*, p. 123): as will be illustrated shortly, semantic decomposition must proceed in stages and be minimal at each stage. This rule is not logically necessary, but it is crucial from a methodological viewpoint because it precludes decompositions of arbitrary depths. A consequence of the systematic application of the Maximal Block Rule is the obligatory use (wherever possible) of "intermediate" semantemes – that is, semantemes that are not semantic primitives but semantic molecules.

4.1.2   Recursive Character of Semantic Decomposition

Here is an example of recursive decomposition, featuring the semanteme '[to] heat**2**' (as in *John is heating the soup*; in the left column, the boldface indicates the element being decomposed, and in the right column its decomposition) (*Table 3.1*).

Table 3.1 Recursive decomposition of the semanteme '*[to] heat***2**'

1	'X **heats2** Y'	'X **causes2** Y to **heat up**'
2	'X causes2 Y to **heat up**'[6]	'X causes2 Y to **become hotter or hot**'
3	'X causes2 Y to become **hotter or hot**'	'X causes2 Y's **temperature** to become **higher (than it is or) than the norm for Y**'
4	'X cause2 Y's temperature to **become** higher than the norm for Y'	'X causes2 Y's temperature to **begin being** higher than the norm for Y'
5	'X causes2 Y's temperature to **begin being** higher than the norm for Y'	'X causes2 Y's temperature, which **was not** higher than the norm for Y **at moment *t*, to be** higher than the norm for Y **after *t*'**
6	'X causes2 Y's **temperature**, which at moment *t* was not higher than the norm for Y, to be higher than the norm for Y after *t*'	'X causes2 **the value Z of the magnitude characterizing Y's heat**, which at moment *t* was not higher than the norm for Y, to be higher than the norm for Y after *t*'
7	'X causes2 the value Z of the magnitude characterizing Y's **heat**, which at moment *t* was not higher than the norm for Y, to be higher than the norm for Y after *t*'	'X causes2 the value Z of the magnitude characterizing **Y's property perceivable at distance by the surface of the human body**, which at moment *t* was not higher than the norm for Y, to be higher than the norm for Y after *t*'
8	'X **causes2** the value Z of the magnitude characterizing Y's property perceivable at distance by the surface of the human body, which at moment *t* was not higher than the norm for Y, to be higher than the norm for Y after *t*'	'X **does something to Y, which entails** that the value Z of the magnitude characterizing Y's property perceivable at distance by the surface of the human body, which at moment *t* was not higher than the norm for Y, to be higher than the norm for Y after *t*'

---

[6] Semanteme [to] heat**1**' is seen in such sentences as *The Sun heats the Earth unevenly*, etc.

| 9 | 'X does something to Y, which entails that the value Z of the magnitude characterizing Y's property perceivable at distance by the **surface** of the human body, which at moment *t* was not higher than the norm for Y, to be higher than the norm for Y after *t*' | 'X does something to Y, which entails that the value Z of the magnitude characterizing Y's property perceivable at distance by the **exterior limiting part** of the human body, which at moment *t* was not higher than the norm for Y, to be higher than the norm for Y after *t*' |

 The semanteme 'cause1' stands for involuntary, non-agentive causation (*Humidity can cause1 chronic fatigue.*), and the semanteme 'cause2', for voluntary, agentive causation (*John caused2 the accident by driving on the wrong side of the road.*). 'X causes1 Y' = 'X is the cause of Y'; 'X causes2 Y' = 'X is the causer of Y'.

For the meaning '[to] heat2', which is not particularly complex, after nine decomposition cycles, we get down to very general (= very abstract) meanings, yet we do not reach the level where all the meanings are semantic primitives (the semantemes 'magnitude', 'exterior', 'human', 'distance' and 'norm', for instance, are not). But since we only want to illustrate the recursiveness of semantic decomposition, we can stop here.

4.1.3   Semantic Primitives

In the Meaning-Text approach, semantic primitives must be the end result of a description of the lexical stock of a language. For us, then, determining the set of semantic primitives of a language is a matter of empirical analysis. And this applies as well to the question of universality of semantic primitives: to determine whether or not the same primitives exist in all the world's languages, we first have to completely describe and compare their respective lexical stocks. Anna Wierzbicka and other proponents of the *Natural Semantic Metalanguage* paradigm take a converse approach. Whereas for us semantic primitives represent a goal, for Wierzbicka they are a starting point: she posits several dozens of universal primitive meanings called semantic primes (such that they have lexical – or at least morphological – expressions in all the languages of the world) and uses them to describe all lexical and grammatical meanings in all languages. Here are Wierzbicka's universal semantic primes:

Table 3.2 Sixty-five semantic primes proposed by A. Wierzbicka *(Goddard & Wierzbicka 2014: 12)*

Substantives	I, YOU, SOMEONE, PEOPLE, SOMETHING/THING, BODY
Relational Substantives	KIND, PART
Determiners	THIS, THE_SAME, OTHER/ELSE
Quantifiers	ONE, TWO, SOME, ALL, MANY/MUCH, LITTLE/FEW
Evaluators	GOOD, BAD
Descriptors	BIG, SMALL
Mental and Experiential Predicates	THINK, KNOW, WANT, DON'T_WANT, FEEL, SEE, HEAR
Linguistic Communication	SAY, WORDS, TRUE
Actions and Events	DO, HAPPEN, MOVE, TOUCH
Existence and Possession	BE [SOMEWHERE], THERE IS/EXIST, BE [SOMEONE'S], BE [SOMEONE/SOMETHING]
Life and Death	LIVE, DIE
Time	WHEN/TIME, NOW, BEFORE, AFTER, A_LONG_TIME, A_SHORT_TIME, FOR_SOME_TIME, MOMENT
Space	WHERE/PLACE, HERE, ABOVE, BELOW, FAR, NEAR, SIDE, INSIDE
Logical Concepts	NOT, MAYBE, CAN, BECAUSE, IF
Intensifiers	VERY, MORE
Similarity	LIKE/WAY/AS

4.2   What Is Semantic Decomposition Necessary For?

Semantic decomposition is needed in order to: (1) determine the semantic identity of any linguistic expression (*4.2.1*), (2) establish the semantic equivalence between linguistic expressions (*4.2.2*) and (3) determine the hierarchy of semantic actants of a semanteme (*4.2.3*).

4.2.1   Determining the Semantic Identity of a Linguistic Expression

Given the overwhelming presence of equinomy (Ch. 1, *2.1*, Ch. 6, *1.3* and Ch. 9, *2.4*, Definition 9.8), in natural languages, a "bare" semanteme label can correspond to several lexical meanings. For example, if we write just 'table', it is unclear whether we mean an object we sit at for meals (*The table is set.*), a group of people sitting around this object (*His stories kept the whole table amused.*) or a particular graphical or numerical representation of data (*Table 3 shows historical emission levels up to 2008.*), etc. By revealing the internal organization of meanings, semantic decomposition helps us clarify which one we have in mind; thus:

(10) a. 'table$_{(N)}$**1a** [of X]'   = 'manufactured object designed for X to eat on it – a rigid plane surface supported by (four) legs …'

   b. 'table$_{(N)}$**1b**'   = 'group of people sitting around a table$_{(N)}$**1a**'

   c. 'table$_{(N)}$**2** [of Xs]'   = 'table$_{(N)}$**1a** for X in a restaurant as a unit of service'

   d. 'table$_{(N)}$^{2} [of Y]'   = 'list of symbolic data (on) Y arranged in columns and rows …'

Once the decomposition of a semanteme is completed, the semanteme is assigned a lexicographic (= distinctive) number, corresponding to this decomposition. This number, which indicates the precise wordsense that is being targeted (in our case, 'table$_{(N)}$**1a**', 'table$_{(N)}$**1b**', 'table$_{(N)}$**2**' and 'table$_{(N)}$^{2}'), is a pointer towards a description of this lexical meaning – that is, its semantic decomposition. Such descriptions are stored in the dictionary of a language: the lexicographic definition of an LU (Ch. 5) is simply a decomposition of its meaning.

4.2.2   Establishing Semantic Equivalence between Linguistic Expressions

We have in mind a particular type of paraphrastic link, which cannot be discovered and described without recourse to semantic decomposition. Such links underlie some semantic paraphrases (Ch. 9, *2.1* and Ch. 12, *2.1*), illustrated in (11):

(11) a. *John fully expects this.*
   b. *According to John, this can very well happen.*

If we want to produce sentence (11b) starting from (11a), we need to decompose the meaning of the LU EXPECT – in order to "discover" the semantemes 'believe' and 'probable', which serve as a bridge between the two sentences: 'expect an event' means, roughly, 'believe that this event is probable'. There are no obvious lexical links between the sentences in (11). In (11a), the semantemes 'believe' and 'probable' do not have explicit lexical correspondences (since they are "inside" the meaning of EXPECT); in (11b), 'believe' has a communicatively conditioned realization: *according to* N$_X$ [= 'as X believes'], and 'probable' is expressed as CAN$_{(V)}$ (CAN$_{(V)}$4 in LDOCE). Thus, the paraphrastic link between (11a) and (11b) is not visible at the syntactic level, where LUs appear as such (= without being decomposed), but at the semantic level, provided there is semantic decomposition, all semantic links are explicit.

4.2.3   Determining the Hierarchy of Actants of a Semanteme

Let us illustrate the task at hand with the semanteme 'return$_{(V)}$**1**' (*Penelope is sure that Ulysses will return to Ithaca.*). This is a predicate describing an action, more precisely a movement; it controls three semantic actants: X, the living being who is returning; Y, the place to which X is returning; and Z, the place from which X is returning. This much an English speaker knows intuitively. But how do we determine the hierarchical order of these actants – X, Y, Z? As the "performer" of the action in question, X clearly must be the SemA **1**. What about the point of departure and the point of arrival, though? Should we consider that X_1 is returning from Z_2 to Y_3, or the other way around – to Y_2 from Z_3? To find the answer, we need to look at the way these two actants are expressed in sentences. The more important an actant of a semanteme 'σ' is in the situation described by 'σ', the more likely its obligatory expression. However, in our case neither Y nor Z need to be expressed: a sentence like *Ulysses$_X$ has returned*, where only X, i.e., the SemA **1** of 'return$_{(V)}$**1**', is expressed, is perfectly correct. Note that this sentence means that *Ulysses* has returned 'here', in other words, to the place where the Speaker (or an imaginary observer "created" by the Speaker) is located. If we ask a question about the point of arrival Y – *Where has he returned to?* – , the answer *I don't know* is unacceptable. In contrast, this answer is possible to the question *Where has he returned from?*, concerning the point of departure Z. Which indicates that, in the situation described by the semanteme 'return$_{(V)}$**1**', the point of arrival is more important than the point of departure and is, therefore, the SemA **2**.

All this becomes clearer once we have decomposed the meaning 'return$_{(V)}$**1**'. The central (= generic) component of this meaning is 'come'; 'return$_{(V)}$**1**' is, therefore, a particular case of 'come'. In addition, one can return only to a place where one has been before, which is expressed by the component '[living being X] who had left place Y'. The decomposition of the semanteme 'return$_{(V)}$**1**' is thus as follows (the central component is underlined):

> 'X returns$_{(V)}$**1** to Y from Z' = '⟦⸢living being⸣ X having left place
> Y and being located at place Z,⟧
> X <u>comes</u> to Y from Z'

☞   The part of the meaning enclosed in double brackets – '⟦ … ⟧ – is a presupposition: it remains asserted when the expression containing the LU in question is negated or questioned; see Ch. 5, *3.4*, Ch. 9, *2.3* and Ch. 10, *3.1.2.4*.

The hierarchy of actants of 'come', which is the central component in the decomposition of 'return$_{(V)}$**1**', is easy to determine: it is the point of arrival that is the SemA **2**, since it is possible to say *Come!*, and this means 'come HERE', i.e., to the place where the Speaker is. The semanteme 'return$_{(V)}$**1**' inherits the actantial hierarchy from its central semantic component. In conclusion:

> The hierarchy of SemAs of a semanteme 'L' (or the corresponding LU L) is established primarily by a decomposition of the meaning 'L'.

Another way to distinguish the actants of a semanteme, very popular in linguistics, is to specify their semantic roles such as Agent, Patient, Beneficiary, Goal, Instrument, etc.[7] For example, semantic roles associated with the semantic actants of 'cut' are Agent, Patient and Instrument (*Max*$_\text{Agent}$ *is cutting bread*$_\text{Patient}$ *with a dull knife*$_\text{Instrument}$.), while the actants of the semanteme 'give' appear in the roles of Agent, Patient and Beneficiary (*Max*$_\text{Agent}$ *gave a piece of bread*$_\text{Patient}$ *to Henry*$_\text{Beneficiary}$.).

In spite of their obvious intuitive appeal, semantic roles raise the following logical problem. Semantemes used to identify semantic roles are themselves semantic predicates (e.g., 'X is the agent of Y'); therefore, their own actants have to be specified, then, possibly, the actants of their actants, etc., which leads to an infinite regression. By way of illustration, consider the following SemS: 'Ulysses←1–return$_{(V)}$1–2→Ithaca'. If we decide to semantically flag all semantic dependencies, we have to write something like this (the semantic roles are shown in boldface): 'Ulysses←1–**Agent**–2→return$_{(V)}$1←2–**Arrival_point**–1→Ithaca'. The names of Sem-roles are themselves two-argument predicates: 'be the agent of', 'be the arrival point of'. Therefore, they have to be linked to their arguments by semantic dependencies – that is, by Sem-roles, which are also predicates, so they will require new semantic dependencies, etc. Moreover, some of these Sem-role names can easily appear on the nodes of a SemS: *Ithaca was the destination* [= 'arrival_point'] *of his journey*. How should we then treat these Sem-role names? The same way whether they stand at a node or on an arrow – or in a different way? No satisfying answer is available.

Another difficulty lies in the fact that no reliable criteria can be established allowing for distinguishing individual semantic roles and determining a definitive set of roles.[8] This, we think, is indicative. In fact, the "semantic role" of an argument Ψ of a predicate 'σ' is determined by the predicate 'σ_1' which is part of the decomposition of 'σ' and whose immediate argument is Ψ. For instance, the Sem-role Causer refers to SemA **1** of the semanteme 'cause**2**', the Sem-role Experiencer, to SemA **1** of the semantemes 'believe', 'feel', and 'perceive'; the Sem-role Patient refers to SemA **1** of the change-of-state-denoting semanteme which is SemA **2** of 'cause**1/2**'; and so on. In point of fact, a semantic role can

---

[7] This approach was initiated by Charles Fillmore as an attempt to compensate for the deficiencies of an overly syntactic perspective dominating the linguistics of the day; see Fillmore (1968).

[8] Varying descriptions in terms of semantic roles are possible even in such seemingly trivial cases as the 'give' example adduced above, where *Max* can be assigned the role of the Agent or that of the Source, *a piece of bread* can be the Patient or the Theme, and *Henry* the Direction/Goal or the Recipient/Beneficiary of the giving (Source: Wikipedia's article on *thematic relations*, which is another term for *semantic roles*.)

be thought of as a handy abbreviation for a semantic configuration inside a decomposed meaning.

 For these reasons, we do not use semantic roles in semantic descriptions – neither in semantic networks, nor in lexicographic definitions. The different actants of a predicate semanteme 'σ' are distinguished by asemantic [= meaningless] numbers that ensure the correct association of each actant with "its" semanteme within the decomposition of 'σ'. Semantic roles, however, can be used in informal descriptions as a way to simplify presentation.

Further Reading

Linguistic meaning: Lyons 1995: 40–45; Carston 2002; [neurolinguistic perspective] Plebe & De La Cruz 2016: 113–129. See also Further Reading for Chapter 1.

Semantic predicates, as used in lexical semantics (vs. logical semantics), in a way similar to ours: [qualia structures] Pustejovsky 1995; [predicates] Goddard 2011; [frames] Ruppenhofer *et al.* 2016.

Semantic actants: See Further Reading for Chapter 10.

Semantic decomposition: Wierzbicka 1980; Wierzbicka & Goddard 2005; Pustejovsky 1995 and 2006.

Semantic primitives: Wierzbicka 1977 and 2011; Goddard & Wierzbicka 2014; Mel'čuk 1989.

Natural language-based languages used for meaning representation: [Basic English] Ogden 1930; [language of lexicographic definition, Moscow branch of MTT] Apresjan 2000: 215–230; [controlled vocabulary of LDOCE] Herbst 1986; [Natural Semantic Metalanguage] see the already provided references to the work of A. Wierzbicka and her colleagues.

Logical languages used for meaning representation: see Further Reading for Appendix.

4 Lexical Meaning, Lexical Items and Lexical Units

Lexical meanings, or semantemes (Ch. 3, *3.1*), of language **L** are, as a rule, expressed by lexical units [LUs].[1] These are: (1) lexemes, or single words, each taken in one well-specified sense (EAT$_{(V)}$**2**, ARGUMENT**2**, LOVE$_{(N)}$**2**, INTERESTING$_{(ADJ)}$, WOW$_{(INTERJ)}$, etc.), and (2) idioms, non-compositional multiword expressions, these too taken each in one well-specified sense (⌐SIT ON THE FENCE⌐ 'avoid communicating which side of the argument you support', ⌐TRIP THE LIGHT FANTASTIC⌐ 'dance nimbly or lightly', etc.).

A set of all LUs of language **L** constitutes the core of the lexical stock of **L**. The lexical stock of **L** is usually described in, or modeled by, a dictionary of **L**. Each LU is the headword of a dictionary article, a.k.a. lexical entry, where its meaning and combinatorial properties are stored.

The lexical stock also contains lexical items that are not LUs but are part of restricted lexical cooccurrence of full-fledged LUs: collocations (*compelling ARGUMENT*, *hot PURSUIT*, *fall in LOVE*, etc.) and clichés (*as mentioned above*, *Yours truly*, *All good things come to an end*, etc.). Collocations and clichés are similar to idioms in that they too are multiword expressions that are in some way constrained (= not free); this is why, together with idioms, they form the class of phrasemes.[2] However, collocations and clichés are not treated in the same way as idioms in the dictionary. That is, they do not have their own lexical entries: a

---

[1] We ignore cases where configurations of semantemes are expressed by morphological means (affixes and meaningful operations), as well as by meaningful syntactic constructions.

[2] Phrasemes include yet another variety: nominemes, or complex proper names, such as *Ernest Hemingway*, *Jehovah's Witnesses* or *Middle East*. Given their special nature, nominemes belong more to an encyclopedia than to a language dictionary and are less interesting for us than other phraseme types; they will be briefly characterized in Subsection *2.2.2.2* below.

collocation is described within the entry of its base (thus, the collocation *compelling ARGUMENT* is described in the lexical entry for ARGUMENT**2**, and so on), and a cliché – within the entry of its anchor (the cliché *Yours truly* is described in the entry for LETTER$_{(N)}$**1** ['correspondence'], etc.).

The part of semantics that deals with the meaning properties of LUs and with the semantic relations they entertain within the lexical stock is lexical semantics. Lexical semantics has close ties with lexicology and its sister discipline, lexicography. We start by explaining these links (Section *1*); then we characterize LUs and other lexical items constituting the lexical stock of a language (Section *2*).

As for other lexical stock-related issues, the lexicographic definition, the central tool for describing lexical meanings, is considered in Ch. 5, semantic-lexical relations and their description in terms of lexical functions are taken up in Ch. 6 and Ch. 7, and the overall organization of the lexical stock and its modeling, in Ch. 8.

1   Lexical Semantics, Lexicology and Lexicography

Lexical semantics is, as we have just said, a subfield of semantics, along with morphological semantics, propositional (= sentence-level) semantics and text/discourse semantics. It overlaps with lexicology and lexicography.

In order to delimit the domain of lexical semantics and that of lexicology/lexicography we first need to make the distinction between the lexical stock and the dictionary more precise.

As indicated above, the lexical stock of language **L** is a structured set of lexical items – lexemes and phrasemes – of **L**; it can be thought of as a union of all lexical items known to **L**'s speakers, i.e., as being part of their individual mental lexicons. As such, the lexical stock is a psychological and neurological reality, namely, particular information stored in the brains of speakers. At the same time, it is an abstraction, because, on the one hand, no speaker knows all the lexical items in the stock and, on the other, the boundaries of the lexical stock are fuzzy and its exact size is difficult to pin down, due to its constant state of flux (with some items disappearing from and others being added to it).

A dictionary of **L** is a model of **L**'s lexical stock or of its part(s). Such a model can assume different shapes, depending on the goals it sets out to achieve (theoretical lexicon vs. commercial dictionary), the profile of its users (learners' vs. general public dictionary), the part of the lexical stock being modeled (general language dictionary vs. dictionary of collocations, of idioms, of borrowings, etc.), and so on. We do not know whether any dictionary model faithfully reflects the organization of the mental lexicon, i.e., the actual way lexical items are stored in speakers' brains; this is in fact quite unlikely.[3] Be that as it may, these two concepts – lexical stock and dictionary – are quite distinct, just like, say, an atom and its model.

---

[3] Some contemporary models, in the form of lexical networks, may have a stronger claim to psychological reality; see, for instance, Polguère 2014.

Back to the distinction we seek to establish – that between lexical semantics and lexicology/lexicography – we can say that lexical semantics studies the meanings of the lexical items of a language independently of the way its findings are presented. (Although these two aspects – the method of studying and the method of presenting the results – can never be completely separated: a particular conceptualization entails a particular formalization, or at least limits the possibilities of formalization.) On the other hand, lexicology is a theory of dictionary making, or more generally, a theory of lexical stock modeling, including all types of models – not only dictionaries, but also databases, lexical networks, etc. As for lexicography, it is the practice of dictionary making – that is, the actual construction of user-oriented models. (So lexicology = theoretical lexicography; or lexicography = practical lexicography.) Lexicology and lexicography are also broader in scope than lexical semantics, because they consider lexical items in all their aspects – semantic, of course, but also syntactic, morphological and phonological.

Lexicology is unlike any other branch of linguistics in the following respect. While each branch of linguistics targets a particular component of language (or of its model) and considers all objects of this component exclusively at two particular adjacent levels of linguistic representation, lexicology considers only one type of object – lexical items – at all representation levels. In this sense, lexicology "cuts across" the four major divisions of linguistics: it is, as it were, a complete linguistic study – semantic, syntactic, morphological and phonological – projected on individual lexical items.

As we can see, lexicography, lexicology and lexical semantics deal with the same data – the lexical stock, but they do so from different, albeit complementary, perspectives. The division is far from being airtight; the three disciplines "talk to and inform one another": thus, lexicography is a testing ground for lexicology, and lexicology supplies material for lexical semantics.

Our perspective in Chapters 4–8 is that of both lexical semantics and lexicology. We base our discussion on a particular theoretical model of the lexical stock, the *Explanatory Combinatorial Dictionary* (ECD), which plays an important role in Meaning-Text models of semantics$_1$.

2   Lexical Items and Lexical Units

Two major types of lexical items – lexemes and phrasemes – are characterized in Subsections *2.1* and *2.2*, respectively. The lexicographic status of lexical items – a lexical unit or not? – is specified in Subsection *2.3*.

2.1   Lexemes

We have already mentioned lexemes in informal discussion. Now it is time to offer a formal definition of the concept.

> **Definition 4.1:** Lexeme
> A lexeme of language **L** is the set of **L**'s wordforms and phrases of special type (= analytical forms) whose signifieds differ only by inflectional meanings (= grammemes) and whose signifiers include the signifier of the same common stem which expresses their shared lexical meaning.

☛   For the concepts of *wordform*, *inflectional meaning* and *radical*, see Ch. 2, *3*.

REMARK. The formulation "the common stem [of all the elements of a lexeme]" is a simplification; in fact, the stem can appear in several morphological forms and may be difficult to specify in the case of an analytical form. However, in a textbook on semantics, these formal details can be ignored.

For example, the wordforms **dog** (*I could hear my **dog** bark.*) and **dogs** (*a pack of stray **dogs***) belong to the same lexeme, DOG$_{(N)}$**I.1**, since they have the same lexical meaning ('domestic animal that ...') and differ only in their inflectional meanings (SINGULAR VS. PLURAL); the phrases **a dog, the dog** and **the dogs** also belong to this lexeme, as analytical forms (INDEFINITE VS. DEFINITE). Similarly, the lexeme LEAVE$_{(V)}$**1** (*Leave the motorway at Junction 7.*) includes the following wordforms and analytical forms: **leaves, left, will leave, has been leaving, having left, was left,** etc., all with the same lexical meaning, roughly, 'X causes_oneself to cease being at location Y'.

However, the wordform **dog** that we see in *You dirty dog!* does not belong to the lexeme DOG$_{(N)}$**I.1**, since its meaning is ≈ 'dishonest man'; it is an element of the lexeme DOG$_{(N)}$**II.1**, metaphorically related to DOG$_{(N)}$**I.1**. In the same way, the wordform **left** in *I left my keys in the front door* is not included in the lexeme LEAVE$_{(V)}$**1**, since its meaning is different, something like '[leaving1 location Z,] X lets Y stay at location Z'; it is part of a semantically related, but distinct, lexeme, LEAVE$_{(V)}$**4**.

Thus, **a lexeme is monosemic by definition**, i.e., it cannot have more than one meaning. A distinctive lexicographic number (Ch. 3, *3.1*), which is assigned to a lexeme L, uniquely identifies L within the vocable (= polysemous word) to which L belongs.

Here are additional examples of English lexemes: BE**I.1** (copula/auxiliary verb: *John **is** tall.* | *Don't disturb me while I **am** working.*); BE**II** (locative verb: *I **am** in Paris right now.*); THINK**1** (*I **think** that you are being unfair.*); THINK**2** (*Wait a moment, I am **thinking**.*); LOVE$_{(N)}$**3** (*my first **love***); ON$_{(PREP)}$**1** (***on** the table*); BUT$_{(CONJ)}$**1** (*Peter left, **but** Mary stayed*).

From the viewpoint of its morphological makeup, a lexeme can be one of the following:

- A simple lexeme, containing a single simple stem (= radical); all the lexemes we have cited so far in this subsection are simple lexemes.
- A (synchronically) derived lexeme, containing a radical and at least one derivational means, expressing a derivateme (Ch. 2, *3.2.2*); for instance, *RE*+APPLY 'apply ⊕ again'; READ+*ABLE* 'read ⊕ such that one can ... it'; etc.

☞   Derivatemes are printed in *HELVETICA ITALICS UPPER CASE LETTERS*.

- A (synchronically) compound lexeme, containing at least two stems; for instance, Ger. PARTIKEL+SYSTEM 'particle⊕system'; UNIVERSITÄT+S+GEBÄUDE 'university ⊕ building'; etc.

> **NB:** 1. The opposition "synchronic (= productive, compositional) ~ diachronic (= non-productive, phraseologized) word formation" was introduced in Ch. 2, *3.3*.
> 2. For derivational relations between LUs, see Ch. 6, *1.2*.

2.2   Phrasemes

The notion of phraseme is taken up in Subsection *2.2.1*, major types of phrasemes are presented in *2.2.2*, and degree of frozenness, an important, albeit non-definitorial, property of phrasemes, is discussed in *2.2.3*.

2.2.1   The Notion of Phraseme

Informally, a phraseme is a complex expression (= an expression that consists of several linguistic signs) that is not free, or is constrained. In what follows, only phrasemes that are phrases (Ch. 2, *2.1.2*) will be considered, such as *To be continued* 'The continuation of the preceding text will appear soon', *launch an attack* 'start an attack', ⌜*curry favor*⌝ [with N by V_GERUND] 'ingratiate oneself with N by V_GERUND', ⌜*red herring*⌝ 'a piece of information introduced into a discussion in order to divert attention away from the main point', etc. This is the best-known family of phrasemes; they can be called lexemic phrasemes (since they are formed by lexemes), or else phrasal phrasemes (since they are phrases).[4]

---

[4] The two other major families of phrasemes are left out: (1) Morphological phrasemes, i.e., phraseologized lexemes, such as CARRIER 'military ship designed for planes to take off from and land on' and BLACKBOARD 'device designed to be used in a classroom ...'. (2) Syntactic (= constructional) phrasemes, such as *Xs will be Xs* 'Xs have typical properties, which you should expect to find in each X' (*Boys will be boys.* | *Linguists will be linguists.*); a syntactic phraseme consists of lexemic variables linked by structural (≈ grammatical) words; it is a phraseologized syntactic construction.

NB: Given the fact that here we are interested only in lexemic phrasemes, the adjective *lexemic* will be omitted.

A phrase that is a phraseme is, first of all, not free – it is, so to speak, bounded. The bounded character of a phraseme is manifested on both paradigmatic and syntagmatic axes.

Let there be a non-free phrase **AB**, consisting of lexemes **A** and **B**.

1. "**AB** is not free on the paradigmatic axis" means that the selection of the components **A** and **B** by the Speaker is constrained. This can happen in two ways: (a) at least one of the two components is not selected exclusively as a function of its meaning, the choice being controlled by the other component; or (b) both components are selected together as one piece. As a result, the Speaker cannot use instead of **A** any sufficiently synonymous **A'**; the same is true of **B**: it cannot be replaced by any synonymous **B'**. For instance:

   $milk_A\ run_B$ 'regular uneventful journey' $\not\equiv dairy_{A'}\ run_B,\ milk_A\ race_{B'}$
   $hit_A\ the\ hay_B$ 'go to bed' $\not\equiv strike_{A'}\ the\ hay_B,\ hit_A\ the\ stack_{B'}$

2. "**AB** is not free on the syntagmatic axis" means that the combination of the components **A** and **B** is not regular: **A** and **B** are not combined according to some general rules of the language. In other words, the phrase **AB** is not compositional (Ch. 2, *1.1.3*). For instance, the expressions *hit the guy* [*in the face*] and *hit the nail* [*with a hammer*] are compositional, while *hit the hay* is not: in the latter expression, the meaning of HIT and that of HAY are not combined according to some general rules. Below, we consider only semantic compositionality – that is, the compositionality of complex signs in their signified:

   'AB' = 'A ⊕ B'.

 Recall that "⊕" is the symbol of the operation of linguistic union, which combines the signs in conformity with their syntactics (Ch. 2, *1.1.1*) and general rules of the language – by combining their components; here, linguistic union is applied to combine two signifieds.

The freedom of selection (= paradigmatic freedom) and the regularity of combination (= syntagmatic freedom) are not mutually independent properties:

- If the Speaker's selection of neither **A** nor **B** is constrained, then the phrase **AB** must be semantically compositional. (The inverse is not true: a semantically compositional **AB** can arise as a result of constrained selection, as in *DO* ⟨**MAKE*⟩ *a favor.*)
- If **AB** is semantically non-compositional, the selection of **A** or that of **B** is necessarily constrained, or else **A** and **B** are selected only together – as a whole.

This gives rise to four possible major classes of phrasemes, shown in *Table 4.1*.

Table 4.1 Major phrase types

	NON-CONSTRAINED SELECTION	CONSTRAINED SELECTION
COMPOSITIONAL	FREE PHRASES	1. collocations (e.g., *pay* ATTENTION, *EASY* as pie) 2. clichés (e.g., *What time is it?*, *To begin with* …)
NON-COMPOSITIONAL	**Impossible case**	3. idioms (e.g., ⌜*call it a day*⌝, ⌜*under the weather*⌝) 4. nominemes (e.g., *Tom Jones*, *Big Salt Lake*)
		PHRASEMES

The property of paradigmatic freedom (= non-constrained selection) is thus stronger: for a phrase **AB** to be a phraseme it is necessary and sufficient that the selection of **A**, **B** or both is constrained. Therefore, the property of semantic compositionality defines not the phrasemes as such, but two major subclasses of phrasemes: compositional phrasemes, which fall into collocations and clichés, and non-compositional phrasemes, further divided into idioms and nominemes. We will return to the notion of compositionality in *2.2.2.1* below.

Phrasemes are extremely frequent in natural languages: they run into millions in a given language. This number can be explained, at least in part, by two independent factors: the use of ready-made blocks and the insufficient quantity of elementary signifiers.

The existence of compositional phrasemes hinges upon speakers' strong preference for using "prefabricated" speech fragments: this is the well-known principle of least effort. It is easier to extract a ready-to-use complex expression from one's memory than to synthesize it, step by step, on each particular occasion. The observation of this principle gives rise to collocations and clichés.

As far as the non-compositional phrasemes – idioms and nominemes – are concerned, they appear because the stock of elementary signifiers available in language is not sufficient to accommodate a huge – and constantly growing – quantity of signifieds. The number of possible elementary signifiers is severely limited by our articulatory and acoustical capabilities,[5] while the number of possible signifieds is unlimited. Therefore, some free phrases are, so to speak, hijacked – in order to be loaded with a new signified and thus become idioms and nominemes.

---

[5] Natural languages have a rather small inventory of phonemes (between 15 and 80) and strong constraints on their combinations.

> **Definition 4.2:** Phraseme
> A phraseme is a phrase consisting of at least two lexemes that is para-
> digmatically constrained.

The constrained character of a phrase can manifest itself at one of the two
stages of speech production, namely:
- If the constraints apply in the transition SemR ⟺ DSyntR, i.e., between
  the semantic level and the deep-syntactic level of representation, the resulting expression is a lexemically constrained phraseme, or lexemic phraseme
  for short. The complex meaning of a lexemic phraseme (= its signified)
  is constructed freely by the Speaker, but the complex lexemic expression
  of this meaning (= the signifier of the phraseme) is not. This is the best-
  known and the best-studied class of phrasemes, which includes idioms and
  collocations.
- If the constraints apply in the transition ConceptR ⟺ SemR, i.e., between
  the conceptual, or prelinguistic, level of representation (Ch. 1, *2.4*) and the
  semantic level, we get a semantic-lexemic phraseme – such that its meaning
  is already not constructed freely. A phraseme of this type is "prefabricated"
  by the language, as it were: a particular meaning coupled with a particular lexical expression that the Speaker must use "ready-made." These are
  nominemes and clichés, extremely numerous, but poorly studied from the
  theoretical viewpoint and even insufficiently recorded.

2.2.2   Types of Phrasemes

Lexemic phrasemes, as more "idiomatic," are considered first (*2.2.2.1*), followed by the less idiomatic, semantic-lexemic phrasemes (*2.2.2.2*).

2.2.2.1   Lexemic Phrasemes: Idioms and Collocations

> **Definition 4.3:** Lexemic Phraseme
> **A** and **B** are lexemes.
> A lexemic phraseme is a phraseme **AB** whose signified is not con-
> strained, but whose signifier is constrained with respect to the sig-
> nified: at least one of the components **A** and **B** is not selected by the
> Speaker independently – that is, strictly for its meaning and without
> regard for the other component.

In other words, the meaning of a lexemic phraseme is constructed by the
Speaker without any constraints; what is constrained is the selection of lexemes for the expression of this meaning.
There are two major types of lexemic phrasemes, distinguished as a function of their semantic compositionality: non-compositional phrasemes (such

as the notorious ⌜KICK THE BUCKET⌝) are called idioms, and compositional phrasemes (of the type *wield AUTHORITY* or *exercise CONTROL*) are known as collocations.

In order to make the notion of compositionality as applied to collocations clearer, on the one hand, and be able to distinguish between subtypes of idioms, on the other, we need the concept of semantic pivot (within the meaning of a phrase).

> **Definition 4.4:** Semantic Pivot
>
> Let there be a phrase L_1—L_2 with the meaning 'σ', 'σ' having the following property: 'σ' can be divided in two parts, 'σ_1' and 'σ_2' ['σ' = 'σ_1' ⊕ 'σ_2'], such that 'σ_1' corresponds to L_1 and 'σ_2' corresponds to L_2, and one of the parts is an argument of the other [for instance, 'σ_1'('σ_2')].
>
> The semantic pivot of the meaning 'σ' is:
>
> 1. Either the argument meaning 'σ_2' – iff
>   (a) 'σ_2' is or contains the communicatively dominant component of 'σ'
>   or
>   (b) L_2 semantically implies L_1.
> 2. Or the predicate meaning 'σ_1' – iff Condition 1 is not satisfied.

In the examples below, the semantic pivot is identified by shading and the communicatively dominant component (Ch. 10, *3.3.1*) is <u>underscored</u>.

Examples

Condition 1a: The meaning of the phrase *sea dog* is 'σ' = '[man].$_{\sigma_2}$, [whose profession is to navigate the seas and who is very experienced].σ_1'; it has as its semantic pivot the semanteme 'man' because (1) this semanteme is the argument of the compound predicate 'whose profession is to navigate the seas and who is very experienced' and (2) it is the communicatively dominant component of the meaning 'σ'.

Condition 1b: The meaning of the phrase *keep a secret* is 'σ' = '[not <u>divulge</u>].$_{\sigma_1}$, [a secret].$_{\sigma_2}$,', where the semantic pivot of 'σ' is 'secret'; the lexeme SECRET 'secret' semantically implies the lexeme KEEP 'not <u>divulge</u>'. (A piece of information can be called *a secret* precisely because it is not supposed to be divulged; on semantic implication, see Ch. 9, *2.2*.)

Condition 2: The meaning of the phrase *war game* is 'σ' = '[<u>exercise</u>].$_{\sigma_1}$, [in war expertise …].$_{\sigma_2}$,', where the meaning 'war expertise' is an argument of the predicate 'exercise'. The semantic pivot of 'σ' is '[<u>exercise</u>].σ_1:

'σ₂' does not contain the communicatively dominant component and the lexeme WAR does not imply GAME.

Now idioms and collocations can be defined.

Idioms

> **Definition 4.5:** Idiom
> An idiom is a lexemic phraseme that is not compositional.

The signified 'σ' of an idiom **AB** includes neither the signified 'A', nor the signified 'B' as the semantic pivot. Symbolically: 'σ' $\not\supset$ 'A' **and** 'σ' $\not\supset$ 'B'. As we shall see below, 'σ' may very well include one or even both of the components 'A' and 'B', but neither may be in the pivotal position!

☞   Recall that idioms are indicated by raised half-brackets: ⌜...⌝.

For instance, ⌜GO TO THE DOGS⌝ is an idiom because its meaning 'σ' = 'deteriorate a lot' does not contain either of the meanings of the lexemic expressions making up its signifier, 'A' = 'go' and 'B' = 'to the dogs'. The same holds for ⌜DOG'S DINNER⌝ 'a complete mess', ⌜DOG IN THE MANGER⌝ ≈ 'a stingy person who ...', and so on.

An idiom is strictly monosemic (just like a lexeme is); thus, the boldfaced phrases in (1) are both elements of the idiom ⌜GO TO THE DOGS⌝ since they have the same lexical meaning and differ only in their inflectional meanings (PRESENT VS. PAST).

(1) a.   *The country **is going to the dogs*** [a book title].
  b.   *For a long time, many English speakers felt that the language **was going to the dogs***.

An idiom, like a lexeme, can belong to a polysemous "word" – that is, be part of an idiom vocable (although polysemous vocables happen much more rarely with idioms); thus:

(2) a.   **Br. informal** X ⌜COMES A CROPPER⌝
  X ⌜COMES A CROPPER⌝**I**: 'X falls heavily on the ground' (*Supermodel Naomi Campbell came a cropper last week on the catwalk of a Paris fashion show.*)
  X ⌜COMES A CROPPER⌝**II**: 'X fails completely in what X is trying to accomplish – ⌜as if⌝ X ⌜came a cropper⌝**I**' (*The leading actor came a cropper when he forgot his lines halfway through the second act.*)

  b.   X ⌜BRINGS DOWN⌝ Y
  X ⌜BRINGS DOWN⌝**I** Y: 'X causes2 Y to fall on the ground' (*Pratt surged into the penalty area, where he was brought down by Liam Francis.*)

X ⌜BRINGS DOWN⌝II Y: 'X causes2 Y to lose Y's public office – ⌜as if⌝ X ⌜brought down⌝I Y (*Anyone who understands democracy knows that he was brought down by the Left.*)

What we see more often, on the other hand, is the homonymy of a free phrase and an idiom. For instance, *tone-deaf* can either be interpreted literally (= compositionally), as 'unable to distinguish tones', or idiomatically (= non-compositionally), as 'unable to discern nuances in …'; the same is true for *take someone for a ride, hit the nail on the head*, etc.

The degree to which the meanings of an idiom's components are present in its own meaning characterizes its semantic transparency/opacity. According to this feature, idioms range from totally non-transparent (= opaque), e.g., ⌜*hair of the dog that bit you*⌝ 'alcoholic beverage consumed as a remedy in a hangover' to quite transparent, e.g., ⌜*baking powder*⌝ 'substance in the form of **powder** used in **baking** …'. (An idiom cannot, of course, be fully – 100 percent – transparent: in that case, it would not be an idiom, but a compositional phrase: a free phrase, a collocation or a cliché.) Three major subclasses of idioms can be distinguished as a function of their transparency/opacity.

Minimal transparency/Maximal opacity

The signified 'σ' of the idiom **AB** includes neither the signified 'A' nor the signified 'B':

'σ' ⊅ 'A' **and** 'σ' ⊅ 'B'

These are strong [= full] idioms; their semantic transparency is minimal or zero. **Examples:** ⌜*kick the bucket*⌝, ⌜*shoot the breeze*⌝, ⌜*hit the hay*⌝, ⌜*take wing*⌝, ⌜*Cat got your tongue*⌝, ⌜*jump the gun*⌝, ⌜*the call of nature*⌝, ⌜*wet blanket*⌝, ⌜*vicious circle*⌝, ⌜*red tape*⌝, ⌜*Jack of all trades*⌝, ⌜*in the wink of an eye*⌝, etc.

Middle transparency/opacity

The signified 'σ' includes just one of the two signifieds 'A' and 'B'; for instance, 'A', but not in the position of semantic pivot, plus another signified 'C', which is the semantic pivot:

'σ' ⊃ 'A', **and** 'σ' ⊅ 'B', **and** 'σ' ⊃ 'C'

These are half-idioms, featuring middle semantic transparency. **Examples**: ⌜*sea dog*⌝, ⌜*take on water*⌝, ⌜*private eye*⌝, ⌜*war game*⌝, etc. Thus, the meaning of the idiom ⌜*sea dog*⌝ includes 'sea', but not in the position of semantic pivot, as explained above; the same is true of all half-idioms.

Maximal transparency/Minimal opacity

The signified 'σ' includes the signified 'A' and the signified 'B', but also an additional signified 'C' (different from 'A' and 'B'), which plays the role of semantic pivot:

'σ' ⊃ 'A', **and** 'σ' ⊃ 'B', **and** 'σ' ⊃ 'C' | 'C' ⊄ 'A' **and** 'C' ⊄ 'B'

These are weak idioms, and they feature maximal semantic transparency. **Examples**: ⌐solar panel⌐, ⌐shopping mall⌐, ⌐bacon and eggs⌐, ⌐expect a child⌐, ⌐under the influence⌐, etc. ⌐Solar panel⌐ means '<u>device</u> designed to absorb the **Sun's** rays and transform their energy into electricity and having the form of a **panel** ...'; the components 'designed to absorb the Sun's rays ...' and 'having the form of a panel ...' are complex semantic predicates that take the component 'device' as their argument; 'device', the communicatively dominant component of the configuration, constitutes its semantic pivot.

Weak idioms (as well as some half-idioms) closely resemble collocations, so much so that in some cases it is easy to confound them; we will briefly address this question after having characterized collocations.

Collocations

> **Definition 4.6:** Collocation
> A collocation is a lexemic phraseme that is compositional.

In a collocation **AB** with the meaning 'σ', the property of non-constrained selection is violated minimally – by just one of the components. For instance, **A** is selected for its meaning independently of **B**, while **B** is selected as a function of **A** in order to express the semantic difference 'C' between 'σ', the global meaning of **AB**, and 'A'. Thus, in the collocation **AB** 'σ', the meaning 'σ' is the sum 'A' ⊕ 'C', and **B** is selected as a function of **A** to express 'C'.

For example, the expression $heavy_B$ $traffic_A$ is a collocation. Its meaning is 'σ' = '[intense].$_C$, [<u>traffic</u>].$_A$'; the component '<u>traffic</u>'.$_A$ is expressed by the noun $TRAFFIC_A$, freely selected, and the component 'intense'.$_C$ is expressed by the adjective $heavy_B$, whose selection is contingent upon the noun. $TRAFFIC_A$, the freely chosen element, is called the base of the collocation **AB**, and $heavy_B$ is the collocate. Note that the base of a collocation is also its semantic pivot (as shown above by underscoring).

More examples of collocations follow (the base is indicated by UPPER CASE ITALICS): passionate LOVE; greatly ⟨much, really⟩ APPRECIATE; UGLY as sin; a compelling ARGUMENT; CRIME scene; flames of PASSION; run into RESISTANCE; undergo SURGERY; make an ERROR; discharge a DUTY; pass an EXAM; place an ORDER; a HURRICANE strikes; PRICES skyrocket; etc.

The compositionality of a collocation is not always obvious. One could argue, for instance, that the collocation pay ATTENTION is not compositional, since its meaning – 'X pays attention to Y' ≈ 'X causes2 X's attention to be directed towards Y' – is not a regular composition of 'pay$_{(V)}$' and 'attention'. However, this reasoning is flawed: the meaning 'pay attention' is expressed compositionally, since 'attention' is expressed by the lexeme ATTENTION and the rest of this meaning – i.e., 'cause2 to be directed towards' – by PAY. The fact that the verb PAY expresses this meaning only in this collocation does not mean that compositionality is violated. We observe here a well-known distinction between inherent meaning, which a lexeme has in the language in an autonomous way and independently of its lexical "partners," and contextual meaning, which a lexeme carries only in combination with another particular lexeme (or several particular lexemes). The meaning of the verb PAY in the collocation *pay ATTENTION* is precisely contextual; the same is true for BREAK in *break the LAW*, for HEAVE in *heave a SIGH*, etc.

The distinction "inherent ~ contextual meaning" is linked to the constrained character of collocations: if the cooccurrence of a collocate is reduced to one or two bases, its meaning in this collocation is contextual. This is obvious in the case of a unique cooccurrence, as in *black COFFEE/TEA*, with *black* having the meaning 'without addition of dairy products' only within this collocation. The meaning 'without addition of dairy products' need not appear in the dictionary as a particular wordsense of the adjective BLACK (since it will never be used outside the collocation in question), and neither do its other contextual meanings, found in the collocations *black FLAG*, *black HUMOR*, *black LIST*, *black MARKET*, etc.

Collocations come in two varieties: standard vs. non-standard.

In a standard collocation, the semantic relation between the base and its collocate is regular in that it holds for a high number of collocations. For instance, the meaning 'intensification', as seen in *LAUGH one's head off*, *great PERIL* or *POOR as a church mouse*, is found in thousands of collocations; 'produce the typical sound' appears with a couple hundred nouns: *a BANNER flaps*, *a BULLET zips*, *an ELEPHANT trumpets*, *a SIREN wails*, *the SNOW creaks/crunches/squeaks* [under somebody's steps], etc. A language has, as a rule, a few dozen types of standard collocation. Standard collocations are described by means of standard lexical functions (Ch. 7, *2*).

A non-standard collocation features a non-regular, often unique, semantic link between the base and the collocate: *black COFFEE* 'coffee without addition of a dairy product', *blow* [one's] *NOSE* 'clean one's nose from mucus by blowing through it', *alternating CURRENT* 'current that cyclically changes direction', *WAR of attrition* 'war aimed at exhausting the resources of the adversary', etc. There are thousands of non-standard collocations, which are described by non-standard lexical functions (Ch. 7, *3*).

Now, closing Subsection *2.2.2.1*, we can explain how collocations, standard as well as non-standard, are different from half-idioms and weak idioms:

> In a collocation, one component – namely, the base – expresses the semantic pivot of the collocation, while in an idiom, none of its components corresponds to its semantic pivot.

As a result, the collocation *heavy traffic* or *black coffee* refers, respectively, to traffic and to coffee; in contrast, the idioms ⌐sea dog⌐ or ⌐solar panel⌐ do not refer to dogs and panels.

2.2.2.2 Semantic-Lexemic Phrasemes: Nominemes and Clichés (Including Pragmatemes)

Just like lexemic phrasemes, semantic-lexemic phrasemes can be non-compositional or compositional, which gives two subclasses: nominemes and clichés.

Nominemes

> **Definition 4.7:** Nomineme
> A nomineme is a semantic-lexemic phraseme that is non-compositional.

A nomineme is a complex proper name – a multiword "label" attached to a particular (individual) entity or fact: *Leo Tolstoy*, *Medicine Hat* [a city in Canada], *the French Riviera*, *Seventh-Day Adventists*, *Crystal Night*, *Little Red Riding Hood*, etc. A proper name has no meaning whatsoever – it is directly "pasted" on its referent; therefore, a complex proper name cannot be said to have a compositional meaning.

> **NB:** Since a nomineme can include normal common nouns, it can have perceivable "etymology"; thus, *the French Riviera* is somehow related to France, etc.

The number of nominemes in a language is not limited; however, they belong to an encyclopedia, rather than to a dictionary of language.

Clichés

> **Definition 4.8:** Cliché
> A cliché is a semantic-lexemic phraseme that is compositional.

In a cliché, the property of non-constrained selection is violated at the semantic level: its complex meaning is not constructed in the given speech act but exists in the language (that is, it is stored in the mental lexicon) as a ready-made whole. The lexical expression of this meaning is also constrained: none of the lexemic components of a cliché can be selected for its meaning independently of other components. Thus, a cliché is a lexemic whole that expresses a given meaning, but each of its lexemic components keeps intact its own meaning that constitutes a part of the cliché's meaning. As a result, clichés are semantically compositional (and fully transparent): their components are combined with each other according to the general rules of the language, and each cliché means exactly what it says. A few examples follow (the last three clichés are pragmatemes; see immediately below): *A picture is worth a thousand words.* | *A woman's work is never done.* | *What is your name?* | *How can I help you?* | *to put it differently* | *in other words ⟨terms⟩* | *Sorry, we are closed* [**sign on the door of a business**]. | *No parking* [**traffic sign**]. | *Wrong way* [**traffic sign**].

NB: Interestingly, most clichés are full-fledged sentences – that is, complete communication units.

Clichés are a heterogeneous lot, comprising greetings, speech formulas, some proverbs and sayings, and so on. An important subclass of clichés are pragmatemes.

Pragmatemes

> **Definition 4.9:** Pragmateme
> A pragmateme is a cliché that is constrained by the speech act situation.

In addition to having a fixed meaning and a fixed expression (as do **all** clichés), a pragmateme must be used strictly in a particular extralinguistic situation [sɪᴛ]. It is the sɪᴛ that determines the selection of the meaning (= the pragmateme's signified) by which a given informational content is to be conveyed; most often, it also determines the linguistic form that expresses this meaning (= the pragmateme's signifier). Thus, in a situation where you say *Hold the line (please)*, it would be linguistically inappropriate to use an expression with a different meaning, for instance, *#Wait a minute (please)*, even if it carries roughly the same information. And it would be equally inappropriate to change the form of the expression, saying, for instance, *#Don't hang up (please)*.

The information about the speech act situation is pragmatic in nature; hence the term pragmateme. The sɪᴛ is characterized, in the first place, by the communication medium: this can be a telephone conversation, a letter, a road sign, etc. Information about the sɪᴛ is specified for each pragmateme in its syntactics; here it is indicated [**in boldface, between brackets**]. **Examples**: *Store hours: Num₁:00 – Num₂:00'* [**on a store entrance**]. | *Yours truly* [**closing a formal letter**]. | *Hold the line (please)* [**in a telephone conversation**]. | *Merry Christmas!* [**Christmas greeting**]. | *Present arms!* [**military command**].

> REMARK. Not only a cliché, but also a lexeme and any type of phraseme can be constrained with respect to the situation of its use. This is the case, for instance, with the lexeme *Love* [**closing of an intimate letter**], the idiom ⌜*To whom it may concern*⌝ [**heading of an official letter**], and the collocation *Wet paint* [**on a sign**]. Just like pragmatemes, these lexical items have the indication of their sɪᴛ in their syntactics. In order to set them off from genuine pragmatemes, we will call these lexical items pragmatically constrained.

To conclude this subsection, here is a recapitulation of phraseme types discussed above:

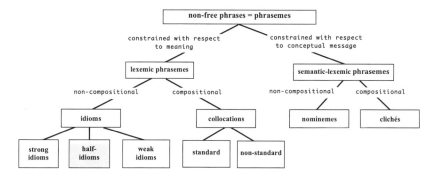

Figure 4.1 A typology of phrasemes

As we have seen, phrasemes form a hierarchy according to decreasing degree of opacity (≈ degree of phraseologization):

full idioms > half-idioms > weak idioms > collocations > clichés

2.2.3   Degree of Frozenness of a Phraseme

A few words are in order about an important property of all phrasemes: their degree of frozenness, or the extent to which they are resistant to modification in speech.

 Note the important difference between the terms phraseologiza- tion and frozenness: phraseologization is a **process** by which a free phrase becomes a phraseme, while frozenness is a **characteristic** of a phraseme.

Contrary to compositionality, which either exists or not (for a given item), frozenness is a gradable property, varying from 0 to 100 percent. The degree of frozenness of a phraseme **P** is determined according to the six features below.

1. The possibility of replacing at least one of **P**'s components by another – synonymous – lexical unit. For instance, the idioms ⌜*kick the bucket*⌝ and ⌜*shoot the breeze*⌝, where no component is replaceable, are 100 percent frozen; by contrast, the following idioms have variants: ⌜*hit the hay* ⟨*the sack*⟩⌝, ⌜*be caught red-handed* ⟨*pants down*⟩⌝. Similarly, the collocation *pay* (someone) *a* VISIT is frozen solid, while the similar collocations of JOURNEY vary: *make* ⟨*take, do*⟩ *a* JOURNEY.

2. The possibility of adding a syntactic modifier at least to one of **P**'s compo- nents different from its syntactic head (Ch. 2, *1.3.2*). For instance, the French idiom ⌜*prendre une veste*⌝ lit. 'take a jacket' = 'suffer a defeat' allows for internal modification: *Le Parti Socialiste a pris une **sacrée** veste aux munic- ipales* 'The Socialist Party suffered a **resounding** defeat in the municipal elections'.

3. The possibility of applying to **P** some syntactic transformations, such as passivization or relativization: ***Accounts*** *have finally **been settled** ⟨**squared**⟩* (from ⌜*settle* ⟨*square*⟩ *accounts*⌝ [*with* N_Y] 'take revenge of Y') vs. ****The beans were spilled*** *by Peter* (from ⌜*spill the beans*⌝ [*to* N_Y] 'divulge a secret to Y'); Fr. *la veste **que Jean a prise*** lit. 'the jacket that Jean has taken' = 'the defeat that Jean suffered' (from ⌜*prendre une veste*⌝ 'suffer a defeat') vs. **la tangente **que Jean a prise*** lit. 'the tangent that Jean has taken' = 'the evasion that Jean made' (from ⌜*prendre la tangente*⌝ 'evade, escape').

4. The possibility of linearly inserting a lexical expression between **P**'s components; this is possible, for instance, for ⌜*move heaven and earth*⌝, and impossible for ⌜*give up*⌝: *He **has moved**, as Mary is telling everyone, **heaven and earth** in order to get this ticket.* vs. **He **gave**, as Mary is telling everyone, **up**.*

5. The possibility of changing the linear order of **P**'s components (in a language where the word order is flexible enough). Consider the Russian idiom ⌜BIT′ BAKLUŠI⌝ 'X who is supposed to do something is not doing anything' (literally, '[to] beat ??': the noun BAKLUŠI has no meaning of its own, since it does not exist outside this idiom). No component of ⌜BIT′ BAKLUŠI⌝ can be replaced; BAKLUŠI cannot accept a modifier and can only be used in this particular inflectional form. Nonetheless, one can invert the linear order of components: *A on b′ët bakluši. ~ A on bakluši b′ët* 'But he, he is twiddling his thumbs'. But then in the collocations *papa rimskij* 'Pope', lit. 'Pope Roman', or *šut goroxovyj* 'miserable buffoon', lit. 'buffoon of.peas', the linear order should not be modified (while normally in Russian an adjective precedes the modified noun).

6. The broadness of cooccurrence of **P**'s components. Within a collocation, the verb MAKE combines with hundreds of bases (*MAKE an apology, an attack, a call, impact, a speech, an arrest, an offer, …*), while the verb HEAVE accepts only a few bases (*HEAVE a sigh, a sob, anchor*). The more the set of possible bases for a given collocate is restricted, the more the collocation is frozen.

The less variation a phraseme tolerates, the more frozen it is. Thus, the cliché *Good night!* is completely invariable and therefore more frozen than, say, *Everybody makes mistakes*, which allows for much variation: *Everybody makes mistakes, **sometimes quite serious**. | Everybody, **as you know**, makes mistakes. | Mistakes? **But** everybody makes **them**.* Clichés – with the exception of pragmatemes – are the least frozen phrasemes.

2.3   Lexicographic Status of Different Types of Lexical Items

As mentioned at the beginning of this chapter, not all lexical items are treated in the same way from a lexicographic point of view, i.e., they do not have the same status in the dictionary. Here are the solutions adopted in the ECD.

Lexemes and non-compositional phrasemes, i.e., idioms and nominemes, are LUs of the language. This means that each lexeme, each idiom and each nomineme featured in the ECD is described in a separate dictionary article – it has its own full-blown lexicographic entry, of which it is the headword. Note, however, that nominemes, as peripheral lexical items, are mentioned here only for completeness (because they fill a spot in our typology of phrasemes) and will not be considered beyond the present chapter.

Definition 4.10: Lexical Unit
A lexical unit of language **L** is either a lexeme or an idiom.

NB: We leave aside the nominemes, which, as we said, are primarily units of an encyclopedia, and therefore of little interest for lexicology.

For a formal description of a lexical unit [LU] in an ECD, see Ch. 8, *2.2*.

Compositional phrasemes – collocations and clichés – are not LUs of the language and do not have dictionary articles of their own.

A collocation is described in the article of its base, as part of the restricted lexical cooccurrence of the base.

A cliché (including a pragmateme) is described in the article of its lexical anchor: an LU that either is part of this cliché or identifies the corresponding situation. For instance, the cliché *What time is it?* has as anchor the lexeme $\text{TIME}_{(N)}$**2**; for the pragmateme *Hold the line, please* [**in telephone conversation**] the anchors are $\text{TELEPHONE}_{(N)}$ and (*telephone*) $\text{CALL}_{(N)}$. Along the same lines, the pragmateme *Emphasis added*, used when someone writing a text quotes another person and wants to indicate that he has somehow emphasized a fragment of the quotation, has three anchors – TEXT, QUOTATION and EMPHASIZE – and appears in the three dictionary articles.[6]

On formal description of collocations and clichés in an ECD – by means of lexical functions – see Ch. 7, *2 & 3*.

Table 4.2 sums up the lexicographic status these four types of lexical items are given in the ECD.

Table 4.2 Lexical items and lexical units

	Lexical item	
A lexical unit: Headword of a dictionary article	**Lexeme**	
	Idiom	**Phraseme**
NOT **a lexical unit**: Described in the dictionary article of its base/anchor	**Collocation**	
	Cliché	

---

[6] An interesting comparison: in this case, French uses the pragmateme *C'est moi qui souligne* 'It is me who underscores', Spanish – the pragmateme *El subrayado es mío* 'The underscoring is mine', German – *Hervorhebung des Autors* 'Emphasis of.the author', Russian – *Kursiv moj* 'Italics [are] mine', and Serbian – *Podvukao*[a male] ⟨*Podvukla* [a female]⟩ [NN] 'Has.underlined [the author's initials]'.

REMARK. In traditional lexicographic approaches, an idiom does not normally get its own dictionary article (= it is not treated as an LU in our sense) but is listed within the article of one of its components. For example, ⌜spill the beans⌝ 'tell everyone something that was supposed to be kept secret' is listed in LDOCE under SPILL¹3, while under BEAN1 one finds a pointer towards SPILL¹3 [→ *spill the beans* under SPILL¹3]. This can be tedious for a dictionary user trying to look up an idiom. Of course, with the advent of computational lexicography and electronic dictionaries, the access to lexicographic information, and thus the way it is stored, is becoming less of an issue. Yet if the user wants to find the idiom to express the meaning ≈ 'divulge a secret', the current practice of storing idioms does not allow him to do so.

Further Reading

Lexical meaning and lexical semantics: [articles] Johnson 2008 and Aquaviva *et al.* 2017; [monographs] Apresjan 2000; Murphy 2010; Geeraerts 2010; Hanks 2013.

Relation between lexicology and lexicography: Wierzbicka 1993; Atkins 2008. For more on lexicology and lexicography see Further Readings for Chapter 8.

Lexical items: Sinclair 2004: 131–148.

Semantic compositionality: Partee 1995; Szabó 2017.

Phraseology: [articles] Becker 1975; Nunberg *et al.* 1994; (NLP perspective) Sag *et al.*, 2002; Gledhill 2011; Mel'čuk 2012a and 2015b; Polguère 2015; [monographs] Cowie 1998; Fellbaum 2007; Granger & Meunier 2008. See also Further Reading for Chapter 7.

5   Lexicographic Definition

The present chapter is dedicated to the description of meanings of lexical units [LUs]. Most LUs have non-elementary meanings, with only a handful of LUs corresponding to semantic primitives (Ch. 3, *4.1.3*). The meaning of an LU L can be made explicit by semantic decomposition. We already talked about this technique in Ch. 3, *1.1* and *4*, where it was said that the canonical representation of the meaning of an LU L, in terms of meanings simpler than that of L, constitutes L's lexicographic definition.

The lexicographic definition of an LU L describes L's propositional meaning (Ch. 3, *1.3*), and in this way specifies L's denotation. In addition to this, L may have a number of connotations – meanings that are not part of its definition but are commonly associated with its denotation by the language. Thus, 'stubbornness' is a connotation of the lexeme DONKEY (cf. *stubborn **as a donkey***), 'diligence' is a connotation of BEE (cf. *busy **as a bee***), 'persistence' a connotation of DOG (cf. ***dogged** determination*), and so on. A description of these two semantic aspects of L – its definition and its connotations – constitutes the semantic zone of a dictionary entry in an *Explanatory Combinatorial Dictionary* (ECD) (for the structure of an ECD entry, see Ch. 8, *2.2*).

The construction of lexicographic definitions is one of the most challenging tasks faced by lexical semantics and lexicology/lexicography, given the very large number of items to be defined – about one million in a language of a contemporary society (Ch. 2, *1.6.2*, Footnote 7) – and their multiple links that must be considered in the process. The meaning of an LU is not defined in isolation, but taking into account, on the one hand, other LUs paradigmatically and syntagmatically related to it (its partners within the same semantic field as well as its derivatives and collocates), and, on the other hand, LUs related to it by polysemy (its partners within the same vocable). In this complex task, we are guided by some general principles that apply also to other aspects of lexicographic description and will be presented in Ch. 8, *2.1.2*: Formality Principle, Internal Coherence Principle and Uniform Treatment Principle.

This chapter begins with a general presentation of the lexicographic definition (Section *1*); then follow: rules for formulating definitions, i.e., rules that ensure the formal correctness of definitions (Section *2*); the types of components of a lexicographic definition and their structuring (Section *3*); criteria for elaborating definitions, ensuring their linguistic ($\approx$ factual) correctness (Section *4*); the distinction "lexicographic definition vs. lexicographic connotation" (Section *5*); lexicographic definition checklist, detailing the steps involved in the construction of a lexicographic definition (Section *6*).

1 General Presentation of a Lexicographic Definition

The lexicographic definition of an LU L is a description of L's meaning – i.e., a semantic representation of L. In our framework, a lexicographic definition can be written in either of the following two logically equivalent formats: as a linear (i.e., textual, or verbal) definition, just like a traditional dictionary definition, or as a semantic network (Ch. 2, *1.6.1* and Ch. 10, *2*).

> REMARK. For pseudo-definitions, approximate but compact and well-formalized descriptions of lexical meanings in terms of semantic labels, see Ch. 8, *1.2*.

For example, here (in *Figures 5.1* and *5.2*) is the definition of the lexeme $\text{LIE}_{(V)}{}^2\mathbf{1}$ (*The accused lied to the authorities about his military record.* | *Mary did not lie about her emails.* | *Have I ever lied to you?*) in both formats.

$\text{LIE}_{(V)}{}^2\mathbf{1}$

X lies to Z about Y: 'X <u>communicates1</u> to Z a piece of false1 information1 α about Y
and X knows1 that α is^{2}1 false1,
X's communication1 being caused1 by the fact that
X wants1 Z to believe1 that α is^{2}1 true1,
(X's desire being caused1 by the fact that
Z believing1 that α is^{2}1 true1 ⌐is^{2}1 in X's
interests$_{(N)}$5'⌐)'

Definiendum:	Definiens:
Propositional form	DEFINITION proper (minimal semantic decomposition of the definiendum)

Figure 5.1 Textual definition of the lexeme $\text{LIE}_{(V)}{}^2\mathbf{1}$

We will provide an explanation for the components of this definition in *3.6* below, once the different types of definition components have been introduced; here it suffices to indicate that parentheses around the last component of the definition show its weak character – it is not necessary for the verb $LIE_{(V)}{}^2\mathbf{1}$ to be used; this allows for covering the cases of "white" lies (told for the benefit of the Addressee), exaggerated friendly compliments and jokes.

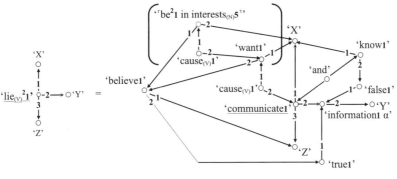

Definiendum:	Definiens:
The semanteme '$lie_{(v)}{}^2\mathbf{1}$'	The minimal semantic decomposition of the semanteme '$lie_{(v)}{}^2\mathbf{1}$'

Figure 5.2 Definition of the lexeme $LIE_{(v)}{}^2\mathbf{1}$ in terms of a semantic network

> **NB:** Some words – structural words – are used in textual definitions just for better readability and do not appear in the semantic network-style definitions because they do not correspond to semantemes (Ch. 3, *3.1*); in our case, these are the conjunction THAT, the prepositions OF, ABOUT, TO, BY and IN, as well as the noun FACT.

Both definition types are couched in specific formal languages (Appendix, *4*). Textual definitions use a standardized defining language (Ch. 3, *2*), a subset of the natural language being described (in our case, English). The defining language is completely disambiguated (by means of distinctive lexicographic numbers, as explained in Ch. 3, *3.1*), standardized (in particular, some elements of the object language are excluded from the defining language) and has a tightly controlled syntax (certain constructions are reserved for certain types of components of the definition, etc.). The language of semantic networks – also used for representing meanings of sentences – is a hybrid, combining the natural language and that of predicate calculus (Appendix, *5.2*).

While these two ways of representing the meaning of an LU are logically equivalent, each has specific practical advantages over the other. Thanks to its precision, a semantic network allows the lexicographer to visualize the links between the components of the definition and easily spot incoherencies or omissions, but it is not ideal for a dictionary user, who may feel intimidated by the formalism. A textual definition is not as precise as one in the form of a semantic network, but is more accessible to the linguistic intuition of both the lexicographer and the dictionary user.

In what follows, we will be referring to the textual lexicographic definitions, leaving aside the semantic network type definitions. This allows us to drop the qualifier *textual* and speak simply of (lexicographic) definitions.

The lexicographic definition of an LU L consists of two major parts. The definiendum features the L to be defined, i.e., the headword. If this L expresses a semantic (quasi-)predicate (Ch. 3, *3.1.2*), it appears within a propositional form, where it is accompanied by variables (X, Y, Z ...), representing its semantic actant slots (Ch. 3, *3.2.2*). The definiens, or the definition proper, is a decomposition of L's meaning in terms of simpler meanings; it consists of hierarchically organized configurations of semantemes – semantic components (see immediately below). In fact, this is the familiar Aristotelian definition (a.k.a. analytical definition), structured in terms of *genus proximum et differentiae specificae*; in our terms, a lexicographic definition consists of the central (= generic) component and a set of peripheral (= specific) components.

An LU stored in an ECD is supplied with a definition of the type illustrated in *Figure 5.1*, except for:

1. LUs expressing the semantic primitives. A primitive is identified as such and supplied, if needed, with informal explanations:

   GOOD, adjective, evaluation, ¦ semantic primitive ¦
   '[X is] good'

2. LUs expressing grammatical significations (Ch. 2, *1.4*), such as the conjunction THAT or the substitute pronouns HE (with the forms *he, him*), WHO(Relative Pronoun) (with the forms *who, whom*), etc. For LUs of this type, syntactic characteristics are provided. For example, the substitute pronoun IT is described along the following lines:

   ITı, nominal pronoun, ¦refers to a lexical unit that has been mentioned and¦ ¦that does not denote a person¦
   ([Where is your office?] *It* [= OFFICE] *is on the third floor.*)

   REMARK. LUs L, L₁, L₂, ..., Lₙ belonging to a series of (exact) synonyms are supplied with identical definitions; for example:

   COUGAR, N, wild animal   ¦**Definition**: A large wild cat¦ ¦living in the mountains¦

   ˹MOUNTAIN LION˺, N, wild animal ¦**Definition**: A large wild cat¦ ¦living in the mountains¦

PUMA, N, wild animal   **Definition**: A large wild cat living in the mountains

Alternatively, a definition can be featured only in the lexical entry of L, the most common LU of the synonymic series (in our case, COUGAR), the entries of the other members of the series L_1, L_2, ..., L_n being supplied only with pointers towards the definition of L (PUMA, N, wild animal **Definition**: $\Rightarrow$ COUGAR, etc.) This is a matter of practical needs arising during the construction of the dictionary (the necessity to save space or the desire to make the dictionary more user-friendly, etc.).

2   Rules for Formulating Lexicographic Definitions

Rules 1–4 target the formal correction of definitions, without addressing their linguistic accuracy (a formally correct definition can still be factually incorrect): (1) propositional form rule, (2) decomposition rule, (3) standardization rule and (4) maximal block rule. Rule 5 – mutual substitutability rule – is aimed at the linguistic accuracy of definitions.

1. Propositional Form Rule

> For a (quasi-)predicative LU L, the definiendum must be a propositional form in which variables X, Y, Z, ... represent L's semantic actant slots.

Thus, in the definition of the verb $\text{LIE}_{(V)}{}^2\mathbf{1}$ (*Figure 5.1*), the definiendum is the propositional form *X lies to Y about Z*. But for the noun COUGAR, which expresses a semantic name, there is no propositional form.

2. Decomposition Rule

> The definition proper of an LU L, i.e., its definiens, must be written in terms of LUs L_1, L_2, ..., L_n (more precisely, the meanings of these LUs, or semantemes: 'L' = '$L_1 \oplus L_2 \oplus ... \oplus L_n$'), each of them being semantically simpler than L.

 Recall (Ch. 3, *4.1.1*) that the meaning 'σ_1' is considered simpler than the meaning 'σ_2', iff in order to decompose 'σ_2' we need to use 'σ_1', while 'σ_2' cannot be used in the decomposition of 'σ_1'. For instance, the meaning '[to] walk' is simpler than the meaning '[to] stroll', because 'stroll'$_{\sigma_2}$ $\approx$ 'walk$_{\sigma_1}$ slowly in a relaxed way', but 'walk$_{\sigma_1}$' $\neq$ 'stroll$_{\sigma_2}$ ...'.

Semantic decomposition is necessary for isolating and organizing the meaning components of individual definitions and for avoiding circularity, or vicious circles, in the system of definitions (i.e., in the dictionary), which represents a serious problem for most existing dictionaries. A vicious circle is the result of an inconsistent application of the decomposition rule. Suppose, for instance, that A is defined (= decomposed) as B + C, B as K + L + M, and C as P + A. If we proceed to substitutions according to these definitions (absolute mutual substitutability of a meaning and its decomposition is another rule which must be observed; see Rule 5 below), we get: $A = \mathbf{B} + C = \mathbf{K} + \mathbf{L} + \mathbf{M} + C = K + L + M + \mathbf{P} + \mathbf{A}$. It turns out that $A = A + K + L + M + P$, which is absurd: nothing can be equal to itself plus something else. Two examples of circularity found in the *Merriam-Webster's Learner's Dictionary* [MWLD online] follow.

Example 1

DAUGHTER: a female **child2**
CHILD**2**:   a son or a **daughter**

The definition of DAUGHTER has 'child2' as the central component and, at the same time, 'daughter' appears as a disjunctive element in the central component of the definition of CHILD**2**. But this is absurd, as shown by the following substitutions (and elimination of redundant elements):

'daughter' = 'a female son or a daughter'; and 'child2' = 'a son or a female child2'.

The erroneous definition is that of CHILD**2**, which should read as follows:

'[X,] **child** of Y and Z' = '[X,] **human being** whose mother is Y and father is Z'.

Note the correct form of the definiendum, i.e., the propositional form, since the lexeme CHILD**2** corresponds to a semantic quasi-predicate (Ch. 3, *3.1.2*). This is also true of other lexemes denoting interpersonal relations, such as DAUGHTER (it is necessarily **someone's** daughter) as well as for lexemes denoting body parts, such as FIN below (it is a fin **of some aquatic animal**).

Example 2

FISH**1**:   a cold-blooded animal that lives in water, breathes with gills and usually has **fins** and scales.

FIN: a thin flat part that sticks out from the body of a **fish1** and is used in moving or guiding the **fish1** through the water.

The error causing the vicious circle in this pair of definitions is the mention of 'fish' in the definition of 'fin', which is unnecessary: fish are aquatic animals, and it is sufficient to state just that. After all, whales also have fins! (And eels do not.) We suggest the following corrections of the definition of FIN that avoids the vicious circle and improves its accuracy:

'**X's** fin' = 'a thin flat body part that sticks out from the body of an **aquatic animal X** and is used in moving or guiding **X** through the water'

By the way, the definition of FISH**1** should contain two additional elements – 'elongated body' and 'tail'. And it is debatable whether the semanteme 'cold-blooded' is necessary, as this information may not be part of linguistic knowledge that should be reflected in lexicographic definitions (see lexicographic vs. encyclopedic knowledge, Section *4* below, Criterion of linguistic relevance).

In some cases, circularity in lexicographic definitions cannot be avoided. For example, the definition of the lexeme BLOOD must contain the component '**red** liquid',[1] and at the same time RED has to be defined as 'that has the color of **blood**'. Consider also 'see' and 'eyes': the meaning of SEE is 'perceive by the **eyes**', and that of EYES, '**vision** [= 'see'] organ'. (True, we could avoid including 'see' in the definition of 'eye', limiting ourselves to the eye's physical description, but this would be unnatural.) Fortunately, cases such as these are rather limited; they concern the meanings related to basic human physiology (such as 'hear' and 'ear' or '[to] smell' and 'nose'); if explicitly marked as such, these "legitimate" vicious circles will pose no problem.

3. Standardization Rule

> Lexicographic definitions should be written in such a way as to avoid either ambiguous elements in any given definiens or synonymous elements in different definienses.

The standardization rule concerns the defining language, mentioned earlier in this chapter: a formalized controlled language used to write definitions, which constitutes one of a number of lexicographic metalanguages (cf. Ch. 8, *2.1.2.1*, Formality Principle).

Avoiding ambiguity in definitions is relatively simple: it is enough to use lexical meanings that have distinctive lexicographic numbers. This was what we did in the definition of $LIE_{(V)}{}^2\mathbf{1}$.

Avoiding synonymy – that is, representing, in any definition, the same semantic fragment by the same sememe – is not that easy, at least judging by several alternative formulations of a single meaning that pop up in the definitions of most common dictionaries. Thus, in the OED one finds the following synonymous formulations: 'a **drinking** container' (GLASS) ~ 'container **for drinking** from' (CUP) or 'container **...** **used for** storing food' (JAR) ~ 'container **for** liquids' (FLASK). The corresponding semantic fragment should be formulated in the four cases in the same way: '**designed for** [drinking/storing]'.

4. Maximal Block Rule

This rule was mentioned in Ch. 3, *4.1.1*, when the semantic decomposition was first discussed. Here is its formal presentation:

---

[1] There are, of course, animals whose blood is not red. However, we speak here not of the physiological liquid called "blood," but of the current English lexeme BLOOD. For a naïve speaker, 'blood' is the epitome of red.

> The definition of an LU L should be written in terms of LUs L_1, L_2, ..., L_n such that no configuration of these LUs can be replaced by a single L' semantically equivalent to this configuration.

In other words, if a lexical configuration in a definition can be replaced by a single LU – that is, if it is lexicalized in the given language, this replacement is obligatory.

The Maximal Block Rule stipulates that decompositions within ECD definitions should be minimal, or the most shallow possible – into "immediate semantic constituents." Given the fact that a semantic decomposition can go on till the level of semantic primitives is reached, the question arises of where exactly to stop decomposing in any given case. On the one hand, decompositions done exclusively in terms of semantic primitives make definitions difficult to understand; on the other hand, decompositions of arbitrary depth cannot be allowed. This means that a gradual, minimal depth decomposition in compliance with the Maximal Block Rule is the best policy to follow.

For example, the definition of the lexeme BROTHER (*I have two brothers and a sister.*) in (1a) violates the Maximal Block Rule because the component 'person having the same parents as Y' corresponds to the meaning of the lexeme SIBLING; consequently, BROTHER should be defined as shown in (1b).

(1) a. *[X is] Y's brother* : '[X is] a male **person having the same parents as Y**'

b. *[X is] Y's brother* : '[X is] Y's male **sibling**'

 In a language where the noun corresponding to SIBLING does not exist (French, German, Russian and many other languages), the definition of 'brother' has to be formulated as in (1a).[2]

The Maximal Block Rule does not affect the factual accuracy of definitions; since a definition that does not conform to the Maximal Block Rule is equivalent to the one that does. The rule has methodological value: a definition which is written in conformity with it is more legible and shows some important lexical links explicitly. Thus, the definition in (1b), which follows the maximal block rule, indicates clearly the link between BROTHER and SIBLING, unlike the definition in (1a), which transgresses it.

5. Mutual Substitutability Rule

The lexicographic definition of L should reflect in the closest way possible the linguistic intuition that native speakers have as to the meaning of L. However,

---

[2] Interestingly, exact equivalents for 'sibling' are found, for instance, in Hungarian (*testvér*) and Finnish (*sisarus*), as well as in several languages of India.

this informal requirement is difficult to check. More formally, the definition of L should satisfy the following general condition:

> An LU L and its definition must be mutually substitutable in all contexts *salva significatione* – that is, without modification of the meaning expressed; stylistic elegance and even correct lexical co-occurrence may be violated.

This rule is also known as the substitutability test (see Ch. 9, *2.4*).[3]

A definition that meets the substitution requirement in a sufficiently high number of different types of contexts can be considered to be valid even though the validity of a definition cannot be proven in the strict sense, since it can never be tested in **all** possible contexts. (The non-validity of a definition, on the other hand, is relatively easy to prove – it is enough to find a single context where is it not substitutable for the LU being defined.)

Let us see how the definition of LIE$_{(V)}$[2]**1**, *Figure 5.1*, p. 118, fares under substitution:

(2) a. *The accused lied to the authorities about his military record.* ≡
      The accused communicated to the authorities false information α about his military record and he knew that α was false; he did this because he wanted the authorities to believe that α was true, this desire being caused by the fact that it was in his interests that the authorities believed that α was true.

   b. *Mary did not lie about her emails.* ≡
      Mary did not communicate [to anyone] *false information about her emails* [she told the truth or she said nothing] *or Mary communicated false information but did not know it was false.*

In both instances, the result of the substitution of the lexeme LIE$_{(V)}$[2]**1** by its definition is a semantically acceptable paraphrase of the starting sentence. True, these paraphrases are not idiomatic (they are so clumsy that neither could ever be used in natural speech), but since the substitution test is aimed at preserving semantic correctness, at the expense of elegance and even proper lexical cooccurrence, such effects must be tolerated. We leave it to the reader to continue with the exercise if he so desires.

 Mutual substitutability of an LU and its definition includes, of course, substitutability within the definitions themselves.

Here is an example of substitutions of semantic elements by their own definitions within the definition of the verb DRINK$_{(V)}$**2** (*How to stop drinking on*

---

[3] It was Anna Wierzbicka who established the substitutability test half a century ago as a major tool of semantic research (Wierzbicka 1972 and 1980: 20).

your own.); namely, the elements 'drink$_{(V)}$**1**' and 'excessively' are replaced with their own definitions:

(3) a. 'X drinks$_{(V)}$**2**' =
'X drinks$_{(V)}$**1** liquids containing alcohol**2** excessively,
which may cause**1** X to become ill or die' =

  b. 'X introduces into X's mouth and_then swallows liquids containing alcohol**2** more than is normal for liquids containing alcohol**2**,
which may cause**1** X to become ill or die'

As we can see, after this "first round" of substitutions, the definition remains valid.

For another, more extensive, example of such substitutions within a semantic decomposition, see Ch. 3, *4.1.2.*

A successfully passed substitutability test indicates that the definition being tested is adequate: each of its elements is necessary and all of its elements taken together are sufficient to describe all possible uses of the lexical item being defined. Two examples of inadequate definitions from *Oxford Australian Junior Dictionary* (cited in Wierzbicka 1993: 49–51) follow.

APPOINTMENT: 'time when you have agreed to **go and** see someone'.

This definition is too specific; the boldfaced elements are not necessary because one can have an appointment without going anywhere – for instance, in one's office.

SECRET: 'something that must be hidden from other people'.

This definition is too general, i.e., it lacks some necessary elements. There are many things that one never does in front of other people which nonetheless do not constitute a secret. This lexeme should be defined rather as 'something that one **knows** and must not **tell** the people who don't know'.

3   Structuring of a Lexicographic Definition: Different Types of Semantic Components

We characterize the different types of semantic components making up a lexicographic definition. Some of these components are obligatory, i.e., present in each definition; others only appear in some definitions.

3.1   The Central Component vs. Peripheral Components

The definition of an LU L is made up of two main blocks: the central component and a set of peripheral components.

The central component of L's definition denotes L's genus proximum, or the closest superordinate term, and is, therefore, also known as L's generic component; it underlies L's possible semantic labels (Ch. 8, *1.2*). The central, or generic, component of L's definition can be thought of as L's minimal paraphrase. Thus, in a lexicographic definition,

central component ≡ generic component

Being a minimal paraphrase of 'L', the central component of L's meaning must be such that the LU L' expressing it is of the same part of speech as L itself: L' is a verb in the definition of a verbal lexeme, a noun in the definition of a nominal lexeme, and so on. This is necessary in order to be able to check the validity of the definition by substituting it for the LU defined in the text.

The central component of a definiens necessarily contains the communicatively dominant semanteme (see Ch. 10, *3.1.1*).

To isolate the central component of the definition of L, it is useful to insert L into the frame *'L' is an instance ⟨a kind⟩ of 'L'*: for example, 'strolling' is an instance of 'walking', 'happiness' is an instance of 'feeling', 'teacher' is a kind of 'person [having a particular profession]', 'car' is a kind of 'motor vehicle', and so on.

Peripheral components flesh out specific differences that distinguish L from all other LUs that have the same central component. The verbs STROLL, STRIDE and MARCH share the central component 'walk' and, therefore, are co-hyponyms. According to LDOCE, their specific differences (boldfaced) are, roughly, as follows: STROLL is 'walk **in a slow relaxed way**', STRIDE – 'walk **quickly with long steps**', and MARCH – 'walk **with firm regular steps**'. The nouns CAR, TRUCK and MOTORCYCLE are also co-hyponyms sharing the central component 'motor vehicle'; they have the following specific differences: CAR is '**a four-wheeled** motor vehicle **that is designed to carry a small number of passengers**', TRUCK is '**a large** motor vehicle **that is designed to carry goods**', and MOTORCYCLE is '**a two-wheeled** motor vehicle **that is designed to carry one or two people**'.

3.2 Simple Components vs. Conjunctive/Disjunctive Components

Besides simple components, such as most of those seen so far in this chapter, lexicographic definitions may contain two types of complex components: conjunctive and disjunctive ones.

A conjunctive component contains a logical conjunction (symbolized as "∧"), which corresponds to the English lexeme AND (as in *John and Mary*). An example of this type of component is the central component of the definition of the lexeme LIE$_{(V)}$²1, *Figure 5.1*. Consider also the definition of the lexeme WIDOW (*Lana Turner stars as a devastated young widow who struggles to make it on Broadway.*):

X, a widow: 'woman1 X [whose husband1 died] **and** [who has not remarried1]'.

Both conjunctive components need to be applicable for a woman to be called a *widow*.

A disjunctive component contains a logical disjunction (symbolized as "V"), which corresponds to the English lexeme OR (*Wine or beer?*). To demonstrate the necessity of such components, let us consider the verb PURIFY in sentences (4a) and (4b):

(4) a.   *We partially purified the water*   : 'We made the water purer'.
     b.   *We completely purified the water*   : 'We made the water pure'.

As can be seen from these examples, its definition must be disjunctive:

'X purifies Y' = '[X causes2 that Y becomes purer] **or** [X causes2 that Y becomes pure]',

which is naturally abbreviated as 'X causes2 that Y becomes [purer **or** pure]', with the disjunctive component 'purer **or** pure'.

Logically, one could speak about two lexemes PURIFY, one of them meaning '... X becomes purer' and the other, '... X becomes pure'. Linguistically, however, this is not warranted: in both uses, PURIFY behaves in the exactly same way. The disjunctive components technique allows us to formally preserve its lexemic unity.

If the definition of L includes a component '... A or B ...', this LU can be used to express, in a given sentence, the meaning 'A' or the meaning 'B' – or even both meanings at the same time, as in (5):

(5) *We purified the water partially and then completely.*

> **NB:** Sentence (5) illustrates the application of the Green-Apresjan criterion, which is called for in case of disjunctive definitions (Mel'čuk 2013: 330); if the hypothetical LU L* '...σ_1 or σ_2 ...' (in (5) L* is PURIFY) can be syntactically linked to a conjoined phrase (in our case, *partially and completely*) such that one of its components bears on 'σ_1' [= 'Y becomes purer'] and the other on 'σ_2'[= 'Y becomes pure'], L* should not be split in two LUs, but must have a disjunctive definition.

Definitions that contain complex components present a higher degree of complexity and require special tools for testing their validity; see Appendix 5, *1* for De Morgan rules, used to verify the coherence of conjunctive and disjunctive definitions. For instance, one of these rules, "Negation of a conjunction results in disjunction of two negations," applies correctly to our definition of WIDOW: *Mary is not a widow* means that either Mary's husband is alive, or he died but she has remarried.

3.3   Regular Components vs. Weak Components

A special case of disjunctive definition for L is a definition of the form 'AB or
A': L can be used to express either the meaning 'AB' or the poorer meaning 'A';
the component 'B' is called weak. A weak component in the definition of L is
not realized in each instance of L's use. For example, the component 'employed
by an educational institution W' in the definition of the lexeme TEACHER is
weak: a teacher does not need to be working in a school, etc. to be called so
(even if this is the default case), since he could be giving private lessons.

A weak component of the definition of certain LUs can "disappear," or "be
ignored," if such an L is used in a particular way. For instance, a Russian masculine noun denoting a profession or nationality, when used in the singular,
denotes a male person; but in the plural it can cover both men and women: *Ja
znaju ètogo poèta*$_{SG}$ 〈*ispanca*$_{SG}$〉 'I know this poet 〈Spaniard〉 [a man]' vs. *Ja
znaju ètix poètov*$_{PL}$ 〈*ispancev*$_{PL}$〉 'I know these poets 〈Spaniards〉 [men (and
women)]'. The definitions of such nouns must contain the weak component
'of masculine sex'. The same is true for the corresponding nouns in several
languages (other Slavic languages, Romance languages, German, etc.).

    Weak semantic components are put in parentheses. In a case where a weak
        component of a definition is "suppressed" only in a particular context,
        this context is explicitly indicated: thus, in Rus. ISPANEC 'Spaniard' =
        '(male)$_{PL/GENERIC}$ person of the ethnicity «Spaniards»', the $_{PL/GENERIC}$ sub-
        script tells the user that this weak component does not appear in the plural or
        in a generic use.

3.4   Presupposition Components vs. Assertion Components

A peripheral component can be presupposed: a presupposed component of
a meaning, which is not negated or questioned when the whole meaning
including it is negated or questioned, contrasts with an asserted component,
which is. To illustrate the opposition, here is Charles Fillmore's well-known
example (Fillmore 1971): *Sue is accused of* 〈*is criticized for*〉 *slamming her
husband*. While ACCUSE asserts that Sue slammed her husband and presupposes that doing so is reprehensible, CRITICIZE asserts that the act was reprehensible and presupposes that Sue was responsible for it. The ECD-type
definitions of the two verbs follow (note, by the way, that the presupposed
component is conjunctive):

X accuses Y of Z: '⟦X believing that fact Z took place and that Z is
                                reprehensible,⟧
                                X declares that Y is **responsible** for Z'.

X criticizes Y for Z: '⟦X believing that fact Z took place and that Y is
                               responsible for Z,⟧
                               X declares that Z is **reprehensible**'.

     In addition to being indicated by special typography (double brackets: ⟦ ... ⟧),
the presupposed part of a lexicographic definition has special syntax: a parti-
cipial phrase. (Alternatively, a relative clause can be used, which, in our case,
would give: 'X, **who believes that…**, declares…'. The first way of indicating
a presupposition is preferable, because it is more explicit.)

This is borne out by the negation test: 'X does not accuse Y of Z' means
'⟦X believing that fact Z took place and that Z **is reprehensible**,⟧ X **does not
declare** Y **responsible** for Z', the belief in the reprehensible nature of the act
being outside the scope of the negation. In the same vein, 'X does not criticize
Y of Z' means '⟦X believing that fact Z took place and that Y **is responsible** for
Z,⟧ X **does not declare** Z **reprehensible**', Y's responsibility for the act being
unaffected by the negation.

Not every definition has a presupposed part, and, as stated above, the central
component of a definition is always asserted.

We will return to the notion of presupposition in Ch. 9, *2.3*, where sentence-
level presuppositions are discussed, and in Ch. 10, *3.1.2.4*, for a more
detailed description of the treatment of presuppositions in the Meaning-Text
framework.

3.5   The Metaphoric Component

In order to provide a formal link (the so-called semantic bridge, see below)
between two co-polysemous LUs – that is, between two LUs belonging to
the same vocable – the definition of one of these may need a component that
indicates a metaphor perceived by the speakers. For instance, ARM$_{(N)}$**II** (*arm
of a crane/of a disk player*) is defined as 'long mobile part of a manufactured
object X designed for X to perform physical actions with – ⌜as if⌝ it were an
arm$_{(N)}$**I.1a** of a person'. This component, marked off by a dash and introduced by the idiom ⌜as if⌝, reflects the fact that a regular speaker of English
feels that this part of a machine is called this way because of its functional
resemblance to a human arm. However, this metaphoric component is not
needed for semantic manipulations of the text, so it can be absent from the
correspondent semantic structure and can be safely ignored in the {SemS} ⇔
{DSyntS} transition.

3.6   An Illustration: A Structured Lexicographic Definition

Let us see how the definition of the verb LIE$_{(V)}$²**1** (Section *1, Figure 5.1*) is
structured.

X lies to Z about Y:	'X communicates1 to Z a piece of false1 information1 α about Y **and** X knows1 that α is²1 false1	Central = generic component	A s s e
	X's communication1 being caused1 by the fact that X wants1 Z to believe1 that α is²1 true1,	Peripheral component = specific difference 1	r t
	(X's desire being caused1 by the fact that Z believing1 that α is²1 true1 'is²1 in X's interests$_{(N)}$5')'	Peripheral component = specific difference 2	i o n

Definiendum:	**Definiens:**
Propositional form	Definition proper (minimal semantic decomposition of the definiendum)

Figure 5.3 The structure of the definition of the lexeme LIE$_{(V)}$²1

In this definition, only the assertion is present (there are no presupposed components); the assertion contains, besides the central component, two peripheral ones, stating the specific differences of the meaning of the lexeme LIE$_{(V)}$²1 with respect to that of its near-synonyms (MISINFORM, MISLEAD, FIB, PERJURE ONESELF, etc.).

Since LIE$_{(V)}$²1 is a communication verb, the central (= generic) component of its definition contains the communicatively dominant semanteme 'communicate1', a genuine three-actantial predicate: 'a person X communicates1 information Y to a person Z'.

The central component is conjunctive; its negation gives a disjunction of two negations (De Morgan rule): *John did not lie about this* means that either that John did not give false information, or that John was himself mistaken.

Specific difference 1 is necessary since some untrue statements, like jokes and compliments, are not meant to be taken at face value (see Wierzbicka 1996: 152).

Specific difference 2 states the reason for which X wants Z to believe that the information he is conveying is true (whereas, in fact, it is not). This component is also weak, as stated above, in *1*, p. 119.

4   Criteria for Elaborating Lexicographic Definitions

These criteria are intended to help a researcher select the semantic components to be included into, or be excluded from, a definition (the most delicate part of the defining process). Four criteria will be presented:

1. Criterion of linguistic relevance
2. Criterion of cooccurrence with qualifying modifiers
3. Criterion of cooccurrence with quantifiers
4. Criterion of cooccurrence with negation

The first criterion targets the internal semantic coherence in the diction-ary, namely, the explicit links between the definition of L and semantically related definitions. The remaining three criteria target the factual accuracy of definitions (since any given definition must correspond to the facts of language **L**).

1. Criterion of Linguistic Relevance
This criterion allows for making a linguistically justified decision in cases where the necessity of a semantic component in a lexicographic definition is not straightforward.

> A contentious semantic component 'σ' may be included in the defi-nition of an LU L if language **L** has at least one other LU L' that is formally related to L and has 'σ' in its meaning.

NB: As should be clear from the formulation of this criterion, it does not require an obligatory acceptance of 'σ' as a component in the definition of L and is applicable to dubious components only.

The existence in **L** of LU L' with the indicated characteristics demonstrates the linguistic relevance of 'σ' in the definition of L.

L' can be formally linked to L through

1. polysemy (L' and L belong to the same vocable),
2. derivation (L' is derived from L) or
3. phraseology (L' is a phraseme that contains L).

In all these cases, the inclusion of 'σ' in the definition of L ensures an explicit specification of the semantic link – formally speaking, a semantic bridge (Ch. 6, *1.3.1*, Definition 6.6) – perceived by speakers between L and L'. For example, 'white' is a linguistically relevant component for the defi-nition of the lexeme SNOW**I** 'white**1a** cold$_{(ADJ)}$**1** substance**1** …' because it provides a semantic bridge between this lexeme and four other lexical items:

• the lexeme SNOW**II** 'cocaine in powder form – **white as sₙowI**' (polysemy)
• the lexeme SNOWY**II** 'pure **white**', as in *snowy hair* (derivation)
• the collocations *white **as snow*** and ***snow**-white* (phraseology).

In contrast, the definitions of SUGAR, SALT and RICE do not contain the component 'white', even if these substances are factually white, since English lacks linguistic evidence of its relevance for these lexemes (there are no expressions like **salt white*, **white **as rice***, and so on).

> REMARKS
> 1. The semantic bridge between L and L' can be a connotation, rather than a component in the definition of L; see Section *5* below.
> 2. Linguistic relevance is language-specific. Thus, unlike the defini-tion of its English equivalent, the definition of Rus. SAXAR 'sugar'

must contain the component 'white' because of the collocation ***saxarnye*** *zubki* lit. 'sugary (i.e., sugar-white) nice.little.teeth'.

Thus, an ECD-type definition of L does not reflect all the facts speakers might know about L's referents, but only those that are linguistically relevant: our approach is strictly lexicological, not encyclopedic. In other words, we maintain that lexicographic definitions must reflect the naïve worldview, that of a layman speaker, and should contain no information related to encyclopedic, extralinguistic or expert knowledge. It should be a description of the **meaning** of a word, not a precise and detailed description of the **thing** we name when we use this word. The following definition of HORSE**1**, taken from OED, contains encyclopedic, linguistically non-relevant information (shaded):

HORSE**1** a solid-hoofed plant-eating domesticated mammal with a flowing mane and tail, used for riding, racing and to carry and pull loads. *Equus caballus*, family *Equideae* (the horse family), descended from the wild Przewalski's horse. The horse family also includes the asses and zebras.

The fact that the horse is a plant-eating animal is not reflected elsewhere in the lexical stock of English (i.e., there are no LUs related to HORSE through this presumed semantic component); its being a mammal is not something a non-expert speaker would likely know just because he speaks English. For him, a horse is simply a domestic animal, used for riding, racing and to carry and pull loads – very strong (*strong as a horse*), having a mane (*her mane of hair*) and a characteristic tail (*a pony tail*). The encyclopedic character of the remaining components is self-evident.

The criterion of linguistic relevance applies to LUs with concrete meaning, designating objects and substances, because it targets observable properties of real objects. The remaining three criteria, which address the combinatorial possibilities of LUs, are of more general applicability.

2. Criterion of Cooccurrence with Qualifying Modifiers
This criterion is helpful when it comes to systematically accounting for the correspondence between the definition and the lexical cooccurrence of L (cf. Ch. 8, *2.1.2*, Internal Coherence Principle).

> The definition of an LU L must explicitly reflect L's cooccurrence with qualifying modifiers – that is, it must include a semantic component 'σ' capable of "accepting" the modifiers in question.

For example, the noun APPLAUSE readily accepts adjectival modifiers expressing intensification/attenuation (`Magn`/`AntiMagn` in lexical-functional terms, see Ch. 7, *2.2.1*): *deafening* ⟨*frenetic, frenzied, thunderous*⟩ or *scant* ⟨*scattered, subdued, thin*⟩ *applause*. Therefore, the definition of APPLAUSE must include a semantic component 'σ' that admits this kind of qualification. Here is a tentative definition ('σ' is shown in capitals):

X's applause to Y for Z: 'clapping$_{(V)}$2 by X as a sign4 of approval1 by X of Y's Z, THE FORCE1 AND/OR RATE$_{(N)}$2 of clapping$_{(V)}$2 being²3 proportional2 to the degree1 of the approval1'

(CLAP$_{(V)}$2: 'clap1 one's hands repeatedly thereby expressing joy1 or happiness1'.)

3. Criterion of Cooccurrence with Quantifiers

This criterion helps, among other things, to select the central component of a definition.

> The definition of an LU L must explicitly reflect L's cooccurrence with quantifiers – especially with plural markers and numerals.

Consider the lexemes ONION (*Finely chop two small onions.*) and GARLIC (*Add some crushed garlic.*) from the perspective of selecting the central component of their respective definitions. At first sight, it might seem that 'vegetable' is an appropriate choice in the case of both lexemes. However, their different cooccurrence with quantifiers indicates that this is incorrect. ONION can be freely quantified: *two ⟨several, a few⟩ onions*; but GARLIC accepts quantification only by means of special classifiers: **two ⟨*several, *a few⟩ garlics* vs. *two heads ⟨a clove⟩ of garlic*. This shows that ONION is conceptualized in English as a unit and GARLIC as a substance. (The plural in *South African Quality Garlics* means '**different sorts of**', rather than 'several units of'.) Therefore, 'vegetable' is fine as the central component of the definition of ONION, but for the definition of GARLIC we need a different one: 'seasoning', which has the same cooccurrence with quantifiers (*some seasoning*, **two seasonings*), is a good candidate.

4. Criterion of Cooccurrence with Negation

> The definition of an LU L must explicitly reflect the way L combines with the negation.

Negation is an important tool for lexicographers, as it helps establish the semantic content and the semantic structure of an LU; here are two examples.

Example 1

In *I do not love John* we see a trivial negation: I state that I do not feel what is called LOVE towards John. However, *I do not like John* is not simply a negation: it is a positive statement about the presence of a particular negative feeling – DISLIKE. Which means that ⌐DO NOT LIKE⌐ is an LU (an idiom) of English: an antonym of LIKE. Similarly, *I don't want to see him* actually means 'I want to not see him'; ⌐DO NOT WANT⌐ is also an antonym of WANT (rather than a simple negation).

Example 2

This example shows how the present criterion is used in order to determine the hierarchical status of some components of a definition.

Take the sentence [The horse broke his leg.] *I had to **put** him **out of** his **misery***; what does it mean? He is in a terrible state – injured and agonized; I have to kill him. Which can be formalized as follows:

⌜*X puts Y out of Y's misery*⌝: '⟦Y being in agony because of sickness or injury and suffering too much,⟧ X kills Y ⌜in order to⌝ stop Y's suffering'

But how do we know that the semantic component '⟦Y being in agony because of Y's sickness or injury and suffering too much⟧' is a presupposition? Because if we say *I did not put him out of his misery*, we still assert that he was in agony, while negating only 'I killed him'.

> REMARK. Not every part of a meaning immune to negation is a presupposition. Thus, PINE is 'evergreen coniferous tree that is P [P stands for a set of *differentiae specificae* characterizing pines]'; saying *This is **not** a pine*, the Speaker continues to affirm that this is a tree, probably evergreen and coniferous – he negates only 'P', believing that this is a cedar, a spruce or a fir. But the generic component 'evergreen coniferous tree that...' is not a presupposition: as said earlier, the generic component cannot be presupposed – only a peripheral component can. A similar case: *They were drinking kumis*, where KUMIS is 'fermented drink prepared from a mare's milk'; 'X drinks Y' = 'X introduces in X's mouth and then swallows liquid Y'. Now, *They were **not** drinking kumis* affirms that KUMIS is a liquid: semantic characterizers of actants are not available for negation, either. The negation criterion must, as one can see, be applied with utmost care.

Also, negation plays an important part in testing the validity of a disjunctive or conjunctive definition; see the already-mentioned De Morgan rules (Appendix, *5.1*).

5   Lexicographic Definition vs. Lexicographic Connotation

The lexicographic connotation of an LU L is a semantic characteristic which, in language **L**, is attributed to the entities denoted by L but which does not constitute a part of L's meaning and, consequently, is not a component of L's lexicographic definition. Simply put, a connotation of L is a piece of information associated with L in **L**, but never expressed in an instance of L's use.

For example, the meanings 'stubborn' and 'stupid' are associated with the referents of the lexeme ASS₁ 'domestic animal ...', which is reflected in language; cf.: *Your ass [= ASS**II**] of a husband never listens to other people's advice and acts quite stupidly.*[4] However, we can say without contradiction *This ass**I** is not at all stubborn ⟨stupid⟩*, which proves that the corresponding

---

[4] ASS**I** is old-fashioned; not ASS**II**, though.

meanings are not part of the definition of this lexeme. Thus, the meanings 'stubborn' and 'stupid' are the connotations of the lexeme ASSI, which we define as follows: 'large domestic animal having gray skin, long hanging ears and mane, used for carrying things'.

> **Definition 5.1:** Lexicographic Connotation
>
> A semanteme 'σ' is a lexicographic connotation of the LU L of language **L** iff 'σ' simultaneously satisfies the following two conditions:
> 1. 'σ' is associated by **L** with the entities denoted by L.
> 2. 'σ' is not a part of the definition of L.

 The question of whether the meaning 'σ' is or is not part of the definition of a given LU must be considered and answered prior to, and independently of, any discussion of connotations of this LU.

Lexicographic connotations of L are indicated in the semantic zone of L's dictionary entry, under the heading **Connotations**.

An intuitively perceived connotation link between 'σ' and L needs to be supported by linguistic evidence: in order to treat 'σ' as a connotation of L, there has to be at least one LU L' that is semantically linked to L via 'σ'. The link can be that of polysemy, derivation or phraseology – as was stated above when discussing semantic bridges between the definitions of lexemes belonging to the same vocable (Section *4*, Criterion of linguistic relevance). In other words, an LU L' that supports the connotation 'σ' of L can be:

1. An LU L' belonging to the same vocable as L, and, therefore, being in the polysemy relation with L. Thus, the vocable ASS contains, along with assι 'domestic animal …', the lexeme ASSII, 'stupid person …' (*that assII of a young man*), linked to ASSI via the connotation 'stupid' of the latter.
2. An LU L' derived from L; thus, the adjective WINDYII 'lacking substance' (*windy generalizations ⟨promises, rhetoric⟩*) is semantically linked to the noun WIND$_{(N)}$, from which it is formally derived, via the connotation 'emptiness' of the latter.
3. A phraseme L' including L; thus, the idioms ⌜*as an ass*⌝ (intensifying the adjective STUBBORN), which is linked to ASSI via the connotation 'stubborn', and ⌜MONKEY BUSINESS⌝ 'mischievous or deceitful behavior', built upon the corresponding connotations of the noun MONKEY.

Here again, linguistic relevance is at stake, only this time it concerns L's connotations, rather than components of L's definition.

While the components of a lexicographic definition of L determine its use in the text, more precisely, its selection by the Speaker to express a given meaning, L's connotations only serve to make L's semantic links with other lexemes in the dictionary explicit.

6   Lexicographic Definition Checklist

In order to give our presentation a more practical feel, in this final section we indicate – in the form of a lexicographic definition checklist – the necessary steps involved in the construction of a lexicographic definition.

Items 15–18 are specific to English and other languages that have the particular grammemes involved; all the others are universally applicable.

All Lexical Units

1. Is the LU L a semantic (quasi-)predicate?

    If the answer is yes, L's definiendum must appear as a propositional form.

2. If L is a semantic (quasi-)predicate, how many semantic actants does it control?

    The answer determines the structure and the formulation of the definiendum and the definiens. As a minimal well-formedness requirement, all the actantial variables mentioned in the definiendum must also be mentioned in the definiens.

3. What is the generic component of L's definiens?

    The answer determines the general orientation of the definiens; thus, if CHANGE$_{(V)}$**1** (*You've changed a lot since then.*) is defined as 'X becomes different (than X was before)', the generic component 'become different' makes it into an inchoative verb, and this property must be borne out in all contexts.

4. Are there weak components in the definition?

    If so, they must be explicitly identified (by parentheses).

5. Are there conjunctions or disjunctions in the definition?

    This question is linked, for instance, to the problem of sense discrimination, or lexemization. Thus, the following question can legitimately be asked: do the instances of *aunt* in **aunt** *Anne, my father's sister* and **aunt** *Joan, my uncle's wife* correspond to two LUs or to a single LU with a disjunctive definition? According to criteria to be discussed in Ch. 8, *2.3.1*, these are instances of a single LU.

6. What are the semantic constraints on L's actants?

    In other words, does the semantic classes (Ch. 8, *1.2*) to which belong L's semantic actants need be specified? Consider LEARN**1** (*I learned English as a boy.*) vs. LEARN**4** (*I learned the truth the hard way.*). The second semantic actant (what is learned) is some knowledge or competence in the first case and a piece of information in the second. As we can see, semantic classes of actants may help us distinguish different wordsenses of a polysemous word.

7. What semantic relations hold between L's actants?

    • For instance, is there a hierarchical relation between (some of) the actants? Thus, FORBID$_{[\text{person X} \sim \text{s action Y to person Z}]}$ presupposes X's authority over Z, BAN$_{[\text{person X} \sim \text{s person Z from action Y}]}$ presupposes that X has institutional or legal authority over Z, and both presuppose that Z wants to do Y. Definitions of these lexemes must contain the components that explicitly state these facts: '⟦X having authority over Z⟧' (the former), '⟦X having institutional or legal authority over Z⟧' (the latter) and '⟦Z wanting to do Y⟧' (both).

- Or else, is there a personal relationship/involvement between the actants? REPROACH$_{[\text{person X ~es fact Y to person Z}]}$ presupposes that X and Z are at least acquainted because you cannot reproach a perfect stranger for something. Therefore, the definition of this verb must contain the semantic component 'Z belonging to the personal sphere of X'.

8. How are the peripheral components of L's definition distributed between presupposed and asserted parts of the definition?

   This question is related, among other things, to Lexicographic Definition Criterion 4 (Section 3 above): cooccurrence with the negation.

9. What is the attitude of the Speaker with respect to the facts and the participants involved (approval/disapproval, personal involvement/distancing, etc.)?

   While the definition of CAR does not include any evaluative component, that of LEMON2 does: 'a car <u>that the Speaker finds old and useless</u>'. Similarly, [a] GERMAN is an objective characterization, but the meaning of **offensive** KRAUT incorporates the Speaker's negative evaluation of its referent.

10. How does L behave with respect to negation and interrogation?

    This question is useful when it comes to determining the logical structure of L's definition: among other things, it helps distinguish between the asserted and the presupposed elements, as well as to identify the constraints on actants.

11. What are temporal relations between the facts implicated in L's meaning?

    All temporal relations between the facts involved – 'simultaneously' or 'after'/'before' – must be explicitly indicated. Thus, 'X inherits Y from Z' ≈ 'X obtains the possession of Y **after** the death of Y's previous possessor Z'.

Verbal Lexical Units

12. Can LU be used performatively and, if yes, what consequences does this have on its cooccurrents?

    A performative verb – or, more precisely, a verb used performatively – denotes the action that the Speaker performs by uttering this verb (Ch. 10, *3.1.2.5*). Among other things, when used performatively, a verb does not accept free modifiers: it requires constrained collocates. For instance, the intensifier *profusely* is possible with APOLOGIZE only if the verb is not used performatively: *He apologizes profusely and leaves* vs. **Excuse me, I apologize profusely.*

13. Is L factive?

The meaning of a factive verb V includes a presupposed component '⟦this being true⟧', which bears on the V's complement P, implying the truth of P. Thus, the sentences *It was revealed that John had left* and *It was not revealed that John had left* both imply 'It is true that John left'. The property of factivity should be reflected in L's definition.

14. Does L denote a state, an event, an activity or an accomplishment in terms of Vendler's aspectual classes (Ch. 8, *1.2.2*)?

L's membership in an aspectual class implies that L will or will not have certain properties; this needs to be reflected in its definition.

15. Can L be used in the progressive aspect?

This information is important for choosing the correct central component of the definition. Consider, for instance, the following LDOCE definition: HEAR$_{(V)}$**2** (*I want to hear his answer* ⟨*what the doctor has to say*⟩.) 'to **listen** to what someone is saying, the music they are playing, etc.' In an accompanying grammar note it is indicated that HEAR$_{(V)}$**2** "is not usually used in the progressive"; yet, the verb chosen as the central component of its definition is freely used in the progressive aspect. A better central component would be 'come to know [about N$_Y$]'; here is a sketch of the definition of HEAR$_{(V)}$**2**: 'come to know about (some aspects of) Y by listening to someone's communicating something about Y'.

16. Can L be used in the passive voice?

Some transitive verbs may not admit passivization; for instance, MEASURE$_{(V)}$**3** (*The flask measures 101 mm.*), or GET**1** (*I got lots of presents for my birthday.*). The central component of their definitions should have the same characteristics. For the verb MEASURE$_{(V)}$**3**, which denotes a property, an appropriate generic component would be '[to] be (of particular size)'. For GET**1**, which denotes a change of state, we could use something like 'begin to own'. Both of these central components do not allow for passivization.

Nominal Lexical Units

17. Can L be used in both grammatical numbers (singular and plural)?

Some nouns have no singular: GLASSES, PANTS, SCISSORS, … (*pluralia tantum*), some others, no plural: ADVICE, NEWS, FURNITURE, … (*singularia tantum*). The definition of such a noun must account for this property. Thus, ADVICE and NEWS should be defined as 'information that …'; this generic component is itself not pluralizable.

18. Should L be defined in the singular or in the plural?

As a general rule, a noun that has both numbers is defined in the unmarked one – the singular. But there are many special cases. Thus, EYES 'organ of sight' must be defined in the plural (i.e., the definiendum should be in the plural form), while [an] EYE is 'one of the eyes'; similarly, EARS 'organ of hearing'. The same reasoning applies to SKIS: 'device designed for moving over the snow…'. Names of ethnicities must also be defined in the plural: GERMANS, RUSSIANS, SPANIARDS …

19. Does L combine with numeral modifiers?

For instance, *three garlics is impossible, while GARLIC in the sense of 'kind of garlic' (a different lexeme) can be pluralized: Indian garlics. The generic component of the definition of GARLIC should be such as to account for this property: 'seasoning' (rather than 'vegetable').

This presentation of the lexicographic definition checklist is not exhaustive. Nevertheless, we hope it is useful to get the reader started. Learning how to define words requires lots of practice. See Exercises for this chapter.

Further Reading

Lexicographic definition: Benson et al. 1988; Wierzbicka 1992 and 1993; Hanks 1993; Mel'čuk 1988b and 2013: 279–307; Mel'čuk & Polguère 2018.

Lexicographic connotation: Allan 2007; Iordanskaja & Mel'čuk 2009.

6   Lexical Relations

This chapter is dedicated to one important aspect of the organization of the lexical stock of a language: relations between LUs from the viewpoint of their meaning and cooccurrence – lexical-semantic relations (for short, lexical relations). In fact, the lexical stock can be seen as a network made up of lexical items linked by multiple and variegated links. These are, on the one hand, paradigmatic links (in the lexical stock), such as synonymy ($WET_{(ADJ)}1$ ~ $DAMP_{(ADJ)}$), antonymy ($WET_{(ADJ)}1$ ~ $DRY_{(ADJ)}1$), derivation ($DRY_{(ADJ)}1$ 'without liquid …' ~ $DRY_{(V)}1$ 'cause1 to become $dry_{(ADJ)}1$' ~ $DRYER_{(N)}$ 'machine designed to $dry_{(V)}1$ clothes after washing'), polysemy ($DRY_{(ADJ)}1$ 'without liquid …' ~ $DRY_{(ADJ)}6$ 'without humor … – ⌐as if⌐ $DRY_{(ADJ)}1$'), and so on. On the other hand, these are various syntagmatic, or collocational, links (in the text), such as, for instance, intensification (*soaking* $WET_{(ADJ)}1$ 'very wet' and $DRY_{(ADJ)}1$ ⌐*as a bone*⌐ 'very dry'). (Another important aspect of the organization of the lexical stock – various paradigmatic groupings of LUs – will be taken up in Ch. 8.)

> REMARK. Lexical relations between LUs have to be strictly distinguished from conceptual relations between their denotations. A standard example of the latter is the "kind ~ species," or hyponymy, relation: DOG ~ POODLE, DOG ~ ⌐GERMAN SHEPHERD⌐, DOG ~ HUSKY, etc. Another one is the "whole ~ part," or meronymy, relation: COMPUTER ~ ⌐HARD DISK⌐, COMPUTER ~ SCREEN, COMPUTER ~ MOUSE, COMPUTER ~ MEMORY, etc. A purely conceptual relation

between two LUs reflects our encyclopedic knowledge about their denotations, rather than linguistic knowledge about the LUs themselves – that is, about their behavior in texts.

L's lexical relations to other LUs tell us a great deal about L: the totality of L's lexical relations constitute what could be called L's paraphrastic and combinatorial potential; they are also highly revealing of L's meaning and instrumental in establishing L's definition.

Lexical relations have been widely investigated both in theoretical linguistics and Natural Language Processing, where their formal description has been a pressing issue. To that effect, Meaning-Text theory has proposed the formalism of lexical functions: a cross-linguistically valid descriptive tool able to account for all types of lexical relations in a systematic way.

Paradigmatic lexical relations are presented in Section *1*, and syntagmatic relations, in Section *2*; lexical functions are dealt with in the next chapter.

1   Paradigmatic Lexical Relations

This section deals with the core semantic-lexical relations of synonymy, antonymy and conversion (*1.1*), the relation of derivation in a broad sense (*1.2*), as well as the relation of equinomy, which manifests itself in the lexicon as polysemy and homonymy (*1.3*).

1.1   The Core Paradigmatic Lexical Relations: Synonymy, Antonymy, Conversion

Synonymy, antonymy and conversion are the most salient lexical relations; they are the first to have been discovered and studied in linguistics.

1.1.1   Synonymy

Definition 6.1: (Exact) Synonymy

Two LUs L_1 and L_2 stand in the relation of exact synonymy and are called exact synonyms [Syn], iff the following four conditions are simultaneously satisfied:

1. The meanings of L_1 and L_2 – that is, their signifieds – are identical: 'L_1' = 'L_2'.
2. The signifiers of L_1 and L_2 are different.
3. L_1 and L_2 belong to the same part of speech.
4. If L_1 and L_2 have semantic and deep-syntactic actants, the actants $i, j, k, \ldots$ of the one correspond one-to-one to the actants $i, j, k, \ldots$ of the other.

For example, the lexemes DRUNK and INTOXICATED, as in *The driver stopped in Denville was drunk* ⟨≡ *intoxicated*⟩, are exact synonyms, since their signifiers are different, while their meanings, parts of speech and actantial structures are identical: both are adjectives meaning '[person X] unable to control X's behavior because X has drunk too much alcohol'. This is true also of the nouns COUGAR and ⌜MOUNTAIN LION⌝, whose meanings are also identical: 'a large brown wild cat living in the mountains'.

Exact synonyms should be mutually substitutable in most contexts *salva significatione* (that is, with the preservation of the meaning expressed); see the substitutability rule, alias substitutability test, Ch. 5, *2* and Ch. 9, *2.1.3*.

LUs that satisfy the four conditions of Definition 6.1 but differ stylistically, e.g., DRUNK ~ **formal** INTOXICATED or KILL ~ **colloq.** WHACK, are substitutable *salva significatione* and are therefore exact synonyms.

Exact synonyms are often said to be extremely rare, even nonexistent. Exact synonymy, the argument goes, contradicts the language economy principle; on closer examination, semantic differences, however subtle, can always be found between putative exact synonyms. This, we think, is an exaggeration: while exact synonymy is indeed much less frequent at the lexical level than approximate synonymy, it is by no means nonexistent. To take just one example, Sanskrit has series of exact synonyms for the most "normal" semantemes; thus, the meaning 'water' is expressed by nine nominal lexemes (j = /ʒ/): AP, JALA, JĪVANA, NĪRA, PĀTHAS, ŚAMBARA, TOYA, UDAKA, VĀRI. Such series are quite frequent in Sanskrit. (Exact synonymy of sentences, i.e., exact paraphrase, is not rare at all, thanks to the phenomenon of semantic neutralization, which manifests itself in a sentential context; see Ch. 9, *2.1.2*.)

Two lexemes whose propositional meanings are identical but which do not belong to the same part of speech are synonymous, but by no means synonyms. This is the case, for instance, with a verb and the corresponding deverbal noun: $KISS_{(V)}$ and $KISS_{(N)}$ are synonymous, but they are of course not synonyms. The same is true for $LOVE_{(V)}$ and $LOVE_{(N)}$, $STEAL_{(V)}$ and $THEFT_{(N)}$, etc.

Alongside exact synonyms, we consider near-synonyms, or quasi-synonyms, much more frequent than the former.

Definition 6.2: Quasi-Synonymy

Two LUs L_1 and L_2 whose meanings are not identical are quasi-synonyms [QSyn] iff the following six conditions are simultaneously satisfied:

1. The meanings 'L_1' and 'L_2' are in the relation of strong inclusion or strong intersection.
2. The signifiers of L_1 and L_2 are different.
3. L_1 and L_2 belong to the same part of speech.
4. The semantic difference 'L_1' − 'L_2' is not regular in the language.
5. If L_1 and L_2 have semantic and deep-syntactic actants, the actants $i, j, k, \ldots$ of the one correspond one-to-one to the actants $i, j, k, \ldots$ of the other.
6. They are mutually substitutable *salva significatione* in at least some contexts.

For the set-theoretical notions of inclusion and intersection, see Appendix, *3.1*.

Strong meaning inclusion obtains just in case the included lexical meaning is the central (= generic) semantic component of the including meaning ('devour' strongly includes 'eat', since 'devour' = '<u>eat</u> quickly and voraciously'); otherwise, the meaning inclusion is weak ('digest' weakly includes 'eat', since 'digest' = '<u>process</u> the food you have eaten into substances that your body can use').

For instance, the verbs [to] LOOK and [to] STARE are quasi-synonyms related by strong inclusion since the meaning of the former is included in that of the latter, where it is the central component: 'stare at Y' ≈ '<u>look</u> at Y for some time without moving one's eyes …'. When you stare at someone, you necessarily look at him (#*She stared at us without looking at us.*), but not the other way around (*She just looked at us, she did not stare* is quite acceptable). MURDER and ASSASSINATE are also quasi-synonyms by strong inclusion, since 'assassinate' = '<u>murder</u> for political reasons', and so are RAIN and DOWNPOUR 'strong <u>rain</u> that falls in a short time', WIND and GALE 'very strong <u>wind</u>', ANIMAL and BEAR 'wild <u>animal</u> that …' (cf. *The bear attacked, but the hunter took aim and shot the animal.*).

Strong meaning intersection obtains if the two meanings have the same central component and each has peripheral components that are not shared with the other one (otherwise – i.e., if the shared component is not the central component in either of the two meanings – the intersection is weak). The nouns PORTRAIT [of X] '<u>pictorial representation</u> of person X's face' and PHOTO [of X] '<u>pictorial representation</u> of entity X created by using photography' are quasi-synonyms related by strong intersection, sharing the central component '<u>pictorial representation</u>': *I saw John's portrait* ⟨≡ *photo*⟩, *so I can recognize him.* And the same is true for STARE and PEEP, the latter meaning '<u>look</u> at Y quickly and secretly (through a hole or opening)'.

Staring is a kind of looking, and assassinating is a kind of murdering; this is meaning inclusion. A portrait and a photo are both kinds of pictorial representation, and stare and peep are both kinds of looking; this is meaning intersection.

As for Condition 4, it is necessary to separate quasi-synonyms from derivatives. See Definition 6.5 (p. 150): a derivative D(L) of L is supposed to express a semantic difference 'D(L) – L' that is regular in the language under consideration.

1.1.2   Antonymy

Definition 6.3: (Exact) Antonymy

Two LUs L_1 and L_2 stand in the relation of exact antonymy and are called exact antonyms [Anti], iff the following three conditions are simultaneously satisfied:

1. The only difference between the meanings of L_1 and L_2 is either the presence of the semanteme 'no' in one but not in the other, or the presence, in the same position, of the semanteme 'more' in one and the semanteme 'less' in the other.
2. L_1 and L_2 belong to the same part of speech.

> 3. If L_1 and L_2 have semantic and deep-syntactic actants, the actants $i, j, k, \ldots$ of the one correspond one-to-one to the actants $i, j, k, \ldots$ of the other.

Definition 6.3 predicts two major types of antonym: negation antonyms (or contraries) and inverse (or "more ~ less") antonyms; cf.:

(1) Negation Antonyms
   a. 'X refuses Y' ≈ 'X says that X opposes Y' (*John refused our offer.*)
   b. 'X accepts Y' ≈ 'X says that X **does not** oppose Y' (*John accepted our offer.*)
   Additional examples: FRIEND ~ ENEMY, MARRIED ~ SINGLE, OBEY ~ DISOBEY, etc.

(2) Inverse Antonyms
   a. '[X is] heavy' ≈ 'X's weight is **bigger** than the normal weight for Xs'
   b. '[X is] light' ≈ 'X's weight is **smaller** than the normal weight for Xs'
   Additional examples: HEAT UP ~ COOL DOWN, INCREASE ~ DECREASE, YOUNG ~ OLD, etc.

Each of these two antonym types can be further subdivided; however, we will not elaborate further on this topic here.

Note that, as a general rule, 'Anti(L)' ≠ '**non** L': an antonym of an LU L and the "external" negation of L do not necessarily have the same meaning. This is true even in the case of negation antonyms. Thus, Anti(*refuse*$_{(V)}$) = *accept*, but ***not** to refuse* does not mean 'accept': *John didn't refuse to pay but didn't accept, either: he was non-committal.* The sentence *John didn't refuse to pay* means 'John did **not** say that he opposed his paying (something)', and this is a real negation, but the meaning of *John accepted to pay* is 'John said that he did **not** oppose his paying (something)', and this sentence has a contrary, i.e., antonymic, meaning with respect to *John refused to pay*. The position of negation within a meaning is indeed crucial: in order for an Anti(L) to be produced from L, the negation (that is, the semanteme 'no') has to be embedded into the meaning 'L'. In many cases, the position of negation gives rise to lexical triplets of the following type:

L		Negation of L		Antonym of L	
refuse	['X says that he opposes']	*not refuse*	['X **does not** say anything']	*accept*	['X says that he **does not** oppose']
heavy	['weight is more than norm']	*not heavy*	['weight is **not** more than norm']	*light*	['weight is less than norm']
constipation	['functioning is insufficient']	*no constipation*	['functioning is **not** insufficient']	*diarrhea*	['functioning is excessive']

In addition to exact antonyms, there are also near-antonyms, or quasi-antonyms [QAnti], which differ not only by negation or the 'more' ~ 'less' opposition, but also feature other semantic differences. As an example, here are two antonym pairs, CONSTRUCT$_{(V)}$1 ~ DEMOLISH and PRAISE ~ DENIGRATE.

(3) a.   'X constructs$_{(V)}$1 Y using Z' ≈ 'X <u>causes</u>2 in a particular way **α** by
                                   using Z that Y begins <u>to exist</u>'
     b.   'X demolishes Y' ≈ 'X <u>causes</u>2 in a particular way **β** that a **con-**
                                   structed$_{(V)}$**1** Y begins **not** <u>to exist</u>'

With respect to DEMOLISH, the verb CONSTRUCT$_{(V)}$1 has an additional semantic component (and an additional semantic actant): 'using `material` Z' (*construct a house **out of bricks** Z*); DEMOLISH, in its turn, has its own additional semantic component: 'a constructed$_{(V)}$1 [Y]'. Note also that **α** and **β** – methods of constructing and demolishing – are not inverse with respect to each other: they are simply different.

(4) a.   'X praises Y for Z(Y)' ≈ 'X <u>speaks</u> **positively** about Y because of Y's
                                   actions or characteristics Z'
     b.   'X denigrates Y for Z(Y)' ≈ '⟦**X wanting Y to appear less good**
                                   or less important than Y really is,⟧ X
                                   <u>speaks</u> **negatively** about Y because of
                                   Y's actions or characteristics Z'

The meaning of the verb DENIGRATE differs from that of the verb PRAISE not only by the semanteme 'no', but also by a presupposed component (identified by the double brackets "⟦...⟧": Ch. 5, *3.4*).[1]

A pair of antonyms always has a marked, semantically more complex, member – the one including the component 'no' or the component 'less'. As a result, the conditions for mutual substitution of antonyms (even exact antonyms) in a sentence are more stringent than is the case with synonyms.

1.1.3   Conversion

> **Definition 6.4:** Conversion
>
> Two LUs L$_1$ and L$_2$ stand in the relation of exact conversion and are called exact conversives [Conv], iff the following three conditions are simultaneously satisfied:
> 1. The propositional meanings of L$_1$ and L$_2$ are identical.
> 2. L$_1$ and L$_2$ belong to the same part of speech.
> 3. The communicative structures of the meanings of L$_1$ and L$_2$ are different – that is, the SemAs of L$_1$ are inverted with respect to the

---

[1] The necessity of this presupposed component is shown by the uneasy cooccurrence of *denigrate* with such adverbs as *unwittingly* or *unconsciously*.

SemAs of L$_2$: at least one SemA *i* of L semantically corresponds to the SemA *j* of L$_2$ (*i* ≠ *j*), and vice versa; their DSyntAs behave accordingly.

For instance, the verbs [to] FEAR and [to] SCARE, illustrated in (5), are exact conversives: they satisfy the three conditions of the above definition.

(5) a. *Some people fear new technologies.* ≡
     b. *New technologies scare some people.*

As can be seen from the semantic decompositions of the two verbs, given in (6), their propositional meanings are equal (they are composed of the same semantemes related in the same way) and their communicative meanings are different – among other things, because they have different dominant nodes: FEAR is a verb of feeling, while SCARE is a verb of causation.

(6) a. 'X fears Y'   = 'person X feels fear, which is caused1 by fact Y'
     b. 'X scares Y'   = 'fact X causes1 person Y to feel fear'

SemA 1 [⇔ X] of FEAR, the Experiencer, is expressed as the DSyntA I (= the surface-syntactic subject), and its SemA 2 [⇔ Y], the Cause, as the DSyntA II (= the surface direct object). With SCARE, the situation is exactly inverse: its SemA 1 [⇔ X] is the Cause and it is expressed as the syntactic subject, while its SemA 2 [⇔ Y] is the Experiencer and is expressed as the direct object.

For the formal encoding of the relation of conversion, see Ch. 7, *2.1.1*.

Additional examples of exact conversives: HUSBAND ~ WIFE, BOYFRIEND ~ GIRLFRIEND, TEACH [person X teaches **subject or skill Y to person Z**] ~ **formal** INSTRUCT [person X instructs **person Y in subject or skill Z**], FOLLOW ~ PRECEDE, 'IN FRONT' [*of* N] ~ BEHIND [N], etc.

Just like synonyms and antonyms, conversives can be approximate [QConv]; such are, for example, commercial transaction verbs BUY, SELL, PAY and COST. They all describe the same situation involving the same four participants: an individual who cedes his possession rights over some goods to another individual for an amount of money. But their propositional meanings are not identical. BUY and SELL have different presuppositions: the Buyer wants the goods, while the Seller wants the money. PAY and COST cover other situations as well: you can pay fines or debts, and something that you have produced yourself can cost you money. At the same time, these four participants play different communicative roles within the definitions of the above verbs and are expressed differently – as different complements – at the deep-syntactic level (or cannot be expressed at all, as is the case of the Beneficiary of the transaction with COST).

(7) a. <u>John</u> **bought** *this car* <u>from Peter</u> *for 1000 dollars.*
     b. <u>Peter</u> **sold** *this car to* <u>John for</u> *1000 dollars.*
     c. <u>John</u> **paid** *1000 dollars* <u>to Peter</u> *for this car.*
     d. <u>This car</u> **cost** <u>John</u> *1000 dollars* *to Peter/*to Peter's benefit.*[2]

All the preceding examples illustrate interlexical conversion – that is, the relation of conversion between two different LUs. But the relation of conversion can hold between two different wordforms of the same LU, more precisely, between forms of the same verb: this is intralexical conversion. Intralexical conversion comes in two varieties: unmarked and marked. If intralexical conversion is unmarked, we are dealing with different Government Patterns (Ch. 2, 1.3.3) for the same LU; if it is marked (= indicated by an affix or an auxiliary), we speak of inflectional conversion, resulting in different grammatical voices. These two cases are illustrated in (8) and (9), respectively.

A Lexeme with Two Government Patterns (GP)

(8) a. *Greenpeace* **criticized** <u>the Government</u>$_{Y, DirO}$ <u>for its position</u>$_{Z, OblO}$ *on deforestation.*
     b. *Greenpeace* **criticized** *the Government's* <u>position</u>$_{Z, DirO}$ *on deforestation.*

Semantic actants of the verb CRITICIZE have two different syntactic realizations. In (8a), we have 'X criticizes **Y for** Y's **Z**', with 'Y' expressed as a direct object and 'Z' as an oblique object, while in (8b) it is rather 'X criticizes Y's **Z**', with 'Z' expressed as a direct object and 'Y' expressed not as a direct dependent of the verb but of the lexeme realizing 'Z'. This kind of alternative actant implementation is possible also with CONDEMN, BLAME, etc.

   The existence of variable GPs is also known as verbal alternations; see, for instance, Levin 1993. Stock examples: *load the hay on the truck ~ load the truck with hay, spray the paint on the wall ~ spray the wall with paint*, etc. (There is a semantic difference between the two uses of LOAD, of SPRAY, etc.: the first implies that all of the hay/all of the paint was loaded/sprayed, while the second implies nothing regarding the amount of hay or paint that might be left over after the action is terminated. This could be a reason to consider each of these lexical items as representing two different lexemes. On the other hand, the identity of the rest of the lexicographic information strongly argues for monolexemic treatment.)

   Another way to change the GP is by the syntactic operation of Possessor Raising: *My right leg was injured in a car accident. ~ I was injured in my right leg in a car accident.* (In the second sentence, the Possessor has a higher syntactic rank than in the first one: it is expressed by the subject.)

---

[2] We have indicated only the conversions with respect to BUY; of course, it is possible to relate in the same way SELL and PAY, SELL and COST, PAY and COST, etc.

Different Grammatical Voices

(9) a. $\boxed{John}$ **bought** $\boxed{this\ car}$ *from Peter for 1000 dollars.*
     b. *This car* **was bought** $\boxed{by\ John}$ *from Peter for 1000 dollars.*

Passive forms of a verb are converse with respect to the corresponding active forms, and vice versa. (Passive forms of two interlexical converses are also mutually converse, just as their active forms are.)

While interlexical conversion affects both the SemAs and DSyntAs of two conversives, only DSyntAs are affected with intralexical conversion: the semantic actants remain the same since the lexeme has only one lexicographic definition, covering all its forms. Intralexical conversives are thus necessarily exact, being forms of the same lexeme.

Any two conversives, whether exact or approximate, differ by their communicative orientation; the reason for using one conversive rather than the other is exactly the communicative promotion or demotion of a given SemA by implementing it as a particular "higher" or "lower" DSyntA. (An element is "higher" or "lower," of course, in the syntactic tree.)

REMARKS

1. **Conversives vs. antonyms**. Certain conversives, for instance, HUSBAND and WIFE, are sometimes considered to be antonyms. But this cannot be correct, because the meanings of these LUs are not opposed either by 'no' or 'more' ~ 'less'. Generally speaking, two LUs can simultaneously be antonyms and conversives only in some special cases. Thus:
• Antonymic parametric adjectives (BIG ~ SMALL, WIDE ~ NARROW, etc.) in the comparative degree are also conversives of each other; if A is bigger/wider than B, then B is smaller/narrower than A.
• Some verbs and their derivatives form antonymic-conversive pairs, such as FOLLOW vs. PRECEDE (*The letter Č follows the letter C.* ~ *The letter C precedes the letter Č.*), WIN (against somebody) vs. DEFEAT (*Surely they will win against an ill-prepared adversary.* ~ *Surely an ill-prepared adversary will not defeat them.*), as well as their derivatives, VICTORY and DEFEAT (*our army's victory over the enemy* ~ *the enemy's defeat by our army*).
2. **Signifiers in conversives and antonyms**. Contrary to synonyms (Definitions 6.1 and 6.2), as well as LUs related by polysemy (Definition 6.7) and homonymy (Definition 6.10), conversives and antonyms can have identical signifiers: so-called auto-conversives and auto-antonyms are possible. Thus, $RENT_{(V)}1$ (*rent* N_Y *from* N_Z) and $RENT_{(V)}2$ (N_Y *to* N_Z) are conversives, similarly to $LOAD_{(V)}1a$ (*load* N_Y *on* N_Z) and $LOAD_{(V)}1b$ (*load* N_Z *with* N_Y); still another well-known case of auto-conversives is Fr. HÔTE**I** 'host' and HÔTE**II** 'guest'. The verb

CLIP$_{(V)}$**I** 'fasten Y on Z' = 'cause2 Y to be on Z' is quasi-antonymous with respect to CLIP$_{(V)}$**II** ≈ 'remove Y from Z' ≈ 'cause2 Y **not** to be on Z by cutting whatever is attaching Y to Z', the same as Lat. SACER**I** 'accursed, damned' and SACER**II** 'sacred, holy'.

1.2   Derivational Relations

> **Definition 6.5:** Derivation
>
> Two LUs L$_1$ and L$_2$ stand in the relation of derivation iff the meaning of L$_2$ includes that of L$_1$ plus a component that represents a regular semantic difference in language **L** (i.e., the presence/absence of this component characterizes many lexical pairs and has – at least in some cases – a standard expression).

L$_1$ is the base of derivation, and L$_2$ is called a derivative of L$_1$.

For example, the lexeme EATER '**person who** eats' is derived from EAT: its meaning includes 'eat' and an additional component – 'a person who …', this component differentiating also the lexical pairs LIAR ~ LIE, MURDERER ~ MURDER, OPERATOR ~ OPERATE, SINGER ~ SING, TALKER ~ TALK, WALKER ~ WALK, etc. and having a regular expression in English: the suffixes **-er**, **-or**, etc. Each of these nouns is a typical name of the first participant of the fact in question – i.e., the one who does, is in the state, etc. Traditionally, they are called Agent Names (*nomina agentis*), even though not all of them are derived from action verbs.

Formally – that is, morphologically – semantic derivation is not necessarily regular. Thus, in addition to pairs like the ones above, where the semantic difference between the derivative and the base is expressed by a morphological means (an affix, an alternation, a reduplication, etc.), we encounter pairs such as TRAITOR [not *BETRAYER] ~ BETRAY, PLAINTIFF [not *SUER] ~ SUE, THIEF [not *STEALER] ~ STEAL, etc., whose semantic difference is not marked by an affix or another morphological means. (Even more than that: these derivatives may have, as we see, different radicals – that is, be suppletive.)

Other patterns of derivation are:
- Patient names (*nomina patientis*): EMPLOYEE 'the person employed by …', derived from EMPLOY by means of the suffix **-ee**; the same relation holds between NOMINEE and NOMINATE, PAYEE and PAY$_{(V)}$, TRAINEE and TRAIN$_{(V)}$, and so on. (But ATTENDEE 'person who attends a meeting' and REFUGEE 'person who has fled his country' are not patient names in the sense characterized above but agent names.)
- Location names: ⌐CRIME SCENE⌐ ~ CRIME, ⌐THEATER OF WAR⌐ ~ WAR, BATTLEFIELD ~ BATTLE, ⌐OPERATING ROOM⌐ ~ SURGERY, ⌐MOVIE THEATER⌐ ~ FILM, etc.
- Instrument names: ⌐MURDER WEAPON⌐ ~ MURDER$_{(V)}$, COMPUTER ~ ⌐INFORMATION PROCESSING⌐, TOASTER ~ TOAST$_{(V)}$, LAWN MOWER ~ MOW [lawns], DRYER ~ DRY$_{(V)}$ [laundry], BROOM ~ SWEEP, ⌐CRYSTAL BALL⌐ ~ PREDICT, etc.

- Result names: ILLUSTRATION**2** ~ ILLUSTRATE, BUILDING**2** ~ BUILD, TRANSLATION**2** ~ TRANSLATE, KNOWLEDGE/SKILL ~ LEARN, COPY$_{(N)}$ ~ COPY$_{(V)}$, etc.

> **NB:** ILLUSTRATION**1** is 'fact of illustrating' – that is, an exact nominalization, or the action name, of ILLUSTRATE. This type of polysemy – action name and result name – is quite common; it is seen as well in BUILDING**1** ~ BUILDING**2** and TRANSLATION**1** ~ TRANSLATION**2**.

In the same vein, the adjective EXCUSABLE '**that can be** excus**ed**' is derived from EXCUSE$_{(V)}$, the meaning of the adjective including that of the verb plus the regular semantic difference 'that can be …ed'. This semantic difference characterizes numerous other pairs: ADMIRABLE ~ ADMIRE, AVOIDABLE ~ AVOID, ENVIABLE ~ ENVY$_{(V)}$, READABLE ~ READ$_{(V)}$, DEFENSIBLE ~ DEFEND, REDUCIBLE ~ REDUCE, etc., where it is regularly expressed by means of the suffix -/əbl/ (spelled mostly as **-able** and – in some special cases – as **-ible**[3]).

Some pairs "derivative ~ base" manifest no semantic difference while belonging to different parts of speech: ADMIRATION$_{(N)}$ ~ ADMIRE$_{(V)}$ (*John's admiration for linguistics* ≡ *John admires linguistics.*), STELLAR$_{(A)}$ ~ STAR$_{(N)}$, (*stellar light* ≡ *light from stars*), HONESTLY$_{(ADV)}$ ~ HONEST$_{(ADJ)}$ (*He behaved honestly.* ≡ *His behavior was honest.*), etc. This is a particular case of derivation: exact nominalization, verbalization, adjectivalization and adverbialization. It is called structural derivation, because the difference between the base LU and the derived one is purely structural, i.e. syntactic, in nature (= it is only the part of speech – that is, the syntactic combinability – that changes). Other examples:

Nominalization:	PURCHASE$_{(N)}$ ~ PURCHASE$_{(V)}$, OBSERVATION ~ OBSERVE**1**, OBSERVANCE ~ OBSERVE**5**; PROFUNDITY ~ PROFOUND; RELIANCE ~ RELY
Verbalization:	PURCHASE$_{(V)}$ ~ PURCHASE$_{(N)}$, OBSERVE**1** ~ OBSERVATION
Adjectivalization:	DOMESTIC ~ HOME, FRATERNAL ~ BROTHER, TEMPORAL ~ TIME, TERRESTRIAL ~ EARTH, TRAGIC ~ TRAGEDY
Adverbialization:	⌜BY CHANCE⌝ ~ ACCIDENTAL, CLOSE/NEARBY ~ NEIGHBORING

Here are some other semantic derivations:

'cause to become':	MODERNIZE ~ MODERN, PRIVATIZE ~ PRIVATE$_{(ADJ)}$ [the suffix **-ize**]; PURIFY ~ PURE, CLARIFY ~ CLEAR, LIQUEFY ~ LIQUID$_{(ADJ)}$ [the suffix **-ify**]

---

[3] Mainly after truncated or alternating Latinate radicals: *poss+ible*, *horr+ible*, *indivis+ible* (cf. *undivid+able*), *defens+ible* (cf. *defend+able*), etc. Note that *-ible* is just a spelling variant of *-able*; linguistically, this is one suffix.

'regular set of':	POD *of whales*, PRIDE *of lions*, SCHOOL *of fish*; *a* PACK ⟨*a* TISSUE⟩ *of lies*, *a* CHORUS *of criticisms*; *a* BUNCH *of keys*, *a* DECK *of cards*
'unit/element of':	*a* BAR *of soap*, *a* CLOVE *of garlic*, *an* EAR *of corn*, *a* BLADE *of grass*, *a* GRAIN *of dust*, *a* GUST *of wind*, *a* FLASH *of lightning*

Derivational relations are extremely variegated; what we have cited above is but a tiny fragment of the whole set. Some further derivational relations will be presented in the next chapter when speaking about lexical functions.

1.3   Polysemy vs. Homonymy

Below we discuss polysemy and homonymy as lexical-level manifestations of equinomy (Ch. 1, *2.1*) in natural language; for equinomy at the sentential level, see Ch. 9, *2.4*.

1.3.1   Polysemy

In order to define polysemy, we need to characterize the underlying notion of semantic bridge (informally introduced in Ch. 5, *4*).

> **Definition 6.6:** Semantic Bridge
> A semantic component 'σ' shared by LUs L_1 and L_2 is called the semantic bridge between L_1 and L_2 iff the following two conditions are simultaneously satisfied:
> 1. 'σ' contains enough semantic material.
> 2. Either 'σ' is part of the lexicographic definitions of both L_1 and L_2, or it is part of the lexicographic definition of one and of a lexicographic connotation of the other.

Condition 1

The lexemes LEG[1]**I.1a** 'body part …' (*John's leg*) and LEG[1]**I.2** 'part of pants that covers person's **leg[1]I.1a**' (*the legs of John's pants*) share enough semantic material: the meaning of the former is completely included in that of the latter; this is an obvious semantic bridge.

The same holds for the lexemes CHILD**1** 'young human …' (*a 5-year-old child*) and CHILDISH**1** 'related to or typical of a **child1**' (*a childish laugh*). The lexemes of the first pair stand in the relation of polysemy and those of the second are related by derivation. In contrast, LEG[1]**I.1a** and LEG[2]**1** 'a **part** of a long journey or a race' (*the last leg of our trip*) cannot be said to share a semantic bridge because the component 'part', in spite of belonging to the central component in both lexemes' definitions, is not specific (= rich) enough, due to its very general (= poor) meaning; these two lexemes stand in the relation of homonymy.

Condition 2

The lexeme PIG**I** 'farm animal ...' has the connotations 'voracious' and 'dirty', which serve as a basis for a metaphorical transfer towards PIG**II.1** 'a person who eats too much' (*I made a bit of a pig of myself at dinner.*) and PIG**II.2** 'a person who is untidy and unpleasant' (*Look at this mess! You're such a pig!*), respectively. Both PIG**II.1** and PIG**II.2**, related to PIG**I** by polysemy, include the component 'ᴬas if ᴬ... were a pig**I**'.

As we can see, the notion of semantic bridge underlies lexical relations of polysemy and derivation. (We mentioned this fact in Ch. 5, *4*, when discussing the notion of linguistic relevance: what components can/should be included in a lexicographic definition of an LU L in order to account for L's relations with other LUs in the lexical stock.) The presence of a semantic bridge also defines the membership of LUs in the same semantic class and the same semantic field (Ch. 8, *1.2 & 1.3*).

Two additional remarks on the notion of semantic bridge are in order.

1. How do we decide that the quantity of shared semantic material is sufficient (or not) to constitute a semantic bridge? The answer, by no means straightforward, depends on at least two factors:

    *   The way lexicographic definitions are formulated: some semantic links may be transparent for some speakers and not for others. Thus, do the lexemes FRONT 'extreme part of X in the direction where X is facing/moving' (*the front of the museum*) and FRONT 'war zone where actual fighting happens' (*All Quiet on the Western Front* [a novel by E. M. Remarque]) have enough semantic links to warrant a semantic bridge? Different speakers will probably have different answers to this question.

    *   The types of semantic components involved, their number and their structural positions within the definitions of the LUs in question. Thus, certain semantemes cannot constitute a semantic bridge by themselves, because they are too general and therefore too common. This is the case of taxonomic semantemes (Ch. 8, *1.2*), such as 'part.of', seen above; other examples include 'cause1/2', 'happen', 'state', 'person', 'substance', etc. For example, the definitions of both CHANGE$_{(V)}$**1** (*change one's eating habits*) and CLEAN$_{(V)}$**1** (*clean one's room*) contain 'cause2' as the central component: 'X causes2 Y to become different', respectively, 'X causes2 Y to become clean'; in spite of this, the two verbs cannot be considered as linked by a semantic bridge.

        The capacity of a semantic component 'σ' to serve as a semantic bridge can be measured by two parameters (Apresjan 2000: 222–223):

    *   The **importance** of 'σ', specified by the number of semantic primitives included in the decomposition of 'σ'; the higher this number, the more important 'σ' is.

    *   The **semantic value** of 'σ', specified by the number of semantemes of the language that include 'σ'; the higher this number, the less important 'σ' is (its semantic value is lower, since it is less distinctive).

2. The semantic bridge between two LUs does not necessarily appear at the first
    level of semantic decomposition: it can be "embedded further down" within
    components of their definitions. To illustrate this, here are two examples.
(10) a. X ⌐BRINGS UP⌐¹I Y: 'X suggests Y for discussion'
     (*The President brought the matter up again today.*)
     X ⌐BRINGS UP⌐¹II Y: 'X causes2 Y to appear on a computer screen'
     (*Please, bring up the file Z-1932.*)
   b. X ⌐MAKES SENSE⌐1: 'X is intelligible'
     (*Those words do not make sense together.*)
     X ⌐MAKES SENSE⌐2: 'X is sensible'
     (*It makes sense to buy now and pay later.*)

The idioms in (10a) are clearly semantically related, but the semantic bridge
they share – roughly, 'X causes2 that Y becomes present' – is not visible without further semantic decomposition. The same is true for the idioms in (10b),
which share the embedded semantic bridge 'corresponds to reason'.

The size of the semantic bridge and its position within the definition of the
concerned LUs, together with the regularity of the semantic link (see regular
polysemy immediately below), determines the semantic distance between these
LUs. Thus, GLASS2a 'container ... made from glass1' (*a wine glass*) is closer
to GLASS1 'transparent material ...' (*a piece of broken glass*) than GLASS2b
is 'quantity of liquid that can be contained in a glass2a' (*a glass of wine*); at
the same time, GLASS2a is closer to GLASS2b than to GLASS1. Or, to take
another example, WOMAN1b 'wife or girlfriend' (*My woman is gone* [Bob
Marley].) is closer to WOMAN1a 'adult female person' (*an interesting woman*)
than WOMAN2 'woman employed to do housework' (*How to hire a cleaning
woman.*) is.

We are now ready to define polysemy.

> **Definition 6.7:** Polysemy
> Two LUs L_1 and L_2 stand in the relation of polysemy iff they simulta-
> neously satisfy the following three conditions:
> 1. They have identical signifiers.
> 2. Their signifieds [= lexicographic definitions] share a semantic
>   bridge.
> 3. They belong to the same part of speech.

In the lexical stock, two LUs standing in the relation of polysemy belong to the
same vocable (traditionally called *polysemous word*); see Ch. 8, *1.1*.

> REMARK. According to Definition 6.7, a noun and its semantically
> identical verbalization, e.g., LOVE$_{(N)}$ (*love felt for someone*) and
> LOVE$_{(V)}$ (*to love someone*), are not related by polysemy – because
> they fail Condition 3 (rather, they are related by derivation); conse-
> quently, such lexemes belong to different vocables. The same holds
> for the pairs like HARD$_{(ADJ)}$ (*hard work*) ~ HARD$_{(ADV)}$ (*to work*

hard), BLUE$_{(ADJ)}$ (*a perfectly blue sky*) ~ BLUE$_{(N)}$ (*the blue of the sky*), etc.

Polysemy can be characterized along three independent axes.

1. Radial vs. Chain Polysemy

First, according to the orientation of semantic links, there are two major types of polysemy.

In the case of radial polysemy (*Figure 6.1a*), all LUs L$_i$ related by polysemy share a semantic bridge 'σ_j' with one and the same LU L$_1$ (called the basic LU of the corresponding vocable); the semantic links are "in parallel." In the case of chain polysemy (*Figure 6.1b*), LUs L$_i$ are linked one to another by a series of semantic bridges, so that some links are indirect: for instance, L$_1$ has a semantic bridge 'σ_1' with L$_2$, which, in its turn, has a semantic bridge 'σ_2' with L$_3$, and so on; the semantic links are "in series." Both types of polysemy can be based on strong inclusion or intersection of meanings; both types can cooccur within one vocable.

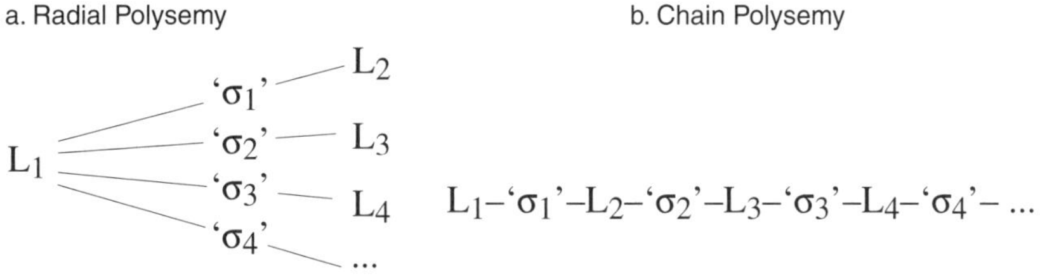

a. Radial Polysemy   b. Chain Polysemy

$$L_1\text{–}'\sigma_1'\text{–}L_2\text{–}'\sigma_2'\text{–}L_3\text{–}'\sigma_3'\text{–}L_4\text{–}'\sigma_4'\text{–} \ldots$$

Figure 6.1 Two major types of lexical polysemy

A good example of radial polysemy based on semantic intersection is found with the different lexemes of the vocable FIELD (boxing shows the semantic bridges):

L$_1$ = FIELD**I.1** 'area of ground where crops are grown' [*corn fields*]
L$_2$ = FIELD**I.2** 'area of ground where sports are played' [*baseball field*]
L$_3$ = FIELD**I.3** 'area of ground where some mineral resources are found' [*oil field*]
L$_4$ = FIELD**II** 'domain of activity – ⌐as if¬ this domain were a field**I.1**' [*the field of fish physiology*]
L$_5$ = FIELD**III** 'part of space where each point is affected by a force – ⌐as if¬ this part of space were a field**I.1**' [*magnetic field*]

Chain polysemy based on semantic inclusion can be illustrated by the following example:

L$_1$ = BUG$_{(N)}$**I.1** 'insect'
L$_2$ = BUG$_{(N)}$**I.2** 'invisible small harmful organism – ⌐as if¬ it were a bug**I.1**'
L$_3$ = BUG$_{(N)}$**II** 'error in a computer program – ⌐as if¬ the error were a bug**I.2**'

2. Non-figurative vs. Figurative Polysemy

Second, from a substantive viewpoint, polysemy links can be non-figurative or figurative, the latter subdividing into metonymic links, based on contiguity (= spatial, temporal or functional proximity) of the denotations of both LUs, and metaphoric links, based on the similarity of their denotations.

Non-figurative polysemy links (based on inclusion or intersection of meanings)

BAKE**I.1a**   'X cooks1 Y by submitting it to indirect action of dry heat …' ~
          (*Mother is baking my favorite cake.*)
BAKE**I.1b**   'Y cooks2 as a result of being $\boxed{\text{baked}\textbf{I.1a}}$ …'
          (*The cake is baking in the oven.*)
MAN$_{(N)}$1   'adult male human' ~
          (*the men's semi-finals*)
MAN$_{(N)}$5   '$\boxed{\text{man1}}$ who works for an employer'
          (*There was a protest from the men at the factory.*)

Figurative polysemy links

Metonymic links

> **Definition 6.8:** Metonymy
> The meaning 'σ_2' stands in a relation of metonymy to the meaning 'σ_1' [= 'σ_2' is a metonymy of 'σ_1'] iff the following two conditions are simultaneously satisfied:
> 1. 'σ_2' includes 'σ_1'.
> 2. The entity/fact denoted by 'σ_2' is physically contiguous in space, time or function to that denoted by 'σ_1'.

For example, the lexeme GLASS**2a** 'container … made from $\boxed{\text{glass1}}$' stands in a relation of metonymy with the lexeme GLASS**1** 'transparent material …', and the lexeme GLASS**2b** 'quantity of liquid that can be contained in a $\boxed{\text{glass2a}}$' stands in a relation of metonymy with the lexeme GLASS**2a** 'container …'; in other words, GLASS**2a** is a metonymy of GLASS**1**, and GLASS**2b** a metonymy of GLASS**2a**.

Metaphoric links

> **Definition 6.9:** Metaphor
> The meaning 'σ_2' stands in a relation of metaphor to meaning 'σ_1' [= 'σ_2' is a metaphor of 'σ_1'] iff the following two conditions are simultaneously satisfied:
> 1. 'σ_2' includes 'σ_1'.
> 2. The entity/fact denoted by 'σ_2' bears a resemblance to that denoted by 'σ_1', so that it is possible to say 'σ_2' ≈ '… – ⌜as if⌝ it were σ_1'.

For example, BUG**I.2** 'invisible small harmful organism – ⌜as if⌝ it were a bug**I.1**' is in a metaphoric relation with (= is a metaphor of) BUG**I.1** 'insect', and BUG**II** 'error in a computer program – ⌐as if⌐ the error were a bug**I.2**' is a metaphor of BUG**I.2**.

Metonymically related LUs are semantically closer to the basic LU than metaphorically related ones, because metonymic links are more objective.

3. Regular vs. Irregular Polysemy
Finally, according to the frequency of occurrence, a polysemy link can be regular (if it holds for a large number of lexical pairs) or not (if it does not). This is a language-specific feature, although some regular polysemy links are shared by several, not necessarily related, languages.

The polysemy links observed between GLASS**2a** 'container' and GLASS**2b** 'quantity of liquid ...' and between BAKE**I.1a** 'cook$_{(V)}$**1** ...' and BAKE**I.1b** ≈ 'be cooked$_{(V)}$**1** ...' are regular. Other regular polysemy links include (for English and a good number of other languages):

- 'teleological (= goal-oriented) action' ~ 'result of this action'
  *The **construction** is under way.   ~ This is a huge **construction**.*
  *The **translation** was done by a computer. ~ I accidentally tore up the **translation** of the certificate.*
- 'body part' ~ 'piece of clothing covering this body part'
  *My **back** hurts. ~ There is a tear in the **back** of your vest.*
- '[someone] having a feeling' ~ '[something] manifesting this feeling' ~ '[something] causing this feeling'
  *a **sad** person ~ a **sad** look ~ a **sad** event*
- 'animal' ~ 'meat of this animal'
  *free-range **chicken** ~ **chicken** burgers*

Metonymic links tend to be more regular than metaphoric links; this too can be explained by the fact that the former are more objective.

1.3.2   Homonymy

> **Definition 6.10:** Homonymy
> Two LUs L_1 and L_2 stand in the relation of homonymy and are called homonyms, iff the following two conditions are simultaneously satisfied:
> 1. They have identical signifiers.
> 2. Their signifieds do not share a semantic bridge (= they are semantically unrelated).

Unlike co-polysemous LUs, homonymy-related LUs are not united in the same vocable: each LU constitutes or belongs to a separate vocable.

Examples

FILE$_{(N)}$[1]   'set of documents containing information on a particular Y'
FILE$_{(N)}$[2]   'line of people ...'
FILE$_{(N)}$[3]   'tool designed to rub a surface with in order to make it smooth'

LIE(V)[1]	'be in a position in which the body is flat on a surface'
LIE(V)[2]	'deliberately say something that is not true'
⌐BRING UP⌐I	'suggest for discussion' (*The problem was brought up at the meeting.*)
⌐BRING UP⌐2	'raise(V)**8** [children]' (*Has she brought up her children well?*)
⌐BRING UP⌐3	'vomit' (*The dog was sick and brought up the food he had eaten.*)

Some cases of homonymy are less clear-cut. Take, for instance, CRANE 'bird' and CRANE 'machine'. We do not believe that the resemblance link between the denotations of these lexemes (the long arm of the machine reminiscent of the elongated neck of the bird) is prominent enough to "prove" their semantic relatedness, but a claim to the contrary would not be outright unacceptable either. Semantic links between LUs may become opaque over time, for some or all speakers, and descriptions of the same lexicographic data may vary in different dictionaries.

Both polysemy and homonymy arise from the insufficiency of formal means that can serve as signifiers for an ever-growing number of signifieds in a language: borrowing an existing signifier and giving it a new signified (thus creating a distinct linguistic sign) allows for getting around the problem. We mentioned this "shortage" of signifiers when discussing phraseologization as a way to get new complex signifiers from free phrases (Ch. 4, *2.2.1*, p. 104).

While homonymy is logically parallel to polysemy and equally pervasive in language, polysemy is more important by far as a basis for word formation. Both relations, however, are exploited for creative purposes: puns, plays on words, different language games and so on.

2   Syntagmatic Lexical Relations

Syntagmatic lexical relations are more variegated than paradigmatic ones. In fact, they form an open set, but we consider here only "institutionalized" syntagmatic lexical-semantic relations, i.e., those that are treated by language in a special way. These include the relations corresponding to intensification (the meaning of one lexeme intensifies the meaning of another), syntagmatic "verbalization" (a support verb verbalizes a non-verbal LU), indication of phase (a phasic verb indicates the phase of a dynamic fact), etc. Such relations are normally expressed in the form of set phrases known as collocations. Collocations, a particular type of phraseme, were characterized in Ch. 4, *2.2.2.1* (Definition 4.6, p. 109); here are additional examples (as before, the collocation base appears in caps):

Intensification

SKINNY as a bone ⟨*as a rake, as a stick*⟩; *abundantly* CLEAR;
strong ACCENT·pronunciation; *inveterate* LIAR; *complete* STRANGER; *sheer* LUCK;
DENY *categorically*; ADMIT *readily*; APOLOGIZE *profusely*

Syntagmatic Verbalization

take a TRIP; *use* CAUTION; *commit a* CRIME; *supply (a piece of)* INFORMATION; *the* RAIN *falls; a* BAN *is imposed* [*on Y*]; [*X*] *undergoes an* ANALYSIS

Indication of Phase

Beginning   : *sink into* DESPAIR; *fly into a* FURY; VIOLENCE *breaks out*
Continuation   : *stay on a* MEDICATION; *maintain a* HYPOTHESIS; [*a*] MEMORY
                     lingers
Cessation   : *lose* PATIENCE; *drop a* HABIT; [*a*] HOPE *fades*

Most importantly, the institutionalized lexical-semantic relations are universal in the sense that different languages institutionalize the same relations; this is the case for the three relation types above. At the same time, concrete collocations corresponding to these relations are extremely varied; the choice of a collocate is language-specific and "capricious." *Table 6.1* illustrates the expressions that correspond to the English collocations SKINNY *as a bone* ⟨*as a rake, as a stick*⟩ and *take a* TRIP in seven typologically different languages.

Table 6.1 Two families of collocations in seven languages

	Intensification	**Syntagmatic Verbalization**
Arabic	//*kaʔannahu žild ʕalā ʕazm* lit. 'as.if.he.were skin on bones'	*qāma bi* SAFAR lit. 'go on trip'
Chinese (Mandarin)	*gǔ*SHÒU*rúchái* lit. 'skinny as sliver of.firewood'	*tàshàng* LÙTÚ lit. 'march.on trip'
French	MAIGRE *comme un clou* lit. 'skinny as a nail'	*faire un* VOYAGE lit. 'make a trip'
German	DÜNN *wie ein Spargel* ⟨*wie ein Strich*⟩ lit. 'skinny as an asparagus ⟨as a thin. line⟩'	*eine* REISE *machen* lit. 'a trip make'
Hungarian	VÉKONY *mint egy cérnaszál* ⟨*mint az aprófa*⟩ lit. 'skinny as a thread ⟨as the wood. sliver⟩'	UTAZÁST *tenni* lit. 'trip make'
Russian	XUDOJ *kak ščepka* ⟨*kak skelet*⟩ lit. 'skinny as wood.sliver ⟨as skeleton⟩'	*soveršit'* PUTEŠESTVIE lit. 'accomplish trip'
Turkish	//*iskelet gibi olmak* lit. 'skeleton as be'	YOLCULUK *yapmak* lit. 'trip make'

REMARK. In the Arabic and Turkish examples, we see a fused expression of intensification – the meaning 'very' is expressed together with the meaning 'skinny' ('[be] very skinny' = '[be as] skin on bones'; '[be as] skeleton'). The fusion is marked by the symbol "//". See Ch. 7, *1*: 163.

Further Reading

General: Apresjan 2000.

Paradigmatic lexical-semantic relations: Murphy 2003; Storjohann 2010.

Synonymy: Miller *et al*. 1990; Edmonds & Hirst 2002; Janda & Solovyev 2009.

Antonymy: Lehrer & Lehrer 1984; Cruse 1992; Fellbaum 1995; Paradis & Willners 2007.

Derivation: Wierzbicka 1982; Comrie & Thompson 2007; Bosch *et al*. 2008.

Polysemy and homonymy:

• Lexical ambiguity: [psycholinguistic perspective] MacDonald *et al*. 1994; Klepousniotou 2002; [NLP perspective] Miller & Gurevych 2015.
• Polysemy: Apresjan 1974; Cowie 1982; Pustejovsky 1995; Ravin & Leacock 2000: 1–29; Falkum & Vicente 2015.

Metaphor and metonymy: Lehrer 1978; Lakoff & Johnson 1980; Panther *et al*. 2009.

See also Further Reading for Chapter 9.

Syntagmatic lexical relations: see Further Reading for Chapters 4 (phraseology, collocations) and 7.

7   Lexical Functions

This chapter presents lexical functions [LFs] – a formal tool used in the Meaning-Text framework to describe lexical relations, dealt with in the preceding chapter. The structure of the chapter is as follows: the notion of lexical function and details of the LF formalism are introduced in Section *1*; standard LFs, which describe systematic, cross-linguistically represented lexical relations and constitute the core of the LF system, are discussed in Section *2*; non-standard LFs, describing non-systematic lexical relations, are the focus of Section *3*; finally, some applications of LFs in Natural Language Processing are illustrated in Section *4*.

 To fully understand lexical functions and appreciate their descriptive power, the reader needs to be familiar with Meaning-Text deep syntax. It is therefore advisable to refer to Ch. 11 of this textbook while reading the present chapter.

1   What Is a Lexical Function?

> **Definition 7.1:** Lexical Function
>
> A lexical function **f** is a function (in the mathematical sense) which associates with an LU L of language **L** a (possibly empty) set of linguistic expressions $\{L_1, ..., L_n\}$ that have the meaning 'f' bearing on the meaning of L [= on 'L'] and are selected for use in an utterance as a function of L:
>
> $$f(L) = \{L_1, ..., L_n\} \mid L_i('f') \text{ and } 'f'('L')$$

A lexical function **f** must be semantically compatible with L; L is called the keyword of **f** and the set of linguistic expressions $\{L_1, ..., L_n\}$ associated with L by **f** is called the value of the application of **f** to L.

> **NB:** The term *keyword* is used for the argument of an LF in order to avoid the annoying ambiguity of the latter term, which can stand for both 'argument of a semantic predicate' and 'argument of a function.'

The meaning 'f' can be very general or even empty, as it is, for instance, in the case of support verbs (see below).

We speak of **lexical** functions, because the keywords of these functions (that is, their arguments) and the values they return for the keywords in question are lexical entities, cf.:

$f_{\text{'one who L-s'}}(L) = \{L_1, ..., L_n\}$		$f_{\text{'intense'}}(L)$	$= \{L_1, ..., L_n\}$
$S_1(employ)$	= *employer*; **informal** *boss*	Magn(*agreement*)	= *full*
$S_1(steal)$	= *thief*	Magn(*apology*)	= *strong*
$S_1(sue)$	= *plaintiff, complainant*	Magn(*rain*$_{(V)}$)	= *in torrents,* ⌐*cats and dogs*⌐

The LF $S_1(L)$ 'individual who does [what is designated by] L' has different values with different keywords and these values are typically not predictable by a general rule; the same is true for the LF Magn(L), corresponding to the meaning 'intense(L)'. In other words, the expression of an LF is phraseologically bound by the keyword L.

Lexical entities constituting the value of an LF, called elements of this value, are synonymous (since they express one and the same LF with one and the same keyword), without necessarily being exact synonyms; in our examples, the elements of value of an LF that feature semantic differences are separated by a semicolon.

The names of LFs come from Latin (thus, Anti comes from *antonymum* 'antonym', S_i from *substantivum* 'noun', Magn is from *magnus* 'grand', etc.), which reflects their universality, see below.

☞   The names of LFs are printed in Courier New.

As we have just said, an LF must be semantically compatible with the LU L to which it is applied; otherwise, L cannot be this LF's keyword. For instance, Anti combines only with LUs whose meaning can accept the component 'no' or 'more'/'less', Magn can only be applied to LUs whose meaning accepts intensification, and so on. This means that expressions such as *Anti(*horse*) or *Magn(*geography*) are absurd.

On the other hand, an LF can be applicable to an LU but return an empty value; for example, V_0(*ultimatum*) = $-$, which means that English has no verb with the meaning 'to give an ultimatum'.

Lexical functions can be classified according to three mutually independent axes.

Paradigmatic/syntagmatic LFs

Depending on whether they can appear in the text instead of or together with their keyword, paradigmatic LFs and syntagmatic LFs are distinguished (cf. paradigmatic and syntagmatic lexical relations, Ch. 6, *1* and *2*).

Paradigmatic LFs describe, for an LU L, its paradigmatic lexical correlates – roughly, L's (quasi-)synonyms, (quasi-)antonyms, (quasi-)conversives and (quasi-)derivatives (Ch. 6, *1.1* & *1.2*). These LFs have to do with selection/substitution; they are supposed to answer the question "What do we call the entity ⟨the fact⟩ X related to Y in a certain way?"

Syntagmatic LFs describe, for an LU L, its syntagmatic lexical correlates, i.e., LUs which, when combined with L in a text, form collocations (Ch. 4, *2.2.2.1* and Ch. 6, *2*). These LFs have to do with the combination of LUs; they are supposed to answer the question "What can we call an action ⟨a characteristic, an attribute, etc.⟩ X of Y that you want to express alongside Y?"

Among the LFs seen so far, S_1 is a paradigmatic LF, while Magn and Oper$_1$ are of the syntagmatic variety.

In some cases the distinction between paradigmatic and syntagmatic lexical functions is blurred; this is mainly because of syntagmatic lexical functions with fused elements of their values. Normally, elements of the value of a syntagmatic LF **f** applied to a lexeme L are separate lexemes corresponding to the meaning of **f** and forming a phrase with the keyword L; for instance, *rain* ⊕ Magn(*rain*) = *heavy rain*. However, sometimes an element of **f**'s value expresses at the same time (= cumulatively) the meaning of **f** and that of L: *rain* ⊕ Magn(*rain*) = //*downpour* (i.e., 'downpour' ≈ 'heavy rain'). Such an element of value **f**(L) of a LF **f** is called a fused element of the value of **f**(L) or the fused expression of **f**(L). Fused elements are identified by means of a double slash "//" preceding them all: Magn(*drunk*) = ⌜*as a lord*⌝, ⌜*as a sailor*⌝, *dead-* //*loaded, wasted*.

A fused element of the value of a syntagmatic LF is used instead of its keyword, just like an element of the value of a paradigmatic LF. However, the distinction between the two LF types is more profound: it is semantic in nature and does not depend on the use of their values in texts.

Standardness of LFs

With respect to their generality and universality, we distinguish standard LFs, which have both of these characteristics, and non-standard LFs, which have neither.

The generality of a standard LF is manifested in its potential to combine with a large number of keywords and have several elements of its value for a given keyword.

Magn(*applause*)   = *lengthy*; *loud* < *thunderous* < *deafening*;
                                enthusiastic < *frenetic*
Oper₁(*conclusion*)   = *make, reach* [ART ~]; *arrive* [*at* ART ~]

1. The symbol "<" indicates the degree of intensification: *thunderous applause* is more intense than *loud applause*, etc.
2. The expression in square brackets following an element of LF value is the "mini"-Government Pattern (Ch. 2, *1.3.3*) of this element. It indicates the way in which it combines with the keyword (represented by a tilde "~").

Standard LFs are linguistically universal – i.e., they are applicable to the description of lexical relations in any language. They appear as deep LUs in deep-syntactic structures of sentences (Ch. 11, *2.2*) and are used in deep-syntactic paraphrasing (Ch. 12, *2.2*). The LFs cited so far in this chapter are standard LFs.

A non-standard LF has few keywords, possibly just one, and few different elements of value, the lower limit being, again, just one. Here are three such LFs, their respective keywords being COFFEE (beverage), YEAR and NOSE (part of the face):

COFFEE
  without a dairy product   : *black*
YEAR
  having one day more than a normal year   : *leap*
NOSE
  thin and curving like an eagle's beak   : *aquiline*

As we can see, the name of a non-standard LF is actually a description of the meaning of its value by means of a natural language paraphrase – i.e., a lexicographic definition thereof.

The number of non-standard LFs cannot be foreseen even for an individual language; these LFs must be empirically discovered for each language. On the positive side, they have rather concrete meanings and tend to belong to specific domains, which facilitates their discovery.

Non-standard LFs are not used in paraphrasing and, therefore, do not appear in deep-syntactic structures, where only elements of their values can be seen. They are thus used to ensure an idiomatic lexical selection in the transition between the starting SemS and the DSyntS of the sentence under synthesis.

Formal constitution of LFs

According to their formal constitution, LFs fall into simple LFs, complex LFs and configurations of LFs.

Simple LFs. All LFs cited above are simple LFs. Other examples:

Anti·$_{antonym of}$'($drunk$)	= $sober$
Able$_{2}$'$_{such that can be L-ed}$'($trust_{(V)}$)	= $trustworthy$
Bon·$_{such that pleases the Speaker}$'($mind_{(N)}$)	= $beautiful$
Incep·$_{begin}$'($cry_{(V)}$)	= //$burst into tears$
Mult·$_{a standard set of}$'($fish$)	= $school$ [$of \sim$]
Propt·$_{caused by}$'($habit$)	= by, ⌐$out of$⌐ [$\sim$]
Real$_{2}$'$_{realize}$'($challenge_{(N)}$)	= $meet$ [ART $\sim$]
Sing·$_{a regular instance of}$'($luck$)	= $stroke$ [$of \sim$]

A **complex LF** is a combination of syntactically linked LFs having a unique keyword for which it returns a unified lexical expression covering the meaning of the entire combination:[1]

AntiMagn($doubt_{(N)}$)	= $slight$
IncepOper$_{2}$($challenge_{(N)}$)	= $encounter$ [ART $\sim$]
AntiReal$_{2}$($challenge_{(N)}$)	= $fail$ [ART $\sim$] //⌐$drop the ball$⌐

A **configuration of LFs** is a combination of syntactically not linked LFs having a unique keyword for which it returns a unified lexical expression covering the meaning of the entire combination:

[Magn + Oper$_{1}$]($laughter$)= $roar$ [$with \sim$]
$roar with laughter \approx$ 'do [= Oper$_{1}$] intense [= Magn] laughter'
[too.Magn$_{1}$^{quant} + IncepOper$_{1}$]($market$) = $flood$ [ART $\sim$]
$flood the market \approx$ 'too many [= too.Magn$_{1}$^{quant}] begin to be [= IncepOper$_{1}$] on the market'
E.g.: *Chinese-made toys laced with lead flooded the domestic market.*

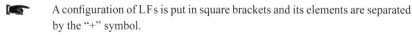 A configuration of LFs is put in square brackets and its elements are separated by the "+" symbol.

Table 7.1 gives a summary of the LF types, illustrating them from the LFs applicable to the lexeme LOVE$_{(N)}$**1** ('individual X's love for individual Y',

---

[1] In the deep-syntactic structure, AntiMagn can be written also as Anti←ATTR–Magn, IncepOper$_{2}$ as Incep–**I**→Oper$_{2}$, etc.

Table 7.1 Types of LFs illustrated from LFs applicable to the lexeme LOVE$_{(N)}$[1]

	LEXICAL FUNCTIONS		
	Standard		Non-standard
	Paradigmatic	Syntagmatic	
simple	S_2 : *love$_{(N)}$*[3], *loved one* A_1 : *in* [~] Adv_1 : *lovingly* $Sing$: *(love) affair* $Propt$: ⌐*out of*⌐ [~]	$Oper_1$: *be [in ~ with N$_Y$]* $Magn$: *strong; passionate, boundless; unconditional*	Strong but transient L. between adolescents: *puppy* [~] Such that X and Y are very young: *young* [~]
complex	$MagnAble_1$: *full [of ~]* *//affectionate*	$IncepOper_1$: *fall [in ~ with N$_Y$]* *// fall [for N$_Y$]* $FinOper_1$: *fall [out of ~ with N$_Y$]*	Such that X and Y start feeling L. from the moment they first meet: [~] *at first sight* Not reciprocated by S_2: *unrequited, one-sided* [~]
configurations	$[Magn+S_2]$: *//idol; love$_{(N)}$*[3] *of [N$_X$'s] life* $[Magn+A_1]$: *//crazy [about N$_Y$]*	$[Adv_2+Oper_1]$: *return [N$_Y$'s ~]*[2]	Love makes you overlook the defaults of your beloved one: *Love is blind.* The rules of fairplay do not apply when it comes to defeating your rival in love or war: *All is fair in love and war.*

2 $[Adv_2+Oper_1]$: 'being loved $[Adv_2]$ by Y, have $[Oper_1]$ love for Y'.

e.g., *Tara is madly in love with you.*), as they would appear in an English *Explanatory Combinatorial Dictionary* (Ch. 8, *2.2.4*).

These are by no means all LFs applicable to the keyword in question. The reader is invited to have another look at this table after reading through the chapter.

Standard simple LFs (≈ 60) constitute the core of the LF system. All LF types combined allow for a large coverage of lexical relations, both derivational and collocational. The formalism of LFs has been used in several applications in lexicography, language teaching and NLP, in particular multilingual sentence generation, machine translation and text reformulation (≈ paraphrasing) and abstracting; for an illustration of its use in the translation of collocations, see Section *4*).

2   Standard Lexical Functions

This section presents in more detail the most frequent standard LFs, both simple and complex; paradigmatic LFs are presented first (*2.1*), followed by syntagmatic LFs (*2.2*).

For some LFs, examples are provided which illustrate how they can participate in text reformulation, i.e., paraphrasing (for the corresponding paraphrasing rules, see Ch. 12, *2*).

2.1   Paradigmatic Lexical Functions

As we have said, a paradigmatic LF applied to an LU L returns different semantic derivatives of L that can be used instead of L in an appropriate context.

2.1.1   LFs Describing Core Lexical Relations: **Syn**, **Anti** and **Conv**

For the corresponding lexical relations, see Ch. 6, *1.1*, Definitions 6.1– 6.4.

No. 1   Syn(L): synonym of L

The LF Syn applies to LUs of any meaning and belonging to any part of speech.

Exact synonyms:

Syn(*buy*$_{(V)}$)   = *purchase*
Syn(*prison*)   = *jail*
Syn(*hurdle*)   = *obstacle*
Syn(*crazy*)   = **colloq.** *bananas*, **colloq.** *crackers*, **colloq.** *nuts*
Syn(*Thank you!*)   = *Thanks!*

Quasi-synonyms (= near-synonyms):

Syn$_⊃$(L): richer synonym of L [its meaning includes 'L']

Syn$_⊃$(*aircraft*)   = *airplane*

AIRPLANE is a richer synonym of AIRCRAFT because its meaning includes that of AIRCRAFT along with other meanings: 'airplane' = 'aircraft that has wings and at least an engine'. Note that as far the denotations of both terms are concerned, the relation is inverse: the class of aircraft strictly includes that of airplanes.

| $\text{Syn}_{\supset}(change_{(V)})$ | = *modify* |
| $\text{Syn}_{\supset}(respect)$ | = *veneration* |

$\text{Syn}_{\subset}$(**L): poorer synonym of L [its meaning is included in 'L']**

| $\text{Syn}_{\subset}(airplane)$ | = *aircraft* |

    AIRCRAFT is a poorer synonym of AIRPLANE because its meaning is included in that of AIRPLANE along with other meanings. Some aircraft, for instance helicopters, are not airplanes, but the inverse is not true.

| $\text{Syn}_{\subset}($ ⌐*break away*⌐ $)$ | = *escape* |
| $\text{Syn}_{\subset}(turkey)$ | = *poultry* |

$\text{Syn}_{\cap}$(L): intersecting synonym of L

$\text{Syn}_{\cap}(escape_{(V)})$	= *elude; avoid*
$\text{Syn}_{\cap}(astonish)$	= ⌐*raise some eyebrows*⌐
$\text{Syn}_{\cap}(protection)$	= *defense*

Set-theoretic subscripts "$\supset$", "$\subset$" and "$\cap$" (Appendix, *3.1*) have the same meaning when used with Anti, Conv_{ijkl} and other LFs.

(1) a.   *If found guilty, he faces some serious **prison**$_L$ time.* ≡
           *If found guilty, he faces some serious **jail**$_{\text{Syn(L)}}$ time.*
     b.   *This decision is bound to **astonish**$_L$ some people.* ≡
           *This decision is bound to **raise some eyebrows**$_{\text{Syn}_{\cap}(L)}$.*

No. 2 Anti(L): antonym of L

LF Anti is applicable to LUs of any part of speech provided their meaning contains a component able to accept either the negation or the predicate 'more/less'.

$\text{Anti}(hire)$	= *fire*, ⌐*let go*⌐
$\text{Anti}(prohibit)$	= *authorize*
$\text{Anti}(praise)$	= *criticize*
$\text{Anti}(friend)$	= *enemy*; **liter.** *foe*
$\text{Anti}(dry_{(ADJ)})$	= *wet*
$\text{Anti}(always)$	= *never*

Anti_(*praise*)   = *denigrate*
Anti_n(*astonishingly*)   = *predictably*
Anti_n(*married*)   = *single* ['neither married nor common-law']
Anti_n(*prohibit*)   = *allow; let*

(2) a. *Smoking **is prohibited**_L on campus.* ≡ *Smoking is not **allowed**_Anti(L) on campus.*

    b. *Ian is **single**_L.* ≡ *Ian is not **married**_Anti(L).*

No. 3 Conv_{ijkl}(L): conversive of L

LF Conv_{ijkl} is applicable to LUs of any part of speech provided they have Sem-/DSynt-actants.

Numerical subscripts following the Conv symbol show the permutations of the DSynt-actants of the conversive with respect to the basic order (= order of the DSynt-actant of the keyword), which is by definition "1234." Thus, Conv_{21}(L) stands for an LU L' whose DSyntA **I** corresponds to the DSyntA **II** of L, its DSyntA **II** corresponding to L's DSyntA **I**.

Conv_{21}(*fear*_(V) 'X fears Y')   = *scare*_(V)
Conv_{21}(*cause*_(N) 'X is the cause of Y')   = *consequence*
Conv_{21}(*above* 'X is above Y')   = *below*
Conv_{321}(*give* 'X gives Y to Z')   = *receive*
Conv_{3214n}(*buy*_(V) 'X buys Y from Z for W')   = *sell*
Conv_{231_}(*opinion* 'X's opinion of Y is Z')   = *reputation*

REPUTATION is a richer conversive of OPINION because with REPUTATION the opinion is necessarily held by a group of people such as family members, colleagues, public at large, etc., while an opinion can well be individual.

In order to correctly compute the value of an LF **f** whose keyword L corresponds to a semantic predicate, it is necessary to establish L's actantial structure – that is, the number and hierarchy of its semantic actants (cf. Ch. 3, *4.2.1*), as we did above for the keywords of LF Conv_{ijkl}. We indicate the actantial structure of keywords on LFs in all cases where it is not straightforward.

(3) a. *The Stone Age_{X ⇔ I} **precedes**_L the Bronze Age_{Y ⇔ II}.* ≡
    *The Bronze Age_{X ⇔ I} **follows**_{Conv21(L)} the Stone Age _{Y ⇔ II}.*
    b. *The defendant's negligence_{X ⇔ I} was the **cause**_L of the accident_{Y ⇔ II}.* ≡
    *The accident_{X ⇔ I} was a **consequence**_{Conv21(L)} of the defendant's negligence_{Y ⇔ II}.*

2.1.2   LFs Describing Derivational Relations

For the corresponding lexical relations, see Ch. 6, *1.2*, Definition 6.5.

2.1.2.1   Structural (= Syntactic) Derivations: S_0, V_0, A_0 and Adv_0

These LFs specify, respectively, the noun [= S(ubstantive)], the verb, the adjective and the adverb having the same meaning as the keyword L. For instance, 'S_0(L)' = 'L' [L = ASSASSINATE, S_0(L) = ASSASSINATION]; syntactically, S_0(L) [ASSASSINATION] and L [ASSASSINATE] have, of course, different distribution (Ch. 2, *1.3.3*).

No. 4 S_0(L): nominalization of L	
S_0(*during*)	= *duration*
S_0(*intrude*)	= *intrusion*
S_0(*legitimate*$_{(V)}$)	= *legitimacy*
S_0(*permit*$_{(V)}$)	= *permission*
S_0(*read*$_{(V)}$)	= *reading*$_{(N)}$; *read*$_{(N)}$
S_0(*swear*$_{(V)}$1)	= *swearing*$_{(N)}$ [*He's written some good tunes but the swearing is just juvenile.*]
S_0(*swear*$_{(V)}$5)	= *oath* [*an oath of allegiance to the country*]

No. 5 V_0(L): verbalization of L	
V_0(*contest*$_{(N)}$)	= *compete*
V_0(*intrusion*)	= *intrude*
V_0(*joyful*)	= *rejoice*
V_0(*reading*$_{(N)}$)	= *read*$_{(V)}$

No. 6 A_0(L): adjectivalization of L	
A_0(*brother*)	= *fraternal*
A_0(*cat*)	= *feline*
A_0(*Earth*)	= *terrestrial*
A_0(*finances*)	= *financial*
A_0(*space*)	= *spatial*
A_0(*Sun*)	= *solar*

No. 7 Adv_0(L): adverbialization of L	
Adv_0(*honest*)	= *honestly*
Adv_0(*last*$_{(V)}$)	= *during*
Adv_0(*quick*)	= *quickly*
Adv_0(*accidental*)	= ⌜*by chance*⌝
Adv_0(*hard*$_{(ADJ)}$)	= *hard*$_{(ADV)}$
Adv_0(*heavy*)	= *heavily*

REMARK. An element of the value of a derivational LF does not necessarily entertain a regular morphological link with its keyword; cf. the pairs $SWEAR_{(V)}5 \sim OATH$, $CAT \sim FELINE$, etc., above, which represent cases of suppletion. This fact was first mentioned in Ch. 6, *2.1*, where a distinction between semantic and morphological derivation was drawn.

These four LFs – Nos. 4–7 – are reversible, in the sense that if $S_0(L_{1(V)}) = L_{2(N)}$, then $V_0(L_{2(N)}) = L_{1(V)}$; in plain English, if $OATH_{(N)}$ is a nominalization of $SWEAR_{(V)}5$, then $SWEAR_{(V)}5$ is a (paradigmatic) verbalization of $OATH_{(N)}$, etc.

(4) a. *What are you supposed to **prepare**$_L$ for the literature course?* ≡
         *What **preparations**$_{S_0(L)}$ are you supposed to make for the literature course?*
     b. *Such is the nature of **cats**$_L$.* ≡ *Such is **feline**$_{A_0(L)}$ nature.*
     c. *The Dry Dock experienced **heavy**$_L$ use during the world wars.* ≡
         *The Dry Dock was **heavily**$_{Adv_0(L)}$ used during the world wars.*

2.1.2.2 Nominal actantial semantic derivations: S_i

No. 8 S_1, S_2, etc.: typical name of L's DSynt-actant **I, II**, …

These are actantial names: Agent name 'the one who L-s', Patient name 'the one who is L-ed', etc.

$S_1(sleep$ ·X sleeps')	$= sleeper$
$S_1(assassinate$ ·X assassinates Y')	$= assassin$
$S_2(assassinate)$	$= victim\ [of\ assassination]$
$S_1(course$ ·X's course in subject Y to Z (in institution W)')	$= teacher$
$S_2(course)$	$= subject$
$S_3(course)$	$= student$
$S_1(buy$ ·X buys Y from Z for W')	$= buyer$
$S_2(buy_{(V)})$	$= buy_{(N)}; purchase_{(N)}$
$S_3(buy_{(V)})$	$= seller$
$S_4(buy_{(V)})$	$= price$

(5) a. *Mr. Smith **teaches**$_L$ us Linguistics 101.* ≡
         *Mr. Smith is our Linguistics 101 **teacher**$_{S_1(L)}$.*
     b. *We **bought**$_L$ our car for 5000 dollars.* ≡
         *The **price**$_{S_4(L)}$ of our car was 5000 dollars.*

2.1.2.3 Adjectival actantial semantic derivations: A_i

No. 9 A_1, A_2, etc.: adjective characterizing L's DSynt-actant **I, II**, …['such as…']

$A_1(illness$ ·X's illness')	$= stricken\ [with\ illness]$

$A_1(know$ ‘$_{X \text{ knows } Y}$’)   = *aware* [*of* N_Y]

$A_1(nourish$ ‘$_{X \text{ nourishes } Y}$’)   = *nourishing*

$A_1(tire_{(V)}$ ‘$_{X \text{ tires } Y}$’)   = *tiring* [*for* N_Y]

$A_2(construction$ ‘$_{X\text{'s construction of } Y}$’)   = *under* [*construction*]

$A_2(trial$ ‘$_{X\text{'s trial of } Y}$’)   = *on* [*trial*]

> **NB:** What is meant here are **deep** adjectives; on the surface, *under construction* and *on trial* are not adjectives, but prepositional phrases.

(6) a. *Did you **know**$_L$ this?*   ≡ *Were you **aware**$_{A_1(L)}$ of this?*

  b. *The walk **tired**$_L$ the kids.* ≡ *The walk was **tiring**$_{A_1(L)}$ for the kids.*

2.1.2.4 Adverbial actantial semantic derivations: Adv_i

No. 10 Adv_1, Adv_2, etc.: adverb characterizing L's DSynt-actant **I, II,** …
['in such a way as…']

$Adv_1(contrast_{(N)}$ 'contrast between X and Y')   = *by* [*contrast*]

$Adv_1(distance_{(N)}$ 'distance between X and Y')   = *at* [ART *distance*]

$Adv_1(surprise_{(N)}$ 'X's surprise at Y')   = *with* [*surprise*]

$Adv_2(surprise_{(N)})$ = *to* [N_Y's *surprise*]

$Adv_2(cause1_{(V)}$ 'X causes Y (by Z(X))')   = *in the wake* [*of* N_X]

$Adv_2(attack_{(N)}$ 'X's attack on Y')   = *under* [*attack*][3]

(7) *The Alberta crop crisis **caused1**$_L$ a sharp increase in wheat prices.* ≡ *Wheat prices increased sharply **in the wake of**$_{Adv_2(L)}$ the Alberta crop crisis.*

2.1.2.5 Potential adjectival actantial semantic derivations: $Able_i$

No. 11 $Able_1, Adv_2$, etc.: adjective characterizing L's "potential" DSynt-actant **I, II,** …
['such that can L'; 'such that can be L-ed'; etc.]

$Able_1(terrify$ ‘$_{X \text{ terrifies } Y}$’)   = *terrible; terrifying*

$Able_1(ask$ ‘$_{X \text{ asks } Y \text{ about } Z}$’)   = *inquisitive*

$Able_1(irritation$ ‘$_{\text{irritation of } Y \text{ by } X}$’)   = *irritating* [*irritating behavior*]

$Able_1(burn$ ‘$_{X\text{'s burns}}$’)   = *combustible, flammable*

$Able_2(irritation$ ‘$_{\text{irritation of } Y \text{ by } X}$’)   = *irritable* [*irritable skin*]

$Able_2(trust$ ‘$_{X \text{ trusts } Y}$’)   = *trustworthy*

$Able_2(laugh_{(V)}$ ‘$_{X \text{ laughs at } Y}$’)   = *ludicrous*

$Able_2(burn$ ‘$_{X\text{'s burns } Y}$’)   = *combustible, flammable*

(8) a. *This idea **terrifies**$_L$ me.*   ≡ *This idea is **terrifying**$_{Able_1(L)}$ to me.*

  b. *Can one **trust**$_L$ him?*   ≡ *Is he **trustworthy**$_{Able_2(L)}$?*

---

3. The phrase *under attack* is both A_2 and Adv_2 of ATTACK$_{(N)}$: *The city under attack is the birthplace of Boko Haram.* ~ *The governor fled under attack.*

The LF Able_i combines easily with the LF Anti to form a complex LF (*2.2.2*):

$\text{AntiAble}_1(fear_{(V) \cdot X \sim_s Y'}) = brave$; $\text{AntiAble}_2(burn) = fire\text{-}proof$; etc.

2.2 Syntagmatic Lexical Functions

Syntagmatic LFs are designed to supply idiomatic cooccurrents to their keywords.

2.2.1 Adjectival and Adverbial Lexical Functions: **Magn, Ver, Bon**

No. 12 Magn: adjectival or adverbial modifier meaning 'intense'/'very'

$\text{Magn}(accent)$	= *heavy, strong; dreadful*
$\text{Magn}(alike)$	= ⌜*as two peas in a pod*⌝
$\text{Magn}(easy)$	= ⌜*as pie*⌝
$\text{Magn}(rain_{(V)})$	= *hard, heavily, in torrents,* ⌜*cats and dogs*⌝

No. 13 Ver: adjectival or adverbial modifier meaning 'such'/'in such a way as it should be'

$\text{Ver}(argue)$	= *convincingly, strongly*
$\text{Ver}(argument)$	= *convincing, strong, valid; sound*
$\text{Ver}(measure)$	= *effective*
$\text{Ver}(popularity)$	= *well-deserved*

No. 14 Bon: adjectival or adverbial modifier meaning 'good'/'well' as a subjective evaluation on the part of the Speaker

$\text{Bon}(different)$	= *refreshingly*
$\text{Bon}(future)$	= *bright*
$\text{Bon}(idea)$	= *great; promising*
$\text{Bon}(smile_{(N)})$	= *dazzling*
$\text{Bon}(smile_{(V)})$	= *dazzlingly*

LFs Magn, Ver and Bon are linked to their keyword (in the DSyntS) via the DSyntRel ATTR:

$$\text{L–ATTR}{\rightarrow}\text{Magn/Ver/Bon}$$

These LFs form complex LFs with the LF Anti, for instance:

$\text{AntiMagn}(applause)$	= *faint, polite, reluctant, scattered*
$\text{AntiMagn}(defeat_{(V)})$	= *narrowly*
$\text{AntiVer}(argument)$	= *invalid*

AntiVer(*promise*$_{(N)}$)   = *empty*
AntiBon(*car*)   = //*lemon*^{2}
AntiBon(*start*$_{(N)}$)   = *rocky*

2.2.2   Support Verbs: Oper$_i$, Func$_{0/i}$, Labor$_{ij}$

The values of these LFs are support, or light, verbs. Such a verb is semantically empty (or at least semantically "bleached") in the context of its keyword L, which is necessarily a predicative noun (= such that its meaning corresponds to a semantic predicate – that is, denotes a fact and has semantic and deep-syntactic actants).

Support verbs of L are used to link L with one of its DSyntAs; in other words, they serve to "verbalize" L, by expressing the mood and tense. (This phenomenon was referred to earlier as syntagmatic verbalization.) These verbs thus have a purely syntactic function; they differ among themselves only by the syntactic role played with respect to them by L itself and L's DSyntAs. As an illustration, here are some support verbs (boldfaced) used with the noun ANALYSIS:

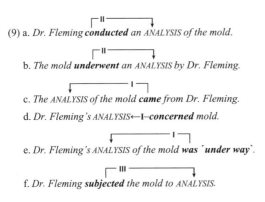

(9) a. *Dr. Fleming **conducted** an ANALYSIS of the mold.*

 b. *The mold **underwent** an ANALYSIS by Dr. Fleming.*

 c. *The ANALYSIS of the mold **came** from Dr. Fleming.*

 d. *Dr. Fleming's ANALYSIS←I–**concerned** mold.*

 e. *Dr. Fleming's ANALYSIS of the mold **was** ˹**under way**˺.*

 f. *Dr. Fleming **subjected** the mold to ANALYSIS.*

Given a collocation of the form "V$_{support}$→L$_{(N)}$," how do we decide by means of which LF this collocation is to be described? The first and absolutely essential step is to correctly determine L's actantial structure. This is not always straightforward; and since our linguistic intuition functions better with verbs, it is helpful to take a verb synonymous with L as a starting point. Thus, the actantial structure of the noun ANALYSIS is determined with respect to that of its verbal counterpart, ANALYZE; starting from (a), we establish (b):

(a) $_{individual}$**X**$_{[\Leftrightarrow I]}$ analyzes $_{phenomenon}$**Y**$_{[\Leftrightarrow II]}$

(b) analysis **of Y**$_{[\Leftrightarrow II]}$ **by X**$_{[\Leftrightarrow I]}$.

No. 15 Oper$_i$: Support verb taking L as its main object, i.e., Oper$_i$–**II**→L.
        L's DSyntA$_i$ appears as the syntactic subject of Oper$_i$.

With a transitive verb, the main object is the direct object, and with an intransitive verb, it is the "strongest" object.

Oper$_1$(*analysis* $_{\text{'X's analysis of Y'}}$)   = *conduct, make* [ART ~]
Oper$_2$(*analysis*)   = *undergo* [ART ~]
Oper$_1$(*order* $_{\text{'X's order to Z to do Y'}}$)   = *give* [ART ~]
Oper$_3$(*order*)   = *receive* [ART ~]
Oper$_1$(*resistance* $_{\text{'X's resistance to Y'}}$)   = *offer*, ⌜*put up*⌝ [ART ~]
Oper$_2$(*resistance*)   = *encounter, hit* [ART ~], *meet* [*with* ART ~]
Oper$_1$(*joke* $_{\text{'X's joke about Y told to Z'}}$)   = *crack, make* [ART ~]; *tell* [ART ~]

For the noun ANALYSIS, the designation of the person who conducts an analysis is the DSyntA **I**, and the designation of the entity being analyzed is its DSyntA **II**. Therefore, the verb CONDUCT, or MAKE, which takes ANALYSIS as its main object, is Oper$_1$ of this noun; UNDERGO, also taking ANALYSIS as the main object, is this noun's Oper$_2$.

No. 16   Func$_{0/i}$: Support verb taking L as its subject, i.e., Func$_{0/i}$–**I**→L.
              L's DSyntA$_i$ appears as the main object of Func$_i$.

Func$_1$(*analysis*)   = *comes* [*from* N$_X$]
Func$_2$(*analysis*)   = *concerns* [N$_Y$]
Func$_1$(*responsibility* $_{\text{'X's responsibility for Y'}}$)   = *lies, rests* [*with* N$_X$]
Func$_2$(*thanks* $_{\text{'X's thanks to Y for Z'}}$)   = *go* [*to* N$_Y$]
Func$_2$(*change* $_{\text{'X's change of Y'}}$)   = *affects* [N$_Y$]

With the verbs COME and CONCERN, the noun ANALYSIS is the syntactic subject. COME takes the DSyntA **I** of ANALYSIS as its main object and is therefore Func$_1$ of ANALYSIS, while CONCERN, which takes the DSyntA **II** of ANALYSIS as its main object, is Func$_2$ of ANALYSIS.

If Func$_i$ does not have objects – that is, if it is an "absolutely" intransitive verb expressing, roughly, the meaning ⌜"take place"⌝, a zero is used as the subscript:

Func$_0$(*analysis*)   = *is* ⌜*under way*⌝
Func$_0$(*accident*)   = *happens*, ⌜*takes place*⌝
Func$_0$(*wind*)   = *blows*
Func$_0$(*situation*)   = *unfolds*
Func$_0$(*rumors*)   = *circulate*

The verbal expression BE ⌜UNDER WAY⌝ is Func$_0$ of ANALYSIS: it takes the noun ANALYSIS as its syntactic subject and neither of the noun's DSyntAs is expressible as its direct dependent.

No. 17   Labor$_{ij}$: Support verb taking L as its most oblique object, i.e.,
              Labor$_{ij}$– **III**→L.
              L's DSyntA$_i$ appears as the subject of Labor$_{ij}$ and L's DSyntSj as its main object.

Labor$_{12}$(*analysis*) = *subject* [N$_Y$ *to* ART ~]
Labor$_{12}$(*consideration* $\cdot$X's consideration of Y$\cdot$) = *take* [N$_Y$ *into* ~]
Labor$_{12}$(*result*$_{(N)}$ 'X's result is Y') = *have* [N$_X$ *as a* ~]
Labor$_{21}$(*surprise* $\cdot$X's surprise at Y$\cdot$) = *catch* [N$_X$ *by* ~]

Again with the noun ANALYSIS, the situation is as follows: the verb [to] SUBJECT takes it as its secondary object, the DSyntA **I** of ANALYSIS as its syntactic subject, and the noun's DSyntA **II** as its main object; this verb is, then, Labor$_{12}$ of ANALYSIS.

We can now return to example (9) and identify the different support verbs used with the noun ANALYSIS: *conducted* [an A.] = Oper$_1$ (9a); *underwent* [an A.] = Oper$_2$ (9b); [the A.] *came* = Func$_1$ (9d); [the A.] *concerned* = Func$_2$ (9c); [the A.] *was* ⌐*under way*⌐ = Func$_0$ (9e); and *subjected* [to A.] = Labor$_{12}$ (9f).

The following table recapitulates the syntax of support verbs; for the sake of simplicity, we have limited ourselves to LUs having no more than two DSyntAs, so that the support verb in question has no more than three DSyntAs (that is, L itself and its two DSyntAs).

Table 7.2 The syntax of support verbs

DSynt-role with respect to V^{LF} / Support verb V^{LF}	DSynt-actant I of V^{LF} is:	DSynt-actant II of V^{LF} is:	DSynt-actant III of V^{LF} is:
Oper$_{1/2}$	DSyntA **I/II** of L	L	—
Func$_{0/1/2}$	L	DSyntA **I/II** of L	—
Labor$_{12/21}$	DSyntA **I/II** of L	DSyntA **II/I** of L	L

Note that if the LU L, the keyword of a support verb V^{LF}, has two DSynt-actants, then the support verb itself – that is, V^{LF} – can or must (in case it is a Labor$_{ij}$) have three DSynt-actants, because V^{LF} takes L itself as an actant plus L's actants. For instance, the noun RESULT has two DSyntAs, but its Labor$_{12}$ has three: *This condition*$_I$ *is the* **result** *of eating*$_{II}$ *too much fatty food.* ~ *Eating*$_I$ *too much fatty food* **has** *this condition*$_{II}$ *as a result*$_{III}$.

Let us now draw the DSyntSs corresponding to different support verb constructions that have ANALYSIS [of Y by X] as the keyword.

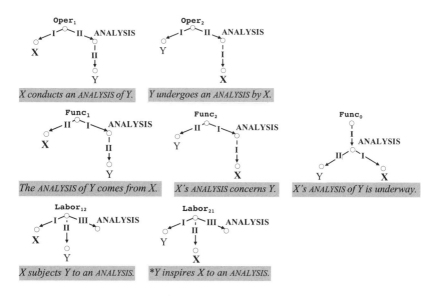

Figure 7.1 Support verb constructions with the noun ANALYSIS

In English, the LF $Labor_{21}$ does not have a value for the noun ANALYSIS; the asterisked hypothetical realization is given for the purpose of illustration. Note the following equalities:

$Oper_1(L) = Conv_{321}Oper_2(L)$,
$Func_1(L) = Conv_{132}Func_2(L)$,
$Oper_1(L) = Conv_{213}Func_1(L)$,
etc.

For instance, with the noun *[phone]* CALL$_{(N)}$ (*X's call to Y*), we have:

$Oper_1(call_{(N)}) = make$ [ART ~ *to* N$_Y$]
$Oper_2(call_{(N)}) = get$ [ART ~ *from* N$_X$]
$Func_1(call_{(N)}) = comes$ [*from* N$_X$ *to* N$_Y$]

```
      ┌─III ────────┐                    ┌─III ────────┐
      │             ↓                    │             ↓
```
John←**I**–*made*–[*a*]–**II**→*call* [*to*] *Mary.* ≡ *Mary*←**I**–*got*–[*a*]–**II**→*call* [*from*] *John.* ≡

```
          ┌────III ────────┐
          │                ↓
```
[*A*] *call*←**I**–*came*–[*from*]–**II**→*John* [*to*] *Mary.*

The above equalities mean that the support verbs from each family are, on the one hand, conversive with respect to each other, and, on the other hand, conversive with respect to the verbs of other families. (For lexical-syntactic paraphrasing rules involving conversives, see Ch. 12, *2.2.2.3.*) These facts show the special importance that the conversion relation has within a Meaning-Text linguistic model.

2.2.3   Realization Verbs: $\texttt{Real}_i$, $\texttt{Fact}_{0/i}$, $\texttt{Labreal}_{ij}$

The values of these LFs are semantically full verbs meaning, roughly, 'realize the objectives inherent to the denotation of L' $\approx$ 'do with L what is supposed to be done with it' and differing only by their syntax. They are applicable to predicative and quasi-predicative nouns whose meaning includes a component 'designed for ...'/'that is supposed to ...'. For instance, the noun CAR combines with realization verbs since a car is designed to be driven by X in order to transport Y; the same is true for MEDICATION, which is designed to alleviate or heal Y's sickness, for SAW, designed to cut Y with, and so on.

$$\texttt{Real}_1(car) \qquad\qquad = drive\ [\text{ART} \sim]$$
$$\texttt{Fact}_3(medication) \quad\ = is\ effective\ [against\ \text{N}_Z]$$
$$\texttt{Labreal}_{12}(saw_{(\text{N})}) \quad = cut\ [\text{N}_Y\ with\ \text{ART} \sim]$$

The actantial structures of LFs $\texttt{Real}_i$, $\texttt{Fact}_{0/i}$ and $\texttt{Labreal}_{ij}$ are identical, respectively, to those of $\texttt{Oper}_i$, $\texttt{Func}_{0/i}$ and $\texttt{Labor}_{ij}$. In other words, with $\texttt{Real}_i$ the keyword L and its DSyntAs play the same roles as with $\texttt{Oper}_i$, and so on. Therefore, these LFs are linked to their keywords as follows:

$$\texttt{Real}_i\text{–}\textbf{II}{\rightarrow}\text{L}; \ \texttt{Fact}_{0/i}\text{–}\textbf{I}{\rightarrow}\text{L}; \ \texttt{Labreal}_{ij}\text{–}\textbf{III/IV}{\rightarrow}\text{L}.$$

No. 18 $\texttt{Real}_i$: semantically full verb meaning $\approx$ 'to do with L what one is supposed to do with it' and taking L as its main object, i.e., $\texttt{Real}_i$–$\textbf{II}{\rightarrow}$L.

L's DSyntA$_i$ appears as the syntactic subject of $\texttt{Real}_i$.

$\texttt{Real}_1(promise_{(\text{N})}$ 'X's promise to Y to do Z') $= fulfill, keep\ [\text{ART} \sim]$,
cf. $\texttt{Oper}_1(promise_{(\text{N})})= give\ [\text{ART} \sim]$

$\texttt{Real}_2(exam$ 'exam by X of Y on Z') $= pass\ [\text{ART} \sim]$,
cf. $\texttt{Oper}_2(exam) = sit\ [\text{ART} \sim]$

$\texttt{Real}_2(challenge$ 'X's challenge to Y to do Z') $= accept\ [\text{ART} \sim]$,
cf. $\texttt{Oper}_2(challenge) = face\ [\text{ART} \sim]$

$\texttt{Real}_3(order$ 'X's order to Z to do Y') $= execute\ [\text{ART} \sim]$,
cf. $\texttt{Oper}_3(order) = have\ [\text{ART} \sim]$

The LF $Real_i$ combines easily with Anti:

$AntiReal_1(\ulcorner red\ light\urcorner)$	$= run$ [ART ~]
$AntiReal_2(rule)$	$= break$ [ART ~]
$AntiReal_3(demand)$	$= reject$ [ART ~]

No. 19 $Fact_{0/i}$: semantically full verb meaning ≈ 'L does what it is supposed to do' and taking L as its subject: $Fact_{0/i}$–**I**→L.

$\qquad\qquad$ L's $DSyntA_i$ appears as the main object of $Fact_{0/i}$.

$Fact_0(dream)$	$= \ulcorner comes\ true\urcorner$
$Fact_0(film)$	$= is\ playing,\ is\ showing$
$Fact_1(fear$ 'X's fear of Y'$)$	$= grips,\ overcomes,\ possesses$ [$_{N_X}$]
$Fact_2(shot$ 'X's shot at Y'$)$	$= hits$ [$_{N_Y}$]
$Fact_2(prize$ 'prize W by X to Y for Z(Y)'$)$	$= goes$ [$to\ _{N_Y}$]

No. 20 $Labreal_{ij}$: semantically full verb meaning ≈ 'to use L in the way in which L is supposed to be used' and taking L as its secondary object: $Labreal_{ij}$–**III/ IV**→L.

$\qquad\qquad$ L's $DSyntA_i$ appears as the subject of $Labreal_{ij}$ and L's $DSyntA_j$ as its main object.

$Labreal_{12}(phone$ 'X's phone for communicating with Y'$)$	$= reach$ [$_{N_Y}\ by$ ~]
$Labreal_{12}(knife$ 'X's knife for cutting Y'$)$	$= cut$ [$_{N_Y}\ with$ ART ~]
$Labreal_{12}(prison$ 'prison run by X where Y is kept'$)$	$= keep$ [$_{N_Y}\ in$ ~]
$Labreal_{12}(prize$ 'prize W by X to Y for Z(Y)'$)$	$= honor,\ reward$ [$_{N_Y}\ with$ ART ~]

2.2.4 Phasal Verbs: **Incep**, **Fin**, **Cont**

The LFs of this family indicate the phase of the action, state or process denoted by the keyword L; these verbs are thus semantically full.

No. 21 Incep: semantically full verb meaning 'begin [doing L]'.

No. 22 Fin: semantically full verb meaning 'cease [doing L]'.

No. 23 Cont: semantically full verb meaning 'not cease [doing L]' = 'continue [doing L]'.

Phasal verbs are related by the following semantic links:

Fin(L) 'cease doing L'	= IncepNon(L) 'begin not doing L'
Cont(L) 'continue doing L'	= NonFin(L) 'do not cease doing L'
	= NonIncepNon(L) 'do not begin not doing L'

Given their semantic nature, phasal LFs are applicable only to verbs and verbal expressions. In English, phasal meanings are expressed with verbs mostly in a regular fashion – $\text{Incep}(L_{(V)})$ can always be realized as *start* ⟨≈ *begin*⟩ *to* $L_{(V)}/L_{(V)}$-*ing*, $\text{Fin}(L_{(V)})$ yields the value *stop* ⟨≈ *cease*⟩ *to* $L_{(V)}/L_{(V)}$-*ing*, etc. – so that, in this context, phasal meanings are not interesting from a lexicographical viewpoint. On the other hand, phasal LFs have a rich cooccurrence with predicative nouns. Incep, Fin and Cont do not have an actantial structure of their own, which means that, in order to use them with a noun, the latter has to be "verbalized" by means of a support or realization verb. This results in complex LFs; for instance:

'begin performing an attack':
$\text{IncepOper}_1(attack \text{ 'attack against Y by X'})$ = *launch* [ART ~ *against* N$_Y$]

'begin following an approach':
$\text{IncepReal}_1(approach \text{ 'X's approach Z to Y'})$ = *take* [ART ~]

'the hope ceases to exist':
$\text{FinFunc}_0(hope \text{ 'X's hope of Y'})$ = *fades*

2.2.5   Causative Verbs: Caus, Liqu, Perm

The values of LFs in this family are semantically full verbs expressing the following three types of causation:

No. 24 Caus: semantically full verb meaning 'cause L'
        [≈ 'cause the fact denoted by L to begin taking place']
No. 25 Liqu: semantically full verb meaning 'liquidate L'
        [≈ 'cause the fact denoted by L to cease taking place']
No. 26 Perm: semantically full verb meaning 'allow L'
        [≈ 'do nothing to cause that the fact denoted by L ceases taking place']

Causative verbs entertain the following semantic links:

$\text{Liqu}(L)$ 'liquidate L'   = $\text{CausNon}(L)$ 'cause non L'
$\text{Perm}(L)$ 'allow L'   = $\text{NonLiqu}(L)$ 'do not liquidate L' =
                    $\text{NonCausNon}(L)$ 'do not cause non L'

They are most often found in combination with other verbal LFs:

$\text{CausOper}_1(position)$ = *put* [N$_X$ *in* ART ~]
$\text{CausOper}_2(arrest)$ = *place* [N$_Y$ *under* ~]
$\text{CausOper}_1(free)$ = *set* [N$_X$ ~]
$\text{Perm}_1\text{Fact}_0(imagination)$ = *let* [ART ~] ⌜*run wild*⌝
$\text{LiquFunc}_0(fears)$ = *allay* [N$_X$'s ~s]
$\text{LiquFunc}_1(appetite)$ = *cut* [N$_X$'s ~]
$\text{Perm}_1\text{AntiReal}_2(hospital)$ = *release* [N$_Y$ *from the* ~]
$\text{CausFact}_0(engine)$ = *start*, ⌜*turn on*⌝ [ART ~]

These LFs can also be used alone, that is without other verbal LFs, but then their keyword must be a verb:

Caus($break_{(Vintr)}$) = //$break_{(Vtr)}$; Liqu($sleep_{(V)}$) = //⌐$wake\ up$⌐; etc.

Unlike all other verbal LFs, which do not change the actantial structure of (the situation denoted by) L, a causative LF introduces a new actant – the Cause/Causer, expressed as the DSyntA **I** of the causative LF; this results in the displacement of L's inherent actants with respect to the causative LF **f**(L). If the Cause/Causer is external (= an actant different from L's own actants), the causative LF is not subscripted with an actantial number (cf. the Caus and Liqu complex LFs above). However, if the Cause/Causer coincides with one of L's actants, the corresponding actantial subscript appears with the causative LF. Thus, Liqu$_2$Func$_0$($rebellion$) = $suppress$ [ART ~] means that the Causer corresponds to the second actant of REBELLION – that is, the authority against which the rebellion is launched; in the case of Perm$_1$NonOper$_1$($hope_{(N)}$) = ⌐$give\ up$⌐ [~], the Causer is at the same time the first actant of HOPE (cf. LiquOper$_1$($hope_{(N)}$) = $crush$ [N_X's ~], where the Cause/Causer is external to the situation of hope); and so on.

3   Non-Standard Lexical Functions

Non-standard LFs are used in ECD-type dictionaries to describe the following three types of lexical entities: non-systematic word formation, non-systematic collocations and clichés (Ch. 4, *2.2.2.2*).

3.1   Non-Standard LFs Describing Non-Systematic Word Formation

CAR

which uses too much gas	: //*gas-guzzler*
having power on all four wheels	: //⌐*all-wheel drive*⌐; ⌐*four-wheel drive*⌐
safety device – belt fixed to a seat of a C. and designed to be fastened around the occupant's body to protect him from injury in case of accident	: *seat belt*
plaque with the registration number of the C.	: *(license) plate* [(*of* ART ~)]

SAILBOAT

tall vertical pole which supports the sail	: *mast* [(*of* ART ~)]

BICYCLE

main component of a B. on which all other components are fitted	: *frame* [*of* ART ~]

3.2   Non-Standard LFs Describing Non-Systematic Collocations

COFFEE

`without a dairy product added`	: *black* [~]
`with a dairy product added`	: *white* [~]

STEAK

`minimally cooked`	: *rare* [~]
`moderately cooked`	: *medium* [~]
`normally cooked`	: *well-done* [~]

LIE(N)

`told in order not to hurt someone by telling the truth`	: *white* [~]

WHISKEY

`served with ice cubes in it`	: [~] ⌜*on the rocks*⌝

NOSE

`flat and short`	: *pug, snub* [~]
`flat and round`	: *bulbous* [~]
`thin and curving like an eagle's beak`	: *aquiline* [~]
`curving out near the top`	: *Roman* [~]

3.3   Non-Standard LFs Describing Clichés

Since clichés, including pragmatemes, keep their literal meaning, what is given in the lexical entry of their anchors is not the meaning, but their conceptual characteristics (shown by special double quotes « … »).

LETTER (mail); X is the author of the letter]

«`being devoted to you [X]`»	: **formal** *Yours sincerely, Yours truly*	**[closing of a letter]**
«`I[X] wish you something good`»	: **informal** *All the best; Cheers!*	**[closing of a letter]**

BUSINESS2 (outlet)

«`Do you want something else?`»	: *Anything else?*	**[salesperson to a client]**
«`Is this all that you want?`»	: *Would that be all?*	**[salesperson to a client]**
«`This B. is open from T₁ to T₂`»	: *Business hours: T_1 to T_2*	**[sign at the entrance]**

GOVERNMENT (of a country)

«department of the
US G. responsible
for foreign policy»   : *State Department*

CAR

«It is forbidden to
park here»   : *No parking* **[on a sign]**

4   Applications of Lexical Functions in Natural Language Processing: An Illustration

In this last section we illustrate the use of LFs for the translation of collocations.

To translate collocations with ease and efficiency, we need to have a monolingual dictionary of the ECD type (Ch. 8) for both the source and the target language, where collocations are encoded in terms of the universally valid formalism of LFs. In some cases, we also need to use the lexical-syntactic paraphrasing system (Ch. 12, *2.2*), whose rules are formulated in terms of LFs, but our examples here do not have recourse to such rules.

Example 1

Consider English sentence (10a) and its Russian translation (10b):

(10) a. *Igor **draws huge** satisfaction from this success.*
      b. *Igor´* **ispytyvaet** *po povodu ètogo uspexa* **glubokoe** *udovletvorenie*
          lit. 'Igor experiences in connection.with this success deep satisfaction'.

If we had just a traditional bilingual English–Russian dictionary (which does not usually have a uniform description of collocations), how could we establish a correspondence between the boldfaced expressions above? We would have to postulate strange equivalences $\text{DRAW}_{(V)} \equiv \text{ISPYTYVAT}´$ '[to] experience' and $\text{HUGE} \equiv \text{GLUBOKIJ}$ 'deep', which are valid only in the given context (and in a few similar ones). With this translation method, we would need a list of translations for all stored collocations and would theefore end up with tens (if not hundreds) of thousands of spurious equivalences of this type. In sharp contrast, if we use two monolingual ECDs, an English one and a Russian one, the task becomes really simple, because the choice of the collocate is made intralinguistically – that is, within one language, with no regard for another language. Here are fragments of ECD dictionary entries for SATISFACTION and its Russian equivalent, UDOVLETVORENIE:

SATISFACTION$_{(N)}$	UDOVLETVORENIE$_{(N, neu)}$
'satisfaction of X with Y'	'udovletvorenie X-a po povodu Y-a'
Oper$_1$: *draw* [~ *from* ART N$_Y$]	Oper$_1$: *ispytyvat'* [~$_{acc}$ *po povodu* N$_Y$]
Magn : *huge < complete*	Magn : *glubokoe < polnoe*

All we need is establish the legitimate equivalence SATISFACTION ≡ UDOV-LETVORENIE; the correspondences between their respective collocates, expressed in terms of lexical functions, are obtained mechanically.

The deep trees (= the DSyntS) of sentences (10b), shown in *Figure 7.2*, demonstrate that these two sentences, seemingly so different at the surface, are very similar at the DSynt-level.

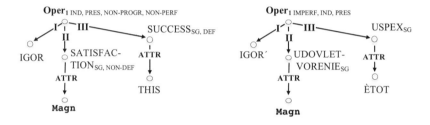

Figure 7.2 Deep-syntactic trees of sentences (10a) and (10b)

Example 2

Now let us consider a more difficult case – the English sentence in (11a); its closest (= most literal) Russian translation is (11b):

(11) a. *The book thief struck again.* ≡
     b. *Knižnyj vor snova soveršil kražu*
        lit. 'Book thief again committed theft'.

In this sentence, we could not possibly translate STRIKE$_{(V)}$ as UDARJAT' 'strike': the result would be incomprehensible. The correct choice is the collo-cation *soveršit' kražu* 'commit a theft'. But where and how do we establish the equivalence *strike ≡ soveršit' kražu*? In different contexts, the verb STRIKE has lots of other equivalents in Russian, for instance:

(12) a. *The hurricane **struck** the island again.* ≡
     *Uragan snova **obrušilsja** na ostrov*
     lit. 'Hurricane again fell.down on island'.
   b. *The bullet **struck** him in the shoulder.* ≡
     *Pulja **popala** emu v plečo*
     lit. 'Bullet hit to.him in shoulder'.

c. *A suicide bomber **struck** in the market.* $\equiv$
*Terrorist-smertnik **podorval sebja** na rynke*
lit. 'Suicide bomber exploded himself in market'.

However, if we think of LFs, the answer comes immediately: all the illustrated uses of STRIKE are elements of the values of LF Fact; and $\text{Fact}_0(\text{L})$ roughly means 'perform the action that (the denotation of) L is supposed to perform in conformity with its nature'. A Russian ECD must have:

$\text{Fact}_0(vor$ 'thief')	: *krast'* 'steal', *soveršat' kražu* 'commit a theft'
$\text{Fact}_2(uragan$ 'hurricane')	: *obrušit'sja* [na N_Y] 'strike [N_Y]'
$\text{Fact}_2(pulja$ 'bullet')	: *popast'* 'hit' [N_{YDAT} v N_Z]
$\text{Fact}_0(terrorist\text{-}smertnik$ 'suicide bomber')	: *podorvat' sebja* lit. 'explode oneself'

An English ECD gives similar indications for the above uses of STRIKE:

$\text{Fact}_0(thief$)	: *strike*
$\text{Fact}_2(hurricane$)	: *strike* [ART N_Y] etc.

Given the regular translation equivalents THIEF $\equiv$ VOR, HURRICANE $\equiv$ URAGAN, etc., the equivalences between the corresponding values of the LF Fact_0 are obtained automatically.

To sum up: lexical functions allow for an elegant and precise formal lexicographic description of lexical relations, in particular of all irregular derivations and all types of compositional phrasemes (collocations and clichés).

Further Reading

Collocations: [articles] McKeown & Radev 2000; Kennedy 2003; Petruck & Ellsworth 2016; [monographs] Sinclair 1991; Bartsch 2004; [dictionaries] Benson *et al.* 1997; Iordanskaja & Paperno 1995.

Lexical functions: Wanner 1996; Mel'čuk 2015a: 155–279.

See also Further Reading for Chapter 4.

8 The Lexical Stock of a Language and the Dictionary

Knowledge about words, or lexical knowledge (as opposed to grammatical knowledge: Ch. 2, *1.6.2*, p. 54), is a very important part of our linguistic competence. A speaker stores in his brain – that is, in his mental lexicon – information about lexical units [LUs] necessary to properly select and use them in speech. The union of the mental lexicons of all the speakers of a language **L** constitutes the lexical stock, or vocabulary, of **L** (Ch. 4, p. 98*ff*).

Within the lexical stock, the following types of information are associated with each individual LU L (a lexeme or an idiom): L's meaning, L's connotations and semantic label, L's register, L's syntactic and morphological behavior, L's phonemic and prosodic features, as well as various relations L entertains with other LUs in the lexicon and in the text. Some of these properties are shared among several LUs, which allows for their grouping within the lexical stock – into semantic classes or semantic fields, for instance. Therefore, we have to consider two major levels of organization of the lexical stock: the micro-level, that is, the organization of data on one individual LU, and the macro-level, or the overall organization of the lexical stock in terms of specific subsets of LUs.

Some aspects of the micro-organization of the lexical stock – namely, the meaning of an individual LU and its paradigmatic and syntagmatic relations with other LUs – were considered in Chapters 5–7. Its macro-organization is the topic of Section *1* of the present chapter. Section *2* addresses lexical stock modeling in linguistics by means of a dictionary: we present one particular type of dictionary, developed within the Meaning-Text framework – the *Explanatory Combinatorial Dictionary*, or ECD.

1   Lexical Stock and Its Structure

The lexical stock of a language is not a mere list of its LUs with corresponding lexicographic information, but a structured whole: LUs are linked by multiple and variegated relations, so that they form a complex network. It is therefore legitimate to speak about the structure, or even the structures, of the lexical stock of a language, because it is structured – that is, its LUs are grouped – in several ways.

Thus, grouping of LUs based on their semantic content results in the following divisions (the list is by no means exhaustive):

- **Synonymic series**: *house* ~ (*place of*) *residence, home; homestead;* ⌐*a roof over one's head*⌐; **formal** *habitation, dwelling* (*place*), *abode, domicile; cottage, cabin, lodge; bungalow,* ⌐*country house*⌐; *shack, chantey;* etc.
- **Antonymic series**: *benefit* ~ *detriment, disadvantage, drawback,* etc.
- **Semantic classes**: sensations [*hunger, cold, pain, tickling* ...], illegal actions [*murder, robbery, fraud, embezzlement* ...], farm animals [*horse, cow, goat* ...], etc.
- **Semantic fields**: COOKING [*cook, chop, marinate, simmer; bowl, caldron, fork, knife, plate;* [*a*] *cook,* [*a*] *chef, kitchen-aid; restaurant, eatery; meal, entrée, dessert; cuisine; healthy, lean, tasty* ...]; CRIME [*crime, criminal,* ⌐*drug lord*⌐, *smuggler; rob, steal, smuggle, robbery; court, judge, sue, defend; prison, sentence, execution* ...]; etc.

Another, orthogonal, way of grouping of LUs, based on their use, results in different subvocabularies: [according to scope] general vs. specialized;

[according to register] standard vs. colloquial vs. slang vs. formal vs. poetic, etc.; [according to geographic/social distribution] literary/national vocabulary vs. dialect/local variety vocabulary, etc.

This does not exhaust all the possibilities of LU groupings, but we have presumably made our point and can go on to discuss four specific types of groupings of LUs: vocables (*1.1*), semantic classes (*1.2*), semantic fields (*1.3*) and lexical fields (*1.4*).

1.1   Vocables

We will characterize the notion of vocable (Ch. 3, *3.1*, p. 79 and Ch. 6, *1.3.1*, p. 154) without addressing the question of how vocables are constituted, i.e., the way individual LUs are distinguished and distributed into vocables; for this, see Subsection *2.3.1* below.

> **Definition 8.1:** Vocable
> A vocable is the set of all LUs related by polysemy.

REMARKS

1. It is possible for a vocable to contain only one LU; however, in general language (as opposed to specialized lexicons – technical, scientific, etc.), vocables with two or more LUs are much more common, which can be explained by a "shortage" of signifiers in a language (cf. Ch. 4, *2.2.1*, p. 104). The average number of LUs per vocable in a language is referred to as its polysemy ratio; for languages like English, it is about 2.

2. In traditional terminology, a vocable is called a polysemous word, and the LUs belonging to it, its wordsenses.

3. In lexicographic terms, a vocable corresponds to a lexical super-entry; see *2.3* below.

Polysemy and the underlying notion of semantic bridge were introduced in Ch. 6, *1.3.1*. For instance, the lexemes $\text{TABLE}_{(N)}$**1a**, $\text{TABLE}_{(N)}$**1b** and $\text{TABLE}_{(N)}$**2** are related by polysemy, since their signifiers are identical (/téꞌbəl/) and their signifieds are linked by semantic bridges (boxed); therefore, they all belong to the same vocable, $\text{TABLE}_{(N)}$**1** ($\text{TABLE}_{(N)}$**2** is 'list of pieces of information arranged in columns and rows'):

$\text{TABLE}_{(N)}$**1a**	manufactured object designed for X to eat on it – a rigid plane surface supported by (four) legs …' (*Set the table, please.*)
$\text{TABLE}_{(N)}$**1b**	'group of people sitting around a $\boxed{\text{table}_{(N)}\text{1a}}$' (*The whole table laughed.*)

TABLE$_{(N)}$¹2   '$\boxed{\text{table}_{(N)}\text{¹1a}}$ for X in a restaurant as a unit of service'
                        (*I booked a table for four at Moishe's.*)

The meaning of the noun TABLE$_{(N)}$¹**1a** is completely included in those of
TABLE$_{(N)}$¹**1b** and of TABLE$_{(N)}$¹**2**. The lexeme TABLE$_{(N)}$¹**1a**, being semanti-
cally simpler (Ch. 3, *4.1.1*) than the other two lexemes, constitutes the basic
LU of the vocable.[1]

As we have repeatedly pointed out, LUs of a vocable are assigned distinctive lexicographic numbers, which serve as pointers towards their lexicographic
definitions (in a dictionary of language). Different dictionaries have different ways of assigning lexicographic numbers; for the system used within our
approach, see Subsection *2.3.2* below.

Two additional examples of vocables follow, illustrating two different types
of polysemic links: radial and chain polysemy (Ch. 6, *1.3.1*).

The vocable HEAD$_{(N)}$ has HEAD$_{(N)}$**I.1a** as the basic LU, the other LUs
being linked to it by radial polysemy:

HEAD$_{(N)}$**I.1a**   'human body part'   (*my head*)
HEAD$_{(N)}$**I.1b**   'animal body part'   (*head of a fly*)
HEAD$_{(N)}$**II**   'chief officer ... – ⌐as if⌐ head**I.1a** ...' (*head of a bank*)
HEAD$_{(N)}$**III.1** 'upper part'   (*head of a hammer*)
HEAD$_{(N)}$**III.2** 'front part'   (*head of a convoy*)

The vocable BODY provides a good example of chain polysemy:

BODY**I.1**   'human body'   (*All my body ached.*)
BODY**I.2**   'main part of the body**I.1**' (*The limbs were severed*
              [≈ torso]   *from the body.*)
BODY**II**   'group of humans'   (*a large body of unemployed*)
BODY**III**   'organization'   (*governing body*)
BODY**IV**   'main part'   (*body of a plant/a text*)

BODY**I.2** has a semantic bridge with the BODY**I.1** ('body**I.1**'), but BODY**II**
has a semantic bridge with BODY**I.2** ('human'); BODY**III** shares a semantic
bridge with BODY**II** ('group of humans'), and BODY**IV** is linked to BODY**I.2**
('main part').

> REMARK. The same types of semantic links found within vocables
> can hold between LUs belonging to different vocables; however, in
> that case we speak about derivational (rather than polysemic) semantic
> links. Thus, for instance, the meaning of INCREASE$_{(V, \ intrans)}$**1**

---

[1] While some approaches use historic or etymological considerations to determine the basic
lexeme within a vocable, we use strictly synchronic considerations.

(*The prices have increased1*.) is completely included in that of INCREASE$_{(V, trans)}$**2**, with which it shares a vocable, and in the meaning of RAISE$_{(V, trans)}$**2**, which belongs to a different vocable (*All the shops have increased2* ⟨≡ *raised2*⟩ *their prices* '... have caused2 their prices to increase1'.).

Homonymous LUs (Ch. 6, *1.3.2*), that is, LUs which have identical signifiers but whose signifieds do not share a semantic bridge, are distributed among different vocables, identified by distinctive numbers placed in superscript:

BANK$_{(N)}$[1] (*river bank*) vs. BANK$_{(N)}$[2] (*the National Bank lending rate*)

TABLE$_{(N)}$[1] (*dining tableI.1a, the tableI.1b that fell silent* and *restaurant tableI.2*) vs. TABLE$_{(N)}$[2] (*Results are presented in Table 4.*)[2]

PEN$_{(N)}$[1] 'writing implement' vs. PEN$_{(N)}$[2] 'enclosure for animals' vs. PEN$_{(N)}$[3] 'penitentiary'

DATE[1] 'sweet fruit' vs. DATE[2] 'indication of a time moment – the name of the day, month, and year' vs. DATE[3] 'romantic meeting of two people'

The concept of vocable is of great utility in lexicography. On the one hand, it allows for important generalizations: LUs belonging to the same vocable have largely the same morphology, at least some common Government Pattern characteristics, and some shared lexical functions; on the other hand, it reflects the intuition of speakers, who perceive a vocable as one polysemous "word."

1.2   Semantic Classes of Lexical Units

The semantic classification of LUs has been a matter of considerable interest both in philosophy of language and linguistic semantics/lexicology. The appeal of such classifications lies in the fact that it is possible to foresee some of an LU's linguistic properties from its membership in a given semantic class. In other words, the concept of semantic class makes possible some interesting generalizations about the behavior of LUs.

We start with an overview of the semantic classifications of LUs denoting facts, proposed by the American philosopher Zeno Vendler (*1.2.1*), then we present the taxonomic semantic classes of LUs (*1.2.2*) and their possible uses for the description of the lexical stock (*1.2.3*).

1.2.1   Vendler's Aspectual Classes

There are four major semantic classes of LUs denoting facts, often called aspectual classes (Vendler 1957) (*Table 8.1*).

---

[2] TABLE$_{(N)}$[1] and TABLE$_{(N)}$[2] were diachronically connected – both are from Old English *tabule* 'flat slab, inscribed tablet' < Lat. *tabula* 'plank, tablet, list'. However, in modern English the meanings of these lexical units do not feature convincing semantic bridges.

Table 8.1 Vendler's aspectual classes

Semantic class	Properties of class members	Examples of class members
state	static, continuous, atelic [= open-ended]	'believe', 'love', 'understand', 'have'
activity	dynamic, continuous, atelic	'run', 'swim', 'push [a cart]', 'drive [a car]'
accomplishment	dynamic, continuous, telic [= having an inherent limit][3]	'build [a house]', 'bake [a cake]', 'recover [from an illness]'
achievement	dynamic, punctual, telic	'find', 'recognize', 'explode', 'die'

States and achievements do not have stages – the former because they are homogeneous, and the latter because they denote near-instantaneous changes of state, whose internal structure is inaccessible for description. For this reason, verbs denoting states and achievements normally cannot be used in the progressive aspect (*Max was *believing in God/*finding his keys.*). However, activities and accomplishments, which do have stages, are compatible with the progressive aspect (*Max was running/building a house.*). States and activities, which are atelic, cooccur with the expression *for time T* (*John loved Mary for years/swam for hours.*), while accomplishments and achievements, being telic, combine with *in time T* (*John baked a cake in half an hour/ recognized me in a second.*).

 A verbal vocable can contain two lexemes, one atelic and the other telic; e.g.: *How to **read** in French* [atelic]. ~ *How to **read** a novel* [telic], cf. *He read **for** hours.* ~ *He read this novel **in** a few hours.*

Vendler's classification, widely popular in linguistics, has served as a basis for many modern semantic classifications.

> **NB:** However, the term *aspectual classes* itself is rather infelicitous. The semantemes 'state', 'activity', 'accomplishment' and 'achievement', which identify these classes, are by no means **verbal aspects**, taking these latter term in the sense of several inflectional categories of aspect, found in various languages: cf. the oppositions "progressive ~ non-progressive

---

[3] The meaning of a telic verb (*telic* comes from Greek *télos* 'goal/limit') includes an inherent limit, which, once attained, entails the cessation of the corresponding fact; e.g., [to] *dress* is telic because *being dressed* is the inherent limit of the action of dressing. The meaning of an atelic verb includes no such limit; e.g., [to] *sleep* is atelic because the state it denotes can in principle go on *ad infinitum*.

aspect" in English (*He smokes.* ~ *He is smoking.*) or Spanish and "perfective ~ imperfective aspect" in Russian (*On po+stroil dom* 'He has. built a.house' ~ *On stroil dom* 'He was.building a.house') and other Slavic languages. Nevertheless, Vendlerian semantic classes and inflectional aspectual meanings are intimately related: as indicated above, state/achievement verbs do not have the progressive aspect, state verbs do not have the perfective aspect, etc. Therefore, when speaking of Vendlerian classes, it is preferable to use the term *lexical aspect*, as opposed to *inflectional aspect*.

1.2.2 Semantic Labels and Taxonomic Semantic Classes of Lexical Units

The notion of semantic class of LUs is built, in an essential way, on that of semantic label of an LU; therefore, we will begin with the latter.

> **Definition 8.2:** Semantic Label of a Lexical Unit
> The semantic label of an LU is its approximate semantic characterization, based on a condensed and normalized formulation of the central, or generic, component of its lexicographic definition and perhaps some (parts) of its peripheral components.

An LU's semantic label is the name of the semantic class of which it is an instance; it is chosen in such a way as to specify the semantic class of LUs having identical or at least highly similar lexicographic properties, see *Table 8.2*.

☞   Semantic labels appear in `Courier New` font.

Table 8.2 Generic component of an LU's definition vs. its semantic label

Lexical Unit	Generic Component of the LU's Definition (shaded)	LU's Semantic Label
TRUCK	'a large motor vehicle1 designed to carry goods'	`motor vehicle1`
DOCTOR(N)1	'a person2 whose profession1 is to treat people who are ill'	`person2 practicing a profession1`
MURDER(N)	'the action2 of murdering1 someone'	`criminal action(N)2`
MURDER(V)1	'kill2 illegally and deliberately'	`act(V)2 criminally`
KILL(V)2	'do1 something to Y which causes1 Y to die'	`act(V)2 causing2 something`

> **Definition 8.3:** Taxonomic Semantic Class of Lexical Units
> A taxonomic semantic class is the set of all LUs (of language **L**) identified by a common semantic label.

Here are a few examples of semantic labels and the semantic classes of LUs they identify, together with some instances of each class.

Table 8.3 Semantic labels for English and some instances of the corresponding semantic classes

	Semantic label/class	Some LUs belonging to the semantic class
1.	act$_{(V)}$**2** criminally	MURDER$_{(V)}$**1**, DEFRAUD, EMBEZZLE, …
2.	psychological charac-teristic$_{(N)}$ of a person**2**	BRAVERY, COWARDICE, GENEROSITY, HONESTY, …
3.	child**1**	BABY$_{(N)}$**1**, INFANT$_{(N)}$**1**, KID$_{(N)}$**1**, TODDLER, …
4.	confront verbally	ARGUE**1**, 'FALL OUT'**1**, SQUABBLE$_{(V)}$, …
5.	experience a feeling$_{(N)}$**2**	HATE$_{(V)}$**1/2**, LOVE$_{(V)}$**1/2**, …
6.	experiencing a sensation**1**	COLD$_{(ADJ)}$**3**, HUNGRY, ITCHY**1**, …
7.	feeling$_{(N)}$**2**	HAPPINESS, LOVE$_{(N)}$**1/2**, PAIN$_{(N)}$**2**, SORROW$_{(N)}$**1**, …
8.	criminal action$_{(N)}$**2**	MURDER$_{(N)}$, FRAUD$_{(N)}$**1**, EMBEZZLEMENT$_{(N)}$; ARSON, …
9.	illness	CHOLERA, FLU, MEASLES, …
10.	[person**2**] hav-ing a psychological characteristic	BRAVE$_{(ADJ)}$**1**, COWARDLY, GENEROUS**1**, HONEST**1/2**, …
11.	'living being'	BIRD**1**, FISH$_{(N)}$**1**, INSECT, 'HUMAN BEING', …
12.	manufactured object	CONSTRUCTION**4**, TOOL$_{(N)}$**1**, VEHICLE**1**, …
13.	person**2** practicing a profession**1**	CARPENTER, LAWYER, DOCTOR$_{(N)}$**1**, TEACHER, …
14.	person**2** having acted criminally	MURDERER, FRAUDSTER, THIEF, EMBEZZLER, …
15.	process$_{(N)}$**1** of changing	FERMENTATION, OXYDATION, FOSSILIZATION, …
16.	sensation**1**	DIZZINESS, HUNGER**2**, PAIN$_{(N)}$**1**, …
17.	tending to cause**1** a feeling$_{(N)}$**2**	DISGUSTING, HATEFUL, LOVABLE, …
18.	undergo a process$_{(N)}$**1** of changing	FERMENT$_{(V)}$, 'GROW UP'**1/2**, SOLIDIFY**1**, …
19.	motor vehicle**1**	CAR**1**, TRUCK$_{(N)}$**1**, VAN**1/2**, …
20.	verbal confrontation	ARGUMENT**1**, QUARREL$_{(N)}$**1**, …

Let us emphasize the following fact:

> A semantic label (or its central element) is itself an LU of language **L**, i.e., a lexical meaning of **L**, identified by a lexicographic distinctive number.

From this, three corollaries follow.

1. A semantic label is language-specific since it corresponds to a seman-teme or a configuration of semantemes: recall the discussion of the "language-specific" character of semantemes, Ch. 3, *3.1.1*.
2. A semantic label belongs to a specific part of speech; consequently, the LUs in a given semantic class necessarily have one and the same part of speech. Semantic labels that correspond to genuine predicates (Ch. 3, *3.1.2*) have four "variants": verbal, nominal, adjectival and adverbial. Thus, as can be seen in *Table 8.3*, in addition to the label act $_{(V)}$ 2 criminally [No. 1], we have the nominal labels criminal action $_{(N)}$ 2 [No. 8] and person2 having acted criminally [No. 14]; the nominal label psychological characteristic $_{(N)}$ of a person2 [No. 2] has the label person2 having a psychological characteristic [No. 10] as its adjecti-val counterpart, and so on. Members of the corresponding lexical classes are related by obvious lexical-functional links (Ch. 7, *2.1*): V_0, $S_{0/i}$, $A_{0/i}$, etc.

    > **NB:** The union of these related semantic classes constitutes a semantic field (Subsection *1.3* below).

    Semantic labels corresponding to quasi-predicates and semantic names have, of course, only the nominal form.
3. A semantic label itself can receive a more general, hyperonymic, semantic label; thus, feeling $_{(N)}$ 2 is an instance of state $_{(N)}$ 1, which is an instance of fact; motor vehicle1 is an instance of vehicle1, an instance of manufactured object, the latter an instance of object $_{(N)}$ 1, which is an instance of entity; and so on. This means that semantic labels can be hierarchized, inducing a hierarchy of corresponding semantic classes of LUs.

Figure 8.1 (next page) shows a small fragment of a hierarchy of semantic labels for English; only its "higher end" is shown, displaying only nominal labels.

The hierarchy starts from an all-embracing class {something}, which imme-diately dominates the two subclasses {entity 'something that exists'} and {fact 'something that takes place'}, each further subdivided as shown. (Note that the semantic labels identifying these three classes correspond to semantic primes of the *Natural Semantic Metalanguage* approach; cf. Ch. 3, *4.1.3*.)

A hierarchy of semantic labels, as envisaged in Meaning-Text approach, has the following two essential characteristics.

*   It is a lexical hierarchy and not a real-world ontology in the philosophical sense. In other words, our hierarchy is about classifying LUs of a lan-guage rather than classifying the corresponding things in the extralinguistic

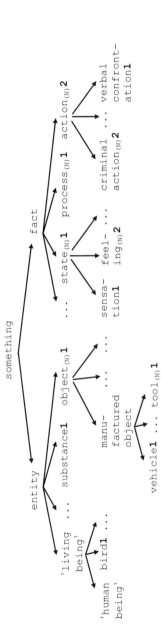

Figure 8.1 Hierarchy of semantic labels for English (fragment)

universe; cf. the remarks on the naïve worldview (Ch. 5, *4*, p. 132, Criterion of Linguistic Relevance), embodied in the lexicon, which our lexicographic descriptions should reflect. A lexicological classification thus differs from scientific and other technical classifications of things and/or concepts. Here is an example that illustrates this fact. For a layman, MURDER$_{(N)}$ is a type of criminal action, which itself is a type of action, the latter being a type of fact; this is the perspective of an average English speaker, that is, of the English language. But for a lawyer, in his professional dealings, an entirely different classification is relevant: thus, in a jurisdiction that has the option of the death penalty, murder $\subset$ capital felony $\subset$ felony $\subset$ personal crime $\subset$ criminal offence. While in a general public dictionary of English **the word** *murder* will not be defined as 'a capital felony that ...', in a specialized legal dictionary or encyclopedia **the corresponding action** (= the corresponding concept) is defined exactly in that way.

- A hierarchy of semantic labels, which are lexical meanings of language **L**, is specific to **L**, and has to be arrived at inductively, as a final result of a description of **L**'s lexical stock. Even if closely related languages are likely to have similar semantic label hierarchies (sharing, in particular, labels with very general meaning, like the ones in *Figure 8.1*), this similarity cannot be taken for granted. For a hierarchy of semantic labels specific to French, as elaborated within Meaning-Text lexicology, see Further Reading.

1.2.3   Semantic Labels in Lexical Descriptions

Semantic labels have at least three important uses in lexicology. First, they allow for better standardization of lexical descriptions, through the mechanism of lexical inheritance that they help specify. Second, semantic labels allow for the construction of "pseudo-definitions" – compact descriptions of the meanings of LUs that can be used in various natural language treatment tasks, such as, for instance, wordsense discrimination. Finally, semantic labels are useful for specifying conditions for the surface realization of LU's actants.

1.2.3.1   Semantic Labels and Lexical Inheritance

Inheritance of lexical properties, or lexical inheritance for short, is a well-known phenomenon: LUs belonging to the same taxonomic semantic class, that is, having the same semantic label, can share semantic, syntactic and restricted lexical cooccurrence properties. In other words, properties of an LU L are in part deducible, or inherited, from its semantic label (more precisely, from the corresponding hyperonymic LU). For instance, nouns denoting illnesses inherit a sizeable part of their cooccurrence from the semantic label illness: *contract, get, suffer from, get over, succumb to* an ILLNESS ⟨FLU, CHOLERA, MENINGITIS, etc.⟩. Most of the action-denoting nouns, like ANALYSIS, EXPERIMENT, OPERATION, etc. share support verbs with their semantic label action**2**: *perform, carry out, conduct*; feeling-denoting nouns, such as LOVE, RESPECT, ANIMOSITY, etc., combine with several support verbs required also by the corresponding label, feeling $_{(N)}$ **2**: *experience, have*; and so on. LUs from the same semantic class also tend to have similar government patterns; thus, the DSyntA **II** of feeling-denoting LUs is often implemented by the prepositional phrase *for ⟨towards⟩ N*, which also expresses the DSyntA **II** of the noun FEELING.

 Lexical inheritance is not 100 percent automatic. In many cases, a particular LU does not inherit a property of its semantic class or has a property not foreseen by it: *feel* LOVE ⟨RESPECT, ANIMOSITY⟩, but **feel a* FEELING; IRRITATION *at her rudeness*, but [*unpleasant*] FEELING **at her rudeness*; HATRED *of war*, but [*unpleasant*] FEELING **of war*, etc.

Thanks to lexical inheritance, the dictionary entry for an LU corresponding to a semantic label can be used as a "template" for elaborating entries of LUs carrying this label. As an illustration, consider a fragment of the cooccurrence zone in the dictionary entry of the semantic label process $_{(N)}$ 1 – that is, the lexeme PROCESS$_{(N)}$1 (No. 15 in *Table 8.3*).

Table 8.4 Some lexical functions of the semantic label process $_{(N)}$ 1

$A_{1\text{-actual}}$	⌜*under way*⌝
Oper$_1$	*undergo* [ART ~]
Func$_0$	*be* ⌜*under way*⌝
IncepFunc$_0$	*start*$_{(V, intransitive)}$
ContFunc$_0$	*continue,* ⌜*go on*⌝
FinFunc$_0$	*cease, come to an end*
LiquFunc$_0$	*interrupt, stop* [ART ~]

This data can be reused in the entries for the instances of process $_{(N)}$ 1 – such as OXIDATION (*oxidation of metals*), FERMENTATION (*fermentation of wine*), OSSIFICATION (*ossification of ligaments*), and LIQUEFACTION (*liquefaction of gases*), which are very likely to have not only the same lexical functions but also identical values for these functions. (However, since the inheritance of lexical properties is never completely automatic, it is necessary for a lexicographer to check whether the values of lexical functions applied to an instance of the label do indeed correspond to those applied to the label.)

1.2.3.2 Semantic Labels and "Pseudo-Definitions"

A global characterization of the meaning of an LU L by means of a semantic label taken together with the semantic "typing" of L's actants constitutes a compact, albeit approximate, lexical description that can be termed pseudo-definition; cf. the pseudo-definition of RESPECT$_{(N)}$**I**:

> `favorable emotional attitude:` person X's respect for person Y because of `qualities/actions` Z(Y)

Without being genuine definitions, such descriptions nevertheless provide good identification of LUs; namely, they can differentiate the LUs within a vocable. As an illustration, here are the pseudo-definitions of five lexemes belonging to the vocable LEARN (the distinctive numbers are ours).

(1) a. LEARN**I.1** 'find out'
[*He learned about the indictment from his lawyer ⟨from the newspapers⟩.*]
`event:` person X learns `information` Y (from `person` or `text` Z)

  b. LEARN**I.2** 'understand'
[*I have learned this the hard way. | Will they ever learn?*]
`process:` person X learns `fact` Y (from `fact` Z)

  c. LEARN**II.1** 'memorize'
[*Learn your math lesson ⟨the poem, the lines⟩!*]
`activity:` person X learns `text` Y

  d. LEARN**II.2** 'acquire [a skill]'
[*I learned how to write all by myself. | Learn how to run from coach Travis.*]
`activity:` person X learns a `skill` Y (from `person` Z)

  e. LEARN**II.3** 'acquire [knowledge of]'
[*He learned Spanish from Pablo ⟨from an old textbook⟩.*]
`activity:` person X learns `information` Y (from `person` or `text` Z)

As we can see, each LU L is uniquely identified, either by the global semantic label attributed to it (examples (1a) vs. (1b) vs. (1c–e)) or by the labels attributed to L's actants, if its global label and that of another lexeme of the vocable coincide (examples (1c) vs. (1d) vs. (1e)).

1.2.3.3 Semantic Labels and Lexicalization

Semantic labels are also convenient for specifying conditions for the choice of the surface means that will be used to implement the actants of LUs. For instance, consider the government of the lexeme BUY$_{(V)}$**III** (≈ 'bribe') in the following examples:

(2) a. *He understood that sometimes loyalty had to be bought **by** ⟨*for⟩ favors$_Z$ and presents.*

  b. *I$_X$ could've bought his loyalty$_Y$ **for** ⟨*by⟩ 200 dollars$_Z$ but missed the date.*

Z, the SemA **3** of BUY$_{(V)}$**III**, is implemented by a prepositional phrase *by* N if N denotes an `action` of X (SemA **1**); otherwise, Z is implemented by a prepositional phrase *for* (NUM) N.

We will now move on to the notion of semantic field.

1.3   Semantic Fields

> **Definition 8.4:** Semantic Field
> A semantic field $\mathbf{F}_{'\sigma'}^{sem}$ is the set of LUs whose definitions share a semantic bridge 'σ' and are, for this reason, perceived as belonging to the same semantic "family."

The semantic bridge 'σ', shared by all LUs of a semantic field, is called the semantic field identifier [SFI]. An SFI is either the generic (= central) component in the definitions of the LUs of the field or is linked to the generic component by a more or less regular semantic link: the SFI 'σ' can be a Sem-actant of the generic component in the definition of an LU belonging to the given $\mathbf{F}_{'\sigma'}^{sem}$, or a constraint on an actant, or underlie an institutionalized lexical relation (which corresponds to an LF), such as 'begin/continue/cease' [`Incep/Cont/Fin`], 'designed to ...' [`Real`], 'sound produced by ...' [`Son`], etc.

> **NB:** Following Definition 8.4, a semantic field $\mathbf{F}_{'\sigma'}^{sem}$ includes the corresponding semantic class of LUs – {L$_i$('σ'') | 'σ'' ⊃ 'σ'}.

Thus, the semantic field of sleeping $\mathbf{F}_{'sleep'}^{sem}$, includes all the LUs whose generic component is 'sleep$_{(V)}$' – that is, all the LUs that belong to the semantic class `sleep`$_{(V)/(N)}$ (DOZE, ⌜DOZE OFF⌝, ⌜DROP OFF⌝, NAP$_{(V)}$, SNOOZE$_{(V)}$, SLUMBER$_{(V)}$, ...) – and also many LUs whose generic component is not 'sleep', but which have the component 'sleep' elsewhere in their definitions, as in the following examples (the generic component is in caps and the SFI is in boldface):

⌜WAKE UP⌝**1**	'X CEASES to **sleep**'
BED$_{(N)}$**1**	'MANUFACTURED OBJECT designed for X to **sleep** in'
SNORE**1**	'X, who is **sleeping**, PRODUCES NOISE with X's mouth and nose'
SLEEPY	'[X] who FEELS THE NEED to **sleep**'
ALARM CLOCK	'CLOCK designed to make an alert sound at a set moment in order to ⌜wake up⌝**2** X [= 'to cause**1** that X ceases to **sleep**']'

The definitions of members of the same semantic field do not have the same structure; still they may show certain parallelisms. For instance, all these LUs appear in the lexical relations zone of the dictionary entry of the LU corresponding to their SFI – in this case, SLEEP $_{(V)/(N)}$.

As follows from Definition 8.4 (and can be seen from the examples above), a semantic field can contain LUs of different parts of speech; at the same time, an LU can belong to several semantic fields. Thus, the lexemes $\text{SWIM}_{(V)/(N)}$ belong to $\mathbf{F}^{\text{sem}}_{\text{'moving'}}$ (together with WALK, RUN, CRAWL, FLY, RIDE, DRIVE, etc.), $\mathbf{F}^{\text{sem}}_{\text{'sports \& recreation'}}$ (with JOG, WORKOUT, GYM, $\text{BIKE}_{(N)/(V)}$, $\text{TRAIL}_{(N)}$, etc.) and $\mathbf{F}^{\text{sem}}_{\text{'beach'}}$ (with SEASIDE, $\text{BATHE}_{(V)}$, NUDIST, LIFEGUARD, 'SWIM SUIT', SUNSHADE, TANNED, etc.). This is due to the fact that semantic fields are created in a rather flexible way, according to the specific needs of the Speaker or the researcher.

A description of LUs done by semantic fields highlights their semantic similarities and helps achieve a degree of descriptive coherence much higher than would be possible if the choice of LUs to describe were arbitrary (according to alphabetical order, for instance).

1.4   Lexical Fields

Definition 8.5: Lexical Field

A lexical field $\mathbf{F}^{\text{lex}}_{\sigma'}$ is the set of all vocables whose basic LUs belong to the same semantic field $\mathbf{F}^{\text{sem}}_{\sigma'}$.

For example, the lexical field $\mathbf{F}^{\text{lex}}_{\text{'bodyparts'}}$ includes the following vocables: $\text{HEAD}_{(N)}$, $\text{ARM}_{(N)}$, $\text{LEG}_{(N)}$, $\text{BELLY}_{(N)}$, $\text{BACK}_{(N)}$, etc. – that is, among others, it contains "indirectly" such lexemes as HEAD**II** [*of a party*] and [*research*] ARM**IV** [*of a company*]. Or, to take another example, the lexical field $\mathbf{F}^{\text{lex}}_{\text{'weather'}}$ is made up of the vocables WEATHER, $\text{RAIN}_{(N)/(V)}$, $\text{SNOW}_{(N)/(V)}$, $\text{STORM}_{(N)}$, CLOUDY, $\text{FORECAST}_{(N)}$, etc., but, in addition to the basic, weather-event denoting lexemes, it contains such lexemes as $\text{RAIN}_{(N)}$**II** [*of bullets*], $\text{SNOW}_{(N)}$ **II** 'cocaine', [*political*] STORM**II**, STORMY**II** [*relationship*], CLOUDY**II** [*memories*], and so on.

In a dictionary, all the vocables within a given lexical field need to be described in a uniform way; see the Uniform Treatment Principle, Subsection *2.1.2* below.

1.5   Vocables, Semantic Classes, Semantic Fields and Lexical Fields Compared

In summary, we will compare the four groupings of LUs within the lexical stock discussed in this section.

The "vertical" grouping of LUs into vocables cuts across the two "horizontal" ones: different LUs from the same vocable normally do not belong to the same semantic class or the same semantic field. And lexical fields represent a mixture where "vertical" and "horizontal" groupings are superimposed.

LUs belonging to the same semantic class are necessarily of the same part of speech and no LU can belong to more than one semantic class. In sharp

Table 8.5 Vocables vs. semantic classes vs. semantic fields vs. lexical fields

VOCABLES				SEMANTIC CLASS	SEMANTIC FIELD
HAND, noun	ARM, noun	LEG¹, noun	BACK, noun		
HAND_(N)I 'body.part'	ARM_(N)I.1a 'body.part'	LEG¹_(N)I.1a 'body.part'	BACK_(N)I.1a 'body.part'	body part	'human body'
	ARM_(N)I.3 'of a chair'	LEG¹_(N)I.2 'of a chair'	BACK_(N)I.3 'of a chair'	part of furniture	'furniture'; 'interior design'
HAND_(N)III 'help'				action	'human relations'; 'help/assistance'
	ARM_(N)I.2 'of a vest'	LEG¹_(N)I.3 'of trousers'	BACK_(N)I.2 'of a vest'	part of clothing	'clothing'; 'fashion'
HAND_(N)II 'of a clock'	ARM_(N)II 'of a crane'			part of device; part of machine	'household'; 'construction'
			BACK_(N)II 'a defending player'	sports player	'sports & recreation'

LEXICAL FIELD "BODY PARTS"

contrast, LUs belonging to the same semantic field can be of different parts of speech, and an LU can simultaneously belong to several semantic fields. Thus, the verb SWIM$_{(V)}$**1** belongs, as indicated above (*1.3*), to at least three semantic fields: $F^{sem}_{'moving'}$, $F^{sem}_{'sports \& recreation'}$ and $F^{sem}_{'beach'}$.

- A semantic class 'L' is defined "objectively," as the set of all LUs {L$_i$} whose definitions include 'L' as (part of) the generic component.
- A semantic field $F^{sem}_{'L'}$ is vaguer and more "subjective"; it is the set of all LUs {L$_j$} that the researcher has decided to consider in parallel and whose definitions include 'L' in a sufficiently prominent, but not necessarily central, position.
- A lexical field $F^{lex}_{'L'}$ is the "loosest" grouping; it consists of all vocables whose basic LUs belong to the same semantic field.

 An LU cannot be an element of a lexical field, since a lexical field is a set of vocables rather than of LUs.

Table 8.5 recapitulates and illustrates the relation between the four modes of organization of the lexical stock.

2   A Model of the Lexical Stock: The *Explanatory Combinatorial Dictionary* (ECD)

In the Meaning-Text approach, the lexical stock of a language is described by means of a dictionary of a special type, called the *Explanatory Combinatorial Dictionary* (ECD). We have already mentioned this dictionary on several occasions, insisting on its crucial role within our model of linguistic synthesis, in particular in the semantic-to-syntax transition. The time has now come to consider it in a more detailed way: first, the general characteristics of an ECD are presented (*2.1*), followed by a description of its microstructure, i.e., the organization of an individual entry, which describes a lexical unit (*2.2*), and, finally, that of its macrostructure, i.e., the organization of entries into superentries, each describing a vocable (*2.3*).

Table 8.6 shows the correspondences of terms designating the basis units of description as used in lexicology and lexicography:

Table 8.6 Units of lexical stock and corresponding dictionary units

	Lexicological perspective	Lexicographic perspective
Microstructure	**lexical unit**	**dictionary entry**
Macrostructure	**vocable**	**dictionary superentry**

2.1   General Characterization of the ECD

This subsection presents the main features of the ECD (*2.1.1*) and the most important principles according to which an ECD is compiled (*2.1.2*).

    The expression "**the** ECD" (with a definite article) stands for the corresponding dictionary type, i.e., any ECD compiled in accordance with the underlying linguistic theory; "**the/an** ECD of language **L**" (with a definite or an indefinite article) stands for a particular ECD, as in *The 4th volume of the French ECD has been published.* | *Is there an ECD for Swahili yet?*

2.1.1   Main Features of the ECD

The *Explanatory Combinatorial Dictionary* is a theoretical dictionary, anchored in a linguistic theory – namely, Meaning-Text theory – and making use of its conceptual tools. More specifically, the ECD is compiled in compliance with the methodological principles of the MTT's lexicological branch, called Explanatory Combinatorial Lexicology. The ECD is, above all, a research tool, providing a standardized framework for the description of the lexical stock of any language.[4]

The ECD has the following three general characteristics.

1. It is an **active dictionary**, oriented towards speech production: the main question it is supposed to answer is *How can this meaning be expressed in this language?*, rather than *What is the meaning of this expression?* In other words, an ECD should enable its user to find all appropriate lexical means to express any intended meaning; it is thus geared to reformulation, or paraphrasing (Ch. 9, *2.1* & Ch. 12, *2*). Since the active orientation of the ECD means that it pays special attention to the semantic and combinatorial properties of LUs, the remaining two characteristics follow naturally from the first.

2. It is a **semantic** (= explanatory) **dictionary**: the definition of an LU L, i.e., a description of L's meaning, is elaborated according to a set of strict conditions which guarantee its coherence (Ch. 5, *2* & *4*). L's definition underlies

---

[4]   As of the time of writing (2019), there are two published ECDs: a Russian ECD (1984 [2nd corrected edition: 2016]; around 300 vocables) and a French ECD (1984–1999; 4 volumes, some 500 vocables), both embodying the "classical" ECD version. In addition, there is a series of pedagogically oriented dictionaries, such as *Lexique actif de français* [LAF] (2007) and *Diccionario de colocaciones en español* [DiCE] (2004), characterized by relaxed lexicographic formalisms adapted to specific learners' needs; for pointers to some of these, see Further Reading. So far, only fragments of an English ECD have been elaborated in individual lexicological projects or as part of scientific articles, as well as a fragment of a bilingual French–English ECD. See Further Reading.

the description of all other features of L – in other words, all other information elements contained in L's entry conform to the definition (for a concrete illustration of this state of affairs, see *2.1.2* below). As a result, ECD definitions must be more precise than those of conventional dictionaries.

3. It is a **combinatorial dictionary**: for each LU L listed, the ECD describes its syntactic cooccurrence (its Government Pattern) and its restricted lexical cooccurrence (semantic derivations and collocations) in a systematic way. Thus, the correspondence between L's semantic and deep-syntactic actants is explicitly indicated, as well as their possible surface expressions; this is something conventional dictionaries rarely attempt to do. Also, L's derivatives and collocates are not only listed or implicitly illustrated through examples of L's use, as they are in a conventional dictionary, but each is supplied with a mini-definition (see *2.2* below).

2.1.2   Principles for Compiling an ECD

In order to provide a rigorous and coherent description of the lexical stock of the language under study, ECD lexicographers observe a number of principles, of which we present the following: the Formality Principle, the Descriptive Coherence Principles, the Uniform Treatment Principles and the Internal Exhaustiveness Principle.

2.1.2.1   The Formality Principle

This principle can be formulated as follows.

> **Formality Principle**
> A description of each LU must be formal, that is:
> 1. written in a pre-established formal language, and
> 2. explicit – not leaving anything to be guessed at by the user.

Lexicographic metalanguages

The ECD makes use of several specialized formal languages which cover different aspects of the lexicographic description of an LU L. Thus, L's semantic description, i.e., the definition, is formulated in a pre-established defining language (Ch. 5, *1*), its syntactic active valence is described by means of the Government Pattern formalism (Subsection *2.2.1.2* below), and its lexical relations – in terms of lexical functions (Ch. 7).

Full explicitness

As for the explicitness requirement, the definition of an LU L should spell out all semantic properties of L so as to allow the user to infer (rather than guess at) its correct uses. Thus, an ECD-style definition of the noun HUNGER (*The feeling of hunger is different for everybody.*) must explicitly account for the uses of this lexeme illustrated in (3a) and the semantic links it entertains with the expressions in (3b):

(3) a.   ***My stomach is growling*** ⟨≡ ***rumbling*⟩ *with hunger*.** | ***Weak with hunger****, she staggered up to the cabin door.* | *Do you start getting **hunger pangs** at 11:50 in anticipation of lunch?*

  b.   *You cannot work properly on an **empty stomach*** '…while you feel hunger'. | *The poor man wants to **eat his fill*** '…eat until his hunger is satisfied'. | *I **was dying for some food*** 'I was feeling hunger intensely – ⌐as if⌐ I were going to die from it'.

Such a definition could look like this (the components of the definition providing the link with the expressions in (3) are boldfaced):

> *X's hunger*: X's **feeling** of **emptiness** in X's **stomach** caused1 by the **need** of X's body for **nutrients**, such that (a) X must **satisfy** it by **eating** something and (b) if not satisfied, this need may cause1 X's **discomfort or death**.

For comparison, here are the definitions of HUNGER from three English dictionaries, each failing to account, to a different extent, for the data in (3):

> [LDOCE]   the **feeling** that you **need** to **eat**
> [MWLD]   an **uncomfortable feeling** in your **stomach** that is caused by the **need for food**
> [OED]   a **feeling of discomfort or weakness** caused by **lack of food**, coupled with **a desire to eat**

2.1.2.2   Descriptive Coherence Principles

There are two aspects to descriptive coherence: internal coherence – that is, coherence inside an LU L's lexicographic entry; and external coherence – that is, coherence at the level of the semantic class/field to which L belongs. These two types of coherence are to be achieved by upholding the next two lexicographic principles.

> **Lexical Unit Internal Coherence Principle**
> Descriptions of different properties of an LU L must be completely harmonized: L's semantic, syntactic and lexical cooccurrence data must be treated in parallel, highlighting their interrelatedness.

For instance, if L cooccurs with intensifiers, its definition must contain a component (or components) that can accept intensification. Thus, the lexeme EVIDENCE$_{(N)}$**1**, illustrated in (4a–b), accepts the intensifying adjectives listed in (4c):

(4) a. *The emergency constitutes **ample evidence** that the city needs backup water sources.*

   b. *The publicity encountered in the lay press is **clear evidence** of public concern.*

   c. *ample, overwhelming; clear, unambiguous; compelling, convincing*

The adjectives *ample* and *overwhelming* bear upon the quantitative side of evidence: they are elements of the value of the LF $\text{Magn}^{\text{quant}}$. The other intensifiers target the qualitative aspect of the evidence and are elements of the value of the LF Magn. Therefore, the ECD-style definition of $\text{EVIDENCE}_{(N)}\mathbf{1}$ looks as follows (semantemes targeted by intensifier LFs are shaded; the corresponding LF is given as the subscript):

$$\text{`X, evidence}_{(N)}\mathbf{1} \text{ that/that not Y'} = \text{`facts and/or entities X}_{\text{Magn}^{\text{quant}}} \text{ that show}_{\text{Magn}}$$
$$\text{that Y is/is not the case'.}$$

Facts and entities can be numerous, so that the component 'facts and/or entities X' accepts $\text{Magn}^{\text{quant}}$; something can be shown more or less clearly and be more or less compelling (Magn). In this way, L's definition is "tuned" to L's restricted lexical cooccurrence.

Since the central component of its definition denotes a plurality of facts and/or entities, the lexeme $\text{EVIDENCE}_{(N)}\mathbf{1}$ cannot be pluralized (**evidences*), and to "singularize" it a special singulative is needed (specified by means of the LF Sing): ***a piece of** [evidence]*; thus, the definition also agrees with the morphological properties of the noun $\text{EVIDENCE}_{(N)}\mathbf{1}$.

Finally, the definition and syntactic cooccurrence of an LU need to be in harmony as well – and the disjunction in the above definition ['that Y **is or is not** the case'] accounts for the following two realizations of the SemA Y of $\text{EVIDENCE}_{(N)}\mathbf{1}$:

Y is the case: *evidence that* V_{FIN}*, of* ⟨*for, pointing to*⟩ *N*
                      (*evidence **that** aliens **exist**; evidence **of** ⟨**for**⟩ the **existence** of aliens*)

Y is not the case: *evidence that not* V_{FIN}*, against N*
                      (*evidence **that** aliens **do not exist**; evidence **against** the **existence** of aliens*)

> **Semantic Class Coherence Principle (= Lexical Inheritance)**
> An LU L's entry should be in agreement with the entry for L′ that expresses the central, or generic, component in L's definition.

Inheritance of L's SemAs and DSyntAs from the LU L′ corresponding to the central component of L's definition can be illustrated with the verb DECLARE (*Lord Aberdeen declared to Parliament that the system worked well.*). This is a communication verb – the central component of its definition is 'communicate'.

COMMUNICATE has three semantic actants and three deep-syntactic actants: 'X_I communicates that Y_{II} to Z_{III}'; consequently, DECLARE also has three SemAs and three DSyntAs:

$$\text{'}X_I \text{ declares that } Y_{II} \text{ to } Z_{III}\text{'} = \text{'}X_I \text{ officially and publicly communicates } Y_{II} \text{ to } Z_{III}\text{'}$$

Such inheritance is not absolute, but can be expected in a good number of cases.

The same is true for LFs; see *Table 8.4*, Subsection *1.2.3* above, for examples of LFs inherited by an LU L from its generic component (≈ its semantic label).

2.1.2.3 Uniform Treatment Principles

Similarly to coherence principles, there are also two uniform treatment principles: uniform treatment of LUs within a semantic class/semantic field and uniform treatment of vocables within a lexical field.

> **Lexical Unit Uniform Treatment Priniciple**
> All LUs of the same semantic class/field must be described in a similar way – of course, "similar" to the degree allowed by their genuine lexical properties.

This principle seems obvious enough, and yet it is far from always observed. Examples: names of professions from LDOCE and ethnicity names from OED.

CARPENTER	someone whose job is making and repairing wooden objects
COOK$_{(N)}$1	someone who prepares and cooks food as their job
DOCTOR$_{(N)}$1	someone who is trained to treat people who are ill
GUARD$_{(N)}$1	someone whose job is to protect a place or person
MECHANIC	someone who is skilled at repairing motor vehicles and machinery
AMERICAN$_{(N)}$1	a native or citizen of the United States
CANADIAN$_{(N)}$	a native or inhabitant of Canada
CHINESE$_{(N)}$2	a native or inhabitant of China or a person of Chinese descent
FRENCH$_{(N)}$2	[as plural noun: *the French*] the people of France collectively

If applied systematically, the Lexical Unit Uniform Treatment Principle allows the lexicographer to create template entries for LUs belonging to the same semantic class/field and make important generalizations concerning their combinatorial properties.

The template entries for profession and ethnicity denoting nouns could look like this:

[*the*] L$_{\text{PLnationality name}}$: 'ETHNICITY native of [country/region] whose mother tongue is [language]'

L$_{\text{profession}}$: 'PERSON1 whose PROFESSION1 is to [...]'

Here are two individual entries elaborated according to the nationality names template:

[*the*] ENGLISH: 'ETHNICITY native of England whose mother tongue is English'

[*the*] CHINESE: 'ETHNICITY native of China whose mother tongue is Chinese'

A template will not fit each member of the class, so that modifications will be required in specific cases; for example, the following ethnicity names, among others, have a different definition structure:

[the] SWISS	citizens of Switzerland
[the] AMERICANS	citizens of the USA
[the] BRITISH	citizens of the United Kingdom
[the] WELSH	ethnicity native of Wales whose ancestral language is Welsh
[the] JEWS	ethnicity whose origin can be traced to the ancient Hebrew people

> **Vocable Uniform Treatment Priniciple**
> Two vocables belonging to the same lexical field should be presented according to the same schema: the related LUs of either vocable should be described in a parallel fashion with respect to the definition, ordering and the distinctive numbers assigned.

Thus, templates for superentries should be foreseen, as well.

2.1.2.4 Internal Exhaustiveness Principle

This last principle concerns the amount of data that is supposed to go into one lexical entry.

> **Internal Exhaustiveness Principle**
> The description of an LU L must contain **all** the information necessary to
> 1. use L correctly in any possible context
> and
> 2. find any other LU semantically related to L.

Two examples can illustrate this principle.

1. For an LU that denotes a sensation or a feeling, the lexical entry must supply interjections normally used to signal the corresponding sensation or feeling. Thus, for PAIN$_{(N)}$ and for HURT$_{(V)}$, an ECD will give *Ouch!* and *Ow!*, for AMAZEMENT, *Ha!* and *Whoa!*, and for RELIEF, *Phew!*
2. For an LU that denotes an animal, the lexical entry must supply the verb used to denote its cry – the LF Son:

Son(*crow*) = *caws*   Son(*duck*) = *quacks*   Son(*horse*) = *neighs*; *whinnies*

Son(*cat*) = *mews*, *meows*; Son(*elephant*) = *trumpets* Son(*mosquito*) = *whines*
         purrs

Son(*dog*) = *barks*; *howls* Son(*frog*) = *croaks*   Son(*sheep*) = *bleats*

The corresponding onomatopoeias should also be indicated: *hee-haw* for DONKEY, *cha-caw* for HEN, *cock-a-doodle-doo* for ROOSTER, *ribbit* for FROG, etc. More than that, the LF Son must be specified for all LUs whose denotations are supposed to produce a typical sound:

Son(*banknote*) = *rustles*   Son(*coins*) = *chink*   Son(*flag*) = *flaps*

Son(*bell*) = *tolls*   Son(*door*) = *creaks*; *slams* Son(*shot*) = ⌜*rings out*⌝

Son(*bullet*) = *buzzes*, *zings* Son(*fire*) = *crackles*   Son(wind) = *whispers*
                  < *whistles* < *howls* <*roars*

And what about external exhaustiveness? In principle, an exhaustive description of the entire lexical stock of a language is quite within reach; however, it is difficult for practical reasons: a lack of financial and other resources.

Let us now see what a lexical entry elaborated according to these principles looks like.

2.2   The ECD Lexical Entry

Each LU featured in an ECD possesses its own lexical entry; conversely, a lexical entry in an ECD describes one and only one LU, called the headword (of that entry). The latter appears in its lexicographic (= citation) form, which is the one that is least marked morphologically; in English, this is the infinitive for verbs, and the singular for nouns.

Lexemes and idioms are described in the same way, i.e., their entries contain the same type of lexicographic information, presented in the same format – with only one difference: an idiom has its SSynt-tree indicated, with additional data necessary for its implementation.

2.2.1   The Structure of an ECD Entry

An ECD entry consists of five zones; the first three zones correspond to the components of the linguistic sign and are logically necessary, while the remaining two are useful for pedagogical purposes.

1. The SEMANTIC ZONE, where the signified of the headword L is described; it
   contains three sub-zones:
   (a) L's definition
   (b) L's semantic label
   (c) L's connotations
2. The PHONOLOGICAL ZONE, which describes L's signifier (including prosody, where needed).
3. The COOCCURRENCE ZONE, where L's syntactics is described, with four
   sub-zones:
   (a) L's morphological cooccurrence (part of speech, conjugation or declen-
       sion class, defective paradigm, irregular forms, etc.)
   (b) L's stylistic cooccurrence, indicating situational contexts appropriate for
       the use of L (usage label, or register: **literary, colloquial, archaic, vulgar**, etc.)
   (c) L's syntactic cooccurrence:
       • Active valence syntactic cooccurrence, i.e., the types of actantial
         dependents that L can have, specified in L's Government Pattern.
       • Passive valence syntactic cooccurrence, i.e., the types of syntactic con-
         structions in which L can participate as a dependent member; this
         cooccurrence is specified by L's part of speech and its syntactic fea-
         tures: «temporal [noun]» (*He was absent for a **week**.*), «atelic [verb]»
         (*1.2.1*, Footnote 2), «postposed [adjective]» (*prince **charming***), etc.
   (d) L's restricted lexical cooccurrence, described in terms of lexical functions
4. The ILLUSTRATION ZONE, with examples of sentences illustrating typical uses
   of L.
5. The IDIOM ZONE, containing pointers towards idioms that include (the signifier of) L.

Below we will present the three core zones of an ECD entry: semantic, syntactic and lexical relations zones, illustrating them with fragments of different concrete entries. For illustrations of complete ECD entries, see Subsection
2.3.3 below.

2.2.2   The Semantic Zone

An entire chapter, Ch. 5, was dedicated to the lexicographic definitions and
lexicographic connotations of LUs. Here, we will simply quote the definitions
and connotations for two lexemes and one idiom.

BABY$_{(N)}$	(*a three-month-old baby*)
Definition	'a very young child1 who is unable to walk or speak'
Semantic Label	`child1`
Connotations	'helpless'; 'innocent'; 'open-minded'; 'unreasonable'

HOPE(N)   (*It is my hope that we will end up with a bipartisan solution.*)

X's hope that Y

Definition   'X's pleasant feeling(N)2 caused1 by X's thoughts about a
                        `fact` Y desirable for X, X believing that Y is likely to take
                        place'

Semantic Label `feeling`(N)`2`

Connotations   'optimism'

⌐PUT UP⌐(V)   (*I won't put up with this nonsense any longer!*)

X puts up with Y

Definition   'X accepts without complaining a situation or person Y that is
                        unpleasant for X'

Semantic Label `attitude`

Connotations   —

2.2.3   The Syntactic Cooccurrence Zone

The main part of the syntactic zone of a dictionary entry for an LU L corresponding to a semantic predicate or a quasi-predicate is dedicated to the description of L's active syntactic valence (Ch. 2, *1.3.3*, Definition 2.8) – the inventory of its deep- and surface-syntactic actants. More specifically, it is a description of the syntactic and morphological implementation of L's semantic actants by means of the formalism of Government Pattern (Ch. 2, *1.3.3*, Definition 2.10). To illustrate the concept, here is the Government Pattern (GP) of the verb BAKE**I.1a**, as in *Jane baked the apples* (*in the oven/over the coals*):

DIATHESIS	X ⇔ I	Y ⇔ II	Z ⇔ III
IMPLEMENTATION OF ACTANTS	1. –**subjectival**→N	1. –**direct-objectival**→N	1. –**oblique-objectival** →PREP$_{\text{LOC}}$ N

Figure 8.2 Government Pattern of the verb BAKE**I.1a**

In a GP, each semantic actant of the headword L is attributed a column. The heading of the GP indicates L's lexicographic (or basic) diathesis: the correspondence between its semantic actants (variables X, Y, Z, …) and its deep-syntactic actants (Roman numerals **I, II, III**, …). The latter represent, so to speak, generalizations over surface-syntactic dependents, since each deep-syntactic actant covers an entire family of surface-syntactic roles.[5]

Each line of a GP specifies a surface-syntactic construction and, when needed, morphological means (nominal case, verbal mode, etc.), which, together, express the deep-syntactic actant [DSyntA] in question. Thus:

- Square 1 of column I of the GP above (Square $C_{I.1}$) indicates that the DSyntA **I** of BAKE**I.1a** is the dependent member of the **subjectival** SSyntRel, i.e., the subject, implemented by a prepositionless noun or a pronoun in the nominative case (*I*, *he*, …):

  –subjectival→N.

- Square $C_{II.1}$ specifies that the DSyntA **II** of this lexeme is realized as a direct object, implemented by a prepositionless noun or a pronoun in the oblique case (*me*, *him*, …):

  –direct-objectival→N.

- Square $C_{III.1}$ indicates that the DSyntA **III** is realized as a prepositional phrase (= an oblique object) headed by a locative preposition.

  REMARK To save space, we do not always indicate SSyntRels in the GP; for instance, instead of **–subjectival**→N, we write simply "N," instead of **–direct-objectival**→*that* CLAUSE, we write "*that* CLAUSE," etc.

A GP can contain conditions which specify the admissible semantic type(s) of actants, on the one hand (e.g., this or that actant should/should not belong to a particular semantic class, etc.) and the expression of actants, on the other. In the latter case, conditions may concern either the expressibility of actants (expression of an actant is obligatory, impossible or optional) or their cooccurrence (simultaneous expression of two actants is obligatory, impossible or non-desirable). The GP in *Figure 8.2* does not contain conditions.

Additional illustrations

STOP**1a**, verb, transitive: 'person X stops doing action or activity Y'

Y ⇔ **I**	Y ⇔ **II**
1. **–subjectival**→N	1. **–direct-objectival**→V_{GER}

C_I + C_{II} : *My **father** stopped **smoking** years ago.*

---

[5] Thus, a DSyntA **I** can correspond, at the SSynt-level, to the subject of a finite verb [*The **President** arrived.*], a noun complement [*the arrival of the **President***]), an adjectival modifier of a noun [***presidential** arrival*], etc. A DSyntA **II** can correspond at the SSynt-level to a direct or indirect object of a verb [*like **the cinema**, listen **to the music***], a noun complement [*translation **of the Bible***]), etc. See Ch. 11, *2.4.*

SURE**1**, adjective: '[person X,] sure of fact Y'

$Y \Leftrightarrow \mathbf{II}$
1. **–oblique-objectival**→*of* N
2. **–oblique-objectival**→*that*-CLAUSE

$C_{II.1}$: N = S_0(Y)

C_{II} : *Mary is sure **of** her **success** ⟨**that** she **will** succeed⟩.*

NEGOTIATIONS$_{(pl!)}$, noun: 'negotiations of person X with person Y concerning Z'

$X \Leftrightarrow \mathbf{I}$	$Y \Leftrightarrow \mathbf{II}$	$Z \Leftrightarrow \mathbf{III}$
1. **–possessive**→N's	1. **–oblique-obj**→*with* N	1. **–oblique-obj**→*over* N
2. **–oblique-objectival**→*between* N_X *and* N_Y		2. **–oblique-obj**→*for* N
3. **–modificative**→$A_0(N_X)$-$A_0(N_Y)$		3. **–compositive**→N
4. **–determinative**→$A_{(poss)}(N_X + N_Y)$		

$C_I + C_{II}$: ***England's** negotiations with **France**; negotiations between **England** and **France**; **Anglo-French** negotiations; **their** negotiations*

C_{III} : *negotiations **over Falkland Islands** ⟨**for** a closer economic **partnership**⟩; **peace** negotiations*

$C_I + C_{II} + C_{III}$: ***England's peace** negotiations with **France**; negotiations between **England** and **France over Channel Islands***

CONDEMN**1**, verb, transitive: 'person X condemns person Y because of fact Z(Y)'

GP 1

$X \Leftrightarrow \mathbf{I}$	$Y \Leftrightarrow \mathbf{II}$	$Z \Leftrightarrow \mathbf{III}$
1. **–subj**→N	1. **–direct-obj**→N obligatory	1. **–oblique-obj**→*for* N

GP 2

$X \Leftrightarrow \mathbf{I}$	$Z \Leftrightarrow \mathbf{II}$
1. **–subj**→N	1. **–direct-obj**→N obligatory

$C_I + C_{II} + C_{III}$: ***We** condemn the **Government for** its flagrant **disregard** of human rights.*

$C_I + C_{II}$: ***We** condemn the Government's flagrant **disregard** of human rights.*

Figure 8.3 Government Patterns of four English lexemes

The GPs of the lexemes $SURE_{(ADJ)}\mathbf{1}$ and NEGOTIATIONS mention the lexical functions S_0 (deverbal noun) and A_0 (denominal adjective); see Ch. 7, *2.1.2*. The fact that lexical functions appear in GPs highlights the idiosyncratic nature of syntactic cooccurrence that this formalism describes.

The GP of CONDEMN**1** involves multiple lexicographic diatheses (or, more precisely, diathetic variants allowed for a single lexeme), which results in two distinct (but obviously paraphrastically related) GPs, noted **GP 1** and **GP 2**.

The Government Pattern reflects the interdependence of lexical and grammatical information in speech production, where a particular lexical choice determines the choice of possible syntactic constructions (the selected LU brings along its syntactic environment) and, conversely, the choice of a particular structure imposes certain lexical choices. Thus, we could say that the GP functions as a "bridge" between the lexical stock and the grammar.

2.2.4   The Lexical Relations Zone

Below we illustrate how semantic derivations, collocations and clichés are described in the entries of their keywords (bases in the case of derivations and collocations, anchors in the case of clichés, Ch. 4, *2.3*).

Semantic Derivations

They are described by means of standard and non-standard paradigmatic LFs (Ch. 7, *2.1* & *3*). For instance:

$ROB_{(V)}$, *X robs Y of Z*

S_0	: robbery
S_1	: robber
S_2	: victim (of robbery)
S_3	: booty; loot

$CONTEMPT_{(N)}$, *X's contempt for Y because of Z(Y)*

V_0	: despise
A_1	: contemptuous
$Able_2$	: contemptible
$[Magn+Able_2]$	: beneath [~]

Collocations

Collocations are described by means of standard and non-standard syntagmatic LFs, including complex LFs and LF configurations (Ch. 7, *2.2* & *3*). For instance:

$LOSSES_{(N)PL}$ 'dead, injured and captured in a military confrontation' [*X's losses in Z caused2 by Y*]

Magn	: grievous, heavy < devastating, huge, staggering
AntiMagn	: light, minor < insignificant
$Oper_1$	: suffer, take [~]
$Caus_2Func_1$	: inflict [~ (up)on N_X]

$SWEAT_{(N)}$ 'physiological liquid that …' [$X's$ sweat]

Sing	: bead [of ~]
$Real_1$	: //$sweat_{(V)}$
$IncepReal_1$	: **Brit** break [into a ~]
$[Magn+A_1Real_1]$	: drenched [in/with ~], dripping [with ~]
$[Magn+IncepReal_1]$	: ⌜break out⌝ [in ~]
$Fact_1$	: pours, runs, streams, trickles [down N_X's Ξ] | Ξ is a part of X's body

$REACTION_{(N)}$ 'psychological response that…' [Z, $X's$ reaction to Y]

automatic and immediate	: knee-jerk [~]
not immediate	: delayed [~]
very intuitive	: gut [~]
There is no reaction	: //⌜Nary a peep⌝

Clichés

Clichés are described by means of non-standard LFs.

 As indicated in Ch. 7, *3.3*, p. 182, the specification of an LF that corresponds to a cliché does not describe its meaning (since a cliché is semantically compositional); rather it gives the cliché's informational content, which is shown by putting the formulation of the LF between double quotes.

For instance:

$DISEASE_{(N)}$

«of the brain in old people, causing1 the loss of memory and other mental functions and eventually death»	: Alzheimer's
«of the brain in people, causing1 the loss of muscular coordination»	: Huntington's
«of the bowels in people, causing1 their inflammation»	: Crohn's

$BIRTHDAY_{(N)}$

«I wish you everything good in connection with your birthday»	: Happy birthday (to you)!

ITALICS$_{(N)}$

```
«It is me who uses the
italics in this quotation»
```
: Italics (are) mine. | Italics added. | Emphasis mine. | Emphasis added.

We now turn to the macrostructure of the ECD: its organization into super-entries, or, to put it differently, lumping certain entries together to form one superentry.

2.3   The ECD Lexical Superentry

As mentioned earlier, an ECD superentry describes a vocable, a set of LUs hav-ing phonologically identical signifiers and signifieds related by polysemy. One of the most important and most difficult lexicographic tasks is to determine how many different LUs there are in a vocable. This task, known as sense discrimi-nation, is normally accomplished in parallel with, rather than prior to, the actual description of the isolated LUs, by using the method of trial and error: more often than not, sketching a definition of a presumed LU of a vocable will reveal that it needs to be split into two LUs or, on the contrary, united with another one. At the same time, the LUs of the vocable are assigned distinctive lexicographic numbers, as a function of semantic distances between them (see below).

Sense-discrimination techniques underlying the ECD superentries are presented in Subsection *2.3.1*, and our system of lexicographic numbers, in Subsection *2.3.2*. We conclude with a detailed illustration of an ECD super-entry, in Subsection *2.3.3*.

2.3.1   Distinguishing Entries within a Superentry

Quite often, when presented with lexicographic data, the lexicographer has to determine whether he is dealing with two (or more) semantically related LUs, i.e., a case of polysemy, or with a single LU with a more general or disjunctive definition (Ch. 5, *3.2*), i.e., a case of semantic vagueness.[6] Consider, for exam-ple, the bolded wordforms in (5a), respectively (5b) and (5c): how many LUs should we postulate in each of these cases?

(5) a. *The soup **cooled** ['became cooler'], but it is still quite hot.*
         vs.
         *The soup **cooled** ['became cool'] completely.*
     b. *Alain **painted** the ceiling blue*
         'Alain covered the ceiling with blue paint'.
         vs.
         *Alain **painted** the ceiling with biblical scenes*
         'Alain covered the ceiling with artistic images of biblical scenes'.

---

[6] Another choice the lexicographer faces is that between polysemy and homonymy: are two (clearly distinct) lexical units semantically related or not? This question was briefly touched upon in Ch. 6, *1.3.2* and will not be revisited here.

c. *This is my **aunt** Dora, my father's sister.*
   vs.
   ***Aunt** Ann, my uncle's wife, is coming to visit.*

To help the lexicographer with sense discrimination, Explanatory Combinatorial Lexicology has come up with the following two criteria.

> **Criterion of Differentiating Lexicographic Information**
> If a perceived semantic difference between two uses of an LU is correlated with different syntactic, morphological and phonological behavior, then we are dealing with differentiating lexicographic information.

The presence of differentiating lexicographic information is an indication that a split of the lexical item under analysis into two (or more) LUs may be warranted. The ultimate decision (to split or not) will depend both on the quantity and the quality of differentiating information, but we cannot delve into this matter here.

For the two uses of $PAINT_{(V)}$ illustrated in (5b), there is differentiating lexicographic information. Thus, the Agent Name PAINTER – in our terms, $S_1(PAINT_{(V)})$ – shows different cooccurrences:

in case if 'paint' = 'cover with paint', there are *house painter* and *painter and decorator*;

in case if 'paint' = 'cover with artistic images', we have *landscape ⟨portrait⟩ painter* or *watercolor ⟨oil, …⟩ painter*.

This is a clear indication that it is necessary to split $PAINT_{(V)}$ into two lexemes.

> **Criterion of Unifying Cooccurrence**
> If two instances of use of the lexical item under scrutiny that exhibit apparent semantic differences can be coordinated without producing a zeugma effect, there should be no split, i.e., a single LU should be postulated. If there is a zeugma, then a split into two LUs is warranted.

Applied to our LUs in (5), these criteria give the following results:

$COOL_{(V, intrans)}$ *X cools*:   'X becomes cooler OR cool'
The mixture cooled first just a little, but in an hour completely: no zeugma.

$PAINT_{(V)}1$ *X paints Y*:   'X covers Y with paint'

$PAINT_{(V)}2$ *X paints Y*:   'X covers Y with artistic images'
**Alain painted the ceiling pink and with biblical scenes*: an obvious zeugma.

AUNT   *Y's aunt*:   'sister of X's father OR sister of X's mother OR wife of X's uncle'
My aunties, Father's sister Dora and Uncle Aaron's wife Ann, were good friends: no zeugma.

So, for COOL$_{(V)}$ and AUNT, there is no split – each is a single lexeme with a disjunctive definition, but PAINT gets split into two co-polysemous lexemes.

The disjunctive character of the definitions proposed for COOL$_{(V)}$ and AUNT is formally demonstrated by the application of the corresponding De Morgan rule (Ch. 5, *3.2* and Appendix, *5.1*):

'X did not cool'   = 'X did not become cooler AND X did not become cool'
'X is not Y's aunt' = 'X is not Y's father's sister, AND X is not Y's mother's
            sister, AND X is not Y's uncle's wife'

2.3.2   Ordering and Numbering Lexical Entries within a Superentry

The ordering and numbering of LUs belonging to the same vocable is done according to their semantic distances (Ch. 6, *1.3.1*: 154), measured in terms of the size and regularity of the semantic bridge(s) they share.

Three levels of semantic distance are distinguished, to which correspond three levels of numbering:

- Roman numerals (**I, II, III**, …) are used to mark the greatest semantic distances.
- Arabic numerals (**1, 2, 3**, …) mark less important distances.
- Lower-case letters (**a, b, c**, …) mark the minimal semantic distances.

By using the three levels of numbering, we can show that a larger grouping of LUs contains several smaller groupings. We can have, for instance, lexicographic number combinations such as **IV.1, IIa, I.2b**, etc., which allow for fine semantic distinctions between the LUs within a vocable.

> REMARK. While this three-degree system of lexicographic distinctions manages to show major semantic distances relatively accurately, it is not fine-grained enough to reflect them perfectly. And it is not meant to do so: the main indication of semantic closeness/remoteness are the components of the definitions of the LUs within a vocable.

Here are four simple rules for using the three-level lexicographic numbering.

1. Metaphoric LUs within one vocable are numbered by Roman numerals: ARM$_{(N)}$**I.1a** (*my arm*) vs. ARM$_{(N)}$**III** (*of a river*).
2. Metonymic LUs, semantically less distant from the basic LU than metaphoric LUs, are normally – but by no means always (see the vocable ARM$_{(N)}$, immediately below) – numbered by Arabic numerals and lower-case letters: LEG$_{(N)}$^{1}**I.1a** (*my leg*) vs. LEG^1**I.2** (*the left leg of my trousers*).
3. Very regular metonymic LUs, which are quite close semantically to the basic LU, are distinguished by lower-case letters: LEG^1**I.1b** (*pig's left hind leg*) vs. LEG^1**I.1c** (*roasted pork leg*) or GLASS$_{(N)}$**I.b** (*a broken wine glass*) vs. GLASS$_{(N)}$**I.2b** (*two glasses of wine*).

4. Non-figurative wordsenses are numbered, as a rule, also by Arabic numerals and lower-case letters: WOMAN**1a** 'adult female person' (*an interesting woman*) vs. WOMAN**1b** 'wife or girlfriend' (*My woman is gone* [Bob Marley].) vs. **obsolete** WOMAN**2** 'woman employed to do housework' (*How to hire a cleaning woman?*).

To illustrate the use of ECD lexicographic numbers, *Table 8.7* shows the superentry of the vocable $ARM_{(N)}$; semantic bridges are boxed.

Table 8.7 Superentry of the vocable $ARM_{(N)}$

$\mathbf{ARM_{(N)}}$		
I.1a	body part	(*A broken **arm** is usually caused by a fall onto an outstretched **arm**.*)
	'arms of a person X' =	'organ of X's physical actions – two lateral long upper parts of person X's body, mobile and articulated at the end'.
I.1b	body part	(*The chimp folded his **arm** a little.*)
	'arms of an ape /a monkey X' =	'organ of X's physical actions – two lateral and long upper parts of ape X's body, similar in form and function to human arms**I.1a**'.
I.1c	body part	(*The ring of eight limbs around the mouth in squids and octopuses are called **arms**.*)
	'arms of an aquatic animal X' =	'organ of X's physical actions – long upper parts of an aquatic animal X's body, similar in function to human arms**I.1a**'.
I.2	part of clothing	(*The pocket stitched in the **arm** of my jacket managed to rip with very little wear and tear.*)
	'arm of a piece of clothing X' =	'a part of a piece of clothing X designed for a person to wear on that person's upper body, this part covering that person's arms**I.1a**'.
I.3	part of manufactured object	(*An **arm** of the chair has a tear where a dog ripped it.*)
	'arm of a manufactured object X' =	'a part of a manufactured object X designed for a person to sit on, this part designed for that person to place that person's arms**I.1a** on'.
II	part of device/machine	(*An **arm** is attached to one of the sides of the capsule container.*)
	'arm of a device/machine X' =	'long, mobile part of a device/machine X designed for X to perform physical actions with – 'as if' it were an arm**I.1a** of a person'.

III	part of ⌐body of water⌐	(*We row on the picturesque North West **Arm** of the Halifax Harbor.*)
	'arm of a ⌐body of water⌐ X' =	'a $\boxed{long}$ narrow part of a ⌐body of water⌐ X – $\boxed{⌐as\ if⌐\ it\ were\ an\ arm\mathbf{I.1a}\ of\ a\ person}$'.
IV	part of organization	(*Egypt court dissolves the political **arm** of Muslim Brotherhood.*)
	'arm Y of organization X' =	'$\boxed{part}$ of an organization X that deals with specific activity Y – $\boxed{⌐as\ if⌐\ X\ were\ an}$ $\boxed{arm\mathbf{I.1a}\ of\ a\ person\ performing\ a\ physical}$ $\boxed{action\ Y}$'.

The vocable $ARM_{(N)}$ contains eight lexemes, all of which denote a part of something (with other minor components shared by some lexemes). The basic lexeme is $ARM_{(N)}\mathbf{I.1a}$, denoting a human body part; four lexemes are linked to it by metonymy (Roman numeral **I**), and three by metaphor (Roman numerals **II**, **III** and **IV**). Within the metonymic LUs, two denote animal body parts corresponding to human arms in form and/or function (**I.1b** and **I.1c**) and two denote manufactured objects designed for coming in physical contact with human arms (**I.2** and **I.3**). Each of these LUs completely includes the meaning of $ARM\mathbf{I.1a}$. The first metaphoric LU (**II**) denotes manufactured objects whose function is similar to that of a human arm; it partially includes the meaning of $ARM\mathbf{I.1a}$. The remaining metaphoric LUs denote parts of entities, the first one resembling human arms physically (**III**), and the second functionally (**IV**). Each metaphoric lexeme includes the meaning of $ARM\mathbf{I.1a}$ within the configuration ' – ⌐as if⌐ it were …', standardly used to indicate metaphoric links.

Table 8.8 Semantic bridges between the lexemes of the vocable $ARM_{(N)}$

$ARM_{(N)}$ **I.1a**	$\Rightarrow ARM_{(N)}\mathbf{I.1b}$	'part … similar in form and function to human $\boxed{arms_{(N)}\mathbf{I.1a}}$'
	$\Rightarrow ARM_{(N)}\mathbf{I.1c}$	'part … similar in function to human $\boxed{arms_{(N)}\mathbf{I.1a}}$'
	$\Rightarrow ARM_{(N)}\mathbf{I.2}$	'part … designed to cover a person's $\boxed{arm_{(N)}\mathbf{I.1a}}$'
	$\Rightarrow ARM_{(N)}\mathbf{I.3}$	'part … designed for X to place X's $\boxed{arm_{(N)}\mathbf{I.1a}}$ on'
	$\Rightarrow ARM_{(N)}\mathbf{II}$	'part … designed for X to perform physical actions with – ⌐as if⌐ it were an $\boxed{arm_{(N)}\mathbf{I.1a}}$ of a person'
	$\Rightarrow ARM_{(N)}\mathbf{III}$	'part … – ⌐as if⌐ it were an $\boxed{arm_{(N)}\mathbf{I.1a}}$ of a person'
	$\Rightarrow ARM_{(N)}\mathbf{IV}$	'part … – ⌐as if⌐ it were an $\boxed{arm_{(N)}\mathbf{I.1a}}$ of a person performing a physical action'

This is a case of radial polysemy (Ch. 6, *1.3.1.1*), as all the lexemes of the vocable have semantic bridges with the basic lexeme.

2.3.3   Three Superentries from an English ECD

We cite below the superentries for the vocables $COMPLIMENT_{(N)}$, $COMPLIMENT_{(V)}$ and ⌐RETURN THE COMPLIMENT⌐$_{(V)}$, the last two each consisting of a single LU. Due to lack of space, only a minimum of explanations is given as to the constitution and/or the content of these superentries.

COMPLIMENT$_{(N)}$, noun

I.   Statement by which X compliments Y …
II.   Fact Z that tends to cause**1** people's positive opinion of Y …
IIIa. The Speaker X's praise addressed to Y …
IIIb. The Speaker X's ⌐good wishes⌐ to Y …

COMPLIMENT$_{(N)}$**I**, countable

Definition

X's compliment to Y for Z(Y): Statement by which X compliments Y for Z(Y)
$$[= S_{instr}(COMPLIMENT_{(V)})].$$

Semantic Label

`verbal communication of an attitude`

Government Pattern

X ⇔ **I**	Y ⇔ **II**	Z ⇔ **III**	
1. N's	1. *to* N	1. *for*	N/V$_{GERUND}$
2. *from* N	2. *for* N	2. *on*	N
		3. *on*	WH-CLAUSE

$C_{II.2} + C_{III.1}$	: **impossible**
$C_I + C_{II}$	: *Her first compliment for ⟨to⟩ me was, "I like the color of your car."*
$C_I + C_{III}$	: *Luis Manzano's compliment on her looks ⟨on how she looked during the Star Magic Ball⟩*
$C_I + C_{II} + C_{III}$	: *Chef's compliment to the pair of diners for using their knife and fork correctly*

Impossible   : **his compliment for me for my new blouse*

Lexical Functions

Syn$_\subset$	: praise$_{(N)}$
Syn$_\cap$	: flattering remark; commendation; flattery
Anti$_\cap$	: ⌐backhanded ⟨left-handed⟩ compliment⌐ (*Oh, you are quite competent for someone so inexperienced!*); insult; slight; criticism
A$_0$	: complimentary[1] (*John's complimentary remark*)
V$_0$	: compliment$_{(V)}$
Adv$_2$	: at [ART ~] (*Mrs. Felson seemed to melt at his compliment.*)
person-S$_{1\cap}$	: sweet-talker

Magn	: big, great < enormous, high, huge
AntiMagn	: small
Ver_1	: sincere
$Ver_{2/3}$	: well-deserved
AntiVer	: hollow
Bon	: fine, kind, nice, pretty
AntiBon	: awkward; doubtful, dubious
$Oper_1$	: give, make, pay, present [N_Y ART ~]; bestow [ART ~ on N_Y]
[$Magn^{quant}$ + $Oper_1$]	: lavish, shower [~s on N_Y] | C. in pl
$Oper_2$	: get, receive, take [ART ~]
$Caus_{(2)}Func_2$	: draw [ART ~] (*I could show you more effective ways to draw a compliment from your husband.* | *This perfume is sure to draw compliments each time it is worn.*)
$try.Caus_2Func_2$	: fish [for ~s] | C. in pl
[$Magn^{quant}$ + $Labor_{12}$]	: lavish, shower [N_Y with ~s] | C. in pl
$Real_2^I$	: accept [ART ~]
$Real_2^{II}$	: return [the ~] ['pay a C. as a reaction to a received C.']

◊ ⌜return the compliment⌝

Examples

If people are enjoying their stay in the country, the usual comment is a compliment on the country's beauty or its delicacies. | *With such a compliment from Mr. Perfectionist himself, what else do you need?* | *Tedious waste of time to sit and hear so many hollow compliments and lies.* | *I got three compliments on my perfume.* | *Make sure to lavish him with compliments for his service!* | *I am compelled to present you my compliments on your work.*

COMPLIMENT$_{(N)}$**II**, sg only

Definition

[Z,] X's compliment to Y: [Z,] X's action or a fact caused2 by X that tends to cause1 people's positive opinion of Y – ⌜as if⌝ Z were X's compliment**I** to Y.

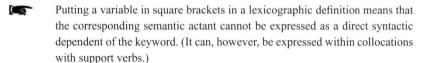   Putting a variable in square brackets in a lexicographic definition means that the corresponding semantic actant cannot be expressed as a direct syntactic dependent of the keyword. (It can, however, be expressed within collocations with support verbs.)

Semantic Label

`action/behavior expressing an attitude`

Government Pattern

X ⇔ I	Y ⇔ II	Z ⇔ III
1. N's 2. *from* N	1. *to* N	—

$C_I + C_{II}$: *That McCormick accepted the deal was his highest compliment ⟨the highest compliment from him⟩ to our team.*

Lexical Functions

Magn   : fine, great, high, huge
Pred   : $[N_Z]$ is [ART ~]
$Oper_1$: pay $[N_Y$ ART ~ by N_Z/by $V_{Z\text{-ING}}]$

Examples

Coming all the way to meet Mrs. Belafonte was a huge compliment the writer was paying her. | *When a patient falls asleep, it is a great compliment to a massage therapist.* | *Mandela paid Castro a huge compliment by visiting him in Havana after his release.* | *I was paid a high compliment when my writing was compared with his.* | *The nickname "Mad Dog" is a high compliment in Marine culture* [The phrase *the nickname "Mad Dog"* here is an ellipsis from 'giving someone the nickname...', so that it denotes an action – cf. the semantic label].

COMPLIMENT$_{(N)}$**IIIa**, pl only

Definition

X's compliments to Y on Z: The Speaker X's praise addressed to Y ⌐in connection with⌐ Z – ⌐as if⌐ they were X's compliments**I** to Y.

Semantic Label

`verbal communication of an attitude`

Government Pattern

X ⇔ I	Y ⇔ II	Z ⇔ III
1. N's 2. *from* N 3. *on behalf of* N	1. *to* N	1. *for* N/V$_{GERUND}$ 2. *on* N

Syntactic Constructions

Can be used performatively: *Compliments to the chef!*

Lexical Functions

$\text{Syn}_\cap$: congratulations

Oper_1 : give, send, transmit [N_X's ~s to N_Y]; extend [N_X's ~s to N_Y]; offer, express [N_X's ~s to N_Y]

Magn : best

Examples

Our compliments on the most entertaining cookbook ever! | *My compliments to Mr. Pradier for his excellent report.* | *This message is to express best compliments on behalf of my wife/myself on this motel.* | *Dad, our best compliments on the launch of your website.*

COMPLIMENT$_{(N)}$**IIIb**, pl only

Definition

X's compliments to Y on Z: The Speaker X's ⌐good wishes⌐ addressed to Y ⌐in connection with⌐ Z – ⌐as if⌐ they were X's complimentsI to Y.

Semantic Label

verbal communication of an attitude

Government Pattern

X $\Leftrightarrow$ I	Y $\Leftrightarrow$ II	Z $\Leftrightarrow$ III
1. *of* N	1. *to* N	1. N [~]
2. $A_{(poss)}$(N)		2. N's
		3. *of* N

If Z = 'Christmas' or 'New Year', then $C_{III} = C_{III.2} = $ *Season's* or $C_{III} = C_{III.3} = $ *of the Season*

C_I : *Our warmest compliments!*
C_{II} : *Best compliments to you!*
$C_I + C_{III}$: *With our holiday compliments.*
$C_I + C_{II} + C_{III}$: *Our New Year compliments to your parents!*

Syntactic Constructions

Can be used performatively: *My best compliments (to you)!*

Lexical Functions

Syn : ⌐good ⟨best, warmest⟩ wishes⌐

Oper_1 : give, send, transmit [N_X's ~s to N_Y]; extend [N_X's ~s to N_Y]; offer, express [N_X's ~s to N_Y]

Magn : best, warmest

X signals that X
Oper₁ C. to you   : **formal** With the ~s of N_X **[on something sent by X free of charge]**
                            [*With the compliments of Benjamins Publisher*]

I signal that I ask
you to Real₂ my C.   : Accept $[A_{(poss)}(N_X)$ ~s]!

Examples

Please give Professor Langston my compliments. | Please accept these tickets with our compliments. | Compliments of the season.

COMPLIMENT$_{(V)}$, transitive

Definition

X compliments Y on Z(Y): X praises Y for Z(Y) because X wants to please Y.

Semantic Label

communicate an attitude

Government Pattern 1

$X \Leftrightarrow I$	$Y \Leftrightarrow II$	$Z \Leftrightarrow III$	
1. N	1. N	1. *for*	N/V_{GERUND}
	obligatory	2. *on*	N

$C_I + C_{II} + C_{III}$: *Lafleur complimented our scouting team for bringing O'Kelly to his attention. | Not everyone likes to be complimented on his looks.*

Government Pattern 2

$X \Leftrightarrow I$	$Z \Leftrightarrow II$
1. N	1. N
	obligatory

$C_I + C_{II}$: *Lafleur complimented Lisa's hairstyle.*

GP 2 = Conv₁₃(GP 1)

[*Lafleur complimented Lisa's hairstyle.* ≡ *Lafleur complimented Lisa on her hairstyle.*]

Lexical Functions

Anti   : criticize; attack$_{(V)}$, insult$_{(V)}$
A₁   : complimentary[1]2 (*He was very complimentary on the work of the government.*)
S$_{instr}$: compliment$_{(N)}$I
Magn   : highly

Examples

When he complimented the girl on her dress, his friends laughed at him. | Sir Archibald Alison addressed the Riflemen, and complimented them on the soldier-like qualities they had shown in the field while under his orders. | They were highly complimented by the inspector.

⌜RETURN THE COMPLIMENT⌝, **verbal idiom, intransitive**

Definition

X returns Y the compliment: '⟦Y having acted/behaved towards Y in a way α,⟧ X acts/behaves towards Y in a way Z similar to α – ⌜as if⌝ α were Y's complimentⲒ to X and X were returning α with Z'

Semantic Label

`act/behave to express an attitude`

Government Pattern

X ⇔ I	Y ⇔ II	Z ⇔ III
1. N	1. N	1. *with* N
		2. (*by*) V_{GERUND}
		3. *and* CLAUSE

C_{II}: **rare**

$C_I + C_{II}$: *If they have done us wrong, we will return the compliment.*

$C_I + C_{III}$: *The rebels returned the compliment by shelling our position.*
      The rebels returned the compliment and shelled our position.

Surface-Syntactic Structure

RETURN–**dir-obj**→COMPLIMENT$_{SG}$–**determ**→THE

Lexical Functions

> Syn   : ⌜return the favor⌝
> Syn$_∩$: ⌜get even⌝
> Magn   : fully

Examples

I was the lucky recipient of this 'salute' and I duly returned the compliment with a flicked V and a barrage of choice expletives. | The batter was thrown out of the game so he returned the compliment by calling the umpire a fool. | They fired two or three more shots and I returned the compliment, wounding one of their horses. | Turchynov, Ukraine's interim president, has returned the compliment – and called Russian president Vladimir Putin a fascist. | Marx regarded them with withering contempt and they, in turn, to the extent that they knew him at all, returned the compliment.

We have now finished our presentation of lexical semantics. The next chapter takes on sentence-level semantics.

Further Reading

Lexical stock and its structure: Handke 1995; Lipka 2002: 148–186; Zareva 2007.

Semantic classes: Vendler 1957 and 1967: 122–146; Kiparsky & Kiparsky 1970; Malt *et al.* 1999; Hirst 2009; Polguère 2011 [in French; presents a hierarchy of semantic labels for French].

Semantic fields: Kittay 1987; [case studies] Fillmore & Atkins 1992; Wierzbicka 1994.

Lexicology & lexicography: [Explanatory Combinatorial Lexicology] Steele & Meyer 1990; Mel'čuk 2006b and 2013: 259–376; Apresjan 2008; [other frameworks] Landau [1984] 2001; Béjoint 2000; Atkins & Rundell 2008; Halliday & Yallop 2007; Fontenelle 2008.

Dictionaries & lexical databases/networks: [based on explanatory combinatorial lexicology] Russian ECD, Mel'čuk & Žolkovskij 1984 [2016]; French ECD, Mel'čuk *et al.* 1984–1988–1992–1999; *DiCo – Dictionnaire de combinatoire* http://olst.ling .umontreal.ca/dicouebe, cf. Polguère 2000a; DiCE – *Diccionario de colocaciones en español* www.dicesp.com, cf. Alonso Ramos 2004; *RLF–Réseau lexical du français*, www.atilf.fr, cf. Lux-Pogodalla & Polguère 2011; [other frameworks] Dictionary of English Speech Act Verbs, Wierzbicka 1987; WordNet https://wordnet.princeton.edu, cf. Miller *et al.* 1990; FrameNet, https://framenet.icsi.berkeley.edu, cf. Ruppenhofer *et al.* 2016.

Principles for compiling an ECD (Descriptive Coherence Principle): Iordanskaja & Polguère 2005.

Structure of an ECD lexical entry: Steele 1986; [Government Pattern] Mel'čuk 2015a: 108–154; L'Homme 2010.

9 Sentential Meaning and Meaning Relations between Sentences

So far, we have mainly been concerned with lexical meaning and semantic relations between lexical units [LUs]. In this chapter, we turn to sentential meaning and semantic relations holding between sentences, reserving a separate section for each of the two topics.

Differences between lexical and sentential meanings stem from a fundamental distinction between LUs and sentences:

> In any given language **L**, the set of LUs, although huge (about one million), is finite, but the set of **L**'s sentences is infinite.

Sentences of **L** are not stored in the brains of its speakers (they cannot be, because, as we have just said, their set is infinite): a normal sentence is constructed out of LUs according to the general rules of **L**.

> **NB:** A notable exception are phraseologized sentences – that is, sentential idioms (⌜*The cat is out of the bag*⌝, ⌜*The fat is in the fire*⌝, ⌜*The fur will fly*⌝, ⌜*The jig is up*⌝) and sentential clichés (*A stitch in time saves nine.* | *Better late than never.* | *What time is it?*). However, these sentences, although quite numerous (tens of thousands) constitute a finite set and represent a particular type of lexical entity.

228

At the same time, LUs of **L** (including, of course, phraseologized sentences) are stored in its speakers' brains. Because of this essential difference, sentential meanings are different from lexical meanings in at least the following three respects. Namely, for a normal sentence:

- Its meaning is compositional (on the notion of compositionality, see Ch. 2, *1.1.3* and Ch. 4, *2.2.1* & *2.2.2*). If it weren't for phraseologized sentences, we could say that a semantically non-compositional sentence is a contradiction in terms. In sharp contrast, the meaning of complex LUs is in most cases non-compositional – except for productive derivations, such as diminutives in Spanish and Italian, as well as in Slavic languages, which are in finite numbers.
- Its meaning can be ill-formed: a sentence can turn out to be semantically bizarre, illogical or outright absurd; this is impossible for an LU.
- Its meaning can correspond to a logical proposition (see *1.2* below & Appendix, *5.1*) and, therefore, it can be true or false in the real or an imaginary world – while no LU can.

As far as semantic sentential relations are concerned, in this book we only discuss semantics at the level of individual sentences, without taking into account discourse semantics (*Preface*, p. xviii). Therefore, only paradigmatic relations between sentences will be considered; their possible syntagmatic relations – rhetorical and anaphoric links they maintain within a text, as well as their textual organization, in particular, in terms of thematic progression – will be left aside.

Some of the paradigmatic semantic relations that hold between sentences are the same as those holding between LUs (Ch. 6, *1*). Thus, just like two LUs, two sentences can be related by synonymy, antonymy, conversion or equinomy ($\approx$ being ambiguous). This is only natural: after all, sentences are made up of LUs. However, there are also notable differences: thus, sentential synonymy and equinomy can also have syntactic, i.e., non-lexical, sources; unlike an LU being derived from another, a sentence cannot be derived from another sentence; nor do we speak about polysemous sentences.

Linguistic semantics must identify and describe sentential meaning properties and semantic relations between sentences; it must also ensure that these properties and relations are adequately reflected in formal representations of sentences. In other words, a semantic representation of sentence *S* must preserve all the relevant properties of *S* as well as the relations between *S* and other similar expressions. This topic will be taken up below, in Subsections *1.3* & *2.1.4*, as well as in Ch. 10, *2.3*.

1 Sentential Meaning Properties

Two types of semantic properties of sentences are considered: semantic normalcy/anomaly (*1.1*), and semantic truth/falsehood (*1.2*).

1.1   Semantic Normalcy/Anomaly of a Sentence

A sentence can have one of the two mutually contrary core semantic properties: being semantically normal or being semantically anomalous.

> **Definition 9.1/2:** Semantically Normal/Anomalous Sentence
> Sentence S is semantically normal/anomalous iff its meaning 'S' is well-formed/ill-formed.

The meaning of a sentence can be well- or ill-formed either from an extralinguistic viewpoint – that is, independently of any particular language, or from a linguistic viewpoint – within a given language **L**, being in accordance or not with **L**'s semantic formation rules.

1.1.1   Extralinguistically Well-/Ill-Formed Sentences

The extralinguistic well-/ill-formedness of a sentence's meaning is determined by its interpretability in terms of extralinguistic reality – that is, in physical, psychological and social terms. This interpretability hinges upon extralinguistic knowledge, which is encyclopedic (knowledge about the world), pragmatic (understanding of the situation in which the linguistic exchange is taking place) and logical (ability to draw simple conclusions, etc.), rather than upon linguistic knowledge. The language-independent character of the extralinguistic normalcy/anomaly of a sentence is proven by the fact that it is preserved under translation. Let us take, as an illustration, N. Chomsky's famous sentence:

(1) #*Colorless green ideas sleep furiously.*

☞   The # symbol indicates the semantic anomaly or pragmatic unacceptability of
         a linguistic expression.

From an extralinguistic viewpoint, sentence (1) expresses an ill-formed meaning, which suffers from logical absurdities: the meaning of the phrase *colorless green ideas* is contradictory; the meaning 'ideas' is incompatible with the meanings 'colorless' and 'green', as well as with 'sleep'; and 'sleep' is incompatible with 'furiously'. (This is an example of violation of free, or semantic, cooccurrence.) However, linguistically, this absurd meaning is quite well expressed: if the Speaker really wants to say 'colorless green ideas sleep furiously', sentence (1) serves his purpose perfectly.

Extralinguistic anomaly can have as its source two specific phenomena that pertain to logic: absurdity and tautology.

A sentence is absurd if it expresses a logical contradiction – if it asserts and negates a given state of affairs at the same time. For example, the absurd sentence (2a) first communicates that the number of cars is one (*a car*) and then contradicts this information by saying that it is three. The absurd sentence (2b) presents two cases of meaning incompatibility (sincerity is not countable, nor is it drinkable), which can be reduced to contradiction.

(2) a. #*I saw a car in the quantity of three.*
     b. #*I drank three sincerities.*

A sentence is tautological if it asserts the same state of affairs twice:

(3) a. #*If he is dead, he is not alive.*
     b. #*Half an hour before he died, he was still alive.*

Both sentences in (3) illustrate a particular case of tautology, the so-called truism; this is an indirect tautology, and is therefore somewhat less obvious.

It is important to note that there are expressions that may look like tautologies without in fact being tautologies; this is the case of sentence (4):

(4) *Linguists are ⟨≡ will be⟩ linguists.*

What we see here is an instance of a phraseologized syntactic construction *Xs are ⟨will be⟩ Xs*, which means something like 'Xs in general have some specific properties, and it is to be expected that the particular X we are talking about does too'.

1.1.2   Linguistically Well-/Ill-Formed Sentences

The meaning of a sentence of language **L** is linguistically well-formed if it respects the constraints on possible semanteme configurations holding in **L** (Ch. 3, *3.1.1*); otherwise, it is ill-formed. The following sentences are linguistically ill-formed because they violate some such constraints of English and French, respectively:

(5) a. #*Forbidden direction.*
         [**as a road sign**]; the correct expression: *Wrong way.*
     b. Fr. #*Méfiez-vous du chien* 'Beware of the dog'
         [**as a warning sign**]; the correct expression: *Chien méchant* 'Vicious dog'.

Both these examples illustrate the construction of meaning "gone wrong." While the attempted expressions are transparent and fully grammatical, they are not idiomatic: you simply do not conceive the corresponding conceptual message in this way in these two languages. The intended expressions are pragmatically constrained clichés – pragmatemes (Ch. 4, *2.2.2.2*), whose meaning or expression cannot be altered.

In the situation corresponding to (5a), the French will say exactly *Sens interdit* 'Forbidden direction'. Similarly, in the situation corresponding to (5b), the English would use *Beware of the dog*, preferring a direct suggestion to an implicit warning. These are two different ways of conceptualizing one and the same situation.

Speakers react differently to utterances whose meaning is ill-formed for extralinguistic reasons and those that have linguistically ill-formed meaning.

In the first case – e.g., sentences (1)–(3) – the reaction could be: "What do you mean? This makes no sense!" But utterances of the second type – e.g., those in (5) – provoke an altogether different reaction: "That's not how you say it," and the Addressee will suggest a correct, more idiomatic, formulation. Reactions to linguistically ill-formed sentences are similar to those provoked by sentences which are incorrect only from the viewpoint of linguistic realization, such as sentence (6a):

(6) a.   *?Three adult females of Chinese origin exited the residence running.*
    b.   *Three Chinese women ran out of the house.*

Sentence (6a), uttered by a native speaker who is recounting an accident on television, is deficient because certain semanteme configurations that should have been expressed synthetically (i.e., within a single LU) were expressed analytically (by several LUs). Namely, the semantic configuration 'movement' + 'means of movement' + 'direction of movement', expressible simply as ⌜*ran out*⌝, was expressed too verbosely, as *exited the residence running* (cf. the discussion on language-specific structural complexity and "packaging" of semantemes in Ch. 3, *3.1.1*). Also, in this neutral context, the meaning 'adult female' should have been expressed by the lexeme WOMAN. A correct implementation of the meaning underlying (6a) is, therefore, (6b). An extreme case of incorrectness of this type amounts to ungrammaticality.

1.2   Semantic Truth/Falsehood of a Sentence

The semantic anomaly of sentences is closely related to their truth/falsehood. In order to speak about logical truth in general, we need the concept of logical proposition (Appendix, *5.1*).

> **Definition 9.3:** Logical Proposition
> A logical proposition is a symbolic expression (including a linguistic expression) to which a truth-value can be assigned: it can be TRUE or FALSE.

Thus, the expression *2 + 3 = 8* corresponds to a logical proposition (which happens to be false), and so does the expression *The Earth revolves around the Sun* (this one being true). But the expressions *2 + 3* and *Be quiet!* do not express logical propositions since they cannot be assigned a truth-value.

A few words on the correlation "(logical) proposition ~ (syntactic) clause" are in order. In the prototypical case, a logical proposition is expressed in a language by a single clause. (A simple clause is, roughly, an utterance that contains a finite verb; a simple independent clause is equivalent to a simple sentence, see Ch. 2, *2.1.3*.) But the converse does not hold, since some types of clause do not express logical propositions; this is the case, for instance, of all imperative and interrogative clauses.

REMARKS

1. A declarative sentence of the type *The biggest natural number is even* does not express a logical proposition, either, because it is neither true nor false: since the biggest natural number does not exist, this sentence cannot be assigned a truth-value. This is due to the false presupposition of existence expressed by this sentence, see Subsection *2.3* below.

2. For brevity's sake, we will speak about truth-values of clauses and sentences, rather than of truth-values of logical propositions expressed by these utterances.

Linguistic semantics should not be concerned with the truth of utterances: horrendous falsehoods and the most brazen lies can be expressed in impeccable English, French, Russian, etc. The only cases in which the truth becomes relevant in semantics are those of contradiction (the Speaker is asserting and negating one and the same logical proposition) and tautology (the Speaker is asserting the same proposition twice). Thus, sentence (7a) asserts and negates the proposition 'X is married' at the same time, and the sentence (7b) does so with the proposition 'Ducks are birds'; sentences (8a) and (8b) assert, respectively, each of these two propositions twice.

(7) a.   *#John, who is a bachelor* [= 'an **unmarried man** …'], *is married*.
     b.   *#These ducks* [= '**birds** that …'] *are plants*.

(8) a.   *#John, who is a bachelor* [= 'an **unmarried man** …'], *is not married*.
     b.   *#These ducks* [= '**birds** that …'] *are birds*.

By virtue of its linguistic meaning and independently of extralinguistic reality, a contradictory sentence is always false, and a tautological sentence is always true. In other words, without any relation to the world, and simply because they mean what they mean, the sentences in (7) are of necessity false and the sentences in (8) are necessarily true. Assigning them a truth-value does not require any real-world knowledge; it is enough to know the language.

> **Definition 9.4:** Semantically True/False Sentence
> A sentence *S* is semantically true/false iff its truth/falsehood can be established solely by virtue of *S*'s linguistic meaning (without taking into consideration the real-world fact to which *S* refers).

REMARK. In philosophy, a distinction is made between analytical and synthetic sentences (or statements): for instance, *All bachelors are unmarried* is an analytic statement (true by virtue of its meaning, i.e., by definition) while *All bachelors are unhappy* is a synthetic one (true [or false] by virtue of how its meaning relates to the world).

1.3   Treatment of Anomalous Sentences in a Formal Linguistic Model

In discourse one finds a whole range of sentences whose meaning is, extralinguistically speaking, more or less anomalous (speakers being not necessarily aware of their deficiency). A linguistic model should not reject such sentences, for at least the following four reasons.

1. A semantic representation is not concerned with the process of meaning construction, the latter being a prelinguistic task, the purview of conceptics (Ch. 1, *2.4*). A semantic representation presents an already constructed meaning and serves as a starting point for the expression of this meaning, whatever its quality.

   However, since semantic properties of sentences must be reflected in their semantic representations, the semantic representation of a sentence perceived as linguistically anomalous (for instance, absurd) should be such as to allow the linguistic model to detect this anomaly; and this holds also for tautology. To put it differently, an adequate linguistic model should be able to recognize the incompatibilities/redundancies in the meaning of sentences like (1)–(3), (7) and (8).

2. A semantically anomalous sentence – contradictory or tautological – can receive a non-literal, in particular poetic, interpretation and be used for the expression of a figurative meaning (metaphorical or ironic, for instance). Anomalous sentences are used in order to insist on something, make a joke, and so on.

3. A sentence which is anomalous in one particular world (= in a given state of affairs) may not be so in another: think of works of fiction where people can fly, animals can talk, etc., or of the fact that a sentence like *John flew over London yesterday* would have been absurd three centuries ago.

4. Even if tautologies are not informative in the strict sense of the term, they have a crucial role to play in metalinguistic terms: a lexicographic definition, such as 'X is a bachelor' = 'man X who is able to be married, and who is not and has never been married', is in fact a tautology. In contrast, contradictory sentences are anomalous without exception.

Thus, extralinguistically ill-formed sentences should be dealt with in (almost) the same way as normal ones. In contrast, linguistically ill-formed expressions, such as those in (5), should be rejected by a linguistic model; more specifically, their semantic representations should be filtered out – by means of special, language-specific rules – and discarded or corrected, since such expressions contravene well-formedness rules which apply to semantic representations of specific languages. For an illustration of rules filtering out linguistically ill-formed semantic representation, see Ch. 10, *2.2*.

2   Meaning Relations between Sentences

We present four types of semantic paradigmatic relations between sentences –
synonymy, or paraphrase (*2.1*), implication (*2.2*), presupposition (*2.3*), and
equinomy, which is the relation between two homophonous sentences (*2.4*).
Since, as announced at the beginning, the only sentential relations considered are paradigmatic relations, in what follows we will omit the adjective
paradigmatic.

2.1   Synonymy of Sentences = Paraphrase

The crucial role that synonymy of sentences, or paraphrase, plays in language
has already been mentioned (Ch. 3, *1.1*). In particular, it has been pointed out
that the ability to paraphrase is an integral part of speakers' linguistic competence: an average speaker knows how to produce and recognize paraphrases.
A Speaker needs paraphrasing as soon as he wants to tackle subjects of a certain level of complexity or abstraction. First, he needs it simply in order to be
able to say anything at all. If it were not for paraphrasing, our Speaker would
get stuck soon enough, unable to overcome the many obstacles (restricted
lexical and syntactic cooccurrence, lexical gaps, irregular or missing forms,
etc.) he inevitably faces in speech production. Second, paraphrasing is necessary in order to speak well and find the most suitable and effective way to
express a semantic content in a given speech situation. Thanks to paraphrasing, it is possible to avoid repetitions, clarify, elaborate, change one's style,
etc. Thus, being fluent in a language means, to a great extent, being able to
paraphrase.

 An important corollary: language models must take into account the
capacity of ordinary speakers to manipulate paraphrase. See Ch. 10, *1*,
paraphrastic potential of Meaning-Text semantic structures.

This subsection is organized as follows: characterization of the notion of paraphrase (*2.1.1*); types of paraphrase (*2.1.2*); testing paraphrastic equivalence:
substitution test (*2.1.3*); and semantic representation of paraphrases (*2.1.4*).

2.1.1   The Notion of Paraphrase

> **Definition 9.5:** (Linguistic) Paraphrases
> Sentences S_1 and S_2 of language **L** are linguistic paraphrases iff they
> are (quasi-)synonymous.

In the discussion that follows we consider only linguistic paraphrases, and will
therefore drop the adjective.

NB: In Chapter 3, p. 74, we mentioned that the other type of paraphrase – so-called cognitive paraphrases, based on encyclopedic and/or pragmatic knowledge – are not considered in this book.

(9) a. S_1: *John's comfortable income$_X$* ***allows*** *him$_Y$ to travel$_Z$ frequently.* $\equiv$

    b. S_2: ***Thanks to*** *his comfortable income$_X$, John$_Y$* ***can afford*** *frequent travel$_{Z'}$.*

☞   A prime *'* attached to the symbol of a variable indicates that the LU involved is a syntactically induced modification of the LU specified by the variable.

The sentences in (9) are mutual paraphrases, semantically linked in the following way:

(9a): 'X **allows2** Y to do Z'   = 'X **causes1** Y **to be able** to do Z' =
                                     'Y **is able** to do Z, **which is caused1 by** X'[1]
(9b): '**Thanks to** X, Y **can afford** to do Z' = '**Caused1 by** X, Y **is able** to do Z' =
                                       'Y **is able** to do Z, **which is caused1 by** X'

One can see that the two sentences in (9) have the same meaning.

Definition 9.5 calls for four comments.

1. The relation of paraphrase is a particular case of the synonymy relation – synonymy of sentences, two other particular cases of this relation being lexical synonymy, i.e., synonymy of LUs (PHYSICIAN ~ (*medical*) DOCTOR, PUMA ~ ⌜MOUNTAIN LION⌝), and syntactic synonymy, i.e., synonymy of constructions (*persons* ***who seek*** *asylum* ~ *persons* ***seeking*** *asylum*).

    Synonymy is a core semantic relation, the foundation of linguistic semantics. It represents a particular case of the relation of equivalence;[2] two sentences are said to be synonymous iff they are equivalent from the viewpoint of their linguistic meaning, i.e., they are semantically equivalent. The synonymy of sentences is based upon semantic relations between LUs, such as synonymy, antonymy (used with negation), conversion (with an appropriate permutation of actants), and so on; these relations were presented in Ch. 6, *1*.

2. While the paraphrase relation has been traditionally construed as holding between sentences, this definition can be extended to cover synonymous expressions smaller than a sentence (= clauses and phrases) and those containing more than one sentence (= chains of semantically related sentences

---

[1] Recall that the semanteme '[to] cause**1**' represents non-agentive causation (*Humidity can cause headaches.*) and the semanteme '[to] cause**2**' stands for agentive causation (*Cops say that militants caused the riots.*).

[2] Logical equivalence of two propositions, or equality of their truth-values, and mathematical equivalence of two arithmetical expressions, or equality of their numerical values, are two other cases of this relation.

that form a whole). Such an extended definition of paraphrase would reflect actual linguistic behavior, in which paraphrasing a phrase by a clause (or vice versa) is fairly frequent (e.g., *No entry* ≡ *Do not enter*) and, on the other hand, a single sentence often gets paraphrased by two or more sentences (e.g., *Could you bring my glasses from the kitchen?* ≡ *Could you bring my glasses? They are in the kitchen.*).

3. Along with INTRAlinguistic paraphrases, i.e., synonymous sentences belonging to the same language, it is possible to consider INTERlinguistic paraphrases, i.e., synonymous sentences coming from different languages. From this perspective, translation is a particular case of paraphrasing – interlinguistic paraphrasing. Here is an example.

(10) English ~ French [notice in the Montreal subway]
    a. ***Use** the intercom **to contact** the train operator.* ≡
    b. ***Communiquez*** *avec le conducteur **à l'aide de** l'interphone*
       lit. 'Communicate with the driver with the aid of [= 'by using'] the intercom'.

The two sentences feature the paraphrastic link 'X uses Y to do Z' ~ 'X fait Z en utilisant Y' (= 'X does Z by using Y'); this is a case of inversion of subordination, or head switching: '[to] use' is the communicatively dominant meaning in (10a), subordinating '[to] contact', the purpose of using, as its SemA **3**; in (10b), 'communiquer' is communicatively dominant, subordinating 'utiliser'. The same paraphrasing link could very well be used for English-to-English paraphrasing of (10a), as is apparent from the gloss for (10b).

While translational equivalence cannot be reduced to semantic equivalence,[3] there are a large number of cases in which the two equivalence types coincide. Thus, rules designed for paraphrasing within a language (Ch. 12, 2) can be efficiently used for paraphrasing between languages – that is, for translation.

4. In addition to exact paraphrases, semantics considers approximate paraphrases. For example, sentences (11) are approximately, or quasi-, synonymous: *pool of unemployed* and *job seekers* do not, of course, mean the same thing, and neither do *can* and *be sufficient*. But in spite of these differences,

---

[3] On the one hand, some sentences that are translational equivalents are not mutual paraphrases; for instance, *Sound of Music*, the title of a well-known movie, and its Spanish translation, *Sonrisas y lágrimas* 'Smiles and tears', or the clichés Eng. *Hard to believe* and Sp. *Parece mentira* 'It.looks.like lie'. On the other hand, some paraphrases, in specific context, can fail to be translational equivalents; thus, Serb. *Njen auto troši nešto više od 2 galona na sto milja* is an exact paraphrase of Eng. *Her car uses over 2 gallons per 100 miles* but not a good translational equivalent of this sentence, since the target audience is used to talking about liters and kilometers, not gallons and miles.

the two sentences are semantically close enough to be perceived as saying more or less the same thing.

(11) a. S_1: *The available pool of unemployed cannot provide the needed labor.* $\cong$
    b. S_2: *The number of job seekers is not sufficient to provide the needed labor.*

☞   Recall that the symbols « $\equiv$ » and « $\cong$ » stand for, respectively, exact and approximate equivalence.

Approximate synonymy (= near- or quasi-synonymy) is actually much more widespread in speech than exact synonymy. Semantic differences can practically always be found between expressions that at first glance appear to be exactly synonymous. However, in everyday communication, such differences are normally ignored; in appropriate contextual conditions, sentences that are only approximately synonymous will be treated as paraphrases by most speakers.

Due to the phenomenon of neutralization of semantic differences, or semantic neutralization for short, semantic differences between near-synonymous or even non-synonymous sentences can be "switched off" or become irrelevant in an appropriate linguistic or pragmatic context. Thanks to this, exact synonymy is more frequent at the level of sentences than at the lexical level. Three examples of semantic neutralization follow.

(12) a. *Penelope is sure that Ulysses* **will come back**. $\equiv$
    b. *Penelope is sure of Ulysses' eventual* **coming back**.

The verbal form *will come back* is semantically richer than its nominalization, *(his) coming back*, since the noun cannot express the time of the event, in this case, the future. However, this semantic difference is neutralized in the context of the adjective EVENTUAL, which situates the *coming back* in the future.

(13) a. *He* **was assassinated** *in a conspiracy.* $\equiv$ *He* **was killed** *in a conspiracy.*
    b. *He* **was assassinated** *during a hunting party.* $\not\equiv$ *He* **was killed** *during a hunting party.*

The semantic differences between ASSASSINATE 'kill an important person deliberately and illegally' and KILL can be neutralized in a context like (13a), which highlights the intentional and illegal nature of the act. In contrast, the difference persists in a vague context like (13b).

While in these two cases the conditions allowing for semantic neutralization are linguistic in nature, in (14) they are pragmatic:

(14) ***Hurricane*** *in Manhattan.* ≅ ***Mayhem*** *in Manhattan.* ≅ ***Destruction*** *in Manhattan.*

The nouns HURRICANE, MAYHEM and DESTRUCTION exhibit important semantic differences and it is difficult to consider them as even quasi-synonymous. However, the three phrases above can be used to indifferently describe the same extralinguistic reality: the "superstorm" Sandy that hit Manhattan and the east coast of the United States in November 2012. Here, the semantic differences in question are of little relevance.

2.1.2 Types of Paraphrase

Several types of paraphrase can be distinguished, according to the axes laid out in *Table 9.1*.

Table 9.1 Types of paraphrase

1. ASPECT OF MEANING	2. EXACTNESS OF THE PARAPHRASING LINK	3. LINGUISTIC EXPRESSIVE MEANS	4. DEPTH OF THE PARAPHRASING LINK	5. MODE OF PRODUCTION
Propositional	Exact	Lexical	Semantic	Virtual
Communicative	Approximate	Syntactic	Lexical-syntactic	Reformulating
Rhetorical		Morphological	Syntactic	
		Prosodic	Morphological	

Let us briefly comment on each of the five axes of classification.

Axis 1. As a function of the aspect of meaning (Ch. 3, *1.3*) involved in their production, we distinguish: propositional paraphrases (cf. the variants in (15a): 'sure' vs. 'certain', 'come back' vs. 'return'), communicative paraphrases (cf. (15a–b) vs. (15c)) and rhetorical paraphrases (cf. (15a, c) vs. (15b)).

☞ **Sem-Rheme**, **Sem-Theme** and **Focalized** are markers of communicative oppositions of Thematicity and Focalization. Contextualization, by means of an underlying question or statement, is used in order to elicit the Theme of the utterance. **Neutral** and **colloquial** are rhetorical, or stylistic, markers. For more on these notions, see Ch. 10, *1* and *3.1.2*.

(15) [**Q**: What about Penelope?]
  a. **neutral** $[Penelope]_{\textbf{T}_{Sem}}$ [*is sure ⟨certain⟩ that Ulysses will come back ⟨return⟩*]$_{\textbf{R}_{Sem}}$.

b. **colloq.** [*Penelope*]_T**Sem** [*KNOWS that Ulysses will show up again*]_R**Sem**.

c. **neutral** [*As for Penelope*]_T**Sem, FOCALIZED** [*she is sure that Ulysses will come back*]_R**Sem**.

[**Q**: What about Ulysses' return?]

d. **colloq.** [*That Ulysses will show up again*]_T**Sem** [*is a no-brainer for Penelope*]_R**Sem**.

Sentence (15d) differs from sentences (15a) and (15c) in all the three aspects of meaning:

	(15a) and (15c)	(15d)
propositional differences	'sure'	'no-brainer'
	'comeback/return'	'show up again'
communicative difference	'Penelope' is the Sem-Theme	'Ulysses' showing up again' is the Sem-Theme
rhetorical difference	**Neutral**	**Colloquial**

Axis 2. The following example illustrates both exact and approximate paraphrases.

(16) a. *I* **expect** *him to come.*
   b. *I* **think** *he'll* **probably** *come.*
   c. *I* **wouldn't be surprised** *if he came.*
   d. *When he comes, I'll be* **ready**.

Sentences (16a) and (16b) are exact propositional paraphrases, since 'X expects Y' means 'X believes that Y is probable'. These sentences are approximate paraphrases of both (16c) and (16d).

The examples in (16) also illustrate the fact that approximate paraphrases can be more or less semantically distant: (16d) is a more remote paraphrase of (16a–b) than is (16c).

Axis 3. Paraphrases can vary according to the linguistic expressive means (Ch. 2, *1.5*) used in their production; here are examples of four types of expressive means variation:

(17) a. Lexical means ~ lexical means
      He **left**. ~ *He* **did not stay**.
      In both paraphrases the meaning in question is expressed by lexical means: the verb LEAVE and its negated antonym, STAY.
   b. Lexical means ~ syntactic means
      Rus. (i) *Nas bylo* **okolo** *10 čelovek* lit. 'We were about 10 people'. ~
         (ii) *Nas bylo* **čelovek** *10* lit. 'We were people 10'. = 'We were maybe 10 people'.
      In (17b–i), the semanteme 'approximately' is expressed by the lexeme OKOLO 'about', while in (17b–ii), the expressive means is the

approximate-quantitative construction, specific to Russian, in which the numeral must follow the quantified noun.

c. Lexical means ~ morphological means
*They **used to** go fishing every Sunday. ~ They **would** go fishing every Sunday.*
The habitual past is expressed either lexically, by means of the lexeme USE$_{(V)}$ [to V$_{INF}$], or morphologically – by the conditional mood of the verb.

d. Morphological means ~ prosodic means
*I **did tell** him. ~ I TÓLD him.*
Emphasis is expressed by means of a special inflectional form of the verb (assertorial) or by emphatic prosody (symbolized by capitalization and the accent symbol).

Axes 4 and **5** are related to the specifics of our framework, which will be addressed in Ch. 12, *2*. Here, it suffices to say that Axis 4 has to do with the fact that formal paraphrastic links between sentences are established at different levels of representation of utterances: some are already "visible" at the level of syntactic representation, while others can only be discovered by semantic decomposition, at the semantic level. Axis 5 concerns two major ways in which paraphrases can be produced: by parallel synthesis from a common source, with no paraphrasing rules proper (virtual paraphrasing), or by application of paraphrasing rules to the representation of a sentence in order to produce a representation of a synonymous sentence (reformulating).

Any pair of paraphrases can exhibit differences along any or all of the five classification axes in *Table 9.1*; the nature and the number of these differences is a measure of the semantic distance between the paraphrases. This topic will be taken up in Ch. 10, *4.2*, where a distinction will be made between paraphrases in the broad sense and paraphrases in the narrow sense – according to formal criteria having to do with the interaction of the propositional and communicative aspects of meaning in the production of paraphrases.

2.1.3   Testing Paraphrastic Equivalence: Substitution Test

In order to check whether two sentences are mutual paraphrases, we use the substitution test (presented in Ch. 5, *2* under the name of mutual substitutability rule):

> Two exactly synonymous sentences (= two exact paraphrases) must be substitutable *salva significatione* – that is, with the preservation of meaning – in any context.

 The result of the substitution need not be impeccable from a stylistic viewpoint – we do not require mutual substitutability *salva correctione*.

For near-synonymous sentences, we allow for a partial substitutability: certain contexts can block the substitution, while it is possible in some others. Thus:

(18) a. *Smoking increases the risk of cancer.*
      b. *For smokers, the risk of cancer is higher.*
      c. *Incidence of cancer is higher in smokers.*

Table 9.2 Substitutability of paraphrases (18) in context

Contexts (preceding)	✓	?	✗
What are some consequences of smoking?	(18a), (18b)	(18c)	
What about the risk of cancer?	(18c)	(18a), (18b)	
What increases the risk of cancer?	(18a)	(18b), (18c)	

These are fairly close paraphrases, and they are easily substitutable for one another. The following ones are more remote, so there are fewer contexts where all of them fit well.

(19) a. *The guy wearing a bizarre hat entered the bar.*
      b. *The guy who entered the bar wore a bizarre hat.*
      c. *The hat worn by the guy who entered the bar was bizarre.*

Table 9.3 Substitutability of paraphrases (19) in context

✓	?	✗	Contexts (following)
(19a)	(19b)	(19c)	*He* [= The guy] *ordered a beer.*
(19a)		(19b), (19c)	*It was a shabby bar with ...*
(19b), (19c)		(19a)	*It was a shabby hat that resembled ...*

The substitution test is frequently resorted to in other areas of linguistics: syntax, morphology and phonology. For instance, substitutability is required of syntactic subtrees controlled by the same surface-syntactic relation and of nouns having the same gender and/or case characteristics.

2.1.4   Semantic Representations of Paraphrases

The substitution test is intended to corroborate in a more or less informal way the researcher's intuition about whether two sentences are mutual paraphrases. But we also have to be able to formally demonstrate that this is (or is not) the case. At the beginning of this chapter it was mentioned that a formal representation of a linguistic object must faithfully reflect that object's properties and the relations it has with other similar objects. So, we can ask ourselves the following question: what do the semantic representations of mutual paraphrases have to look like in order for us to be able to assert that they are paraphrases?

From a formal viewpoint, we posit the following requirements for semantic representations [SemRs] of paraphrases.

For exact paraphrases

> If sentences S_1 and S_2 are exact paraphrases, their SemRs must be identical or equivalent.

Two representations are equivalent if they can be reduced to one another by means of linguistic rules. In our case, these are equivalence, or paraphrasing, rules (Ch. 1, *2.3* & Ch. 12, *2*).

Let us illustrate the above requirement by two simple examples.

(20) [**Q**: And the rain?]
   a. *The rain **continued** (**to fall**) for the next two days.*
   b. *The rain **kept falling** for the next two days.*

Sentences (20a) and (20b) are exact paraphrases of each other, differing only in their means of lexicalization: CONTINUE vs. KEEP for the expression of the main predication; the infinitive vs. the *-ing*-form for the implementation of the main verb's complement, with the possibility of omitting the latter altogether if the Main Verb is CONTINUE. These paraphrases have the same SemR, shown in *Figure 9.1*.

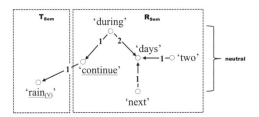

Figure 9.1 (Partial) SemR of the exact paraphrases in (20)

☞   "Neutral" is a rough indication representing the rhetorical structure, see Ch. 10, *1*: p. 257).

This SemS can be literally read as 'Raining continued during the next two days'; all other paraphrases are obtainable by deep-syntactic paraphrasing rules. (For rules of this type, see Ch. 12, *2*.)

(21) a. *A strange noise **awakened** me in the middle of the night.*
   b. *A strange noise **made** me **wake up** in the middle of the night.*

The SemSs of these sentences differ only in the degree of decomposition: the SemS of (21a) is not decomposed at all, while that of (21b) features the decomposition of the semanteme 'X awakens Y', which is 'X causes**1** Y to ⌐wake up⌐**1**' (the causation semanteme is expressed in (21b) by the verb MAKE).

This decomposition corresponds to the definition of 'X awakens1 Y', i.e., to a semantic paraphrasing rule of a particular type (expansion-reduction rules, yielding exact propositional paraphrases; see Ch. 12, *2.1.1.1*). Other structures of the SemRs of the two sentences are identical; thus, overall, their SemRs are identical, as can be seen in *Figure 9.2*.

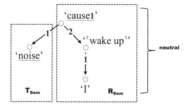

Figure 9.2 (Partial) SemR of the exact paraphrases in (21)

For approximate paraphrases

> If sentences S_1 and S_2 are approximate paraphrases, the difference between their SemRs must correspond to the semantic difference intuitively perceived between them.

Here is an illustration.

(22) [**Q**: What about the next two days?]
    The next two days heavy rain fell nonstop.

Sentence (22) and the sentences in (20) are approximate paraphrases, differing in propositional content, communicative orientation and style. Propositionally, sentence (22) adds the qualification of the rain as intense. Communicatively, the sentences in (20) present as their semantic Theme the fact of <u>raining</u> and as the semantic Rheme – the fact of its <u>continuing</u> during the next two days, while in sentence (22) the $\mathbf{T_{Sem}}$ is '<u>during</u> the next two days', and the $\mathbf{R_{Sem}}$ communicates that during this time it was <u>raining</u> continually and heavily. As for the style of expression, the adverb NONSTOP used in sentence (22) makes it informal, while the sentences in (20) are stylistically neutral. The SemR of sentence (22) is shown in *Figure 9.3*.

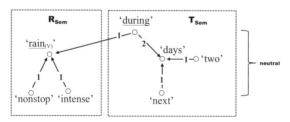

Figure 9.3 (Partial) SemR of sentence (22)

All the indicated differences are small and can easily be accounted for by semantic paraphrasing rules (namely, semantic quasi-equivalencies, see Ch. 12, *2.1*, p. 237*ff*), which means that here we are dealing with fairly close approximate paraphrases. For comparison, in (23) we give a sample of sentences representing more remote approximate paraphrases of both (20) and (22):

(23) *For the next two days, there was a sustained rainfall* ⟨≡ *it was raining and raining* | *there was no end to the rain* | *it seemed as if the rain would never stop*⟩.

We will now turn to the semantic relation of implication.

2.2 Implication

Definition 9.6: Implication
Sentence S_1 semantically implies sentence S_2 [= S_2 is a semantic implication of S_1] iff by admitting the truth of S_1 the Speaker commits himself to the truth of S_2; the converse is not necessarily the case.

For example, sentence (24a) semantically implies sentence (24b):

(24) a. S_1: *John plays bridge* ['bridge' = 'a card game which …']. →
　　b. S_2: *John plays cards*.

If John plays bridge, it is necessarily true that he plays cards, so negating this implication amounts to a contradiction: #*John plays bridge* [*S*], *but he does not play cards* [**non** *S'*]. In contrast, if John plays cards, it does not follow that he plays bridge (he may play poker, canasta or whatever – but not bridge), which is demonstrated by the normalcy of the sentence *John plays cards* [*S'*]*, but he does not play bridge* [**non** *S*]. In negating the truth of *S* the speaker does not commit himself to anything: *John does not play bridge* does not entail either *John does not play cards* or *John plays cards*.

REMARKS

1. In point of fact, the relation of implication does not hold between sentences but between the logical propositions (see above, Subsection *1.2*) expressed by those sentences. However, for simplicity's sake, we will continue to speak about sentences implying other sentences.
2. A term synonymous with implication is entailment; thus, we can also say that (24a) entails (24b).

Let us give two additional examples of implication.

(25) a. S_1: *The President has been assassinated* ['assassinate' = 'kill [≈ 'cause**2** to die'] an important person deliberately and illegally']. →
　　b. S_2: *The President is dead*.

(26) a. S_1: *John plays tennis well.* →
   b. S_2: *John plays tennis.*

Phenomena similar to, but distinct from, semantic implication have been studied in pragmatics; conversational implicature is a case in point. This is a procedure whereby the Speaker introduces a piece of implicit information – which he is said to conversationally imply – that the Addressee is supposed to pick up based on some general rules governing conversation (conversational maxims and cooperation principle, Grice 1975). As an example, consider the following exchange between A and B (McCawley 1981: 218):

A: – *I am almost out of gas.*
B: – *There is a gas station just around the corner.*

Not only does B state that there is a gas station nearby, but he also conversationally implies that he believes the station is open at the moment of the exchange and that one can get some gasoline there. He does so by virtue of the Maxim of relevance, according to which one should not be giving information that is useless in the given speech situation.

This is a fascinating subject, but one that lies outside of the field of linguistics: we are dealing here with the construction of meaning, rather than with the expression of meaning. Only the latter problem is within the scope of linguistics.

2.3   Presupposition

> **Definition 9.7:** (Semantic) Presupposition
> Sentence S_1 semantically presupposes sentence S_2 [= S_2 is a semantic presupposition of S_1] iff, when S_1 is stated, negated or interrogated, the Speaker cannot negate S_2 without contradicting himself.
>
> REMARK. This is a broad and generally accepted definition of the notion of presupposition. In the Meaning-Text framework, a somewhat narrower definition is used, which does not cover all the types of presupposition considered in the literature: in our approach, presuppositions are indicated as part of the communicative structure of lexical meanings (Ch. 5, *3.4*) and of the semantic-communicative structure of sentences (Ch. 10, *3.1.2.4*).

For example, the sentences in (27a–b) both presuppose (27c):

(27) a. S_{1-1} : *Max knows ⟨does not know⟩ that Mary left.*
   b. S_{1-2} : *Does Max know ⟨Doesn't Max know⟩ that Mary left?*
   c. S_2 : *Mary left.*
   d. **non** S_2 : *#Max knows ⟨does not know⟩ that Mary left but, in fact, she did not leave.*

If someone states (27a) or asks (27b), he cannot add *but, in fact, she did not leave* without contradicting himself; cf. sentence (27d), which is contradictory and, therefore, absurd.

Presuppositions have various sources, which fall into three major types.

1. Presuppositions carried by the meanings of lexical units (that constitute the sentence)

Here are three examples of LUs that bring their presuppositions to the meaning of the sentence.

Factive verbs

The meaning of a factive verb includes a presupposed component 'this being true' bearing on the meaning of the verb's complement; for instance:

'X knows that P' ≈ 'X has in his mind information P [[, P being true]]'.

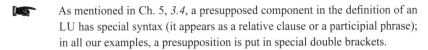 As mentioned in Ch. 5, *3.4*, a presupposed component in the definition of an LU has special syntax (it appears as a relative clause or a participial phrase); in all our examples, a presupposition is put in special double brackets.

Therefore, a factive verb in the main clause presupposes the truth of the logical proposition expressed by its completive clause; cf. [*that*] *Mary left* in (27a–b). Verbs like REGRET, REVEAL and REALIZE [*that* P] are factive; in contrast, BELIEVE, SUPPOSE and DECLARE [*that* P] are not: *Max believes ⟨does not believe⟩ that Mary left* does not presuppose *Mary left*, since it is possible to say without contradiction *Max believes ⟨does not believe⟩ that Mary left, but ⟨and⟩, in fact, she did not leave.*

Phasal verbs of continuation and cessation

A phasal verb indicates the phase of a dynamic non-punctual fact (= process, action, activity, etc.) – its beginning, its continuation or its end. A phasal verb indicating the continuation or the cessation of a fact presupposes, by virtue of its meaning, the existence of this fact. For example, to stop doing something presupposes that one was doing this something before; cf. the lexicographic definition of the verb [to] STOP:

'X stops doing P' ≈ '[[X having done P before moment **t**,]] X does not do P after **t**'.

(28) a. S_1: *You have ⟨You have not⟩ stopped drinking?*
      b. S_2: *You drank* (≡ *You were an alcoholic*).

Sentence (28a) presupposes (28b).

LUs that impose semantic constraints on their actants

The meaning of an LU may contain components that act as constraints on its semantic actants – for instance, on the role an actant plays with respect to another. This is the case with the verbs like PUNISH and EXILE, as well as with some communication verbs, such as REPRIMAND and FORBID: the person who punishes or reprimands someone has an institutionally granted power to do so. The person who forbids someone to do something also has an authority to do so. As a consequence, the meaning '[person X having an authority over Z]' is presupposed by a sentence in which such an LU appears. For example, *John$_X$ forbade ⟨did not forbid⟩ Mary$_Z$ to leave* presupposes that John has the authority to forbid (because Mary is his employee, his teenage daughter, etc.); cf. the ungrammatical sentence **The toddler$_X$ forbade ⟨did not forbid⟩ his mother$_Z$ to take the toy* (for the meaning 'The toddler communicated/signaled to his mother that he did not want her to take the toy'), which violates the presupposition carried by FORBID, since normally a young child has no authority over his parents.

This meaning of FORBID contains yet another presupposed component, of a different type: the Speaker's belief that Y (= the one who is forbidden by X to do Z) wants to do Z (= action which is the target of X's forbidding); cf. the unacceptability of *#John$_Y$ did not want to leave$_Z$, but I$_X$ forbade him$_Y$ to do$_Z$* so, where the explicit negation of Y's will to do Z clashes with the presupposed component in the definition of FORBID: '[Y wanting to do Z,] ...'. This presupposed component is found in the meaning of other semantically close verbs, such as PROHIBIT, BAN, ALLOW1, APPROVE, DISAPPROVE, and so on.

Here is the definition of the verb FORBID, with two presuppositions of different types:

'X forbids Y to do Z' = '[Y wanting to do Z]$_{\text{Presupposition 1}}$ and
[X having authority over Y,]$_{\text{Presupposition 2}}$
X communicates to Y that X is against Y's
doing Z'.

(Cf. the definition of FORBID in Wierzbicka 1987: 90–91.)

2. Presuppositions induced by the syntactic role of a linguistic expression
Syntactic modification (in a broad sense)

In a sentence of the form "ADJ N V$_{\text{FIN}}$" (e.g., *A smart$_{\text{(ADJ)}}$ boy$_{\text{(N)}}$ is reading$_{\text{(V)}}$.*), the meaning of ADJ is presupposed – simply by virtue of ADJ's being a modifier. This is a defining property of a modifying construction, which opposes it to a predicative construction: put succinctly, while predication states (= asserts), modification presupposes.[4]

(29) a. S$_1$:   *The **red** pencil is ⟨is not⟩ on the table*   presupposes
         S$_2$:   *The pencil is red.*
     b. S$_1$:   *This **scoundrel** John has ⟨has not⟩ come*   presupposes
         S$_2$:   *John is a scoundrel.*

---

[4] The expressions *an interesting book* and *a book that costs a lot* illustrate the modifying construction; expressions of the type *The book is interesting* and *The book costs a lot* represent the predicative construction.

3. Presuppositions induced by the referential status of a linguistic expression

Definite description

A definite description is an expression whose meaning – in the given utterance – uniquely identifies its referent. In a sentence, a definite description presupposes the existence of its referent; for instance:

(30) S_1: ***Our cat** is ⟨is not⟩ sad* presupposes
  S_2: ***Our cat** exists* ≅ *We have a cat.*

Just as with implication (*2.2*), here too we need to distinguish between semantic presupposition, characterized above, and pragmatic presupposition. The latter refers to background assumptions of the Speaker that he believes are shared by his Addressee: propositions whose truth is taken for granted and which do not have to be stated. A pragmatic presupposition targets extralinguistic reality, i.e., roughly speaking, the speech situation. For example, the sentence *Close the door!* pragmatically presupposes that at the moment it is uttered the door in question is open; otherwise, it would be inappropriate in this particular speech situation. See Keenan (1971), where the distinction between semantic and pragmatic presupposition is established.

2.4   Equinomy

> **Definition 9.8:** Equinomy
> Two sentences S_1 and S_2 are equinomous [= stand in the relation of equinomy] iff their signifiers are identical and their signifieds are different.

For example, sentences (31a) and (31b) are equinomous:

(31) a. *John is an English history teacher*
      'John is a teacher of English history [= history of England]'.
   b. *John is an English history teacher*
      'John is English [= an English national] and a history teacher'.

> REMARK. Sentences (31a) and (31b) are equinomous only in writing; when uttered, their signifiers can be distinguished by prosody (pauses and intonation contours).

Equinomy is a term that we introduce as logically parallel to synonymy: while synonymy is a relation between two different texts whose meanings are identical, equinomy is a relation between two identical texts whose meanings are different. Just like synonymy, equinomy is applicable to all linguistic entities – lexical units, phrases, clauses and sentences.

> REMARK. No term currently available has the exact extension of *equinomy*, hence our need to coin it. Ambiguity designates not a

relation between texts but a **property** of a text that alternatively corresponds to at least two meanings. In point of fact, saying that a sentence is ambiguous is an abbreviation: what this actually means is that its signifier coincides with the signifier of another sentence, their respective meanings, i.e., signifieds, being different. Homonymy and polysemy designate a relation, but are too specific (too narrow): the former covers only cases where the signifieds involved do not have semantic bridges, and the latter, only cases with different, but semantically related, signifieds. Equinomy, when applied to LUs, covers both: if two LUs are equinomous, they stand either in relation of homonymy (BOX^1**I.a** [container] ~ BOX^2 [sport]) or in that of polysemy (BOX^1**I.a** [container] ~ BOX^1**I.b** [quantity: boxful]). (However, for equinomous phrases or sentences there is no distinction between homonymy and polysemy.) This being said, in what follows we will not dispense altogether with the terms ambiguous sentence and ambiguity because of their familiarity.

Equinomy, viz. ambiguity, is pervasive in language; taken out of context, most linguistic forms are ambiguous. In fact, ambiguity, along with synonymy, is a fundamental feature of natural language; together, they conspire to make the language – that is, the Meaning-Text correspondence – highly complex and its description extremely difficult (Ch. 1, *2.1*).

The ambiguity of a sentence can have lexical or syntactic sources.

Lexical ambiguity

(32) a. *Did he reach the **bank** in time?*
     b. *Close this **window**, please.*

Lexical ambiguity is due to lexical homonymy or lexical polysemy (Ch. 6, *1.3*). Thus, the text in (32a) corresponds to two different and unrelated meanings because of lexical homonymy: BANK$_{(N)}$^{1}**1a** 'business that keeps and lends money…' vs. BANK$_{(N)}$^{2} 'land along the side of a river or a lake'. The text in (32b) corresponds to two different, but related, meanings because of lexical polysemy: WINDOW**I** 'an opening in the wall of a building … that lets the light in' vs. WINDOW**II** 'a separate area on a computer screen … – ⌜as if⌝ it were a window**I**'.

Syntactic ambiguity

(33) *Giant poster sale.*

Syntactic ambiguity is due to the fact that the same linear arrangement of lexemes can correspond to different syntactic structures. The text in (33) is either the signifier of the phrase whose meaning is 'sale of very big posters' or that of the phrase with the meaning 'a very big sale of posters'; the two phrases have different syntactic structures, the adjective GIANT modifying the noun SALE in the former and the noun POSTER in the latter:

GIANT←ATTR–SALE$_{SG}$–II→POSTER$_{PL}$ VS.

SALE$_{SG}$–II→POSTER$_{PL}$–ATTR→GIANT

The syntactic structures of sentences (31) are also different: while the adjective *English* expresses an actant of the noun *history* in (31a), it is a modifier of the noun *teacher* in (31b).

> REMARK. An ambiguous text always corresponds to at least two distinct syntactic structures, regardless of the source of ambiguity: in the case of lexical ambiguity, the nodes of the syntactic tree carry different labels (lexemes with different distinctive numbers), and in the case of syntactic ambiguity, the links between the nodes, i.e., syntactic relations, are different. (This, of course, is in addition to corresponding to different semantic structures; for the semantic structures of the phrases in (33), see Ch. 10, *2.1.3, Figure 10.9.*)

Lexical and syntactic ambiguity can combine, as they do in the following example, borrowed from Hockett (1987: 32):

(34) [telegraphic style] *Ship sails today.*

Speakers tend to be unaware of ambiguities in their speech, which can lead to unintended humorous effects. Here are just a few examples, randomly taken from the Internet:

(35) *For anyone who has children and doesn't know it, there is a day care on the first floor. | Gene Autry is better after being kicked by a horse. | Children make delicious snacks. | Squad helps dog bite victim. | Astronaut takes blame for gas in spacecraft.*

On the other hand, ambiguity is often used on purpose – to create puns and word play. This is exactly what Groucho Marx does when he declares:

(36) *One morning I shot an elephant in my pajamas; how he got in my pajamas I do not know.*

Either Groucho was wearing his pajamas at the moment of shooting the elephant (which was at an undisclosed location), or an elephant was wearing Groucho's pajamas when it was shot at, or else Groucho shot an elephant located in his [Groucho's] pajamas. The second sentence cancels the normal interpretation of the first one, and this creates a comic effect.

Creative usage of ambiguity is no less frequent in advertising. As a way of illustration, consider the advertisement for garbage bags of the brand GLAD that used to be seen on CBC television:

(37) *Don't get mad, get GLAD.*

The commercial tries to persuade the viewer that the bags in question are extraordinarily solid and reliable. It exploits the ambiguity of the expression *get* GLAD, which can mean either 'come into possession of garbage bags GLAD' [where *get* is a semantically full verb] or 'become satisfied' [where *get* is a support verb for *glad*], as well as extralinguistic knowledge, in order to create a complex message whose meaning is more or less as follows (the implicit components of the message are in square brackets): 'Instead of *getting mad* [which will happen if you buy the bags from the competition, because they are bad], *get* GLAD [i.e., buy ours] *and you will be glad* [because they are good]'.

This concludes Part II of the book. We now go on to Part III, where a formal model of semantics is presented.

Further Reading

Compositionality: See Further Reading for Chapter 4.

Tautology and contradiction: Snider 2015.

Paraphrase: [Concept of paraphrase] Harris 1979; Vila *et al.* 2014; [Aspects of paraphrasing competence] Parret 1989; Hagaman & Reid 2008; Walker 2008; Milićević & Tsedryk 2011; Russo 2014; [Paraphrase in philosophy and literary studies] von Solodkoff 2014; Keller 2015. See also Further Reading for Chapter 12.

Presupposition and implication: Keenan 1971; Horn 2006; Potts 2015; Domaneschi 2016.

Equinomy (i.e., sentence-level ambiguity): Berry *et al.* 2003.

Part III

Meaning-Text Model of Semantics

10 Semantic Representation

This chapter opens the last part of the book, which describes a formal model of semantics$_1$ as envisaged in the Meaning-Text framework. Recall (Ch. 1, *2.3*) that *semantics$_1$* means 'the set of rules of the semantic module of a language or of a Meaning-Text linguistic model'. Semantic representations, the topic of this chapter, serve as the input for the application of the semantic rules, their output being deep-syntactic representations, presented in Ch. 11, with the rules themselves dealt with in Ch. 12.

In the Meaning-Text framework, we use the same basic formalism – semantic networks (Ch. 1, *2.2.2* & Ch. 2, *1.6.1*) – to represent the propositional meaning of LUs and that of utterances, in particular, sentences. Lexical meaning representations (i.e., lexicographic definitions) were considered in Ch. 5; we do not return to this subject here and devote the present chapter exclusively to the semantic representation of sentences.

Due to the abundance of synonymic means in language (Ch. 2, *1.5* & Ch. 9, *2.1.2*), the meaning encoded by a semantic representation can, in principle, be expressed in several different ways, i.e., by several alternative sentences. This is why we say that a semantic representation encodes the meaning of a set of synonymous sentences (= paraphrases, Ch. 9, *2.1*), rather than the meaning of an individual sentence.

In our discussion so far, we have already shown some semantic representations of sentences, relying on an intuitive grasp of the formalism on the part of the reader. Now is the time to introduce the notion of semantic representation formally and with the appropriate level of detail. We proceed as follows: Section *1* characterizes the semantic representation in terms of its major components, called structures; Sections *2* and *3* present two of these structures in more detail: the semantic structure and the semantic-communicative structure; Section *4* illustrates the way in which the structures making up the semantic representation interact during sentence production.

1   General Characterization of the Semantic Representation

Linguistic representations of utterances at all levels are organized in the same way, each being made up of several structures: see Ch. 1, *1.2.2*. In particular, the semantic representation [SemR] of a set of synonymous sentences is an ordered set consisting of four structures:

- One basic structure, which reflects the linguistic entity central to this representation level – a chunk of linguistic meaning that corresponds to the sentence(s) to be synthesized. This is the semantic structure [SemS]; it models the propositional aspect of meaning (Ch. 3, *1.3*) and appears as a configuration of lexical meanings, or semantemes. From a formal viewpoint, the SemS is a semantic network (Section *2* below).
- Three peripheral structures, superimposed on the basic structure and providing additional characterization thereof: a semantic-communicative structure [Sem-CommS], a rhetorical structure [RhetS] and a referential structure [RefS].

The Sem-CommS and the RhetS, which model, respectively, the communicative and rhetorical aspects of meaning (Ch. 3, *1.3*), do not concern the propositional content as such but the way this content is "packaged" for communication.

The Sem-CommS, a.k.a. information structure, specifies the Speaker's communicative intent, namely the way he wants to orient his "scanning" of the SemS in a given speech situation, while he is verbalizing it. We could say that the communicative structure traces the Speaker's itinerary through the propositional space, organizing the propositional content into a specific message. For example, the sentences in (1), which have the same propositional content, correspond to two distinct messages due to their different communicative orientations: the first is a message about the opposition (criticizing the First Lady's dress style), while the second one is about the First Lady's dress style (being criticized by the opposition).

(1) a. *The Opposition criticizes the First Lady's expensive designer dresses.*

   b. *The First Lady's expensive designer dresses draw flak from the Opposition.*

Formally, the Sem-CommS is a division of the SemS into communicative areas – subnetworks, such that each subnetwork has a communicatively dominant node and is labeled with a value of one or more communicative oppositions, such as **Rheme** vs. **Theme** vs. **Specifier**; **Given** vs. **New**; **Asserted** vs. **Presupposed**; etc. (Section *3*).

The RhetS specifies the Speaker's rhetorical intent, i.e., the style in which the starting SemS is to be expressed. For example, the sentences in (2) both say the same thing (= they are propositionally identical), but they do so using different styles: (2a) is stylistically unmarked, and (2b) is colloquial.

(2) a. **neutral** *Give me a call!*

   b. **colloq.** *Give me a shout!*

The RhetS consists in specifying stylistic labels, such as **neutral, formal, colloquial, vulgar, slang, poetic**, etc., which characterize specific subnetworks of the SemS.

As for the RefS, it is the set of pointers from semantic configurations towards their referents (Ch. 2, *1.1.2*), which are entities and facts in the real world.

The SemR is defined as follows:

> **Definition 10.1:** Semantic Representation
> The Semantic Representation SemR (of a set of synonymous sentences) is a quadruplet
>
> $$\text{SemR} = \langle \text{SemS, Sem-CommS, RhetS, RefS} \rangle,$$
>
> where SemS stands for semantic structure, Sem-CommS for the semantic-communicative structure, RhetS for the rhetorical structure, and RefS for the referential structure.

Figure 10.1 shows the SemR that underlies sentence (1a) above (and all sentences synonymous to it; for some of these, see Section *4*).

 For simplicity's sake, we do not represent the nominal inflectional meanings (values of number and definiteness); instead, we have indicated the corresponding semantemes in the "plural form" ('dresses' and 'designers'), which is, strictly speaking, incorrect (since the meaning of grammemes should be described explicitly: cf. *Figure 10.3* below).

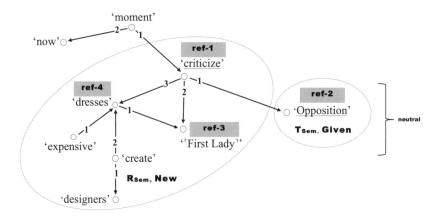

Figure 10.1 Semantic representation of sentence (1a) and all sentences synonymous with it

The four structures of the SemR interact in a complex way during sentence construction.

The SemS (= the basic structure of a semantic representation) ensures the production of the highest possible number of more or less synonymous expressions: this is what we will call the paraphrastic potential of the SemS. A high paraphrastic potential of the SemS is necessary for successful sentence production because of numerous obstacles that may arise in the process of synthesizing a sentence – restricted lexical cooccurrence, lexical gaps, defective paradigms, LUs being incompatible with a selected syntactic construction, etc. Such difficulties can block the synthesis if no "spare" paraphrastic variants are available. For example, imagine an English speaker who wants to express the meaning 'The army attacked the city with all the means available'. If he attempts to implement the semanteme 'attack' by the verb [*to*] ATTACK, he will run into a dead end, since no adverbial intensifier carrying the meaning 'with all the means available' exists in English: *The army attacked the city __???__*. Our speaker will need to "backtrack" and implement the semanteme 'attack' as a noun (in the appropriate collocation with a light verb), for which there is a corresponding intensifying adjective (bolded): *The army launched a **full-scale** attack on the city*. Even if not completely blocked, sentence synthesis could still result in a clumsy formulation, were it not for the paraphrasing potential of the SemS. Thus, tedious repetition of the noun CIGARETTE in *Light cigarettes are as lethal as any other **cigarettes*** can be avoided thanks to the availability of a generic expression,

TOBACCO PRODUCT$_{(N)}$: *Light cigarettes are as lethal as any other **tobacco products***.

The peripheral structures, superimposed on the basic structure, ensure that the selection of the expression that conveys the propositional content provides the closest possible fit for the Speaker's intent and the given speech context. More precisely, Sem-CommS and RhetS constrain lexicalization (choice of LUs that express meanings present in the SemS) and arborization (choice of syntactic constructions that express, often indirectly, semantic relations present in the SemS), while RefS, through control of pronominalization and ellipsis, impacts the shape of the syntactic tree being constructed. In this way, the peripheral structures reduce the paraphrastic potential of the SemS. As one can see, the peripheral structures are "peripheral" only in that they do not exist independently of the basic structure; from the viewpoint of their role in synthesis, they are absolutely necessary (for more on the interaction SemS ~ Sem-CommS, see Section *4*).

2   Semantic Structure

The basic structure of the SemR is defined as follows:

> **Definition 10.2:** Semantic Structure
> The Semantic Structure 'S' (of a set of synonymous sentences) is a network whose nodes are labeled with semantemes and whose arcs are labeled with distinctive numbers identifying semantic relations between a (quasi-)predicative semanteme and the semantemes functioning as its arguments (or semantic actants).
>
> **NB:** A network is a connected, fully directed and fully labeled graph, Ch. 2, *1.6.1*.

A SemS is written in a special, hybrid metalanguage (Ch. 3, *2*), containing elements of two types: the network's nodes and arcs, along with the actantial numbers which label the arcs, are the **formal elements** of the SemS, while the semantemes labeling the nodes are its **linguistic elements**.

These elements are manipulated by rules of three types:

1. Formation rules indicate how to construct formally correct, or well-formed, expressions of the SemS formal language – that is, well-formed SemSs. In other words, these rules specify the meanings that are "correct" from the viewpoint of the language being described. (Only this rule type will be considered in this chapter – see Subsection *2.2* below.)
2. Transformation rules indicate how to manipulate expressions written in the SemS formal language in order to obtain equivalent expressions – that is,

semantically equivalent SemSs. Thus, they model the synonymy, in a broad sense, that exists in the language considered. (These are semantic para-phrasing rules, described in Ch. 12, 2.)

3. Interpretation rules indicate how to interpret the expressions of the SemS formal language in order to link them to the real linguistic objects that we want to describe by means of this language. These explanations, both for-mal and informal, allow us to grasp the informational content of the formal symbolic expressions used. For instance, we have to explain what is the "human" meaning of formal expressions such as 'John←1–love–2→Mary': the word meanings are treated as semantic predicates and semantic names, the arrows show predicate ~ argument relations, numbers on the arrows distinguish arguments of the same predicate, etc. A substantial part of the present book is actually an informal presentation of the SemS formal lan-guage interpretation rules.

2.1   Elements of the Semantic Structure

We consider in turn the SemS graph (*2.1.1*), SemS node labels (*2.1.2*) and SemS arc labels (*2.1.3*).

2.1.1   The Graph: A Semantic Network

A SemS appears as a connected, (fully) directed and (fully) labeled graph, called a network. The graph of a SemS is connected because we only want to represent meanings where all elements are properly linked. It is directed because a SemS contains elements of two types, which are not equal: (quasi-) predicates have arguments (Ch. 3, *3.1.2*), which they control. The orientation of the arcs shows the hierarchy of the elements: an arc points from a (quasi-) predicate towards one of its arguments. Finally, the graph of a SemS is labe-led for an obvious reason: it is the labels on the nodes and arcs that carry the semantic content the network is supposed to represent (the numbers on the arc do so in an indirect way, see Subsection *2.1.3* below). *Figure 10.2* shows an abstract schema of a semantic network.

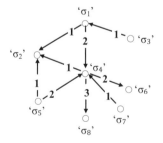

Figure 10.2 Schema of a semantic network

A semantic network is not linearly ordered: the physical disposition of its nodes on a diagram has no logical relevance.

2.1.2   Node Labels: Semantemes

As indicated in Ch. 3, *3.1*, in most cases, a semanteme corresponds to the signified of a lexical unit, but the converse does not hold: some LUs do not correspond to any semanteme – that is, these LUs are not represented in a SemS.

> Only semantically full, or meaning-carrying, lexical units are reflected in a SemS; these LUs are freely chosen by the Speaker because of their meaning.

Some LUs that we see in a sentence do not reflect the Speaker's free choices; rather, they are imposed by the grammar of his language. These LUs are semantically empty – they are introduced into the sentence for syntactic reasons. A SemS does not include (the image of) the following lexical items:

- Governed adpositions (= prepositions and postpositions) and governed conjunctions: *count **on**(PREP) somebody, hint **at**(PREP) something, insist **that**(CONJ) this is the case.*
- Support verbs: ***perform** an analysis, **commit** an error, **exercise** caution.*
- Substitute pronouns – i.e., 3rd person pronouns such as ***he/she, the former/ the latter** or **who/ which/that***, devoid of meaning and only cross-referencing a semantically full noun.

Semantemes are also used to represent semantic inflectional significations, or semantic grammemes; for instance, in English, these are the grammemes of verbal tense (PRESENT, PAST, FUTURE), nominal number (SINGULAR, PLURAL) and determination (DEFINITE, INDEFINITE, NON-DEFINITE). *Figure 10.3* shows how three grammemes of English are represented in a SemS.

verbal PAST	nominal SINGULAR	nominal PLURAL
'moment' 'X' 'before'	'one' 'X'	'more than one' 'X'

Figure 10.3 Semantic representations of three English grammemes

Syntactic grammemes, such as those of verbal number and person or of adjectival number and gender, are not represented by any semanteme: they are semantically empty and do not appear at all in a SemS. They are thus treated in the same way as empty LUs.

> REMARK. As indicated in the *Preface*, semantic inflectional meanings are the domain of morphological semantics (as opposed to lexical semantics); their description thus belongs to grammar. In this book, we consider these morphological meanings to the extent that they are relevant for the semantic representation of sentences that appear in our illustrative examples.

2.1.3   Arc Labels: Semantic Actantial Numbers

Actantial numbers that label the arcs of a SemS indicate semantic dependency relations linking a (quasi-)predicative semanteme to its actants (Ch. 4, *2.2*). A predicative semanteme can have up to six semantic actants, whence the actantial numbers ranging from 1 to 6. The maximum number of possible semantic actants has been determined empirically; for instance, the semanteme 'exile' has six semantic actants: 'X exiles Y from Z to W because of P for duration D' (*The KGB$_X$ exiled Igor$_Y$ for five years$_D$ from Moscow$_Z$ to Vladivostok$_W$ for having insulted$_P$ their chief.*). While semantemes having one, two or three actants are quite common in most languages, those with four actants or more are rather infrequent.

 Theoretically, nothing precludes the existence of lexemes with more than six semantic actants.

Figure 10.4 shows three predicative semantemes and one quasi-predicative semanteme ('mother') of English with their respective actants.

'X is.happy'	'X returns to Y from Z'	'X buys Y from Z for W'	'[X,] mother of Y'
'happy' ○ ⁝1 ↓ ○ 'X'	'return' ○ 1 2 3 ○ ○ ○ 'X' 'Y' 'Z'	'buy' ○ 1 2 3 4 ○ ○ ○ ○ 'X' 'Y' 'Z' 'W'	'mother' ○ ⁝2 ↓ ○ 'Y'

Figure 10.4 Semantic representations of four English (quasi-)predicative semantemes

Actantial numbers in a SemS are "asemantic" – in the sense that they themselves do not carry meaning. Their only task is to distinguish different actants of a predicative semanteme 'σ'; they tell us nothing about the semantic nature of the relations between these actants and 'σ'. As we have explained, in order to determine the role that a semantic actant [SemA] of 'σ' plays with respect to 'σ' in a SemS, we need to analyze the semanteme 'σ' – i.e., proceed to its semantic decomposition. This technique was illustrated in Ch. 3, *4.2.1*, with the semanteme 'return$_{(V)}$**1**'. Here is another example.

Consider the English SemS (3a), underlying the sentence *Jean likes Marie*, and the French SemS (3b), corresponding to the sentence *Jean plaît à Marie* lit. 'Jean pleases (≈ is.likeable to) Marie' = 'Marie likes Jean'.

(3) a. 'Jean←**1**–like–**2**→Marie'
     b. Fr. 'Jean←**1**–plaire–**2**→Marie'

How do these SemSs formally show that the SemA **1** of 'like' is the person who experiences a particular feeling (for someone), while the SemA **1** of 'plaire' is the person for whom this feeling is experienced (by someone)? Well, they don't: these facts are not explicitly shown in (3), but it is possible to "establish" them thanks to the semantic decomposition of the two predicates ('Ψ' stands for a complex feeling that can loosely be called *liking*; the semanteme 'cause**1**' represents non-agentive causation, as explained in Ch. 3, *4.1.2*, p. 92):

(4) a. 'X likes Y'   ≈ 'X <u>feels</u> Ψ for Y, which is caused**1** by (some properties of) Y'
     b. Fr. 'X plaît à Y' ≈ 'X <u>causes</u>**1** (by some properties of X) that Y feels Ψ for X'

> **NB:** Semantic decomposition of semantemes of language **L** should be done in terms of other semantemes of **L**. However, for simplicity's sake, decompositions of semantemes from languages other than English will be presented in English (as we just did with the French semanteme 'plaire').

The semanteme 'like', which has 'feel' as its central component, inherits from it the Experiencer of the feeling as its SemA **1** ['X'], which puts the Cause of the feeling in the position of its SemA **2** ['Y']. But 'plaire', which has 'cause**1**' as the central component, inherits the Cause of the feeling as its SemA **1** ['X'], therefore having the Experiencer of the feeling as its SemA **2** ['Y']. Thus, while both semantemes denote the same extralinguistic situation, with the same participants, these participants do not have the same communicative prominence in their respective decompositions: the SemAs of 'like' are inverted with respect to those of 'plaire', and the same holds for DSyntAs of the corresponding verbs, which stand in the relation of lexical conversion (Ch. 6, *1.1.3*, Definition 6.4).

This example has shown that the semantic decomposition of a semanteme induces the hierarchy of its actants, and that, consequently, SemAs must be numbered for each particular predicate according to this hierarchy.

The numbering of the actants of a semanteme 'σ' is crucially related to the correspondence between the semantic and syntactic actants of L('σ'), known as linking (Ch. 2, *1.3.3*), and, as has just been demonstrated, to lexical conversion.

2.2   Formal Requirements on Semantic Structures

In order to be formally correct (and therefore apt to be manipulated by linguistic rules), a SemS must satisfy a number of requirements, known as well-formed-ness rules. These concern: the organization of the graph, i.e., semantic network, itself; the labeling of the network – its nodes by semantemes and its arcs by actantial numbers; and the assignment of referential pointers to specific nodes. Let us illustrate each of these types of rules.

1. Semantic network organization rules

> The graph of the SemS must be (1) connected, (2) directed and (3) labeled.

Examples of ill-formed semantic networks, which violate these constraints, are shown in *Figure 10.5*.

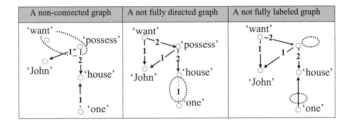

Figure 10.5 Three ill-formed semantic networks

2. Semantic network labeling rules

We have here, on the one hand, language-independent rules that specify the number of arcs leaving a node (labeled by a semanteme), and, on the other hand, language-specific rules that constrain the cooccurrence of some specific semantemes.

Rules constraining the number of arcs leaving a node

Let there be a node (of a SemS) labeled with a semanteme 'σ'.

> 1. If 'σ' is a semantic (quasi-)predicate, the number of arcs leaving this node should be equal to the number of actants of 'σ'.
> 2. If 'σ' is a semantic name, there should be no arc leaving the node.

In a SemS, all actantial positions of a (quasi-)predicative semanteme must be saturated, even if the corresponding actants are not specified or will not be expressed in the sentence under construction. If the Speaker chooses not to specify a semantic actant, an indeterminate variable (α, β, …) or a very general constant ('people', 'plant', 'substance') is used in the SemS. For example, SemSs of sentences in (5) are indicated in *Figure 10.6*.

(5) a. *John is reading.* ['John is.reading something'.]
     b. *Smoking kills.* ['Smoking tobacco by.people kills [those] people'.]

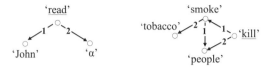

Figure 10.6 (Incomplete) SemSs of sentences (5a) and (5b)

> **NB:** Note that a predicative semanteme can function as an actant of another
> predicative semanteme, and two semantemes can share one or several actants.
> Thus, in the SemS of (5b), 'smoke' is the first actant of 'kill', while 'smoke'
> and 'kill' share the SemA 'people'.

Why do we need to indicate, in a SemS, all semantic links, including those
with actants that are unspecified or remain unexpressed? Many of these links
would be redundant in a sentence but are necessary in the network to allow a
speaker (or a computer program) to make inferences and paraphrase. Thus, if it
weren't for the underlying, unexpressed, semantemes in the SemS of (5b), how
could we link this sentence to its more elaborate paraphrases, such as *Smoking
can kill you* or *If you smoke tobacco, this will kill you*?

Rules constraining the cooccurrence of some specific semantemes

These constraints are needed to identify semantic configurations that are not
admissible in the SemSs of a particular language **L**. In other words, their role is
to tease out the SemSs of sentences that will end up being linguistically ill-formed
(Ch. 9, *1.1.2*). Being language-specific, these constraints cannot be postulated
theoretically and must be discovered empirically. Here are three examples.

Example 1

French does not allow a motion-denoting semanteme whose decomposition
includes a manner of motion component ('marcher' ≈ 'se déplacer **à pied**'
['walk' ≈ 'move on foot'], 'conduire' ≈ 'se déplacer **en véhicule** ['drive' ≈
'move in a vehicle']', 'voler' ≈ 'se déplacer **en avion**' ['fly' ≈ 'move by plane'])
to cooccur with a semanteme expressing the destination (6a):

(6) a. Fr. **marcher à la maison* 'walk home'; **conduire au travail* 'drive to
         work'; **voler à Paris* 'fly to Paris'.
     b. Fr. *rentrer à la maison* (*à pied*) 'return home (on foot)'; *aller au tra-
         vail* (*en voiture*) 'go to work (by car)'; *aller/se rendre/voyager à Paris*
         (*en avion*) 'to get/travel to Paris (by plane)'.

The manner of motion can be expressed in French by a separate lexeme, but
this happens only if one wants to insist on it; otherwise, it is dropped: (6b). In
English, however, these expressions are perfectly normal.

In the same vein, while French does not allow a motion-denoting semanteme which includes the component 'manner of motion' to cooccur with a semanteme denoting direction of motion, English allows them to cooccur freely; cf. the following translations from English, where we see again that the manner of motion is dropped (except in a marked, contrastive context): *walk **away*** ⇒ Fr. *s'éloigner (à pied)* 'to get.away from ... (on foot)'; *walk up to* ⇒ Fr. *s'approcher (à pied)* 'to get closer to ... (on foot)'; *walk **back*** ⇒ Fr. *rentrer/revenir (à pied)* 'to return/get back'; etc.

> **NB:** Similar examples, comparing constraints on the expression of motion in English, Spanish and Russian verbs, were given in Ch. 3, *3.1.1*, when discussing the structural complexity of semantemes and their language-specific character.

Rules specifically designed for modeling constraints such as these are known as filter rules. Here is a sketch of a filter rule for the French case illustrated in (6):

$$\text{Fr. } *['\sigma' = '\sigma_1 \supset \text{'manner of motion'} \overset{\mathbf{i}}{\rightarrow} \sigma_2 \supset \text{'destination'}']$$

Example 2

To indicate the time of the clock, languages (even those closely related) may resort to different constructions. For instance, while *thirteen to five* is translated into German almost literally, as *dreizehn vor fünf* '13 before 5', in French and Russian you have to say *cinq heures moins treize* 'five hours less 13' and *bez trinadcati pjat'* 'without 13 five'. The expressions #*treize minutes avant cinq* and #*trinadcat' minut do pjati*, although fully grammatical, would immediately be recognized as non-native productions. In order to preclude these, we need rules such as the following one.

Time of the clock, a moment before a given hour 'H'

      Allowable semanteme configurations

L_1: 'm_{minutes} before H_{hours}' (e.g., German, English, etc.)

L_2: 'H_{hours} minus m_{minutes}' (e.g., French, Russian, etc.)

Example 3

A configuration of semantemes (in a starting SemS) that is quite correct as such may be blocked by pragmatic considerations (see Ch. 9, *1.1.2*). Thus, the SemR 'This is freshly painted' expressed verbatim as a warning sign is unacceptable in English, because the standard official expression – a pragmatically constrained collocation – is 'wet paint' ⇔ | WET PAINT |. (However, in Russian the SemR 'This is freshly painted' corresponds to a pragmatically constrained lexeme: OKRAŠENO 'painted' [**on a sign**], which should be used in this situation.) To account for such cases, a special semantic filter rule is needed:

If a configuration of semantemes '$\tilde{\sigma}$' is to be used in pragmatically constrained circumstances,
then '$\tilde{\sigma}$' must be identical to '$\tilde{\sigma}'$', which is the signified of the expression E('$\tilde{\sigma}'$'), prescribed by the language for these circumstances.

3. Semanteme ~ referent correspondence rules

These rules, which establish correspondences between semantemes labeling SemS nodes and their referents, concern primarily the RefS; however, the referential status of semantemes impacts the way we draw semantic structures, and this is why we present the semanteme ~ correspondence rules here.

> 1. A semanteme (or a semanteme configuration) used in the SemS of an utterance should or should not have a referent, depending on its nature and its role in a given SemS.
> 2. Two identical semantemes used in the SemS of an utterance can correspond to two distinct referents; two different semantemes can have the same referent.

(7) a. *my book$_i$ and John's book$_j$ ⟨and that$_j$ belonging to John⟩*
    b. *Mary phoned John$_i$, but the rascal$_i$ did not reply.*

☞   Co-referentiality of clause elements is indicated in (7) by supplying them with the same referential index: $_i$, $_j$, etc.

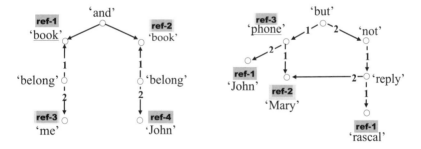

Figure 10.7 SemSs of phrase (7a) and of sentence (7b), with referential pointers

> **NB:** The arcs leaving a node labeled with the semanteme 'and' (logical conjunction) are not labeled because the number of its SemAs is theoretically unlimited: they all play the same semantic role and therefore cannot be distinguished. The same holds for 'or' (logical disjunction); however, 'but' (opposition) is different, since it has only two semantic actants, which are unequal: 'X, but Y' ≠ 'Y, but X'.

Certain semantemes, such as logical connectors 'and', 'but' and 'not', as well as the semanteme 'belong', never have referents; the action semanteme 'reply', being negated, does not have one either.[1] The semanteme 'phone$_{(V)}$', however, which refers here to a specific telephone call, must be supplied with a referential pointer.

If a semanteme appears twice in a SemS, as does 'book' in (7a), then we are talking about two different books; if two different semantemes have the same referent, as do 'John' and 'rascal' in (7b), we are obviously dealing with one and the same person.

A single referential semanteme that has multiple governors is featured in the SemS only once, i.e., is not repeated. For example, the SemS of the sentence *John* said that he [**John**] *would take his* [**John**'s] *wife to dinner* contains just one semanteme 'John' (unless we consider a less plausible interpretation that John promised to take to dinner the wife of another person also named John, in which case there would be two distinct semantemes 'John').

2.3   Substantive Requirements on Semantic Structures

In addition to being formally correct, a symbolic representation of an object must accurately reflect that object's relevant features. In other words, it has to be faithful to the represented object "not only in letter but also in spirit." The SemS, which represents the meanings of linguistic expressions, must reflect the semantic properties and organization of these expressions; this point has been raised in connection with the formal treatment of semantically anomalous sentences and the semantic representation of synonymous sentences, i.e., paraphrases (Ch. 9, *1.3* & *2.1.4*). To make sure that this is the case, the following two requirements are imposed on SemSs (of any language).

> **Requirement 1**
> The SemS of a linguistic expression ***E*** must accurately reflect ***E***'s semantic properties and ***E***'s semantic relations with other expressions {***E'***}.

For instance, the SemS(***E***) must reflect ***E***'s property of being (or not) semantically compositional, as well as ***E***'s being related to some {***E'***} by synonymy, equinomy, and so on.

Semantic compositionality of a linguistic expression (Ch. 2, *1.1.3* & Ch. 4, *2.2.1*)

If speakers perceive an expression ***E*** as compositional, the SemS of ***E*** must preserve this feature. Thus, the meaning of a compositional expression $X = Y$

---

[1] The semanteme 'designers' in the SemR of sentence (1a), *Figure 10.1*, p. 258, is also non-referential: it functions as a qualifier of 'dresses', rather than pointing to specific people. (In another context, it could of course be referential.)

⊕ *Z* must be represented by a compositional SemS: SemS(*X*) = SemS(*Y*) ⊕ SemS(*Z*).

 Recall that the symbol "⊕" stands for the operation of linguistic union (Ch. 2, *1.1.3*).

For example, the meaning of the compositional expression [*a*] *clever child* is represented as 'clever child' = 'clever' ⊕ 'child'. But the meaning of the non-compositional expression ⌜*know one's onions*⌝ 'be very knowledgeable about the subject in question' cannot be represented in this way: "'X knows X's onions" ≠ 'X knows' ⊕ 'X's onions'; ⌜*know one's onions*⌝ is an idiom (Ch. 4, *2.2.2.1*).

Synonymy of linguistic expressions (Ch. 6, *1.1.1* & Ch. 9, *2.1*)

If two expressions **E₁** and **E₂** are perceived as (exactly) synonymous, their SemSs must be identical. If their synonymy is only approximate, the respective SemSs must be (quasi-)equivalent (= it should be possible to link them by some linguistic rules). Thus, the two synonymous sentences in (2) – *Give me a call!* and *Give me a shout!* – have the same SemS and the same Sem-CommS, indicated in *Figure 10.8* (they have different RhetSs, which is not reflected here).

 Signaled is an element of the Sem-CommS, which appears within the illocutionary frame of the SemS; see immediately below.

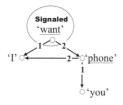

Figure 10.8 SemS of synonymous sentences (2a) and (2b), p. 257

Equinomy of linguistic expressions, i.e., ambiguity of their respective signifiers (Ch. 9, *2.4*)

If the signifier of **E** is ambiguous, **E**'s semantic analysis must result in (at least) two different SemSs, such that one corresponds to **E** and the other to an **E'** equinomous with **E**. For instance, the expression *Giant poster sale*, ambiguous between 'sale of posters of very big size' and 'sale of a very big quantity of posters' corresponds to the two SemSs, indicated in *Figure 10.9*.

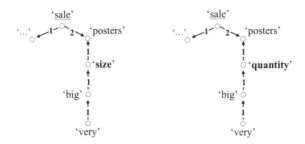

Figure 10.9 Two SemSs corresponding to the ambiguous expression *giant poster sale*

This semantic difference is reflected at the syntactic level as different dependencies of GIANT, which depends on the noun POSTERS in the first interpretation (GIANT←ATTR–POSTER$_{PL}$), and on the noun SALE in the second (Magn$_2^{quant}$←ATTR–SALE$_{SG}$).[2]

> **Requirement 2**
> Each SemS of a full-fledged sentence must have an illocutionary frame.

The illocutionary frame is a semanteme configuration which indicates the type of communication act encoded by a given SemS; for instance: 'I communicate to you [= I want you to know] that P' (the Speaker is declaring something); 'I want you to do P' (the Speaker directs his Addressee to do something); etc. The illocutionary frame is closely linked to the communicative opposition of Locutionality and will be further discussed in Subsection 3.2.1.5 below.

This concludes our presentation of the SemS, the basic structure of the SemR; we now turn to one of its peripheral structures, the Sem-CommS.

3   Semantic-Communicative Structure

Let us start by formally defining the Sem-CommS.

> **Definition 10.3:** Semantic-Communicative Structure
> The Semantic-Communicative Structure is a division of the Semantic Structure into communicative areas – subnetworks, such that each of them
> 1. has a communicatively dominant node, and
> 2. is marked with a value of one or several semantic-communicative oppositions.

The elements of the Sem-CommS are presented first (*3.1*), followed by the rules of formation of this structure (*3.2*).

---

[2] The LF Magn$_2^{quant}$, a variety of Magn, is a quantifying intensifier bearing on the second deep-syntactic actant of the keyword.

3.1   Elements of the Semantic-Communicative Structure

These are, as we just said, the communicatively dominant node (of a communicative subnetwork) and the values of communicative oppositions.

3.1.1   Communicatively Dominant Node

In each communicative area, which corresponds to a semantic subnetwork, one semanteme is chosen by the Speaker as the communicatively dominant node (CDN). The CDN of a semantic subnetwork is the semanteme to which the entire subnetwork can be reduced – without distortion of the information involved (although, of course, with losses). In other words, the CDN sums up the meaning of the subnetwork and functions as its "minimal paraphrase." For example, the subnetwork (a) in *Figure 10.10* can be reduced to 'return', and the one in (b) to 'Ulysses', these being the contents of their respective CDNs (underscored).

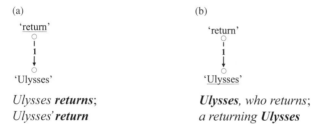

(a)

'return'

'Ulysses'

Ulysses **returns**;
Ulysses' **return**

(b)

'return'

'Ulysses'

Ulysses, *who returns*;
a returning **Ulysses**

Figure 10.10 Two semantic subnetworks with communicatively dominant nodes specified

 Note that communicative and semantic dominance can go in opposite directions, as is the case in subnetwork (b).

The CDN of a semantic subnetwork plays an important role in determining the structure of the resulting linguistic expression. Thus, subnetwork (a) can be expressed as a full sentence, while (b) can only give rise to a nominal phrase.

3.1.2   Semantic-Communicative Oppositions

Semantic-communicative oppositions characterize communicative areas, which are superposed on a SemS. A Sem-Comm opposition consists of mutually exclusive communicative values; these values are analogous to the values of an inflectional category (Ch. 2, *3.2.1*).

Communicative areas labeled with different values of one communicative opposition exhaustively divide the SemS but do not partition it: they can overlap, i.e., a semanteme configuration (in a given SemR) can belong to two different communicative areas at the same time. This is the case for the semanteme ⸢First Lady⸣[3] in the SemRs in *Figures 10.13* and *10.14*, p. 282, which is part of both the Thematic and the Rhematic communicative areas. Also, a communicative area can be further subdivided: a primary area may contain another, secondary, area; in what follows, we will not consider such subdivisions.

Out of the eight Sem-Comm oppositions distinguished in our framework, five will be presented here; for each opposition, we indicate the values and the means for expressing them (Ch. 2, *1.5*).

 Bear in mind that the Sem-Comm oppositions apply to the **meaning** of sentences, rather than to the sentences themselves, even if in what follows the Sem-Comm oppositions will be illustrated by means of sentences.[4]

Let there be sentence *S*, having the meaning 'S'.

3.1.2.1 Thematicity

> **Definition 10.4:** Semantic Rheme
> That part of the meaning 'S' that the Speaker presents as the information being supplied is called the semantic rheme of 'S'.

> **Definition 10.5:** Semantic Theme
> That part of the meaning 'S' that the Speaker presents as the information about which the Sem-Rheme is stated is called the semantic theme of 'S'.

> **Definition 10.6:** Semantic Specifier
> That part of the meaning 'S' which belongs neither to the Sem-Rheme nor the Sem-Theme is called the semantic specifier of 'S'; semantic-communicative specifiers indicate different circumstances either of the fact represented or of the corresponding speech act.

> REMARK. The "Theme ~ Rheme" opposition is also known as the "Topic ~ Comment" opposition.

Thematicity is the most important communicative opposition; its presence is mandatory in the meaning of each full sentence of each language. A full sentence must have at least a Sem-Rheme; it can additionally have a Sem-Theme and a theoretically unlimited number of Sem-Specifiers. Sentences whose Sem-CommS consists only of a Sem-Rheme, like (8a) below, are called all-rhematic, or thetic; they state that an event is taking place.

---

[3] The phrase ⸢*First Lady*⸣ is an idiom: 'the wife of a non-monarchical head of state or chief executive'.

[4] In Ch. 11, *3*, we will consider syntactic-communicative structure and syntactic-communicative oppositions: these oppositions do apply to sentences, or, more precisely, to the syntactic structure of sentences.

(8) a.   [**Q**: What is going on?]
           [*There has been an accident*]$_{\textbf{RSem}}$.
     b.   [**Q**: What about the price of gas?]
           [*Gas prices*]$_{\textbf{TSem}}$ [*continue to soar*]$_{\textbf{RSem}}$.
     c.   [**Q**: And Ulysses?]
           [*According to Penelope*]$_{\textbf{SPECSem}}$ [*Ulysses*]$_{\textbf{TSem}}$
           [*will come back*]$_{\textbf{RSem}}$.

In order to determine the distribution of Thematicity values in the meaning
'S' of a sentence *S*, we normally use an underlying question (identified above as
Q): this is a question to which *S* can be an appropriate answer. The underlying
question thus provides a minimal context for *S*. (A declarative sentence immediately preceding or following *S* can also be used for this purpose.) A question
of the type "What can be said about X?" identifies the part of the meaning 'S'
which corresponds to X as *S*'s semantic Theme, while a question like "What is
going on?" serves to identify an all-rhematic *S*.

The means for expressing the values of Thematicity are: word order, prosody, grammatical particles and morphological markers (affixes).

Word order as a communicative means

In many languages featuring so-called flexible word order, such as Latin,
Ancient Greek and the Slavic languages, word order is actively exploited to
mark the Theme ~ Rheme contrast. Thus, in Russian the meaning 'I love you'
can be expressed by six different linear arrangements:

(9) a.   *Ja tebja ljublju*   'I$_{\textbf{TSem}}$ {you love}$_{\textbf{RSem}}$' = 'I love you'
                                        [with neutral declarative intonation].
     b. i.   *Ja* LJUBLJÚ *tebja*   'I$_{\textbf{TSem}}$ {do love you}$_{\textbf{RSem}}$' [with empha-
                                        sis on *ljublju*].
         ii. *Ja ljublju* TEBJÁ   '{It is you}$_{\textbf{RSem}}$ who(m) {I love}$_{\textbf{TSem}}$'
                                        [with emphasis on *tebja*].
     c. i.   TEBJÁ *ja ljublju*   '{It is you}$_{\textbf{RSem}}$ who(m) {I love}$_{\textbf{TSem}}$'
                                        [with emphasis on *tebja*].
         ii. *Tebja* JÁ *ljublju*   '{It is me}$_{\textbf{RSem}}$ {who loves you}$_{\textbf{TSem}}$'
                                        [with emphasis on *ja*].
     d. i.   TEBJÁ *ljublju ja*   '{It is you}$_{\textbf{RSem}}$ who(m) {I love}$_{\textbf{TSem}}$'
                                        [with emphasis on *tebja*].
         ii. *Tebja ljublju* JÁ   '{It is me}$_{\textbf{RSem}}$ {who loves you}$_{\textbf{TSem}}$'
                                        [with emphasis on *ja*].
     e.   LJUBLJÚ *ja tebja*   '{Do love}$_{\textbf{RSem}}$ {I you}$_{\textbf{TSem}}$' [with
                                        emphasis on *ljublju*].
     f.   LJUBLJÚ *tebja ja*   '{Do love}$_{\textbf{RSem}}$ {you I}$_{\textbf{TSem}}$' [with
                                        emphasis on *ljublju*].

NB: We do not indicate all possible interpretations of the expressions in (9)
as a function of prosody – they are more numerous.

While in Indo-European languages the Theme of a neutral-style declarative sentence is normally expressed clause-initially, followed by the expression of the Rheme, in Salishan and Algonquian languages the phrases expressing the Theme and the Rheme appear in the inverse order. Thus, in Lushootseed (a Salishan language), the element of the clause corresponding to the syntactic predicate (which is not necessarily a verb but can belong to any word class) expresses the Rheme and occupies clause-initial position; cf.:

(10) Lushootseed

Sʔuladxʷ	*tiʔəʔ*	*suʔələd*	*ʔə*	*tiʔił*	*pišpiš*
salmon	the	eating	of	the	cat

lit. 'Salmon [is] the eating of the cat'. = 'The cat eats/is.eating salmon'.

Prosody as a communicative means

Prosody is the most widespread means for the expression of the Rheme ~ Theme contrast. Clause elements expressing the Rheme and the Theme normally have different intonation contours: in languages where the Theme precedes, it usually carries a rising intonation, and the Rheme, a falling one: [*This book↗*]**THEME** [*is very interesting↘*]**RHEME**. However, in practice, as a function of word order, the Rheme and the Theme can have contours other than these default ones: for instance, [*Only in "Crazy Kris"↗*]**RHEME** [*can one | find such pickles↘*]**THEME**. The expression of the Theme and that of the Rheme can be separated by a major pause.

Particles and affixes as a communicative means

In Tagalog, the element of the clause that expresses the Theme and precedes the main predicate is marked – in formal style – by the postposed particle AY; for example:

(11) Tagalog

Ana	*ay*	*maganda*
lit. 'Ana	THEME	be.pretty-PRES' = 'Ana, [she] is.pretty'.

Japanese marks the thematic sentence element by means of the suffix **-wa**:

(12) Japanese

Taroo+ **wa**	*gakusei*	*des+u*
Taro	THEME student	be	PRES

lit. 'Taro, [he] student is'. = 'Taro is a student'.

3.1.2.2 Givenness

> **Definition 10.7:** Given
> That part of the meaning 'S' that the Speaker presents as already active in the mind of the Addressee is called Given in 'S'.

In other words, the Addressee is presumed capable of identifying the referent of what is Given.

> **Definition 10.8:** New
> That part of the meaning 'S' that the Speaker presents as not yet active in the mind of the Addressee is called New in 'S'.

The Addressee is presumed incapable of identifying the referent of what is New.

(13) a. [**Q**: Where is the book you are talking about?]
    [*The book*$_{GIVEN}$ *is*]$_{T_{Sem}}$ [*on the table*$_{GIVEN}$]$_{R_{Sem}}$.
   b. [**Q**: Where is the book you are talking about?]
    [*The book*$_{GIVEN}$ *is*]$_{T_{Sem}}$ [*on a table*$_{NEW}$]$_{R_{Sem}}$.
   c. [**Q**: What is there on the table?]
    [*On the table*$_{GIVEN}$ *there is*]$_{T_{Sem}}$ [*a book*$_{NEW}$]$_{R_{Sem}}$.

Givenness can be expressed by word order, special function words (articles) and morphological markers (affixes).

The oppositions of Thematicity and Givenness are logically mutually independent so that the four combinations shown in *Table 10.1* are possible.

Table 10.1 The interplay of Thematicity and Givenness

THEME Given ~	[*Now I'd like to talk about the poem "Evasion."*]
RHEME New	[*This poem*]$_{T_{Sem}}$, **GIVEN** [*offers a nice example of his mature style*]$_{R_{Sem}}$, **NEW**
THEME Given ~	[*For a long time, John was trying to solve that problem.*]
RHEME Given	[*Finally,*]$_{Sem-Spec}$ [*he*]$_{T_{Sem}}$, **GIVEN** [*did it*]$_{R_{Sem}}$, **GIVEN**.
THEME New ~	[The first sentence of a newspaper article]
RHEME New	[*A tourist*]$_{T_{Sem}}$, **NEW** [*was injured in a hiking expedition*]$_{R_{Sem}}$, **NEW**.
THEME New ~	[*For five years, John has tried to solve that problem.*]
RHEME Given	[*But one of his colleagues*]$_{T_{Sem}}$, **NEW** [*just did it*]$_{R_{Sem}}$, **GIVEN**.

By default, the Theme is Given and the Rheme, New; all other combinations are marked (= non-neutral).

3.1.2.3 Focalization

> **Definition 10.9:** Focalized
> That part of the meaning 'S' that the Speaker presents as being logically salient is called Focalized in 'S'.

> **Definition 10.10:** Non-Focalized
> That part of the meaning 'S' that the Speaker does not present as being logically salient is called Non-focalized in 'S'.

By convention, the value **Non-focalized** is not indicated.

(14) a. [**Q**: What is there on the table?]
        [*It's a book*]$_{R_{Sem}}$, **FOCALIZED** [*that is on the table*]$_{T_{Sem}}$.
   b. [**Q**: What is there on the table?]
        [*A BÓOK*]$_{R_{Sem}}$, **FOCALIZED** [*is on the table*]$_{T_{Sem}}$.
   c. [**Q**: Where are the book and the magazine?]
        [*As for the book,*]$_{T_{Sem}}$, **FOCALIZED** [*it is on the table*]$_{R_{Sem}}$.
   d. [**Q**: What about the book?]
        [*The book*]$_{T_{Sem}}$ [*is on the table*]$_{R_{Sem}}$.

Focalization can be expressed by the following means:

1. Special lexical units – for instance, LUs used to indicate the focalized character of the Theme, such as Eng. ⌜SPEAKING OF⌝, ⌜WHEN IT COMES TO⌝, ⌜AS FOR⌝, etc.
2. Syntactic constructions – clefts (*It's X that* ...; *What X is/does is* ...) for Rheme focalization, as in (14a), and prolepses, for Theme focalization (Fr. [*Le livre,*]$_{T_{Sem}}$, **FOC** [*il est sur la table*]$_{R_{Sem}}$ lit. 'The book, it is on the table'.).
3. Prosody, as in (14b).

3.1.2.4 Assertivity

> **Definition 10.11:** Asserted
> That part of the meaning 'S' that is presented by the Speaker as communicated and can therefore be negated and questioned is called Asserted in 'S'.

> **Definition 10.12:** Presupposed
> That part of the meaning 'S' that is presented by the Speaker not as communicated but as taken for granted and which is therefore unaffected even if all of 'S' is negated or questioned is called Presupposed in 'S'.

The opposition of Assertivity is used mostly (but not exclusively) to describe LUs whose meaning, in addition to an asserted part, contains a presupposed part (Ch. 5, *3.4*).

The communicative value **Presupposed** does not cover all cases of presupposition considered in the literature. A broader concept of presupposition, which applies to meanings of sentences, was introduced and illustrated in Ch.

9, *2.3*. It was pointed out that presupposition-carrying LUs are just one possible source of sentence-level presupposition, which can also be induced by the syntactic structure or referential properties of the sentence or its elements. Using the terminology of this chapter, we could say that the communicative opposition of Assertivity is expressed by lexical means or syntactic constructions; this is illustrated in (15) and (16), respectively.

(15) a.   *Bob regrets ⟨does not regret⟩ that he did not work harder.*
     b.   *Does Bob regret that he did not work harder?*

The presupposed meaning in the sentences in (15) – 'Bob did not work harder' – is expressed lexically, by the verb REGRET, which is factive (Ch. 9, *2.3*, p. 247): even if Bob does not feel regret or his feeling that way is questioned, it remains true that he did not work harder.

(16) A: – *This controversial report was published in* National Geographic.
     B: – *No, it wasn't.*

The meaning 'this report is controversial' is expressed as presupposed by an adjectival modifier (*controversial*). While rejecting A's statement, B continues to accept A's presupposition that the report in question is controversial.

3.1.2.5   Locutionality

The opposition of Locutionality concerns enunciation modes, i.e., the ways in which the content of an utterance is conveyed. The Speaker can choose to either (1) communicate something to somebody, or (2) signal something without explicitly communicating it, or else (3) perform, by uttering a sentence, the very action that this sentence describes. These three enunciation modes correspond to the three values of this opposition:

> **Definition 10.13:** Communicated
> That part of the meaning 'S' that the Speaker presents in a form geared to the transmission of information (in particular, it allows for negation and interrogation) is called Communicated in 'S'.

> **Definition 10.14:** Signaled
> That part of the meaning 'S' that the Speaker presents in a form geared to the expression of his interior state or of the type of his speech act (i.e., it does not allow for negation and interrogation) is called Signaled in 'S'.

> **Definition 10.15:** Performative
> That part of the meaning 'S' whose enunciation constitutes the action denoted by 'S' is called Performative.

(17) a. [*This is delicious!*]_{**Communicated**} [said upon tasting some food]
    b. [*How delicious!*]_{**Signaled**} | [*Yummy!*]_{**Signaled**} [said on the same occasion]
    c. [*I promise*]_{**Performative·**} | [*I give you my word*]_{**Performative·**}

To communicate is taken here in a technical sense (much narrower than its usual meaning): 'to explicitly express the informational content in the form of an utterance that corresponds to a logical proposition' (Ch. 9, *1.2*).

To signal means 'to express *tout court* – without constructing logical propositions'. The Speaker can signal his opinion (e.g., he finds curious the state of affairs he is talking about: *Funny thing ⟨Curiously (enough)⟩*) or his rhetorical action (e.g., he is going to give an example illustrating what he just said: *Say, … ⟨For instance, …⟩*).

A performative utterance normally contains a performative LU, most often a verb, which denotes an act accomplished by the enunciation of a particular form of this LU. To be used performatively, a verb must be in the present indicative and the 1st person; thus, to accomplish the act of promising, the Speaker has to say *I promise*. (The utterance *I promised* is not performative – it communicates the meaning 'I promised', i.e., describes an act of mine.)

REMARKS

1. Not all performative utterances contain just one performative lexeme; there are more complex performative expressions: for instance, *I now pronounce you man and wife*, used to perform the act of marrying.
2. Not all performative LUs are verbs: *Thanks!* is a noun, but by uttering it the Speaker performs the act of thanking.
3. The study of performative utterances has been a staple of pragmatics; see Further Reading.

The first enunciation mode – communication – produces descriptive utterances whose content concerns the state of affairs in the world, which includes the Speaker himself. The other two modes of enunciation – signaling and performing speech acts – result in non-descriptive utterances, centered upon the Speaker. For this reason, non-descriptive utterances have specific syntactic behavior: they cannot be negated, interrogated or freely modified (**It is **not** true that yuck!* ~ ***Is it** true that yuck?* ~ ***Very** yuck!*).

Each of the enunciation modes corresponds to a particular semanteme configuration in the SemS indicating the Speaker's enunciative goals:

- '**I communicate to you** that …';
- '**I signal** that I want/I feel/I believe that …', '…that I am explaining …', '…that I am justifying …', '…that I am illustrating …';
- 'By pronouncing **E, I am doing that which is denoted** by **E**'.

These semanteme configurations represent illocutionary frames, mentioned in Subsection *2.3* above as obligatory elements of our semantic representations.

REMARKS

1. Note that the illocutionary frames must themselves be marked as **Signaled** since they are not meant to be realized lexically ("verbatim"), but are needed in order impose a particular sentence type – declarative vs. expressive – to the sentence under construction. Thus, the configuration '[I communicate that]**Signaled** the minister has been arrested' yields the declarative sentence *The minister has been arrested* (rather than *I communicate that the minister has been arrested.*); the configuration '[I feel]**Signaled** disgusted by this' gives rise to the expressive sentence *How disgusting! ⟨Disgusting!, Yuck!⟩.* To produce the declarative sentence *This disgusts me*, the illocutionary frame of its SemS must be 'I communicate that ...' and be marked as **Signaled**.
2. Since declarative sentences represent the non-marked (= default) case, by convention, we omit the illocutionary frame 'I communicate that ...' from their semantic structures.

The opposition of Locutionality is expressed by special lexical means: signalatives for the expression of **Signaled** (e.g., *Wow!* or *Phew!*) and performatives for the expression of **Performative** (e.g., *I promise to ...* or *I am cursing you!*).

3.2   Formal Requirements on Semantic-Communicative Structures

Three Sem-CommS formation rules will be presented, all having to do with the most important semantic-communicative opposition – Thematicity.

> **Sem-Comm-Structure Constitution Rule**
> The Sem-CommS superposed on a SemS representing a full clause must contain a Rhematic area; it can additionally contain a Thematic area and one or several Specifier areas.

For examples, see *3.1.2.1* above.

> **Sem-Comm-Structure Connectedness Rules**
> **Rule 1: Obligatory connectedness of Rheme and Theme dominant nodes**
> The CDN of the Sem-Rhematic area and that of the Sem-Thematic area (distinguished in a SemS) must be directly connected by a semantic link.

The presence of such a link is necessary because, in a message articulated into a Sem-Rheme and a Sem-Theme, the Sem-Rheme provides information about the Sem-Theme. Without a direct link between the two communicatively dominant nodes, which, as we know, sum up the semantic content of their respective subnetworks, the SemR could not be realized as a coherent message.

NB: Some "transparent" semantemes – such as the negative semanteme 'no' or modal semantemes 'can'/'possible' – can intervene between the CDNs of the rhematic and thematic areas. This, however, is too technical a question to be elaborated upon here.

> **Rule 2: No semantic discontinuities within a communicative area**
> The Sem-Rhematic and the Sem-Thematic communicative areas should not be semantically discontinuous – that is, they should not contain semantemes that are not semantically linked to other semantemes in the area.

Within a discontinuous communicative area it is impossible to isolate a unique CDN and, as a result, to produce a coherent sentence.

4   Interaction of Semantic and Semantic-Communicative Structures in Linguistic Synthesis

We now turn to the interaction between the structures of a SemR during sentence synthesis; to simplify our task, we only consider the interaction between the SemS and Sem-CommS. First we show how these two structures can be "put together" to form a SemS ~ Sem-CommS pairing (*4.1*); then we explain how sentence synthesis can be controlled by superposing on an initial SemS different Sem-CommSs (*4.2*).

4.1   SemS ~ Sem-CommS Pairings and the Well-Formedness of the SemR

There are few constraints as to what Sem-CommSs can be superposed on a SemS.

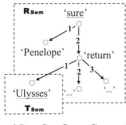 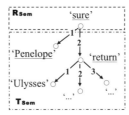 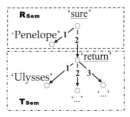

*SemS ~ Sem-CommS Pairing 1	*SemS ~ Sem-CommS Pairing 2	SemS ~ Sem-CommS Pairing 3
Q: What about U.?	**Q**: # What about P. and the return of U.?	**Q**: What about the return of U.?

Figure 10.11 illustrates three pairings, two of which are bad and one of which is good.

Pairing 1 in *Figure 10.11* is deficient because of the ill-formed Sem-CommS: it features a discontinuity between the Sem-Theme and the Sem-Rheme; and there is no coherent underlying question for it. Pairing 2 has a discontinuous Sem-Theme ('Penelope' and 'return' are not semantically linked within the Sem-Thematic area), so it cannot be assigned one CDN; note also the "non-unique" underlying question. Pairing 3, however, is well-formed and has grammatical realizations: *Ulysses' return* ⟨≡ *That Ulysses will come back*⟩ *is certain* ⟨≡ *a certainty, a sure thing*⟩ *for Penelope.*

4.2   SemS ~ Sem-CommS Pairings and the Paraphrastic Potential of the SemS

We indicate the pairings of a single SemS with four different Sem-CommSs and compare their respective realizations from the viewpoint of their semantic closeness.

SemS ~ Sem-CommS Pairing 4

[**Q**: And the Opposition?]

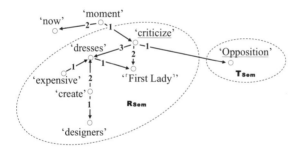

Figure 10.12 SemS ~ Sem-CommS pairing underlying sentences in (18)

This pairing, featured within the SemR in *Figure 10.1* above, yields, for instance, the following realizations (sentence (18a) was already cited as (1a)):

(18) a. [*The Opposition*]**T**Sem [*criticizes the First Lady's expensive designer dresses*]**R**Sem.
     b. [*The Opposition*]**T**Sem [*voices criticism of the First Lady's costly designer clothes*]**R**Sem.

SemS ~ Sem-CommS Pairing 5

[**Q**: What is the Opposition criticizing the First Lady for?]

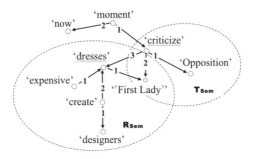

Figure 10.13 SemS ~ Sem-CommS pairing underlying sentences in (19)

This pairing can be realized by the following sentences:

(19) a. [*The Opposition **criticizes** the First Lady*]**T**$_{\textbf{Sem}}$ [*for her high-priced designer dresses*]**R**$_{\textbf{Sem}}$.

  b. [*The Opposition is critical of the First Lady*]**T**$_{\textbf{Sem}}$ [*on account of her pricey designer apparel*]**R**$_{\textbf{Sem}}$.

NB: The **R**$_{\textbf{Sem}}$ ~ **T**$_{\textbf{Sem}}$ overlap ("First Lady") observed at the Sem-level (Fig. 10.13) gives rise, in the sentences (19a–b), to two occurrences of the phrase *First Lady*, the second one being pronominalized.

SemS ~ Sem-CommS Pairing 6

[**Q**: And the First Lady?]

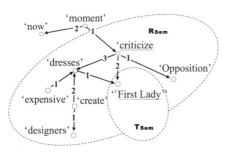

Figure 10.14 SemS ~ Sem-CommS pairing underlying sentences in (20)

Two possible realizations of this pairing follow:

(20) a. [*The First Lady*]**T**$_{\textbf{Sem}}$ [*gets criticized by the Opposition for her expensive designer dresses*]**R**$_{\textbf{Sem}}$.

  b. [*The First Lady*]**T**$_{\textbf{Sem}}$ [*is under fire from the Opposition over her costly designer dresses*]**R**$_{\textbf{Sem}}$.

SemS ~ Sem-CommS Pairing 7

[**Q**: What about the First Lady's outfit?]

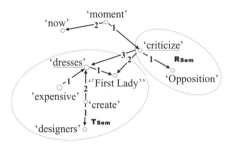

Figure 10.15 SemS ~ Sem-CommS pairing underlying sentences in (21)

This pairing can be implemented, for example, by the sentences in (21); (21b) was already cited as (1b).

(21) a. [*The First Lady's pricey designer dresses*]**TSem** [*are criticized by the Opposition*]**RSem**.

b. [*The First Lady's expensive designer dresses*]**TSem** [*draw flak from the Opposition*]**RSem**.

Since sentences produced from the four pairings above only have their SemSs in common, they are paraphrases in a broad sense; while such paraphrases are not mutually substitutable in all contexts, they must be so in at least some. Paraphrases produced from a specific pairing are paraphrases in a narrow sense: they should be substitutable in all contexts.

As these examples show, Sem-CommS plays a decisive role in sifting out close paraphrases from more remote ones, thus reducing the paraphrastic potential of the SemS on which it is superposed.

Further Reading

Semantic structure: Mel'čuk 2012b: 161–288; Polguère 1997.

Semantic representation [NLP perspective]: Abend & Rappaport 2017.

Semantic actants: Mel'čuk 2004a; see also, in other frameworks, argument structure and linking: Grimshaw 1990; Pustejovsky 1991; Bencini & Goldberg 2000; Givón 2001: 105–173; Van Valin 2004; Lehman 2006; Suihkonen *et al.* 2012.

Semantic-communicative structure: [articles and book chapters] Halliday 1967; Chafe 1987; Iordanskaja 1992; Polguère 1997; Beyssade *et al.* 2004; Féry & Krifka 2008; Zimmermann & Onea 2011; Mel'čuk 2012b: 289–394; [monographs] Lambrecht 1994; Mel'čuk 2001; Krifka & Musan 2012.

Performatives: Austin 1962.

Semantic Structure ~ Semantic-Communicative Structure Pairings: Milićević 2013.

11 Deep-Syntactic Representation

In the previous chapter we introduced the Semantic Representation [SemR] of utterances, the **input** for the semantic rules of a Meaning-Text linguistic model. The present chapter is dedicated to the Deep-Syntactic Representation [DSyntR], which is the result of the application, or the **output**, of these rules. DSyntR, the interface between semantics and syntax, could also, in fact, be considered in a book titled "Introduction to Syntax," as the input for the rules of the syntactic module. However, the DSyntR must be introduced before the rules of the semantic module – hence its presentation in this book.

As has been stated (Ch. 10, p. 256), a SemR encodes the meaning shared by a set of paraphrases and normally yields (under synthesis) several alternative DSyntRs. In contrast, as a rule, a DSyntR reflects the organization of a concrete individual sentence (or a few structurally very close sentences).

The very general concept of sentence – the central unit in syntax – was introduced in Ch. 2, *2.1.4*. Let us add here that a sentence is perceived by speakers as a "complete utterance" that carries a prosody belonging to a small set of specific prosodies, called *sentence prosodies*; these include two major pauses which can always surround the sentence and a final intonation contour, specific to language **L**. Sentence prosodies minimally include declarative, interrogative and exclamative prosodies.

A given DSyntR reflects the first step of the verbalization of a SemR, the most complex stage of linguistic synthesis, laden with consequences: it is here that lexical and syntactic choices are made that largely determine the final shape of the sentence to be produced. (Technically speaking, the operations taking place in this phase of synthesis are lexicalization and arborization, plus, in some languages, morphologization; more will be said on these in the next chapter.) A DSyntR thus encodes what might be called the structural frame of the sentence, while allowing for finer-grained choices at closer-to-surface representation levels.

In keeping with the distinction "deep (sub)level ~ surface (sub)level" of linguistic representations (Ch. 1, 2.2.2), the DSyntR of a sentence S is oriented towards the meaning of S, i.e., the content to be expressed by S; it is supposed to make all essential semantic contrasts explicit, through the choice of appropriate LUs, grammemes and syntactic links. Details relevant only from a formal viewpoint are dealt with at the level of Surface-Syntactic Representation [SSyntR], oriented towards the form of expression. For instance, the expressions (a) [*the*] *President's speech* and (b) [*the*] *speech by the President*, being semantically identical and syntactically very close, are represented in the same way at the DSynt-level; however, given their constructional differences, at the SSynt-level they are assigned two distinct structures (cf. a similar example on p. 15).

DSynt-level	SSynt-level	
SPEECH$_{SG}$–**I**→PRESIDENT$_{SG}$	⇔ SPEECH$_{SG}$–**possessive**→PRESIDENT$_{SG}$	(a)
	⇔ SPEECH$_{SG}$–**agentive**→BY–**prepositional**→	(b)
	PRESIDENT$_{SG}$	

Only the deeper one of these representations, the DSyntR, is relevant for semantics. To describe it, we proceed as follows: Section *1* offers a general characterization of the DSyntR; Sections *2* and *3* present Deep-Syntactic Structure, the basic structure of the DSyntR, and one of its peripheral structures – Deep-Syntactic-Communicative Structure; finally, Section *4* illustrates the role the DSyntS plays in sentence synthesis, in particular, its usefulness for the description of important phenomena taking place in the transition from semantics to syntax.

1 General Characterization of the Deep-Syntactic Representation

Definition 11.1: Deep-Syntactic Representation
The Deep-Syntactic Representation [DSyntR] of a sentence is a quadruplet
DSyntR = ⟨DSyntS, DSynt-CommS, DSynt-AnaphS, DSynt-ProsS⟩, where DSyntS stands for deep-syntactic structure, DSynt-CommS for the deep-syntactic-communicative structure, DSynt-AnaphS for the deep-syntactic-anaphoric structure, and DSynt-ProsS for the deep-syntactic-prosodic structure.

The DSyntR of a sentence S characterizes S according to its four aspects, each corresponding to a distinct structure:

1. Deep-Syntactic Structure, the basic structure of the DSyntR, is a dependency tree (Ch. 2, *1.6.1*); its nodes are labeled with deep (≈ semantically full) LUs subscripted with deep grammemes (Ch. 2, *3.2.1*) and its branches are labeled with the names of deep-syntactic relations.

2. Deep-Syntactic-Communicative Structure is the counterpart of the communicative structure at the semantic level, the Sem-CommS (Ch. 10, *3*). Its presence in the DSyntR is necessary in order to control lexical and grammatical choices, as well as the linear ordering of lexemes in the subsequent transitions towards the morphological string.

3. Deep-Syntactic-Anaphoric Structure encodes anaphoric relations between LUs in the sentence. Thus, the sentence *A Montreal **man**$_i$ wants you to manage **his**$_i$ website for **him**$_i$* contains three wordform occurrences that refer to the same person; they are shown by boldface and the subscript $_i$. At the DSynt-level, the corresponding lexical nodes are linked by the anaphoric relation: MAN ◄┄┄► MAN ◄┄┄► MAN. (Since anaphora is an equivalence relation between lexical expressions that have the same referent, it is represented by a double-headed arrow.) The DSyntR does not allow for pronouns and ellipses; DSynt-AnaphS is thus necessary for computing pronominalizations and ellipses in the transition towards the surface-syntactic representation.

4. Deep-Syntactic-Prosodic Structure [DSynt-ProsS] specifies semantically induced prosodies. These are the prosodies which come from the SemR (they express certain semantemes present in the initial Semantic Structure), such as neutral, emphatic, ironic prosody, or declarative, interrogative, exclamatory prosody, etc. (Syntactically induced prosodic elements, for instance, obligatory pauses and breath groups, are not represented at the syntactic level: they appear only in the deep-morphological string.)

As an illustration, the DSyntR of sentence (1) appears in *Figure 11.1* below:

(1) *John bitterly regrets his stupid error.*

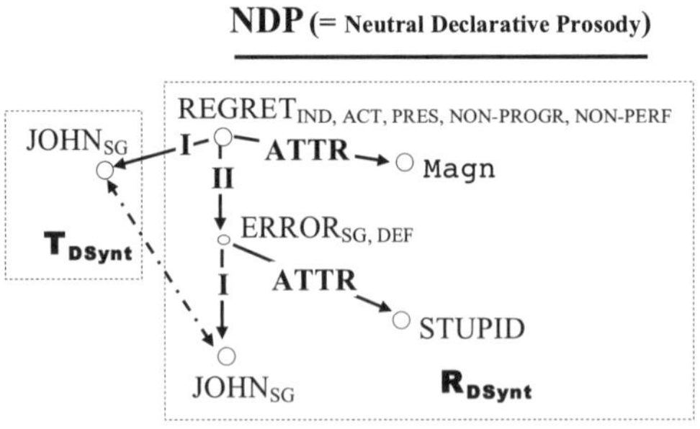

Figure 11.1 DSyntR of sentence (1)

Magn is the name of the lexical function (Ch. 7) representing intensification; INDICATIVE, ACTIVE, PRESENT, NON-PROGRESSIVE, NON-PERFECTIVE and SINGULAR, DEFINITE are deep grammemes; **I, II** and **ATTR** are the names of three deep-syntactic relations; **RHEME**$_{\text{DSynt}}$ and **THEME**$_{\text{DSynt}}$ are the markers of the communicative opposition of Thematicity at the DSynt-level.

The formalism of the DSyntR, and, in particular, that of the DSyntS, is valid cross-linguistically: it is sufficient to represent the overall structural and lexical organization of any sentence in any language. This point will be looked at in more detail below.

2   Deep-Syntactic Structure

The basic structure of the SemR is defined as follows:

> **Definition 11.2:** Deep-Syntactic Structure
> The Deep-Syntactic Structure (of a sentence) is a dependency tree whose nodes are labeled with deep LUs, subscripted with deep grammemes, and whose branches are labeled with names of deep-syntactic relations.

We now present the elements of the DSyntS: the graph itself, i.e., a dependency tree (*2.1*), and the linguistic elements that label it: deep LUs (*2.2*), deep grammemes (*2.3*), and deep-syntactic dependency relations (*2.4*).

2.1   Dependency Tree

Syntactic dependency, a particular type of linguistic dependency, was introduced in Ch. 2, *1.3.2*, Definition 2.4.

 Syntactic dependency is shorthand for *syntactic dependency relation*.

The characterization of the dependency tree from Ch. 2, *1.6.1*, p. 51 is repeated here (slightly rephrased):

> **Definition 11.3:** Dependency Tree
> A dependency tree is a directed connected graph that simultaneously satisfies the following two conditions:
> 1. The uniqueness of the governor: each node accepts no more than one entering branch.
> 2. The existence of the top node (or the summit): there is one and only one node that accepts no entering branches.

An abstract schema of the dependency tree is shown in *Figure 11.2*.

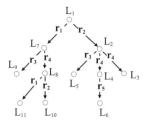

Figure 11.2 Schema of a dependency tree

 The nodes of a dependency tree are not linearly ordered; this fact should always be borne in mind in order for our examples of syntactic structures to be understood correctly.

While the dependency tree formalism is used at both deep- and surface-syntactic sublevels of representation, the two sublevels differ with respect to the types of LUs labeling the nodes of the tree and the types of syntactic dependency relations labeling its branches.

2.2   Deep Lexical Units

A deep LU is either a genuine, semantically full LU (*2.2.1*), a lexical function (*2.2.2*), or a fictitious lexeme (*2.2.3*).

The opposition "(semantically) full ~ (semantically) empty" LU was introduced in Ch. 3, *3.1*. A full LU, which corresponds directly to a seman-teme (a configuration of semantemes) in the starting semantic structure, appears legitimately in the DSyntS, since, as explained at the beginning of this chapter, this syntactic structure is oriented towards meaning, i.e., sup-posed to express all relevant meaning distinctions. In contrast, an empty LU – a substitute pronoun (HE, SHE, WHICH(relative pronoun), …), a gov-erned preposition/conjunction (a*gree **with** Z **that** Y, ask Y **whether** Z*), etc. – which has no direct correspondent in the semantic structure, cannot appear in the DSyntS (it is only inserted into the SSyntS, the syntactic structure oriented towards the form of expression, i.e., supposed to reflect all relevant formal distinctions).

A deep LU can belong to one of the following five parts of speech (Ch. 2, *2.2*): verb [V], noun [N], adjective [A = ADJ], adverb [ADV], and clausative [CLAUS]. (Full conjunctions and prepositions are considered as a subclass of adverbs.)

2.2.1   Semantically Full Lexical Units

A semantically full LU is either a semantically full lexeme or an idiom.

• **Full lexemes** (Ch. 4, *2.1*) are simple, derived or compound.

A simple lexeme, i.e., one that is non-derived and non-compound, appears at the DSynt-level as a simple node label: GIRL1, LOVE$_{(N)}$2, UNDERSTAND4, FAST$_{(ADJ)}$1, QUICKLY3, etc.

A derived lexeme is represented at the DSynt-level as a combination of a simple lexeme, constituting the base of the derivation, with a derivational means, which expresses a derivateme (Ch. 2, *3.2.2*); for instance, Sp. CIELITO 'nice little sky' is represented in the DSyntS as one node: [*DIM* ⊕ CIELO], where *DIM* stands for "diminutive suffix," and CIELO is the lexeme meaning 'sky').

A compound lexeme is represented at the DSynt-level as a combination of two or more full lexemes (more precisely, two or more stems); for instance, Ger. BERLINREISE lit. 'Berlin trip' = 'trip to Berlin' appears in the DSyntS as [BERLIN ⊕ REISE 'trip'].

• **Idioms** (Ch. 4, *2.2.2.1*)

An idiom, or a non-compositional lexemic phraseme, such as ⌈RED TAPE⌉, ⌈LAME DUCK⌉1, ⌈TAKE THE BULL BY THE HORNS⌉, ⌈SPILL THE BEANS⌉, ⌈BY HEART⌉, etc., is represented in the DSyntS as a single node, that is, in the same way as a simple lexeme. (The node labeled with an idiom is developed into the corresponding surface dependency subtree at the SSynt-level.)

2.2.2   Lexical Functions

We saw earlier, in *Figure 11.1*, the symbol of a lexical function: Magn. Lexical functions [LFs], formal tools used for modeling semantic-lexical relations (Ch. 6) – that is, the "conventionalized" relations between LUs, such as synonymy, antonymy, nominalization, intensification, etc. – were described in Ch. 7. We can therefore limit ourselves to a few additional examples of simple standard LFs (Ch. 7), as a way to refresh the reader's memory.

Examples of paradigmatic LFs (semantic derivations)

Syn$_{\text{'synonym of L'}}$($assist_{(V)}$*1*)	≈ *help*$_{(V)}$, *aid*$_{(V)}$, **coll.** ⌈*give a hand*⌉
Anti$_{\text{'antonym of L'}}$($like_{(V)}$*1*)	= ⌈*do not like*⌉, *dislike* < *hate*
Conv$_{21\text{'conversive of L'}}$($preceding$)	= *following*
S$_{0\text{'fact of being L'}}$($serious$*1*)	= *seriousness*
S$_{1\text{'person who L-s'}}$($escape_{(V)}$)	= *escapee; fugitive*
S$_{2\text{'that which is L-ed'}}$($cause_{(V)}$)	= *result*$_{(N)}$*1*
A$_{1\text{'characteristic of the person who L-s'}}$($know_{(V)}$*1*)	= *aware* [*of* N$_Y$]

Examples of syntagmatic LFs (collocations)

Magn·'intensely'(care(V))	= *deeply, really,* **coll.** ⌈*like hell*⌉
Bon·'good'(*criticism*)	= *constructive; fair*
Ver·'such as it should be'(*definition*)	= *rigorous*
Oper1·'do'(*activity*)	= *perform* [ART ~], *engage* [*in* ART ~]
Oper2·'undergo'(*humiliation*)	= *suffer* [~]
Func0·'there.be'(*rumors*)	= [ART ~] *circulate*
Real1·'do what one is supposed to do with'(*problem*)	= *solve* [ART ~]

As noted before, the use of LFs is twofold. On the one hand, they are used in *Explanatory Combinatorial Dictionaries* (Ch. 8) for the description of lexical relations; this description ensures the correct selection of derivationally and collocationally bound surface lexemes to be introduced into the SSyntS. On the other hand, LFs underlie the lexical-syntactic paraphrasing system incorporated into the Meaning-Text linguistic models (Ch. 12, *2.2*). Lexical-syntactic paraphrasing rules establish equivalences between configurations of LFs; their domain of application is the Deep-Syntactic Structure.

2.2.3   Fictitious Lexemes

A fictitious lexeme does not exist in language **L**, but is posited (by the researcher) to represent, in the DSyntS, a meaning-bearing syntactic construction of **L**. Such constructions constitute a special case: a "normal" syntactic construction does not carry meaning itself (= does not correspond directly to a configuration of semantemes in the SemS).

A meaning-bearing syntactic construction is, generally speaking, specific to a given language (and does not have correspondents in other languages). For this reason, in order to preserve the universality of deep-syntactic relations (see below, *2.4.1.1*), we represent such specific constructions by means of fictitious lexemes. Here are three examples, taken from English and Russian.

    A fictitious lexeme appears (in the DSyntS) between double angular quotes: «L».

Example 1

Eng. *X V-s* **Z** [*an*] *Y*: She_X baked **me**_Z a cake_Y.
        I_X made **Jane**_Z a dress_Y.

In the above construction, where V is a creation verb, X the Creator, Y the Creation and Z the Beneficiary, Z is not an element of the Government Pattern (Ch. 2, *1.2.2* and Ch. 8, *2.2.1*) of the verb: since the Beneficiary is not an obligatory participant of the corresponding situation, it is not one of the verb's semantic actants and, consequently, cannot be one of its deep-syntactic actants, either (for the notion of deep-syntactic actant, see below, Subsection *2.4.2.1*, Definition 11.2). To represent the Beneficiary in the above contexts at the DSynt-level, we use the fictitious lexeme «FOR»:

$$L_{(V\text{ 'creation'})}-\mathbf{ATTR}\rightarrow\text{«FOR»}-\mathbf{II}\rightarrow L_{(N)}$$

Example 2

Eng. X V-s (NUM) **Z**: I_X walked 3 ***blocks***$_Z$.

John$_X$ backpacked 300 ***miles***$_Z$ on the Appalachian Trail.

John$_X$ drove the car 150 ***miles***$_Z$.

Australia ships its bauxite 3000 ***miles***$_Z$ to New Zealand.

The ***ball***$_X$ is thrown 5 ***meters***$_Z$ upward.

The construction contains a verb V whose meaning includes a semantic component "directed motion": it can be intransitive (*to walk, to backpack*) or transitive (*to drive [a Volvo]*), it can denote the causation of directed motion (*to ship [the materials]*), it can be in the active or the passive (*to be thrown*). Z is a noun denoting a distance – as a rule, a measure noun such as MILE or KILOMETER, but not necessarily: *I drive a large **stretch**$_Z$ of highway every day*; it specifies the distance covered by the moving entity. In the DSynt-structure, this construction is represented by the fictitious lexeme «DISTANCE». (In the SSyntRel, the noun Z is subordinated to V by the **distance-circumstantial** SSynt-relation.)

Example 3

Rus. N + NUM: *metrov desjat'* lit. 'meters ten' = 'maybe ten meters';

čelovek sto lit. 'people hundred' = 'maybe a hundred people'

This is the Russian approximate-quantitative construction, which contrasts semantically with the "normal" numeral construction NUM + N (*desjat' metrov* 'ten meters', etc.). In the approximate construction the meaning 'maybe' is expressed by the anteposition of the noun with respect to the numeral (whereas in the "normal" construction the noun follows the numeral, just like in English). Here is the DSyntS of the approximate construction, featuring the fictitious lexeme «PRIMERNO» 'maybe' (lit. 'approximately'):

$$\text{«PRIMERNO»}\leftarrow\mathbf{ATTR}-L_{(NUM)}\leftarrow\mathbf{ATTR}-L_{(N)PL}.$$

The DSyntS of the constructions of the type *desjat' metrov* is, of course, different: $L_{(NUM)}\leftarrow\mathbf{ATTR}-L_{(N)PL}.$

See also example (17b), Ch. 9, *2.1.2.*

2.3   Deep Grammemes

The notion of grammeme was introduced in Ch. 2, *3.2.1*, along with the opposition "deep ~ surface grammemes." Grammemes are language-specific inflectional significations, a particular subset of grammatical significations, such as PLURAL, ACCUSATIVE, INDICATIVE, FUTURE, etc. Specific grammemes characterize LUs of a given part of speech, and their expression is obligatory with all LUs belonging to this part of speech. Mutually opposed grammemes are united into (inflectional) categories: the grammemes PLURAL and SINGULAR form the inflectional category of nominal number; PRESENT, PAST and FUTURE constitute the category of verbal tense, etc.

Deep, or semantic, grammemes express semanteme configurations present in the initial SemS. (On the semantic representation of deep grammemes, see Ch. 3, *1* and Ch. 10, *2.1.2, Figure 10.3*). In English, these are:

- the grammemes of number and determination for the noun (as in *pencil+Ø* ~ *a pencil+Ø* ~ *the pencil+Ø* ~ *pencil+s* ~ *the pencil+s*)
- the grammemes of degree of comparison for the adjective (*large+Ø* ~ *larg+er* ~ *larg+est*)
- the grammemes of voice, mood, aspect and tense for the verb ([*they*] *build+Ø* ~ *was buil+t* ~ [*if it*] *were buil+t* ~ *am building* ~ *build!*, etc.)

Surface, or syntactic, grammemes do not express semanteme configurations; they are induced by the syntactic phenomena of agreement and government. Typical syntactic grammemes are those of adjectival agreement with the noun in gender and number (lacking in English but present in a host of other languages – Romance, Slavic, Semitic, etc.), and verbal agreement in person and number with the subject.

| Only deep grammemes appear with deep LUs in the DSyntS.

Table 11.1 gives examples of English deep grammemes accompanying deep LUs in the DSyntS, along with their sentence-level realizations.

Table 11.1 Some deep grammemes of English and their sentence-level realizations

BOOK$_{SG, INDEF}$	*a book+Ø*
BOOK$_{PL, DEF}$	*the book+s*
S$_1$(TEACH)$_{PL, INDEF}$	*teacher+s*
LARGE$_{COMPAR}$	*larg+er*
[$_{RE-\oplus}$ESTABLISH]$_{PRES, PART}$	*re-establish+ing*
SELL$_{ACT, IND, PRES, PROGR, NON-PERF}$	e.g., [*he*] *is selling*
SELL$_{PASS, IND, FUT, NON-PROGR, PERF}$	e.g., [*it*] *will have been sold*
Oper$_1$(MISTAKE)$_{ACT, IND, PAST, NON-PROGR, NON-PERF}$	e.g., [*they*] *made* [*a mistake*]

REMARK. In the right-hand column, for the last three examples we have arbitrarily chosen the values for verb agreement with the subject (hence the "e.g."), as the corresponding grammemes – the number and the person of the syntactic subject – are surface grammemes and therefore not present in the DSyntS.

2.4 Deep-Syntactic Dependency Relations

We begin with a general characterization of syntactic dependency relations, or syntactic relations for short (*2.4.1*), followed by an inventory of deep-syntactic relations (*2.4.2*).

2.4.1 General Characterization of Syntactic Relations

Two topics will be addressed: properties of syntactic relations (*2.4.1.1*) and major types of syntactic relations (*2.4.1.2*). Most of what will be said below is valid for both deep- and surface-syntactic relations; where there are differences between the two, this will be specifically indicated.

2.4.1.1 Properties of Syntactic Relations

Logical properties of syntactic relations

Syntactic dependency is an "anti-relation": it is antireflexive, antisymmetric and antitransitive (on properties of binary relations, see Appendix, *3.2*).
<u>Antireflexivity</u>. No LU L can be its own syntactic governor:

Substantially, this means that no LU can be linearly positioned and inflected with respect to itself.
<u>Antisymmetry</u>. If L_1–**synt**→L_2, then, in the same syntactic structure, it cannot be the case that L_2–**synt**→L_1 (an LU L_1 cannot govern an LU L_2 and be governed by it at the same time):

$$* \quad \overset{\text{synt}}{\underset{\text{synt}}{L_1 \quad L_2}}$$

This translates into the following substantive requirement: if an LU L_1 controls the linear positioning of another LU L_2, L_1's own linear placement cannot be controlled by L_2 at the same time.

<u>Antitransitivity</u>. If L_1–**synt**→L_2 and L_2–**synt**→L_3, then, in the same syntactic structure, it cannot be the case that L_1–**synt**→L_3:

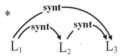

In substantive terms, an LU cannot have two direct syntactic governors: this would violate the condition of the uniqueness of the syntactic governor in Definition 11.1, p. 285.

Semantic dependency is different: while also being antireflexive and anti-symmetric, it is only **non**-transitive (Ch. *3, 3.2.1*).

Number and types of syntactic relations

In syntax, it is necessary to distinguish several types of dependency relations – that is, give them distinct names. This is so because the syntactic constructions that dependency relations are supposed to describe are quite varied, even in a single language. Thus, a construction of the type [*X's*] *nice looks* is different from that of the type [*X*] *looks nice*, the construction *John sees* [*Y*] differs from the construction [*X*] *sees John*, etc. Deep-syntactic relations are "gener-alized" syntactic relations, each subsuming several concrete surface-syntactic relations. For instance, the DSyntRel ATTR subsumes all the relations between a syntactic governor and its modifier (among others, N–**determinative**→DET, N–**modificative**→ADJ, V–**circumstantial**→ADV); the DSyntRel **II** sub-sumes all the relations between a verb and its primary object (e.g., V–**direct-objectival**→N; V–**oblique-objectival**→PREP); and so on. There are far fewer relations at the deep-syntactic level, but at both levels they are distinct and typed. In contrast, semantic relations are distinguished only by the num-bers assigned to the arguments of the same predicate and can all be reduced to the same type: the "predicate ~ argument" relation.

Universality of deep-syntactic relations

We want the DSyntRels to be universal, i.e., valid for the description of syn-tactic structures in any language. In order to be able to represent syntactic phenomena in different languages in a natural way, DSyntRels must be rather general. At the same time, in order to allow for an economic and elegant descrip-tion, they must be few in number (currently, we posit thirteen DSyntRels, see below, *2.4.2*). Trying to reconcile these two opposing requirements – general-ity and economy – we make use of the technique of fictitious lexemes, described earlier (Subsection *2.2.3*): a meaning-bearing syntactic construction specific to a single language (or a small number of languages) is represented at the deep-syntactic level by means of a fictitious lexeme rather than by means of an additional DSyntRel. As for surface-syntactic relations, they are language-specific (for instance, English features fewer than a hundred such relations).

2.4.1.2 Major Types of Syntactic Relations

Syntactic dependencies in the world's languages can be characterized according to three oppositions : coordination ~ subordination; weak subordination ~ strong subordination; modification ~ actancy. These are the three most fundamental distinctions in syntax. Let us examine them in turn.

1. Coordination vs. Subordination
This opposition divides all syntactic dependencies into two subsets: coordinate dependencies (known also as parataxis) and subordinate dependencies (or hypotaxis).

Coordination links sentence elements – LUs, phrases and clauses – in an "egalitarian" way. Informally speaking, coordination is about making lists, "flat" sequences of elements, which, in a sense, all play the same syntactic role with respect to an external element. Most often, coordinate links are expressed explicitly, by means of coordinate conjunctions, e.g., *Peter **and** Paul*; *Peter, Paul **and** Mary*; *read **or** write*; *in Paris **as well as** in London*; ***either** his **or** mine*; *Peter left, **but** Paul stayed*. Coordination can also be asyndetic, i.e., expressed only by word order and prosody; e.g., *Peter left, Paul stayed.* (In addition to genuine coordination, we distinguish pseudo-coordination, which links sentence elements in a way that resembles genuine coordination while being distinct from it; see below, *2.4.2.4*.)

Subordination links sentence elements in a hierarchical way: L_1 subordinates L_2 means that only L_1 plays a dependent syntactic role with respect to an external governor, while L_2 cannot appear in that role. Here are some stock examples (the subordinating element is in small caps): *READ a book*; *READ while eating*; *GIVE an apple to the boy*; *loud MUSIC*; *INTRODUCE them to him*.

2. Weak Subordination vs. Strong Subordination
This opposition divides subordinate dependencies into two subsets. Weak subordination describes elements that are not solidly anchored in the syntactic structure of the sentence; these elements lack a fixed position and/or do nor interact syntactically and morphologically with the rest of the sentence: vocatives (***Peter**, come here!*), parentheticals (*Peter has, **for all I know**, declined the offer.*), interjections (***Ouch**, it hurts!*), prolepses (***Peter**, now there's a nasty fellow!*), etc. Strongly subordinated elements are well integrated into the sentence; all the examples in the preceding paragraph illustrate strong subordination.

3. Modification vs. Actancy
This opposition divides strong subordinate dependencies into two subsets again. Modification (in a broad sense) covers all the relations between the syntactic governor and its modifiers/circumstantials whose passive valence (Ch. 2,

1.3.3, Definition 2.7) allows them to be subordinated to this governor. Actancy covers all the relations between the governor and its actants, the latter saturating the active valence (Ch. 2, *1.3.3,* Definition 2.8) of the governor.

Modification is, in a way, the inversion of a semantic relation, namely the semantic dependency between a predicate and one of its arguments. During the arborization of a SemS, in the case of modification, a "modifying" predicate, which is necessarily a semantic governor, is expressed syntactically by an adjective/adverb, i.e., by a syntactic dependent. In contrast, in the case of actantial dependents, the orientation of the semantic relation is preserved: a typical semantic actant is expressed by a syntactic actant. The choice between expressing a semantic dependency by a modifying or an actantial construction is made according to the indication – in the SemS – of the communicatively dominant node (Ch. 10, *3.1.1*). These two situations are illustrated in *Figure 11.3* (the communicatively dominant node is underscored, the syntactic dependent is in bold).

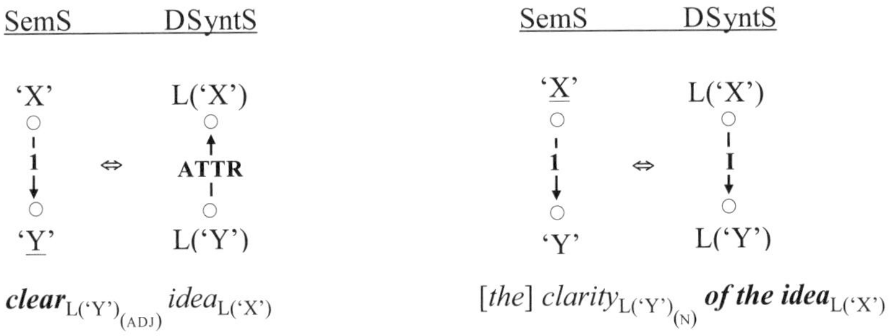

SemS	DSyntS		SemS	DSyntS
'X'	L('X')		'<u>X</u>'	L('X')
1	↑ ATTR	⇔	1	1
'Y'	L('Y')		'Y'	L('Y')

$$\textit{clear}_{L(`Y`)_{(ADJ)}} \quad \textit{idea}_{L(`X`)} \qquad [\textit{the}] \ \textit{clarity}_{L(`Y`)_{(N)}} \quad \textit{of the idea}_{L(`X`)}$$

Figure 11.3 Modification vs. actancy

The opposition "modification ~ actancy" can be summarized as follows: actants of an LU L are controlled by L, but L's circumstantials/modifiers are not. More specifically:

- The PRESENCE of an actant of L in the sentence is determined by the meaning of L, i.e., the slots opened for L's actants must be foreseen in L's lexicographic definition. In contrast, L's modifiers/circumstantials are free adjuncts, whose presence in the sentence is not determined by L.
- The FORM of expression of L's actants is also determined by L – that is, their form is idiosyncratically linked to L and has to be specified in L's dictionary entry, more precisely – in L's Government Pattern. The form of a modifier/circumstantial, on the other hand, does not depend on a particular L that is its syntactic governor.

- L's actants are NON-REPEATABLE with L; in a given sentence, the main verb can have just one subject, one direct object, and so on. However, modifiers/circumstantials are repeatable with the same governor; for example, a noun can have several qualifying modifiers (*a **new bisyllabic inflectional nominal** suffix*), a verb can have several time circumstantials (***On November 29** John will arrive **in the evening before 9** PM.*), etc.

Actantial relations are thus strongly bound to the lexical properties of the governor, while non-actantial ones are practically independent of those properties.

While theoretically clear, the distinction "actants ~ modifiers/circumstantials" is not always easy to make in practice: there are borderline cases. Moreover, what is an actant at the deep-syntactic level of representation may be a circumstantial at the surface-syntactic level, and vice versa. However, we cannot go into further detail about these points here.

2.4.2   Inventory of Deep-Syntactic Relations

The inventory of DSyntRels is given in *Table 11.2*, starting with the strongest subordinate dependencies and going towards the weakest coordinate links.

We now illustrate these relations. For each DSyntRel, we indicate the surface-syntactic constructions that it describes and give linguistic examples; where necessary, brief explanations are provided.

1. In the examples, the elements that do not illustrate the central point are within square brackets.
2. Governed prepositions and conjunctions, such as ON in *depending on many factors* and THAT in *I assume that this is true*, which do not appear in the DSyntS, are not featured in the examples.
3. DirO = Direct Object; IndirO = Indirect Object; OblO = Oblique Object; MV = Main Verb

2.4.2.1   Actantial DSyntRels

Let us start with a definition of deep-syntactic actant.

> **Definition 11.4:** Deep-Syntactic Actant (approximate formulation)
> In the DSynt-subtree $L_1{\rightarrow}L_2$, L_2 is a deep-syntactic actant of L_1 iff L_2 corresponds to a semantic actant of L_1.

For example, the idiom ⌐FALL SHORT⌐ (*His skills fell short of the required standard.*) has two SemAs: 'X←**1**–⌐falls short'–**2**→Y'; consequently, it has two deep-syntactic actants [DSyntAs]: SKILL$_{PL}$←**I**–⌐FALL SHORT'–**II**→STANDARD$_{SG}$.

Table 11.2 Inventory of deep-syntactic relations

SUBORDINATE DSyntRels									COORDINATE DSyntRels	
STRONG						Attributive DSyntRels		WEAK		
Actantial DSyntRels						$ATTR_{restr}$	$ATTR_{descr}$	APPEND	ADDRESS	COORD	PSEUDO-COORD
I	II	III	IV	V	VI	$II_{dir.speech}$	8	9	10	11	12	13
1	2	3	4	5	6	7						

REMARK. The above definition characterizes, in fact, what can be called a **prototypical** deep-syntactic actant, because it does not cover several special cases, of which we will mention the following two.

CASE 1

L_2 can correspond not to a SemA of L_1 but to a SemA of a different LU, which itself is a SemA of L_1. This situation obtains, for instance, in the case of Possessor Raising, a syntactic operation frequent in Romance languages (among others); cf.: Fr. *Maman **lui**$_{L2}$ changera$_{L1}$ la coiffure* lit. 'Mom **to.him** will.change the hairstyle' = 'Mom will change **his** hairstyle'. The clitic pronoun *lui* 'to.him' is a SSynt-actant (more precisely, the indirect object) of CHANGER. At the DSynt-level (where pronouns are not allowed), it corresponds to a noun (e.g., PAUL) functioning as the DSyntA **III** of the verb. However, this DSyntA **III** does not correspond to a SemA of CHANGER, because the latter has only two inherent SemAs: '$X_{cause(r)}$←1–changer–2→$Y_{affected}$', expressed in our sentence as DSyntA **I** (*maman*) and DSyntA **II** (*coiffure*). The clitic *lui* corresponds in fact to SemA **1** of 'coiffure', i.e., the possessor of the hairstyle, which has undergone "raising" to its governor's governor. Thus, we go from 'changer–2→ **coiffure**–1→**de.Paul**' at the Sem-level to À.PAUL←**III**–CHANGER–**II**→COIFFURE at the DSynt-level to finally obtain at the SSynt-level IL$_{(Pron.pers)}$←**indirect-object**–CHANGER–**direct-object**→COIFFURE.

CASE 2

L_2 can be a DSyntA "by promotion," as with the English prepositional passive: L_2 corresponds to a circumstantial of the verb in the active voice. Thus, we have ***This dress**$_{L2}$←**I**–cannot$_{L1}$ be sat down in* from *One cannot sit.down*–ATTR→***in this dress***; ***This lawn**$_{L2}$←**I**– has been barbecued on by the Royal Family* from *The Royal Family has barbecued*–ATTR→***on this lawn***, and so on. Similar phenomena exist in Malagasy, Nez Perce, a number of Australian languages, etc.

Six basic DSynt-actantial relations are known, as illustrated in sentence (2):

(2)   *The Emperor$_I$ exiled Ovid$_{II}$ from Rome$_{III}$ to Tomis$_{IV}$ for life$_V$ for his erotic poetry$_{VI}$.*

The seventh actantial DSyntRel (**II**$_{dir\text{-}speech}$) is close to, but distinct from, the DSyntRel **II**: it represents a Direct Speech complement of a communication verb.

DSyntRel I

- $V_{FIN}\to$Subject construction

ARRIVE$_{FIN}$–I→JOHN	: *John arrives.*
END(V)$_{FIN}$–I→STORY	: *The story ended.*

- Different "transforms" of $V_{FIN}\to$Subject construction with an infinitival/nominal governor and analogous constructions

ARRIVE–I→JOHN	: [*for*] *John* [*to*] *arrive*
S$_0$(ARRIVE)–I→JOHN	: *John*[*'s*] *arrival*
END$_{(N)}$–I→STORY	: *end* [*of the*] *story*
CROWD$_{(N)}$–I→STUDENT$_{PL}$	: *crowd* [*of*] *students/student crowd*
ATTACK$_{(V)}$–I→S$_1$(USA)$_{PL}$	: [*The*] *Americans attacked.*
ATTACK$_{(N)}$–I→S$_1$(USA)$_{PL}$	: [*an*] *attack* [*by the*] *Americans*
ATTACK$_{(N)}$–I→A$_0$(USA)	: [*an*] *American attack*

DSyntRel II

- $V\to$DirO construction

SEND–II→LETTER	: *send* [*a*] *letter*

- Different "transforms" of $V\to$DirO construction with a nominal governor

SENDING–II→LETTER	: *sending* [*of this*] *letter*
MURDER–II→JOHN	: *John's murder*
EXPULSION–II→WE	: *our expulsion*

- $L\to$OblO construction – only if L has neither a DirO nor an IndirO

COUNT–II→WE	: *count* [*on*] *us*
RETURN–II→LONDON	: *return* [*to*] *London*
RESPECT$_{(N)}$–II→JOHN	: *respect* [*for*] *John*
DIFFERENT–II→I	: *different* [*from*] *me*

- $V_{PASSIVE}\to$Agentive Complement construction

EAT$_{PASSIVE}$–II→WOLF	: *be eaten* [*by the*] *wolf*

- ADJ/ADV$_{COMPAR}\to$THAN construction

LARGE$_{COMPAR}$–II→N	: *larger* [*than*] *life*
BEAUTIFUL$_{COMPAR}$–II→N	: *more beautiful* [*than*] *Mary*

- PREP$\to$N/V$_{INF}$ construction

FOR–II→MARY	: *for Mary*
⌜IN ORDER TO⌝–II→WIN	: *in order to win*

- $CONJ_{(SUBORD)} \rightarrow V_{FIN}$ construction

SINCE–**II**→LEAVE	: *since [we] are leaving*
WHEN–**II**→LEAVE	: *when [we] left*

- $CONJ_{(COORD/COMPAR)} \rightarrow L$ construction

AND–**II**→LEAVE	: *[got up] and left*
BUT–**II**→LEAVE	: *but left*

DSyntRel III

- L→IndirO Construction – only if L has a DirO

SEND–**III**→JOHN	: *send John [a letter]*
SEND–**III**→JOHN	: *sending [a letter to] John*

- L→OblO construction – only if L has a DirO or an IndirO

EXILE$_{(V)}$–**III**→SIBERIA	: *[to] exile [Ivan to] Siberia*
EXILE$_{(N)}$–**III**→SIBERIA	: *[the] exile [of Ivan to] Siberia*

DSyntRels IV-VI

- Different L→OblO constructions

LEASE$_{(V)}$–**IV**→DOLLAR$_{PL}$	: *[to] lease [for a thousand] dollars*
LEASE$_{(N)}$–**IV**→DOLLAR$_{PL}$	: *[a] lease [for a thousand] dollars*
EXILE$_{(V)}$–**V**→YEAR	: *[to] exile [for ten] years*
EXILE$_{(V)}$–**VI**→YEAR	: *[to] exile [for antigovernment] activity*

DSyntRel II$_{dir\text{-}speech}$

The DSyntRel **II**$_{dir.speech}$ corresponds to the Direct Speech complement and represents a quoted utterance; it contrasts semantically with the DSyntRel **II**, as the following example shows:

(3) *Alain said: "You should*$_{IIdir.speech}$ *go there".* ~
     Alain said you should$_{II}$ *go there.*

The governing element of this relation is prototypically a speech verb, but it can also be a verb meaning 'mean' or 'signify'.

- V→Direct Speech Complement construction

[ALAIN] SAY–**II**$_{dir.sp}$→HELLO	: *Alain said: "Hello."*
[THIS] MEAN–**II**$_{dir.sp}$–[I]→BE [HUNGRY]	: *This means: "I am hungry."*

Figure 11.4 shows some of the actantial constructions presented above within two full-fledged DSyntSs.

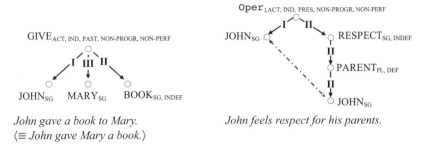

John gave a book to Mary.
⟨≡ *John gave Mary a book.*⟩

John feels respect for his parents.

Figure 11.4 Two DSyntSs featuring some actantial DSyntRels

2.4.2.2 Attributive DSyntRels

Two attributive DSyntRels are distinguished: one restrictive and the other descriptive.

ATTR$_{restr}$ DSyntRel (for short, ATTR)

This relation links an LU to a "normal" (= restrictive) modifier of any kind; for instance, *news→good for Canada* 'not all news, but only news that is good for Canada'. Since this DSyntRel represents the default (= unmarked) case of modification, we omit the subscript "restr".

- N→ADJ construction

BOY–**ATTR**→LITTLE	: [*a*] *little boy*
BOY–**ATTR**→THIRD	: [*the*] *third boy*
FREEZE–**ATTR**→Magn	: *deep freeze*

- N→DET construction

BOY–**ATTR**→THIS	: *this boy*
BOY–**ATTR**→ANY	: *any boy*

- N→NUM construction

BOY–**ATTR**→THREE	: *three boys*
DOLLAR–**ATTR**→THOUSAND	: [*three*] *thousand dollars*

- N→Relative Clause construction

BOY–**ATTR**–[BOY]→IS [CUTE]	: [*a*] *boy* [*who*] *is* [*cute*]
GUY–**ATTR**–[GUY I]→KNOW	: [*a*] *guy* [*whom I*] *know*

- V→ADV construction

ARRIVE–**ATTR**→LATE	: *arrive late*
ARGUE–**ATTR**→Ver	: *argue convincingly*

- ADJ→ADV construction

NICE–**ATTR**→VERY	: *very nice*
SKINNY–**ATTR**→Magn	: *skinny ⌜as a rake⌝*

- PARTICLE←L construction

YOU–**ATTR**→ONLY	: *only you*
THERE–**ATTR**→EVEN	: *even there*

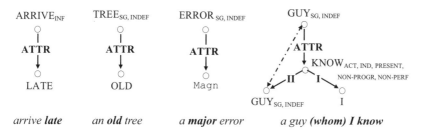

Figure 11.5 Four DSyntSs featuring the DSyntRel ATTR

ATTR_{descr} DSyntRel

This relation links an LU to its descriptive modifier; for instance, *this news→good for Canada,* 'this news, previously identified, which is good for Canada'.

- N→ADJ construction

[THIS] NUMBER–**ATTR**_{descr}→ACCURATE	: *[this] number, accurate and precise, can be used...*

- N→Relative Clause construction

[THIS] NUMBER–**ATTR**_{descr}–[NUMBER]→IS [ACCURATE]	: *[this] number, which is accurate, ...*

2.4.2.3   APPEND and ADDRESS DSyntRels

These are the two weak subordinate DSyntRels. Their dependent members have similar linear positioning and prosodic properties, but **APPEND** is repeatable (with the same governor): *Well,*←**APPEND**–[*Mary*]–*is*–**APPEND**→⌜*of course*⌝ *right!*, while **ADDRESS** is not.

APPEND DSyntRel

This relation links to the Main Verb [MV] a sentential adverb, an interjection, etc.

- MV→Sentential Adverb (= Parenthetical) constructions

⌜OF COURSE⌝←**APPEND**–COME   : *Of course,* [*we*] *will come.*
OBVIOUSLY←**APPEND**–LIE   : [*He*] *is, obviously, lying.*

- MV→Interjection construction

OUCH←**APPEND**–HURT   : *Ouch,* [*it*] *hurts!*

ADDRESS DSyntRel

- MV→Address construction

MARY←**ADDRESS**–LOVE   : *Mary,* [*I*] *love* [*you*].

[DEAR] FRIEND_{PL}←**ADDRESS**–[I]–INVITE [YOU]: [*I*] *invite* [*you*], [*dear*] *friends,…*

COME_{ACT, IND, PAST, NON-PROGR, NON-PERF}   INVITE_{ACT, IND, PRES, NON-PROGR, NON-PERF}

JOHN ○ ←I ATTR→ ⌜ON TIME⌝   I ○ ←I II→ ○ YOU
        APPEND   **ADDRESS**
          ↓   FRIEND_{PL, NON-DEF}
          ○   ATTR
    SURPRISINGLY   ↓
                                 DEAR

Surprisingly, John came on time.   I invite you, **dear friends**, …

Figure 11.6 Two DSyntSs featuring the DSyntRel APPEND and ADDRESS

2.4.2.4 Coordinate DSyntRels

As indicated earlier, we distinguish genuine coordination and pseudo-coordination.

COORD DSyntRel

This relation links a conjunct (= element of a coordinate phrase) either with a coordinate conjunction or another conjunct.

☞   Ψ stands for a lexical unit of any part of speech.

- Ψ_1→Conjunction[→Ψ_2] construction

PETER–**COORD**→AND[–**II**→PAUL]   : *Peter and* [*Paul*]
STAY–**COORD**→OR[–**II**→LEAVE]   : *stay or* [*leave*]
SLOWLY–**COORD**→BUT[–**II**→SURELY]   : *slowly but* [*surely*]

- Ψ_1→Ψ_2→Ψ_3 constructions

PETER–**COORD**→PAUL–**COORD**→MARY   : *Peter, Paul, Mary*
BEAUTIFUL–**COORD**→NICE–**COORD**→SMART   : *beautiful, nice, smart*

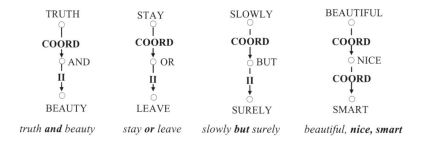

Figure 11.7 Four DSyntSs featuring the DSyntRel **COORD**

PSEUDO-COORD DSyntRel

Pseudo-coordination represents elaboration; the elements it links are syntactically not equal, since each element that is added semantically elaborates on the previous one: *Paul arrived **Tuesday**, **at** 3PM.* | *I am from **Montreal**, **Quebec**, **Canada**.* | *I live **in** the USA, **in** New York, **on** 5th Avenue, **at** Paul's.* In pseudo-coordination, no conjunctions are possible (**Paul arrived **Tuesday** $\boxed{and}$ at 3PM.*).

- $\Psi_1 \rightarrow \Psi_2 \rightarrow \Psi_3$ constructions

MONTREAL–**PSEUDO-COORD**→QUEBEC–**PSEUDO-COORD**→CANADA
Montreal, Quebec, Canada

This concludes our survey of deep-syntactic relations.

3   Deep–Syntactic-Communicative Structure

Just like its counterpart at the semantic level (the Sem-CommS), the Deep-Syntactic-Communicative Structure [DSynt-CommS] consists of communicative areas specified on the DSyntS, each of which is marked with an element (= value) from the set of communicative oppositions. Of course, the communicative areas and communicative oppositions of these two representation levels are different in nature (even though their names are the same, since they fulfill similar functions).

At the DSynt-level, communicative areas completely partition the syntactic structure (on which they are superposed) so that there are no overlaps between them; in contrast, overlaps can exist at the Sem-level. Thus, unlike a semanteme, a lexeme cannot be in two different communicative areas. Let us compare the communicative structures of the Sem- and DSynt-levels in the corresponding representations of sentence (4), *Figure 11.8.*

(4) [**Q**: And the First Lady?]

The First Lady is being criticized by the Opposition for her expensive
designer dresses.

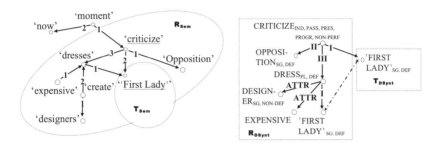

Figure 11.8 SemR and DSyntR of sentence (4)

In the SemR of (4), there is an overlap (more precisely, inclusion)
between the thematic and rhematic areas, the semanteme 'ʿFirst Lady" being
part of both. But in the DSyntS of (4) we see two occurrences of the LU
(idiom) ˹FIRST LADY˺, located in different communicative areas. This is
understandable, since a semanteme associated with a single referent cannot
appear in the SemS more than once, but can be lexicalized several times – by
co-referential LUs.

There are fewer communicative oppositions at the DSynt-level than at the
Sem-level. This is because some semantic-communicative oppositions are
expressed in the DSyntS by lexical and/or syntactic means. Thus, out of the
five semantic-communicative oppositions introduced in Ch. 4, *3.1.2*, only
three remain at the DSynt-level:

1. DSynt-Thematicity
2. DSynt-Givenness (lacking in some languages, see below)
3. DSynt-Focalization (also lacking in some languages).

The oppositions of Assertivity and Locutionality no longer exist at the DSynt-
level because they are always expressed in the DSyntS through choices of LUs
and syntactic constructions. Therefore, these oppositions are embodied in the
DSyntS, as it were.

Moreover, two of the oppositions appearing at the DSynt-level can in
some languages be "consummated" during lexicalization and arborization,
which means that they do not appear as such in the DSyntS. Givenness can
be implemented by articles (in languages that have them); as for Focalization,
in some languages it is implemented by syntactic means, and in other by particles (which are lexical means). For example, focalization of the Rheme is
expressed in English by means of clefting, but Russian uses for this purpose the
particle ÈTO ≈ 'it.is' (without modifying the syntactic structure of the clause):

(5) a. Eng. ***It is*** *John **who** brought water.*
    b. Rus. ***Èto*** *Ivan prinës vodu* lit. 'It.is Ivan brought water'.

Thus, Thematicity is the only communicative opposition (among those we have introduced) that is necessarily present at the DSynt-level in all languages.

4   Role of the Deep-Syntactic Structure in Sentence Synthesis

As shown above, the DSyntR and, in particular, its basic structure, the DSyntS, is a generalized representation of sentence syntactic organization, based on the universal formalism of dependency trees. It features restricted lexical and grammatical elements (only semantically full LUs and full grammemes) and uses a small number of cross-linguistically valid syntactic relations. Thanks to this property, the DSyntS makes it possible to maximally reduce superficial differences between synonymous expressions (coming from the same language or from different languages), allowing for their common representation.

Recourse to a representation of this type proves useful for at least the following five reasons.

1. The DSyntS allows for relatively easy representation of phenomena related to phraseology – idioms and collocations (Ch. 4, *2.2.2.1*).

    The way idioms are represented in the DSyntS accounts for their double nature: while at the deep-syntactic level an idiom is represented as one node – an LU, with its own meaning and Government Pattern, at the surface-syntactic level it is an ordinary phrase, just like any other. This particular behavior of idioms has been a stumbling block for most linguistic models that do not posit two levels of representation in syntax.

    Collocations are represented in the DSyntS in a homogeneous and systematic way, so that phrases that on the surface look very different, e.g., *rain* ⌐*cats and dogs*⌐ and *sleep* ⌐*like a log*⌐, when described in terms of lexical functions, appear in a comparable form:

    $RAIN_{(V)}$–**ATTR**→Magn($RAIN_{(V)}$)

    $SLEEP_{(V)}$–**ATTR**→Magn($SLEEP_{(V)}$)

2. The DSyntS allows for a considerable reduction of syntactic synonymy; syntactic constructions superficially quite different, for example "$N_1 + of + N_2$" and "ADJ + N," have, in the case of synonymy of the corresponding phrases, identical DSyntSs. Thus, the phrases *intervention of the United States of America*, *US intervention* and *American intervention* are represented at the DSynt-level in the same way: $INTERVENTION_{SG}$–**I**→USA.

3. The DSyntS facilitates the description of pronominalization, by preserving the sources of all substitute pronouns, while all co-reference links between LUs are indicated by the DSynt-AnaphS. This allows for a separate treatment of two complex operations: lexicalization, taking place in the transition

SemR $\Rightarrow$ DSyntR, and pronominalization, undertaken in the subsequent phase of synthesis – that is, in the transition DSyntR $\Rightarrow$ SSyntR.

4. The DSyntS is the representation level where lexical-syntactic paraphrasing rules (Ch. 12, 2) operate. These rules, which are formulated in terms of lexical functions and, like them, are universal, ensure paraphrasing within a language (INTRAlinguistic paraphrasing) as well as between languages (INTERlinguistic paraphrasing). For example, the same paraphrasing rule can be used to link intralinguistic paraphrases (6a–b) and interlinguistic paraphrases (6b–c).

(6) a. Fr. *Marc*$_{X\Leftrightarrow I}$ ***aime*** *ce roman*$_{Y\Leftrightarrow II}$ 'Marc likes this novel'.
     b. Fr. *Ce roman*$_{X\Leftrightarrow I}$ ***plaît*** *à Marc*$_{Y\Leftrightarrow II}$ lit.'This novel pleases Marc'.
     c. Eng. *Mark*$_{X\Leftrightarrow I}$ ***likes*** *this novel*$_{Y\Leftrightarrow II}$.

French verbs AIMER 'like' and PLAIRE 'please' $\approx$ 'be likeable', just like Eng. LIKE and Fr. PLAIRE, are lexical conversives (Ch. 6, 1.1.3). They have more or less the same meaning, but the distribution of their semantic and deep-syntactic actants (X $\Leftrightarrow$ **I** and Y $\Leftrightarrow$ **II**) is converse with respect to the participants of the corresponding situation: while with AIMER and LIKE, X $\Leftrightarrow$ **I** corresponds to the Experiencer of the feeling and Y $\Leftrightarrow$ **II** to the Cause/Object of the feeling, with PLAIRE it is the other way around. (For the corresponding paraphrasing rule, a particular conversive substitution, see Ch. 12, 2.2.2.3.)

As shown in *Figure 11.9*, differences between the representations of sentences (6b) and (6c), which are considerable at the SSynt-level, are reduced to the permutation of actantial numbers at the DSynt-level.[1] Thanks to this maximal neutralization of structural differences, the DSyntS can be used in translation (in conjunction with paraphrasing rules) to significantly simplify the transfer between source and target languages.

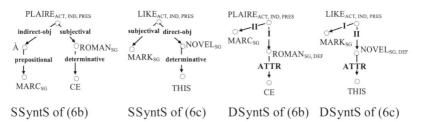

SSyntS of (6b)   SSyntS of (6c)   DSyntS of (6b)   DSyntS of (6c)

Figure 11.9 SSyntSs and DSyntSs of two sentences which are mutual translational equivalents

---

[1] We are taking the liberty of citing some surface-syntactic structures – properly the subject of another book – and are counting on the reader being able to understand them intuitively: the names of the surface-syntactic relations reflect some familiar concepts of traditional grammar.

5. Syntactic phenomena linked to transformations of the type active ~ passive
    (technically called modifications of the diathesis of an LU) are much easier
    to describe at the DSynt-level; namely, their deep representation is more
    homogeneous than the surface one. As an illustration, compare the SSyntSs
    and DSyntSs of the sentences in (7), which are mutual paraphrases featur-
    ing different voices: respectively, active, direct passive and indirect passive.

(7) a. *Granny **told** John a story.*
     b. *A story **was told** to John by Granny.*
     c. *John **was told** a story by Granny.*

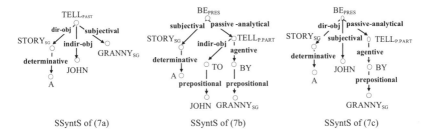

Figure 11.10 SSyntSs of the three synonymous sentences in (7), featuring different
voices

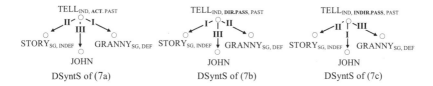

Figure 11.11 DSyntSs of the three synonymous sentences in (7)

Having characterized the two levels of linguistic representation between
which operate the rules of the semantic module of an MTM, we are now ready
for the rules themselves.

Further Reading

Dependency syntax: [general] Tesnière 1959 [2015]; Mel'čuk 1988a and 2015: 387–
505; Polguère & Mel'čuk 2009; [English] Mel'čuk & Pertsov 1987.

Syntactic relations: Cole & Saddock 1977; Haiman & Thompson 1984; Haspelmath 2004.

Syntactic actants: Mel'čuk 2004b. See also Further Reading for Chapter 10 (Argument
structure and linking). "Actant vs. circumstantial" distinction: Kay 2005.

Deep-syntactic structure in Natural Language Processing: Lavoie & Rambow 1997;
Ballesteros *et al.* 2015.

12   Semantic Rules

In this final chapter of the book we characterize the rules that ensure the transition between semantic and deep-syntactic representations of utterances, called semantic rules or, collectively, semantics$_1$ (on the opposition semantics$_1$ ~ semantics$_2$, see Ch. 1, *1*). These rules constitute the semantic module of a linguistic model, in particular a Meaning-Text linguistic model [MTM]; they were introduced in Ch. 1, *2.3*.

The semantic module of an MTM has the task of producing, for a given SemR, all (more or less) synonymous DSyntRs corresponding to it.

From a formal viewpoint, the semantic module contains two major types of rule (this distinction is valid for the rules of all modules of an MTM):[1]

---

[1] In fact, a Meaning-Text model makes use of yet another rule type: filter rules, which specify the formal correctness of linguistic representations; for examples, see Ch. 10, *2.2*, p. 265. For the sake of simplicity, we will not consider these rules here.

1. Transition, or expression, rules are responsible for inter-level correspondences and allow for the construction of several alternative DSyntRs from a single SemR; they are of the following form:

$$X_{\text{Sem-level}} \Leftrightarrow Y_{\text{DSynt-level}} \mid C \textit{(conditions)}.$$

2. Equivalence, or paraphrasing, rules establish intra-level correspondences – between two SemRs or two DSyntRs – while preserving the meaning to be expressed; they are of the form:

$$X_{\text{Sem-level}} \equiv Y_{\text{Sem-level}} \mid C \qquad \text{or} \qquad X_{\text{DSynt-level}} \equiv Y_{\text{DSynt-level}} \mid C$$

☞ X and Y are fragments of the structures of the indicated levels; "$\Leftrightarrow$" means 'corresponds to', and "$\equiv$" means 'is equivalent to'.

As we see from this, there are two formal varieties of semantic equivalence rules: **semantic equivalences proper**, i.e., equivalences between configurations of semantemes ($\text{SemR}_1 \equiv \text{SemR}_2 \equiv \dots$), and **lexical-syntactic equivalences**, i.e., equivalences between LUs and the syntactic constructions they form ($\text{DSyntR}_1 \equiv \text{DSyntR}_2 \equiv \dots$).

Figure 12.1 shows how both types of semantic rules – Transition and Equivalence – can be applied.

	$\text{DSyntR}_{1\text{-}1} \equiv$	$\text{DSyntR}_{1\text{-}1'} \equiv \; \text{DSyntR}_{1\text{-}1''} \equiv \dots \equiv \text{DSyntR}_n$	Equivalences (= paraphrasing)
Transition (= expression)	$\Updownarrow$		
	$\text{SemR}_1 \quad \equiv$	$\text{SemR}_2 \quad \equiv \; \dots \; \equiv \; \text{SemR}_m$	Equivalences (= paraphrasing)

Figure 12.1 Semantic transition and semantic equivalence rules

The above rules fall into additional subtypes, indicated in *Figure 12.2* (partially repeating *Figure 1.4* from Ch. 1, *2.3*).

	Semantic transition (expression) rules [SemR $\Leftrightarrow$ DSyntR]	Semantic Equivalence (paraphrasing) rules	
		Semantic equivalences proper [SemR $\equiv$ SemR']	Lexical-Syntactic equivalences [DSyntR $\equiv$ DSyntR']
Rules operating on basic structures	Lexicalization rules Morphologization rules Arborization rules	Substitution rules Restructuring rules	Substitution rules Restructuring rules
Rules operating on peripheral structures	Communicative rules Prosodic rules Co-reference rules	Communicative restructuring rules	Communicative restructuring rules

Figure 12.2 Major types and subtypes of semantic rules

> **NB:** To avoid confusion, let us indicate that what is called "lexical-syn-tactic equivalences" here are in fact deep-syntactic paraphrasing rules, which are actually part of both the semantic module and the deep-syntactic module of an MTM. This set of rules functions simultaneously at two stages of linguistic synthesis: at the last stage of Sem-synthesis, which is also the first stage of the DSynt-synthesis. Within the Sem-module the DSynt-paraphrasing rules are part of the **semantic rules**, so they have to be called "lexical-syntactic equivalences"; within the DSynt-module, they are part of **deep-syntactic rules** and can appear under their genuine denomination.

All major semantic rule types are universal, i.e., present in any language, with the exception of morphologization rules, lacking in languages without inflectional morphology.

The structure of the present chapter is straightforward: semantic transition rules are considered in Section *1*, and semantic equivalence rules in Section *2*.

1   Semantic Transition (= Expression) Rules

We focus on the rules performing the transition between the basic structures of the two representations involved, i.e., the transition SemS ⇔ DSyntS. Transition rules concerning the peripheral structures of these representations are left aside.

> **NB:** Since semantic rules make use of the information encoded by the Sem-CommS (Ch. 10, *3*), namely, the communicatively dominant node of the SemS, and the communicative role of specific semanteme configurations, these communicative elements will be present in some of the rules below.

The SemS ⇔ DSyntS transition rules can be split into three major families:

1. Lexicalization rules treat configurations of semantemes and select deep lexical units [LUs] (Ch. 11, *2.2*) that express them.
2. Morphologization rules treat configurations of semantemes and select deep grammemes (Ch. 11, *2.3*) that express them – to be assigned to deep LUs.
3. Arborization rules treat semantic relations and select deep-syntactic relations (Ch. 11, *2.4*) that correspond to them.

Rules of the first type are the most numerous; they are consigned to the *Explanatory Combinatorial Dictionary* (ECD) of **L**, which is a model of **L**'s lexical stock (Ch. 8). The rules of the remaining two types belong to the grammar of **L**. (For the opposition "lexical stock ~ grammar," see Ch. 2, *1.6.2*, pp. 54–55.)

1.1 Lexicalization Rules

Lexicalization rules fall into four groups according to their output, that is to say, deep LUs that they introduce into the target structure, the DSyntS. Since deep LUs are of four types – lexemes, idioms, names of lexical functions and fictitious LUs (Ch. 11, *2.2.1*) – we need just as many subsets of lexicalization rules:

- Lexemic rules perform the transition from semantic configurations to lexemes.
- Phrasemic rules are responsible for the transition from semantic configurations to idioms.
- Lexical-functional rules carry out the transition from semantic configurations to lexical functions.
- Lexical-constructional rules take care of the transition from semantic configurations to fictitious LUs, which represent meaning-carrying syntactic constructions.

Let us illustrate each of these types of rules. All the rules given below are approximate; the conditions of application are missing in most cases.

> **NB:** Each rule has an "active" part, which consists of the elements manipulated by the rule, and a "passive" part, or the context, consisting of the elements not treated by the rule itself but necessary for its application; the context is indicated by shading. The notation "L('X')" stands for an LU L that expresses the meaning 'X', and the communicatively dominant node (appearing in the left-hand part of a rule, that is, in the semantic subnetwork) is underscored.

1.1.1 Lexemic Rules

According to the three lexeme subtypes identified in Ch. 11, *2.2.1*, lexemic rules fall into simple, derivational and compounding lexemic rules.

> **NB:** Derivational and compounding lexemic rules treat only productive derivatives and compounds – i.e., those not stored in the dictionary but "dynamically" produced in speech. For idiosyncratic derivations, stored as wholes in the dictionary and treated by lexical-functional rules, see Subsection *1.1.3* below.

Simple Lexemic Rules

The simple lexemic rule shown in *Figure 12.3* links a semantic decomposition of a semanteme 'X' to the corresponding lexeme L('X').

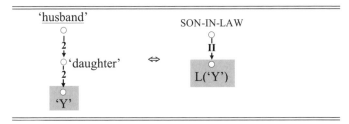

The semantemes 'husband' and 'daughter' are quasi-predicates (Ch. 3, *3.1.2*), whose SemA **1** is "incorporated," so to speak, and therefore does not appear above: '[an individual X,] the husband of [an individual who is] a daughter of an individual Y'.

Figure 12.3 Simple lexemic rule R^{LEX} 1 (English)

Strictly speaking, this rule is a shorthand for a complex of the two rules shown in *Figure 12.4*.

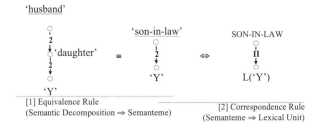

Figure 12.4 Simple lexemic rule R^{LEX} 1 (developed view)

In other words, a simple lexemic rule has a dual nature: on the one hand, it represents the semantic decomposition of a lexical meaning, actually the lexicographic definition thereof (Ch. 5); and, on the other hand, it ensures a mapping from this lexical meaning to the lexeme itself. Thus, it can function both as a semantic equivalence rule [1], performing the reduction (or, conversely, the expansion) of a semantic structure (see below, Subsection *2.1.1*), and as a lexicalization rule [2]; schematically in *Figure 12.5*.

Semantic Decomposition	Semanteme	Lexeme
$'\sigma_1' \oplus '\sigma_2' \oplus ... \oplus '\sigma_n'$ ≡	'σ' ⇔	L('σ')
Semantic Equivalence Rule		
[1]		
	Lexicalization Rule	
	[2]	

Figure 12.5 The schema of a simple lexemic rule

In this subsection, we will focus on the lexicalization function of these rules and will cite them in an abridged form, directly linking the semantic decomposition of the meaning of a lexeme to the lexeme itself.

> **NB:** All that has just been said about the form of simple lexemic rules also holds for phrasemic rules (see immediately below, Subsection *1.1.2*).

Figure 12.6 shows another simple lexemic rule for English.

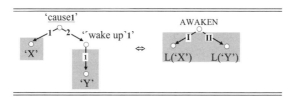

Figure 12.6 Simple lexemic rule R^{LEX} 2 (English)

This rule stipulates that the semanteme configuration '[X] causes**1** that [Y] ⌜wakes up⌝**1**' (the left-hand part of the rule) can be expressed in the DSyntS by means of the lexeme AWAKEN**1**$_{(V, \text{ transitive})}$ (the right-hand part of the rule). It is used, for instance, to produce sentences such as *Suddenly, a noise*$_{L(\text{'X'})}$ ***awakened me***$_{L(\text{'Y'})}$ or *The man*$_{L(\text{'Y'})}$ ***was awakened*** *by the light*$_{L(\text{'X'})}$*flooding in from the hallway.*

Derivational Lexemic Rules

A derivational lexemic rule establishes a correspondence between a semantic configuration and a derivateme, i.e., a derivational signification (Ch. 2, *3.2.2*), such as 'nice little', 'again', 'inhabitant of', etc., assigned to a simple lexeme serving as the base of the derivation.

A derivateme is most often expressed by a derivational affix, but it can also be expressed by a morphological operation, such as conversion; the derivational lexemic rules in *Figures 12.7* and *12.8* illustrate both of these possibilities. In the rules, a derivateme is represented by a symbol standing for a set of synonymous signs that express it (in a particular case, this set can contain just one element).

Figure 12.7 Derivational lexemic rule R^{LEX} 3 (English)

The semanteme 'again' bearing on a meaning 'X' can be realized in the DSyntS by a derivateme *RE-* under the condition that 'X' is expressed by a verb. At the morphological level, this derivateme is expressed by the prefix **re-**: **re**+*assign*, **re**+*run*, **re**+*establish*, etc.

> **NB:** French has a similar rule, also with the derivateme RE-, but in French, this derivateme has several allomorphic realizations; for instance, /re-/ (*ré+inventer* 'reinvent'), /rə-/ (*re+saisir* lit. 'reseize'), and /r-/ (*r+ouvrir* 'reopen').

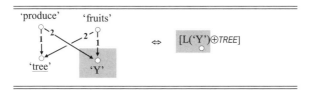

Figure 12.8 Derivational lexemic rule R^{LEX} 4 (Spanish)

In Spanish, the semantic configuration 'tree producing fruits Y' can be realized in the DSyntS by the derivateme TREE, expressed at the DMorph-level by the morphological conversion "feminine ⇒ masculine." This conversion changes the gender indication in the syntactics of N('Y'), which results in the replacement of the gender suffix in the noun: *naranja*$_{(fem)}$ 'orange' ~ *naranjo*$_{(masc)}$ 'orange tree'; *manzana*$_{(fem)}$ 'apple' ~ *manzano*$_{(masc)}$ 'apple tree'; *ciruela*$_{(fem)}$ 'plum' ~ *ciruelo*$_{(masc)}$ 'plum tree'; *cereza*$_{(fem)}$ 'cherry' ~ *cerezo*$_{(masc)}$ 'cherry tree'; etc.

Compounding Lexemic Rules

A compounding lexemic rule unites two stems (Ch. 2, *3.1.3*) into a compound stem; *Figure 12.9* shows one such rule for German.

Figure 12.9 Compounding lexemic rule R^{LEX} 5 (German)

This rule describes the construction of German compound nouns having the nominal stem PLAN- 'plan' as a basic (= communicatively dominant) element: REISEPLAN 'trip plan', KRIEGSPLAN 'war plan', BAUPLAN 'construction plan', AUSFLUGSPLAN 'hike plan', FORSCHUNGSPLAN 'research plan', etc.

> REMARK. The above rule could have been generalized: instead of a particular nominal stem, i.e., PLAN-, we could have used a variable standing for any nominal stem that allows this type of compounding; however, we did not do so in order to keep things simple.

1.1.2   Phrasemic Rules

Two phrasemic rules will be presented, one for an English nominal idiom (*Figure 12.10*), and one for a French verbal one (*Figure 12.11*).

The SemAs **1** and **2** of the semanteme 'procedures' – who performs the procedures ('bureaucracy**2**') and on what – are not shown; they are irrelevant for our illustration and could be instantiated by 'anybody' and 'anything'. The SemA **3** manifests the domain in which the procedures are applied.

Figure 12.10 Phrasemic rule R^LEX 6 (English)

The semantic configuration 'excessive bureaucratic procedures' represents (roughly) the meaning of the idiom ⌐RED TAPE⌐ (e.g., *Eurosceptics cite **red tape** as an example of bureaucratic waste.* | *The Government moves to cut **red tape** for skilled immigrant workers.*).

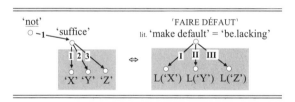

Figure 12.11 Phrasemic rule R^LEX 7 (French)

According to Rule R^LEX 7, the semantic configuration '[X] ne suffit pas [à Y pour Z(Y)]' = '[X] does not suffice [to Y for Z(Y)]' can be expressed in the DSyntS by the idiom ⌐FAIRE DÉFAUT⌐ lit. 'make default' = 'be.lacking': *Les connaissances*$_{L('X')}$ *lui*$_{L('Y')}$ *font défaut pour répondre*$_{L('Z')}$ *à cette question* lit. 'Knowledge to.him is.lacking to reply to this question'. | *Quand la foi*$_{L('X')}$ *vous*$_{L('Y')}$ *fait défaut*… lit. 'When faith to.you is.lacking…'. | *Les idées ne manquent pas, seul l'argent*$_{L('X')}$ *fait défaut* 'Ideas are not in.short.supply, only the money is.lacking'.

1.1.3   Lexical-Functional Rules

These rules exploit the semantic-lexical relations an LU L entertains with other LUs in the lexical stock: semantic derivatives idiosyncratically linked to L (Ch. 7, *2.1*) and restricted lexical cooccurrents of L – lexical elements with which L forms collocations (Ch. 7, *2.2*). These relations are described in an EDC in the LF zone of the dictionary article of which L is the headword.

One derivational and three collocational lexical-functional rules will be cited.

Figure 12.12 Derivational lexical-functional rule R^LEX 8 (English)

In the derivational rule shown in *Figure 12.12*, the semanteme '<u>person</u> [who X-es]', the communicatively dominant meaning of the semantic configuration present in the left-hand side of the rule R^LEX 8 is expressed in the DSyntS by means of the lexical function S_1 [≈ Agent Noun]; for instance, if X = RESIDE [*in Berlin*], then S_1(RESIDE) = **resident** [*of Berlin*]; if X = READ [*the paper*], then S_1(READ) = **reader** [*of the paper*].

Figure 12.13 Collocational lexical-functional rule R^LEX 9 (English)

The rule in *Figure 12.13* shows how the semanteme 'intense' bearing on a communicatively dominant meaning '<u>X</u>' can be expressed in the DSyntS by means of the lexical function Magn(L('X')); for instance, *freezing*_Magn *cold*_L('X') (*a freezing cold afternoon*); *hate*_L('X') *positively*_Magn (*She positively hates me.*); *skinny*_L('X') ⌜*as a rake*⌝_Magn (*Johnny is skinny as a rake.*); etc.

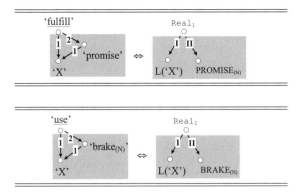

Figure 12.14 Collocational lexical-functional rules R^LEX 10 – 11 (English)

The LF Real$_1$ has several semantic sources – that is, it can correspond to different semantemes in the starting Sem-structure; thus, in *Figure 12.14*, these are the semantemes 'fulfill' (*keep X's word, do X's duty, pay X's debt*) and 'use' (*step on the brake, pilot a helicopter, run a program*).

1.1.4   Lexical-Constructional Rules

Two rules of this type follow, one for English (*Figure 12.15*) and one for Russian (*Figure 12.16*).

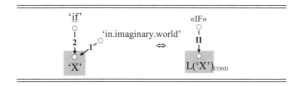

Figure 12.15 Lexical-constructional rule R^{LEX} 12 (English)

The configuration of semantemes 'in.imaginary.world' encodes the meaning of the conditional mood, seen in *If I **were** a rich man, ...* ('if in an imaginary world I am a rich man – while in the real world I am not, ...') and *If he **had** **told** me in time, ...* ('if in an imaginary world he told me in time – while in the real world he did not, ...'). The semanteme 'if' taken together with this configuration can be expressed by the meaningful syntactic construction "V$_{\text{COND}}$ + N" – with the inversion of the subject and the main verb in the conditional, as in ***Were I** a rich man, ...* and ***Had he** told me, ...* This construction is represented at the DSynt-level by the fictitious lexeme «IF».

The notation '$\underline{X}$' ⊃ '<u>number</u>' means "X contains the semanteme 'number' as the Comm-dominant node – that is, '$\underline{X}$' denotes a number."

Figure 12.16 Lexical-constructional rule R^{LEX} 13 (Russian)

The semanteme 'maybe' bearing on a semanteme 'X' that denotes a number can be expressed in Russian by so-called approximate construction (Ch. 11, *2.2.3*, p. 291): Russian opposes phrases of the type *desjat' dnej* 'ten days' (with the numeral preceding the noun) and *dnej desjat'* 'maybe ten days' (with the numeral following the noun). At the DSynt-level, the approximate construction is encoded by means of the fictitious lexeme «PRIMERNO» lit. 'approximately' = 'maybe'.

A given semanteme configuration can be lexicalized in several different ways. Thus, the semantic configuration in the left-hand part of the rule R^LEX 2 can be realized in the DSyntS by the phraseme ⌐WAKE UP⌐2_(V, transitive). Similarly, the left-hand part of the rule R^LEX 7 can be expressed in the DSyntS by the lexeme MANQUER 'be.lacking'. Sometimes it is possible to express the same semanteme configuration by a lexical means (= a lexical unit) or by a morphological means (= a derivational affix). Thus, in Russian, the semanteme 'small' is expressed by the adjective MALEN´KIJ 'small' (introduced by a lexemic rule) or, in an appropriate context, by the diminutive derivational suffix -IK/-ČIK/-K/-C (introduced by a morphologization rule); in this way, we can obtain quasi-synonymous pairs *malen'kij stol* ~ *stol+ik* 'small table', *malen'kaja pugovica* ~ *pugovič+k(+a)* 'small button', etc. And the semanteme 'maybe' seen in R^LEX 13 can be realized in Russian not only by a fictitious lexeme, which will appear on the surface as a particular syntactic construction, but also by the genuine lexeme PRIMERNO 'approximately'.

1.2   Morphologization Rules

Semantic morphologization rules are inflectional rules; they establish correspondences between semantic configurations and full grammemes, which they assign to deep LUs. As noted earlier, not all languages have inflectional rules (Mandarin Chinese and Vietnamese do not) and in those that do these rules may be more or less abundant (Slavic languages have much richer inflectional morphology that Romance languages, for example). We cannot properly present these rules here: they belong to morphological semantics and should be described in a monograph on morphological significations.

Figures 12.17 and *12.18* show two inflectional rules specific to English.

Figure 12.17 Inflectional rule R^INFLECT 1 (English)

This rule associates the semantic configuration 'more.than.one' to the grammeme PLURAL, assigned to nouns (for example, CAT_PL ⇔ *cats*).

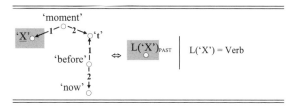

Figure 12.18 Inflectional rule R^INFLECT 2 (English)

The rule R^INFLECT 2 ensures the expression of the semantic configuration 'moment [of X] is *t*, *t* being before now' by the grammeme PAST, assigned to verbs (for example, SLEEP_PAST ⇔ *slept*).

1.3   Arborization Rules

Arborization rules are of two types: rules that establish the top node (Ch. 11, *2.1*, Definition 11.1) of the DSynt-tree under synthesis and those that construct its branches and subtrees, starting from the arcs of the semantic network.

1.3.1   Rules Establishing the Top Node of the DSynt-Tree

These rules (*Figures 12.19–12.21*) perform the following three operations:

1. In the starting SemS, they select the candidates for the status of the entry node – that is, the SemS node that can give rise to the top node of the DSyntS.
2. Among the selected candidates, they choose the best possible one(s).
3. If the selected candidate cannot be expressed in L by a verb, arborization rules "verbalize" it by adding to it a support verb (Ch. 7, *2.2.2*) or a copula (= a "linking" verb of type BE, SEEM, APPEAR).

A node labeled with a genuine predicate 'σ' can be the entry node iff 'σ' satisfies one of the following two conditions:

1) Either 'σ' is the communicatively dominant node [CDN] of the **R_Sem** or of the **T_Sem** and can be expressed in **L** by a verb.

2) Or 'σ' is the CDN of the **R_Sem** and cannot be expressed by a verb.

Figure 12.19 Choice of potential entry nodes (arborization rule R^ARBOR 1)

NB: In the following examples, the Sem- and DSynt-structures are partial: inflectional values are not shown and some irrelevant elements are omitted.

Example (for condition 2)

(1) a. [**Q**: What about John?] *John is sick.*

   b. SemS: '[sick]$_{\textbf{RSem}}$–1→[John]$_{\textbf{TSem}}$'

   c. DSyntS: JOHN←**I**–Copul–**II**→SICK

Suppose we want to produce sentence (1a). Condition 2 of the R^{ARBOR} 1 allows for the choice of 'sick', a genuine predicate with no verbal expression, as the entry node of the SemS of (1a), given in (1b); this calls for the application of another arborization rule (R^{ARBOR} 3, *Figure 12.21* below), which adds the copula BE to the DSyntS of our sentence, yielding (1c).

---

1) If the candidate 'σ_1' for the entry node has a verbal expression in **L** and the other candidate 'σ_2' does not, then:

   a) If 'σ_2' is not a genuine predicate and does not belong to the **R**$_{\textbf{Sem}}$, choose 'σ_1'.

   b) If 'σ_1' is a genuine predicate and belongs to the **R**$_{\textbf{Sem}}$, keep both candidates, giving preference to 'σ_1'.

2) If both candidates lack verbal expression, then choose the one in the **R**$_{\textbf{Sem}}$.

Figure 12.20 Ranking of potential entry nodes (arborization rule R^{ARBOR} 2)

Examples (for Conditions 1a and 2)

(2) a. [**Q**: What about John's paper?] *John's paper was accepted for publication.*

   b. SemS: '[...←1–accept$_{\sigma1}$–2→publish]$_{\textbf{RSem}}$–2→[paper$_{\sigma2}$–1→John]$_{\textbf{TSem}}$'

   c. DSyntS: S$_0$(PUBLISH)←**III**–ACCEPT$_{PASS}$–**I**→PAPER–**I**→JOHN

Condition 1a imposes the selection of the semanteme 'accept$_{X \sim Y}$', a genuine predicate, as the entry node, preferring it to the semanteme 'paper$_{X's \sim on\,Y}$', a quasi-predicate. (For the arborization rule involved in the production of sentence (2a), see below: R^{ARBOR} 5, *Figure 12.23*.)

(3) a. [**Q**: What is John's paper about?] *John's paper deals with French.*

   b. SemS: '[John←1–paper$_{\sigma1}$]$_{\textbf{TSem}}$–2→[French$_{\sigma2}$]$_{\textbf{RSem}}$'

   c. DSyntS: JOHN←**I**–PAPER←**I**–Func$_2$–**II**→FRENCH$_{(N)}$

As per Condition 2, the semanteme '<u>French</u>' [language] is selected as the entry node. The support verb Func$_2$ is inserted into the DSyntS by the rule R^{ARBOR} 3.

If the chosen entry node 'σ' has only a non-verbal lexical expression L('σ'),

then it is necessary to replace the lexeme L('σ'), which should serve as the top node of the DSyntS, by one of the following DSynt-configurations:

Copul–II→L('σ'), Oper$_i$–II→L('σ'), Func$_i$–I→L('σ')

or Labor$_{12}$–III→L('σ').

Figure 12.21 "Verbalization" of a non-verbal entry node (arborization rule R^{ARBOR} 3)

Example

(4) a. [**Q**: And the Empire?] *The Empire committed aggression against the Rebel Alliance.*

b. SemS: '[Empire]$_{\textbf{T}_{\textbf{Sem}}}$←1–[aggression$_σ$–2→Alliance]$_{\textbf{R}_{\textbf{Sem}}}$'

c. DSyntS: EMPIRE←I–Oper$_1$–II→AGRESSION–II→ALLIANCE

The meaning 'aggression' does not have a verbal expression in English (*The Empire aggressed the Rebel Alliance* is ungrammatical); in order to realize the SemS (4b) as a full sentence like (4a), the support verb Oper$_1$ (realized as COMMIT) is introduced at the DSynt-level by the above rule, as seen in (4c).

See also examples (1) and (3) above, which illustrate recourse to the rule R^{ARBOR} 3.

1.3.2   Rules Constructing Branches and Subtrees of the DSynt-Tree

Five rules will be presented.

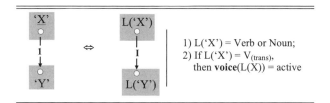

Figure 12.22 Construction of the DSyntRel I of an active verb (arborization rule R^{ARBOR} 4)

The rule in *Figure 12.22* describes the construction of an actantial DSyntRel. It stipulates that the SemRel **1** linking a meaning '<u>X</u>' (both semantically and communicatively dominant) to its semantic actant 'Y' corresponds – at the

DSynt-level – to the DSyntRel **I**, which has L('X') as the governing member and L('Y') as the dependent member. The rule can apply under the condition that L('X') is a verb or a noun; moreover, if L('X') is a transitive verb, it has to be in the active voice.

Examples

(5) a. *The author considers Equation (11).*

   b. SemS: '[author$_Y$←1–consider$_X$]$_{T_{Sem}}$–2→[equation (11)]$_{R_{Sem}}$'

   c. DSyntS: AUTHOR←**I**–CONSIDER$_{IND, ACT, PRES}$–**II**→EQUATION (11)

(6) a. *Mary reacted quickly.* | *Mary's reaction was quick.*

   b. SemS: '[Mary$_Y$←1–react$_X$]$_{T_{Sem}}$←1–[quick]$_{R_{Sem}}$'

   c. DSyntSs: MARY←**I**–REACT$_{(V)IND, ACT, PAST}$–**ATTR**→QUICKLY
   MARY←**I**–S$_0$(REACT$_{(V)})_{(N)}$←**I**–BE$_{IND, PAST}$–**II**→QUICK

In the above rule, the SemRel **1** is "transcoded" into the DSyntRel **I**. However, such a simple, one-to-one correspondence between Sem- and DSynt-dependencies does not always obtain: many arborization rules violate this correspondence, distorting the simple linkage between the SemS and the DSyntS of a sentence. The following three rules illustrate this phenomenon.

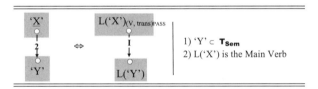

Figure 12.23 Construction of the DSyntRel **I** with a passive verb as the governor (arborization rule R^{ARBOR} 5)

The rule shown in *Figure 12.23* is a passivization rule: it attaches the grammeme PASS(ive) to the Main Verb of the clause, and implements the SemRel **1** as the DSyntRel **II** under the condition that 'Y', the dependent member of the former, belongs to the Semantic Theme of the clause. (This amounts to a demotion of what by default should have been the DSyntA **I** of the Main Verb to its DSyntA **II**.)

Example

(7) a. [**Q**: What about Equation (11)?] *Equation (11) is considered on p. 245.*

   b. SemS : 'author←1–consider$_X$–2→[equation $_Y$ (11)]$_{T_{Sem}}$'

   c. DSyntS: EQUATION (11)←**I**–CONSIDER$_{IND, PASS, PRES}$

R^{ARBOR} 5 does not produce the DSyntA **II** (the surface-syntactic level Agent Complement), so it is good for the so-called short passive. In order to cover the so-called long passive – the passive form with an Agent Complement – another rule is needed, as in *Figure 12.24*.

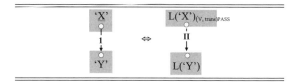

Figure 12.24 Construction of the DSyntRel **II** with a passive verb as the governor (arborization rule R^ARBOR 6)

This rule takes care of the demotion of the presumed DSyntA **I** of $L_{(V)}$ to its DSyntA **II**, provided $L_{(V)}$ is in the passive voice. The DSyntA **II** is expressed at the SSynt-level by a BY-phrase.

Example

(8) a.   [**Q**: What about Equation (11)?] *Equation (11) is considered by the author on p. 245.*

   b.   SemS : '[author$_Y$←**1**–<u>consider$_X$</u>]$_{\textbf{RSem}}$–**2**→[<u>equation (11)</u>]$_{\textbf{TSem}}$'

   c.   DSyntS: EQUATION (11)←**I**–CONSIDER$_{IND, PASS, PRES}$–**II**→AUTHOR$_{SG, DEF}$

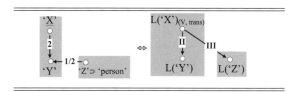

Figure 12.25 Possessor Raising (arborization rule R^ARBOR 7)

The rule R^ARBOR 7 (*Figure 12.25*) describes the syntactic phenomenon known as Possessor Raising, found, for instance, in French:

(9)   Fr. *L'infirmière* **te**$_{L(‘Z’)}$ *lavera*$_{L(‘X’)}$ *les mains*$_{L(‘Y’)}$ lit. 'The nurse to.you will.wash the hands'.

Semantically, 'toi' = 'you$_{SG}$' is the Sem-actant **1** of 'mains' = 'hands' ('toi' is the Possessor of 'mains'). Syntactically, however, in (9), TOI does not depend on the corresponding lexeme MAIN$_{PL}$ 'hands' (if it did, this would give *tes mains* 'your hands'), but is instead "raised," as it were, to become DSynt-actant **III** of the verb that governs MAIN$_{PL}$ in the sentence; literally, this gives 'wash to.you the hands'. This type of raising is common in other Romance languages and in Balkan languages (Serbian and Albanian, for instance).

Raising semantic rules are similar to passivization semantic rules in that they also distort the simple correspondence between semantic and deep-syntactic actants.

To conclude this subsection, *Figure 12.26* is an arborization rule of a different type, describing the construction of a relative clause.

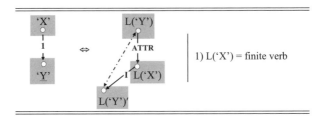

Figure 12.26 Construction of a relative clause (arborization rule R[ARBOR] 8)

The rule R[ARBOR] 8 treats the case in which semantic and communicative dependencies between two semantemes go in opposite directions: in the left-hand part of the rule, 'X' semantically dominates '$\underline{Y}$' via the SemRel **1**, while being communicatively dominated by it. In this case, it is L('Y') that becomes the syntactic governor of L('X'), to which it is linked via the DSyntRel **ATTR**, as indicated in the right-hand part of the rule. L('Y') is duplicated, its copy, L('Y')', being subordinated via the SSyntRel **I** to L('X') and linked to L('Y') by a co-reference arrow, under the condition that L('X') is a verb. This rule can produce, for instance, the structure in *Figure 12.27*.

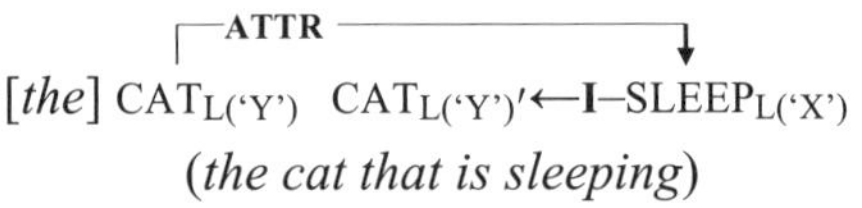

$$[\textit{the}] \ \text{CAT}_{L('Y')} \quad \overbrace{\text{CAT}_{L('Y')'} \leftarrow\!\text{I}\!-\!\text{SLEEP}_{L('X')}}^{\text{ATTR}}$$

(*the cat that is sleeping*)

Figure 12.27 Example of the application of arborization rule R[ARBOR] 8

The pronominalization – implementation of L('Y')' by a relative pronoun (WHICH, THAT or WHO) – happens later, during the transition to the surface-syntactic structure.

What we just presented is a small yet representative sample of semantic transition rules; we hope that they give the reader a clear idea of what the SemS ⇒ DSyntS correspondence looks like. Let us now turn to semantic equivalence rules.

2   Semantic Equivalence (= Paraphrasing) Rules

Equivalence rules are in fact paraphrasing rules, i.e., rules for the production of paraphrases (Ch. 9, *2.1*). They are of two types: semantic equivalences proper (*2.1*) and lexical-syntactic equivalences (*2.2*). Both rule types can be further subdivided; both contain exact equivalences and approximate, or quasi-, equivalences.

    "≡" stands for an exact equivalence, and "≅" is the symbol for an approximate equivalence.

As with the semantic transition rules, we will consider only the semantic equivalence rules operating on the basic structures of the two representations concerned – SemSs for semantic equivalences proper and DSyntSs for lexical-syntactic equivalences.

2.1   Semantic Equivalences Proper

Semantic equivalences proper are based on operations of two types: 1. substitution (of configurations) of semantemes labeling the nodes of the SemS, and 2. restructuring of the graph of the SemS, namely the omission/addition and reconnection/transfer of semantemes and arcs.

2.1.1   Semantic Substitution Rules

These rules either reduce a SemS subnetwork to a node, or expand a SemS node into a subnetwork, or else perform a simple, that is, node-for-node, substitution.

2.1.1.1   Semantic Reduction/Expansion Rules

A rule of this type performs two mutually inverse operations:

- Reduction of a SemS – that is, replacement of a semanteme configuration '$\tilde{\sigma}$' appearing in a SemS by a single semanteme 'σ', of which '$\tilde{\sigma}$' is a decomposition.
- Expansion of a SemS – that is, replacement of a semanteme 'σ' appearing in a SemS by a semanteme configuration '$\tilde{\sigma}$', representing a decomposition of 'σ'.

An example is shown in *Figure 12.28*.

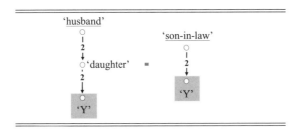

Figure 12.28 Semantic reduction/expansion rule R^EXP-RED 1

Applied to the SemS of (10a), from left to right, the rule works as a reduction rule, producing the SemS of (10b); conversely, if applied to the SemS of (10b), from right to left, the same rule functions as an expansion rule, producing the SemS of (10a).

(10) a. *My **daughter's husband** is a teacher.* ≡
   b. *My **son-in-law** is a teacher.*
   c. SemS of (10a):
       'I←**2**–**daughter**←**2**–**husband**←**1**–profession–**2**→teacher'
   d. SemS of (10b): 'I←**2**–**son-in-law**←**1**–profession–**2**→teacher'

A semantic reduction/expansion rule is actually the equivalence part of a simple lexemic or phrasemic rule (*1.1.1* above, p. 314) – a formalized lexicographic definition of the LU having the corresponding configuration of semantemes as its signified, i.e., an ECD-style definition written in the form of a semantic network (Ch. 5, *1*). The application of such rules produces exact paraphrases.

Semantic reduction/expansion rules are necessary to produce "deep" paraphrases – those whose paraphrastic links are not "visible" without recourse to semantic decomposition. Let us consider the following paraphrases:

(11) a. *The **din** of a truck speeding past my window **woke** me **up** at 5 am.* ≡
   b. *The **loud, unpleasant noise** of a truck speeding past my window **interrupted** my **sleep** at 5 am.*

Four semantic equivalence rules are needed in order to link the SemSs of these sentences: Rules 2–4 expand the starting SemS, producing three intermediate SemSs, and Rule 5 performs a reduction leading to the target SemS. The rules, along with the SemSs they produce, are shown in *Figure 12.29*; the boldface marks the nodes involved in the operation under consideration. (The SemSs are incomplete and the rules not precise enough, but this will suffice to illustrate our point; we cite the rules in the "linear" form of a traditional dictionary definition.)

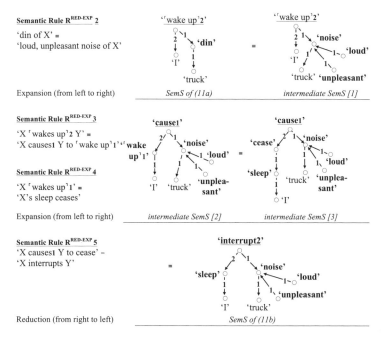

Figure 12.29 Five equivalent SemSs with different degrees of decomposition

The intermediate SemSs allow for getting additional paraphrases, some of which are given in (12):

(12) a.   The **din** ⟨*loud*, ***unpleasant noise***⟩ *of a truck speeding past my window* ***made*** *me* ⌐*wake up*⌐*1 = awake1*⟩ *at 5 am.* ≡
   b.   The **din** ⟨*loud*, ***unpleasant noise***⟩ *of a truck speeding past my window* ***brought*** *my* **sleep to an end** ⟨*= awoke2 me from my* **sleep**⟩ *at 5 am.*

Apart from being used as paraphrasing rules in their own right, reduction/ expansion semantic rules – in particular, expansions – serve as auxiliary rules, as it were: they prepare the terrain for the application of other types of equivalence rules, which perform restructurings of SemSs and whose application often requires SemSs to be decomposed.

2.1.1.2   Global Substitution Semantic Rules

Most global substitution rules produce approximate paraphrases which, in addition to differing propositionally, often feature communicative differences. Four global substitution semantic rules are presented in *Figures 12.30–12.33*, involving relations between some fundamental semantic and logical concepts.

☞   As indicated in Ch. 3, *4.1.2*, 'cause1' stands for non-agentive causation ('being the cause') and 'cause2' for agentive causation ('being the causer').

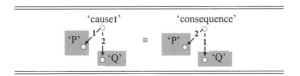

Figure 12.30 Cause ~ consequence (semantic rule R[GLOBAL-SUBST] 1)

(13) a.   *John's comfortable **income**$_P$ **enables** him*$_{['\text{causes1}\ J.\ to\ be\ \textbf{able}\ [=\ Q]']}$ *to travel a lot.* ≅
      b.   *John has a comfortable **income**$_P$; **therefore**$_{['\text{as a consequence}']}$, he is **able**$_Q$ to travel a lot.*

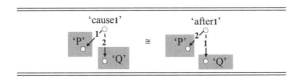

Figure 12.31 Cause ~ temporal succession (semantic rule R[GLOBAL-SUBST] 2)

(14) a.   *The army started **patrolling**$_P$ the streets, **causing** the neighborhood to **calm_down**$_Q$.* ≅
      b.   *The neighborhood **calmed_down**$_P$ **after** the army started **patrolling**$_Q$ the streets.*

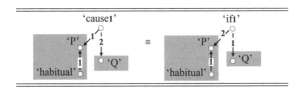

Figure 12.32 Cause ~ condition (semantic rule R[GLOBAL-SUBST] 3)

(15) a.   *(Your) **smoking**$_P$ **increases2**$_{['\text{causes1 to increase1}[=\ Q]']}$ your risk of cancer.* ≅
      b.   *If you **smoke**$_P$, your risk of cancer **increases1**$_Q$.*

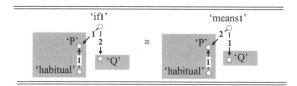

Figure 12.33 Condition ~ means (semantic rule R^{GLOBAL-SUBST} 4)

(16) a. *If you **donate**$_P$ 30 dollars a month, you **can**$_Q$ change the life of a child.* ≅
     b. ***With***$_{[\text{‘by means of’}]}$ *a monthly **donation**$_P$ of 30 dollars you **can**$_Q$ change the life of a child.*

Other verbalizations are also possible. Thus, for (13a), we could have *Because of* ≅ *Given, Due to, Thanks to⟩ his comfortable income, John is able to ⟨*≅ *is in a position to, can (afford to)⟩ travel a lot*; and for (13b), *John has a comfortable income (and) so ⟨*≅ *as a consequence, consequently⟩ he can ⟨is in a position to, can (afford to)⟩ travel a lot.* This is true for the other three rules, as well. The relative simplicity of global semantic rules means heavier involvement of transition (lexicalization and arborization) rules.

2.1.2   Semantic Restructuring Rules

These rules describe sememe omission from, or addition to, the SemS and arc reconnections/transfers; they necessarily result in approximate paraphrases.

2.1.2.1   Semantic Omission/Addition Rules

Consider the approximate paraphrases in (17) and their respective SemSs in *Figure 12.34.*

(17) a. *Fred walked*$_{[\text{‘moved **on.foot**’}]}$ *quickly across the road.* ≡
     b. *Fred hurried*$_{[\text{‘moved **quickly**’}]}$ *across the road.*

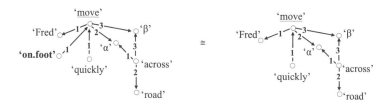

Figure 12.34 SemSs of sentences (17a) and (17b)

The SemS of sentence (17a) features the decomposition of the semanteme 'X walks from point α to point β' ≈ 'X moves on.foot from point α to point β', and that of the sentence (17b) the decomposition of the semanteme 'X hurries from point α to point β' ≈ 'X moves quickly from point α to point β'. The only difference between these two SemSs is the presence of an additional semanteme in the SemS (17a), the semanteme 'on.foot', specifying the manner of locomotion. This difference can be ignored in some contexts. This, in fact, is an entailment, or implication (Ch. 9, 2.2) – 'move on.foot' entails 'move' – which can be modeled by means of the rule in *Figure 12.35*, carrying out the subtraction of the semanteme configuration '[do P] in the manner α'.

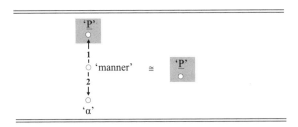

Figure 12.35 Omission of a specific difference (semantic rule R^{RESTRUCT} 1)

The next rule (*Figure 12.36*) adds the semanteme 'can$_{(V)}$' [≈ 'able'] to a predicate semanteme 'P' denoting a habitual action/activity:

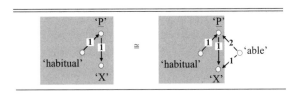

Figure 12.36 Addition of 'can$_{(V)}$' in a habitual context (semantic rule R^{RESTRUCT} 2)

This rule exploits the link existing between habitual/imperfective action and capacity: "X does Y usually" can also be conceptualized as "X can do Y". Its application allows for paraphrases such as these:

(18) a. *At that time, people **were building** [≅ **could build**] stone bridges.*
    b. *Depression and anxiety: Exercise **eases** [≅ **can ease**] symptoms.*

Semantic omission/addition rules are "asymmetric": they are not necessarily applicable in both directions. Thus, if Fred hurried across the road, he did not necessarily walk across: he could have been riding a bike, for example. Similarly, if exercise can ease the symptoms of depression and anxiety, it does not necessarily follow that they effectively do so every time.

Since the equivalences established by semantic omission/addition rules are only approximate, the application of these rules is subject to conditions, which we cannot present here.

2.1.2.2 Semantic Reconnection/Transfer Rules

Let there be the following sentences and their respective SemSs in *Figure 12.37*:

(19) a. *I **hate**$_Q$ the **dryness**$_P$ of this climate$_X$.* $\cong$
      b. *I **hate**$_Q$ this dry$_P$ **climate**$_X$.*

Figure 12.37 SemSs of Sentences (19a) and (19b)

In the SemS of (19a), the semanteme 'hate' takes as its second actant a fact – '[be] dry', while in the SemS of (19b), the second actant of this same semanteme is a participant of this fact, i.e., 'climate'. This is a reconnection – that is, the changing of a connection – of a semantically and communicatively dominant semanteme; the corresponding rule looks like *Figure 12.38* (the reconnected arc is thick):

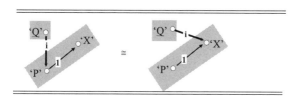

Figure 12.38 Reconnection of a communicatively dominant semanteme (semantic rule R^{RESTRUCT} 3)

At the syntactic level, there is head switching, or inversion of subordination, between L('P') and L('X').

Other examples: *A **lack** of funding ⟨Insufficient **funding**⟩ is slowing down the construction.* | *The tropical island boasts an **abundance** of flora and fauna ⟨an abundant **flora and fauna**⟩.* | *Word repetitions are due to the **poverty** of vocabulary ⟨to poor **vocabulary**⟩.*

This rule is not applicable in all contexts, cf.: *I understand the complexity of this problem* ≠ *I understand this complex problem* (realizing that the problem is complex does not entail the ability to solve it); however, we cannot provide here the conditions under which it applies.

Another similar rule links paraphrases like the following ones:

(20) a.   *John cooks*[P+Y] ***well****ₐ.* ≅ *John makes*ₚ ***good****ₐfood*ᵧ.

b.   *John writes*[P+Y] ***convincingly****ₐ.* ≅ *John's writing* ['texts*ᵧ* which J. creates*ₚ*'] *is* ***convincing****ₐ.*

This quasi-equivalence is possible in the context of creation predicates ('cook' = 'create food', 'write' = 'create texts', etc.), where a characterization can bear either upon the creation itself or upon its result: 'create Y in manner for Y to be α' is quasi-equivalent to 'create Y that is α'. This is a reconnection of a semantically dominant but communicatively dominated semanteme; it is modeled by the rule in *Figure 12.39*.

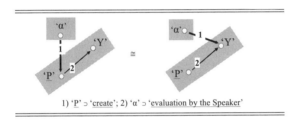

1) '**P**' ⊃ '<u>create</u>'; 2) 'α' ⊃ '<u>evaluation by the Speaker</u>'

Figure 12.39 Reconnection of a communicatively subordinated semanteme (semantic rule R^RESTRUCT 4)

This rule (unlike the preceding one) does not trigger head switching in syntax: 'α', the reconnected semanteme, remains expressed in target sentences as a circumstantial/modifier, i.e., as a syntactically subordinated element.

Wrapping up this subsection, let us note that some paraphrastic links presented as semantic equivalences proper can also be described as lexical-syntactic equivalences. However, only the former allow for establishing "deep" semantic links, for which meaning decomposition is required.

2.2   Lexical-Syntactic Equivalences

Lexical-syntactic equivalences involve (quasi-)equivalences and implications between configurations of LUs. They differ from semantic equivalences proper in that the lexical-syntactic equivalence between two paraphrases is established without recourse to the semantic decomposition of the LUs involved. For a lexical-syntactic equivalence, it is not necessary to have access to that sentence's SemS: all changes are carried out at the level of lexical links (= DSynt-level).

Since lexical-syntactic equivalences are based on the notions of deep-syntactic structure (Ch. 11) and lexical function (Ch. 7), which are linguistic universals, they too have a linguistically universal character: in principle, they are applicable in any language, as well as between any two languages.

Lexical-syntactic equivalences are established by deep-syntactic paraphrasing rules, which belong, as was indicated at the beginning of this chapter, to both the Semantic and the Deep-Syntactic modules of an MTM.

Two major classes of deep-syntactic paraphrasing rules are distinguished:

- Lexical rules specify lexical equivalences that underlie the LU substitutions possible in a DSyntS. They are divided into two subclasses:
  (quasi-)equivalent substitutions, based on lexical relations described in Ch. 6, *1.1 & 1.2* and further split into (1) synonymic substitutions (in the narrow sense, with the use of synonyms); (2) antonymic substitutions; (3) conversive substitutions; (4) derivative substitutions
  implicative substitutions, based on the sentential relation of implication (Ch. 9, *2.2*).
- Restructuring rules specify syntactic transformations of the DSyntS imposed by lexical rules. In a DSyntS, four types of restructuring are possible: (1) fission of a node or, conversely, fusion of two nodes; (2) branch relabeling; (3) branch transfer (to a different governor); and (4) inversion of subordination, or head switching. These are shown in *Figure 12.40*.

While restructurings of types (1)–(3) are elementary operations, type (4) restructuring is complex and can entail the first three.

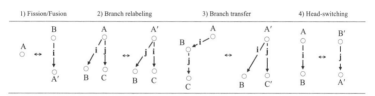

Figure 12.40 Types of restructuring possible at the deep-syntactic level

 The symbol ↔ means 'is re-written as'; the symbol ' (prime) accompanying the name of an LU indicates that it is either the same LU (as previously) or one of its derivatives: A' is either A or a derivative (in the broad sense) of A.

Examples

1. $[to]\,fight_A$ $\equiv [to]\,wage_B-[a]-\mathbf{i}{\rightarrow}fight_{A'}$
2. $I_B{\leftarrow}\mathbf{i}{-}fear_A{-}[her]{-}\mathbf{j}{\rightarrow}anger_C.$ $\equiv Her\,anger_C{\leftarrow}\mathbf{i}{-}frightens_{A'}{-}\mathbf{j}{\rightarrow}me_B.$
3. $A\,violent_C{\leftarrow}\mathbf{i}{-}wind_B\,is.blowing_A.\equiv The\,wind_B\,is.blowing_{A'}{-}\mathbf{j}{\rightarrow}violently_{C'}.$
4. $keep_A{-}\mathbf{i}{\rightarrow}talking_B$ $\equiv still_A{\leftarrow}\mathbf{j}{-}be.talking_{B'}$

In what follows, we will present only lexical paraphrasing rules, leaving aside the reconstruction rules. However, we will indicate, for each lexical rule type, the restructuring rules that accompany them.

> **NB:** The DSyntSs cited below are incomplete; we have omitted the grammemes because they are not involved in the paraphrasing rules presented.

2.2.1   (Quasi-)Equivalent Substitutions

These substitutions establish exact paraphrasing links if the LUs involved are exact synonyms, antonyms, etc. Otherwise, the links are those of approximate paraphrases.

2.2.1.1   Synonymic Substitutions

In the simplest case, a synonymic substitution does not entail any additional change in the syntactic organization of the tree being treated (cf. rule $R^{\text{LEX.SYNT}}$ 1, *Figure 12.41*), but some synonymic substitutions are accompanied by fissions (cf. rules $R^{\text{LEX.SYNT}}$ 2/3, *Figures 12.42* and *12.44*) and may occasionally involve branch transfers.

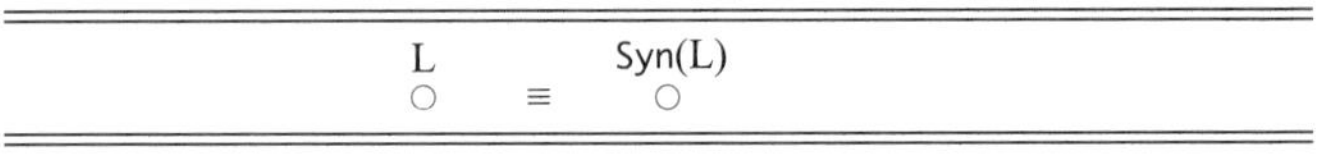

Figure 12.41 Synonymic substitution ($R^{\text{EQ.LEX/SYNT}}$ 1)

The rule in *Figure 12.41* describes a substitution of an LU L by L's exact synonym; for instance:

(21) a.   *To **combat**$_L$ inflation, the Government raised interest rates.* ≡
       b.   *To **fight**$_{\text{Syn}(L)}$ against inflation, the Government raised interest rates.*

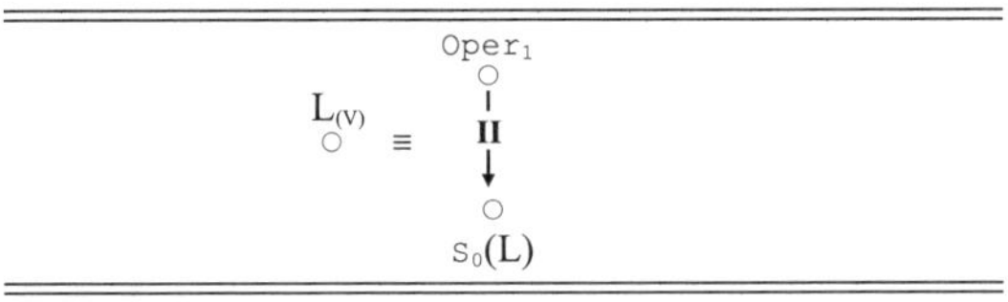

Figure 12.42 Synonymic substitution with light verb fission ($R^{\text{EQ.LEX/SYNT}}$ 2)

Rule $R^{\text{EQ.LEX/SYNT}}$ 2, in *Figure 12.42*, describes a substitution of an LU L by a multi-lexemic expression synonymous with L. More specifically, this rule allows for the replacement of a verbal lexeme L by a configuration made up of L's nominalization – $S_0(L)$ – and an appropriate light verb Oper_1, i.e., by a collocation $\text{Oper}_1(S_0(L))$–$\textbf{II} \rightarrow S_0(L)$; this operation is known as light verb fission. This is illustrated in (22), with its DSyntSs in *Figure 12.43*.

(22) a. *I respect_L Balthazar a lot.* ≡
     b. *I have*$_{\text{Oper}_1(S_0(L))}$ *a lot of respect*$_{S_0(L)}$ *for Balthazar.*

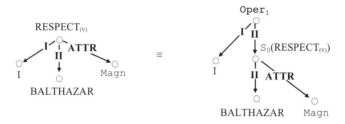

Figure 12.43 DSyntSs of paraphrases (22)

REMARK. The modifier Magn in the target DSyntS bears on the node labeled with $S_0(\text{RESPECT}_{(V)})$ rather than on the node labeled with Oper_1. Attachment of the dependents of a node that has undergone fission (in our case, $\text{RESPECT}_{(V)}$ in the source structure) is taken care of by special rules that will not be presented here.

$$
L_{(V)} \quad \equiv \quad
\begin{array}{c}
\text{Oper}_1 \\
\circ \\
\mid \\
\text{II} \\
\downarrow \\
\circ \\
S_1(L)
\end{array}
$$

Figure 12.44 Synonymic substitution with light verb fission ($R^{\text{EQ.LEX/SYNT}}$ 3)

A verbal LU L can be replaced by a configuration consisting of the standard name of L's DSyntA **I** and the light verb Oper_1 of this noun (another collocation), as seen in *Figure 12.44*. The value of the LF Oper_1 for an agent name is trivial: BE and, sometimes, APPEAR [*as*] or SEEM. This rule also describes light verb fission.

(23) a. *Who wrote_L "Tristram Shandy"?* ≡
     b. *Who is*$_{\text{Oper}_1(S_1(L))}$ *the author*$_{S_1(L)}$ *of "Tristram Shandy"?*

(24) a. *Dr. Jones treats_L my parents.* ≡
     b. *Dr. Jones is*$_{\text{Oper}_1(S_1(L))}$ *my parents' physician*$_{S_1(L)}$.

2.2.1.2 Antonymic Substitutions

An antonymic substitution involves either a single node replacement accompanied by negation fission (cf. rule $R^{\text{LEX.SYN}}$ 4, *Figure 12.45*) or the replacement of a minimal subtree, i.e., two nodes linked by a DSyntRel, in which case, no syntactic reconstruction takes place (cf. rule $R^{\text{LEX.SYNT}}$ 5, *Figure 12.47*).

$$L_{(V)} \equiv \begin{array}{c} \text{Anti}(L) \\ | \\ \text{ATTR} \\ \downarrow \\ \text{NOT} \end{array}$$

Figure 12.45 Antonymic substitution with negation fission (R[EQ.LEX/SYNT] 4)

Rule R[EQ.LEX/SYNT] 4 replaces an LU L by a configuration consisting of L's antonym and the negative polarity lexeme NOT depending on Anti(L) via the DSyntRel ATTR.

(25) a. *The President's proposal is **unlikely**$_L$ to break the deadlock in Washington.* ≡

   b. *The President's proposal is **not likely**$_{Anti(L)}$ to break the deadlock in Washington.*

(26) a. *Johnny behaves fairly well at home but **disobeys**$_L$ his daycare teachers.* ≡

   b. *Johnny behaves fairly well at home but **does not obey**$_{Anti(L)}$ his daycare teachers.*

Partial DSyntSs of sentences (26a) and (26b) are given in *Figure 12.46*.

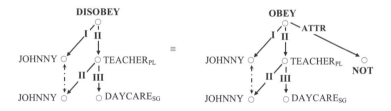

Figure 12.46 Partial DSyntSs of paraphrases (26a–b)

$$\begin{array}{c} L_1 \\ | \\ II \\ \downarrow \\ L_2 \end{array} \equiv \begin{array}{c} \text{Anti}(L_1) \\ | \\ II \\ \downarrow \\ \text{Anti}(L_2) \end{array}$$

Figure 12.47 Antonymic substitution (R[EQ.LEX/SYNT] 5)

In a subtree L_1–**II**→L_2, LUs L_1 and L_2 can be replaced by their antonyms; no restructuring rule is necessary.

(27) a. *John **started**$_{L_1}$ **breaking**$_{L_2}$ the rules.* ≡

   b. *John **stopped**$_{L_1}$ **respecting**$_{L_2}$ the rules.*

Rule R[EQ.LEX/SYNT] 5 needs to be supplied with conditions of application, because it does not work in all cases; cf. *He forbade me to speak.* ≢ *He authorized me not to talk.*

2.2.1.3 Conversive Substitutions

A conversive substitution always entails the syntactic operation of branch relabeling (and sometimes fission and/or transfer).

Figure 12.48 Conversive substitution (R[EQ.LEX/SYNT] 6)

As shown in *Figure 12.48*, an LU L can be replaced by $\text{Conv}_{21}(L)$ provided that the corresponding branch labeling rule is applied. The sentences in (28) illustrate the lexical conversion and those in (29) the grammatical conversion, or passivization, that this rule can perform.

(28) a. *We$_I$ fear$_L$ unforeseen consequences$_{II}$ of this decision.* ≡
     b. *Unforeseen consequences$_I$ of this decision frighten$_{\text{Conv}_{21}(L)}$ us$_{II}$.*

(29) a. *The wolf$_I$ ate$_L$ Little Red Riding Hood$_{II}$.* ≡
     b. *Little Red Riding Hood$_I$ was eaten$_{\text{Conv}_{21}(L)}$ by the wolf$_{II}$.*

> **NB:** A conversive substitution entails a modification of the semantic-communicative structure – namely, the **R$_{\text{Sem}}$** and **T$_{\text{Sem}}$** are inverted. Such substitution is therefore subject to conditions, impossible to discuss here.

An LU L can be replaced by L's Conv_{321} (again under the condition that the corresponding branch labeling rule is applied), as illustrated in (30) and its DSyntSs in *Figure 12.49*.

(30) a. *The general$_I$ gave$_{\text{Oper}_1(L)}$ the troops$_{III}$ the order$_{L, II}$ to advance.* ≡
     b. *The troops$_I$ received$_{\text{Oper}_3(L)}$ the order$_{L, II}$ to advance from the general$_{III}$.*

> **NB:** Oper_1 and Oper_3 of the same LU L are conversives: $\text{Oper}_3(L) = \text{Conv}_{321}\text{Oper}_1(L)$.

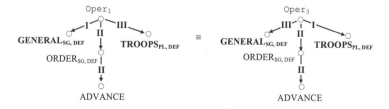

Figure 12.49 DSyntSs of sentences (30a) and (30b)

$$L_{(V)} \quad \equiv \quad \begin{array}{c} \text{Oper}_1(L) \\ \circ \\ | \\ \text{II} \\ \downarrow \\ \circ \\ A_2(L) \end{array}$$

Figure 12.50 Conversive substitution with light verb fission ($R^{\text{EQ.LEX/SYNT}}$ 7)

A verbal LU L can be replaced by a phrase implementing a deep adjective that characterizes L's DSyntA **II** plus the light verb Oper_1 of this adjective (*Figure 12.50*):

(31) a.   *General Wanner* **commanded**$_L$ *the 2nd Division.* ≡
    b.   *The 2nd Division was*$_{\text{Oper}_1(A_2(L))}$ ***under the command***$_{A_2(L)}$ *of General Wanner.*

2.2.1.4   Derivative Substitutions

Derivative substitutions are rather numerous and variegated. We illustrate them with three rules describing distinct derivation types.

$$L_{(N)\text{PL}} \quad \equiv \quad \text{Mult}(L_{(N, \text{ collective})})_{\text{SG}}$$

Figure 12.51 Derivative substitution ($R^{\text{EQ.LEX/SYNT}}$ 8)

According to the rule in *Figure 12.51*, a collective noun, i.e., a noun meaning 'a regular set of Xs' (represented by the LF Mult) can be substituted for a noun with the meaning 'X', if the latter is in the plural.

(32) a.   *The latest President's move doesn't sit well with the **voters**$_L$.* ≡
    b.   *The latest President's move doesn't sit well with the **electorate**$_{\text{Mult}(L)}$.*

Some other lexical equivalences that this rule establishes: READERS ~ READERSHIP; (UNIVERSITY) TEACHERS ~ FACULTY; WORKERS ~ WORKFORCE; etc.

$$L_{(N)} \quad \equiv \quad S_1\text{Real}_1(L_{(N)})$$

Figure 12.52 Derivative substitution ($R^{\text{EQ.LEX/SYNT}}$ 9)

The rule in *Figure 12.52* exploits a common metonymy, "vehicle ~ its driver."

(33) a.   *The **plane**$_L$ was cleared for takeoff.* ≡
    *The **pilot**$_{S_1\text{Real}_1(L)}$ was cleared for takeoff.*

b. *My car*$_\text{L}$ *is not properly parked.*   ≡
    $I_{\text{S}_1\text{Real}_1(\text{L})}$ *am not properly parked.*

The next derivative substitution rule, in *Figure 12.53*, describes a particular case of subordination inversion, or head switching.

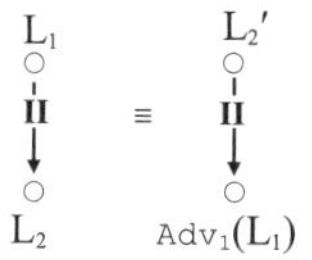

Figure 12.53 Derivative substitution with inversion of subordination (R$^{\text{EQ.LEX/SYNT}}$ 10)

The verb L_1, governor of L_2, becomes the adverb $\text{Adv}_1(L_1)$, while L_2, its actant, turns into the new governor L_2', subordinating $\text{Adv}_1(L_1)$.

(34) a. *The rain* **continued**$_{\text{L}_1}$→*to fall*$_{\text{L}_2}$. ≡
     b. *The rain was falling*$_{\text{L}_2'}$→**continually**$_{\text{Adv}_1(\text{L}_1)}$.

(35) French ~ English
     a. *Il* **a failli**$_{\text{L}_1}$→ *se casser*$_{\text{L}_2}$ *la jambe.* ≡
     b. *He* **almost**$_{\text{Adv1}(\text{L}_1)}$←*broke*$_{\text{L}_2'}$ *his leg.*

> **NB:** Note that in French the meaning 'almost' is expressed by a verb, FAILLIR lit. 'to almost [do something]'.

2.2.2 Implicative Substitutions

Implicative substitutions are unilateral: *S'*, a sentence expressing an implication of *S*, can be a paraphrase of *S*, but the converse does not hold. They give rise to approximate paraphrases: a substitution of *S* by *S'* results in an important loss of information. Consider, for instance, sentence (36a) and its possible implication, (36b), from which the component '[to] cause2' has been omitted, or sentence (36b) and its possible implication, (36c), which lacks the component '[to] begin'.

(36) a. *John turned on the engine* 'John caused2 the engine to begin to run'.
     b. *The engine started up* 'The engine began to run'.
     c. *The engine is running.*

However, this kind of information loss can be compensated for by context (cf. neutralization of semantic differences, Ch. 9, *2.1.1*, p. 238); this is why (some) implications can be used in paraphrasing. Here are three paraphrasing rules making use of implication.

☞   Ξ is a variable standing for LUs and LFs.

Figure 12.54 Attempted causation ~ effective causation (R[IMPLIC.SUBST] 1)

(37) a. *On entering, he **turned** the **switch on***
          [//try.CausFact$_0$(light$_{[\text{'electricity'}]}$)]. $\cong$
    b.   *On entering, he **switched on*** [CausFact$_0$(light)] *the **light**.*

Figure 12.55 Causation of the end of process ~ end of process (R[IMPLIC.SUBST] 2)

(38) a. *He **stopped2*** [LiquFact$_0$(car)] *the **car** close to the entrance.* $\cong$
    b.   *The **car** **stopped1*** [FinFact$_0$(car)] *close to the entrance.*

Figure 12.56 End of process ~ nonexistence of process (R[IMPLIC.SUBST] 3)

(39) a. *Finally, the **wind has subsided*** [FinFunc$_0$(wind)]. $\cong$
    b.   *Finally, **there is no*** [NonFunc$_0$(wind)] ***wind**.*

This concludes our presentation of Meaning-Text paraphrasing rules. We hope to have demonstrated their usefulness for various text-production tasks, as well as their power and elegance.

Further Reading

Lexical choice: [MTT] Polguère 2000b; [other approaches] Matthiessen 1991; Chapter 11 in Horacek & Zock 2015.

MTT semantic correspondence rules: Mel'čuk 2013: 198–258.

MTT paraphrasing rules: Mel'čuk 2013: 137–197; Milićević 2007.

Paraphrase and paraphrasing in NLP applications: [MTT] Iordanskaja *et al.* 1991; Apresjan *et al.* 2009; [other approaches] Bannard & Callison-Burch 2005; Madnani & Dorr 2010; Mallinson *et al.* 2017.

Concluding Remarks

Dear reader, the moment has come to part with you. It is a bit sad, but, at the same time, we are happy – you followed us up to this point and you are going away much more knowledgeable about linguistic semantics than you were at the beginning (or so we hope). Here are, briefly summarized, four fundamental insights into natural language semantics this book has tried to provide.

Interconnectedness of semantics and other parts of the linguistic system

Semantics is a crucial, privileged part of language (and linguistics) for the simple reason that language is, first and foremost, a tool for expressing meaning. However, semantics cannot be studied in isolation, without considering its place within the overall linguistic system and the ways it interacts with other components of it. This is why we have defined semantics as a system of rules ensuring a transition between (semantic representations of) linguistic meanings and their possible expressions (at the deep-syntactic level of representation of sentences).

Functional modeling of semantic phenomena as a basic research tool in modern semantics

Describing natural language semantics is best approached as modeling, or simulation, of the linguistic activity of the Speaker: the way he conveys meaning through linguistic expressions. (This is the synthesis, or language production, viewpoint; from the point of view of analysis, or language comprehension, the question becomes: how does the Addressee extract meaning from linguistic expressions?) The resulting model is verifiable and falsifiable through experimentation: it is possible to correct the model if it does not perform adequately in some of its aspects or even discard it altogether if it proves entirely inadequate.

Importance of conceptual apparatus for the development of semantic models

This approach – the creation of functional formal models – is based upon the development of a deductive system of concepts and terms, just like in the hard sciences. General semantics is actually such a system: a rigorously structured set of definitions based on some basic, non-definable elements, taken as axioms. Have a look at the *Definition Index* and the *Notion and Terms Index/Glossary*.

"Real-world" applicability as the ultimate validity test for semantic models

The value of a scientific theory can be measured, among other things, by its applicability – loosely speaking, by the extent to which it can contribute to making our lives better. Theoretical semantics certainly has this potential; in fact, it has already seen many applications in Natural Language Processing (NLP), Artificial Intelligence, Lexicography and Language Learning/ Teaching. As far as Meaning-Text semantics goes, we mentioned some NLP applications of lexical functions and paraphrasing rules in translation (Ch. 7 and Ch. 10), as well as lexicographic applications of lexical functions and semantic labels (Ch. 8). These and other formal tools can be, and have been, adapted for efficient language learning and teaching; for instance: (1) learner-friendly lexical functions for the systematic acquisition of lexical relations and the self-detection of lexical errors (Alonso Ramos 2004; Polguère 2004; Mel'čuk & Polguère 2007); (2) pedagogical lexicographic definitions for the acquisition and cross-linguistic comparison of word meanings (Milićević 2016); and (3) simplified paraphrasing rules for text reformulation and translation (Milićević 2008 and 2009; Milićević & Tsedryk 2011; Tsedryk 2016). For pointers towards some of these applications, see also Further Reading for Ch. 8.

If this was your first encounter with semantics, we do hope that you liked it, in spite of occasional difficulties, and that you will continue the journey as far as your intellectual curiosity and spirit of adventure takes you. On this note, we say so long – be well, do good work and stay in touch!

Some Mathematical and Logical Notions Useful to Linguistics

This Appendix introduces some notions that came into linguistics from mathematics and logic: sets (*1*), operations (*2*), relations (*3*), formal languages (*4*) and, finally, propositions and predicates (*5*).

The most important contribution of mathematics to linguistics lies not so much in some specific mathematical notions that linguistics borrowed from it (although these can be absolutely vital!) as in the **overall manner of describing** the object under study and **reasoning** about its properties. What we mean is the deductive method, based on strict definitions of concepts and statements that can be "mechanically" derived from these definitions. In this book, we have tried our best to follow the deductive method, abiding by the following proviso: "In any scientific discussion, define each term you use, and define it properly – that is, based on some indefinibilia, specified by a list, and the terms already defined."

We will illustrate the notions that are proposed with examples based on properties of the English language.

1   Sets

A set is a well-specified collection of distinct objects. The objects that make up a set, called elements, or members, of the set, can be anything: numbers, people, abstract ideas, other sets, etc. While a set can be as heterogeneous as one likes, in practice it is homogeneous sets that are most often considered – such that all their elements share some defining properties. A set of this type is called a class.

We say that an element a_i of the set A belongs to A; this is written $a_i \in A$; $a_i \notin A$ means 'a_i is not an element of A' (= 'does not belong to A'). We also say that A contains the element a_i. (The relations of belonging/containing are inverse; the corresponding lexical units – BELONG and CONTAIN – are conversives: Ch. 6, *1.1.3*). A set is indicated by curly brackets: $A = \{a_i \mid 1 \le i \ge n\}$ means 'the set A contains n elements a_1, a_2, ..., a_n'; the curly brackets mean 'contains', and the vertical bar means 'such as ...'.

A set is non-ordered just in case its elements are all "equal," i.e., not distinguishable according to their individual properties. In an ordered set, elements are presented in a specific order, corresponding to their individual properties or different roles within the description where they are used. An ordered set is indicated by angular brackets: $\langle a, b \rangle$ is an ordered pair, $\langle a, b, c \rangle$ is an ordered triplet, and so on.

Examples. A linguistic sign (2, *1.1.1*), a semantic representation (Ch. 10) and a deep-syntactic representation (Ch. 11) are ordered sets.

The most common types of sets are:

1. the empty set (denoted "Λ"), which does not contain any elements.
2. A finite set, which contains a finite number of elements.
3. An infinite set, which contains an infinite number of elements.

Examples. The set of English bilabial fricatives is empty: English has no bilabial fricatives (/v/ ~ /f/ being labiodental fricatives, and /b/ ~ /p/, bilabial stops). The set of English derivational affixes is finite. The set of all English sentences is infinite (if sentences are allowed to be of infinite length).

The set B is a strict subset of (is strictly included in) A if every element of B is also an element of A, but A also contains elements that do not belong to B; this is written $B \subset A$.

Example. The set of meanings of English is a proper subset of significations of English: all English meanings are significations, but the inverse does not hold (Ch. 2, *1.4*, pp. 47–48).

2   Operations

An action on an entity m of a particular type that associates to it the entity n of the same type is called an operation. Depending on m, an operation can be unary (applying to a single entity m), binary (applying to two entities m_1 and m_2), ternary, etc. Thus, logical negation is a unary operation: A ~ ¬A; arithmetic addition is a binary operation yielding the sum of any two numbers: $m_1 + m_2 = n$. Operations allow for all kinds of calculations over different sets. Basic operations on sets include: union of the sets A and B (denoted $A \cup B$); intersection ($A \cap B$); and set difference, or relative complement ($A \setminus B$).

The set $A \cup B$ contains all the elements that are in A and all the elements that are in B:

$A = \{1, 2, 3, 4\}, B = \{3, 4, 5\}, A \cup B = \{1, 2, 3, 4, 5\}$.

The set $A \cap B$ contains all the elements that belong simultaneously to both A and B:

$A = \{1, 2, 3, 4\}, B = \{3, 4, 5\}, A \cap B = \{3, 4\}$.

The set $A \setminus B$ contains all the elements that are in B, but not also in A:

$A = \{1, 2, 3, 4\}, B = \{3, 4, 5\}, A \setminus B = \{5\}$.

Example. A morphonological alternation is an operation; for instance, the alternation /f/ ⟹ /v/ in some English nominal radicals before the plural suffix: *wife* vs. *wive+s*, *wolf* vs. *wolv+es*, etc. See also the operation of linguistic union ⊕, Ch. 2, *1.1.3*.

3   Relations

A relation is a particular correspondence between elements, most often (but not necessarily) – two, which are its members. A relation with two members is binary; a relation with three members is ternary; and so forth.

Examples. 'X is smarter than Y' or 'X loves Y' are binary relations; 'X sits between Y and Z' or 'X gives Y to Z' are ternary relations.

3.1   Set-Theoretical Relations (Relations between Two Sets)

Any two sets A and B can entertain one of the following four relations.

1. A contains all the elements of B, and B contains all the elements of A; A and B are identical, or equal: $A = B$. This is (set) identity.
    Example. The set of morphs of language **L** is equal to the set of segmental elementary signs of **L**.

2. A contains all the elements of B, but B does not contain all the elements of A; A (strictly) includes B: $A \supset B$. We also say that B is included in A: $B \subset A$ (cf. *4.1*). This is (set) inclusion.
    Example. The set of morphs of language **L** strictly includes the set of affixes of **L**.

3. A and B share some elements, but each set also has some elements that the other does not; A and B have non-empty intersection (in the strict sense): $A \cap B \neq \Lambda$. This is (set) intersection.

Example. The set of English consonants and the set of English sonorants have a non-empty intersection: not all consonants are sonorants (a consonant can be an obstruent) and not all sonorants are consonants (a sonorant can be a vowel).

4. *A* and *B* do not share any elements, that is, the intersection of *A* and *B* is empty; *A* and *B* are disjoint: $A \cap B = \Lambda$. This is (set) disjunction.
   Example. The set of English consonants and the set of English vowels are disjoint.

These four major set-theoretical relations are conveniently represented in so-called Venn diagrams (*Figure 1*).

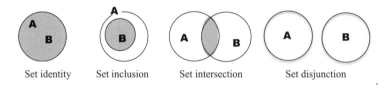

Set identity   Set inclusion   Set intersection   Set disjunction

Figure 1: Venn diagrams

3.2   Properties of Binary Relations

Binary relations are characterized by the properties of reflexivity, symmetry and transitivity. Each of the properties accepts three values: a given relation R can be (1) always true – that is, holding for any possible members; (2) never true (anti-); (3) sometimes true and sometimes false (non-).

The notation R(*a*, *b*) means 'entities *a* and *b* entertain ⟨stand in⟩ the relation R'.

Reflexivity. A relation R over a set *A* (= 'between the elements of *A*') is reflexive iff any element of *A* entertains this relation with itself, that is, iff R(*a*, *a*) is always true; e.g., the relation 'have the same weight as' is reflexive: any object whose weight can be measured has the same weight as itself. A relation R is antireflexive iff R(*a*, *a*) is never true; e.g., 'be heavier than …' (no object can be heavier than itself). A relation R is non-reflexive iff R(*a*, *a*) is sometimes true and sometimes false; e.g., 'be a patient of …' (a physician can treat himself, but this is not at all obligatory).

Examples
Synonymy is a reflexive relation, since each lexeme is synonymous with itself; antonymy is antireflexive: no lexeme can be antonymous to itself.

Symmetry. A relation R over a set *A* is symmetric iff, for all pairs of elements *a* and *b* of *A*, R(*a*, *b*) always entails R(*b*, *a*): R(*a*, *b*) → R(*b*, *a*); e.g., 'be a spouse of'. A relation R is antisymmetric iff, for any *a* ≠ *b*, R(*a*, *b*) never entails R(*b*, *a*): R(*a*, *b*) → ¬R(*b*, *a*); e.g., 'be heavier than'. A relation R is non-symmetric iff R(a, b) → R(b, a) is sometimes true and sometimes false; e.g., 'love' (over the set of humans): if a loves b, it is possible that b loves a as well, but this is not necessary.

Examples

Antonymy is symmetric (if HIGH is an antonym of LOW, then LOW is necessarily an antonym of HIGH; a semantic or syntactic dependency relation is antisymmetric (if A depends on B, then B does not depend on A).

For the symbols → 'entails', ¬ 'no' and ∧ 'and', see *5.1* below.

Transitivity. A relation R over a set *A* is transitive iff, for each triplet ⟨a, b, c⟩ of elements of *A* (such that a ≠ b ≠ c), R(a, b) and R(b, c) are true, then R(a, c) is always true: R(a, b) ∧ R(b, c) → R(a, c); e.g., the relation 'be heavier than' is transitive: if a is heavier than b, and b is heavier than c, then *a* is heavier than c.

A relation R is antitransitive iff, R(a, b) and R(b, c) never entails R(a, c): R(a, b) ∧ R(b, c) → ¬R(a, c); e.g., 'be the mother of'. A relation R is non-transitive iff R(a, b) ∧ R(b, c) → R(a, c) is sometimes true and sometimes false; e.g., 'love' (over the set of humans): if a loves b and b loves c, it is possible but not necessary that a loves c.

Examples

Synonymy is transitive: if MURDER is synonymous with ⌜BUMP OFF⌝, ⌜BUMP OFF⌝ is synonymous with ⌜RUB OUT⌝, and ⌜RUB OUT⌝ is synonymous with ASSASSINATE, then MURDER is necessarily synonymous with ASSASSINATE.

Direct syntactic dependency is antitransitive: if a–**synt**→b and b–**synt**→c, then it follows that ¬ (a–**synt**→c)).

Direct semantic dependency is non-transitive: if a–**sem**→b and b–**sem**→c, then it is possible that a–**sem**→c and ¬(a–**sem**→c); for instance, in 'John wants to leave' we have 'want–**sem**→leave', 'leave–**sem**→John' and 'want–**sem**→John', but in 'John is deeply asleep', 'deeply–**sem**→asleep', 'asleep–**sem**→John', but ¬('deeply–**sem**→John').

For a characterization of semantic and deep-syntactic relations in terms of the above properties, see Ch. 3, *3.2.1* and Ch. 11, *2.4.1.1*.

Two families of binary relations have a special importance for linguistics: equivalence relations and order relations.

Equivalence relations. An equivalence relation is reflexive, symmetric and transitive; for instance, 'X has the same length as Y' and 'X is in the same room as Y'. A and B are equivalent according to a given parameter iff they have an identical value of this parameter. In language, synonymy is an equivalence relation.

Order relations. An order relation is antireflexive, antisymmetric and transitive; for instance, 'X is longer than Y' and 'X is an ancestor of Y'. (X cannot be his own ancestor; if X is an ancestor of Y, then Y is not an ancestor of X; if Y is an ancestor of Z, Y's ancestor X is necessarily an ancestor of Z.) In language, syntactic dependency is an order relation.

3.3   A Very Special Relation: Isomorphism

Let there be two sets A and B; they have a structure – namely, the elements $\mathbf{a_i} \in A$ are linked by the relation $\mathbf{r_1}$ and the elements $\mathbf{b_j} \in B$ are linked by the relation $\mathbf{r_2}$; for instance:

$$A = \{\mathbf{a_1, a_2, a_3} \mid \mathbf{r_1(a_1, a_2)}, \mathbf{r_1(a_1, a_3)}\} \text{ and}$$
$$B = \{\mathbf{b_1, b_2, b_3} \mid \mathbf{r_2(b_2, b_1)}, \mathbf{r_2(b_2, b_3)}\}$$

A and B are called isomorphic iff there is a one-to-one correspondence between their elements such that if a pair of $\mathbf{a_i}$ is linked by $\mathbf{r_1}$, then the elements $\mathbf{b_j}$ corresponding to this pair are linked by $\mathbf{r_2}$. In this example, A and B are isomorphic, the correspondence being $\mathbf{a_1 \leftrightarrow b_2}$, $\mathbf{a_2 \leftrightarrow b_1}$ and $\mathbf{a_3 \leftrightarrow b_3}$. In other words, isomorphism is a one-to-one correspondence between two sets that preserves the structure of the sets – that is, correctly reflects the relations between elements inside the sets.

The relation of isomorphism plays an important role in linguistics: crucially, a representation of a given linguistic expression and the expression itself must be isomorphic.

4   Formal Languages

A formal language is created by humans in order to manipulate with precision a limited set of concepts. The main characteristic of a formal language is that it serves as a basis for some calculations – in a very broad sense of the term. Thus, logical languages are used to model deductive reasoning; the language of arithmetic is used to model arithmetic calculus; programming languages serve to give instruction to computers (which do calculations based on programs); and so on.

A formal language $\mathbf{L_f}$ is a triplet of sets $\langle V, R, R^* \rangle$, where:

1. V is a finite set of symbols, called the vocabulary, or alphabet, of $\mathbf{L_f}$.
2. R is a couple of sets $\langle R_1, R_2 \rangle$, called the grammar of $\mathbf{L_f}$; we will refer to R simply as the rules of $\mathbf{L_f}$.
   - R_1 are formation rules: they indicate how to construct, using elements of V, expressions of $\mathbf{L_f}$ that are formally correct, or well-formed.
   - R_2 are transformation rules: they indicate how to manipulate the expressions of $\mathbf{L_f}$ in order to obtain equivalent expressions.

3. R* are interpretation rules: they indicate how to interpret expressions of $\mathbf{L_f}$ in order to link them to real objects that we want to describe by means of $\mathbf{L_f}$.

Formation and transformation rules constitute the syntax of $\mathbf{L_f}$, while interpretation rules are its semantics.

As a simple example, let us consider a formal language $\mathbf{L_{f\text{-}AR}}$ constructed for a fragment of arithmetic consisting only of addition.

<u>1. Vocabulary of $\mathbf{L_{f\text{-}AR}}$</u>:

$V = \{\mathbf{N}: 0, 1, 2, ..., 9; +, =\}$; $\mathbf{N}$ is here a meta-symbol for 'number'.

<u>2. Rules of $\mathbf{L_{f\text{-}AR}}$</u>:

Formation rules of $\mathbf{L_{f\text{-}AR}}$:

R1: $\mathbf{N} \rightarrow \mathbf{NN}$. This rule allows for the construction of numbers of infinite length: 01012, 3475910922, etc.

F: $\mathbf{N} + \mathbf{N} = \mathbf{N}$; **F** is a meta-symbol for 'correct formula'. Using this rule, we can construct any addition formula we want, for instance: $2 + 2 = 4$, $236 + 7 = 764$, $12345 + 6789 = 00123456890$, etc. (Note that a correct formula is not necessarily true!)

Transformation rules of $\mathbf{L_{f\text{-}AR}}$:

R2: $\mathbf{N1} + \mathbf{N2} = \mathbf{N2} + \mathbf{N1}$. This rule establishes the equivalence between any two formulas; it expresses what is known as the commutativity law for addition: "changing the order of two added numbers does not change their sum."

<u>3. Interpretation Rules of $\mathbf{L_{f\text{-}AR}}$</u>:

0 denotes the absence of anything; 1 denotes a single object: |; 2 denotes two objects: ||; etc.

+ denotes the action of "uniting" or "putting together"; thus, $| + | = ||$; $|| + |$ $= |||$; etc.

Two formal languages widely used for meaning representation, with a long tradition in logic, are the languages of propositional calculus and predicate calculus (see immediately below). Our own formalism for meaning representation, the semantic network (Ch. 2, *1.6.1* and Ch. 10, *2.1.1*), is a hybrid language, based on a subset of natural language meanings and a version of predicate calculus.

> REMARK. In logic and computer science the term *formal language* refers to a set of strings generated by a (formal) grammar starting from elements of an input set.

5   Propositions and Predicates

We now briefly characterize two essential logical instruments mentioned above: propositional calculus and predicate calculus. In logic, they target valid inferences; in linguistics, they have multiples uses, from meaning representation to the formulation of conditions on linguistic rules to the construction of linguistic argumentation.

5.1   Propositional Calculus

Propositions. A logical proposition is a symbolic expression that possesses a truth-value, i.e., for which it is natural to say *It is true* or *It is false*. (For the relation between logical propositions and natural language expressions, see Ch. 9, *1.2*, p. 232.) A proposition that does not contain other propositions is called elementary. Such a proposition is non-analyzable within propositional calculus: it is considered atomic, i.e., lacking an internal structure. Atomic propositions are designated by propositional variables: $p, q, \ldots$

Logical operations. Elementary logical propositions can be united into complex propositions by means of logical operations; for instance: $p \wedge q; p \rightarrow q;$ $\neg p \wedge (q \vee r)$; etc. A logical operation is defined by truth-values that it associates with the proposition it produces as a function of the logical values of the starting propositions. We will mention here the following five logical operations:

$\neg$ negation, $\wedge$ conjunction, $\vee$ disjunction, $\rightarrow$ implication, $\leftrightarrow$ equivalence.

Logical negation corresponds to *not*, conjunction to *and*, disjunction to *or*, implication to *if ... then*, and equivalence to *if and only if ... then*.

Definitions of logical operations are formulated in terms of truth tables; truth-values are notated 1= T(rue) and 0 = F(alse).

Table Appendix-1: Truth table for five logical operations

p	q	$\neg p$	$p \wedge q$	$p \vee q$	$p \rightarrow q$	$p \leftrightarrow q$
1	1	0	1	1	1	1
1	0	0	0	1	0	0
0	1	1	0	1	1	0
0	0	1	0	0	1	1

Some Basic Laws of Propositional Calculus. Propositional calculus operates based on several fundamental equivalences, or laws, of which we will cite the following ones, most useful for linguistics. (These laws are actually transformation rules of the language of propositional calculus; see Section *4* above.)

1. $p \equiv \neg\neg p$ — Double negation
2. a. $p \wedge q \equiv q \wedge p$ — Commutativity of conjunction and disjunction
   b. $p \vee q \equiv q \vee p$

3   a. $\neg(p \lor q) \equiv \neg p \land \neg q$ De Morgan laws (= rules)
    b. $\neg(p \land q) \equiv \neg p \lor \neg q$
4. $p \leftrightarrow q \equiv (p \to q) \land (q \to p)$ Equivalence expressed by implication and
                                                                          conjunction

Example. De Morgan laws are recurred to, for instance, in lexicography, when one needs to check the accuracy of a disjunctive or a conjunctive lexicographic definition (Ch. 5, *3.2*). Thus, consider the definition of the verb HARDEN1 (*The mixture hardened a bit, still remaining liquid.* vs. *The mixture hardened completely.*):

'X hardens' = 'X becomes harder **or** hard'

According to De Morgan Law 3a – "Negation of a disjunction is equivalent to the conjunction of two negations" – the negation of the sentence *The mixture hardened*, whose meaning includes a disjunction, must represent a conjunction of two negations, and this is the case:

The mixture did not harden. ≡ *The mixture did not become harder and did not become hard.*

Or take the following definition, a conjunctive one:

'[X is a] bachelor' = 'man X [who is able to be married]
                                  and [who is not and has never been married]'

De Morgan Law 3b – "Negation of a conjunction is equivalent to the disjunction of two negations" – stipulates that the negation of the sentence *John is a bachelor*, whose meaning contains a conjunction, must represent a disjunction of two negations, and this is borne out:

John is not a bachelor. ≡
John is not able to be married (he is a catholic priest or a monk, too young for marriage, etc.)*, or used to be married, or is currently married.*

5.2   Predicate Calculus

Predicates. The concept of predicate makes it possible to analyze the content of a logical proposition, thus allowing for a more precise representation of its content. A logical predicate is a binding meaning, that is, a meaning that requires a specific number of additional elements in order to form a logical proposition. These elements are called arguments of the predicate. For instance, 'sleep' is a predicate with one argument: the creature that sleeps; 'give' has three arguments: the giver, the gift and the recipient of the gift, and so on. A predicate and its arguments indicated with non-saturated variables – 'sleep(X)' or 'give(X, Y, Z)' – constitute a propositional form.

Quantifiers. The meanings 'all' and 'some' correspond to logical quantifiers:

Universal quantifier $\forall$:   'given any ...'/'for all ...'
Existential quantifier $\exists$:   'there exists'/'there is at least one ...'/'for some ...'

A predicate within the scope of the universal quantifier is true of every value of the predicate variable; a predicate within the scope of the existential quantifier is true for at least one value of the predicate variable. For instance:

All politicians are dishonest: $\forall x$('politician(x)' $\rightarrow$ 'dishonest(x)')
'Given any x, if x is a politician, it entails that x is dishonest'.
Some politicians are dishonest: $\exists x$('politician(x)' $\wedge$ 'dishonest(x)')
'There is at least one x such that x is a politician and x is dishonest'.

Two Quantifier Distribution Laws of the Predicate Calculus

1. $\forall x(P(x))$ $\equiv \neg\exists x(\neg(P(x)))$ 'Every x is P' $\equiv$ 'There is no x that is not P'
2. $\exists x(\neg P(x))$ $\equiv \neg\forall x(P(x))$ 'Some x are not P' $\equiv$ 'It is not the case that all x are P'

Example. Using the formalism of predicate calculus, the meaning of the sentence *The spacecraft recorded a strange sound* can be represented as follows (predicates and quasi-predicates are printed with a capital letter):

Recorded(The(Spacecraft) ; Strange(Sound(α)))

Further Reading

Introductory texts on logic: [relations of logic to language and linguistics] Copi & Cohen 2016; [predicate logic] Bonevac 1990; [languages of propositional calculus and predicate calculus] Heil 1994.

Logic and linguistics: McCawley 1981.

Exercises

We will now suggest exercises for Chapters 3 to 12 of this book. Going through these will allow you to apply the linguistic concepts and formalisms that we have introduced and will also help develop your linguistic intuition.

 Some of the exercises are more difficult than would be expected in an introductory textbook, and some lack the full linguistic data essential for their solution. Such data, and all necessary explanations, will be found in "Key to the Exercises" (available at www.cambridge.org/meaning-text). These exercises and their proposed solutions should be considered as additional examples in support of the notions introduced in Chapters 3 to 12.

Chapter 3: Linguistic Meaning

1. Consider the meaning 'That Max left surprised everybody'; give for it as many (near-)synonymous expressions as you can find.

2. Give one linguistic and one extralinguistic paraphrase of the sentence *The President of the USA met his French counterpart in Washington yesterday*.

3. In what aspects of meaning do the following paraphrases differ?

   a. *Max's comfortable income allows him to travel a lot.*
   b. *It's easy for Max to travel around with the big bucks he's making.*

4. For each lexical item below, indicate whether it corresponds to a semantic predicate, a semantic quasi-predicate or a semantic name. For each predicate and quasi-predicate, indicate the number of arguments (= semantic actants) it controls. **NB**: In order to answer this question correctly, you first need to make it more precise.

   REPROACH$_{(V)}$, STAR$_{(N)}$, 'ROUND TABLE', TYPEWRITER, ELEGANT, SEA.

5. Give an example of a semanteme denoting (a) an action, (b) an event, (c) a property, (d) a relation.
   In each case, indicate the actantial structure of the semanteme and supply a sentence in which the corresponding LU is used.

6. Which of the two meanings in each pair is semantically simpler? (a) 'walk' or 'limp'; (b) 'walk' or 'run'
7. The following is a semantic decomposition of an English communication verb, suggested by A. Wierzbicka. Which verb is this?

> I say: something bad is happening (to me)
> I feel something bad because of that
> I say this because I want to cause someone to know about it and to do something because of that that would cause me to feel better.

Chapter 4: Lexical Meaning, Lexical Items and Lexical Units

1. Demonstrate that the bolded expressions in the examples below correspond to three different lexical units [LUs].

> (1) a. *A **youth** in revolt.* [movie title]
> b. *What is happening with our **youth**?* [news article caption]
> c. *Poets in their **youth**: A Memoir.* [book title]

2. What is a semantically full vs. semantically empty LU? Illustrate these two types of LUs.

3. Characterize each of the following LUs in terms of their morphological makeup (i.e., as a synchronically simple, derived or compound LU): RELEGATE, REOPEN, REDIRECT and HONEYBEE, HONEYCOMB, HONEYMOON. Explain your reasoning.

4. Are the following free phrases or set phrases? For all set phrases, indicate their type. Start by supplying a context (a sentence) for each phrase.

> (2) a. *red herring*   ~ *smoked herring*
> b. *drop the ball*   ~ *drop the course*
> c. *fat fingers*   ~ *sticky fingers*

5. Are the following expressions collocations or idioms?

> (3) a. *business end*   ~ *business park*
> b. *family business*   ~ *monkey business*
> c. *storm window*   ~ *storm cloud*

6. For each of the following pragmatemes, indicate its lexical anchor(s) and the pragmatic component of its meaning: BEST BEFORE: [date]; NO TRESPASSING.

7. Suggest approximate semantic descriptions of the following proverbs and indicate their lexical anchors.

(4) a. *Barking dogs seldom bite.*
    b. *Curiosity killed the cat.*

8. Consider the expressions *since time immemorial* and *Prince Charming*. What set phrase types do they belong to? What flags them as being set phrases?

9. The phrase type in the left lower square of *Table 4.1* [Ch. 4, *2.2.1*: 104] is characterized as impossible. Why is this so?

Chapter 5: Lexicographic Definition

1. (a) Sketch the lexicographic definitions for the lexemes FRIEND, ACQUAINTANCE and COLLEAGUE according to the methodology proposed in the textbook. Briefly justify the choice of the components of the definition. (Use relevant indications in the *Lexicographic checklist*, Ch. 5, *6*.)
  (b) Perform the same task for the idiom ⌈TAKE FOR A RIDE⌉.

2. Compare the following definitions of the lexeme SPIDER (*There is a spider in the bath tub.*). Propose an ECD-style definition of this lexeme.

> [OED] An eight-legged predatory arachnid with an unsegmented body consisting of a fused head and thorax and a rounded abdomen. Spiders have fangs that inject poison into their prey, and most kinds spin webs in which to capture insects. | Order Araneae, class Arachnida.
>
> [LDOCE] A small creature with eight legs, which catches insects using a fine network of sticky threads.

3. Find an example of circularity in a dictionary definition; correct the definition so as to eliminate the vicious circle(s).

4. Consider the collocations *devastating* STORM, *debilitating* ⟨*life-altering*⟩ ILLNESS, and *paralyzing* ⟨*petrifying*⟩ FRIGHT. What does this cooccurrence tell us about the meaning of the bases?

5. What semantic-lexical relations hold between the boldfaced lexemes in the examples below? How should these relations be accounted for in an ECD-type lexicographic description?

    (1) a. *Today: scattered **clouds** and light rain.*
       b. *The new study seems to **cloud** the picture even further.*
       c. *This shows how good intentions could be tainted by a **clouded** judgment.*

6. (a)   Should the component 'salt' be part of the definition of SEA (*Sea levels are rising rapidly due to climate change.*)?

   (b)   The same question for 'cunning' and FOX (*Fox hunting was banned in the UK some ten years ago.*).

7. Give some lexicographic connotations of the lexeme WIND1 (*gale force winds in Cape Breton*). Adduce linguistic evidence to support your claim. Explain why these meanings are connotations rather than components of the definition of this lexeme. (A hint: Have a look at our examples featuring the lexeme WINDYII, Ch. 5, 5: 136.)

Chapter 6: Lexical Relations

1. Find four synonyms of the verb ([to] DISMISS, as in *He was dismissed after 10 years of service*, and look up the corresponding definitions in an English dictionary (OED, LDOCE, MWLD, etc.). According to the definitions, are these verbs exact or approximate synonyms? Do you agree with the way they are treated in the dictionary? If not, suggest corrections.

2. Are the lexemes DAY ~ NIGHT and LAND ~ SEA antonyms? Sketch their respective definitions. Start by identifying (by examples of use and/or distinctive lexicographic numbers) the wordsenses of the corresponding vocables that you are considering.

3. Give some examples of adjectives that are (a) negation antonyms; (b) inverse antonyms.

4. Give some examples of (a) interlexical conversion; (b) intralexical conversion. Make sure to specify the actantial structure of the corresponding LUs.

5. Which semantic-lexical relation holds between the pairs of Even lexemes in columns A and B? How is it formally marked? [Even, spoken in Siberia, belongs to the Tungusic branch of the Altaic family.]

	A	**B**	
'[to] forge'	*tava-*	*tava* +*čak*	'[a] forge'
'teach'	*xupku-*	*xupku* +*ček*	'school'
'heal'	*begde-*	*begde* +*ček*	'hospital'

Find examples of the same semantic-lexical relation between English lexemes. By what linguistic means is it expressed ?

6. Give an example of LUs related by (a) metonymy; (b) metaphor. Indicate explicitly the semantic bridges between them.

7. Are the following boldfaced expressions cases of polysemy or homonymy? How many vocables/lexemes are there in each case? What semantic links hold between the lexemes belonging to the same vocable?

(1) a. **overlook** *someone's name*
    b. **overlook** *a spruce forest*
    c. **overlook** *someone's faults*

(2) a. *All* **hands** *on deck!*
    b. *Your* **hand** *is cold.*
    c. *The hour* **hand** *of the clock is the small* **hand** *that tells us what the hour is.*

8. Find as many different collocations as possible of the lexeme PATIENCE (*You'll need patience if you're going to be a teacher.*); try to describe the meaning of each collocation. Example: [collocation] *patience of Job* [meaning] 'a huge amount of patience'.

Chapter 7: Lexical Functions

1. Give your own examples of the application of the following paradigmatic LFs: Syn, $\text{Syn}_\supset$, Anti, $\text{Anti}_\cap$, Conv_{21}, Conv_{321}, S_0, S_1, A_0, A_2, Adv_0, Adv_1, Able_2, and AntiAble_2. (Make sure to identify the LU to which the given LF is applied and to indicate, where necessary, its actantial structure.) Illustrate how an element of the LF value can be substituted for the LF keyword in paraphrasing, as we did in Ch. 7, *2.1*.

2. Describe the following collocations in terms of LFs, indicating, where necessary, the actantial structure of the keyword: *clear evidence, undergo an eclipse, the movie camera is rolling, effective measure, utter threats, responsibility lies with someone, valuable contribution, aid reaches someone, undergo an operation, satisfy one's hunger.*

3. Indicate all the elements of the value of the LFs in the A column as applied to the keywords in the B column.

A	B
AntiMagn	ARGUMENT, RELATED, RISK
AntiVer	ARGUMENT, ATTEMPT, EXCUSE
AntiBon	HOTEL, SMELL$_{(N)}$, START$_{(N)}$
IncepOper_1	EXPENDITURE, INTEREST, OBLIVION
CausOper_2	ATTENTION, CONTROL, DISCUSSION
LiquFunc_0	ASSEMBLY, RESTRICTION, TRACES

4. Complete the following poem[1] with the appropriate values of the LF Real_i.

What Is Life?

Life is a CHALLENGE.	_____ it!	Life is a SONG.	_____ it!
Life is a GIFT.	_____ it!	Life is an OPPORTUNITY.	_____ it!
Life is a PLEASURE.	_____ it!	Life is a JOURNEY.	_____ it!
Life is a SORROW.	_____ it!	Life is a PROMISE.	_____ it!
Life is a TRAGEDY.	_____ it!	Life is a BEAUTY.	_____ it!
Life is a DUTY.	_____ it!	Life is a STRUGGLE.	_____ it!
Life is a GAME.	_____ it!	Life is a GOAL.	_____ it!
Life is a MYSTERY.	_____ it!	Life is a PUZZLE.	_____ it!

> **NB:** We allowed ourselves to replace the original "Life is an ADVENTURE" with "Life is a PLEASURE," since there is no universally accepted value for $\text{Real}_1(\text{ADVENTURE})$.

5. Explain the following LF encoding: $[\text{Magn} + \text{IncepReal}_1](tears) = burst$ [*in ~s*]. What type of LF is this?

> **NB:** Some of the LFs you will be asked to produce in Exercises 6–8 have not been introduced in Ch. 7. Try your best and, if you are unable to come up with the right lexical-functional notation, provide an informal solution (a gloss, an explanation "in prose"). Additional information about these LFs can be found in the Key.

6. Describe the collocations of PATIENCE (Chapter 6, Question 8) in terms of LFs.

7. Look up the collocations of the lexeme APPETITE1 in LDOCE and describe these in terms of LFs. (Start by indicating the actantial structure of APPETITE1.)

8. Here is an excerpt from the article "Honduras' Electoral Court Declares President Election Winner" (*The National Post*, Dec 19, 2017). Identify all the collocations present in the excerpt and describe them in terms of LFs, indicating, where necessary, the actantial structure of the keyword.

> Hernandez, a 49-year-old businessman and former lawmaker, took office in January 2014 and built support largely on a drop in violence in this impoverished Central American country. According to Honduras' National Autonomous University, the nation's homicide rate has plummeted from a dizzying high of 91.6 per 100,000 inhabitants in 2011 to 59 per 100,000 – though Honduras remains among the deadliest places in the world. But corruption and drug trafficking allegations cast a shadow over Hernandez's government, and his

---

[1] Anonymous. *The Gazette* (Montreal daily), September 28, 1985.

re-election bid fueled charges that his National Party was seeking to entrench itself in power by getting a court ruling allowing him to seek a second term.

Chapter 8: The Lexical Stock of a Language and the Dictionary

1. Demonstrate that the vocable ACCOMPANY is polysemic.

2. How many lexemes of the vocable COFFEE do you see in the following examples? Sketch their respective definitions and assign to each lexeme a lexicographic number.

>   (1) a. *Is coffee the most popular drink in the world?*
>   b. *How long does coffee need to rest after roasting?*
>   c. *Coffee needs an annual rainfall of 1500 to 3000 mm.*
>   d. *I much prefer coffee to tea.*
>   e. *People over 65 who drink more than three coffees a day suffer less memory loss.*
>   f. *He wore a zigzag shirt of blue and gold, coffee pants, and silver trinkets.*

3. Give five LUs belonging to the semantic classes (a) `conversations` and (b) `unpleasant sensations`. Sketch a definition template for the LUs of each class.

4. In the examples below, identify different lexemes of the vocable THIRSTY; indicate polysemic links between the lexemes and assign them lexicographic numbers; for each lexeme, sketch its pseudo-definition (in terms of semantic labels).

>   (2) a. *Emerging markets thirsty for oil and gas.*
>   b. *I'm always thirsty for Coke. How can I stop?*
>   c. *"Thirsty for justice" campaign takes aim at First Nation water issues.*
>   d. *Is my plant thirsty? Know when to water plants.*
>   e. *Are you always thirsty, even when drinking lots of water?*

5. (a)   Distribute the following LUs into (i) semantic fields and (ii) semantic classes:
       BOOK$_{(N)}$, COMMUTE, JANITOR, KINDERGARTEN, PUBLISH, SCHOOLBUS, SCHOOL$_{(N)}$, STUDENT, STUDY$_{(V)}$, TEACH, TRAIN$_{(N)}$, TRAVELER

   (b)   Give the semantic class of the lexeme RIFLE (*cleaning an old rifle barrel*) and as many semantic fields as you can think of to which it belongs.

6. Consider the sentence #*Max swallowed his coffee and his pride*; why is it funny?

7. The LDOCE definitions below transgress some ECD lexicographical rules and principles – which ones? Correct the definitions.

UTENSIL   : a thing such as knife, spoon, etc. that you use when you are cooking
SPOON_{(N)}1 : an object that you use for eating, cooking, or serving food; it has a small bowl-shaped part and a long handle
KNIFE_{(N)}1 : a metal blade fixed onto a handle, used for cutting or as a weapon
FORK_{(N)}1 : a tool you use for picking up and eating food, with a handle and three or four points

8. Give the Government Pattern for each of the following LUs: BLAME_{(V)} (*The French blamed the crisis on Anglo-American actions they had approved only reluctantly.*), CONVERSATION (*What was the conversation about?*), DANGEROUS (*a virus dangerous to humans*).

9. Propose a full-fledged ECD-type lexicographic entry for the lexeme REVENGE (*Louise wanted revenge for the insult.*).

Chapter 9: Sentential Meaning and Meaning Relations between Sentences

1. Give examples of sentences ill-formed for extralinguistic reasons.

2. Give an example of a sentence that is (a) linguistically true; (b) linguistically false.

3. The expression Lat. *Festina lente* lit. 'Hurry.up slowly' (usually translated as *make haste slowly*) is only seemingly semantically anomalous. How so?

4. What stylistic device has been used in the expression Fr. *Un sou est un sou* lit. 'A penny is a penny'? Give the meaning of the expression and its English equivalent (if there is one).

5. What's wrong with the following notice [in an Austrian lodge catering to hikers and mountain climbers]: *No perambulation in boots of ascension*?

6. Are the following sentences exact or approximate paraphrases? Substantiate your answer.

    (1) a. *The victim was stabbed to death.*
        b. *The victim was killed with a knife.*

7. Give an example of neutralization of semantic differences between paraphrases (a) in a linguistic context; (b) in an extralinguistic context.

8. Indicate the presupposition(s) of each of the following sentences, along with the source of the presupposition.

   (2) a. *It's Max who's bringing a dessert.*
       b. *Max didn't realize that he was lied to.*
       c. *Why are they persecuting Max?*

9. (a) Demonstrate that sentence B is an implication (= an entailment) of sentence A.

A	B
Max got well.	*Max is not sick.*
Max kissed Lea passionately.	*Max kissed Lea.*

   (b)   Give an implication of each of the following sentences:

   (3) a. *A strange noise awoke Max.*
       b. *The noise stopped.*

10. Demonstrate that each of the following texts (examples (34) and (35), Ch. 9: 251) corresponds to two sentences that stand in the relation of equinomy; or, to put it differently, resolve the ambiguity of these texts.

   (4) a. [telegraphic style] *Ship sails today.*
       b. [newspaper caption] *Squad helps dog bite victim.*

Chapter 10: Semantic Representation

1. Here is a partial semantic representation [SemR] with a semantic structure whose nodes are not labeled. Complete it in such a way as to get a SemR that is (a) well-formed and (b) corresponds to a set of paraphrases that "make sense." Indicate some of the paraphrases. (**NB**: Do not represent inflectional meanings.)

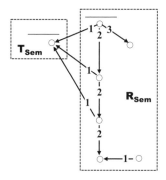

Figure Ex.1: A SemS with unlabeled nodes

2. Give as many verbalizations as you can of the following SemR. (Assume a past tense reading.)

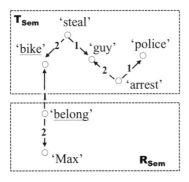

Figure Ex.2: A SemR to verbalize

3. Draw the SemS of the sentence *The city changed a lot during my absence*, decomposing the meaning of the lexeme CHANGE$_{(V)}$. Give at least one paraphrase of the sentence in question possible only thanks to the decomposition of its meaning.

4. (a) Specify the semantic-communicative structure of each of the following sentences by indicating an underlying question for which it could be an appropriate answer:

(1) a. *1492 saw the discovery of America.*
    b. *America was discovered in 1492.*
    c. *It was America that was discovered in 1492.*

(b) Indicate the semantic-communicative structure of each of the following sentences according to the preceding context (in square brackets):

(2) a. [It's -25 °C in downtown Halifax, -30 °C with wind chill.] *These frigid temperatures should not last.*
    b. [Is the movie any good?] *To my mind, it is very bad.*
    c. [I've decided to go.] *As for Max, he is still thinking about it.*
    d. [What is it?] *There is a gentleman looking for you.*

(c) The marked word order that we observe in the following English sentence expresses some semantic-communicative values – which ones? Give a context to substantiate your answer.

(3) *That I do not know.*

5. (a) Give some examples of signalatives. What are the particular properties of expressions of this type?

    (b) Which verbs in the examples below are used performatively? Are there some that cannot be used performatively at all?

        (4) a. *And I **quote**: "No person should be ..."*
            b. *I often **quote** that passage.*
            c. *I **am telling** you to stop.*
            d. *I'm **telling** you the truth.*
            e. *I **quit**!*
            f. *I am going to **quit**.*
            g. *We **are defending** our right to strike.*

6. Superpose two different semantic-communicative structures onto the semantic structure below. For each pairing of structures thus obtained, indicate some sentences that can be produced out of it. What kind of para-phrases are the sentences produced from the two pairings? Can you find a context in which they are mutually substitutable?

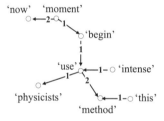

Figure Ex.3: A SemS to be paired with different Sem-CommSs

7. Draw the SemR of the sentence *Thanks to this program, young adults are able to travel.* (You may omit the Referential structure.) Give some other sentences that can be produced from the same SemR.

Chapter 11: Deep-Syntactic Representation

1. Why do we need a syntactic representation in semantics?

2. (a) What types of LUs can appear in a deep-syntactic structure? Give some examples of such LUs.
    (b) Give a list of deep grammemes of English and distribute them into the appropriate inflectional categories.

3. (a)   Determine the direction of the syntactic dependency between the elements of each phrase below.

   (1) a. *symbol sequence*
       b. *fast access memory*
       c. *a different proposal from this*

   (b)   Is the following graph a tree or a network? Why?

Figure Ex.4: A graph

4. (a)   What type of syntactic dependency relation (coordination/subordination, complementation/modification) is featured in the following examples? How is the relation marked?

   (2) a. Lat. *Venī, vidī, vicī.* [Julius Caesar]
       '[I] came, [I] saw, [I] won'.
       b. Tsakhur   *jedi*   +*s*   +*jī   dakki*   +*s*
                    mother   DAT and   father   DAT = 'to father and
       mother'
       c. Sp. *Queríamos dártelo.* Cf.: *Te lo queríamos dar.*
       'We.wanted to.give=you_{DAT}=it_{ACC}' = 'We wanted to give it to
       you'.
       d. Ancient Greek
       Molõn labé! [King Leonidas to King Xerxes]
       'Coming_{MASC, SG, NOM} take!' = 'Come and take [our weapons]!'
       e. *Try and catch the wind.* [Donovan]

   (b)   In the following sentences, determine the deep-syntactic role of the bolded element – is it an actant or a circumstantial/modifier?

   (3) a. *Max sings **well**.*
       b. *Max behaves **well**.*
       c. *Have you listened to the **presidential** address?*
       d. *What is a **presidential** look, anyway?*

   (c)   What kind of deep-syntactic actant is illustrated by the examples below? (Consult Ch. 11, 2.4.2.1: 297, Definition of deep-syntactic actant, and the REMARK that follows it.)

(4) a. Fr. *Regarde-**moi** ça!* Cf. *Regarde ça!*
   'Watch to.me this!'
   b. Sp. [...] *un poncho de lana **le** envolvía las piernas.*
   '[...] a wool poncho **to.him** was.covering the legs'
   c. *Max slept a troubled **sleep**.* Cf. **Max slept a sleep.*

5. (a) Draw the deep-syntactic structure for each of the following sentences:

   (5) a. *The defendant made a brief court appearance yesterday.*
      b. *This, of course, depends on the facts and factors relevant for this case, which will be discussed below.*

   (b) Perform the same task for the following sentences (cf. Chapter 10, question 6):

   (6) a. *Physicists are starting to use this method extensively.*
      b. *This method is finding widespread use among physicists.*

6. (a) Each of the following texts is ambiguous, i.e., corresponds to at least two equinomous sentences. In each case, indicate the source of ambiguity and draw the corresponding DSyntSs.

   (7) a. [A sign in a pharmacy] *We dispense with accuracy.*
      b. [A sign in a pharmacy] *Eye Drops off Shelf.*
      c. [Newspaper caption] *Children make nutritious snacks.*

   (b) Draw the DSyntSs corresponding to the two interpretations of the text *Squad helps dog bite victim*, cited in Chapter 9 as example (10b).

Chapter 12: Semantic Rules

1. Draw the common SemS of the sentences in (1) – to do this, a semantic decomposition is necessary! – and their respective DSyntSs; give all lexicalization rules necessary to link the structures of the two levels.

   (1) a. *Max expects the program to run without a hitch.*
      b. *Max thinks the program is likely to run smoothly.*

2. Here are two arborization semantic rules. Explain in your own words what each rule does and give examples of its application. (A hint: Rule (b) is very similar to Arborization Rule R^{ARBOR} 8, Ch, 12, *1.3.2*: 326.)

(a)
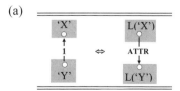

Figure Ex.5: Arborization rule 1

(b)

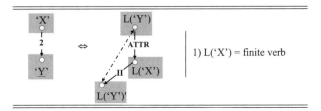

Figure Ex.6: Arborization rule 2

3. Consider the pairs of paraphrases below. For each pair, determine if its sentences are semantic or lexical-syntactic paraphrases and propose the corresponding paraphrasing rule.

(2) a. *They attacked at dawn.*
      ~ *Their attack took place at dawn.*
   b. *Max analyzed the sentence correctly.*
      ~ *Max was able to analyze the sentence correctly.*
   c. *This is a morph.*
      ~ *This is an elementary segmental sign.*
   d. *We like eating out.*
      ~ *We often eat out.*

4. For each of the following paraphrasing rules give two pairs of paraphrases it allows to produce:

(a) $L_{(V)} \equiv \texttt{Real}_1 \text{–}\mathbf{II}\rightarrow S_0(L_{(V)})$;

(b) $L_{(V)} \equiv \texttt{Oper}_1 \text{–}\mathbf{II}\rightarrow S_2(L_{(V)})$.

5. Why does the synonymic substitution *to smoke ~ to be a smoker* give an acceptable result in (3a) but not in (3b)? The same question for the synonymic substitution [my] *daughter's husband ~* [my] *son-in-law* in (3c) and (3d).

(3) a. *Max has smoked all his life.*
      ~ *Max has been a smoker all his life.*
   b. *Max has smoked all day long.*
      ~ **Max has been a smoker all day long.*
   c. *Max is my daughter's husband.*
      ~ *Max is my son-in-law.*
   d. *Max is my youngest son-in-law.*
      ~ *#Max is my youngest daughter's husband.*

6. Have another look at paraphrases (1)–(8) in Ch. 7, repeated here as (4)–(15) [some of the paraphrases accountable for by the same paraphrasing rules have been omitted]. Among the paraphrasing rules introduced in Ch. 12, identify the ones involved in the production of these paraphrases. For the paraphrases that cannot be covered by these rules, propose the rules yourself.

     (4) *If found guilty, he faces some serious **prison** time.* ≡
        *If found guilty, he faces some serious **jail** time.*

     (5) *Smoking **is prohibited** on campus.* ≡ *Smoking **is not allowed** on campus.*

     (6) *The Stone Age **precedes** the Bronze Age.* ≡
        *The Bronze Age **follows** the Stone Age.*

     (7) *What are you supposed to **prepare** for the literature course?* ≡
        *What **preparations** are you supposed to **make** for the literature course?*

     (8) *Such is the nature **of cats**.* ≡ *Such is **feline** nature.*

     (9) *The Dry Dock **experienced** heavy **use** during the world wars.* ≡
        *The Dry Dock **was** heavily **used** during the world wars.*

    (10) *Mr. Smith **teaches** us Linguistics 101.* ≡
        *Mr. Smith **is** our Linguistics 101 **teacher**.*

    (11) *We **bought** our car for 5,000 dollars.* ≡
        *The **price** of our car **was** 5,000 dollars.*

    (12) *Did you **know** this?* ≡ ***Were** you **aware** of this?*

    (13) *The Alberta crop crisis **caused**1 a sharp **increase** in wheat prices.* ≡
        *Wheat prices **increased** sharply **in the wake of** the Alberta crop crisis.*

    (14) *This idea **terrifies** me.* ≡ *This idea **is terrifying** to me.*

    (15) *Can one **trust** him?* ≡ *Is he **trustworthy**?*

References

Abend, Omri & Rappaport, Ari. 2017. The State of the Art in Semantic Representation. In *Proceedings of the 55th Annual Meeting of the Association for Computational Linguistics, July 30 – August 4, 2017*, Vancouver, 77–89.

Akmajian, Adrian, Farmer, Ann, Bickmore, Lee & Harnish, Robert. 2017. *Linguistics: An Introduction to Language and Communication*. Cambridge (MA): MIT Press.

Allan, Keith. 2007. The Pragmatics of Connotation. *Journal of Pragmatics*, 39/6: 1047–1057.

Alonso Ramos, Margarita. 2004. Elaboración del Diccionario de colocaciones en español y sus aplicaciones. In Bataner, P. & de Cesaris, J., eds., *De lexicographia. Actes del I symposium internacional de lexicografía*, Barcelona: IULA – Edicions Petició, 149–162.

Apresjan, Jurij. 1974. Regular Polysemy. *Linguistics*, 12/142: 5–32.

Apresjan, Jurij. 2000. *Systematic Lexicography*. Oxford: Oxford University Press.

Apresjan, Jurij. 2008. Principles of Systematic Lexicography. In Fontenelle, ed., 51–60.

Apresjan, Jurij, Boguslavskij, Igor, Iomdin, Leonid & Cinman, Leonid. 2007. Lexical Functions in Actual NLP Applications. In Wanner, ed., 2007, 203–233.

Apresjan, Jurij, Boguslavskij, Igor, Iomdin, Leonid, Cinman, Leonid & Timoshenko, Svetlana. 2009. Semantic Paraphrasing for Information Retrieval and Extraction. In Andreasen, T., Yager, R., Bulskov, H., Christiansen, H., Legind Larsen, H., eds., *Flexible Query Answering Systems (FQAS 2009)*, Berlin/Heidelberg: Springer, 512–523.

Aquaviva, Paolo, Lenci, Alessandro, Paradis, Carita & Raffaelli, Ida. 2017. Models of Lexical Meaning. In Pirrelli, V., Plag, I. & Dressler, W., eds., *Word Knowledge and Word Usage: A Cross-Disciplinary Guide to the Mental Lexicon*, Berlin: Mouton de Gruyter.

Atkins, Sue. 2008. Theoretical Lexicography and Its Relation to Dictionary Making. In Fontenelle, ed., 2008, 31–50.

Atkins, Sue & Rundell, Michael, eds. 2008. *The Oxford Guide to Practical Lexicography*. Oxford: Oxford University Press.

Austin, John. 1962. *How to Do Things with Words*. Oxford: Clarendon Press.

Ballesteros, Miguel, Bohnet, Bernd, Mille, Simon & Wanner, Leo. 2015. Data-Driven Deep-Syntactic Dependency Parsing. *Natural Language Engineering*, 1/1: 1–38.

Bannard, Colin & Callison-Burch, Chris. 2005. Paraphrasing with Bilingual Parallel Corpora. In *Proceedings of the 43rd Annual Meeting of the Association for Computational Linguistics*, 597–604.

Barsalou, Lawrence, Yeh, Wenchi, Luka, Barbara, Olseth, Karen, Mix, Kelly & Wu, Ling-Ling. 1993. Concepts and Meaning. In *Proceedings of the Annual Meeting of the Chicago Linguistics Society 29, vol. 2*, Chicago: Chicago Linguistics Society, 23–61.

Bartsch, Sabine. 2004. *Structural and Functional Properties of Collocations in English: A Corpus Study of Lexical and Pragmatic Constraints on Lexical Cooccurrence.* Tübingen: Gunter Narr.

Bauer, Laurie. 2004. The Function of Word-Formation and the Inflection-Derivation Distinction. In Aertsen, H., Hannay, M. & Lyall, R., eds., *Words in Their Places. A Festschrift for J. Lachlan Mackenzie*, Amsterdam: Vrije Universiteit, 283–292.

Becker, Joseph. 1975. The Phrasal Lexicon. In *Proceedings of the 1975 Workshop on Theoretical Issues in Natural Language Processing*, Association for Computational Linguistics, 60–63.

Béjoint, Henri. 2000. *Modern Lexicography: An Introduction.* Oxford: Oxford University Press.

Bencini, Giulia & Goldberg, Adele. 2000. The Contribution of Argument Structure Constructions to Sentence Meaning. *Journal of Memory and Language*, 43: 640–651.

Benson, Morton, Benson, Evelyn & Ilson, Robert. 1988. Basic Principles of Lexicographic Definition. In Benson, M., Benson, E. & Ilson, R., *Lexicographic Description of English*, Amsterdam/Philadelphia: John Benjamins, 203–228.

Benson, Morton, Benson, Evelyn & Ilson, Robert. 1997. *The BBI Dictionary of English Word Combinations.* Amsterdam/Philadelphia: John Benjamins.

Berry, Daniel, Kamsties, Erik & Krieger, Michael. 2003. *From Contract Drafting to Software Specification: Linguistic Sources of Ambiguity. A Handbook.* Available at http://se.uwaterloo.ca/~dberry/handbook/ambiguityHandbook.pdf.

Beyssade, Claire, Delais-Roussarie, Elisabeth, Doetjes, Jenny, Marandin, Jean-Marie & Rialland, Annie. 2004. Prosodic, Syntactic and Pragmatic Aspects of Information Structure: An Introduction. In Corblin F. & Swart, H. de, eds., *Handbook of French Semantics*, Stanford (CA): CSLI Publications, 455–475.

Bonevac, Daniel. 1990. *The Art and Science of Logic.* Mountain View (CA): Mayfield Publishing.

Bosch, Sonja, Pala, Karel & Fellbaum, Christiane. 2008. Derivational Relations in English, Czech and Zulu Wordnets. *Literator: Journal of Literary Criticism, Comparative Linguistics and Literary Studies*, 29/1: 139–162.

Carston, Robyn. 2002. Linguistic Meaning, Communicated Meaning and Cognitive Pragmatics. *Mind and Language*, 17/1–2: 127–148.

Chafe, Wallace. 1987. Cognitive Constraints on Information Flow. In Tomlin, R. ed., *Coherence and Grounding in Discourse*, Amsterdam/Philadelphia: John Benjamins, 21–51.

Cole, Peter & Saddock, Jerrold, eds. 1977. *Grammatical Relations. [Syntax and Semantics, 8.]* New York: Academic Press.

Comrie, Bernard & Thompson, Sandra. 2007. Lexical Nominalization. In Shopen, T., ed., *Language Typology and Syntactic Description, vol. 3: Grammatical Categories and the Lexicon*, Cambridge: Cambridge University Press, 334–381.

Copi, Irving M. & Cohen, Carl. 2016. *Essentials of Logic.* London/New York: Routledge.

Cowie, Anthony. 1982. Polysemy and the Structure of Lexical Fields. *Nottingham Linguistic Circular*, 11/2: 51–64. Available at: http://nottingham.ac.uk/research/groups/cral/documents/nlc/nlc-1980-1985/nlc-volume11-number2-dec82.pdf#page=55.

Cowie, Anthony, ed. 1998. *Phraseology: Theory, Analysis, and Applications*. Oxford: Oxford University Press.

Cruse, Alan. 1992. Antonymy Revisited: Some Thoughts on the Relationship between Words and Concepts. In Lehrer, A. & Kittay, E., eds., *Frames, Fields and Contrasts: New Essays in Semantic and Lexical Organization*, Hillsdale (NJ): Lawrence Erlbaum Associates, 289–309.

Cruse, Alan. 2011. *Meaning in Language: An Introduction to Semantics and Pragmatics*. Oxford: Oxford University Press.

Cruse, Alan, Hundsnurscher, Franz, Job, Michael & Lutzeier, Peter, eds. 2005. *Lexicology: An International Handbook on the Nature and Structure of Words and Vocabularies*. Berlin: Mouton de Gruyter.

Cummins, Chris & Griffiths, Patrick. 2016. *An Introduction to English Semantics and Pragmatics*. Edinburgh: Edinburgh University Press.

Domaneschi, Filippo. 2016. Introduction: Presuppositions, Philosophy, Linguistics and Psychology. *Topoi*, 55 (Special Issue on Presupposition): 5–8.

Edmonds, Philip & Hirst, Graeme. 2002. Near-Synonymy and Lexical Choice. *Computational Linguistics*, 28/2: 105–144.

Falkum, Ingrid & Vicente, Agustin. 2015. Polysemy: Current Perspectives and Approaches. *Lingua*, 157: 1–16.

Fellbaum, Christiane. 1995. Cooccurrence and Antonymy. *International Journal of Lexicography*, 8/4: 281–303.

Fellbaum, Christiane, ed. 2007. *Idioms and Collocations: Corpus-Based Linguistic and Lexicographic Studies*. London: Continuum.

Féry, Caroline & Krifka, Manfred. 2008. Information Structure: Notional Distinctions, Ways of Expression. In Sterkenburg, P. van, ed., *Unity and Diversity of Language*, Amsterdam/Philadelphia: John Benjamins, 123–136.

Fillmore, Charles. 1968. The Case for Case. In Fillmore, Ch., *Form and Meaning in Language, vol. 1: Papers on Semantic Roles*, Stanford (CA): CSLI Publications, 2003, 23–122.

Fillmore, Charles. 1971. Verbs of Judging: An Exercise in Semantic Description. In Fillmore & Langendoen, eds., 1971, 273–290.

Fillmore, Charles. 2006. Frame Semantics. In Geeraerts, D., ed., *Cognitive Linguistics: Basic Readings*. Berlin: Mouton de Gruyter, 373–401.

Fillmore, Charles & Atkins, Sue. 1992. Toward a Frame-Based Lexicon: The Semantics of RISK and Its Neighbors. In Lehrer & Kittay, eds., 2000, 75–102.

Fillmore, Charles & Langendoen, Terence, eds. 1971. *Studies in Linguistic Semantics*. New York: Holt, Rinehart & Winston.

Fontenelle, Thierry, ed. 2008. *Practical Lexicography: A Reader*. Oxford: Oxford University Press.

Frege, Gottlob. 1892. Sinn und Bedeutung. In Frege, G., *Funktion, Begriff, Bedeutung*, 1962, Göttingen: Vandenhoeck & Ruprecht, 38–63.

Geeraerts, Dirk. 2010. *Theories of Lexical Semantics*. Oxford: Oxford University Press.

Givón, Talmy. 2001. *Syntax: An Introduction, vol. 1*. Amsterdam/Philadelphia: John Benjamins.

Gledhill, Christopher. 2011. The 'Lexicogrammar' Approach to Analyzing Phraseology and Collocation in ESP Texts. *ASp, la revue du GERAS (Groupe d'études et de recherche en anglais de spécialité)*, 59: 5–23.

Goddard, Cliff. 2011. *Semantic Analysis: A Practical Introduction*. Oxford: Oxford University Press.

Goddard, Cliff & Wierzbicka, Anna. 2014. *Words and Meaning: Lexical Semantics across Domains, Languages and Culture*s. Oxford: Oxford University Press.

Granger, Sylviane & Meunier, Fanny, eds. 2008. *Phraseology. An Interdisciplinary Perspective*. Amsterdam/Philadelphia: John Benjamins.

Grice, Paul. 1975. Logic and Conversation. In Cole, P. & Morgan, J., eds., *Syntax and Semantics, vol. 1, Speech Acts*, New York: Academic Press, 41–58.

Grimshaw, Jane. 1990. *Argument Structure*. Cambridge (MA): MIT Press.

Hagaman, Jessica & Reid, Robert. 2008. The Effects of the Paraphrasing Strategy on the Reading Comprehension of Middle-School Students At-risk for Failure in Reading. *Remedial and Special Education*, 29: 222–234.

Haiman, John & Thompson, Sandra. 1984. "Subordination" in Universal Grammar. In *Proceedings of the Tenth Annual Meeting of the Berkeley Linguistics Society*, 510–523.

Halliday, Michael. 1967. Notes on Transitivity and Theme in English, Parts 1, 2 & 3. *Journal of Linguistics*, 3/1: 37–81; 3/2: 199–244; 4/2: 179–215.

Halliday, Michael & Yallop, Collin. 2007. *Lexicology: A Short Introduction*. London/New York: Continuum.

Handke, Jürgen. 1995. *The Structure of the Lexicon. Man versus Machine*. Berlin/New York: Mouton de Gruyter.

Hanks, Patrick. 1993. Definitions and Explanations. In Sinclair, J. ed., *Looking Up: An Account of the COBUILD Project in Lexical Computing*, London: Harper Collins, 116–136.

Hanks, Patrick. 2013. *Lexical Analysis: Norms and Exploitations*. Cambridge (MA): MIT Press.

Harris, Zellig. 1970. The Two Systems of Grammar: Report and Paraphrase. In Harris, Z., *Papers in Structural and Transformational Linguistics*, Dordrecht: Reidel, 612–692.

Haspelmath, Martin. 2004. Coordinating Constructions: An Overview. In Haspelmath, M., ed., *Coordinating Constructions*, Amsterdam/Philadelphia: John Benjamins, 3–39.

Heil, John. 1994. *First-Order Logic: An Introduction*. Boston (MA): Jones and Bartlett.

Hengeveld, Kees. 1992. Parts of Speech. In Fortescue, M., Harder, P. & Kristoffersen, L., eds., *Layered Structure and Reference in a Functional Perspective*, Amsterdam/Philadelphia: John Benjamins, 29–55.

Herbst, Thomas. 1986. Defining with a Controlled Defining Vocabulary in Foreign Learners' Dictionaries. *Lexicographica*, 2: 101–119.

Hirst, Graeme. 2009. Ontology and the Lexicon. In Staab, S. & Studer, R., eds., *Handbook on Ontologies*, Berlin/Heidelberg: Springer, 269–292.

Hockett, Charles. 1987. *Refurbishing Our Foundations: Elementary Linguistics from an Advanced Point of View*. Amsterdam/Philadelphia: John Benjamins.

Horacek, Helmut & Zock, Michael, eds. 2015. *New Concepts in Natural Language Generation: Planning, Realization and Systems*. London: Bloomsbury.

Horn, Lawrence. 2006. Implicature. In Horn, L. & Ward, G., eds., *The Handbook of Pragmatics*, Malden (MA)/Oxford: Blackwell, 3–28.

Iordanskaja, Lidija. 1992. Communicative Structure and Its Use during Text Generation. *International Forum on Information and Documentation*, 17/2: 15–27.

Iordanskaja, Lidija & Mel'čuk, Igor. 2009. Connotation (in Linguistic Semantics). In Kempgen, S., Kosta, P., Berger, T. & Gutschmidt, K., eds., *The Slavic Languages. An International Handbook of Their Structure, Their History and Their Investigation*, Berlin/New York: Mouton de Gruyter, 875–882.

Iordanskaja, Lidija & Paperno, Slava. 1995. *The Russian–English Collocational Dictionary of the Human Body*. Columbus (OH): Slavica.

Iordanskaja, Lidija & Polguère, Alain. 2005. Hooking Up Syntagmatic Lexical Functions to Lexicographic Definitions. In Apresjan, Ju. & Iomdin, L., eds., *East-West Encounter: Second International Conference on Meaning-Text Theory*, Moscow: Slavic Languages and Cultures Publishing House, 176–186.

Iordanskaja, Lidija, Kittredge, Richard & Polguère, Alain. 1991. Lexical Selection and Paraphrase in a Meaning-Text Generation Model. In Paris *et al.*, eds., 293–312.

Jackendoff, Ray. 1992. *Semantic Structures*. Cambridge (MA): MIT Press.

Jakobson, Roman. 1957 [1971]. Shifters, Verbal Categories and the Russian Verb. In Jakobson, R., *Selected Writings, vol. 2*, The Hague: Mouton, 130–147.

Jakobson, Roman. 1960. Linguistics and Poetics. In Sebeok, T., ed., *Style in Language*, Cambridge (MA): MIT Press, 350–377.

Jakobson, Roman. 1971. Language in Relation to Other Communication Systems. In Jakobson, R., *Selected Writings, vol. 2*, The Hague: Mouton, 697–708.

Janda, Laura & Solovyev, Valerij. 2009. What Constructional Profiles Reveal About Antonymy: A Case Study of Russian Words for SADNESS and HAPPINESS. *Cognitive Linguistics*, 20/2: 367–393.

Jespersen, Otto. 1923. *Language: Its Nature, Development and Origin*. London: George Allen & Unwin.

Johnson, Kent. 2008. An Overview of Lexical Semantics. *Philosophy Compass*, 3/1: 119–134.

Kahane, Sylvain. 2003. The Meaning-Text Theory. In Ágel, V., Eichinger L. M, Eroms, H.-W., Hellwig, P., Heringer, H. J. & Lobin, H., eds., *Dependency and Valency: An International Handbook of Contemporary Research, vol. 1*, Berlin/New York: Mouton de Gruyter, 546–570.

Kay, Paul. 2005. Argument Structure Constructions and the Argument-Adjunct Distinction. In Fried, M. & Boas, H., eds., *Grammatical Constructions: Back to the Roots*, Amsterdam/Philadelphia: John Benjamins, 71–98.

Keenan, Edward. 1971. Two Kinds of Presupposition in Natural Language. In Fillmore & Langendoen, eds., 1971, 44–52.

Keller, John. 2015. Paraphrase, Semantics, and Ontology. *Oxford Studies in Metaphysics*, 9: 89–128.

Kennedy, Graeme. 2003. Amplifier Collocations in the British National Corpus: Implications for English Language Teaching. *Tesol Quarterly*, 37/3: 467–487.

Kiefer, Markus & Pulvermüller, Friedemann. 2012. Conceptual Representations in Mind and Brain: Theoretical Developments, Current Evidence and Future Directions. *Cortex*, 48/7: 805–825.

Kiparsky, Paul & Kiparsky, Carol. 1970. Fact. In Bierwisch, M. & Heidolph, K., eds., *Progress in Linguistics*, The Hague/Paris: Mouton, 143–173.

Kittay, Eva. 1987. Semantic Field Theory. In Kittay, E., *Metaphor: Its Cognitive Force and Linguistic Structure*, Oxford: Clarendon Press, 214–257.

Klepousniotou, Ekaterini. 2002. The Processing of Lexical Ambiguity: Homonymy and Polysemy in the Mental Lexicon. *Brain and Language*, 81/1: 205–223.

Krifka, Manfred & Musan, Renate, eds. 2012. *The Expression of Information Structure*. Berlin/New York: Mouton de Gruyter.

Lakoff, George. 1988. *Cognitive Semantics: Meaning and Mental Representations*. Bloomington (IN): University of Indiana Press.

Lakoff, George & Johnson, Mark. 1980. *Metaphors We Live By*. Chicago: University of Chicago Press.

Lambrecht, Knudt. 1994. *Information Structure and Sentence Form: Topic, Focus and the Mental Representation of Discourse Referents*. Cambridge: Cambridge University Press.

Landau, Sidney. [1984] 2001. *Dictionaries: The Art and Craft of Lexicography*, 2nd edition. Cambridge: Cambridge University Press.

Lappin, Shalom & Fox, Chris, eds. 2015. *The Handbook of Contemporary Semantic Theory*, 2nd edition. Malden (MA)/Oxford: Wiley & Blackwell.

Lavoie, Benoît & Rambow, Owen. 1997. A Fast and Portable Realizer for Text Generation Systems. In *Proceedings of the 5th Conference on Applied Natural Language Processing, Washington (DC)*, 265–268.

Lehman, Christian. 2006. Participant Roles, Thematic Roles and Syntactic Relations. In Tsunoda, T. & Kageyama, T., eds., *Voice and Grammatical Relations. In Honor of Masayoshi Shibatani*, Amsterdam/Philadelphia: John Benjamins, 153–174.

Lehrer, Adrienne. 1978. Structures of the Lexicon and Transfer of the Meaning. *Lingua*, 45/2: 95–123.

Lehrer, Adrienne & Kittay, Eva, eds. 1992. *Frames, Fields and Contrasts: New Essays in Semantic and Lexical Organization*. Hillsdale (NJ): Lawrence Erlbaum Associates.

Lehrer, Adrienne & Lehrer, Keith. 1984. Antonymy. *Linguistics and Philosophy*, 5: 483–501.

Levin, Beth. 1993. *English Verb Classes and Alternations: A Preliminary Investigation*. Chicago (IL): University of Chicago Press.

Levin, Beth & Rappaport Hovav, Malka. 2005. *Argument Realization*. Cambridge: Cambridge University Press.

L'Homme, Marie-Claude. 2010. Designing Terminological Dictionaries for Learners Based on Lexical Semantics: The Representation of Actants. In Fuertes-Olivera, P., ed., *Specialized Dictionaries for Learners*, Berlin/New York: de Gruyter, 141–153.

Lipka, Leonhard. 2002. *English Lexicography: Lexical Structure, Word Semantics and Word Formation*. Tübingen: Gunter Narr.

Longman Dictionary of Contemporary English Online, www.ldoceonline.com. London: Longman.

Löbner, Sebastian. 2013. *Understanding Semantics*. London: Routledge.

Lux-Pogodalla, Veronika & Polguère, Alain. 2011. Construction of a French Lexical Network: Methodological Issues. In *First International Workshop on Lexical Resources (WoLeR 2011)*, 54–61.

Lyons, John. 1995. *Linguistic Semantics: An Introduction*. Cambridge: Cambridge University Press.

MacDonald, Maryellen, Pearlmutter, Neal & Seidenberg, Mark. 1994. The Lexical Nature of Syntactic Ambiguity Resolution. *Psychological Review*, 101: 676–703.

Madnani, Nitin & Dorr, Bonnie. 2010. Generating Phrasal and Sentential Paraphrases: A Survey of Data-Driven Methods. *Computational Linguistics*, 36/3: 341–387.

Mallinson, Jonathan, Sennrich, Rico & Lapata, Mirella. 2017. Paraphrasing Revisited with Neural Machine Translation. In *Proceedings of the 15th Conference of the European Chapter of the Association for Computational Linguistics*, vol. 1, 881–893.

Malt, Barbara, Sloman, Steven, Gennari, Silvia, Shi, Meiyi & Wang, Yuan. 1999. Knowing versus Naming: Similarity and the Linguistic Categorization of Artifacts. *Journal of Memory and Language*, 40/2: 230–262.

Matthews, Peter. 2007. The Scope of Valency in Grammar. In Herbst, Th. & Götz-Votteler, K., eds., *Valency: Theoretical, Descriptive and Cognitive Issues*, Berlin/ New York: Mouton de Gruyter, 3–15.

Matthiessen, Christian. 1991. Lexico(Grammatical) Choice in Text Generation. In Paris *et al.*, eds., 1991, 249–292.

McCawley, James. 1981. *Everything That Linguists Have Always Wanted to Know about Logic but Were Ashamed to Ask*. Chicago: University of Chicago Press.

McKeown, Kathleen R. & Radev, Dragomir. 2000. Collocations. In Dale, R., Mools, H. & Somers H., eds., *Handbook of Natural Language Processing*, New York/Basel: Marcel Dekker, 507–524.

Mel'čuk, Igor. 1982. *Towards a Language of Linguistics: A System of Formal Notions for Theoretical Morphology*. Munich: Wilhelm Fink.

Mel'čuk, Igor. 1988a. *Dependency Syntax: Theory and Practice*. Albany (NY): SUNY Press.

Mel'čuk, Igor. 1988b. Semantic Description of Lexical Units in an Explanatory Combinatorial Dictionary: Basic Principles and Heuristic Criteria. *International Journal of Lexicography*, 1: 165–188.

Mel'čuk, Igor. 1989. Semantic Primitives from the Viewpoint of the Meaning-Text Linguistic Theory. *Quaderni di semantica*, 10/1: 65–102.

Mel'čuk, Igor. 2001. *Communicative Organization in Natural Language*. Amsterdam/ Philadelphia: John Benjamins.

Mel'čuk, Igor. 2004a. Actants in Semantics and Syntax I: Actants in Semantics. *Linguistics*, 42/1: 1–66.

Mel'čuk, Igor. 2004b. Actants in Semantics and Syntax II: Actants in Syntax. *Linguistics*, 42/2: 247–292.

Mel'čuk, Igor. 2006a. *Aspects of the Theory of Morphology*. Berlin/New York: Mouton de Gruyter.

Mel'čuk, Igor. 2006b. Explanatory Combinatorial Dictionary. In Sica, G., ed., *Open Problems in Linguistics and Lexicography*, Monza: Polimetrica, 225–355.

Mel'čuk, Igor. 2012a. Phraseology in the Language, in the Dictionary, and in the Computer. *Yearbook of Phraseology*, 3/1: 31–56.

Mel'čuk, Igor. 2012b, 2013 & 2015a. *Semantics: From Meaning to Text*. Vols 1–3. Amsterdam/ Philadelphia: John Benjamins.

Mel'čuk, Igor. 2015b. Clichés: An Understudied Subclass of Phrasemes. *Yearbook of Phraseology*, 6: 55–86.

Mel'čuk, Igor. 2016. *Language: From Meaning to Text*. Brighton (MA): Academic Studies Press.

Mel'čuk, Igor & Pertsov, Nikolaj. 1987. *Surface-Syntax of English. A Formal Model within the Meaning-Text Framework*. Amsterdam/Philadelphia: John Benjamins.

Mel'čuk, Igor & Polguère, Alain. 2007. *Lexique actif du français. L'apprentissage du vocabulaire fondé sur 20 000 dérivations sémantiques et collocations du français*. Brussels: De Boeck.

Mel'čuk, Igor & Polguère, Alain. 2018. Theory and Practice of Lexicographic Definition. *Journal of Cognitive Science*, 19/4: 417–470.

Mel'čuk, Igor & Žolkovskij, Aleksandr. 1984. *Tolkovo-kombinatornyj slovar' russkogo jazyka. Opyty semantiko-sintaksičeskogo opisanija russkoj leksiki [Explanatory Combinatorial Dictionary of Russian. Essays in Semantic and Syntactic Description of Russian Lexicon]*. Vienna: Wiener Slawistischer Almanach. [Reprinted in 2016, Moskva: Global Kom.]

Mel'čuk, Igor *et al.* 1984–1988–1992–1999. *Dictionnaire explicatif et combinatoire du français contemporain: Recherches lexico-sémantiques I-IV*. Montréal: Presses de l'Université de Montréal.

Merriam-Webster Learner's Dictionary Online, learnersdictionary.com. Springfield: Merriam-Webster Inc.

Milićević, Jasmina. 2007. Semantic Equivalence Rules in Meaning-Text Paraphrasing. In Wanner, ed. 2007, 267–297.

Milićević, Jasmina. 2008. Paraphrase as a Tool for Achieving Lexical Competence in L2. In Van Daele, S., Housen, A., Kuiken, F., Pierrard, M. & Vedder, I., eds., *Proceedings of the Symposium "Complexity, Accuracy and Fluency in Second Language Use, Learning and Teaching"*, Brussels: Royal Belgium Academy of Science and Arts, 153–167.

Milićević, Jasmina. 2009. C'est la définition de quel mot? Tester la validité des définitions lexicographiques pour un dictionnaire d'apprentissage. In Beck, D., Gerdes, K., Milićević, J. & Polguère, A., eds., *Proceedings of the 4th International Conference on Meaning-Text Theory,* Montreal: Université de Montréal, 275–285.

Milićević, Jasmina. 2013. Pairing Semantic and Semantic-Communicative Structures for Paraphrase Generation in a Meaning-Text Linguistic Model. In Apresjan, V., Iomdin, B. & Ageeva, E., eds., *Proceedings of the 6th International Conference on Meaning-Text Theory*, Prague, 113–124.

Milićević, Jasmina. 2016. La définition lexicographique pédagogique: enjeux et difficultés. *Cahiers de lexicologie*, n° 109: 95–117.

Milićević, Jasmina & Tsedryk, Alexandra. 2011. Assessing and Improving Paraphrasing Competence in FSL. In Boguslavskij, I. & Wanner, L., eds., *Proceedings of the 5th International Conference on Meaning-Text Theory*, Barcelona, 176–185.

Miller, George, Beckwith, Richard, Fellbaum, Christiane, Gross, Derek & Miller, Katherine. 1990. Introduction to WordNet: An On-line Lexical Database. *International Journal of Lexicography*, 3/4: 235–244.

Miller, Tristan & Gurevych, Iryna. 2015. Automatic Disambiguation of English Puns. In *Proceedings of the 53rd Annual Meeting of the Association for Computational Linguistics and the 7th International Joint Conference on Natural Language Processing of the Asian Federation of Natural Language Processing*, vol. 1: 719–729.

Murphy, Lynne. 2003. *Semantic Relations and the Lexicon: Antonymy, Synonymy and Other Paradigms.* Cambridge: Cambridge University Press.

Murphy, Lynne. 2010. *Lexical Meaning.* Cambridge: Cambridge University Press.

Nunberg, Geoffrey, Sag, Ivan & Wasow, Thomas. 1994. Idioms. *Language*, 70/3: 491–538.

Ogden, Charles. 1930. *Basic English: A General Introduction with Rules and Grammar.* London: K. Paul & Treber. [Reprinted as The ABC of Basic English. 1944. London: K. Paul.]

Oxford English Dictionary Online, www.oed.com. Oxford: Oxford Dictionaries.

Panther, Klaus-Uwe, Thornburg, Linda & Barcelona, Antonio, eds. 2009. *Metonymy and Metaphor in Grammar.* Amsterdam/Philadelphia: John Benjamins.

Paradis, Carita & Willners, Caroline. 2007. Antonyms in Dictionary Entries: Methodological Perspectives. *Studia Linguistica*, 61/3: 261–277.

Paris, Cecile, Swartout, William & Mann, William, eds. 1991. *Natural Language Generation in Artificial Intelligence and Computational Linguistics.* Boston: Kluwer.

Parret, Herman. 1989. Paraphrase as a Coherence Principle in Conversation. In Conte, M.-E., Petöfi, J. & Sözer, E., eds., *Text and Discourse Connectedness*, Amsterdam/Philadelphia: John Benjamins, 281–289.

Partee, Barbara. 1995. Lexical Semantics and Compositionality. In Gleitman, L. & Liberman, M., eds., *An Invitation to Cognitive Science, vol. 1: Language*, Cambridge (MA): MIT Press, 311–360.

Petruck, Miriam & Ellsworth, Michael. 2016. Representing Support Verbs in FrameNet. In *Proceedings of the 12th Workshop on Multiword Expressions (Berlin, August 7–12, 2016)*, 72–77.

Plebe, Alessio & De La Cruz, Vivian. 2016. Semantic Theories. In Plebe, A. & De La Cruz, V., eds., *Neurosemantics: Neural Processes and the Construction of Linguistic Meaning*, New York: Springer International Publishing, 113–129.

Polguère Alain. 1997. Meaning-Text Semantic Networks as a Formal Language. In Wanner, ed., 1997, 1–20.

Polguère Alain. 2000a. Towards a Theoretically Motivated General Public Dictionary of Semantic Derivations and Collocations for French. In *Proceedings of EURALEX 2000 (Stuttgart)*, 517–527.

Polguère Alain. 2000b. A "Natural" Lexicalization Model for Language Generation. In *Proceedings of the Fourth Symposium on Natural Language Processing 2000 (SNLP'2000), Thailand, 10-12 May 2000*, 37–50.

Polguère, Alain. 2004. La paraphrase comme outil pédagogique de modélisation des liens lexicaux. In Calaque, E. & David, J., eds., *Didactique du lexique: contextes, démarches, supports*, Brussels: De Boeck, 115–124.

Polguère, Alain. 2011. Classification sémantique des lexies fondée sur le paraphrasage. *Cahiers de lexicologie*, 98: 197–211.

Polguère, Alain. 2014. From Writing Dictionaries to Weaving Lexical Networks. *International Journal of Lexicography*, 27/4: 396–418.

Polguère, Alain. 2015. Lexicon Embedded Syntax. In *Proceedings of the 3rd International Conference on Dependency Linguistics, DEPLING 2015 (August 24–26 2015, Uppsala)*, 2–9.

Polguère, Alain & Mel'čuk, Igor, eds. 2009. *Dependency in Linguistic Description.* Amsterdam/ Philadelphia: John Benjamins.

Portner, Paul & Partee, Barbara, eds. 2002. *Formal Semantics: The Essential Readings.* Oxford: Blackwell.

Potts, Christopher. 2015. Presupposition and Implicature. In Lappin & Fox, eds., 2015 168–202.

Pustejovsky James. 1991. The Syntax of Event Structure. *Cognition*, 41: 47–81.

Pustejovsky, James. 1995. *The Generative Lexicon.* Cambridge (MA): MIT Press.

Pustejovsky, James. 2006. Type Theory and Lexical Decomposition. *Journal of Cognitive Science*, 6: 39–76.

Quirk, Randolph, Greenbaum, Sidney, Leech, Geoffrey & Svartvik, Jan. 1985. *A Comprehensive Grammar of the English Language.* London: Longman.

Ravin, Yael & Leacock, Claudia, eds. 2000. *Polysemy: Theoretical and Computational Approaches.* Oxford: Oxford University Press.

Reichenbach, Hans. 1947. *Elements of Symbolic Logic.* New York: Macmillan.

Reimer, Marga & Michaelson, Eliot. 2017. Reference. In Zalta, E., ed., *The Stanford Encyclopedia of Philosophy* (Spring 2017 edition), https://plato.stanford.edu/ archives/spr2017/entries/reference/.

Ruppenhofer, Josef, Ellsworth, Michael, Petruck, Miriam, Johnson, Christopher, Baker, Collin & Scheffczyk, Jan. 2016. *FrameNet II: Extended Theory and Practice.* Berkeley (CA): International Computer Science Institute.

Russo, Mariachiara. 2014. Testing Aptitude for Interpreting: The Predictive Value of Oral Paraphrasing, with Synonyms and Coherence as Assessment Parameters. *Interpreting*, 16/1: 1–18.

Saeed, John. 2011. *Semantics.* Oxford: Wiley-Blackwell.

Sag, Ivan, Baldwin, Timothy, Bond, Francis, Copestake, Ann & Flickinger, Dan. 2002. Multiword Expressions: A Pain in the Neck for NLP. In *Proceedings of the 3rd International Conference on Computational Linguistics and Intelligent Text Processing, Mexico City, Feb. 17–23, 2002*, 189–206.

Sapir, Edward. 1921 [2004]. *Language: An Introduction to the Study of Speech.* Mineola (NY): Dover Publications.

Saussure, Ferdinand de. 1916 [2013]. *A Course in General Linguistics.* London: Bloomsbury Publishing.

Sinclair, John. 1991. *Corpus, Concordance, Collocation.* Oxford: Oxford University Press.

Sinclair, John. 2004. *Trust the Text: Language, Corpus and Discourse.* London/New York: Routledge.

Slobin, Dan. 1996. From "Thought and Language" to "Thinking for Speaking". In Gumperz, J. & Levinson, S., eds., *Rethinking Linguistic Relativity*, Cambridge: Cambridge University Press, 70–96.

Snider, Todd. 2015. Using Tautologies and Contradictions. In Csipak, E. & Zeijlstra, H., eds., *Proceedings of Sinn und Bedeutung*, 19, 590–607.

Steele, James. 1986. A Lexical Entry for an Explanatory Combinatorial Dictionary of English (hope **II.1**). *Dictionaries*, 8/1: 1–54.

Steele, James, ed. 1990. *The Meaning-Text Theory of Language: Linguistics, Lexicography, and Practical Implications.* Ottawa: University of Ottawa Press.

Steele, James & Meyer, Ingrid. 1990. Interlingual Meaning-Text Lexicography: Towards a New Type of Dictionary for Translation. In Steele, ed., 1990: 175–270.

Storjohann, Petra. 2010. Lexico-Semantic Relations in Theory and Practice. In Storjohann, P., ed., *Lexical-Semantic Relations: Theoretical and Practical Perspectives*, Amsterdam/Philadelphia: John Benjamins, 5–15.

Solodkoff, Tatjana, von. 2014. Paraphrase Strategies in Metaphysics. *Philosophy Compass*, 9/8: 570–582.

Suihkonen, Pirkko, Comrie, Bernard & Solovyev, Valerij, eds. 2012. *Argument Structure and Grammatical Relations*. Amsterdam/Philadelphia: John Benjamins.

Szabó, Zoltán. 2017. Compositionality. In Zalta, E., ed., *The Stanford Encyclopedia of Philosophy* (Summer 2017 edition), https://seop.illc.uva.nl/entries/compositionality.

Talmy, Leonard. 1985. Lexicalization Patterns: Semantic Structure in Lexical Forms. In Shopen, T., ed., *Language Typology and Syntactic Description, vol. 3: Grammatical Categories in the Lexicon*, Cambridge: Cambridge University Press, 57–149.

Tesnière, Lucien. 1959 [2015]. *Elements of Structural Syntax*. Amsterdam/Philadelphia: John Benjamins.

Tsedryk, Alexandra. 2016. *La compétence paraphrastique en français langue seconde*. Berne: Peter Lang.

Van Valin, Robert, Jr. 2004. Semantic Macroroles in Role and Reference Grammar. In Kailuweit, R. & Hummer, M., eds., *Semantische Rollen*, Tübingen: Gunter Narr, 63–79.

Vendler, Zeno. 1957. Verbs and Times. *The Philosophical Review*, 6: 143–160.

Vendler, Zeno. 1967. Facts and Events. In Vendler, Z., *Linguistics in Philosophy*, Ithaca (NY): Cornell University Press, 122–146.

Vila, Marta, Martí, Antònia & Rodríguez, Horacio. 2014. Is This a Paraphrase? What Kind? Paraphrase Boundaries and Typology. *Open Journal of Modern Linguistics*, 4/1: 205–218.

Walker, Angela. 2008. Preventing Unintentional Plagiarism: A Method for Strengthening Paraphrasing Skills. *Journal of Instructional Psychology*, 35/4: 387–396.

Wanner, Leo, ed. 1996. *Lexical Functions in Lexicography and Natural Language Processing*. Amsterdam/Philadelphia: John Benjamins.

Wanner, Leo, ed. 1997. *Recent Trends in the Meaning-Text Theory*. Amsterdam/Philadelphia: John Benjamins.

Wanner, Leo, ed. 2007. *Selected Lexical and Grammatical Issues in the Meaning-Text Theory*. In Honor of Igor Mel'čuk. Amsterdam/Philadelphia: John Benjamins.

Weinreich, Uriel. 1961. On the Semantic Structure of Language. In Weinreich, U., *On Semantics*, Philadelphia: University of Pennsylvania Press, 1980, 37–96.

Wierzbicka, Anna. 1977. Mental Language and Semantic Primitives. *Communication and Cognition*, 10/3–4: 155–179.

Wierzbicka, Anna. 1980. *Lingua Mentalis: The Semantics of Natural Language*. Sidney: Academic Press.

Wierzbicka, Anna. 1982. Why Can You "Have a Drink" When You Can't "*Have an Eat"? *Language*, 58/4: 753–799.

Wierzbicka, Anna. 1987. *English Speech Act Verbs: A Semantic Dictionary*. Sydney: Academic Press.

Wierzbicka, Anna. 1992. Back to Definitions: Cognition, Semantics and Lexicography. *Lexicographica*, 8: 146–174.

Wierzbicka, Anna. 1993. What Are the Uses of Theoretical Lexicography? *Dictionaries*, 14: 44–78.

Wierzbicka, Anna. 1994. Cognitive Domains and the Structure of the Lexicon: The Case of Emotions. In Hirschfeld, L. & Gelman, S., eds., *Mapping the Mind: Domain Specificity in Cognition and Culture*, Cambridge: Cambridge University Press, 431–452.

Wierzbicka, Anna. 1996. *Semantics: Primes and Universals*. Oxford: Oxford University Press.

Wierzbicka, Anna. 1997. Lexicon as a Key to Ethno-Sociology and Cultural Psychology; Patterns of "Friendship" Across Cultures. In Wierzbicka, A., *Understanding Cultures Through Their Key Words*, Oxford/New York: Oxford University Press, 31–125.

Wierzbicka, Anna. 2011. Common Language of All People: The Innate Language of Thought. *Problems of Information Transmission*, 47/4: 378–397.

Wierzbicka, Anna & Goddard, Cliff. 2005. Lexical Decomposition: Conceptual Axiology. In Cruse *et al.*, eds., 2005, 256–268.

Zareva, Alla. 2007. Structure of the Second Language Mental Lexicon: How Does It Compare to Native Speakers' Lexical Organization? *Second Language Research*, 23/2: 123–153.

Zimmermann, Malte & Onea, Edgar. 2011. Focus Marking and Focus Interpretation. *Lingua*, 121/11: 1651–1670.

Zimmermann, Thomas & Sternefeld, Wolfgang. 2013. *Introduction to Semantics. An Essential Guide to the Composition of Meaning*. Berlin/New York: Mouton de Gruyter.

Notion and Term Index cum Glossary

This Index/Glossary contains explanations of most important linguistic notions appearing in the book; special pointers are provided towards the spots where these notions are discussed in more detail ("Consult …"); pages on which the most developed characterization of the notion is found are printed in bold.

Since the aim of the Glossary is to serve as a resource for quick reference, the formulations found therein are not necessarily precise and/or complete.

There is, inevitably, some repetition with respect to Chapter 2 ("Some Basic Linguistic Notions") and Definition Index, but redundancy is a necessary feature of any semiotic system (the present book being such a system, and a rather complex one at that). And, as a Latin cliché (for *cliché*, see below) would have it, *Repetitio mater studiorum.*

Actant (of L)
>
> Lexical unit [LU] L' that is foreseen (= implied) by the signified of L and that can be expressed as a syntactic dependent of L.
>
> Cf. modifier (of L).
>
> Consult Ch. 2, *1.3.2*, p. 44.
>
> See pp. 6, **44**, 83, 88, 296–297, 366

—«—, deep-syntactic
>
> LU L' that syntactically depends on the LU L and corresponds to a SemA of L.
>
> Consult Definition 11.4, p. 297.
>
> See pp. 26, 43, 45–46, 88, 142–145, 169, 176, 211–212, 290, **297**, 325, 366

—«—, semantic (of 'σ'/ L('σ'))
>
> • Either the semanteme 'σ'' that depends on the semanteme 'σ' and corresponds to a semantic actant slot in 'L'; e.g.:
>
> $$\text{'John}\leftarrow\textbf{1}\text{–love–}\textbf{2}\rightarrow\text{Mary' } (\textit{John loves Mary})$$
>
> where 'John' and 'Mary' are, respectively, SemA **1** and **2** of 'love'.
> • Or the LU L('σ'') that semantically depends on the LU L('σ').
> Consult Definition 3.4, p. 87.
> See pp. 6, 41, 43, 45–46, 83, **87***ff*, 94–96, 137–138, 142–145, 197, 222, 259, 262, 267, 325, 355

—«—, surface-syntactic (of L)
>
> LU L' that syntactically depends on the LU L and either is L's syntactic subject/direct object or shares several relevant syntactic properties with these clause elements; e.g., indirect object:
>
> GIVE–**indir-objectival**→JOHN [*the permission to leave*].
>
> See pp. 43–**44**, 211–212, 299

actantial number
>
> Name of a Sem-actant.
>
> Consult Ch. 10, *2.1.3*, p. 262.
>
> See pp. 87, 181, 259, **262**, 308

actantial structure (of L)

> Set and nature of all actants of the LU L.
>
> See pp. **88–89**, 169, 174, 178, 180–181, 355, 358–360

adjunct, free (of L)

> Modifier/Circumstantial of the LU L.
>
> Consult Ch. 11, *2.4.1.2*, p. 296.
>
> See pp. 44, **296**

affix

> Morph that is not a radical; e.g.: **-s** in *finger+s*, **-ing** in *formulat+ing*, **re-** in *re+formulate*, etc.
>
> Cf. radical.
>
> Consult Ch. 2, *3.1.3*, p. 62.
>
> See pp. 31, 54, 62–63, 274–275, 315, 320, 346

agreement

> One of the two types of morphological dependency (the other one being government): the wordform w_1 is said to agree with the wordform w_2 if and only if some grammemes of w_1 are determined by:
>
> 1. Some grammemes of w_2:
>
> **this**$_{w_1}$ *stick*$_{w_2}$ ~ **these**$_{w_1}$ *sticks*$_{w_2}$
>
> 2. The agreement class of w_2:
>
> Fr. **beau**$_{MASC-w_1}$ *palais*$_{(masc)w_2}$ 'beautiful palace' ~ **belle** $_{FEM-w_1}$ maison$_{(fem)w_2}$ 'beautiful house'
>
> 3. Some semantemes in the signified of w_2:
>
> Rus. *Ètot vrač*$_{(masc)w_2}$ **prišël**$_{MASC-w_1}$ 'This doctor [male] arrived'. ~
> *Ètot vrač*$_{(masc)w_2}$ **prišla**$_{FEM-w_1}$ 'This doctor [female] arrived'.
> Consult Ch. 2, *1.3.1*, p. 42.
>
> See pp. 42, 48, 50, 62–63, 75, 292–293

analysis, linguistic (= speech understanding)

> Operation whereby the Addressee of a speech act goes from the text received to the linguistic meaning expressed by it: Text $\Rightarrow$ Meaning; cf. synthesis, linguistic.
>
> See pp. xvii, 8, 13, 16–18, 343

analytic expression

> Complex linguistic expression in which a grammeme is realized by a separate lexeme; e.g.: **will** *stay*, where the grammeme FUTURE is expressed by an auxiliary verb; cf. synthetic expression.
>
> See pp. 48, **63**, 101, 232

apophony

> Meaningful alternation; e.g.: $\mathbf{A}_{PAST}^{/ɪ/\Rightarrow/æ/}$, as in *sing* ~ *sang*.
>
> See pp. 33, **48**, 61

approximate-quantitative syntactic construction (in Russian)

> Construction "N + NUM", in which the anteposing of the noun with respect to the numeral expresses the meaning 'the Speaker is uncertain about the number'; e.g., *tonn desjat´* lit. 'tons ten' = 'maybe ten tons' (*desjat´ tonn* means 'ten tons'). In the DSyntS, this construction is encoded by the fictitious lexeme «PRIMERNO» [lit. 'approximately'] 'maybe'.
>
> See pp. 240, 291, **319**

arborization

>Operation whereby the branches of the DSyntS are constructed under synthesis; cf. lexicalization and morphologization.
>See pp. 20, 23, 259, 284, 296, 306, **321ff**, 367–368

aspectual classes

>Major semantic classes of verbs from the viewpoint of their telic/atelic, dynamic/static and punctual/continuous characteristics; first established by Z. Vendler.
>See pp. 139, **190–191**

asyndetic

>Without conjunction; e.g.: the sentence *John entered, Mary left* features an asyndetic coordination of two clauses.
>See p. 295

Base (of a collocation)

>Component of a collocation that is selected by the Speaker freely and that controls the selection of the collocate; e.g.: in *pay attention*, ATTENTION is the base; in *black coffee*, COFFEE is the base.
>See pp. 99, **109–110**, 114–115, 158

base (of derivation)

>Stem of the lexeme L from which a derivative L' is produced by adding a derivateme.
>See pp. **150–151**, 289, 315

basic lexical unit (of a vocable)

>LU to which other LUs of the vocable refer.
>See pp. **155**, 157, 188–189, 199–200, 218

basic structure (of a linguistic representation)

>Structure on which other structures of the representation (= the peripheral ones) are superimposed.
>See pp. **16**, 52, **256**–258, 286, 287, 312, 327

binary relation

>Relation holding between two elements; e.g.: 'X is.equal to Y'.
>See pp. 86, **347–349**

Circularity

>Presence of a vicious circle in a system of definitions.
>See pp. 90, **121–123**, 357

clause (simple)

>Phrase that contains a V_{FIN} and all its direct and indirect dependents—except for another phrase of the same type; e.g.: *John told Mary the news. | that I know the truth | which we found yesterday*
>Consult Definition 2.15, p. 57.
>See pp. **57**–58, 232–233, 237, 279

clause element

>Phrase whose syntactic head either is the syntactic head of a clause or a direct syntactic dependent of the clause head; e.g.: Subject, DirO, …, circumstantial, prolepsis, parenthetical, etc.
>See pp. 13, 274

cleft

>   Syntactic construction used to express Focalization:
>
>   IT←BE→(PREP→)N THAT/WHO-CLAUSE
>
>   E.g.: *It was from John*_{FOCALIZED} *that Mary learnt the news.*
>   See pp. 276, 306.

cliché

>   Compositional semantic-lexemic phraseme; e.g.: *Rome was not built in a day.*
> | *Everybody makes mistakes.* | *No parking.*
>   Consult Definition 4.8, p. 111.
>   See pp. 98–99, 104, **111**–112, 113, 114, 115, 182, 215, 228, 231, 237

co-hyponyms

>   LUs that have the same hyperonym; e.g.: COLLIE, GREYHOUND,
>   ⌐GREAT DANE˥ and ⌐GERMAN SHEPHERD˥ are co-hyponyms with
>   the hyperonym DOG.
>   See p. 127

collocate

>   Component of a collocation that is selected by the Speaker as a function of its
>   base; e.g.: in *pay attention*, PAY is the collocate.
>   See pp. **109**, 110, 114, 138, 159, 183–184, 204

collocation

>   Compositional lexemic phraseme one component of which—the base—is
>   selected by the Speaker freely (according to its meaning and combinatorial
>   properties), while the second component—the collocate—is selected as a
>   function of the base; e.g.: *pay ATTENTION, heavy INVOLVEMENT, under
>   CONSTRUCTION, black COFFEE, leap YEAR.*
>   Consult Definition 4.6, p. 109.
>   See pp. 6, 18, **34**, 98, 104, **109–110**, 113–115, 132, 141, 158–159, 163, 174,
>   182, 183–185, 214, 258, 266, 290, 307, 318–319, 337, 356, 357, 359, 360

communicate

>   To express meanings by clauses that implement logical propositions (describ-
>   ing situations the Speaker targets): these clauses can be negated or questioned.
>   Cf. signal_(V). Consult Definition 10.13, p. 277.
>   See pp. 58, 270, **277**, 278–279

communicatively dominant component (of a meaning)

>   Part 'σ'' of meaning 'σ' to which 'σ' can be reduced without distortion of
>   information; 'σ'' is the minimal paraphrase of 'σ'. Communicative domi-
>   nance is shown by <u>underscoring</u>. E.g.: in the meaning '<u>motor vehicle</u> that is
>   designed to carry a small number of passengers' the communicatively domi-
>   nant component is 'motor vehicle'.
>   See pp. 21, 22, 90, 106, 127, 131, 237, 270, 271, 279, 280, 296, 313, 316,
>   318, 323, 333

compositional (complex linguistic sign **s**)

>   Complex linguistic sign **s** that can be represented as a regular "sum" of signs
> $\mathbf{s}_1$ and $\mathbf{s}_2$: $\mathbf{s} = \mathbf{s}_1 \oplus \mathbf{s}_2$.
>   See pp. **37–38**, 63, 64, 103–104, 106, 109–111, 115, 215, 229, 268–269

concept
>   Designation of an element of extra-linguistic reality by means of LUs of natural language, "freed" as much as possible from linguistic peculiarities.
>   See pp. 27, 28, 182, 231

conceptics
>   Logical device (= set of rules) responsible for the correspondence between conceptual representations and semantic representations:
>
> $$\{\text{ConceptR}_\text{l}\} \Leftarrow \text{conceptics} \Rightarrow \{\text{SemR}_\text{i}\}.$$
>
>   Conceptics is part of a general model of human linguistic behavior.
>   Consult Ch. 1, *2.4*, p. 27.
>   See pp. 15, 27–28, 234

conceptual representation

>   See representation, conceptual

conjunction (in logic and semantics)
>   Logical operator "∧" ('and'):
>>   A ∧ B is true if and only if both A and B are true.
>   Consult Appendix, *5.1*, p. 352.
>   See pp. 78, 84, 127–128, 137, 267, **352**–353

connotation, lexicographic (of an LU L)
>   Meaning associated by the language with the denotation of L that cannot be included in L's lexicographic definition. E.g.: 'strong' is a connotation of HORSE1 `domestic animal`; 'cunning' is a connotation of $FOX_{(N)}\mathbf{1}$ `wild animal`; 'helpless', 'innocent', 'open-minded' and 'unreasonable' are the connotations of $BABY_{(N)}\mathbf{1}$ `child1`.
>   Consult Definition 5.1, p. 136.
>   See pp. 73, 117, 132, 135–**136**, 152, 210–211, 358

context (of a rule)
>   Part of a rule that is not manipulated by the rule itself, but whose presence (in the rule's input) is necessary for the rule to apply.
>   See p. 313

conversion (morphological)
>   Morphological operation consisting in modifying the syntactics of the targeted sign; e.g.: the substitution "N $\Rightarrow$ V," which, applied to the noun $SAW_{(N)}$ 'tool ...', gives the verb $SAW_{(V)}$ 'cut Y with a saw'.
>   See pp. 61, 64, **316**

conversion (lexical and/or syntactic)
>   1. Lexical relation between LUs L_1 and L_2 such that their meanings are identical but the DSynt-actants of the one do not correspond to the same DSynt-actants of the other; e.g.:
>
>> $X\,fears_{L_1}\,Y$ ~ $Y\,frightens_{L_2}\,X$;
>> $X\,is\,Y\text{'s}\,wife_{L_1}$ ~ $Y\,is\,X\text{'s}\,husband_{L_2}$;
>> $X\,is\,before_{L_1}\,Y$ ~ $Y\,is\,after\,X_{L_2}$.
>
>   2. Syntactic operation of replacing an LU L_1 by the conversive LU L_2.
>   Consult Definition 6.4, p. 146.
>   See pp. 39, 89, **146**–**148**, 149, 178, 263, 339, 358

coordination

> One of two major types of semantic/syntactic structure (the other one being subordination), which unites several elements playing the same semantic/ syntactic role; e.g.: *The dresses were **red, blue, and yellow**. | **John and Mary** travel together. | John **awoke, but stayed** in bed.*
> See pp. 84, **295**, 304

criteria for elaborating lexicographic definitions

> Consult Ch. 5, *4*, p. 131*ff*.

De Morgan rules

> Rules (or laws) of formal logic that establish correspondences between conjunction, disjunction and negation.
> Consult Appendix, *5.1*, p. 352.
> See pp. 128, 131, 218, 353

deductive method

> Method of reasoning from more general to more specific, based on rigorous definitions of all notions used. A rigorous definition is formulated strictly in terms of some indefinibilia, specified by a list, and notions previously defined.
> See pp. xvii, 56, 343, 345

deep-syntactic representation

> See representation, deep-syntactic.

definiendum

> Left-hand part of a lexicographic definition that presents the LU L defined, i.e., the headword; if L is a (quasi-)predicate, the definiendum is presented inside its propositional form.
> See pp. 118, 119, 120–122, 137

definiens

> Right-hand part of a lexicographic definition that, in the general case, presents the decomposition of the meaning of the LU defined.
> See pp. 118, 119, 120, **121**, 123, 127, 137

definiteness (of an LU L)

> 1. Characteristic of L's referential status from the viewpoint of its referent's identifiability in a given utterance for the Speaker and/or the Addressee.
> See p. 36
> 2. Morphological category of nouns.
> See pp. 49, 50, 61

definition, lexicographic (of an LU L)

> Formal description of L's meaning by a linguistic expression (of the same language) that is an exact paraphrase of L satisfying six special rules.
> Consult Ch. 5.
> See pp. 6, 23, 90, 94, **117*ff*,** 152–154, 192, 197, 203, 314, 328, 357–358, 361

—«—«—, disjunctive

> Definition that contains at least two semantic components linked by logical disjunction OR [= "V"]; e.g.: 'X ʳcools down" (*The air has cooled down.*) = 'X becomes cooler (than X was before) or cool'.
> See pp. 122, 127–129, 137, 216, 353

denotation (of a linguistic sign)
> Set of all facts or entities of the extralinguistic world that the sign can describe (= all potential referents of this sign).
> See pp. **36**, 141, 156, 168, 178, 185

dependency relation (semantic or syntactic)[1]
> Binary relation between two semantemes or two LUs in an utterance: '$\sigma_1 \rightarrow \sigma_2$' or $L('\sigma_1') \rightarrow L('\sigma_2')$; this relation is antireflexive and antisymmetric, and can be non-transitive (semantic dependencies) or anti-transitive (syntactic dependencies).
> See pp. xviii, 14, **40**–41, 43, 86, **293**–294, 366

diathesis (of an LU L)
> Correspondence between L's Sem-actants and its DSynt-actants (specified in L's government pattern).
> Consult Ch. 3, *1.3.3.*
> See pp. **45**, 211, 309

dictionary article (of an LU L)
> Systematically presented information about L.
> See pp. 98, 115

disjunction
> Logical operator "∨" ('or'):
>
> A ∨ B is true if and only if at least A or B is true.
>
> Consult Appendix, *5.1*, p. 352.
> See pp. 84, 128, 131, 137, 206, 348, **352**–353

distinctive number
> See lexicographic number.

Ellipsis
> Syntactic operation whereby some repeated occurrences of a phrase in the DSyntS are deleted in the SSyntS; e.g.:
> *John travelled to England and Mary [traveled] to Spain. |*
> *John can play the guitar, and Mary [can play the guitar] too.*
> See pp. 75, 259

'entity'
> Class of semantemes denoting objects, living beings, substances, places, etc.; e.g.: 'Sun', 'boy', 'sand', 'water', 'ravine', 'city'.
> Cf. 'fact'.
> See pp. 36, 40, 60–61, 84, 111, 156, **194**

equinomy
> Binary relation between two LUs L_1 and L_2 whose signifieds are different and signifiers identical; equinomy is either homonymy or polysemy.
> Consult Ch. 9 Definition 9.8, p. 249.
> Cf. synonymy.
> See pp. **9**, 93, 152, **249**–**250**, 269, 363

---

[1] Morphological dependencies are not considered here, because their logical properties are too involved to be discussed in this textbook.

equivalence relation
> Relation that is reflexive, symmetric and transitive.
> Consult Appendix, *3.2*, p. 349.
> See pp. 39–40, 74, 94, 184–185, 236–238, 241, 243, 286, 311–312, 334–335, **349**, 351, 352

equivalence rule (= paraphrasing rule)
> See rule, equivalence.

equivalent (semantic representations)
> $SemR_1$ and $SemR_2$ are equivalent if and only if one can be transformed into the other (of course, without affecting the meaning represented) by some rules of the language.
> See pp. 21, 25, 26, 28, 57, 73, 75, 83, 90, 119, 124, 236, 243, 259, 269, 329, 334–336, 349, 353

·**F**act'
> Class of semantemes denoting states, processes, properties, actions, events, etc.; e.g.: 'grief', 'be.located [somewhere]', 'sick', 'expensive', 'write', 'explode'. Cf. 'entity'.
> See pp. 5, 36, 40, 61, 84, 130, 147, 156, 174, 190, 194, 206, 211, 213, 222, 247, 333

factive verb
> Verb that accepts the complement clause *that P* and whose meaning includes a presupposed component '⟦P being true⟧'; e.g.: the sentences *He regrets that John left* and *He does not regret that John left* both imply that John has left because REGRET is a factive verb.
> See pp. 138, **247**, 277

feature of syntactics
> See syntactic feature.

fictitious lexeme
> Lexeme that does not exist in the language but is introduced (by the linguist) into the DSyntS in order to represent a meaningful syntactic construction. E.g.: *Had John not worn* [*the seatbelt, he wouldn't be alive.*], where the syntactic construction with inversion *Had John...* expresses the meaning of an irreal conditional (= 'if John had not worn...'); in the deep-syntactic structure this meaning is represented by the fictitious lexeme «IF_{IRR}».
> See pp. **290**–291, 319–320

Fillmore, Charles
> American linguist (1929–2014), whose contributions are especially influential in semantics and syntax.
> See pp. 96, 129

finite (verbal form)
> See verbal form, finite.

formal language
> Logical system designed for the description of objects and their relations in a particular domain; it is specified by 1) its vocabulary (= list of elementary symbols), 2) formation rules (rules for constructing well-formed formulae), and 3) transformation rules (rules establishing equivalence between formulae).
> Consult Appendix, *4*, p. 350.
> See pp. 7, 10, 77, 79, 119, 204, 259, **350**–351

Frege, Gottlob
> German mathematician, logician and philosopher (1848–1925), known in particular for establishing the distinction between Sense (or, in our terms, linguistic meaning) and Reference (Ger. *Sinn* vs. *Bedeutung*).
> See p. 36

frozenness (of a phraseme)
> Characteristics of a phraseme from the viewpoint of its modifiability, i.e., its (in)ability to accept modification, different inflectional values, different linear arrangements of its elements, etc.
> See p. 113

functional model
> See model, functional

Government

> One of the two types of morphological dependency (the other one being agreement): the wordform $\mathbf{w}_1$ is said to be governed by the wordform $\mathbf{w}_2$ if and only if some grammemes of $\mathbf{w}_1$ are determined by some features of the syntactics of $\mathbf{w}_2$; e.g.:
>
> Fr. *le*$_{\text{ACC-w}_1}$ *remercier*$_{\text{w}_2}$ lit. 'him thank'
> or
> Ger. *ihm*$_{\text{DAT-w}_1}$ *danken*$_{\text{w}_2}$ lit. 'to.him thank',
>
> where the verb determines the case of the object.
> Consult Ch. 2, *1.3.1*, p. 42.
> See p. 42

government pattern [GP] (of an LU L)
> Table that describes the actants of the headword L: L's diathesis, the surface form of L's SSynt-actants, their combinability, etc.
> Consult Ch. 2, *1.3.3*, Def. 2.10, and Ch. 8, *2.2.3*.
> See pp. 45, **46**, 148, 164, 210, 211, 213, 290, 296, 362

governor, syntactic (of an LU L)
> LU L' on which the LU L depends syntactically; e.g.:
>
> *some*←**synt**–*grammemes*; *Chapter*–**synt**→*11*;
> *John*←**synt**–*is*–**synt**→*working*.
>
> See pp. 41–46, 51, 287, 293–296, 326, 341

grammar (of a language)
> One of the two major components of a language description, the other one being the lexicon. (Grammar itself consists of semantics, syntax, morphology, and phonology.)
> Consult *Table 2.4*, p. 54.
> See pp. 17, 18, 53, **54**–55, **312**, 350–351

graph
> Formal object consisting of points (= nodes) connected by lines (= edges); nodes represent elements of a set, and edges, relations between them.
> Consult Ch. 2, *1.6.1*, p. 51.
> See pp. **14**, **51**, 259, **260**, 264, 287, 327, 366

Green-Apresjan criterion
>One of the two criteria used for wordsense discrimination.
>Consult Ch. 5, *3.2*, p. 128, and Mel'čuk 2013, pp. 324–334.

Head, syntactic (of a phrase P)
>LU L on which all other LUs of P depend syntactically—directly or indirectly;
>e.g.: *South Korean warships* **conducted** *live-fire exercises.* | **Hold** *infinity in the palm of your hand* [W. Blake]. | *what wives and children* **say**.
>See pp. **41**–42, 51, 113

head switching
>Operation of transition from a SemS to a DSyntS under which a configuration of semantemes 'σ_1'–**sem**→'σ_2' corresponds to the configuration of lexemes L('σ_1')←**synt**–L('σ_2'); e.g.:

$$\text{'red–}\textbf{sem}\rightarrow\underline{\text{button}}\text{'} \Leftrightarrow \text{RED}\leftarrow\textbf{synt}\text{–BUTTON.}$$

>See pp. 26, 237, 333–**335**, 341

headword (of a dictionary article)
>LU L described by the given dictionary article.
>See pp. 98, 115, 120, **209**, 211, 317

homonymy (of linguistic expressions **E**$_1$ and **E**$_2$)
>Relation between two linguistic expressions **E**$_1$ and **E**$_2$ whose signifiers are identical and signifieds do not share a semantic bridge (a particular case of equinomy); e.g.: BOX$_{(N)}$[1] 'container' ~ BOX$_{(N)}$[2] 'sport'. Homonymy is indicated by superscripts.
>Consult Definition 6.10. p. 157.
>See pp. 9, 108, **157**, 250, 359

hyperonym (of L)
>LU L' of whose denotation L's denotation is a particular case; e.g.: VEHICLE is a hyperonym of TRUCK; MOVE$_{(V)}$ is a hyperonym of FLY$_{(V)}$.
>See p. 194

hyponym (of L)
>LU L' whose denotation is a particular case of L's denotation; e.g.: TRUCK is a hyponym of VEHICLE; FLY$_{(V)}$ is a hyponym of MOVE$_{(V)}$.
>See p. 141

Idiom
>Non-compositional lexemic phraseme; e.g.: ⌐ALL THUMBS⌐ 'very awkward' or ⌐HIT THE ROAD⌐ '[to] leave'.
>Consult Ch. 4, *2.2.2.1*, p. 107.
>See pp. 16, 38, 40, 47, 54, 79, 98, 104, 106, **107**–108, 110, 112, 113, 114, 115, 130, 134, 136, 154, 209, 210, 226, 228, 269, 272, 289, 297, 306, 307, 313, 317, 356

illocutionary frame
>Semanteme configuration that indicates the type of communication act encoded by a given SemS (statement, order, expression of an internal state, etc.).
>Consult Ch. 10, *3.2*, p. 270.
>See pp. 269–**270**, 278–279

inflectional category
> Set of mutually opposed grammemes; e.g.:
> nominal number = {SG, PL}; verbal tense = {PRES, PAST, FUT}.
> See pp. 37, **62**, 191, 271, 292, 365

inheritance, lexical
> Sharing, by LUs that belong to the same taxonomic semantic class, of semantic, syntactic and restricted lexical cooccurrence properties of the LU corresponding to the semantic label of this class.
> Consult Ch. 8, *1.2.3*, pp. 196–197.
> See p. 206

inversion of subordination
> See head switching.

isomorphism
> Binary relation between two structured sets **A** and **B** such that 1) there is a one-to-one correspondence between elements $a_i \in A$ and elements $b_i \in B$ and 2) for any pair a_i–r–a_j, the corresponding pair b_i, b_j is linked by the same relation –r–.
> Consult Appendix, *3.3*, p. 350.
> See p. 10

Jakobson, Roman
> Russian-American linguist, semiotician and literary theorist (1896–1982), whose contributions to linguistics span phonology, morphology, syntax, and semantics.
> See p. 4.

Leibnitz, Gottfried Wilhelm
> German mathematician and philosopher (1646–1716), who created a semantic metalanguage called *Characteristica Universalis*.
> See p. 78

lexeme
> Set of wordforms and phrases (representing analytical forms) that differ only by inflectional significations.
> Consult Ch. 4, Definition 4.1, p. 101.
> See pp. 23, 34, 40, 51, 54, 56, 63–64, 79, **101**–102, 110, 115, 148–149, 188, 266, 278, 289, 305, 313, 315, 359, 361

lexical anchor (of a cliché)
> LU identifying the situation in which this cliché is used; it can be or not part of the cliché; e.g.: the cliché *What time is it?* has the lexeme TIME$_{(N)}$'2 as anchor; the anchors of the cliché *Emphasis added* are the lexemes TEXT, QUOTATION and EMPHASIZE; etc.
> See pp. 99, **115**, 182, 214, 356

lexical entry
> See dictionary article.

lexical field
> Set of all LUs such that the basic LUs of their vocables belong to the same semantic field; cf. semantic field.
> Consult Ch. 8, Definition 8.5, p. 199.
> See pp. 200–202, 208

meaning, linguistic (of an expression **E**)

Invariant of all paraphrases of **E**.

Consult Ch. 3, p. 69*ff* and Definition 3.1, p. 71.

See pp. xvii–xix, 4–12, 18–20, 28, 32, 38, 47–49, 63, **70–72**, 73–74, 77–79, 81, 89, 90, 98*ff*, 101, 111, 117, 133, 135–136, 162, 229–231, 234, 258–259, 268–269, 290, 314, 343

—«—«—, inherent vs. contextual

The meaning of a linguistic entity is inherent iff it is attached to it in any context this entity can appear; it is contextual iff it is attached to it only in a few particular contexts.

See p. 110

—«—«—, propositional vs. communicative vs. rhetorical

The meaning of a linguistic entity is propositional iff it can be expressed by logical propositions; it is communicative iff it identifies the communicative organization of the sentence; it is rhetorical iff it identifies the rhetorical intentions of the Speaker.

See pp. 20, 76–77, 80, 255–257, 291

meaning-bearing (= meaningful) syntactic construction

Construction that itself expresses some meaning; e.g.:

$$N_1 \ by \ N_2 \ \text{'[treating] one N after another'}$$
$$(cleaning \ the \ office \ room \ by \ room)$$

Such a construction is represented in the DSyntS by a fictitious lexeme; in this case, by «ONE.AFTER.ANOTHER».

See pp. 47, 98, 290, 294, 319

metaphor (of 'σ_1')

Relation that links two meanings 'σ_1' and 'σ_2' such that 'σ_2' contains 'σ_1' and the denotation of 'σ_2' is similar to the denotation of 'σ_1'; within 'σ_2', the meaning 'σ_1' is introduced by a semanteme that indicates its role—such as '⌐as if⌐ it were …'. E.g.: 'heart**II.1**' (*of the problem*) is a metaphor of 'heart**I.1**' (*of John*), since 'heart**II.1** of X' = 'central point of X—⌐as if⌐ it were the heart**I.1** of X'.

Consult Ch. 6, Definition 6.9, p. 156.

See pp. 73, 101, 130, 153, **156**, 218, 220, 358

metonymy (of 'σ_1')

Relation that links two meanings 'σ_1' and 'σ_2' such that 'σ_2' contains 'σ_1' and the denotation of 'σ_2' is contiguous to the denotation of 'σ_1'; e.g.: 'heart**I.2**' (*He pressed his hands to his heart.*) is a metonymy of 'heart**I.1**' (*of John*), since 'heart**I.2** of X' = 'part of X's chest were X's heart**I.1** is'.

Consult Definition 6.8, p. 156.

See pp. **156**, 220, 340, 358

model, linguistic (of language **L**)

A logical device (consisting of a set of rules for **L**) that simulates the linguistic activity of speakers of **L** (i.e., speech production and speech comprehension). A linguistic model is necessarily functional, in the following two senses: 1) it represents the functioning, rather than the structure, of **L**; 2) it models **L** as a mathematical function, i.e., a mapping from meanings of **L** to texts of **L** and vice versa.

See pp. xvii, 8, 10–15, 18, 27, 53, 70, 99, 100, 202, 234–235, 312, 343

modifier (of LU L)
> LU L′ that syntactically depends on L, but semantically
> bears on L; e.g.:

$$\overset{sem}{\underset{synt}{\textit{red apple}_L}}, \quad \overset{sem}{\underset{synt}{\textit{seen}_L}} \textit{ after eye surgery}, \text{ etc.}$$

> Cf. actant.
> See pp. 42, 43, 44, 88–89, 113, 133, 138, 212, 294–297, 344, 366

—«—«—, descriptive
> Modifier of an LU L that does not define a subset of entities specified by L,
> but only adds a non-definitorial characterization to 'L'; e.g.:

> *These books*$_L$[, *sold in our bookstore,*]$_{L's\ Descr.Modif.}$ *are affordable.*

> Consult Ch. 11, *2.4.2.2*, p. 303.

—«—«—, restrictive
> Modifier of an LU L that defines a subset of entities specified by L; e.g.:

> *The books*$_L$ [*sold in our bookstore*]$_{L's\ Restrict.Modif.}$ *are affordable.*

> Consult Ch. 11, *2.4.2.2*, p. 302.

module (of a linguistic model)
> Component of a linguistic model: a set of rules ensuring the transition between the
> adjacent levels of representation of utterances (foreseen by the linguistic model).
> See pp. **12, 13**, 14, 18, 53

—«—«—, deep-syntactic
> The module ensuring the transition between the deep-syntactic and sur-
> face-syntactic representations of utterances.
> See pp. 14, 284, 335

—«—«—, morphological
> The module ensuring the transition between the morphological and phonolog-
> ical representations of utterances.
> See p. 14

—«—«—, phonological
> The module of a linguistic model ensuring the transition between the phono-
> logical and phonetic representations of utterances.
> See p. 14

—«—«—, semantic
> The module ensuring the transition between the semantic and deep-syntactic
> representations of utterances.
> See pp. 14, 18–25, 255, 311–312

—«—«—, surface-syntactic
> The module ensuring the transition between the surface-syntactic and
> deep-morphological representations of utterances.
> See pp. 14, 284

mood
> Inflectional category of the verb whose grammemes indicate the way the cor-
> responding fact is viewed/reported by the Speaker: as objective (the indica-
> tive mood), as hypothetical (the conditional mood), as possible or wished for
> (the subjunctive mood), as an injunction (the imperative mood), and so on.
> See pp. 57, 58, 75, 174, 241, 292, 319

morphological module
> See module (of a linguistic model), morphological.

morphological representation
> See representation, morphological.

morphologization
> Semantic operation whereby the inflectional subscripts to lexical nodes (of the syntactic structure) are constructed.
> See pp. 53, 312, 320

N ame, semantic
> Meaning denoting an entity and having no slots for other meanings; e.g.: 'sand', 'Moon', 'girl', 'rhinoceros', 'hill'.
> See pp. 84–**85**, 121, 194, 260, 264, 355

Natural Language Processing
> Interdisciplinary field at the crossroads of computer science, artificial intelligence and computational linguistics, concerned with devising computer programs capable of treating natural language. Some of the NLP tasks include automatic text generation, summarizing and reformulation, machine translation, automatic text analysis (= parsing), speech recognition and synthesis; etc.
> See pp. 7, 8, 28, 142, 183, 344

Natural Semantic Metalanguage
> Semantic metalanguage based on a few dozen semantic primes established by A. Wierzbicka.
> See pp. 7, 78, **92**, 194.

network, semantic
> Graph that is fully connected, fully directed and fully labeled: used to represent the meaning of linguistic expressions.
> Consult Ch. 10, *2.1.1*, p. 260.
> See pp. xvii, 8, 11, 14, 27, 51, 79, 83, 90, 97, 119–120, 259–261, 264–265, 328, 351

nomineme
> Non-compositional semantic lexical phraseme (= a compound proper name); e.g.: *Medicine Hat* (a Canadian city), *Brown shirts* (a paramilitary wing of the Nazi party), *Saint-Bartholomew's Day* (the massacre of Protestants by Catholics in Paris in 1572).
> Consult Ch. 4, Definition 4.7, p. 111.
> See pp. 98, 104, 105, **111**, 114–115

non-finite (verbal form)
> See verbal form, non-finite.

O pacity (of a phraseme)
> See transparency.

P aradigm (of a lexeme L)
> The set of all inflectional forms of L. E.g.: the paradigm of the noun SISTER is as follows: {**sister, sisters, a sister, the sisters, sister's, a sister's, the sister's, sisters', the sisters'**}.
> See pp. **34**, 61, 64, 210, 258

paraphrase (of sentence *S*)

> Sentence *S'* that is synonymous with sentence *S*; e.g.:
>
> S: *Two brothers of Egyptian origin were arrested in France while preparing to commit an attack.* ≡
>
> S': *The French police captured two brothers, originally from Egypt, who were getting ready to perpetrate an attack.*
>
> See pp. 13, 19, 20, 21, 70–72, 94, 125, 127, 143, 164, 235–245, 256, 283, 308, 309, 327–329, 331, 332, 334, 336–338, 341, 355, 362, 363, 364, 368, 369

partition (of a set)

> Division of a set in subsets that do not intersect; e.g.: {1, 2, 3} and {4, 5, 6} represent a partition of the set {1, 2, 3, 4, 5, 6}, while {1, 2, 3, 4} and {4, 5, 6} do not.
>
> See pp. 271, 305

performative expression

> Expression such that uttering it constitutes the act denoted by it; e.g.: by uttering *Thank you!* the Speaker performs the act of thanking the Addressee.
>
> Consult Ch. 10, Definition 10.15, p. 277.
>
> See pp. **138**, 223, 224, 277, 278–279, 365

peripheral structure

> See structure, peripheral (of a linguistic representation).

phone (of **L**)

> An articulated sound of language **L**: e.g.:

$$\text{Eng. [t] } (steak) \text{ and } [t^h] \ (take).$$

> See p. 14

phoneme (of **L**)

> The set of all phones of **L** whose articulatory/acoustical differences are never used in **L** to distinguish signs; e.g.:

$$\text{Eng. } /t/ = \{[t] \ (stick), [t^h] \ (tick), [?] \ (kitten)\};$$
$$/d/ = \{[d] \ (kid), [\mathfrak{r}] \ (kiddy)\}.$$

> See pp. **13**, 32, 61, 104

phonemic representation

> See representation, phonemic.

phonetic representation

> See representation, phonetic.

phonetic (= narrow) transcription

> See transcription, phonetic (= narrow).

phonological module

> See module, phonological.

phonology$_1$

> Component of a language responsible for the correspondence

$$\{DPhonR_{j-1}\} \Leftarrow phonology_1 \Rightarrow \{SPhonR_j\}$$

> See p. 5

phonology$_2$

> Branch of linguistics that is responsible for describing phonologies$_1$ of individual languages.
>
> See p. 5

phrase
>   Utterance that consists of syntactically linked wordforms, features a prosodic unity, but is not necessarily a unit of communication.
>   Consult Ch. 2, Definition 2.14, p. 57.
>   See pp. 4, 13, 18, 37, 41, 55, **57**, 80, 101, 102, 103, 104, 106, 108, 158, 172, 197, 212, 271, 274, 340, 356, 357

phraseme
>   Phrase in which the selection of components is constrained (= phrase that is not free); four major classes of phrasemes are idioms, nominemes, collocations and clichés.
>   Consult Ch. 4, Definition 4.2, p. 105.
>   See pp. 38, 98*ff*, 115, 132, 136, 158, 185, 289

—«—«—, lexemic
>   Phraseme constrained with respect to its meaning (= its semantic representation); lexemic phrasemes come in two varieties: idioms and collocations.
>   Consult Ch. 4, Definition 4.3, p.105
>   See pp. 102–103, **105**, 107, 109, 289

—«—«—, semantic-lexemic
>   Phraseme constrained with respect to its conceptual representation; semantic-lexemic phrasemes come in two varieties: nominemes and clichés.
>   See pp. 105, 111

plurale tantum ('plural only')
>   Noun having only the plural form; e.g.:

$$\text{TROUSERS}_{(PL!)} \text{ or SMITHEREENS}_{(PL!)}.$$

>   Cf. *singulare tantum.*
>   See p. 139

polysemy
>   Relation between two LUs whose signifiers are identical and whose signifieds share a semantic bridge.
>   Consult Ch. 6, Definition 6.7, p. 154.
>   See pp. 9, 118, 132, 136, 141, 149, 151, 152–158, 188, 189, 216, 220, 250, 259

predicate, semantic
>   Meaning denoting a fact and having "slots" for other meanings without which it is incomplete; e.g.: 'intelligent(X)' [*X is intelligent*], 'love(X,Y)' [*X loves Y*], 'under(X, Y)' [*X is under Y*], 'order(X, Y, Z)' [*X orders Y to do Z*], 'buy(X, Y, Z, W)' [*X buys Y from Z for W*], etc.
>   See pp. 40, 41, 43, **83–84**, 86, 87, 89–93, 96, 106, 109, 131, 137, 162, 169, 174, 194, 211, 260, 263–264, 294, 296, 322, 334, 353, 354

predicate calculus
>   Branch of formal logic that deals with propositions consisting of predicates and their arguments.
>   Consult Appendix, *5.2*, p. 535.
>   See pp. 41, 77–79, 119, 351, 353

prefix
>   Affix that precedes the radical; e.g.:

$$\textit{re}+consider \text{ or } \textbf{\textit{un}}+constitutional.$$

>   See pp. 31, 55, 56, 63–64, 82, 316

presupposition

> Part '$[\![\sigma']\!]$' of the meaning 'σ' that is not negated or questioned when the whole 'σ' is negated or questioned—that is, '$[\![\sigma']\!]$' is not accessible to negation or interrogation. E.g.: the sentence *John knows that Mary is in town* presupposes 'Mary is in town'; this presupposed meaning remains unaffected when the sentence is negated or questioned: both sentences *John does not know that Mary is in town* and *Does John know that Mary is in town?* presuppose that Mary is in town.
>
> Consult Ch. 9, Definition 9.7, p. 246.
>
> See pp. 95, 129–130, 135, 137, 138, 146, 147, 233, **246**–249, 276–277, 363

principles for compiling ECDs

> Consult Ch. 8, *2.1.2*, p. 204*ff*.

propositional form

> Expression consisting of the headword L and the variables specifying the Sem-actants of L; e.g.:
>
> X *replaces* Y *with* Z; X, *important to* Y; X*'s bed.*
>
> Consult Ch. 5, *2*, Propositional Form Rule, p. 121.
>
> See pp. 70, 89, 118, 120–122, 137, 354

pronominalization

> Syntactic operation whereby some repeated occurrences of LUs in the DSyntS are replaced by substitute pronouns in the SSyntS.
>
> See pp. 75, 259, 282, 286, 307, 308, 326

pronoun, substitute

> Pronoun used instead of a noun, which is its source; e.g.: HE, SHE, THEY, IT, WHICH, etc.
>
> See pp. 80, 120, **261**, 288, 307

prosody

> Suprasegmental expressive means of language: stress, intonation contours, pauses.
>
> See pp. 39, 49, 50, 52, 57, 210, 241, 249, 273, 274, 276, 284, 286, 295

Quasi-predicate

> Meaning denoting an entity (as a semantic name), but having "slots" for other meanings (as does a semantic predicate); e.g.:
>
> 'brother OF $_{\text{person}}$Y', 'head OF $_{\text{person}}$X', 'roof OF $_{\text{building}}$X', etc.
>
> Consult Ch. 3, *3.1.2*, p. 85.
>
> See pp. **85**–86, 89, 122, 194, 211, 314, 322, 354–355

Radical

> Morph that is obligatorily contained in any wordform[2] and whose syntactics 1) is similar to the syntactics of the majority of morphs of the language and 2) contributes the majority of features to the syntactics of the wordform to which it belongs; e.g.: **finger-** in *finger+Ø* and *finger+s*, **fast** in *fast*, **formulat(e)-** in *formulat+ing*, etc.

---

[2] This formulation leaves out megamorphs – amalgamated realizations of strings of morphemes, such as **me** ⇔ {I}⊕{OBL} or **am** ⇔{BE}⊕{IND.PRES}⊕{1.SG}.

> **NB:** The term *radical* is used in this book strictly in its synchronic sense; *root* is reserved for historical (= diachronic, or etymological) radical. Thus, the radical of the noun EXPRESSION is **expression-**, while its root is **press-** ⇐ Proto-Indo-European ****per**[6]- ≈ 'strike'.[3]

Consult Mel'čuk, I. 1997. *Cours de morphologie générale. Vol. 4, Montréal/ Paris*: Les Presses de l'Université de Montréal/CNRS, 59*ff* [radical ≡ *racine synchronique*].

See pp. 31–34, 52, 56–57, 62, 64, 82, 102, 150

referent (of a linguistic sign **s**)

Fact or entity in the extralinguistic world (real or imaginary) to which the sign **s** refers in the given utterance.

Cf. denotation.

See pp. 35–37, 40, 74–75, 78, 111, 133, 135, 249, 256–257, 264, 267–268, 275, 286, 306

reflexivity

Property of a binary relation **R**: $\mathbf{R}(a, b) \rightarrow \mathbf{R}(a, a)$.

See pp. 86, 293, 348

relation, syntactic

Relation of syntactic dependency between two LUs.

Consult Ch. 2, Definition 2.4, p. 41, and Ch. 11, *2.4*, p. 293.

See pp. 23, 47, 48, 51, 242, 251, 286, 287, 290, 293, 294–305

representation (linguistic)

Formal object designed to represent a particular aspect of linguistic entities; consists of several structures whose character depends on the level of representation.

Consult Ch. 2, *1.6.1*, p. 50.

See pp. xviii, 10–13, 14–16, 50–52, 77, 100, 256, 268, 285, 310

—«—«—, conceptual

Representation of the informational content of a sentence at a prelinguistic level: a network composed of discrete concepts that are as language-independent as possible and of the relations between them.

Consult Ch. 1, *2.4*, p. 27.

See pp. 15, 27–28, 75

—«—«—, deep-syntactic

Representation of the formal organization of sentences at the deep-syntactic level.

Consult Ch. 11, *1*, p. 284*ff* and Definition11.1, p. 285.

See pp. 8, 13, 19, 53, 281, 308, 310, 346, 365

—«—«—, morphological[4]

Representation of the linear organization of sentences in terms of fully inflected lexemes.

Consult Ch. 1, *2.2.2*, p. 13 and Ch. 2, *1.6.1*, p. 52.

See p. 13

---

[3] In diachronic linguistics an asterisk in front of a sign is used to indicate that this sign is reconstructed.

[4] The morphological representations (deep and surface) of wordforms are not considered in this textbook.

—«—«—, phonemic (= phonological)
  Representation of texts in terms of phonemes and prosodemes. Cf. transcription, broad (= phonemic).
  Consult Ch. 1, *2.2.2*, p. 13.
  See pp. 13–14, 32, 77
—«—«—, phonetic
  Representation of texts in terms of allophones and allo-prosodies. Cf. transcription, narrow (= phonetic).
  Consult Ch. 1, *2.2.2*, p. 14.
  See pp. 14, 28, 77
—«—«—, semantic
  Representation of the common meaning of a set of synonymous sentences.
  Consult Ch. 10, *1*, p. 255*ff* and Definition 10.1, p. 257.
  See pp. xix, 13, 18, 21, 27, 49, 72, 75–76, 77–80, 90, 118, 229, 242–243, 292, 343, 363
—«—«—, surface-syntactic
  Representation of formal organization of sentences at the surface-syntactic level.
  Consult Ch. 11 p. 285.
  See pp. 15, 46, 51–52, 83–84, 88–89, 147, 211–212, 226, 288, 293–294, 297, 307–308
rule (linguistic)
  Formal expression specifying a correspondence between linguistic objects.
  Consult Ch. 2, *1.6.2*, p. 52.
  See pp. 4, 11–15, 19, 243, 264, 269, 352
  equivalence (= paraphrasing) —«—«—
    Rule specifying the equivalence between two linguistic objects of the same level of representation: $X \equiv Y \mid C$.
    Consult *Figure 12.1*, p. 311.
    See pp. 19, 21, 22, 184, 243–245, 308, 314*ff*
  filter —«—«—
    Rule specifying the well-formedness of a linguistic entity.
    See pp. 266, 310
  transition (= expression) —«—«—
    Rule specifying the transition between two linguistic objects of two adjacent levels of representation: $X \Leftrightarrow Y \mid C$.
    Consult Ch. 2, Definition 2.11, p. 52 and *Figure 12.1*, p. 311.
    See pp. 19, 22–23, 26, 53, 311, 312*ff*
rules for formulating lexicographic definitions
  Consult Ch. 5, *2*, p. 121*ff*.

Saussure, Ferdinand de
  Swiss linguist and semiotician (1857–1913), one of the founders of modern linguistics and semiotics; see Saussure 1916.
  See pp. 31, 38.

—«—«—, presupposed

> Component (of the definiens) that expresses the presupposed part of the meaning of the LU under description—that is, the part that cannot be negated or questioned.
> See pp. 129, 138, 146, 247, 248

—«—«—, weak

> Component (of the definiens) that becomes suppressed in particular contexts (= whose presence is not necessary for the LU to be used).
> See pp. 129, 137

semantic decomposition

> Representation of a linguistic meaning in terms of simpler linguistic meanings.
> Consult Ch. 3, *4*, p. 89*ff*.
> See pp. 24, 72, 117, 119, 121–122, 124, 126, 153, 241, 243–244, 263, 313–315, 327–328, 332, 334, 356, 364, 367

semantic dependency

> Dependency of an argument of a predicate on this predicate:

$$\text{`}\sigma_1\text{'}\text{--}\mathbf{sem}\rightarrow\text{`}\sigma_2\text{'}, \text{ where `}\sigma_1\text{'}(\text{`}\sigma_2\text{'}).$$

> Consult Definition 2.3, p. 40.
> See pp. **86–87**, 262, 294, 296, 349

semantic distance (between LUs L_1 and L_2)

> Semantic distance between L_1 and L_2 is inversely proportional to the quantity and importance of shared semantic material and directly proportional to the regularity of the semantic difference between them.
> Consult Ch. 8, *2.3.2*, p. 218.
> See pp. 154, 216, **218**, 241

semantic field

> Set of LUs whose definitions share a semantic bridge; e.g.: the $\mathbf{F}^{\text{Sem}}_{\text{cook}}$. contains all LUs carrying the semanteme 'cook' (the names of dishes, of cooking ustensils, of types of cooking, etc.).
> Cf. lexical field.
> Consult Ch. 8, *1.3*, p. 198.
> See pp. 118, 153, 187, 194, 199–202, 207, 361

semantic label (of LU L)

> Expression that, based on the definition of L, determines L's semantic class.
> Consult Ch. 8, *1.2.2*, p. 191.
> See pp. 84, 118, 127, 187, **192**–199, 210, 221, 223, 224, 225, 226, 361

semantic module (of a linguistic model)

> See module, semantic.

semantic pivot

> See Ch. 4, Definition 4.4, p. 106.

semantic primitive/prime

> Simple meaning (= semanteme) of language **L** that cannot be decomposed in terms of other meanings of **L**; e.g.: 'no', 'time1', 'speak', 'feel1', 'good', 'this', etc.
> Consult Ch. 3, *4.1.3*, p. 92.
> See pp. 90, 92, 117, 120, 124, 153, 194

semantic representation

    See representation, semantic.

semantic role

    Semantic relation between an argument of a predicate and this predicate; e.g.: in the sentence *John washed the shirt with soap*, JOHN is the Actor, SHIRT is the Patient, and SOAP, the Means.

    Consult Ch. 3, *4.2.3*, p. 96.

    See pp. 96–97

semantics$_1$

    Component of a language responsible for the correspondence between semantic representations and deep-syntactic representations:

$$\{\text{SemR}_i\} \Leftarrow \text{semantics}_1 \Rightarrow \{\text{DSyntR}_k\}.$$

    See pp. **3–7**, 18, 28, 69, 255, 310

semantics$_2$

    Branch of linguistics responsible for the description of the semantics$_1$ of individual languages.

    See pp. **3–7**

sense discrimination

    Operation performed by the lexicographer in order to distinguish different wordsenses of one polysemous word—that is, to establish different lexemes within a vocable.

    Consult Ch. 8, *2.3.1*, p. 216.

    See pp. 137, 196, **215–216**

sentence

    Maximal utterance that typically consists of clauses and is a complete unit of communication.

    Consult Definition 2.16, p. 58.

    See pp. xvii, 4, 5, 13, 34, 59, 228, 229, 230–234, 241–244, 250, 279, 284

shifter

    Sign whose signified includes a reference to the Speaker; e.g.: **I** 'individual who says *I*', **now** 'moment when I say *now*', **yesterday** 'the day immediately preceding the day when I say *yesterday*', etc.

    See p. 17

sign, linguistic

    Triplet X; Y; Z, where X is the signified, Y the signifier, and Z the syntactics; e.g.:

    page$_{(N)}{}^1$ = '<one side of a piece of paper in...'; /péǯ/; Σ = N, countable, ...>

    Consult Ch. 2, *1.1* Definition 2.1, p. 31*ff.*

    See pp. **31**, 35–36, 37–39, 53–56, 61–62, 80, 102, 158, 209, 346

signal$_{(V)}$

    To express meanings by using clauses that do not that do not implement propositions: the Speaker targets a situation by a clause that cannot be negated or questioned. Cf. communicate.

    Consult Definition 10.14, p. 277.

    See pp. 58, 59, 73, 75, 208, 225, 269, **277–279**, 365

signification, linguistic

> Any type of information carried by a linguistic sign: a genuine meaning, a syntactic feature, a semantically empty grammeme, a stylistic characteristic, etc.
> Consult Ch. 2, *1.4*, p. 46 and *3.2*, p. 62.
> See pp. 46–49, 53, 61–63 120, 261, 291, 315

signifiers, their "shortage"

> Consult Ch. 4, *2.2.1*, p. 104.
> See pp. **104**, 158, 188

simpler, semantically

> Meaning 'σ_1' is simpler than the meaning 'σ_2' if and only if 'σ_2' can be decomposed using 'σ_1', but not vice versa.
> Consult Ch. 3, *4.1.1*, p. 90.
> See pp. 70, 72, **90**, 117, 120–121, 189, 356

singulare tantum ('singular only')

> Noun having only the singular form; e.g.:
> NEWS $_{(sg!)}$ or ⌐CUP OF TEA⌐ $_{(sg!)}$ (as in *It's not my cup of tea.*)
> Cf. *plurale tantum.*
> See pp. 139

source (of a pronoun L)

> LU in the DSyntS that is replaced by L in SSyntS; e.g.:
> *I saw John as ~~John~~ ⟺ he*$_L$ *was crossing the street.*
> (The first occurrence of JOHN is the antecedent of L.)
> See p. 307

Speaker, the

> The initiator of the given speech act; the person who says *I* in this speech act.
> Consult Ch. 1, *2.1*, p. 8.
> See pp. xvii–xviii, **8**, 10, 16–17, 20–21, 36, 38–39, 48, 75–77, 82, 95, 138, 223, 224, 270–272, 274–278

stem

> Radical taken together with derivational affixes; e.g.:
>
> **swimmer-** is the stem of the wordforms *swimmer, swimmers* and *swimmer's*;
> **unlucky-** is the stem of the wordforms *unlucky, unluckier* and *unluckiest*.
> Consult Ch. 2, *3.1.3*, p. 62.
> See pp. 31, 48, 57, 64, 80, 101, 102, 316

stratificational character (of a linguistic model)

> Property of the model consisting in reflecting different aspects of language by different modules related through interface representations.
> Consult Ch. 1, 2.2.2, p. 12*ff.*
> See pp. 10, 13, 15

string

> Tree without branching: each node receives no more than one entering arc and no more than one leaving arc; there is one node that receives no arc. A string is equivalent to a linear sequence.
> See pp. 11, 14, 32, **51**, 61, 77

strong inclusion (of meanings)

'L$_1$' strongly includes 'L$_2$', if and only if 1) 'L$_1$' includes 'L$_2$' and 2) 'L$_1$' and 'L$_2$' share the same central component; e.g.: STARE$_{(V)}$ strongly includes LOOK$_{(V)}$ since 'stare' ≈ 'look in a particular way'.

See pp. 143, **144**, 155

strong intersection (of meanings)

'L$_1$' and 'L$_2$' strongly intersect if and only if 1) 'L$_1$' and 'L$_2$' intersect and 2) 'L$_1$'and 'L$_2$' share the same central component; e.g.: METHOD1 'planned <u>way of doing</u> something, especially one that a lot of people know about and use' and MEANS1 '<u>way of doing</u> or achieving something' strongly intersect.

See p. 144

structural words

Lexical items that have no meaning of their own and are imposed by syntax.

See pp. 39, 48, 119

structure, peripheral

Structure that is a non-autonomous component of a linguistic representation—it is superposed on the basic structure and specifies some of its essential properties.

Consult Ch. 1, *2.2.2*, p. 16.

See pp. 16, 256, 259, 270, 285, 312

subordination

One of two major types of semantic/syntactic structure (the other one being coordination), which unites two elements playing "unequal" semantic/syntactic roles; e.g.: ***red←dresses*** | ***John←left***. | ***very←interesting***.

See pp. 295, 366

substitutability test

Test that allows the researcher to see whether two expressions can be included into the same unit of a higher level or be described by a common representation at some level: these expressions must be mutually substitutable at least in some contexts.

See pp. 121–122, **124**–126, 143, 241–242

suffix

Affix that follows the radical; e.g.: *chair+**s**, read+**ing**, read+**er***.

See pp. 17, 31, 32, 33, 42, 49, 55, 64, 80, 150, 151, 274, 289, 316, 320, 347

superentry

Structured set of lexical entries; it describes a vocable.

Consult Ch. 8, *2.3*, p. 215*ff*.

See pp. 188, 202

suppletion

Roughly, relation between two morphs that belong to the same morpheme but whose signifiers are not related by some alternations of the language; e.g.: **go**- ~ **wen**-(*t*), **good** ~ **bett**-(*er*) or Lat. **fer**-*(ō)* 'I carry' ~ **tul**-*(ī)* 'I carried'.

Consult Mel'čuk 2006: 409.

See p. 171

symmetry

Property of a binary relation **R**: **R**$(a, b) \rightarrow$ **R**(b, a).

See pp. 86, 293, **348**

synonymous (linguistic expressions $\mathbf{E}_1$ and $\mathbf{E}_2$)

Two linguistic expressions $\mathbf{E}_1$ and $\mathbf{E}_2$ such that their meanings are identical; e.g.: DRUNK$_{(ADJ)}$ and INTOXICATED, EYE DOCTOR and OPHTHALMOLOGIST, etc.

See pp. 13, 32, 103, 143, 162, 235–237, 241–242, 256, 257, 258, 269, 307, 348–349

synonyms

LUs 1) that have identical signifieds and different signifiers, 2) whose syntactic actants (if any) correspond one-to-one and 3) that belong to the same part of speech; e.g.:

SOFA ~ COUCH, BEHEAD ~ DECAPITATE, CRAZY ~ NUTS.

Consult Ch. 6, *1.1.1*, p. 142ff.

See pp. 23, 120–121, 142–146, 167–168, 187, 240–241, 289, 355, 358

synonymy (of linguistic expressions $\mathbf{E}_1$ and $\mathbf{E}_2$)

1) Identity of meaning of two linguistic expressions $\mathbf{E}_1$ and $\mathbf{E}_2$ ('$\mathbf{E}_1$' = '$\mathbf{E}_2$').
2) Relation between two LUs L_1 and L_2 that are synonyms (e.g., FILM ~ MOVIE).

Cf. equinomy.

Consult Definitions 6.1 and 6.2, pp. 142 and 143.

See pp. 9, 18, 22, 39, 70, 123, 141, 142–143, 229, 235, 236, 238–239, 269, 307, 348, 349

syntactic feature (of a lexical unit)

Indication of a cooccurrence property of an LU; e.g.: «postposed» is a syntactic feature of the adjectives that can follow the modified noun (*notary public, secretary general,* [*in*] *matters military, times immemorial*). The same as feature of the syntactics of the LU.

See pp. 34, 44, 210

syntactic module

See module, syntactic.

syntactics

One of the three components of a linguistic sign (along with the signified and the signifier) that contains information on the sign's cooccurrence with other signs in the form of a set of features; e.g.: the syntactics of the noun SCISSORS contains the following features:

"noun", "plural only", "quantification by Num *pair(s) of*".

See pp. 31, 33–35, 53, 103, 112, 210, 316

syntax$_1$

Component of a language responsible for the correspondence between deep-syntactic representations and deep-morphological representations:

$$\{DSyntR_k\} \Leftarrow syntax_1 \Rightarrow \{DMorphR_l\}$$

See p. 5

syntax$_2$

Branch of linguistics responsible for description of the syntaxes$_1$ of individual languages.

See p. 5

synthesis, linguistic (= speech production)

Operation whereby the Speaker goes from a meaning he wants to convey to the text that expresses this meaning: Text ⟹ Meaning; cf. analysis, linguistic.

See pp. xvii, 8, 10, 12–13, 16–23, 280, 307, 312, 343

synthetic expression

Expression in which a grammeme is realized by a morphological means; e.g.: Fr. *pardonne+r+a* 'will pardon', where the grammeme FUTURE is expressed by the suffix -**r**. Cf. analytic expression.

See pp. 48, 63

T ext (in the technical sense)

Physical (= superficial) expression of a meaning, in terms of speech sounds or graphic symbols.

See pp. 4, 8–11, 12, 55

transcription, phonemic (= broad)

Transcription showing phonemes; e.g.: /**pít**/ *pit* and /s**pít**/ *spit*.

See pp. 14, 32, 77

transcription, phonetic (= narrow)

Transcription showing allophones; e.g.: [**pʰít**] *pit* and [s**pít**] *spit*.

See pp. 14, 77

transition (= correspondence) rule

See rule, transition.

transitivity

Property of a binary relation **R**: **R**(a, b) ∧ **R**(b, c) → **R**(a, c).

See pp. 86–87, 349

transparency (of a phraseme)

Characteristic of the phraseme from the viewpoint of its comprehensibility by speakers of the language.

See pp. 108–109

tree, syntactic

Network satisfying two additional conditions:

1. Each node receives no more than one entering arc.

2. There is one and only one node that does not receive any arc; this node is the top node of the tree.

See pp. xvii, 14, 51, 251, 287–288

U nderlying question

Question **Q** formulated by the linguist in order to elicit the semantic-communicative structure of sentence *S*; this is a question to which *S* can be an appropriate answer. E.g.:

Q = "What about John?" allows for identification of the semantic Theme ([*John*]_{**TSem**} [*left for the South Pole*]_{**RSem**}.);

Q = "What did John do?" identifies the semantic Rheme ([*John*]_{**TSem**} [*left for the South Pole*]_{**RSem**}.).

See pp. 22, 26, 77, 239, 273, 281, 364

$\mathbf{V}$endler, Zeno

American philosopher of language (1921–2004), a pioneer in the study of semantics of lexical aspects, quantifiers, and modifiers.

See pp. 139, 191

verb, atelic

Verb whose meaning does not include an indication of the necessary limit of the fact denoted; e.g.: the meaning 'X is.sick' does not include a limit for the 'being.sick' process—semantically speaking, X can be sick forever.

See pp. 190–191, 210

—«—, light

Collocational verb that is semantically empty in the context of its base; e.g.: PAY in *pay attention* or LIE in *the responsibility lies with* N. Light verbs are elements of the value of lexical functional verbs Oper_i, Func_i and Labor_{ij}.

See pp. 174, 258, 336–337, 340

— « —, phasal

Verb that denotes a phase of an event—its beginning, continuation or cessation; e.g.: $\mathrm{START}_{(V)}$ or $\mathrm{STOP}_{(V)}$.

See pp. 179–180, 247

—«—, telic

Verb whose meaning includes an indication of the necessary limit of the fact denoted; e.g.: the meaning 'Y is.dying' includes the limit of the 'dying' process—namely 'Y is dead'.

See p. 191

verbal form, finite

Verbal form that expresses mood and, as a result, can constitute the syntactic head of a clause; e.g.: *reads, am, read!*

See pp. 42, 44, 57–58, 59, 212, 232

—«—«—, non-finite

Verbal form that does not express mood and, as a result, cannot constitute the syntactic head of a clause; e.g.: *reading,* [*to*] *be, written.*

See p. 58

vicious circle

Statement in which A is defined through B_1, B_2, ..., B_n and one of B_i contains A in its definition; e.g.: the following definitions, taken from LDOCE, contain a vicious circle (shaded): FRIGHTENED 'feeling afraid' and AFRAID 'frightened because you think that you may get hurt or that something bad can happen to you'.

Cf. circularity.

See pp. 90, 121–123, 357

vocable

Set of LUs related by polysemy. In the dictionary, a vocable is described by a superentry.

Consult Ch. 8, *1.1*, p. 187*ff.*

See pp. 79, 101, 107, 130, 132, 136, 154–155, 188–190, 198, 200–201, 202, 208, 216, 218–220, 358, 359, 361

Wierzbicka, Anna

Polish-Australian linguist, born 1938, one of the founders of modern semantics, creator of Natural Semantic Metalanguage.

See pp. 78, 89, 92–93, 125, 356

wordform

Segmental sign that is more or less autonomous and not representable in terms of other (previously established) wordforms.

Consult Definition 2.13, p. 56.

See pp. 31–34 48, 57, 63, 101

language —«—«—

Wordform that is autonomous enough to appear between two pauses or is similar to such a wordform; a language wordform belongs to a lexeme. E.g.: **computers**, **light**, **good**, **taking**, **them**.

See p. 56

speech   —«—«—

Wordform that is produced by syntactic rules that either:

1. split a language wordform in a particular context; e.g.: Ger. *Mache das Licht **aus**!* 'Switch off the light!', with the verbal lexeme AUSMACHEN 'switch off' (MACHEN means 'make', and AUS- corresponds to 'out'); in this sentence, **mache** and **aus** are speech wordforms, $\Rightarrow$; or

2. amalgamate two language wordforms in a particular context; e.g.: *want to* $\Rightarrow$ **wanna** or Fr. *à le* 'to the' $\Rightarrow$ **au** /o/.

A speech wordform does not belong to a lexeme.

See p. 56

wordsense

One sense of a polysemous word; corresponds to a lexical unit and is described by a lexical entry.

See pp. 54, 94, 110, 137, 188, 196, 358

Zeugma

Syntactic construction of the form "L–**synt**→L_1 *and* L_2," where L represents two homophonous lexemes L′ and L″ such that L′ is supposed to combine with L_1 and L″, with L_2. For instance: *You are free to **execute**$_L$ your laws$_{L_1}$ and your citizens$_{L_2}$*; or *a house where love$_{L_1}$ and money$_{L_2}$ **are made**$_L$*. A zeugma produces a pun.

See p. 217

Definition Index

Since in our approach the notional apparatus is so important (*Preface*, p. xvii, and Ch. 3, *2*, p. 78), we brought together here, for easy consultation, all the seventy-eight definitions of linguistic notions presented in this book.

 Recall that LU stands for "lexical unit" and iff means 'if and only if'.

Chapter 1

Definition 1.1: Natural Language (p. 4)
A (natural) language **L** is a set of rules encoded in the brains of its speakers that establish a correspondence between meanings of **L** and their expressions, or texts, of **L**.

Chapter 2

Definition 2.1: Linguistic Sign (p. 31)
A linguistic sign **s** is a triplet **s** = ⟨'s' ; /s/ ; Σ_s⟩, where 's' is the signified of **s**, /s/ is the signifier of **s**, and Σ_s is the syntactics of the pair ⟨'s' ; /s/⟩.

Definition 2.2: Linguistic Dependency (p. 40)
Linguistic dependency is a hierarchic (= antisymmetric) syntagmatic relation between two LUs in a sentence *S* or two semantemes in the semantic structure of *S*, one called governor and the other dependent.

Definition 2.3: Semantic Dependency (p. 40)
Semantic dependency is dependency between either two semantemes 'L_1' and 'L_2' that stand in a "predicate ~ argument" relation or two corresponding LUs in a sentence, L_1 and L_2: the governor (= predicate) determines the presence and the nature of the dependent (= argument) in the sentence.

Definition 2.4: Syntactic Dependency (p. 41)
Syntactic dependency is a dependency between two LUs in a sentence, L_1 and L_2, such that one, for instance, L_1, called the governor of L_2, determines the syntactic distribution – i.e., types of external syntactic links – of the whole phrase L_1–**synt**→L_2.

Definition 2.5: Morphological Dependency (p. 42)
Morphological dependency is a dependency between two LUs in a sentence, L_1 and L_2, such that at least some inflectional values of one, for instance, L_2, called target (= morphological dependent), are imposed by the other, L_1, which is the controller (= morphological governor).

411

Definition 2.6: Semantic Valence of a Lexical Unit (p. 44)
The semantic valence of an LU L is the set of all L's semantic actants – i.e., the set of L's semantic dependents filling the actantial slots in L's lexicographic definition.

Definition 2.7: Passive Syntactic Valence of a Lexical Unit (p. 44)
The passive syntactic valence of an LU L is the set of all syntactic constructions into which L can enter as a dependent.

Definition 2.8: Active Syntactic Valence of a Lexical Unit (p. 45)
The active syntactic valence of an LU L is the set of all syntactic constructions into which L enters as the governor of its actantial dependents, a.k.a. complements.

Definition 2.9: Diathesis of a Lexical Unit (p. 45)
The correspondence between the semantic actants of an LU L and its deep-syntactic actants is called the diathesis of L.

Definition 2.10: Government Pattern of a Lexical Unit (p. 46)
The Government Pattern of an LU L is a specification of L's basic diathesis, as well as of the surface-syntactic constructions and morphological means implementing L's deep-syntactic actants.

Definition 2.11: Transition Linguistic Rule (p. 52)
A transition linguistic rule is an expression of the form $X \Leftrightarrow Y \mid C$, where X is instantiated by some linguistic content and Y by what expresses this content; the bi-directional double arrow means 'corresponds to', and C represents the set of conditions (possibly empty) under which the correspondence in question is valid.

Definition 2.12: Utterance (p. 55)
An utterance is a linguistic expression that is more or less autonomous: it can appear between two major pauses, can constitute a prosodic unit, and its internal structure is governed by linguistic rules; an utterance is perceived by speakers as "something that exists in the language."

Definition 2.13: Wordform (p. 56)
A wordform is a segmental sign that is more or less autonomous and not representable in terms of other (previously established) wordforms.

Definition 2.14: Phrase (p. 57)
A phrase is an utterance that consists of syntactically linked wordforms supplied with an appropriate prosody and is perceived by the speakers as a unit of their language, but does not necessarily constitute a complete unit of communication.

Definition 2.15: Clause (p. 57)
A clause is a phrase that contains a finite verb with its actants or is syntactically equivalent to such a phrase (that is, it has the same syntactic distribution).

Definition 2.16: Sentence (p. 58)
A sentence is a maximal utterance that typically consists of clauses and is a complete unit of communication.

Definition 2.17: Elementary Sign (p. 61)
An elementary sign of language **L** is a sign that is not representable in terms of other signs of **L**.

Definition 2.18: Segmental Sign (p. 61)
A segmental sign is a sign whose signifier is a segment – a string of phonemes.

Definition 2.19: Morph (p. 61)
A morph is an elementary segmental sign.

Chapter 3

Definition 3.1: Linguistic Meaning (= The Meaning of a Linguistic Expression) (p. 71)
The meaning of an expression **E** of language **L** is a formal description of the invariant of paraphrases of **E** – that is, a description of the meaning of all the expressions of **L** having the same meaning as **E**.

Definition 3.2: Semanteme (p. 79)
A semanteme is a lexical meaning – that is, the signified of a full lexical unit of **L**.

Definition 3.3 (= 2.3): Semantic Dependency (p. 86)
Semantic dependency is dependency between either two semantemes 'L$_1$' and 'L$_2$' that stand in a "predicate ~ argument" relation or two corresponding LUs in a sentence, L$_1$ and L$_2$: the governor (= predicate) determines the presence and the nature of the dependent (= argument) in the sentence.

Definition 3.4: Semantic Actant (p. 87)
A semantic actant of a predicative semanteme 'σ$_1$' is another semanteme 'σ$_2$' that is an argument of the predicate 'σ$_1$': 'σ$_1$(σ$_2$)'; a semantic actant of a predicative LU L$_1$ is another LU L$_2$ that corresponds to an argument of the predicate 'L$_1$'.

Chapter 4

Definition 4.1: Lexeme (p. 101)
A lexeme of language **L** is the set of **L**'s wordforms and phrases of special type (= analytical forms) whose signifieds differ only by inflectional meanings (= grammemes) and whose signifiers include the signifier of the same common stem which expresses their shared lexical meaning.

Definition 4.2: Phraseme (p. 105)
A phraseme is a phrase consisting of at least two lexemes that is paradigmatically constrained.

Definition 4.3: Lexemic Phraseme (p. 105)
A and **B** are lexemes.
A lexemic phraseme is a phraseme **AB** whose signified is not constrained, but whose signifier is constrained with respect to the signified: at least one of the components **A** and **B** is not selected by the Speaker independently – that is, strictly for its meaning and without regard for the other component.

Definition 4.4: Semantic Pivot (p. 106)
Let there be a phrase $L_1 - L_2$ with the meaning 'σ', 'σ' having the following property: 'σ' can be divided in two parts, '$σ_1$' and '$σ_2$' ['σ' = '$σ_1$' $⊕$ '$σ_2$'], such that '$σ_1$' corresponds to L_1 and '$σ_2$' corresponds to L_2, and one of the parts is an argument of the other [for instance, '$σ_1$'('$σ_2$')].
The semantic pivot of the meaning 'σ' is:
   1. Either the argument meaning '$σ_2$' – iff
      (a) '$σ_2$' is or contains the communicatively dominant component of 'σ'
      or
      (b) L_2 semantically implies L_1.
   2. Or the predicate meaning '$σ_1$' – iff Condition 1 is not satisfied.

Definition 4.5: Idiom (p. 107)
An idiom is a lexemic phraseme that is not compositional.

Definition 4.6: Collocation (p. 109)
A collocation is a lexemic phraseme that is compositional.

Definition 4.7: Nomineme (p. 111)
A nomineme is a semantic-lexemic phraseme that is non-compositional.

Definition 4.8: Cliché (p. 111)
A cliché is a semantic-lexemic phraseme that is compositional.

Definition 4.9: Pragmateme (p. 112)
A pragmateme is a cliché that is constrained by the speech act situation.

Definition 4.10: Lexical Unit (p. 115)
A lexical unit of language **L** is either a lexeme or an idiom.

Chapter 5

Definition 5.1: Lexicographic Connotation (p. 136)
A semanteme 'σ' is a lexicographic connotation of the LU L of language **L** iff 'σ' simultaneously satisfies the following two conditions:
   1. 'σ' is associated by **L** with the entities denoted by L.
   2. 'σ' is not a part of the definition of L.

Chapter 6

Definition 6.1: (Exact) Synonymy (p. 142)
Two LUs L_1 and L_2 stand in the relation of exact synonymy and are called exact synonyms [Syn], iff the following four conditions are simultaneously satisfied:
1. The meanings of L_1 and L_2 – that is, their signifieds – are identical: 'L_1' = 'L_2'.
2. The signifiers of L_1 and L_2 are different.
3. L_1 and L_2 belong to the same part of speech.
4. If L_1 and L_2 have semantic and deep-syntactic actants, the actants i, j, k, … of the one correspond one-to-one to the actants $i, j, k,$ … of the other.

Definition 6.2: Quasi-Synonymy (p. 143)
Two LUs L_1 and L_2 whose meanings are not identical are quasi-synonyms [QSyn] iff the following six conditions are simultaneously satisfied:
1. The meanings 'L_1' and 'L_2' are in the relation of strong inclusion or strong intersection.
2. The signifiers of L_1 and L_2 are different.
3. L_1 and L_2 belong to the same part of speech.
4. The semantic difference 'L_1' – 'L_2' is not regular in the language.
5. If L_1 and L_2 have semantic and deep-syntactic actants, the actants i, j, k, … of the one correspond one-to-one to the actants $i, j, k,$ … of the other.
6. They are mutually substitutable *salva significatione* in at least some contexts.

Definition 6.3: (Exact) Antonymy (p. 144)
Two LUs L_1 and L_2 stand in the relation of exact antonymy and are called exact antonyms [Anti], iff the following three conditions are simultaneously satisfied:
1. The only difference between the meanings of L_1 and L_2 is either the presence of the semanteme 'no' in one but not in the other, or the presence, in the same position, of the semanteme 'more' in one and the semanteme 'less' in the other.
2. L_1 and L_2 belong to the same part of speech.
3. If L_1 and L_2 have semantic and deep-syntactic actants, the actants i, j, k, … of the one correspond one-to-one to the actants $i, j, k,$ … of the other.

Definition 6.4: Conversion (p. 146)
Two LUs L_1 and L_2 stand in the relation of exact conversion and are called exact conversives [Conv], iff the following three conditions are simultaneously satisfied:
1. The propositional meanings of L_1 and L_2 are identical.
2. L_1 and L_2 belong to the same part of speech.

3. The communicative structures of the meanings of L_1 and L_2 are different – that is, the SemAs of L_1 are inverted with respect to the SemAs of L_2: at least one SemA i of L semantically corresponds to the SemA j of L_2 ($i \neq j$), and vice versa; their DSyntAs behave accordingly.

Definition 6.5: Derivation (p. 150)
Two LUs L_1 and L_2 stand in the relation of derivation iff the meaning of L_2 includes that of L_1 plus a component that represents a regular semantic difference in language **L** (i.e., the presence of this component characterizes many lexical pairs and has – at least on some cases – a standard expression).

Definition 6.6: Semantic Bridge (p. 152)
A semantic component 'σ' shared by LUs L_1 and L_2 is called the semantic bridge between L_1 and L_2 iff the following two conditions are simultaneously satisfied:
1. 'σ' contains enough semantic material.
2. Either 'σ' is part of the lexicographic definitions of both L_1 and L_2, or it is part of the lexicographic definition of one and of a lexicographic connotation of the other.

Definition 6.7: Polysemy (p. 154)
Two LUs L_1 and L_2 stand in the relation of polysemy iff they satisfy simultaneously the following three conditions:
1. They have identical signifiers.
2. Their signifieds [= lexicographic definitions] share a semantic bridge.
3. They belong to the same part of speech.

Definition 6.8: Metonymy (p. 156)
The meaning 'σ_2' stands in the relation of metonymy to the meaning 'σ_1' [= 'σ_2' is a metonymy of 'σ_1'] iff the following two conditions are simultaneously satisfied:
1. 'σ_2' includes 'σ_1'.
2. The entity/fact denoted by 'σ_2' is physically contiguous in space, time or function to that denoted by 'σ_1'.

Definition 6.9: Metaphor (p. 156)
The meaning 'σ_2' stands in the relation of metaphor to meaning 'σ_1' [= 'σ_2' is a metaphor of 'σ_1'] iff the following two conditions are simultaneously satisfied:
1. 'σ_2' includes 'σ_1'.
2. The entity/fact denoted by 'σ_2' bears a resemblance to that denoted by 'σ_1', so that it is possible to say 'σ_2' $\approx$ '... – ⌜as if⌝ it were σ_1'.

Definition 6.10: Homonymy (p. 157)
Two LUs L_1 and L_2 stand in the relation of homonymy and are called homonyms, iff the following two conditions are simultaneously satisfied:
1. They have identical signifiers.
2. Their signifieds do not share a semantic bridge (= they are semantically unrelated).

Chapter 7

Definition 7.1: Lexical Function (p. 162)
A lexical function **f** is a function (in the mathematical sense) which associates to an LU L of language **L** a (possibly empty) set of linguistic expressions $\{L_1, \ldots, L_n\}$ that have the meaning 'f' bearing on the meaning of L [= 'L'], and are selected for use in an utterance as a function of L:
$$\mathbf{f}(L) = \{L_1, \ldots, L_n\} \mid L_i(\text{'f'}) \text{ and } \text{'f'}(\text{'L'})$$

Chapter 8

Definition 8.1: Vocable (p. 188)
A vocable is the set of all LUs related by polysemy.

Definition 8.2: Semantic Label of a Lexical Unit (p. 191)
The semantic label of an LU is its approximate semantic characterization, based on a condensed and normalized formulation of the central, or generic, component of its lexicographic definition and perhaps some (parts) of its peripheral components.

Definition 8.3: Taxonomic Semantic Class of Lexical Units (p. 192)
A taxonomic semantic class is the set of all LUs (of language **L**) identified by the common semantic label.

Definition 8.4: Semantic Field (p. 198)
A semantic field $\mathbf{F}_{'\sigma'}^{\text{sem}}$ is the set of LUs whose definitions share a semantic bridge 'σ' and are, for this reason, perceived as belonging to the same semantic "family."

Definition 8.5: Lexical Field (p. 199)
A lexical field $\mathbf{F}_{'\sigma'}^{\text{lex}}$ is the set of all vocables whose basic LUs belong to the same semantic field $\mathbf{F}_{'\sigma'}^{\text{sem}}$.

Chapter 9

Definition 9.1/2: Semantically Normal/Anomalous Sentence (p. 230)
Sentence S is semantically normal/anomalous iff its meaning 'S' is well-formed/ill-formed.

Definition 9.3: Logical Proposition (p. 232)
A logical proposition is a symbolic expression (including a linguistic expression) to which a truth-value can be assigned: it can be TRUE or FALSE.

Definition 9.4: Semantically True/False Sentence (p. 233)
A sentence S is semantically true/false iff its truth/falsehood can be established solely by virtue of S's linguistic meaning (without taking into consideration the real-world fact to which S refers).

Definition 9.5: (Linguistic) Paraphrases (p. 235)
Sentences S_1 and S_2 of language **L** are linguistic paraphrases iff they are (quasi-)synonymous.

Definition 9.6: (Semantic) Implication (p. 245)
Sentence S_1 semantically implies sentence S_2 [= S_2 is a semantic implication of S_1] iff by admitting the truth of S_1 the Speaker commits himself to the truth of S_2; the converse is not necessarily the case.

Definition 9.7: (Semantic) Presupposition (p. 246)
Sentence S_1 semantically presupposes sentence S_2 [= S_2 is a semantic presupposition of S_1] iff, when S_1 is stated, negated or interrogated, the Speaker cannot negate S_2 without contradicting himself.

Definition 9.8: Equinomy (p. 249)
Two sentences, S_1 and S_2, are equinomous [= stand in the relation of equinomy] iff their signifiers are identical and their signifieds are different.

Substitution Test (p. 241)
Two exactly synonymous sentences (= two exact paraphrases) must be substitutable *salva significatione* – that is, with the preservation of meaning – in any context.
See also MUTUAL SUBSTITUTABILITY RULE, Ch. 5, p. 124.

Chapter 10

Definition 10.1: Semantic Representation (p. 257)
The Semantic Representation SemR (of a set of synonymous sentences) is a quadruplet

$$\text{SemR} = \langle \text{SemS, Sem-CommS, RhetS, RefS} \rangle,$$

where SemS stands for semantic structure, Sem-CommS for the semantic-communicative structure, RhetS for the rhetorical structure, and RefS for the referential structure.

Definition 10.2: Semantic Structure (p. 259)
The Semantic Structure 'S' (of a set of synonymous sentences) is a network whose nodes are labeled with semantemes and whose arcs are labeled with distinctive numbers identifying semantic relations between a (quasi-)predicative semanteme and the semantemes functioning as its arguments (or semantic actants).

Definition 10.3: Semantic-Communicative Structure (p. 270)
The Semantic-Communicative Structure is a division of the Semantic Structure into communicative areas – subnetworks, such that each of them
  1. has a communicatively dominant node, and
  2. is marked with a value of one or several communicative oppositions.

Definition 10.4: Semantic Rheme (p. 272)
That part of the meaning 'S' (of sentence S) that the Speaker presents as the information being supplied is called the semantic rheme of 'S'.

Definition 10.5: Semantic Theme (p. 272)
That part of the meaning 'S' (of sentence S) that the Speaker presents as the information about which the Sem-Rheme is stated is called the semantic theme of 'S'.

Definition 10.6: Semantic Specifier (p. 272)
That part of the meaning 'S' (of sentence S) which belongs neither to the Sem-Rheme nor the Sem-Theme is called the semantic specifier of 'S'; semantic-communicative specifiers indicate different circumstances either of the fact represented or the corresponding speech act.

Definition 10.7: Given (p. 274)
That part of the meaning 'S' (of sentence S) that the Speaker presents as already active in the mind of the Addressee is called Given in 'S'.

Definition 10.8: New (p. 275)
That part of the meaning 'S' (of sentence S) that the Speaker presents as not yet active in the mind of the Addressee is called New in 'S'.

Definition 10.9: Focalized (p. 275)
That part of the meaning 'S' (of sentence S) that the Speaker presents as being logically salient is called Focalized in 'S'.

Definition 10.10: Non-Focalized (p. 276)
That part of the meaning 'S' (of sentence S) that the Speaker does not present as being logically salient is called Non-focalized in 'S'.

Definition 10.11: Asserted (p. 276)
That part of the meaning 'S' (of sentence S) that is presented by the Speaker as communicated and can therefore be negated and questioned is called Asserted in 'S'.

Definition 10.12: Presupposed (p. 276)
That part of the meaning 'S' (of sentence S) that is presented by the Speaker not as communicated but as taken for granted and which is therefore unaffected even if all of 'S' is negated or questioned is called Presupposed in 'S'.

Definition 10.13: Communicated (p. 277)
That part of the 'S' (of sentence *S*) that the Speaker presents in a form geared to the transmission of information (in particular, it allows for negation and interrogation) is called Communicated in 'S'.

Definition 10.14: Signaled (p. 277)
That part of the meaning 'S' (of sentence *S*) that the Speaker presents in a form geared to the expression of his interior state or of the type of his speech act (i.e., it does not allow for negation and interrogation) is called Signaled in 'S'.

Definition 10.15: Performative (p. 277)
That part of the meaning 'S' (of sentence *S*) whose enunciation constitutes the action denoted by 'S' is called Performative.

Chapter 11

Definition 11.1: Deep-Syntactic Representation (p. 285)
The Deep-Syntactic Representation [DSyntR] (of a sentence) is a quadruplet
$$\text{DSyntR} = \langle \text{DSyntS, DSynt-CommS, DSynt-AnaphS, DSynt-ProsS} \rangle,$$
where DSyntS stands for deep-syntactic structure, DSynt-CommS for the deep-syntactic communicative structure, DSynt-AnaphS for the deep-syntactic anaphoric structure, and DSynt-ProsS for the deep-syntactic prosodic structure.

Definition 11.2: Deep-Syntactic Structure (p. 287)
The Deep-Syntactic Structure (of a sentence) is a dependency tree whose nodes are labeled with deep LUs, subscripted with deep grammemes, and whose branches are labeled with names of deep-syntactic relations.

Definition 11.3: Dependency Tree (p. 287)
A dependency tree is a directed connected graph that simultaneously satisfies the following two conditions:
1. The uniqueness of the governor: each node accepts no more than one entering branch.
2. The existence of the top node (or the summit): there is one and only one node that accepts no entering branches.

Definition 11.4: Deep-Syntactic Actant (Approximate Formulation) (p. 297)
In the DSynt-subtree $L_1 \rightarrow L_2$, L_2 is a deep-syntactic actant of L_1 iff L_2 corresponds to a semantic actant of L_1.

Language Index

While most of the linguistic phenomena discussed in this book were illustrated from English (as is advisable in an introductory text), occasionally we resorted to examples from other languages, either because English lacked the linguistic features being illustrated or these features were more characteristically represented in those languages.

Lexical Unit and Semanteme Index

The list below contains the LUs that have been treated in this book. The word "treated" should be understood in a loose sense, since it covers different types and depths of description: full-fledged lexicographic definitions and/or pseudo-definitions in terms of semantic labels, LUs' Government Patterns and/or LFs controlled by them, as well as, in a few cases, entire lexicographic entries. As for the semantemes, we have listed some fundamental ones, corresponding or close to semantic primitives (such as the causation semantemes) and those for which the actantial structure was explicitly indicated or decompositions were proposed.

 As explained ("Symbols, Abbreviations and Writing Conventions", p. xxv*ff*), the numbering of word-senses follows LDOCE's system where we find it acceptable, and our own system is used elsewhere.